# THINK
## AMERICAN GOVERNMENT

### 2010 Edition

**NEAL TANNAHILL**
Houston Community College

**Longman**

Boston   Columbus   Indianapolis   New York   San Francisco   Upper Saddle River
Amsterdam   Cape Town   Dubai   London   Madrid   Milan   Munich   Paris   Montreal   Toronto
Delhi   Mexico City   São Paulo   Sydney   Hong Kong   Seoul   Singapore   Taipei   Tokyo

Editor-in-Chief: Eric Stano
Assistant Development Manager: David Kear
Associate Development Editor: Donna Garnier
Marketing Manager: Lindsey Prudhomme
Media Supplements Editor: Regina Vertiz
Production Manager: Eric Jorgensen
Project Coordination, Development, Text Design, Photo Research, and Electronic Page Makeup: Pre-Press PMG
Cover Designer: John Callahan
Cover Image: © Beau Lark/Corbis
Manufacturing Manager: Mary Fischer
Printer and Binder: Worldcolor/Dubuque
Cover Printer: Lehigh-Phoenix Color/Hagerstown

For permission to use copyrighted material, grateful acknowledgment is made to the copyright holders on pp. 456–457, which are hereby made part of this copyright page.

Library of Congress Cataloging-in-Publication Data
   Tannahill, Neal R., 1949-
    Think : American government / Neal Tannahill. -- 2nd ed.
      p. cm.
    Includes bibliographical references and index.
    ISBN 978-0-205-71472-8 (alk. paper)
    1.  United States--Politics and government.  I. Title.
    JK275.T36 2010a
    320.473--dc22
              2009047756

1 2 3 4 5 6 7 8 9 10—V042—12 11 10 09

**Longman**
is an imprint of

www.pearsonhighered.com

ISBN-13: 978-0-205-71472-8
ISBN-10:    0-205-71472-2

# >brief CONTENTS

## THINK
**AMERICAN GOVERNMENT**
TANNAHILL 2010

> on the cover:

**p. 229 President Obama's Full Plate**
p. 311–312 Health care
p. 339, 357 The Wars in Iraq and Afghanistan
p. 244 Climate Change
p. 234 The Economy

President Obama's Full Plate
How the administration has addressed health care, the wars in Iraq and Afghanistan, climate change, and the economy

Government 2.0
The Twitter Revolution, the BlackBerry President, and more

**p. 116–118 Government 2.0**
The Twitter Revolution, the BlackBerry President, and more

**p. 321 What's in your wallet?**
Successes and failures of the economic recovery, and what the future holds

What's in your wallet?
Successes and failures in the economic recovery — and what the future holds

www.thethinkspot.com

# >detailed CONTENTS

# >acknowledgments

Many people contributed to the writing and production of this book. Eric Stano, Donna Garnier, Eric Jorgensen, and the whole team at Pre-Press PMG gave me sympathetic and professional help from the beginning of work on the edition to its completion.

I am grateful to my friends and colleagues among the government faculty at Houston Community College for their friendship and support. I have learned most of what I know about teaching from them. Finally, I wish to dedicate this book to the people who are close to me personally, especially Anup Bodhe, Anderson Brandao, Jason Orr, and Kim Galle.

NEAL TANNAHILL

# >about the
## AUTHOR

NEAL TANNAHILL has taught courses in American government and politics at Houston Community College for more than 30 years. The primary focus of his career has been helping students to master course content, successfully complete courses, earn degrees, and achieve their academic goals. He is the author of a series of textbooks including *American Government, Texas Government,* and *American and Texas Government.*

Neal Tannahill welcomes your comments and suggestions about this *Think American Government* text at neal.tannahill@hccs.edu or ntannahill@aol.com.

# GOVERNMENT,

The Americans with Disabilities Act of 1990 (ADA) is a federal law designed to end discrimination against persons with disabilities and to eliminate barriers to their full participation in American society. The ADA protects people with disabilities from discrimination in all employment practices, including hiring, firing, promotions, and compensation. The ADA does not force employers to hire unqualified individuals who happen to be disabled, but it does require companies to make "reasonable accommodation" for otherwise qualified job applicants or current employees who happen to be disabled unless the business can show that the accommodation would put an "undue hardship" on its operation. The ADA also requires that private businesses that are open to the public—such as restaurants, hotels, theaters, retail stores, funeral homes, healthcare offices, pharmacies, private schools, and daycare centers—be accessible to persons with disabilities. Business owners may have to modify their premises or change their ways of doing business so long as these changes do not unduly burden the business or force business owners to alter the fundamental nature of the goods or services they provide.[1]

# POLITICS, AND THE POLICYMAKING PROCESS

3

# ESSENTIALS...

*after studying the Introduction, students should be able to answer the following questions:*

> What is the impact of government on the lives of individuals as well as society as a whole?

> What are the five stages of the public policy approach?

> What was the process for formulation, adoption, and implementation of the Americans with Disabilities Act (ADA)?

# the importance
## OF GOVERNMENT

t he ADA illustrates the importance of government. For millions of Americans with disabilities, the act offers the promise of opportunity to compete in the workplace without discrimination. It guarantees access to restaurants, hotels, shops, and clinics. The ADA forces employers to review their employment practices to ensure compliance with the law and to take reasonable steps to accommodate the needs of workers and customers with disabilities. For society as a whole, the ADA gives millions of people with disabilities the opportunity to become full participants in the nation's economy, both as workers and as consumers.

Government affects individual Americans through regulations, services, and taxes. Government regulates many aspects of daily life, either directly or indirectly. The government sets speed limits and other driving regulations, determines a minimum age to purchase and

consume alcoholic beverages, and establishes the educational and technical qualifications required for practicing many occupations and professions. Government regulations affect the quality of air and water, gasoline mileage performance of automobiles, and working conditions in factories. In addition, regulation attempts to protect consumers from unsafe products, untested drugs, misleading package labels, and deceptive advertising.

Government services provide benefits to all Americans. Public hospitals, schools, and transportation networks serve millions of people. Many college students receive financial aid and attend institutions that benefit from public funding. Government welfare programs assist millions of low-income families. Elderly people and many individuals with disabilities receive Social Security and Medicare benefits.

Rebuilding New Orleans.

Government regulations and services cost money. Federal, state, and local taxes combined represent 29 percent of the nation's **Gross Domestic Product (GDP),** which is the total value of goods and services produced by a nation's economy in a year, excluding transactions with foreign countries.[2] Workers pay income and payroll taxes on the wages they earn. Consumers pay sales taxes on retail purchases, and excise taxes on tobacco, alcohol, tires, gasoline, and other products. Homeowners and business owners pay property taxes on their homes and businesses.

Government not only touches the lives of individual Americans, but also affects the quality of life of the nation as a whole. Few people would want to live, work, or run a business in a country without a fully functioning government. Government regulations and services help ensure safe neighborhoods, a healthy environment, an efficient transportation system, and an educated workforce. The tax system

**These statements have NOT BEEN EVALUATED by the Food and Drug Administration (FDA). These products ARE NOT INTENDED TO DIAGNOSE, TREAT, CURE, OR PREVENT ANY DISEASE.**

provides a mechanism for government to spread the cost of its operation across a broad range of individuals and groups in society. In times of emergency, such as a terrorist attack or a natural disaster, people expect government to respond to the crisis, assist the victims, and rebuild damaged communities.

**gross domestic product (GDP)** the total value of goods and services produced by a nation's economy in a year, excluding transactions with foreign countries.

# government
## AND POLITICS

**g**overnment and *politics* are distinct but closely related terms. **Government** is the institution with authority to set policy for society. Congress, the president, courts, and government agencies, such as the Social Security Administration (SSA) and the Food and Drug Administration (FDA), are all structures of American national government. Each state has a governor, legislature, court system,

and administrative departments, in addition to a series of local governments, such as municipalities, townships, counties, and school districts.

Government is an *institution*, but politics is a *process*. One political scientist says that **politics** is the way in which decisions for a society are made and considered binding most of the time by most of the people.[3] Another scholar declares that the study of politics is "the attempt to

**government** the institution with authority to set policy for society.
**politics** the process that determines who shall occupy the roles of leadership in government and how the power of government shall be exercised.

explain the various ways in which power is exercised in the everyday world and how that power is used to allocate resources and benefits to some people and groups, and costs and burdens to other people and groups."[4] We could add a third definition: Politics is the process that determines who shall occupy the roles of leadership in government and how the power of government shall be exercised.

**think** Do you favor a small government that provides relatively modest services but holds down taxes, or an active government that provides more services but costs more?

# the public
## POLICY APPROACH

the public policy approach is one of the models that political scientists use for studying government and politics. **Public policy** is the response, or lack of response, of government decision-makers to an issue. Government policies can take the form of laws, executive orders, regulations, court decisions, or, in some cases, no action at all. The decision by government decision-makers *not* to act is just as much a policy decision as the choice to take a particular action.

The **public policy approach** is a comprehensive method for studying the process through which issues come to the attention of government decision-makers and through which policies are formulated, adopted, implemented, and evaluated. The public policy approach goes beyond an examination of the content of laws and regulations to consider the broader scope of policymaking. A study of government policy toward persons with disabilities would begin by examining the legal, cultural, socioeconomic, and political factors shaping the environment for the policy. It would consider how the rights of people with disabilities became an issue of public concern, and it would examine the process through which the government formulated and adopted the ADA. The study would also consider the policy's implementation and evaluation.[5]

## The Policymaking Environment

The **policymaking environment** is the complex of factors outside of government that has an impact, either directly or indirectly, on the policymaking process. The types of issues that the government addresses, the set of policy alternatives that government decision-makers are willing to consider, and the resources available to the government depend on the international, cultural, demographic, economic, constitutional, and political environments.

## Agenda Building

**Agenda building** is the process through which problems become matters of public concern and government action. The politics of agenda building involves government officials and groups outside of the government competing to determine which problems government will address. Whereas some interests want to promote the consideration of certain issues, other forces that oppose change work to block discussion by denying that a problem exists or by arguing that the government either cannot or should not address it.[6]

Agenda building not only identifies problems for government attention but also defines the nature of those problems, and therefore the eventual thrust of a policy solution.[7] Consider the issue of disability rights. During the debate in Congress on the ADA, spokespersons for advocacy groups for the disabled, such as the Disability Rights Education and Defense Fund (DREDF) and the Americans Disabled for Attendant Programs Today (ADAPT), noted that the employment rate for persons with severe disabilities was only 23 percent, compared to an employment rate for adults without disabilities of nearly 80 percent.[8] The supporters

**AGENDA BUILDING IS THE PROCESS THROUGH WHICH PROBLEMS BECOME MATTERS OF PUBLIC CONCERN AND GOVERNMENT ACTION.**

**public policy** the response or lack of response of government decision-makers to an issue.

**public policy approach** a comprehensive method for studying the process through which issues come to the attention of government decision-makers and through which policies are formulated, adopted, implemented, and evaluated.

**policymaking environment** the complex of factors outside of government that has an impact, either directly or indirectly, on the policymaking process.

**agenda building** the process through which problems become matters of public concern and government action.

of disability rights argued that discrimination or a lack of access to public facilities prevented many persons with disabilities from working. They proposed passage of federal legislation prohibiting discrimination against people with disabilities and ensuring access to business facilities as a solution to the problem. In contrast, business groups opposed government regulation. They denied that employment discrimination against people with disabilities was a major problem, suggesting instead that the employment rate for people with disabilities was low because many people with disabilities either cannot work or do not want to work. Furthermore, they claimed, individuals with disabilities who have few skills can make more money from government disability payments than they can earn in low-wage jobs.

## Policy Formulation

**Policy formulation** is the development of strategies for dealing with the problems on the official policy agenda. Government officials as well as individuals and organizations outside of government, such as interest groups, political parties, policy experts, and the media, participate in policy formulation. The formulation of ADA legislation, for example, involved negotiations among members of Congress, executive branch officials, business interests, and advocacy groups for people with disabilities. Although most business groups supported the goals of the ADA, they were concerned that the law would require businesses to hire unqualified applicants or make extensive (and expensive) physical modifications to their facilities. Business owners also worried that the new law would subject them to lawsuits and the possibility of expensive jury settlements.

The wording of the ADA reflects a compromise between the supporters of people with disabilities and business interests. The advocacy groups succeeded in writing a broad definition of disability into the law. The ADA declares that an individual with a disability is "a person who

**policy formulation** the development of strategies for dealing with the problems on the official policy agenda.

*Disability rights activists crawl across the plaza of the U.S. Supreme Court building to protest court rulings limiting the scope of the ADA.*

**SUTTON V. UNITED AIRLINES (1999):** The U.S. Supreme Court has weakened the ADA by limiting its applicability and interpreting its provisions narrowly. *Sutton v. United Airlines* involved a lawsuit filed by twin sisters against United Airlines. The airline refused to consider them for employment as pilots because their uncorrected eyesight did not meet the company's minimum standard of 20/100. The sisters could see well with glasses, so they sued the airlines, charging that it discriminated against them because of their disability. The U.S. Supreme Court rejected their lawsuit because, the Court said, their vision was correctable with glasses and they were therefore no longer disabled under the law.

**MURPHY V. UNITED PARCEL SERVICE (1999):** The case of *Murphy v. United Parcel Service* concerned a UPS mechanic who was fired because the company thought that his high blood pressure might interfere with his ability to safely operate a motor vehicle. Murphy said that he was not a safety risk because his blood pressure was controlled by medication. He filed suit under the ADA, but the Supreme Court ruled that he was not covered by the law because doctors testified that his hypertension could be completely controlled by medication. He was therefore not disabled under the law.

**CONGRESS AMENDS THE ADA:** In 2008, Congress passed, and President George W. Bush signed, legislation to make it clear that the courts should interpret the civil rights guarantees of the ADA broadly and that mitigating factors should not be considered in determining whether an individual has a disability. The measure explicitly reversed the Supreme Court's interpretation of the ADA in *Sutton* and *Murphy.*

has a physical or mental impairment that substantially limits one or more major life activities, a record of such an impairment, or is regarded as having such an impairment."[9] Major life activities include the ability of individuals to care for themselves, perform manual tasks, walk, see, hear, speak, breathe, learn, work, sit, stand, lift, and reach. Under the law, persons with learning disabilities, epilepsy, mental illness, muscular dystrophy, HIV infection, cancer, diabetes, mental retardation, alcoholism, and cosmetic disfigurement are considered disabled.

Business groups succeeded in limiting the scope of the law. Although the ADA prohibits discrimination, it does not establish a quota system for hiring people with disabilities. It requires only that employers hire and promote qualified candidates without regard to disability. Furthermore, the ADA declares that a business need make only "reasonable accommodations" for employees and customers with disabilities that do not place an "undue hardship" on its operations.

Political scientists use the term **issue network** to describe a group of political actors actively involved with policymaking in a particular issue area. Issue networks vary from issue to issue. The issue network for disabilities includes advocacy groups for people with disabilities, business organizations, individual spokespersons for disability rights, journalists who focus on disability issues, members of Congress and the executive branch who are involved with the issue, and the courts. Although not all participants in an issue network are equally influential, generally no one individual or group is able to dominate policymaking on the issue. Instead, policy reflects the result of conflict, and occasionally compromise, among the participants.

## Policy Adoption

**Policy adoption** is the official decision of a government body to accept a particular policy and put it into effect. The ADA, for example, was enacted through the legislative process. Congress passed the measure and the president signed it into law.

Not all policies are drafted into formal legislation and adopted through the legislative process. Courts adopt policies when they decide cases. Government agencies, such as the Environmental Protection Agency (EPA), adopt policies

**issue network** a group of political actors that is actively involved with policymaking in a particular issue area.

**policy adoption** the official decision of a government body to accept a particular policy and put it into effect.

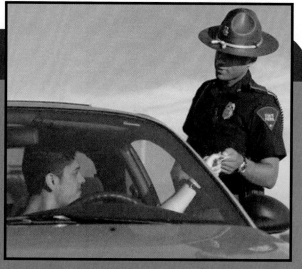

# takeaction

## GOVERNMENT AND YOU >>

Government policies affect each of us every day in ways that are obvious and in ways that may not always be readily apparent. If a police officer stops you for speeding on your way to class, the government has touched you in a fashion that is direct and clear. In contrast, when you pick up a relative at the airport for a holiday visit, it may not occur to you that tax dollars paid to build the airport.

An important goal of this course is for students to recognize the relevance of government to their own lives and to the life of their community. To help achieve that goal, your assignment is to keep a journal documenting the impact of government on your life throughout the semester. You can write in longhand in a notebook or create your journal entries in a computer file to be submitted at the end of the term. Each entry will identify and discuss a daily event in your life that involved your interaction with government, either directly or indirectly.

Your instructor will grade your journal on the following criteria:

• Number and frequency of entries. Your journal must include at least four dated entries for each week of the course.

• Evidence of growth in your understanding of American government. As the course progresses, your journal entries should reveal a higher level of sophistication than entries made in the first few weeks of the term.

• Quality of journal entries. Some of your entries should identify a connection to course materials, citing concepts discussed in your textbook or in the classroom. At least one entry a week should include a personal evaluation of the role of government. You will not be graded on your point of view, but you should display evidence that you have thought critically about the role of government in your life and in society as a whole.

by issuing regulations. The president can adopt policy by issuing executive orders. Government officials also make policy when they decide either to take no action or to continue policies already in place.

## Policy Implementation

**Policy implementation** is the stage of the policy process in which policies are carried out. Implementation involves not just government officials but also individuals and groups outside of the government. Private businesses, individual with disabilities, the Equal Employment Opportunity Commission (EEOC), and the courts participate in the implementation of the ADA. The law requires private businesses to take reasonable steps to accommodate employees and customers with disabilities. If individuals with disabilities believe they have suffered discrimination, the law allows them to file a lawsuit against the offending business and/or file a complaint with the EEOC. Penalties for violators can be as high as $110,000 for repeat offenders.[10] During 2006, the EEOC, which also hears charges of racial, ethnic, gender, and age discrimination, handled 15,575 complaints based on the ADA, more than a fifth of the total complaints filed with the agency.[11]

think

Has the ADA been a success or failure? What is the basis for your answer?

The implementation process often involves supplying details and interpretations of policy that are omitted, either intentionally or unintentionally, during policy formulation. The ADA, as noted, requires businesses to make "reasonable accommodations" for employees and customers with disabilities that do not place an "undue hardship" on their operations. How these terms apply to hundreds of specific circumstances depends on their interpretation by the EEOC and the courts. The EEOC, for example, has ruled that employers may not refuse to hire people with disabilities because of concerns about their impact on health insurance costs.[12] More often than not, the courts have sided with employers, narrowing the scope of the ADA and making it difficult for individuals to prevail in disability discrimination lawsuits filed against businesses. Employers win more than 90 percent of the workplace discrimination cases filed under the ADA.[13]

In 1969, the Cuyahoga River in northeastern Ohio gained national attention when the debris and chemical runoff from industrial pollution caught fire. The images of the burning river were so spectacular that Congress passed the Clean Water Act. The Environmental Protection Agency (EPA) was put in charge of the Cuyahoga River cleanup program. The river drains over 800 square miles and empties into Lake Erie, which it was helping to pollute at an alarming rate. Today, the Cuyahoga River supports 62 species of fish, where there were none in 1962. Several of the Cuyahoga's tributaries have already met some, or all, of the requirements of the Clean Water Act. In spite of this really encouraging progress, the river system still fails to meet many of the mandates of the Clean Water Act. And most environmentalists agree that a complete river recovery is at least 20 years in the future. The EPA and volunteer organizations continue to work for a complete recovery for the Cuyahoga River.

## Policy Evaluation

**Policy evaluation** is the assessment of policy. It involves questions of equity, efficiency, effectiveness, and political feasibility. Equity is the concept that similarly situated people should be treated equally. Efficiency is a comparison of a policy's costs with the benefits it provides. Effectiveness is the extent to which a policy achieves its goals. Political feasibility refers to the ability of a policy to obtain and hold public support. Equitable policies are not always efficient. Similarly, some policies that are effective are not politically feasible, and vice versa.[14]

**policy implementation** the stage of the policy process in which policies are carried out.

**policy evaluation** the assessment of policy.

**normative analysis** a method of study that is based on certain values.

Evaluation can be either normative or empirical. A **normative analysis** is a method of study based on certain values. A normative evaluation of the ADA, for example, might consider the merits of the goals of the law or the wisdom of trying to achieve those goals through government regulation. In contrast, an **empirical analysis** is a method of study that relies on experience and scientific observation. An empirical evaluation might focus on changes in the employment rate for people with disabilities, the number of lawsuits filed under the law, or the average cost of compliance to employers and business owners.

Evaluation studies show that the ADA has had a mixed impact:

- A survey of corporate executives found that the median cost of making the workplace more accessible was only $223 per individual with disabilities. Two-thirds of the executives surveyed reported that the ADA had not spawned an increase in lawsuits.[15]
- A majority of ADA complaints filed with the EEOC have involved issues that members of Congress did not discuss in drafting the law, such as back problems and psychological stress. Only 10 percent of the complaints have come from people with spinal cord injuries or other neurological problems—the conditions most frequently mentioned when the ADA was written.[16]
- Despite the ADA, the employment rate for people with disabilities actually declined between 1992 and 2000.[17]

The impact of the results of policy evaluation on the policy process is known as **feedback**. If a policy is judged successful and the problem solved, officials may terminate the policy. Should the problem persist, the policy process may begin anew as groups and individuals once again push the issue to the forefront of the policy agenda. Evaluation studies frequently result in initiatives to modify policies or improve their implementation. In 1999, for example, Congress passed, and President Bill Clinton signed, legislation making it easier for people with disabilities to keep their government-funded healthcare coverage after taking a job. Despite the ADA, thousands of people with disabilities had been kept out of the job market, because of fear of losing their health coverage. The supporters of the act hoped it would enable them to take jobs.

# Evaluation studies frequently result in initiatives to modify policies or improve their implementation.

**empirical analysis** a method of study that relies on experience and scientific observation.

**feedback** the impact of the results of policy evaluation on the policy process.

# looking FORWARD

The public policy approach provides the basis for the organization of this textbook. The book's first three chapters deal with the international, socioeconomic, and constitutional environments for policymaking. Chapter 1 focuses on the cultural, international, demographic, and economic backgrounds of policymaking in America, whereas the next two chapters explore the constitutional environment for policymaking. Chapter 2 deals with the U.S. Constitution; Chapter 3 focuses on the federal system.

Chapter 4 through Chapter 9 focus on the various elements of the political environment for policymaking: Chapter 4 examines political socialization and public opinion. Chapter 5 discusses individual participation. Chapter 6 considers the media, whereas Chapter 7 looks at interest groups. Chapter 8 deals with political parties, and Chapter 9 discusses political campaigns and elections.

The next four chapters profile the policymaking institutions of American national government: Chapter 10 examines Congress; Chapter 11, the president. The federal bureaucracy is the subject of Chapter 12. Chapter 13 focuses on the federal courts.

The last four chapters of the text deal with the nature of policy and policymaking in four substantive areas: Chapter 14 examines economic policymaking. In Chapter 15, the focus is on civil liberties policymaking, whereas civil rights policymaking is the subject of Chapter 16. Finally, Chapter 17 examines foreign and defense policymaking.

# Beyond Obama-Mania: Will Young People Stay Involved Postelection?

**Diverse Online**
**BY ROBIN CHEN DELOS**
**DECEMBER 1, 2008**

Christopher Carter worked hard up until the presidential election to register and turn out his classmates to vote. Carter, a second-year political science student, attends the country's oldest historically black college, Cheyney University in Pennsylvania.

"Our efforts were very successful; we were able to register almost everyone on campus. It took a lot of work. We had someone sitting in the cafeteria every day registering students to vote and then reminding people to go out and vote," says Carter, a vice president of his school's NAACP chapter, which organized a get-out-the-vote campaign on the school's 1,000-student campus.

Young people like Carter poured out to vote in record numbers during the presidential election but that does not necessarily mean they will stay involved in politics, or even their communities.

Motivating young people during a highly contentious election is one thing, keeping them involved in community organizing and volunteerism is another.

It isn't so easy, says Dr. Pedro Noguera, an urban sociologist at New York University. "The candidacy of Barack Obama really appealed to young people. But whether or not that translates to ongoing involvement remains to be seen," he says. "Getting organized around an election has a very definite goal, but a lot of things this country needs to work on don't have such clear targets."

Nearly 53 percent of young people—those under 30—voted in the election, about 3.4 million more than voted in 2004, according to data released this week by the CIRCLE at Tuffs University.

Experts say youth who do work with organizations are more likely to remain involved for the long term. "Once you get engaged, once you actually do something, the likelihood of doing it again is really high," says Dr. Constance Flanagan, a professor of youth civic development and an expert in youth civic and political development at The Pennsylvania State University. "Organizations are formed and they don't just go away. I'm hopeful lots of young people will continue doing grassroots work in their communities and their colleges."

Carter, the student at Cheyney University in Pennsylvania, says he has a renewed faith in the political system. "The election showed me that maybe there is a lot more hope for the democratic system in this country because the last two elections I felt the same way other people felt," he says, "left out, and that whoever we voted for wouldn't matter."

Carter decided to give the democratic process and activism another chance. Obama's win, he says, shows him that getting involved can make a difference. "When we go all out and do everything we have to do, you can be successful in the system. I would say it inspired me," Carter says.

## CRITICAL THINKING QUESTIONS:

- Did the 2008 presidential election excite and energize the young people you know? Why do you think that happened?
- Why is it important for young people to be involved in politics and the policymaking process?
- Is the continued political involvement of young people dependent on the success of the Obama administration? Why or why not?

>> END

# TEST yourself

1. Which of the following is not a provision of the Americans with Disabilities Act (ADA)?
   A. Employers are required to hire any disabled person who applies for a job as long as that person meets the minimum qualifications.
   B. Private businesses that are open to the public must be accessible to people with disabilities.
   C. Employers must make "reasonable accommodations" for disabled employees who are otherwise qualified for their jobs.
   D. Employers may not discriminate against disabled persons in hiring and promotions.

2. The institution with authority to set policy for society is known as which of the following?
   A. Politics
   B. Political science
   C. Government
   D. Congress

3. Congress, the president, the Federal Communications Commission, and the Supreme Court are all part of which of the following institution?
   A. Politics
   B. Policymaking environment
   C. Government
   D. Feedback

4. The way in which decisions for a society are made and considered binding most of the time by most of the people is a definition of which of the following?
   A. Politics
   B. Political science
   C. Government
   D. Public policy

5. A city council refuses to adopt an ordinance (local law) designed to regulate smoking in public places. Is this decision an example of a public policy?
   A. No. Public policies require the adoption of a policy and the city council rejected the policy proposal.
   B. No. This proposal would have violated the ADA.
   C. Yes. This is an example of a public policy because it would have regulated public places.
   D. Yes. A public policy is the response, or lack of response, by government decision-makers to an issue.

6. Is the ADA an example of a public policy?
   A. Yes, because it is the response of government decision-makers to the issue of discrimination against people with disabilities.
   B. Yes, because it was not done secretly.
   C. Yes, because it affects a lot of people.
   D. No, because it does not involve an election.

7. Which of the following is NOT an example of a public policy?
   A. The decision of the United States government not to grant diplomatic recognition to the nation of Cuba.
   B. The decision of *CBS Nightly News* to name Katie Couric as the anchor of its network evening news.
   C. The decision of the Federal Communications Commission (FCC) to adopt a rule concerning the joint ownership of a newspaper, television, and radio station in the same market.
   D. The decision of the Senate to confirm a presidential appointment to the Fifth Circuit Court of Appeals.

8. "The complex of factors outside of government that has an impact, either directly or indirectly, on the policymaking process" is a definition of which of the following terms?
   A. Agenda building
   B. Policymaking environment
   C. The public policymaking process
   D. Politics

9. "The process through which problems become matters of public concern and government action" is a definition of which of the following terms?
   A. Policy adoption
   B. Policy implementation
   C. Agenda building
   D. Policy formulation

10. Which of the following is a good example of agenda building?
    A. The president meets with advisors to discuss how best to respond to North Korea testing a nuclear weapon.
    B. The Supreme Court rules that the execution of convicted murderers who are mentally retarded violates the U.S. Constitution.
    C. A group of concerned scientists publish a report on the problem of global warming.
    D. An economist publishes a study showing the impact of minimum wage laws on the unemployment rate of low-skilled workers.

**11** The development of strategies for dealing with the problems on the official policy agenda is a definition for which of the following?
A. Policy formulation
B. Policy adoption
C. Policy implementation
D. Policy evaluation

**12** A congressional committee meets to discuss the details of proposed legislation to improve automobile mileage standards. The action best illustrates which of the following stages of the policymaking process?
A. Agenda building
B. Policy formulation
C. Policy adoption
D. Policy evaluation

**13** A group of political actors that is actively involved with policymaking in a particular issue area is known as which of the following?
A. Interest group
B. Issue network
C. Feedback
D. Political party

**14** The official decision of a government body to accept a particular policy and put it into effect is a definition for which of the following?
A. Policy evaluation
B. Policy formulation
C. Policy implementation
D. Policy adoption

**15** The president issues an executive order imposing U.S. sanctions on Sudan, a North African country whose government is accused of human rights violations. This act illustrates which stage of the policymaking process?
A. Agenda setting
B. Policy adoption
C. Policy evaluation
D. Policy implementation

**16** The stage of the policy process in which policies are carried out is a definition for which of the following?
A. Agenda setting
B. Policy adoption
C. Policy evaluation
D. Policy implementation

**17** The president signs legislation establishing a process for trying individuals accused of plotting terror attacks against the United States. This action best illustrates which of the following stages of the policymaking process?
A. Agenda setting
B. Policy adoption
C. Policy formulation
D. Policy implementation

**18** Medicare beneficiaries register for prescription drug benefits. This action illustrations which of the following?
A. Agenda setting
B. Policy adoption
C. Policy evaluation
D. Policy implementation

**19** In which stage of the policymaking process are policies assessed to determine their impact and effectiveness?
A. Agenda setting
B. Policy adoption
C. Policy evaluation
D. Policy implementation

**20** Congress changes the Medicare prescription drug benefit program in response to complaints about coverage. This event best illustrates which of the following?
A. Feedback
B. Issue networks
C. Normative analysis
D. Empirical analysis

KNOW *the* **score**
18–20 correct: Congratulations! You are well informed!
15–17 correct: Your political knowledge is a bit low—be sure to review the key terms and visit TheThinkSpot.
<14 correct: Reread the chapter more thoroughly.

1. A; 2. C; 3. C; 4. C; 5. D; 6. A; 7. B; 8. B; 9. C; 10. C; 11. A; 12. B; 13. B; 14. D; 15. B; 16. D; 17. B; 18. D; 19. C; 20. A

# 1 A CHANGING

> WHAT'S AHEAD

The population of the United States is aging. In 2008, 38.9 million Americans were aged 65 or older. The U.S. Census Bureau estimates that the number of older Americans will increase steadily for at least the next two decades. While the older population is increasing rapidly, the number of people between 16 and 64 years of age, the prime working years, is growing slowly (actually falling as a percentage of the total population).[1]

The aging of the population threatens the financial solvency of the government's major healthcare and pension programs—Medicare, Medicaid, and Social Security. Medicare and Medicaid are healthcare programs. **Medicare** is a federally funded health insurance program for the elderly. As the population ages, the number of people eligible for Medicare will climb and the cost of the program will grow. **Medicaid** is a federal program designed to provide health insurance coverage to low-income persons, people with disabilities, and elderly people who are impoverished. Although older people are a minority of Medicaid recipients, the cost of their healthcare is greater than it is for other groups of beneficiaries. **Social Security** is a federal pension and disability insurance program funded through a payroll tax on workers and their employers. Its costs will rise as an increasing number of people reach retirement age and begin collecting benefits. Because the traditional working age population is growing slowly, payroll tax revenues will be unable to keep up with program expenditures.

Demographic change, such as the aging of the population, is an important element of the policymaking environment. This complex of factors outside of government has an impact, either directly or indirectly, on the policymaking process. The policymaking environment influences the types of issues that appear on the policy agenda, the policy options government

# AMERICA

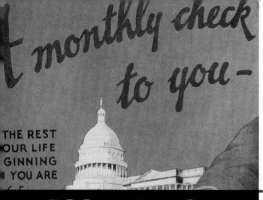

t monthly check
to you —

THE REST
OUR LIFE
GINNING
I YOU ARE

decision-makers consider during policy formulation, the policy alternatives selected during policy adoption, the resources available for policy implementation, and the values that influence policy evaluation. Chapter 1 is the first of a series of chapters that deals with the environment for policymaking. This chapter examines some of the more important aspects of the cultural, international, and socioeconomic environments for policymaking in America. Subsequent chapters address the legal/constitutional environment and the political environment.

# ESSENTIALS...

after studying Chapter 1, students should be able to answer the following questions:

> How would you describe America's political culture?

> How does the global economy affect policymaking in the United States?

> How has the population of the United States changed in terms of size, growth rate, race and ethnicity, and geographic distribution? How do these changes affect the policymaking environment?

> What are the patterns of wealth and poverty in America, and how does the economic status of families and individuals vary based on race, ethnicity, gender, residence, region, and family composition?

> What is the relationship between the cultural, international, demographic, and economic environments and the policymaking process?

# political
## CULTURE

**p**olitical culture refers to the widely held, deeply rooted political values of a society. America's political culture can be characterized as a capitalistic democracy. A **democracy** is a system of government in which ultimate political authority is vested in the people. In the box on the following page, political scientist Robert A. Dahl identifies eight criteria of a democratic society. **Capitalism** is an economic system characterized by individual and corporate ownership of the means of production, and a market economy based on the supply and demand of goods and services. Under capitalism, the marketplace, in which buyers and sellers freely exchange goods and services, determines what goods and services

**Medicare** a federally funded health insurance program for the elderly.

**Medicaid** a federal program designed to provide health insurance coverage to low-income persons, people with disabilities, and elderly people who are impoverished.

**Social Security** a federal pension and disability insurance program funded through a payroll tax on workers and their employers.

**political culture** the widely held, deeply rooted political values of a society.

**democracy** a system of government in which ultimate political authority is vested in the people.

THE GRAYING OF AMERICA

| 1940 | 1950 | 1960 | 1970 | 1980 | 1990 | 2000 | 2010 | 2020 | 2030 | 2040 | 2050 |
|------|------|------|------|------|------|------|------|------|------|------|------|
| 6.8 | 8.1 | 9.2 | 9.9 | 11.3 | 12.6 | 12.4 | 13.0 | 16.3 | 19.6 | 20.4 | 20.6 |

Percent aged 65 and over of the total population (1900–2000, actual; 2010–2050, estimated).

# 8 CRITERIA OF DEMOCRACY

ROBERT A. DAHL POLITICAL SCIENTIST

**1 THE RIGHT TO VOTE.** All or nearly all citizens enjoy the right to vote and have their votes counted equally. In the United States, every adult citizen has the right to vote except people who have lost their voting rights because they have been convicted of a serious crime. Significant restrictions on the right to vote are undemocratic. For example, Saudi Arabia held elections for the first time in 2006 to select members of municipal councils but only allowed men to cast ballots. Although holding an election is a step toward democracy, excluding women is undemocratic.

**2 THE RIGHT TO BE ELECTED.** Citizens have the right to compete for elective office, including people who oppose the policies of the current government. In 2002, Vietnam held elections for the National Assembly with 759 candidates competing for 498 positions. The election fell short of democracy, however, because the only candidates who were allowed to compete were either members of the Communist Party or had been approved by the party organization.[2]

**3 THE RIGHT OF POLITICAL LEADERS TO COMPETE FOR SUPPORT AND VOTES.** Candidates have an opportunity to conduct campaigns in order to win support. If candidates cannot campaign, voters are unable to make informed choices.

**4 FREE & FAIR ELECTIONS.** All candidates compete under the same set of rules, without legal advantage or disadvantage. Democratic governments respect the outcomes of elections, peacefully stepping down from office and allowing opposition political parties and leaders to take power.

**5 FREEDOM OF ASSOCIATION.** Citizens have the right to form political parties and organize groups. They can attend meetings, participate in political rallies, and take part in peaceful demonstrations.

**6 FREEDOM OF EXPRESSION.** People living in a democracy have the right to express their political views without censorship or fear of government retaliation. Governments that jail their critics are not democracies. For example, an Egyptian court sentenced an opposition political leader to five years in prison at hard labor for allegedly forging the signatures on the petition he used to create his own political party, including those of his wife and father.[3]

**7 ALTERNATIVE SOURCES OF INFORMATION.** The citizens in a democracy have access to information sources that are not controlled by the government. Elections cannot be free and fair if the only information voters have about government policies and candidates is information supplied and controlled by the government.

**8 INSTITUTIONS FOR MAKING PUBLIC POLICIES DEPEND ON VOTES & OTHER EXPRESSIONS OF CITIZEN PREFERENCE.** In a democracy, citizens elect policymakers. Free and fair elections are meaningless if military leaders or religious figures that do not answer to the voters are the real policymakers.[4]

are produced, how they are produced, and for whom they are produced. The proponents of capitalism argue that it is good for consumers because businesses compete to provide quality goods and services at prices that consumers are willing to pay. They believe that capitalism promotes economic growth because only the most efficient business enterprises survive the competition of the marketplace.

**capitalism** an economic system characterized by individual and corporate ownership of the means of production and a market economy based on the supply and demand of goods and services.

# the international
## ENVIRONMENT

t he United States is the preeminent nation in the world, militarily, economically, and culturally. Since the collapse of the Soviet Union in 1991, the United States has become the world's only military superpower. The United States alone accounts for 45 percent of world military expenditures, which in 2007 were estimated at $1.34 trillion. The United Kingdom, China, France, and Japan were the countries with the next largest defense budgets, with each accounting for 4 to 5 percent of total world military expenditures."[5]

The United States is also the foremost economic power with the world's largest and most productive economy, which is more closely tied to the global economy than ever before. Furthermore, American culture permeates the world. American fashion, music, and entertainment are pervasive.

A newsstand in Beijing displays the Chinese version of *Rolling Stone* magazine, demonstrating the pervasiveness of American culture around the world.

# the demographic
## ENVIRONMENT

t he United States has more than 300 million people. The figure on page 19 traces the population growth rate of the United States during the twentieth century. The nation's population increased rapidly in the early decades of the century. Then the Depression years of the 1930s slowed the growth rate sharply. The population growth rate accelerated in the late 1940s and 1950s with the birth of the **baby boom generation**, which is the exceptionally large number of Americans born during the late 1940s, 1950s, and early 1960s.

**baby boom generation** the exceptionally large number of Americans born during the late 1940s, 1950s, and early 1960s.

Many American families delayed having children during the Great Depression of the 1930s and also during World War II in the early 1940s. After the war, the birthrate soared because families reunited and people were optimistic about the future. With the end of the baby boom, the rate of population growth slowed in each subsequent decade until the 1990s, when the nation's population increased more rapidly than it had in any decade since the 1950s. Even though birthrates fell during the 1990s, the population growth rate climbed because of increased immigration.

## Immigration

Immigrants constitute an eighth of the nation's population.[6] Whereas earlier waves of immigration to the United States were primarily from Europe, most recent immigrants come from Latin America or Asia. The primary countries of origin for recent legal immigrants to the United States are, in descending order, Mexico, India, Philippines, and China. The states in which immigrants most frequently settle are California, New York, Texas, Florida, New Jersey, and Illinois.[7]

## Illegal Immigration

More than 11 million people live in the United States illegally. The undocumented population is evenly divided between people who entered the country legally but overstayed temporary visas, such as student visas and tourist visas, and people who crossed the border illegally. More than half of the unauthorized immigrants are from Mexico. One of every nine Mexicans now lives in the United States. A quarter of illegal immigrants are from other Latin American countries, particularly Honduras, El Salvador, Guatemala, Nicaragua, and Brazil. The rest come from Canada and various countries in Europe, Africa, and Asia. The Center for Immigration Studies believes that the population of illegal immigrants in the United States has been falling recently be-

**Average Annual Growth Rate of the American Population**   percent annual growth

POPULATION GROWTH RATES WERE DEPRESSED DURING THE GREAT DEPRESSION.

THE BIRTHRATE BOOMED AFTER WORLD WAR II.

A SURGE OF IMMIGRANTS LED TO A RESURGENCE IN THE POPULATION GROWTH RATE.

1900–1910 1.9

1910–1920 1.4

1920–1930 1.5

1930–1940 0.7

1940–1950 1.3

1950–1960 1.7

1960–1970 1.3

1970–1980 1.1

1980–1990 0.9

1990–2000 1.2

2000–2008* 1.0

*The U.S. Census Bureau estimates that the population of the United States increased at a 1 percent annual rate during the first eight years of the 2000s.

cause of stepped-up immigration law enforcement and because of a slump in the U.S. economy.[8]

People migrate to the United States primarily for economic reasons. Unauthorized workers account for 5 percent of the civilian workforce. They are concentrated in low-wage occupations such as farming, cleaning, construction, and food preparation. Although unauthorized workers in the United States earn only about half as much per person as do American citizens and permanent residents, they make substantially more money than they would earn in their home countries. Nonetheless, most unauthorized families live at or near the poverty level and lack health insurance.[9]

Illegal immigration is controversial. Critics charge that undocumented workers drive down wages for American citizens while overcrowding schools and hospital emergency rooms. They argue that unauthorized immigrants undermine the nation's cultural integrity because they create cultural enclaves that resemble their home countries instead of learning English and adopting the customs of the United States. The opponents of illegal immigration favor tighter border controls, strict enforcement of immigration laws, and punishment for American citizens who provide unauthorized im-

## IMMIGRATION ADVOCATES CONTEND THAT THE UNITED STATES BENEFITS FROM IMMIGRATION, EVEN ILLEGAL IMMIGRATION

migrants with jobs, housing, healthcare, and other services.

Immigration advocates contend that the United States benefits from immigration, even illegal immigration. They argue that undocu-mented workers take jobs that citizens do not want and that they pay more in taxes than they receive in government services. An influx of hard-working, well-motivated manual workers enhances the competitiveness of American industry and provides additional jobs for citizens as managers. The defenders of immigration believe that today's immigrants enrich the nation's culture just as did earlier waves of immigrants from Great Britain, Germany, Ireland, Italy, and Poland. Furthermore, the proponents of immigration contend that most recent immigrants are quick to learn English and eager to become citizens so they can participate in the nation's political life. Immigration advocates believe that the United States should grant legal status to undocumented workers who have helped build the nation's economy while enacting a realistic immigration system to enable foreign workers to enter the country legally to find jobs.

Illegal immigrants are concentrated in low-wage occupations such as farming, cleaning, construction, and food preparation.

# Immigration Policy and Politics in France

After World War II, the government of France encouraged immigration to provide labor for postwar reconstruction. France was experiencing a postwar labor shortage because it suffered 600,000 casualties during the war. It also had the lowest birthrate in Europe between World War I and World War II. The steel, mining, and electric power industries, in particular, needed foreign workers to meet the postwar demand. Many foreign workers took jobs in service industries as well. Over the next 30 years, millions of foreign workers migrated to France. Sometimes they were joined by their families. Immigrants came to France from Southern Europe, especially Italy and Portugal, and from North Africa. Algeria, which had been a French colony prior to its independence in 1962, was the most common North African nation of origin.[10]

The presence in France of a large number of North African immigrants has been controversial. Some French see North Africans as a threat to social cohesion and even national security. North Africans, most of whom are Arab Muslims, are ethnically and culturally different from the French European majority, most of which is non-observant Catholic. Some French also consider North Africans a threat to national security because of the association of some European Islamic immigrants with 9/11 and other terrorist acts. Nonetheless, many European French reject anti-immigrant appeals because they believe that anti-immigrant sentiments contradict the fundamental principles of French democracy, which are Liberté, Égalité, Fraternité (liberty, equality, and brotherhood). They believe that France should embrace the cultural diversity of immigrant populations rather than forcing their assimilation.[11]

France has adopted a series of laws and regulations aimed at addressing the issue of non-European immigration. France has halted the immigration of non-European workers but continues to allow family reunification, which has increased the number of North Africans living in France. The government has threatened to fine employers who use illegal workers. To reduce the size of its immigrant population, France has also offered financial incentives for immigrants to return home, but the program has had little success. France has also attempted to pressure North African immigrants to assimilate into French culture. A 2004 law, for example, bans religious symbols from public schools. This law effectively prevents Muslim girls from covering their heads in French classrooms.[12]

> **THIS LAW EFFECTIVELY PREVENTS MUSLIM GIRLS FROM COVERING THEIR HEADS IN FRENCH CLASSROOMS**

Muslim schoolgirls gather in Strasbourg to protest a ruling banning headscarves in French public schools.

## Questions

1. How important is it for immigrants to adopt the culture of the majority of people in their new country?

2. Are Mexican immigrants in the United States as culturally different as North African immigrants in France?

3. Is opposition to non-European immigration in France (and the United States) racist?

## Population Diversity

The United States is a multiracial/multiethnic society. A 2008 U.S. census report found that the nation's population was 66 percent non-Hispanic white, 15 percent Hispanic, 12 percent African American, 4.4 percent Asian American, 0.8 percent American Indian and Alaska Native, 0.1 percent Native Hawaiian and other Pacific Islanders, and 1.5% two or more races.[13] Nearly 15 percent of the nation's population identified as Hispanic (who may be of any race). Hispanics were the most rapidly growing American ethnic group during the 1990s, increasing by more than 50 percent. Demographers predict that Hispanics will make up a fourth of the nation's population by 2050.[14]

# The Face of AMERICA

**66% NON-HISPANIC WHITE**

**15% HISPANIC**
**12% AFRICAN AMERICAN**
**4.4% ASIAN AMERICAN**
**0.8% AMERICAN INDIAN AND ALASKA NATIVE**
**0.1% NATIVE HAWAIIAN AND OTHER PACIFIC ISLANDERS**
**1.5% TWO OR MORE RACES**

The population of the United States has been shifting to the South and the West, the region known as the **Sunbelt**, and away from the Northeast and Midwest, the **Frostbelt**. In 1970, a majority of the nation's population, 52 percent, lived in the Frostbelt. The population has subsequently shifted steadily to the South and West. In 2000, 58 percent of Americans lived in the Sunbelt.[15] The Sunbelt population is growing because of relatively higher birthrates in the region, immigration from abroad, and intrastate migration from the Frostbelt.

Population changes have affected the political balance in the U.S. House of Representatives. Because the Northeast and Midwest have lost population, they have lost seats in the House. After the 2000 U.S. Census, New York and Pennsylvania each lost two House seats, and eight other Frostbelt states lost one seat each. In contrast, the South and West gained seats. Arizona, Texas, Florida, and Georgia gained two seats each in the House. Four other Sunbelt states added one seat apiece.

**Sunbelt** the southern and western regions of the United States.

**Frostbelt** the northeastern and midwestern regions of the United States.

Sunbelt politicians have dominated the race for the White House; every elected president from 1964–2004 was from the Sunbelt.

Ronald Reagan
(1980 and 1984)

Richard Nixon
(1968 and 1972)

Lyndon Johnson
(1964)

George H.W. Bush
(1988)

Bill Clinton
(1992 and 1996)

George W. Bush
(2000 and 2004)

Jimmy Carter
(1976)

# **take**action

## A CHANGING NATION, CHANGING COMMUNITIES >>

Data from the 2000 U.S. Census show that the United States is changing. The population is both aging and growing more diverse. Whereas the huge baby boom generation is aging, immigration, especially from Latin America and Asia, is transforming the face of America. The economy is changing as well. "Smokestack industries," such as automobile manufacturing and steel production, are in decline; high-tech industries, such as biotechnology and robotics, are expanding.

Is your local community changing as well? Your assignment is to research the ways in which your community has changed by interviewing one or more people who are longtime residents. The individuals you interview should be persons who have lived in the community for at least 15 or 20 years. They can be relatives, friends, coworkers, or classmates. Your questions should cover the following topics:

1. **Population change.** Has the population of your area grown? Have people immigrated to your community from other states or other nations? How has the racial/ethnic makeup of the population changed? Has the population as a whole grown younger or older?

2. **Economic change.** Has the mix of businesses and industries changed? Have any major employers gone out of business? Are there new industries?

3. **Cultural change.** Does the community have places of worship for religious faiths new to the area? Are there new types of restaurants? Do grocery stores carry different varieties of produce to match the tastes of new residents? Does the community celebrate different or additional holidays and festivals?

Take careful notes on what you are told because your instructor plans to organize a class discussion around the research that you and other students have completed. The instructor will ask students to relate the information from their interviews and then analyze the impact of socioeconomic change on the policymaking process. Prepare for the discussion by considering the following questions:

1. Would you expect different issues to appear on the policy agenda today as compared with 20 years ago because of the changes that have taken place in your community?

2. Do you think the capacity of government to respond to policy demands has changed?

3. Would you expect that the community's standard for evaluating government performance has changed?

## 1980–2008
## GROWTH OF HISPANIC POPULATION
### HISPANIC POPULATION AND PERCENTAGE OF TOTAL POPULATION

Hispanic Population (millions)

- 1980: 14.6
- 1990: 22.4
- 2000: 35.3
- 2008: 46.9

Hispanic Population (percent)

- 1980: 6.4
- 1990: 9.0
- 2000: 12.5
- 2008: 15.4

Based on the 2008 U.S. Census.

Stock markets in Japan and around the world tumbled during the American financial crisis of late 2008.

# the economic
## ENVIRONMENT

the United States has the largest economy in the world. The **gross domestic product (GDP)** is the total value of goods and services produced by a nation's economy in a year, excluding transac-

U.S. Census Bureau, "Gross National Income (GNI) by Country," *2009 Statistical Abstract*, available at www.census.gov.

tions with foreign countries. The U.S. GDP stood at $13.8 trillion at the end of 2007. No other country's economy is nearly as large. Even though the United States contains only 4.6 percent of the world's population, it generates 21.1 percent of world economic output.[16]

The figure at left shows GDP **per capita** (per person) adjusted for purchasing power differences for Canada, Germany, Japan, Mexico, the United Kingdom, and the United States. Because the cost of goods and services varies from country to

**gross domestic product (GDP)** the total value of goods and services produced by a nation's economy in a year, excluding transactions with foreign countries.

**per capita** per person.

**standard of living** the goods and services affordable to and available to the residents of a nation.

country, the same amount of money does not purchase the same quantity of goods and services from one nation to another. Adjusting GDP per capita to reflect differences in purchasing power is a good measure of a nation's **standard of living**, which is

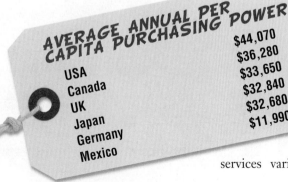

AVERAGE ANNUAL PER CAPITA PURCHASING POWER

| | |
|---|---|
| USA | $44,070 |
| Canada | $36,280 |
| UK | $33,650 |
| Japan | $32,840 |
| Germany | $32,680 |
| Mexico | $11,990 |

a term that refers to the goods and services affordable by, and available to, the residents of a nation. As the figure indicates, the average American enjoys greater purchasing power than people living in the other countries listed in the table. Meanwhile, the standard of living in the United States is substantially higher than it is in Mexico and other **developing countries**, which are nations with relatively low levels of per capita income.

## Global Economy

The United States is part of a **global economy**, which is the integration of national economies into a world economic system in which companies compete worldwide for suppliers and markets. International treaties and agreements have reduced the barriers to trade among the world's countries. The move toward free trade has allowed American companies to compete for business abroad, but it has also forced them to compete at home against overseas competitors.

Some American companies and workers have prospered in the global economy. American agriculture and major retailers such as Wal-Mart have benefited from international trade because their markets (and profits) have grown.[17] Companies that have lowered their cost of doing business through outsourcing or the

> **" American companies have begun to cut costs by outsourcing "**

use of modern technology have also done well. Their investors have profited from higher stock prices, and their managers and executives have reaped the reward in higher salaries and bonuses. Skilled workers who understand and can operate the latest technology in their fields are in high demand, especially workers who have the ability to adapt quickly as technology changes.

In contrast, international trade has been a disaster for workers in fields that have been unable to compete against low-wage competition from abroad. Less expensive transportation and communication systems

make it possible to produce goods in countries where production costs are low and then transport those goods to markets worldwide. How can an American manufacturer afford to pay $15 an hour to low-skill assembly workers in the United States if low-skill workers in Indonesia, China, or the Caribbean will do the same work for less than $2 an hour? The American firm must either move its production process to a country with lower wage costs or lose market share because it cannot compete. American companies have also begun to cut costs by outsourcing information technology work and some business process functions to India, China, and Russia—countries that have a large number of college-educated workers who work for much lower wages

**developing countries** nations with relatively low levels of per capita income.

**global economy** the integration of national economies into a world economic system in which companies compete worldwide for suppliers and markets.

## btw...

Outsourcing may be more prevalent in your daily life than you realize. In 2006, about 50 McDonald's restaurants began experimenting with "remote order-taking." Customers at drive-through windows from Hawaii to Mississippi were, in fact, placing their orders to a call center in California. The call centers take advantage of ever-cheaper communications technology and specially trained minimum-wage employees to field and place the orders over the Internet. Saving just a few seconds on each order can add up in the volume of extra sales, and, thus far, the system appears to be improving accuracy and cutting costs.

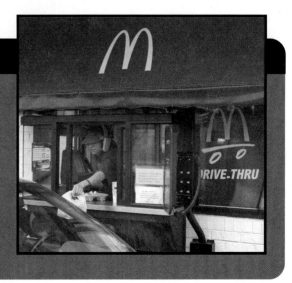

than their counterparts in the United States. Computer programming jobs that pay $60,000 to $80,000 a year in the United States can be performed for as little as $9,000 a year in China, $6,000 in India, and $5,000 in Russia.[18]

Low-skill, poorly educated American workers have also been damaged by technological change. Modern technology has enabled companies to replace low-skill workers with machines, which generate the same output, or more, with fewer workers. Between 1979 and 2000, U.S. factory output nearly doubled even though the number of manufacturing jobs fell by more than 2 million. A quarter century ago, General Motors (GM) employed 454,000 workers to manufacture 5 million vehicles. Today, GM produces the same number of cars and trucks, but its payroll has shrunk to 118,000 employees.[19] American workers who lose their jobs because of international trade and technological change usually find new positions, but these new jobs often come without benefits and typically pay $2 or more an hour less than their old jobs.[20]

## Income Distribution

As the U.S. economy has changed, the gap between the rich and other income groups has widened. The figure below shows the share of national income earned by each of five income groups, from the poorest fifth of American families through the wealthiest fifth. Over a 26-year period from 1980 through 2006, the proportion of national income received by the wealthiest fifth of the population increased from 41.4 percent to 50.5 percent. The rich got richer. In the meantime, the share of national income earned by the four other groups of families declined. In particular, the share of income earned by the poorest families fell by more than 35 percent, from 5.3 percent of the total in 1980 to 3.4 percent in 2006. The poor got poorer.

Economist Robert H. Frank attributes the growth of income inequality to changes in the economy and in tax policy. Professor Frank says that the United States has a

winner-take-all economy in which small differences in performance often translate into huge differences in economic reward. Corporate executives, sports stars, and well-known entertainers earn huge paychecks, many times greater than the earnings of ordinary workers, average athletes, and entertainers without "star power." In the meantime, income tax reductions adopted during the Ronald Reagan and George W. Bush administrations significantly reduced income tax rates for upper-income earners, effectively shifting wealth toward the top of the income ladder.[21]

Household income in the United States varies, depending on race, ethnicity, residence, region, and gender. Whites and Asian Americans/Pacific Islanders are better off than Latinos and African Americans. Incomes vary depending on whether families live in metropolitan or non-metropolitan areas. In 2008, the average household income for families living in metropolitan areas was higher than it was for families located outside big cities. Suburban households had higher incomes than families living in the inner city. Family incomes differ based on region. In 2008, household income was lower in the South than

| DATE | POOREST 5TH | SECOND 5TH | THIRD 5TH | FOURTH 5TH | WEALTHIEST 5TH |
|------|------------|-----------|-----------|------------|----------------|
| 1980 | 5.3 % | 11.6 % | 17.6 % | 24.4 % | 41.4 % |
| 1985 | 4.8 % | 11.0 % | 16.9 % | 24.3 % | 43.1 % |
| 1990 | 4.6 % | 10.8 % | 16.6 % | 23.8 % | 44.3 % |
| 1995 | 4.4 % | 10.1 % | 15.6 % | 23.2 % | 46.5 % |
| 2000 | 4.3 % | 9.8 % | 15.5 % | 22.8 % | 47.4 % |
| 2006 | 3.4 % | 8.6 % | 14.5 % | 22.9 % | 50.5 % |

**SHARE OF NATIONAL INCOME RECEIVED BY EACH FIFTH OF FAMILIES, 1980–2006**

U.S. Census Bureau, *2008 Statistical Abstract*, available at www.census.gov; U.S. Census Bureau, "Income and Earnings Summary Measures by Selected Characteristics: 2005 and 2006," *Income, Poverty, and Health Insurance Coverage in the United States: 2006*, available at www.census.gov.

# Changing Faces of Republican and Democratic Parties

**Do the parties still represent their mid- to late-twentieth-century constituencies? How have they adapted to meet technological and political change?**

**Whom do the parties truly represent? Is there really significant change in whom the parties actually represent and, if so, what is the reason?**

**Overview:** When voting for elective offices, research indicates that voters take their cues from party labels and cast their votes accordingly. The last 15 years, however, have seen significant changes in the American and global political landscape, including the fall of the Soviet Union, the war on terror, the impeachment of a president, and a contested presidential election decided by an arguably partisan Supreme Court. These events have had a striking impact on how Americans have come to view their party loyalties, and the two major parties are attempting to assess the change in the American political arena.

Generally speaking, certain groups of voters are associated with either one of the two major parties, and the parties themselves claim to represent these same voters. Voting studies demonstrate that there is truth to this contention. For example, in the 2006 midterm election, the Joint Center for Political and Economic Studies reports that 89 percent of black Americans who voted, voted for the Democratic Party; and Pew Research shows that 55 percent of those who attend worship services regularly voted for the Republican Party. But with the momentous changes in global and American politics, can office-seekers continue to count on the support of traditional voting blocs?

American politics is now considered to be polarized between the "blue" (Democratic-leaning) and "red" (Republican-leaning) states and precincts, and the country is understood to be in the middle of a historic national dialogue concerning its future and values. The 2006 midterm election is instructive. The Democratic Party ran on a traditional Republican platform of earmark reform and less government spending, and the Republicans ran on a traditional Democratic party platform of benefit provisions, such as the prescription drug bill. With changes such as these, how is a voter to take his or her cue?

## supporting · a demographic shift in party affiliation

**research indicates that American youth may be changing party affiliation.** For example, a 2003 Harvard University poll shows that 31 percent of college students consider themselves Republicans, whereas 27 percent consider themselves Democrats, a reversal of trends over the last 30 years.

**the parties have modified their policy position to represent changes in American political values.** For instance, the Democratic Party's support of welfare reform, limited government, and middle-class tax cuts are much different than the Democratic policies created in Lyndon Johnson's Great Society of the mid-1960s.

**american voters are responding to changes in global and domestic politics.** For example, the war on terror has focused the electorate on foreign affairs, and the results of the 2006 midterm elections may be viewed as a referendum of the Bush administration's management of international policy.

## against · a demographic shift in party affiliation

**in politics, it is normal for there to be temporary shifts in voter allegiance.** Take, for example, the "Reagan Democrats." President Reagan was supported by most Americans—both Republicans and Democrats—in his attempt to end the Cold War, but once the Cold War ended, Reagan Democrats began to vote for the Democratic Party out of concern for domestic politics.

**once the rhetoric used by the major parties is swept aside, one finds that the parties still represent their traditional post–World War II constituencies.** The parties do represent their respective voting blocs. For example, the Democratic Party still champions minority rights, and the Republican Party is still considered to represent religious values.

**an examination of the party platforms shows that the parties are concerned with representing the issue and policy preferences of their members.** For example, the Democratic Party platform advocates the use of international institutions and allies in the prosecution of the war on terror, and the Republican Party platform advocates keeping the Bush administration tax cuts while cutting government spending.

# 2010 Census Count Called Vital for Texas

**DALLAS MORNING NEWS**

**JUNE 9, 2009**

SAN ANTONIO—Texas stands to lose millions of dollars in federal money for health care and schools if the 2010 census undercounts residents as it has in the past, some officials say.

In the last census, 373,567 Texans, or 1.76 percent of the state's population in 2000, were not counted, according to an audit done then. The undercount could have resulted in Texas missing out on $1 billion in federal funds from 2002 to 2012 if a recalculation hadn't been done.

The undercount was most pronounced in border counties, where unincorporated neighborhoods known as *colonias* are located and where residents are often in most need of aid. "We in South Texas were hurt with the 2000 census because the *colonias* were undercounted in a drastic way," Juan Vargas, Webb County economic development director, said in the *San Antonio Express-News*.

Robert Groves, President Barack Obama's nominee for director of the U.S. Census Bureau, has identified multiple-family homes and language barriers as an issue for every census. Return home visits by census-takers, though expensive, are highly successful, he said.

An accurate count is important for other reasons, too. Economic development officials use the data to lure businesses and new jobs. "It's part of our bread and butter," said Patrick Jankowski, vice president of research for the Greater Houston Partnership. "If the census data didn't exist, my job would be nearly impossible." The data allow communities to compare and market themselves with other areas when employers are interested in moving or expanding to a Texas city.

### About the 2010 Census (Available at www.census.gov)

*What:* The census is a count of everyone residing in the United States: in all 50 states, the District of Columbia, Puerto Rico, and the U.S. Island Areas.

*Who:* All residents of the United States must be counted. This includes people of all ages, races, ethnic groups, citizens, and non-citizens. People should be counted where they live and sleep most of the year.

*When:* Every 10 years; the next census occurs in 2010.

*Why:* The U.S. Constitution (Article I, Section 2) mandates a headcount of everyone residing in the United States. The population totals determine each state's congressional representation. The numbers also affect funding in your community and help inform decision-makers about how your community is changing.

*How:* Census questionnaires will be mailed or delivered to every household in the United States in March 2010. Households that still do not respond will be called or visited by a Census Bureau worker.

↗ CRITICAL THINKING QUESTIONS:

- If you were the mayor of a large city, would you be concerned about the possibility of a census undercount? Why or why not?
- Why are some people reluctant to cooperate with census takers?
- Why do some people believe that Latinos in particular are undercounted by the census?

**>> END**

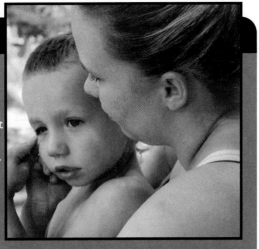

## btw...

In 2008, the Federal government ment defined poverty level for a family of four as $21,200 per year. 19 percent of all American children live below this poverty level. Research indicates that the federal poverty level should actually be raised to about twice the current level. Using that standard, about 39 percent of all children (about 28 million) live in low-income families. Until 1999, the number of low-income families had been declining. Since 2000, however, the number has increased by about 15 percent. As the economy turns downward, a further increase in this number of children living in poverty can be expected.

Source: National Center for Children in Poverty

it was in any other region of the country. Household income was highest in the Northeast. Income also varies by gender. In 2008, the average income of male, full-time, year-round workers was $46,367 compared to $35,745 for women.[22]

Income differences among racial and ethnic groups, and between men and women, reflect disparities in education and training, social factors, and discrimination. As a group, Asian Americans and whites are better educated than African Americans and Latinos. Women often fall behind their male counterparts on the career ladder because many women leave the workforce for years to raise children. Jobs that are traditionally held by women, such as nursing and education, typically pay less than jobs that are traditionally male. Finally, many observers believe that the incomes of women and minorities lag behind those of white males because of employment discrimination.

## Poverty

The government measures poverty on a subsistence basis. The **poverty threshold** is the amount of money an individual or family needs to purchase basic necessities, such as food, clothing, healthcare, shelter,

**poverty threshold** the amount of money an individual or family needs to purchase basic necessities, such as food, clothing, healthcare, shelter, and transportation.

## INCOME AND POVERTY RATE IN THE UNITED STATES, BY ETHNICITY

MEDIAN HOUSEHOLD INCOME, United States 2008

| | 65,000 |
| | 60,000 |
| | 55,000 |
| | 50,000 |
| | 45,000 |
| | 40,000 |
| | 35,000 |
| | 30,000 |

Asian American — White — Hispanic — African American

POVERTY RATE

25% — 20% — 15% — 10% — 5% — 0

Asian American 11.8% — White 8.6% — Hispanic 23.2% — African American 24.7%

the economic environment **29**

and transportation. The actual dollar amount varies with family size and rises with inflation. In 2008, the official government poverty threshold was $21,200 for a family of four.[23] Nearly 40 million Americans lived in poverty in 2007, 13.2 percent of the population.[24]

Although the poverty rate for racial and ethnic minority groups and for families headed by women has declined over the last 50 years, it is still higher than for other groups. In 2008, the poverty rate for Latinos, African Americans, and Asian Americans stood at 23.2 percent, 24.7 percent, and 11.8 percent, respectively, compared with 8.6 percent for whites. Poverty also affects children and families headed by

women in disproportionate numbers. In 2008, 19 percent of the nation's children under 18 lived in families that were poor. The poverty rate for families headed by women was 28.7 percent.[25]

More than 46 million Americans, 15.4 percent of the population, lack health insurance coverage. Government-funded health insurance programs—Medicare, Medicaid, and military healthcare—cover about a fourth of the population. Almost 60 percent of the population enjoy health insurance through their employers, although that figure has been falling because some companies have dropped coverage for existing employees or have

think — What could the government do to reduce poverty?

chosen not to offer coverage to new employees.[26] Most of the people who lack health insurance work in jobs that do not provide coverage. These people also have too much income to be eligible for Medicaid and are too young to qualify for Medicare. Without health insurance, they and their families must do without healthcare, pay for health services out of pocket, or go to hospital emergency rooms.

# CONCLUSION
# the cultural, international,
## & SOCIOECONOMIC CONTEXT FOR POLICYMAKING

the cultural, international, demographic, and economic environments affect every stage of the policymaking process.

## Agenda Building

The policymaking environment creates the context in which individuals and groups raise issues to the policy agenda. Dramatic events can have an immediate impact on the policy agenda. For example, the startling terrorist attacks of September 11, 2001 focused the nation's attention on the issues of national defense and homeland security. Other developments, such as the aging of the nation's population, are less dramatic but nonetheless important. As the baby boom generation reaches retirement, the policy agenda will increasingly reflect the interests and demands of

older adults. Healthcare and retirement income security will claim a higher place on the policy agenda. Patterns of income distribution have an impact on attitudes about government programs. African Americans and Latinos are more likely to favor government healthcare and income security programs than are whites and Asian Americans because the former are more in need of government assistance.

## Policy Formulation and Adoption

The environment has an impact on policy formulation. Political culture limits the range of acceptable policy alternatives available to policymakers. Policy solutions that are widely

**POLITICAL CULTURE LIMITS THE RANGE OF ACCEPTABLE POLICY ALTERNATIVES**

perceived as undemocratic or contrary to the nation's capitalist traditions are not politically feasible. The nation's economy affects policy formulation as well. A healthy economy generates tax revenues that can be used to tackle policy problems, whereas a stagnant economy reduces the options of policymakers. Defense spending reflects the perceived level of threat to American interests in the international environment.

Policy adoption is affected by environmental factors. Consider the impact of the population aging on the budget process. The aging of the population is draining the budget of resources that could be used to support new government pro-

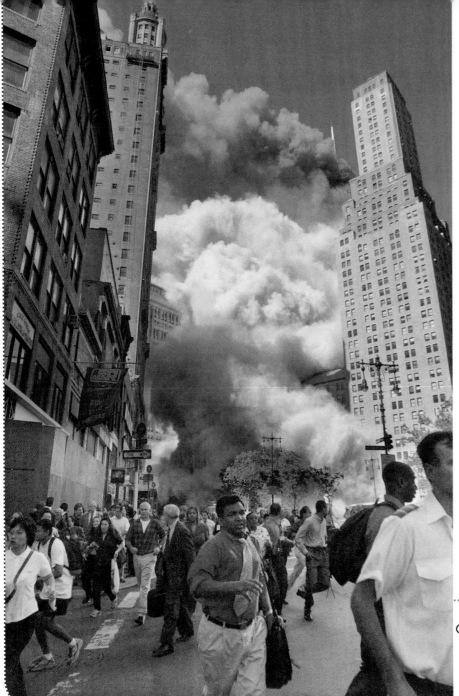

grams. When the baby boom generation retires, the cost of programs targeting the elderly will consume so much of the budget that they will crowd out most other spending.

## Policy Implementation and Evaluation

Cultural, international, demographic, and economic factors affect policy implementation. The ability of the government to implement expensive policies successfully may depend on long-term economic growth sufficient to generate revenue. For example, illegal immigration from Mexico may slow in the next few years because the Mexican economy is growing, while the size of the Mexican population is increasing more slowly. [27]

Environmental factors also influence policy evaluation. Americans evaluate policies from the perspectives of the broad political culture—capitalism and democracy. Groups of Americans that are numerous and groups that are economically advantaged are better positioned to make their voices heard in evaluating policies than smaller groups with relatively fewer resources.

New Yorkers flee as the World Trade Center collapses on September 11, 2001. These events quickly brought issues of national defense and homeland security to the top of the nation's policy agenda.

the THINK SPOT
www.thethinkspot.com

**1** Why is the average age of the American population increasing?

A. The immigration rate is increasing.

B. The large baby boom generation is nearing retirement age.

C. The birthrate is increasing.

D. All of the above

**2** A system of government in which ultimate political authority is vested in the people is the definition of which of the following terms?

A. Policymaking environment

B. Political culture

C. Democracy

D. Capitalism

**3** According to Robert A. Dahl, which of the following is a criterion of democracy?

A. Candidates have the opportunity to conduct political campaigns in order to win political support.

B. All businesses and industry are privately owned.

C. All citizens enjoy a minimum standard of living, including access to healthcare.

D. All of the above

**4** According to Robert A. Dahl's criteria of democracy, which of the following nations would NOT be considered a democracy?

A. In Country A, the government controls the news media and ensures that information damaging to the government is suppressed.

B. In Country B, the government owns and operates the airlines and the railroads.

C. In Country C, the income gap between the wealthiest and poorest sectors of society is huge.

D. All of the above

**5** Which of the following is characteristic of a democracy?

A. People have the right to criticize the government.

B. People have the right to join unions and other interest groups.

C. People have the right to run against current officeholders.

D. All of the above

**6** An economic system characterized by individual and corporate ownership of the means of production, and a market economy based on the supply and demand of goods and services is a definition of which of the following?

A. Constitutional monarchy

B. Capitalism

C. Democracy

D. Absolute monarchy

**7** Which of the following nations spends the most on its military?

A. The United States

B. China

C. Russia

D. India

**8** Which of the following nations has the largest economy?

A. The United States

B. China

C. Russia

D. India

**9** Which of the following statements is true about the baby boom generation?

A. The baby boom generation is smaller than preceding or succeeding generations.

B. The baby boom generation retired just before 2000.

C. The baby boom generation was born during the late 1940s, 1950s, and early 1960s.

D. None of the above

**10** Which of the following statements is true about population growth in the 1990s?

A. The population growth rate increased during the decade largely because of immigration.

B. The population growth rate increased during the decade largely because the birthrate increased.

C. The population growth rate fell during the decade because the baby boom generation began to die off.

D. The population growth rate fell during the decade because the birthrate declined.

**11** Which of the following countries is NOT an important source of recent immigration to the United States?

A. Mexico

B. China

C. Great Britain

D. India

**12** Which racial/ethnic group grew the most rapidly during the 1990s?

A. Latinos

B. Whites

C. African Americans

D. Asian Americans

**13** After the 2000 Census, California gained seats in the U.S. House of Representatives. Knowing that fact, which of the following statements must therefore be true?

A. California is the most populous state in the nation.

B. The population of California increased at a faster rate in the 1990s than did the population of the United States as a whole.

C. California is in the Sunbelt.

D. All of the above

**14** The integration of national economies into a world economic system in which companies compete worldwide for suppliers and markets is the definition for which of the following terms?

A. Capitalism

B. Gross domestic product

C. Democracy

D. Global economy

**15** How have low-skilled workers been affected by the global economy?

A. They have been harmed because global competition has led to price increases for many of the products that they purchase.

B. They have been harmed because American companies cannot afford to pay high wages to low-skill workers and still compete effectively against foreign competitors with lower wage costs.

C. They have been helped because the number of good jobs available to low-skill workers has increased.

D. All of the above

**16** Which of the following statements is true about income distribution in the United States?

A. Since 1980, the proportion of national income received by the wealthiest fifth of the population has increased.

B. Since 1980, the proportion of income received by the poorest fifth of the population has fallen.

C. The income gap between the wealthiest and poorest families has been increasing.

D. All of the above

**17** Median household income in the United States is highest for which of the following groups?

A. Asian Americans

B. Whites

C. African Americans

D. Latinos

**18** Which of the following statements is true?

A. Household income is higher in the South than it is in any other region.

B. On average, women earn more than men.

C. The average income for people living in metropolitan areas is lower than it is for people living outside metropolitan areas.

D. None of the above

**19** How is the official poverty threshold determined?

A. The poverty threshold is set at 30 percent of the average household income. Anyone earning less than 30 percent of the average is considered poor.

B. The official poverty rate was set in 1950 at $8,000 and changes each year based on the inflation rate.

C. The poverty threshold is based on the amount of money an individual or family needs to purchase basic necessities.

D. People declare whether they are poor based on their perception of their ability to buy the things they need.

**20** Which of the following statements is true about poverty in America?

A. Nearly half of African Americans and Latinos live in poverty.

B. Nearly a third of all Americans have incomes below the official poverty level.

C. More than a fourth of families headed by women are below the official poverty level.

D. All of the above

KNOW *the* **score**

18–20 correct: Congratulations! You are well informed!

15–17 correct: Your political knowledge is a bit low—be sure to review the key terms and visit TheThinkSpot.

<14 correct: Reread the chapter more thoroughly.

1. B; 2. C; 3. A; 4. A; 5. D; 6. B; 7. A; 8. A; 9. C; 10. A; 11. C; 12. A; 13. B; 14. D; 15. B; 16. D; 17. A; 18. D; 19. C; 20. C

# 2 AMERICAN

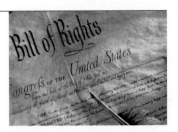

The State Children's Health Insurance Program (SCHIP) is a federal program designed to provide health insurance to children from low-income families. Although both Democrats and Republicans supported SCHIP when it was created, the effort to renew the program proved controversial. Whereas Democrats favored expanding SCHIP to reduce the number of uninsured children, Republicans opposed the expansion as a backdoor attempt to enact government-run healthcare. Congress, which was controlled by Democrats, passed SCHIP expansion legislation in 2008, but Republican President George W. Bush vetoed the measure, and Congress was unable to override the veto. In 2008, the political landscape changed with the election of Barack Obama, a proponent of expanding SCHIP. Congress quickly passed the expansion legislation in early 2009, and President Obama signed it into law.

The battle over SCHIP illustrates the interplay between the U.S. Constitution and contemporary politics. The Constitution establishes the roles officials play in the policy process, determines the powers they can exercise, and outlines the procedures for policy adoption. A measure cannot become law unless it passes both houses of Congress and the president signs it into law or allows it to become law without signature. If the president vetoes a bill, the Constitution provides that it can become law only if both houses of Congress vote to override the veto by a two-thirds margin. SCHIP expansion failed in 2008 because the president vetoed the measure and Congress was unable to override the veto. The measure became law in early 2009 because the election of a proponent of SCHIP expansion as president changed the policymaking environment.

# CONSTITUTION

# background
## OF THE CONSTITUTION

English colonists advertised opposition to the hated Stamp Act on everyday items, such as this teapot.

**a** **Constitution** is the fundamental law by which a state or nation is organized and governed, and to which ordinary legislation must conform. It establishes the framework of government, assigns the powers and duties of government bodies, and defines the relationship between the people and their government. The U.S. Constitution, which is more than 220 years of age, is the oldest written national constitution still in effect in the world today.

## Historical Setting

The Americans who wrote the Constitution of 1787 had lived through two difficult periods: the late colonial period under British rule and the period under the government created by the Articles of Confederation. To a considerable degree, the Constitution was a reaction to these two experiences.

**The Colonial Period.** The American colonists were initially satisfied with the political relationship with Great Britain. Preoccupied with matters at home, the British authorities allowed the Americans a substantial measure of self-government. Each colony had a governor, appointed by the king, and a legislative assembly whose members were locally elected. The colonial assemblies could levy taxes, appropriate money, approve or reject the governor's appointments, and pass laws for their colony. Although the governor had the power to veto legislation, the assemblies exercised considerable leverage over the governor by virtue of their control of the budget. This **power of**

**the purse**, which is the authority to raise and spend money, made the locally elected legislative assemblies the dominant bodies of colonial government.

After 1763, the British chose to reorganize their colonial system. The French and Indian War (1756–1763), in which the British and the Americans fought against the French and their Indian allies for control of North America, left the British with a sizable war debt. The British also faced the problem of governing Canada and enforcing treaties with the Indians, which limited westward expansion by the colonists.

British officials decided that the American colonists should pay part of the cost of defending and administering the empire in North America. The British imposed new taxes, and to enforce their policies, they increased the number of officials in North America and permanently stationed troops in the colonies.

To the surprise of the British, the Americans were outraged. Over the years, the colonists had grown accustomed to self-government and they were unwilling to surrender the privilege. They regarded the new policies as a violation of local traditions and an abridgment of their rights as British citizens. Before 1763, the only taxes the Americans paid to London were duties on trade, and the colonists interpreted the duties as measures to regulate

**constitution** the fundamental law by which a state or nation is organized and governed, and to which ordinary legislation must conform.
**power of the purse** the authority to raise and spend money.

commerce rather than taxes. Now, however, London attempted to impose levies that were clearly taxes. The Americans argued that as English citizens they could be taxed only by their own elected representatives and not by the British Parliament. No taxation without representation, they declared. This argument made no sense to the British. In their view, every member of Parliament represented every British citizen; it was irrelevant that no Americans sat in Parliament. The dispute over taxation and other issues worsened, leading eventually to revolution and American independence.

During the Revolutionary War, the American colonies became the United States, loosely allied under the leadership of the Continental Congress, which was a **unicameral** (one-house) **legislature** in which each state had a single vote. Although the Continental Congress had no official governing authority, it declared America's independence, raised an army, appointed George Washington commander in chief,

coined money, and negotiated with foreign nations. The Continental Congress also drafted a plan for national union. This plan, known as the Articles of Confederation, went into effect in 1781, upon approval by the 13 states.

**The Articles of Confederation.** The Articles of Confederation created a league of friendship, a "perpetual union" of states, with a unicameral congress. Although state legislatures could send as many as seven delegates to the Confederation Congress, each state possessed a single vote, and 9 states (of 13) had to approve decisions. Amending the Articles required unanimous approval of the states. The Articles provided for no independent national executive or national judiciary.

Alexander Hamilton, the first secretary of the Treasury, was one of the strongest critics of the weak central government of the Articles of Confederation. He was one of the leaders of the movement to strengthen the national government.

**unicameral legislature** a one-house legislature.

## btw...

While residents of the District of Columbia do vote in the presidential election, they have only a non-voting delegate in the House of Representatives and no representation in the Senate.

The slogan "Taxation Without Representation" was added to D.C. license plates in 2000 to protest the District's lack of representation in Congress. In 2008, the District also attempted to incorporate the slogan into its design for the 50 State Quarters program, but it was rejected by the U.S. Mint. Do you think the half million residents of the District of Columbia are fairly represented in Congress?

Washington, D.C.
D.C. GOVT.
★★★
Fleet
DC 2368
TAXATION WITHOUT REPRESENTATION

The states were the primary units of government in the new nation rather than the Confederation government. Each of the 13 states had its own state constitution that established a framework for state government. These state constitutions typically provided for a **bicameral (two-house) legislature**, a governor, and a court system. Because Americans feared executive power as a source of tyranny, they adopted state constitutions that limited the powers of state governors, making legislatures the dominant branch of state government.[1]

The Americans who wrote the Articles of Confederation were determined to create a government whose powers would be strictly limited. Having just freed themselves from British rule, they did not want to create a strong national government that might become as oppressive as the British colonial government. The Americans who wrote the Articles apparently went too far, however, because the Confederation proved too weak to deal effectively with the new nation's problems. It lacked the power to collect taxes from individuals, having to rely instead on contributions from the states. When state governments failed to pay—as many did—the Confederation government was left without financial support. The Confederation also lacked authority to regulate commerce, prohibit states from printing worthless currency, enforce the provisions of the peace treaty with Great Britain, or even defend itself against rebellion. When small farmers in western Massachusetts engaged in an armed uprising against the government over debt and taxes in 1786–1787, the Confederation government failed to respond. After a private army finally crushed the insurrection, which was known as Shay's Rebellion after its leader, Daniel Shay, public opinion began to coalesce in favor of a stronger national government than the one provided by the Articles of Confederation.

Popular protest in the United States did not end with Shay's Rebellion. Ironically, a strong central government became the protector of the right to protest. Consider the modern cause of animal rights. Animal rights activists have protested at fashion shows, dumped dead animals on fashionable restaurant tables, and thrown red paint on fur coats. Fashion magazine editors have also been taken to task for encouraging the wearing of furs. A stronger national government has been able to suppress armed rebellions, but it has also taken on the cause of protecting people's right to protest.

**bicameral legislature** a two-house legislature.

# "HERE'S THE REST OF YOUR FUR COAT."

*Singer Shirley Manson and other high-profile celebrities, such as Alicia Silverstone and Pamela Anderson, embrace their constitutional right to protest by engaging in public demonstrations or creating controversial advertisements to protest the wearing of furs.*

# John Locke & American Political Thought

*The colonists used Locke's theories to justify their revolution and inform the creation of their new government.*

## THE REVOLUTION

Locke's theory of revolution offered the perfect theoretical rationale for the American Revolution. In the Declaration of Independence, which is reprinted in the Appendix of this text, the founders used Locke's theory to justify independence from Great Britain. The Americans were justified in revolting against the king, the founders declared, because the king deprived them of their rights to "Life, Liberty, and the pursuit of Happiness."

## THE NEW GOVERNMENT

Locke provided a theoretical basis for the creation of a national government that could be a positive force in society instead of just a necessary evil. According to Locke, the people create government in order to accomplish certain goals, that is, to protect life, liberty, and property from the dangers inherent in a state of nature. In theory, then, government can play an active, positive role in society.

## THE BILL OF RIGHTS

Locke's concept of natural rights offered a theoretical foundation for limiting government authority over the individual. The doctrine of natural rights is the belief that individual rights transcend the power of government. People create government to protect their rights, not to abridge them. Locke's theory of natural rights provided a basis for a bill of rights, which is a constitutional document guaranteeing individual rights and liberties.

Actor Paul Giamatti portrayed John Adams, one of the most influential Founding Fathers, in the HBO miniseries *John Adams*.

## American Political Thought

The Americans who wrote the Constitution were educated people who studied the important political writings of their day. The work of Englishman John Locke (1632–1704) was particularly influential. In his *Second Treatise on Government* (1689), Locke declared that people in their natural state were born free and equal, and possessed certain natural rights, which were life, liberty, and property. Unfortunately, Locke said, evil people disrupt the good life of the state of nature by conspiring to deprive others of their life, liberty, or property. In order to protect their rights, people voluntarily join together to form governments. The power of government, then, stems from the consent of the governed, who entrust the government with responsibility for protecting their lives, liberty, and possessions. Should government fail in this task, Locke declared, the people have the right to revolt and institute a new government.

Although the nation's founders frequently cited the writings of European philosophers such as Locke, they did more than just apply the theories developed in Europe to the United States. They created a nation and wrote a Constitution that was also based on American events, experiences, and ideas.[2]

The most important element of American political thought was the changing conception of the nature of politics and government. At the time of the Revolution, American political theorists believed that politics was a never-ending struggle between the people and the government. In their view, the people were virtuous and united in support of the public good. In contrast, the government, personified by the king, was corrupt and oppressive. After declaring their independence, the Americans knew that they needed a national government, but they did not want a strong one. The government established by the Articles of Confederation fit the bill nicely.

After a few years of independence, many Americans recognized that they were wrong about the nature of the people and the role of government. Instead of society being united behind a common perception of the public good, they saw that it was composed of a variety of interests or factions, which opposed each other on a number of policy issues. Furthermore, practical political experience in the states demonstrated that the people were not so virtuous after all. When one faction gained control of the government of a particular state or locality, it would often use its power to enforce its will over opposing interests.

By 1787, many Americans had decided that a strong national government could play a positive role in society. First, the national government could reconcile the divergent concerns of various groups in society to

A LARGE NATION, SUCH AS THE UNITED STATES, INCLUDES A **WIDE** RANGE OF INTERESTS COMPETING FOR POWER.

produce policies designed to achieve the public good. A large nation, such as the United States, includes a wide range of interests competing for power. Although a particular group or faction might be strong enough to control the government in one state or a local area, no single group would be able to dominate nationwide. A strong national government would provide a forum in which groups would be able to reconcile their differences. The result would be policies that would be acceptable to a broad range of interests.

Second, a strong national government could protect individual liberty and property from the power of

oppressive majorities. At the state or local level, a dominant faction could adopt policies designed to advance its own religious or economic interests at the expense of the minority.

At the national level, however, no one group or faction would be powerful enough to enforce its will on the entire nation. Because every group held minority status in one state or another, it would be in each group's interest to protect minorities against the power of oppressive local majorities.[3] For example, the framers of the Constitution included a provision prohibiting a state-supported church because of the multiplicity of religious sects in America. Although many of the early American religious groups would have liked nothing better than to establish their faith as the official state religion, they lacked the power to achieve that goal. Consequently, they preferred an official government policy of religious freedom to risking the possibility that another religious group would gain official recognition.[4]

# constitutional
## PRINCIPLES

**t**o understand the American Constitution, we must study the principles behind it. Let's look in detail at some of the constitution's most important themes.

### Representative Democracy

A **democracy** is a system of government in which the people hold ultimate political power. Although the framers of the Constitution favored a government that would answer to the people, they did not

want to give too much power to majority opinion. The framers were particularly wary of **direct democracy**, which is a political system in which the citizens vote directly on matters of public concern. The framers of the Constitution worried that ordinary citizens lacked the information to make intelligent policy decisions. They feared that direct democracy would produce policies reflecting hasty, emotional decisions rather than well-considered judgments.

The framers also worried that direct democracy would enable a majority of the people to enact policies

**democracy** a system of government in which ultimate political authority is vested in the people.

**direct democracy** a political system in which the citizens vote directly on matters of public concern.

**think** Assuming that modern technology would overcome any logistical problems, do you think the United States would be better off today with a direct democracy rather than a republic? Why or why not?

that would silence, disadvantage, or harm the minority point of view, thus producing a **tyranny of the majority**, which is the abuse of the minority by the majority. The danger of majority rule is that the majority may vote to adopt policies that unfairly disadvantage the minority. The challenge for the framers of the Constitution was to create a form of government that would provide for majority rule while protecting the rights and liberties of minorities.

Instead of a direct democracy, the framers created a **representative democracy** or a **republic**, which is a political system in which citizens elect representatives to make policy decisions on their behalf. The framers believed that elected representatives would act as a buffer between the people and government policies. Representatives would be more knowledgeable than ordinary citizens about policy issues. They would also be more likely than the general public to recognize the legitimate interests of different groups in society and to seek policy compromises designed to accommodate those interests.

To further guard against the tyranny of the majority, the framers provided that some policy actions could be taken only with the consent of a **supermajority**, a voting margin which is greater than a simple majority. Constitutional amendments must be proposed by two-thirds of the members of both the House and the Senate and ratified by three-fourths of the states. Treaties must be approved by two-thirds of the Senate. Presidential vetoes can be overridden only by a two-thirds vote of each chamber of Congress. Executive and judicial officials can be removed from office only by a two-thirds vote of the Senate. In each of these cases, a simple majority of 50 percent plus one does not prevail. Instead, policy actions require the support, or at least acceptance, of a supermajority of two-thirds or more.

## Rule of Law

The **rule of law** is the constitutional principle that holds that the discretion of public officials in dealing with individuals is limited by the law. The very existence of a written constitution implies the rule of law, but certain constitutional provisions deserve special notice. In Article I, Section 9, the Constitution guarantees the privilege of the writ of *habeas corpus* except in cases of invasion, rebellion, or threat to public

The Fifth Amendment allows private property to be seized for public purposes if compensation is made. In 2005, the Supreme Court's 5–4 ruling in *Kelo v. New London* stretched the definition of eminent domain by allowing a city to seize private property (Susette Kelo's house in New London, Connecticut, as pictured above) to sell to a private real estate developer, with the hopes that tax revenues would benefit the city.

**tyranny of the majority** the abuse of the minority by the majority.

**representative democracy/republic** a political system in which citizens elect representatives to make policy decisions on their behalf.

**supermajority** a voting margin that is greater than a simple majority.

**rule of law** the constitutional principle that holds that the discretion of public officials in dealing with individuals is limited by the law.

**think**

Should the government be allowed to arrest American citizens and hold them without charges and without trial if it believes that they are involved in planning terrorist attacks against the United States?

safety. A **writ of *habeas corpus*** is a court order requiring that government authorities either release a person held in custody or demonstrate that the person is detained in accordance with law. *Habeas corpus* is designed to prevent arbitrary arrest and imprisonment. The Constitution protects Americans from being held in custody by the government unless they are charged and convicted in accordance with the law.

The Constitution prohibits the passage of bills of attainder and *ex post facto* laws. A **bill of attainder** is a law declaring a person or a group of persons guilty of a crime and providing for punishment without benefit of a judicial proceeding. An ***ex post facto* law** is a retroactive criminal statute that operates to the disadvantage of accused persons. It makes a crime out of an act that was not illegal when it was committed.

**Due process of law** is the constitutional principle holding that government must follow fair and regular procedures in actions that could lead to an individual's suffering loss of life, liberty, or property. In both the Fifth and Fourteenth Amendments, the Constitution provides that neither Congress (the Fifth Amendment) nor the states

**writ of *habeas corpus*** a court order requiring government authorities either to release a person held in custody or demonstrate that the person is detained in accordance with law.

**bill of attainder** a law declaring a person or a group of persons guilty of a crime and providing for punishment without benefit of a judicial proceeding.

***ex post facto* law** a retroactive criminal statute that operates to the disadvantage of accused persons.

**due process of law** the constitutional principle holding that government must follow fair and regular procedures in actions that could lead to an individual's suffering loss of life, liberty, or property.

PROTECTIONS GUARANTEED BY THE
# Bill of RIGHTS

**FIRST AMENDMENT** Protects freedom of speech, press, assembly, and petition, and prohibits Congress from creating an established religion or restricting the free exercise of religion.

**SECOND AMENDMENT** Guarantees the right to keep and bear arms.

**THIRD AMENDMENT** Prohibits forced quartering of troops during time of peace.

**FOURTH AMENDMENT** Protects against unreasonable searches and seizures.

**FIFTH AMENDMENT** Guarantees due process, the use of a grand jury for serious crimes, protects against double jeopardy and self-incrimination, and prohibits seizure of private property without compensation.

**SIXTH AMENDMENT** Protects the rights of the accused, including the right to a speedy and public trial and to an impartial jury, the right to be informed of charges, face accusers, and obtain witnesses, and the right to counsel.

**SEVENTH AMENDMENT** Guarantees the right to a civil trial by jury.

**EIGHTH AMENDMENT** Prohibits excessive bail and cruel and unusual punishment.

**NINTH AMENDMENT** Declares that individual rights are not limited to those rights specifically enumerated in the Constitution.

**TENTH AMENDMENT** Stipulates that the powers not delegated to the national government or denied to the states are reserved for the states or the people.

# THE CREATION AND INCORPORATION OF THE BILL OF RIGHTS

**1787** | In order to promote the ratification of the Constitution written in 1787, the Federalists promise to add a bill of rights once the Constitution is approved.

**1868** | The Fourteenth Amendment is ratified, declaring that states may not "deprive any person of life, liberty, or property, without due process of law."

**1963** | *Gideon v. Wainwright* incorporated the Sixth Amendment requirement for courts to provide counsel in criminal cases for indigent defendants.

| 1780 | 1800 | 1820 | 1840 | 1860 | 1880 | 1900 | 1920 | 1940 | 1960 | 1980 |
|------|------|------|------|------|------|------|------|------|------|------|

**1787** | The Constitution is ratified and the Federalists are true to their word, proposing a set of 12 amendments.

**1791** | 10 of the proposed amendments are quickly ratified, and the Bill of Rights becomes part of the Constitution.

**1925** | *Gitlow v. New York* incorporated First Amendment rights protecting freedom of speech and freedom of the press.

**1961** | *Mapp v. Ohio* incorporated the Fourth Amendment protection against unreasonable searches and seizures.

**20th Century** | Throughout the twentieth century, the Supreme Court began selective incorporation of the Bill of Rights against the states.

---

(the Fourteenth Amendment) may deprive any person of "life, liberty, or property, without due process of law." Due process of law generally protects individuals from the arbitrary actions of public officials. Before individuals may be imprisoned, fined, or executed, they must be given their day in court in accordance with law. Among other rights, the Constitution guarantees accused persons the right to a speedy, public trial by an impartial jury, the right to confront witnesses, and the right to legal counsel.

## Limited Government

**Limited government** is the constitutional principle that government does not have unrestricted authority over individuals. The government of the United States is not a dictatorship with absolute authority; its power is limited. Perhaps the most important constitutional restriction on the authority of government is the **Bill of Rights**, the first 10 amendments to the Constitution.

The Bill of Rights was not part of the original Constitution because a majority of the framers of the Constitution believed that such a provision was unnecessary, redundant, useless, and possibly even dangerous. The framers thought that a bill of rights would be unnecessary be-

> A BILL OF RIGHTS BECAME A POLITICAL ISSUE DURING THE DEBATE OVER RATIFICATION

cause each state constitution had a bill of rights, and the national government lacked sufficient power to threaten individual liberty. They considered a bill of rights redundant because the Constitution already contained a number of provisions designed to protect individual liberty, such as the prohibition against *ex post facto* laws and bills of attainder, and the guarantee of due process of law. They thought that a bill of rights would be useless because they believed that a paper guarantee of individual liberty would mean little in the face of public pressure. Finally, the framers resisted the inclusion of a bill of rights in the Constitution because they worried that some rights might be inadvertently left out and that any right omitted from the document would be lost.[5]

After the Constitution was written in 1787, it still had to be approved (or ratified) by 9 of the 13 states. The failure to include a bill of rights became a political issue during the debate over ratification of the proposed Constitution. The **Antifederalists** opposed the ratification of the new Constitution because they thought it gave too much power to the national government. They raised the issue of a bill of rights in hopes of defeating the Constitution and to force the con-

vening of a new constitutional convention. The **Federalists** supported the ratification of the Constitution. Although most Federalists had opposed inclusion of a bill of rights in the constitution, they switched sides in order to secure ratification and to prevent a new convention. They promised to add a bill of rights once the Constitution was ratified and the new government took office.[6]

The Federalists kept their promise. In 1789, the First Congress of the United States proposed 12 amendments, 10 of which were

**limited government** the constitutional principle that government does not have unrestricted authority over individuals.

**Bill of Rights** the first ten amendments to the U.S. Constitution.

**Antifederalists** Americans opposed to the ratification of the new Constitution because they thought it gave too much power to the national government.

**Federalists** Americans who supported the ratification of the Constitution.

ratified by a sufficient number of states to become part of the Constitution by 1791. One of the rejected amendments was a provision that a congressional pay raise could not go into effect without an intervening election. It was finally ratified in 1992 as the Twenty-seventh Amendment.

The authors of the Bill of Rights intended that it would apply only to the national government and not the states because the states already

James Madison is called "Father of the Constitution."

had bills of rights. The U.S. Constitution and the national Bill of Rights would protect individual rights against abuse by the national government. State constitutions and state bills of rights would secure individual rights from infringement by state governments.

The Fourteenth Amendment, which was added to the Constitution immediately after the Civil War, provided the constitutional basis for applying the national Bill of Rights to the states. Congress proposed the Fourteenth Amendment in 1866 to protect the rights of former slaves from infringement by state governments. The amend-

ment defined U.S. citizenship, making it clear that all Americans are citizens of both the United States and the state in which they live. The amendment declared that state governments could not take life, liberty, or property without "due process of law," or deny to any person within their jurisdiction "equal protection of the laws." The Fourteenth Amendment also prohibited states from making laws abridging the "privileges or immunities" of citizens.

The Fourteenth Amendment did not play a major role in the protection of individual rights until the twentieth century. Initially, the Fourteenth Amendment had little impact on individual rights because the Supreme Court of the United States refused to interpret its provisions to protect individual rights. Not until the twentieth century did the Court begin the process known as the selective incorporation of the Bill of Rights against the states. This is the process through which the U.S. Supreme Court interpreted the Due Process Clause of the Fourteenth Amendment of the U.S. Constitution to apply most of the provisions of the national Bill of Rights to the states. Although the Supreme Court has never ruled that the Bill of Rights as a whole applies to the states, it has selectively held that virtually all of its key provisions apply against the states through the Due Process Clause of the Fourteenth Amendment. As a result, the national Bill of Rights now protects individual rights against infringement by both the national government and state governments as well.

## Separation of Powers with Checks and Balances

The framers of the U.S. Constitution adopted separation of powers

## JAMES MADISON WAS THE PRINCIPAL ARCHITECT OF AMERICA'S SYSTEM OF SEPARATION OF POWERS WITH CHECKS AND BALANCES

with checks and balances to control the power of the Federal government. The roots of these concepts went back a century, but they were more fully developed by Baron de Montesquieu, an eighteenth-century French political philosopher. Montesquieu identified three kinds of political power: the power to make laws (**legislative power**), to enforce laws (**executive power**), and to interpret laws (**judicial power**). Montesquieu warned against allowing one person or a single group of people to exercise all three powers because that person or group would pose a threat to individual liberty. Montesquieu advocated **separation of powers**, that is, the division of political power among executive, legislative, and judicial branches of government. He called for a system of checks and balances to prevent any one of the three branches from becoming too strong. **Checks and balances** refer to the

**legislative power** the power to make laws.

**executive power** the power to enforce laws.

**judicial power** the power to interpret laws.

**separation of powers** the division of political power among executive, legislative, and judicial branches.

**checks and balances** the overlapping of the powers of the branches of government designed to ensure that public officials limit the authority of each other.

overlapping of the powers of the branches of government to ensure that public officials limit the authority of each other.

James Madison was the principal architect of America's system of separation of powers with checks and balances. In fact, scholars sometimes refer to the nation's constitutional apparatus as the Madisonian system. Madison and two other proponents of the new constitution, Alexander Hamilton and John Jay, wrote a series of essays known as the **Federalist Papers** to advocate the ratification of the new Constitution. In *The Federalist* No. 51, Madison identified two threats to liberty: 1) **factions**, which are special interests who seek their own good at the expense of the common good, and 2) the excessive concentration of political power in the hands of government officials. Madison's remedy for these dangers was the creation of a strong national government with separation of powers and checks and balances.

Madison believed that the nation needed a strong national government to control the power of factions. In this regard, Madison noted the advantage of a large nation with many diverse interests. At the local or state level, he said, a single faction might be powerful enough to dominate. It could unfairly force its will on the minority, creating a tyranny of the majority. Over the breadth of the entire nation, however, the narrow perspectives of that faction would be checked by the

**Federalist Papers** a series of essays written by James Madison, Alexander Hamilton, and John Jay advocating the ratification of the Constitution.

**factions** special interests who seek their own good at the expense of the common good.

# **take**action

## SERVICE LEARNING >>

Service learning is based on the concept that students can learn more about a subject through participation and experience combined with traditional coursework than they can through classroom instruction alone. Students will gain valuable knowledge and skills from the experience beyond those normally acquired in a classroom.

Use the following checklist to guide you through your service-learning project:

1. Identify a government office or agency that welcomes student volunteers. You may wish to begin with the mayor's office, a county commissioner or county supervisor, school district, hospital district, or state legislator. They can give you suggestions or referrals to agencies that deal with issues related to your career goals.

2. Call the agency or department that interests you and ask to speak to the volunteer coordinator. Explain that you are completing a service-learning project for your college and want to know about volunteer opportunities. You will want to arrange a placement that matches your interests and the needs of the agency.

3. Your instructor will set the number of hours you should volunteer over the course of the term. Normally, students should expect to work from 20 to 40 hours over a long semester to receive full benefit from the activity.

4. As you complete your assignment at the agency, ask the volunteer coordinator to provide you with docu-

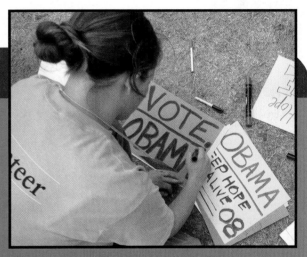

mentation of the hours of your work to present to your instructor.

You will be required to keep a reflective journal documenting your service. Journal entries should discuss your work on the project and your reaction to the experience. Your journal should cover the following topics:

1. What you did for the organization.
2. What you thought of the clients served by the organization.
3. What you thought of the other people working for the organization.
4. What you thought of the work done by the organization.
5. How your experience relates to course materials.
6. How your experience relates to topics in the news.

Write at least one journal entry for every two hours you spend at your placement. Each journal entry should be at least four sentences long. You will be evaluated on the amount of time you spent at your placement, the number and length of your journal entries, and the quality of your entries.

## THE CONNECTICUT COMPROMISE

The precise organization of America's bicameral Congress was the product of an agreement between large-state and small-state forces known as the Connecticut Compromise. Members of the House of Representatives would be chosen by direct popular election to serve two-year terms with the number of representatives from each state based on population. (This pleased large states.) Each state would have two senators chosen by their state legislatures to serve six-year terms. This pleased small states. The adoption of the Seventeenth Amendment in 1913 provided for direct popular election of senators.

interests of other factions entrenched in other areas. A strong national government would provide an arena in which factions would counterbalance each other. National policies, therefore, would reflect compromise among a range of interests.

Madison also favored separation of powers with checks and balances as a means to control the power of government officials. Madison said that the goal of the system was "to divide and arrange the several offices [of government] in such a manner as that each may be a check on the other."[7] In this fashion, the selfish, private interests of officeholders would counterbalance each other to the public good. "Ambition," Madison wrote, "must be made to counteract ambition."[8]

The Constitution contains an elaborate network of checks and balances. The executive branch, for example, checks the judicial branch through the power of the president to appoint members of the Supreme Court and other federal courts. Congress, in turn, checks the president and the courts in that the Senate must confirm judicial appointments. Similarly, the Constitution declares that Congress has the authority to declare war, but it names the president commander in chief of the armed forces. The president negotiates treaties, but the Senate must ratify them.

## Federalism

The framers of the Constitution set out to establish a government that would be capable of effective administration but would not undermine the American tradition of local control. Their solution was to create a federation. A **federation** or **federal system** is a political system that divides power between a central government, with authority over the whole nation, and a series of state governments.

A federation is a compromise between unitary government and a confederation. In a unitary system, the national government is sovereign. **Sovereignty** is the authority of a state to exercise its legitimate powers within its boundaries, free from external interference. The powers of state and local governments (if they exist) are granted to them by the national government. In a confederation, the states are sov-

ereign. The national government's authority flows from the states. In a federal system, both the national (or federal) government and the state governments are sovereign. They derive their authority not from one another but from the Constitution. Both levels of government act directly on the people through their officials and laws, both are supreme within their proper sphere of authority, and both must consent to constitutional change.

A federation offers Americans several advantages. A federal system provides a means of political representation that can accommodate the diversity of American society. Individual Americans are citizens of their states and the nation, and participate in the selection of representatives to both levels of government. In a federal system, local interests shape local policy. The national government, meanwhile, is an arena in which local interests from different regions can check and balance each other, permitting the national interest to prevail.

Federalism can help protect against the tyranny of the majority. The federal system creates a series of overlapping state and district election systems that select both members of congress and the

**Which do you think is the best form of government—a unitary government, a confederation, or a federal government?**

**federation/federal system** a political system that divides power between a central government, with authority over the whole nation, and a series of state governments.

**sovereignty** the authority of a state to exercise its legitimate powers within its boundaries, free from external interference.

# The British Parliamentary System

Most of the world's democracies are patterned after the British parliamentary system rather than the checks and balances system of the United States. A **parliamentary system** is a system of government in which political power is concentrated in a legislative body and a cabinet headed by a prime minister. The British legislature, which is called the **Parliament**, has two chambers, a House of Commons and a House of Lords. Real power is in the hands of the House of Commons, which is composed of 660 members elected from districts. The House of Lords, which includes the bishops of the Church of England and other members appointed for life by the king or queen, is now little more than a debating society with the power only to delay legislation, not to defeat it.

British voters understand that when they vote for members of Parliament that they are also choosing a government. At election time, each British political party presents the voters with a detailed set of policy proposals that it promises to implement. Voters know that a vote for a particular parliamentary candidate is also a vote for the policies offered by that candidate's political party and a vote for the election of that party's leader as prime minister.

In the 1997 national election, the Labour Party won a majority of seats in Commons, ending 18 years of rule by the Conservative Party. The new Parliament elected Tony Blair, the Labour Party leader, prime minister, to replace John Major, the Conservative prime minister. With a majority in Parliament, the Labour government was able to enact its program without worrying about constitutional checks and balances.

The primary check on the government in Great Britain is the electorate. The government must hold a new parliamentary election within five years, giving voters the opportunity to keep the current government in power or to turn the government over to the opposition. Labour has continued in office because it has been able to maintain its parliamentary majority, winning elections in both 2001 and 2005. When Blair resigned as prime minister in 2007, the Labour members of Parliament chose Gordon Brown as their new leader and he became prime minister.

## Questions

1. Which political system is more responsive to citizen demands—the American or the British system?

2. Which political system is more likely to produce dramatic policy change?

3. Which political system is better equipped to protect the rights of minorities?

**parliamentary system** a system of government in which political power is concentrated in a legislative body and a cabinet headed by a prime minister.

**Parliament** the British legislature.

Britain's Queen Elizabeth II named Labor Party leader Gordon Brown (inset) prime minister in June 2007.

IN MAY 2008, THE CALIFORNIA SUPREME COURT RULED THAT SAME-SEX COUPLES COULD NOT BE PREVENTED FROM MARRYING IN CALIFORNIA. OPPOSITION TO THIS DECISION LED TO A BALLOT MEASURE, KNOWN AS PROPOSITION 8, WHICH SAID, "ONLY MARRIAGE BETWEEN A MAN AND A WOMAN IS VALID OR RECOGNIZED IN CALIFORNIA." ROMAN CATHOLIC, MORMON, AND EVANGELICAL CHRISTIAN LEADERS SUPPORTED THE BAN. EPISCOPALIAN AND MANY JEWISH LEADERS, AS WELL AS ALL 10 OF THE STATE'S LARGEST NEWSPAPERS, OPPOSED THE MEASURE. ALTHOUGH PROPOSITION 8 PASSED in NOVEMBER 2008, NUMEROUS LAWSUITS CHALLENGED ITS VALIDITY. IN MAY 2009, THE CALIFORNIA SUPREME COURT UPHELD PROPOSITION 8, BUT ALLOWED EXISTING SAME-SEX MARRIAGES TO STAND. ADDITIONAL LAWSUITS IN FEDERAL COURTS ARE PENDING, AND BALLOT REPEAL EFFORTS ARE ONGOING.

president. The federal election system gives minorities of all kinds—racial, ethnic, religious, regional, local, occupational, social, and sexual—the opportunity to be part of a majority because they may comprise the swing vote in a closely divided state or district. Consequently, they must be consulted; their interests must be considered.[9]

Nonetheless, a federal system imposes certain disadvantages. Local variations confuse citizens and hinder business. Traveling Americans face different traffic laws in each state. People who move from one state to another must adapt to different laws regarding such matters as marriage, divorce, wills, and occupational licensing. A couple approved as foster parents in one state may have to go through the approval process again if they move to another state. Businesses must adjust to variations in

tax laws and regulations. Federalism also sets the stage for conflict. American history is filled with examples of disputes between states and the national government; the Civil War was the most serious. Issues such as the 55-mile-per-hour speed limit requirement and the 21-

# A FEDERAL SYSTEM IMPOSES CERTAIN DISADVANTAGES

year-old minimum legal drinking age are contemporary examples of conflicts between states and the national government.

## Bicameralism

The framers of the Constitution expected the legislative branch to be the dominant institution of Ameri-

can national government because it was the dominant branch of state governments. To prevent the national legislature from becoming too powerful, the framers divided Congress into two houses with different sizes, terms of office, responsibilities, and constituencies.

The framers expected that the popularly elected House would be constrained by a more conservative Senate. With a two-year term, members of the House would be closer to the people and more likely to act hastily in accordance with short-term popular sentiment. In contrast, senators, chosen by state legislatures and serving longer terms, would be insulated from popular pressures, thus enabling them to act more cautiously and to put the national interest ahead of short-term political gain.[10]

# the living
## CONSTITUTION

**think**

**What are the advantages and disadvantages of a less specific Constitution?**

t he Constitution has not merely survived for more than 220 years. It has grown and matured with the nation, serving as the fundamental framework for policymaking to this day. The genius of the Constitution lies in its ability to adapt to changing times while maintaining adherence to basic principles. The Constitution is a brief, generalized document that is full of phrases lacking clear definition. The Eighth Amendment, for example, prohibits "cruel and unusual punishments." Article I, Section 8 gives Congress the power to regulate "commerce." Article II, Section 4 declares that the president may be impeached and removed from office for "treason, bribery, or other high crimes and misdemeanors." The Fourth Amendment prohibits "unreasonable searches and seizures." What do these terms mean? What punishments are

"cruel and unusual?" What is "commerce?" What are "high crimes and misdemeanors"? Which searches and seizures are "reasonable" and which are "unreasonable"?

The Constitution is often vague, and this is what the framers intended. They set down certain basic, fundamental principles, but omitted details in order to allow succeeding generations to supply specifics in light of their own experiences. The basic idea behind the concept of "cruel and unusual punishments," for example, is that government must not go too far in punishing criminals. The prohibition against "unreasonable searches and seizures" places limits on the police. Had the framers of the Constitution decided to spell out everything in detail, they would have produced a document far longer and less satisfactory than the one we have. Even-

tually, the nation would have outgrown it and either cast it aside or been forced to amend it repeatedly.

## Constitutional Change through Practice and Experience

The Constitution has adapted to changing times through practice and experience. Consider the role of the presidency. The historical development of the office has given definition to the powers of the presidency beyond the scope of that office as foreseen by the framers. Other elements of American government have developed despite slight mention in the Constitution. The federal bureaucracy, for example, is barely discussed in the Constitution. Yet its importance in American government has grown to the point that some observers refer to it as the fourth branch of government. Furthermore, some important contemporary features of American government are not mentioned in the Constitution at all, including the committee system in Congress, the executive cabinet, and the political party system. To an important extent, the meaning of the Constitution

In 2002, in *Atkins v. Virginia*, the Supreme Court reversed its previous course and said that the execution of the mentally retarded was cruel and unusual punishment. The ruling benefited Daryl Renard Atkins (shown here) who was convicted of the slaying of an airman from Langley Air Force Base.

# CONSTITUTIONAL CHANGE

**PROPOSING A CONSTITUTIONAL AMENDMENT**

**TWO-THIRDS VOTE OF EACH HOUSE OF CONGRESS**

**A CONSTITUTIONAL CONVENTION CALLED BY CONGRESS UPON PETITION BY TWO-THIRDS OF THE STATES**

**RATIFYING A CONSTITUTIONAL AMENDMENT**

**THREE-FOURTHS OF THE STATES RATIFY IT IN STATE LEGISLATURES**

**THREE-FOURTHS OF THE STATE RATIFY IT IN SPECIALLY CALLED STATES CONVENTIONS**

called by Congress upon petition by two-thirds of the states. The first method has been used many times; Congress proposed all 27 amendments that have been added to the Constitution. The convention procedure has never been used.

After an amendment is proposed, by either Congress or a convention, three-fourths of the states must ratify it. Ratification can be accomplished either by vote of the state legislatures or by specially called state conventions. The former method has been used successfully 26 times, the latter only once, to ratify the Twenty-first Amendment repealing Prohibition.

**constitutional amendment** a formal, written change or addition to the nation's governing document.

is found in its historical development over time as succeeding generations of Americans have addressed policy issues within its framework.

## Constitutional Change through Amendment

A **constitutional amendment** is a formal, written change or addition to the nation's governing document. A major flaw of the Articles of Confederation was that the articles could be amended only by unanimous vote. In practice, this made change impossible because of the obstinacy of only one or a few states. In 1787, then, the Constitution's framers were careful to include a reasonable method of amendment that permitted change but was difficult enough to preclude hasty, ill-conceived changes.

The Constitution provides two methods for proposing amendments and two methods for their ratification. An amendment may be proposed by either a two-thirds vote of each house of Congress or by a constitutional convention

(From left to right) George E.C. Hayes, Thurgood Marshall, and James M. Nabrit, were the NAACP Legal Defense Fund attorneys who represented the Brown family in *Brown v. Board of Education* (1954), the great school desegregation case.

## Constitutional Change through Judicial Interpretation

A final means of constitutional change is judicial interpretation. In fact, it may be no exaggeration to say that what counts most in constitutional law is the interpretation of the Constitution by the courts, particularly the U.S. Supreme Court, rather than the words of the document itself. Many phrases important to constitutional law are not even in the Constitution, including "war power," "clear and present danger," "separation of church and state," "right of privacy," "separate but equal," and "police power." These famous words appear not in the Constitution but in judicial opinions.

Judicial interpretation of the Constitution is inevitable because of the document's generalized nature. Many of the phrases of the Constitution are purposely ambiguous, requiring continuous reinterpretation and adaptation. Indeed, one constitutional scholar says that we have an unwritten constitution, whose history is the history of judicial interpretation.[11]

The power of courts to declare unconstitutional the actions of the other branches and units of government is known as **judicial review**. Although the Constitution is silent about the power of judicial review, many historians believe that the founders expected the courts to exercise the authority. Ironically, the Supreme Court assumed the power of judicial review through constitutional interpretation, first holding an act of Congress unconstitutional in 1803 in the case of *Marbury v. Madison*.[12]

Judicial review is an instrument of constitutional change because the process involves constitutional interpretation. Professor Richard H. Fallon, Jr., says that today's justices interpret the Constitution in light

**judicial review** the power of courts to declare unconstitutional the actions of the other branches and units of government.

Statue of John Adams in Quincy, Mass.

# MARBURY v. MADISON

### CASE

In 1800, President John Adams and his Federalist Party were defeated. In the months of his remaining presidency, Adams appointed a number of loyal Federalists to the judicial branch of government. One of these judicial appointments went to William Marbury, who was named justice of the peace for the District of Columbia.

President Adams signed and sealed Marbury's commission the day before he left office, but the secretary of state neglected to deliver it. The new president, Thomas Jefferson, ordered his secretary of state, James Madison, not to deliver the commission. Marbury sued, asking the Supreme Court to issue a writ of *mandamus* to force Madison to deliver his commission. A writ of *mandamus* is a court order directing a public official to perform a specific act or duty.

### DECISION

The Supreme Court had a problem. Chief Justice John Marshall and the other members of the Court were Federalists. They would have liked to force Madison to deliver the commission. However, Jefferson might well have defied the order, damaging the Court's prestige.

Judicial review provided Marshall and the Court with their way out of the dilemma. Marshall used the Court's opinion to scold Jefferson and Madison for refusing to deliver the commission. Marbury was entitled to his commission, said Marshall, and a writ of *mandamus* was in order.

However, Marshall also ruled that the Supreme Court lacked authority to issue the writ. Marshall pointed out that the Constitution lists the types of cases that may be tried before the Supreme Court in Article III, Section 2. The list does not include the power to issue writs of *mandamus* to federal officials. Congress had given the Court the authority to issue the writ in the Judiciary Act of 1789, but Marshall argued that Congress had no constitutional authority to do this. Therefore, the section of the Judiciary Act that gave the Court the power to issue writs of *mandamus* was unconstitutional. By this means, Marshall was able to attack Jefferson but keep the president from defying the Court.

### SIGNIFICANCE

*Marbury v. Madison* is the first case in which the Supreme Court ruled that acts of Congress can be unconstitutional. In his ruling, Marshall stated that the Constitution is the "fundamental and paramount law of the nation" and that it is the duty of the courts to interpret the law.

"Thus," Marshall continued, "the particular phraseology of the Constitution of the United States confirms and strengthens the principle . . . that a law repugnant to the Constitution is void."

Marshall concluded that it was the Court's duty to enforce the Constitution by refusing to uphold the act of Congress.

of history, precedent (that is, earlier interpretations), and considerations of moral desirability and practical workability.[13] Consider the history of judicial interpretation of the **Equal Protection Clause**, which is the provision found in the Fourteenth Amendment of the U.S. Constitution that declares that "No State shall . . . deny to any person within its jurisdiction the equal protection of the laws." Historians believe that Congress proposed this phrase to safeguard the civil rights of former slaves and their offspring by requiring states to treat all of their residents equally under state law, regardless of race.

The U.S. Supreme Court's initial interpretation of the Equal Protection Clause came in 1896 in *Plessy v. Ferguson*. The case centered on the constitutionality of a Louisiana law that required racial segregation (separation) in passenger railcars. Could a state government prohibit African American travelers from sharing a railcar with white passengers without violating the Equal Protection Clause? The Supreme Court answered that it could as long as the accommodations were equal. "Separate but equal" facilities, said the Court, were sufficient to satisfy the requirements of the Fourteenth Amendment.[14] Almost 60 years later, the Supreme Court addressed a similar issue in the case of *Brown v. Board of Education of Topeka* (1954). The *Brown* case involved a constitutional challenge to a Kansas law requiring racial segregation in public schools. Could a state government prohibit African American youngsters from sharing a school with white children without violating the Equal Protection Clause? In this case, the Supreme Court overruled *Plessy*, holding that the Equal Protection Clause of the Fourteenth Amendment prohibits state laws requiring racial segregation in public schools. The Court declared that "separate but equal" was a contradiction because the legal requirement of separation placed the stamp of inferiority on the black race.[15] And so the Constitution was changed, not through the adoption of a constitutional amendment (the wording of the Equal Protection Clause remained the same), but because of changing judicial interpretation.

> **Equal Protection Clause** a provision of the Fourteenth Amendment of the U.S. Constitution that declares that "No State shall . . . deny to any person within its jurisdiction the equal protection of the laws."

# the constitution, politics,
## AND PUBLIC POLICY

t he U.S. Constitution affects the policymaking process by fragmenting political power. Separation of powers divides power at the national level among legislative, executive, and judicial branches. Bicameralism splits power between the House and Senate. Federalism distributes power between the national government and the states.

The fragmentation of political power in the United States produces slow, incremental change. Presidents need the cooperation of Congress to have their programs enacted. In turn, Congress has difficulty acting without presidential initiative. Both the president and Congress need the support of the bureaucracy if their policies are to be faithfully executed. Frequently, they require the cooperation of state and local officials as well. The courts, meanwhile, can reverse or delay policies adopted at other levels or by other branches of

California Governor Arnold Schwarzenegger asked the federal government for financial aid during a state budget crisis in 2008.

# Constitutional Principles

**What is the best way of understanding the Constitution? Does it embody universal values, or should it be understood in terms of contemporary society?**

**Is there a difference between the founding conceptions of equality and those of today? Does a natural rights understanding assume more individual freedom?**

**Overview:** When the Constitution was ratified in June 1788, the United States had a population of roughly 3.9 million, with an urban population of less than 500,000 citizens (approximately 11 percent). The overwhelmingly dominant religion was Protestantism, and the right to vote was held principally by those who owned property. In 2005, the United States had a population of nearly 300 million, with an urban population of roughly 225 million (75.2 percent). How is it that the

Constitution can incorporate the differing social and political views of a multicultural and diverse nation?

Some scholars argue that the Constitution has been a successful document because it is based upon the principles of natural law and natural rights—principles holding that all human beings are created equal and endowed with certain inalienable rights, that these principles do not change over time, and that political institutions can be created to reflect natural equality and human dignity.

Others argue that the Constitution is a flexible instrument created to adapt to social, historical, and political change. This view—positivism—holds that constitutions and laws should reflect prevailing social convention and thought, and it is in this way that the Constitution has been able to be interpreted to allow for equality and social justice.

Just what does the Constitution mean, and how will this question determine the near future of American history?

## supporting | a natural rights interpretation of the Constitution

**natural rights theory assumes a higher moral law.** The founders were correct in their supposition that it is through liberty and justice that individuals can realize their potential and approach happiness, and the Constitution was created to embody these values. These values do not change over time.

**a natural rights interpretation assumes the use of reason.** Alexander Hamilton argues in the *Federalist Papers* that the Constitution represents "good government" created by "reflection and choice." The founders used reflection and reason to create a new form of government based on the natural rights principle that all political power is derived from the people exercising their right to create government and to live under laws of their own choosing.

**natural rights theory embodies the principle of political equality.** The Constitution should be interpreted as incorporating the principle found in the Declaration of Independence that "all men are created equal" and should have equal political rights. This allows the rich and the poor, the highly educated and the ignorant, the secular and the religious, and the interested and the apathetic to have a say and a share in government.

## against | a natural rights interpretation of the Constitution

**the founders simply used the prevailing philosophies of their times.** There is no way to determine if natural rights theory is true. The founders lived in a certain moment in history and they had no way of knowing what the future held in the way of new philosophies and science of government. For example, they did not consider that government could be used for social purposes, such as ensuring social welfare through government policy.

**the Constitution must be interpreted in light of advances in technology and social organization.** The United States of 2008 is a different nation than the America of 1788. It is highly unlikely that the founders could envision the complex evolution of human society and technology—how could they consider freedom-of-speech issues and the Internet? To apply constitutional law to Internet speech issues necessarily means interpreting the Constitution in a way undreamed of by the founders.

**natural rights theory as understood by the founders leads to inequality.** For example, the Declaration of Independence declares all men are equal, yet it allowed for slavery and unregulated free markets. The Constitution must be interpreted with a view to new understandings of social and political equality.

government. When policy changes occur, they are generally incremental and gradual, reflecting compromise among the various political actors involved in the process.

The framers of the U.S. Constitution were cautious people, wary of rapid change and none too confident about the judgment of popular majorities. Consequently, they created a constitutional apparatus that would work slowly. The founders feared that rapid, major change would too often produce more harm than good.

The Constitution promotes policy stability.[16] The election of a new president or a change in control of Congress is unlikely to produce dramatic policy change. A new president with bold new ideas must convince both Congress and the federal courts that the policy ideas are not only wise but constitutional.

President John F. Kennedy confers with his brother, Attorney General Robert Kennedy, during the 1962 Cuban Missile Crisis.

The framers of the Constitution wanted to ensure that the diversity of political interests in American society would be represented in the policy process. During the debates at the constitutional convention of 1787, one of the major issues was how best to protect the small states from large-state domination. The authors of the Constitution established a system that would provide opportunity for the varied groups and interests of American society to participate in policymaking.

America's constitutional arrangements have their critics. The oldest complaint is that the Constitution favored the rich and wellborn over the common people. In the early twentieth century, historian Charles Beard argued that the framers of the

Constitution had been members of a small group of wealthy Americans who set out to preserve and enhance the economic and political opportunities of their class.[17] Although modern historians have refuted most of Beard's research, a number of contemporary observers nonetheless believe that the Constitution benefits special interests. The constitutional fragmentation of power that presents a range of forums in which different groups may be heard also provides a series of power centers that interest groups can control. Entrenched groups can frequently muster the influence to halt policy changes, sometimes overriding the wishes of a majority in Congress and the nation.

The most basic criticism of the Constitution is that it is a blueprint for political deadlock among the branches and units of government. By dividing government against itself, the founders ensured that all proposals for policy change must pass through a maze of power centers. The complexity of the arrangement not only slows the policymaking process but also gives most of the trump cards to the forces opposing whatever measure is under consideration. It is easier to defeat policy proposals than to pass them.

Professor James Sundquist believes that American history is filled with the failures of the system to respond effectively to policy crises. Consider the dilemma of the Vietnam War. Congress and the president were unable to agree either to withdraw American forces or do what was necessary to win the war. As a result, the nation was condemned to a half-in, half-out compromise policy that satisfied no one. Sundquist says the same constitutional paralysis hindered the nation's ability to deal with secession in the 1860s, the Great Depression in the 1930s, and federal budget deficits of the 1980s.[18]

Nonetheless, constitutional stalemate is not inevitable. The nation did eventually rise to the challenge of secession and preserved the Union. The constitutional deadlock over the Great Depression ended. The budget deficit of the 1980s was finally eliminated. Furthermore, we can point to national crises such as World War II and the Cuban Missile Crisis that the American government was able to address in a forthright, spirited manner.

Policy deadlocks are as much political as they are constitutional. The Constitution structures the policy process by setting the ground rules. It does not dictate the outcome of the policy process. The failure of American government to resolve the Vietnam War reflected a lack of political consensus rather than a constitutional breakdown.[19] We could say the same about the failure of Congress to dictate the withdrawal of American combat forces from Iraq. Whereas public opinion polls showed that a majority of Americans believed that the war was a mistake, they found the public conflicted on the best course to end American involvement.[20]

# constitutional
## ENVIRONMENT FOR POLICYMAKING

the U.S. Constitution has an impact on every stage of the policymaking process.

## Agenda Building

Constitutional principles often define issues during the agenda setting stage of the policymaking process. Because of the Constitution, Americans debate the role of religion in public life from the perspectives of the First Amendment, considering both the constitutional guarantee of free exercise of religion and the prohibition against an establishment of religion. Discussions of the wisdom of state-sponsored prayers in public-school classrooms inevitably revolve around issues of constitutionality. Constitutional considerations frame the abortion controversy as well, with a constitutional "right to life" counterbalanced against a "right to choose."

## Policy Formulation and Adoption

The Constitution limits the policy options available to policymakers during the policy formulation stage to those policy approaches that are consistent with the Constitution. A policy aimed at shielding children from offensive materials on the Internet must be formulated with the Constitution in mind because it will likely face legal challenge from critics who believe that it violates the free speech provision of the First Amendment. Similarly, policies designed to control illegal immigration must be formulated to pass constitutional scrutiny because the Constitution protects all *persons* in the United States, not just citizens.

The Constitution sets the ground rules for policy adoption. Legislative policies require passage by both houses of Congress and the signature of the president. If the president vetoes a measure, the Constitution provides that it dies unless the House and Senate pass it again by a two-thirds margin. Not all policies are adopted through the legislative process. The Constitution also establishes procedures, either explicitly or implicitly, for the adoption of policies through treaties, constitutional amendments, executive orders, judicial decisions, and rulemaking by government agencies.

## Policy Implementation and Evaluation

The Constitution influences the implementation of policy. At the national level of government, policy implementation is primarily the responsibility of the executive branch. State and local governments also participate in policy implementation because of the federal system.

Finally, the Constitution affects policy evaluation. The separation of powers system with checks and balances ensures that each branch of government can evaluate policies adopted by the other branches. Congress oversees policy implementation by the executive branch. The judicial branch evaluates policies adopted by the other branches by interpreting laws and reviewing the constitutionality of executive and legislative policies.

> The Constitution sets the ground rules for policymaking

Congressional supporters of the bill watch as President George W. Bush signs the No Child Left Behind bill into law.

# TEST yourself

1. The fundamental law by which a state or nation is organized and governed, and to which ordinary legislation must conform, is the definition of which of the following?
   A. Bicameralism
   B. Separation of powers
   C. Constitution
   D. Federalism

2. Which of the following can be defined as a political system in which the citizens vote directly on matters of public concern?
   A. Representative democracy
   B. Direct democracy
   C. Republic
   D. Confederation

3. Suppose that the majority of the people of a particular political district adhere to the same religion. The majority uses its control of government to adopt policies that limit public office to members of that religion, and they seriously disadvantage people who do not share their belief. The framers of the Constitution would use which of the following terms or phrases to describe that situation?
   A. Tyranny of the majority
   B. Representative democracy
   C. Direct democracy
   D. Separation of powers with checks and balances

4. Which of the following can be defined as a political system in which citizens elect representatives to make policy decisions on their behalf?
   A. Federalism
   B. Direct democracy
   C. Unitary government
   D. Representative democracy

5. Congress passes a law that criminalizes past actions that were taken before the law was passed. This law would be an example of which of the following?
   A. *Ex post facto* law
   B. Bill of attainder
   C. *Habeas corpus*
   D. Separation of powers

6. The Constitution guarantees accused persons the right to a speedy, public trial by an impartial jury, the right to confront witnesses, and the right to legal counsel. These provisions embody which of the following constitutional principles?
   A. Separation of powers
   B. Tyranny of the majority
   C. Checks and balances
   D. Due process of law

7. The constitutional principle that government does not have unrestricted authority over individuals is the definition for which of the following terms?
   A. Limited government
   B. Due process of law
   C. Separation of powers
   D. Bicameralism

8. The first 10 amendments to the Constitution are known as which of the following?
   A. Declaration of Independence
   B. Articles of Confederation
   C. Bill of Rights
   D. Bill of attainder

9. Do the provisions of the Bill of Rights apply to state governments?
   A. No. The Bill of Rights applies only to the actions of the federal government.
   B. Yes. The Supreme Court has ruled that the entire Bill of Rights applies to state governments as well as the national government.
   C. Yes. The Supreme Court has ruled that the Bill of Rights applies to the states but not to the national government.
   D. Yes, for the most part. The Supreme Court has ruled that most of the provisions of the Bill of Rights apply to the states.

10. The selective incorporation of the Bill of Rights to the states is based on which of the following constitutional provisions?
    A. The Due Process Clause of the Fourteenth Amendment
    B. The Equal Protection Clause of the Fourteenth Amendment
    C. The Privileges and Immunities Clause of the Fourteenth Amendment
    D. The Thirteenth Amendment

11. The political thought of Baron de Montesquieu is associated most closely with which of the following constitutional principles?
    A. Bill of Rights
    B. Separation of powers
    C. Federalism
    D. Due process of law

12. According to James Madison, what constitutional principle was designed to prevent the concentration of power in the hands of one government official or set of officials?
    A. Separation of powers with checks and balances
    B. Federalist Papers
    C. Tyranny of the majority
    D. Bill of Rights

13 The president nominates Person A to the U.S. Supreme Court, but the Senate rejects the nomination. This scenario is an example of which of the following?

A. Federalism

B. Bicameralism

C. Checks and balances

D. Tyranny of the majority

14 The state of California has tougher automobile emissions standards than the national government. This situation reflects which of the following constitutional principles?

A. Representative democracy

B. Bicameralism

C. Separation of powers with checks and balances

D. Federalism

15 Why did the framers of the Constitution create a bicameral legislative branch?

A. They wanted to ensure that the executive branch would be the dominant branch of government.

B. They wanted to prevent the legislative branch from becoming too powerful.

C. They wanted to prevent the judicial branch from becoming too powerful.

D. They wanted to strengthen the legislative branch.

16 Which of the following statements is true of the British parliamentary system?

A. It is undemocratic because it does not have separation of powers.

B. The House of Lords and the House of Commons are equally powerful.

C. The prime minister is chosen by the queen.

D. None of the above

17 Which of the following is a means through which the Constitution changes?

A. Practice and experience

B. Constitutional amendment

C. Judicial interpretation

D. All of the above

18 Which of the following is NOT a step in the process of amending the Constitution?

A. The House votes to propose the amendment by a two-thirds vote.

B. The Senate votes to propose the amendment by a two-thirds vote.

C. The president signs the proposed amendment.

D. Three-fourths of the states ratify the proposed amendment.

19 What was the significance of *Marbury v. Madison?*

A. It was the first case in which the U.S. Supreme Court declared an act of Congress unconstitutional.

B. The U.S. Supreme Court ruled that racial segregation was constitutional.

C. The U.S. Supreme Court ruled that state laws requiring racially segregated schools were unconstitutional.

D. The U.S. Supreme Court ruled that federal law takes precedence over state law.

20 How does the U.S. Constitution affect the policymaking process?

A. Change often comes slowly because the Constitution fragments political power.

B. Public policies often reflect compromise among various interests and groups.

C. Drastic policy changes are unlikely to occur.

D. All of the above

KNOW *the* **score**

18–20 correct: Congratulations! You are well informed!

15–17 correct: Your political knowledge is a bit low—be sure to review the key terms and visit TheThinkSpot.

<14 correct: Reread the chapter more thoroughly.

1. C; 2. B; 3. A; 4. D; 5. A; 6. D; 7. A; 8. C; 9. D; 10. A; 11. B; 12. A; 13. C; 14. D; 15. B; 16. D; 17. D; 18. C; 19. A; 20. D

the THINKSPOT
www.thethinkspot.com

# 3 THE FEDERAL

No Child Left Behind (NCLB) is a federal law that requires state governments and local school districts to institute basic skills testing in reading and mathematics for students in grades three through eight, and to use the results to assess school performance. Schools must assess student progress not just for the entire school but also by subgroups based on race/ethnicity, income level, English proficiency, and special education status. Even if a school's overall performance is good, it will receive a failing grade under the law if, for example, the performance of Latino or special-education students lags.[1] The goal of NCLB is to make schools regularly improve their performance so all students, including low-income and minority students and students with disabilities or with limited English proficiency, will be proficient in reading and math by 2014.

NCLB, which was named for a slogan used by the George W. Bush presidential campaign, substantially increases the role of the federal government in public education.[2] Historically, state and local governments operated the nation's public education system and provided more than 90 percent of education money.[3] NCLB forces states to neglect their own education reform plans to concentrate instead on creating an intricate system of high-stakes basic skills testing. Instead of learning to read, write, and do math, students will learn how to take multiple-choice exams to pass a particular test. The school may even pressure weak students to drop out of school before the test is administered in order to inflate school test scores.[4]

The controversy over the federal role in public education demonstrates the relevance of the federal system to the policymaking process.

# SYSTEM

59

after studying Chapter 3, students should be able to answer the following questions:

> What powers does the Constitution delegate to each of the three branches of the federal government, and what powers are implied? What is the status of the federal system in light of both *McCulloch v. Maryland* and recent Supreme Court rulings?

> How are federal programs adopted? What are the different kinds of grants, and what are the restrictions Congress places on the receipt of federal money?

> What is the impact of the federal system on each stage of the policymaking process?

# the constitutional
## BASIS OF FEDERALISM

t he United States has a **federal system**, which is a political system that divides power between a central government with authority over the whole nation and a series of state governments.

## Powers of the National Government

The powers explicitly granted to the national government by the Constitution are known as the **delegated** or **enumerated powers**. The Constitution grants each branch of the national government certain powers. It gives the legislative branch the most extensive list of powers and the judicial branch the least extensive.

**Powers of the Legislative Branch.** The Constitution vests the **legislative power**, the power to make laws, in Congress. In Article I, Section 8, the Constitution gives Congress broad legislative authority. Congress has the **power of the purse**, the authority to raise and spend money.

The Constitution charges Congress with providing for the "common defense and general welfare." It authorizes Congress to borrow money and to repay the nation's debt. Congress can regulate commerce among the states and trade with other nations. It can coin money, enact laws governing bankruptcy, set standards for weights and measures, provide for

**federal system** a political system that divides power between a central government, with authority over the whole nation, and a series of state governments.

**delegated or enumerated powers** the powers explicitly granted to the national government by the Constitution.

**legislative power** the power to make laws.

**power of the purse** the control of the finances of government.

**Checking Judicial**
• Appoint federal judges
• Enforce federal laws and court orders
• Grant reprieves and pardons

**Checking Executive**
• Declare executive branch actions unconstitutional

**Checking Legislative**
• Propose legislation to Congress
• Negotiate foreign treaties
• Serve as commander in chief of the armed forces
• Veto bills

## SEPARATION OF POWERS AND CHECKS AND BALANCES

EXECUTIVE BRANCH

JUDICIAL BRANCH

LEGISLATIVE BRANCH

**Checking Legislative**
• Declare acts of Congress unconstitutional

**Checking Executive**
• Pass all federal laws
• Pass the federal budget
• Declare war
• Ratify treaties and confirm presidential appointments
• Override presidential vetoes
• Impeachment

**Checking Judicial**
• Establish courts and set the number of judges
• Amend the Constitution
• Impeachment

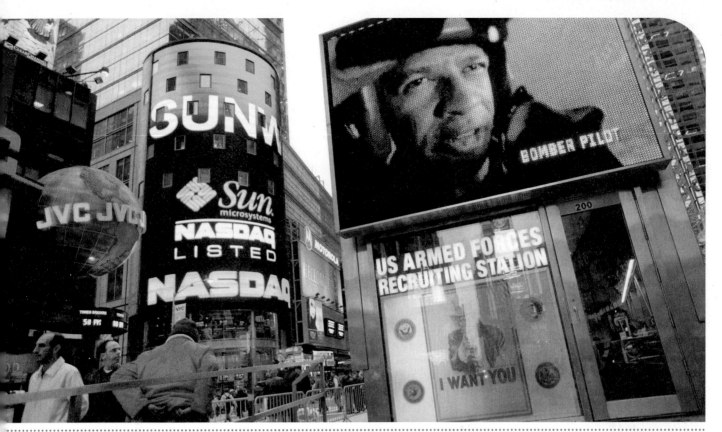

An Army recruiting center in New York City. In Article I, Section 8, the Constitution gives Congress the authority to "raise...Armies."

the punishment of counterfeiters, create post offices and post roads, and establish rules for copyright and patent protection. The Constitution also gives Congress an important role in foreign affairs and the nation's defense. Congress can suppress insurrection and repel invasion. It can declare war, raise and support armies, and maintain a navy.

Article I, Section 8 concludes with the **Necessary and Proper Clause or Elastic Clause**. "[Congress shall have the power] to make all laws which shall be necessary and proper for carrying into execution the foregoing powers, and all other powers vested by this Constitution in the government of the United States, or

> THE NECESSARY AND PROPER CLAUSE IS THE BASIS FOR MUCH OF THE LEGISLATION PASSED BY CONGRESS BECAUSE IT GIVES CONGRESS THE MEANS TO EXERCISE ITS DELEGATED AUTHORITY

in any department or office thereof." The Necessary and Proper Clause is the basis for much of the legislation passed by Congress because it gives Congress the means to exercise its delegated authority.

The Necessary and Proper Clause is the constitutional basis for the doctrine of **implied powers**, which are those powers of Congress not explicitly mentioned in the Constitution but derived by implication from the delegated powers. Because the Constitution explicitly grants Congress the authority to raise armies, for example, the power to draft men and women into the armed forces would be an example of an implied power. The authority to draft is not explicitly granted as a delegated power, but it can be inferred as an action "necessary and proper" for carrying out one of the delegated powers—raising armies.

**Powers of the Executive Branch.** The Constitution grants **executive power**, the power to enforce laws, to the president, declaring that the

**Necessary and Proper Clause/Elastic Clause** the Constitutional provision found in Article I, Section 8 that declares that "[Congress shall have the power] to make all laws which shall be necessary and proper for carrying into execution the foregoing powers, and all other powers vested by this Constitution in the government of the United States, or in any department or office thereof." It is the basis for much of the legislation passed by Congress because it gives Congress the means to exercise its delegated authority.

**implied powers** those powers of Congress not explicitly mentioned in the Constitution, but derived by implication from the delegated powers.

**executive power** the power to enforce laws.

the constitutional basis of federalism **61**

president should "take Care that Laws be faithfully executed." In Article II, the Constitution says that the president shall be commander in chief of the nation's armed forces. It states that the president may require reports from the heads of the executive departments, grant pardons and reprieves, make treaties with "the Advice and Consent" of the Senate, and appoint ambassadors, judges, and other officials. The president may make policy recommendations to Congress, receive ambassadors, and convene special sessions of Congress.

**Powers of the Judicial Branch.** The Constitution vests **judicial power**, the power to interpret laws, in a Supreme Court and whatever other federal courts Congress sees

"we know we're unfair ...but if Oregon's angry, who really cares?"

"GORDON SMITH JOHN ASHCROFT KEVIN MANNIX THREE PEAS IN A POD"

An Oregon campaign flyer groups three Republicans, claiming all three would end Oregon's Death With Dignity Law and undermine the Tenth Amendment to the Constitution.

fit to create. In Article III, the Constitution declares that the judicial power extends to all cases arising under the Constitution, federal law, and treaties. The Constitution gives the Supreme Court of the United States the authority to try a limited range of cases, such as cases affecting ambassadors and cases in which a state is a party. Congress determines the types of cases that may be appealed to the Court.

**National Supremacy.** The Constitution addresses the question of the relative power of the national and state governments in Article VI in a passage known as the **National Supremacy Clause**. This is the constitutional provision that declares that the Constitution and laws of the United States take precedence over the constitutions and laws of the states. The U.S. Constitution is superior to national law, state constitutions, and state laws. National law is superior to state constitutions and state laws.

## The Constitutional Status of the States

The Constitution discusses the relationship of states with one another and with the national government. The **Full Faith and Credit Clause** is the constitutional provision requiring that states recognize the official acts of other states, such as marriages, divorces, adoptions, court orders, and other legal decisions. The **Privileges and Immunities Clause** is a constitutional provision prohibiting state governments from discriminating against the citizens of other states. This provision ensures that visitors to a state are accorded the same legal protection, travel rights, and property rights as a state's own citizens. **Extradition** is the return from one state to another of a person accused of a crime. A person charged with a crime in California who flees to

**judicial power** the power to interpret laws.

**National Supremacy Clause** the constitutional provision that declares that the Constitution and laws of the United States take precedence over the constitutions and laws of the states.

**Full Faith and Credit Clause** the constitutional provision requiring that states recognize the official acts of other states, such as marriages, divorces, adoptions, court orders, and other legal decisions.

**Privileges and Immunities Clause** the constitutional provision prohibiting state governments from discriminating against the citizens of other states.

**extradition** the return from one state to another of a person accused of a crime.

**republic** a representative democracy in which citizens elect representatives to make policy decisions on their behalf.

Nevada, for example, could be extradited back to California.

The Constitution prohibits states from taking certain actions. States may not negotiate international treaties, form alliances with foreign countries, or engage in war unless they are invaded. States may not create their own currency or levy taxes on commerce with other states or foreign nations.

The Constitution includes a number of guarantees to the states. It declares that states may not be divided or consolidated without their permission. The Constitution also promises states defense against invasion, protection from domestic violence when requested, equal representation in the U.S. Senate, and a republican form of government. A **republic** is a representative democracy in which citizens elect representatives to make policy decisions on their behalf. The Eleventh Amendment prohibits foreign residents or the citizens of other states from suing a state in federal court.

The best-known constitutional guarantee given the states is the Tenth Amendment: "The powers not delegated to the United States by the Constitution, nor prohibited by it to the states, are reserved to

Which side more closely reflects your point of view: the supporters of a strong national government or the advocates of states' rights? Why?

the states respectively, or to the people." The powers of the national government are enumerated in the Constitution—the delegated powers. According to the Tenth Amendment, the powers not delegated to the national government are reserved to the states or to the people. **Reserved,** or **residual powers**, then, are the powers of government left to the states. In other words, the national government may exercise only those powers granted to it by the Constitution, whereas state governments possess all the powers not given to the national government, except those that are prohibited to the states by the Constitution.

## The States' Rights/ National Government Supremacy Controversy

The supporters of states' rights and the proponents of national government supremacy have long debated the role of the states and the national government in the federal system. The doctrine of **states' rights** is an interpretation of the Constitution that favors limiting the authority of the federal government while expanding the powers of the states. The advocates of states' rights believe that the Constitution is a compact among the states that restricts the national government to those powers explicitly granted to it

by the Constitution, that is, to the delegated powers. They would question, for example, whether the federal government should be involved in public education at all. The advocates of states' rights argue that the scope of the implied powers should be strictly limited. In contrast, the supporters of national government supremacy contend that the Constitution is a contract among the people rather than the states. They note that the document begins with the following phrase: "We the people..." The supporters of a strong national government believe that the implied powers should be construed broadly in order to further the interests of the people. The federal government has a role to play in public education, they say, because it has a duty to "promote the general Welfare."

## The Federal System and the Supreme Court

The Supreme Court of the United States first addressed the controversy over the relationship between the states and the national government in the famous case of *McCulloch v. Maryland* (1819), when the Court ruled that states do not have the right to interfere in the constitutional operations of the national government. (See box on next page.)

## NATIONAL POWERS
### (ENUMERATED)

- COIN MONEY
- CONDUCT FOREIGN RELATIONS
- REGULATE COMMERCE WITH FOREIGN NATIONS AND AMONG THE STATES
- RAISE AND SUPPORT ARMIES
- PROVIDE AND MAINTAIN A NAVY
- DECLARE AND CONDUCT WAR
- ESTABLISH A NATIONAL COURT SYSTEM
- MAKE LAWS NECESSARY AND PROPER TO CARRY OUT THE DELEGATED POWERS

## CONCURRENT POWERS
### (SHARED)

- TAX
- BORROW MONEY
- MAKE AND ENFORCE LAWS
- CHARTER BANKS AND CORPORATIONS
- SPEND MONEY FOR THE GENERAL WELFARE
- TAKE PRIVATE PROPERTY FOR PUBLIC PURPOSES, WITH JUST COMPENSATION

## STATE POWERS
### (RESERVED)

- ESTABLISH LOCAL GOVERNMENTS
- REGULATE COMMERCE IN THE STATE
- CONDUCT ELECTIONS
- RATIFY AMENDMENTS TO THE FEDERAL CONSTITUTION
- TAKE MEASURES FOR PUBLIC HEALTH, SAFETY, AND MORALS
- EXERCISE POWERS THE CONSTITUTION DOES NOT DELEGATE TO THE NATIONAL GOVERNMENT OR PROHIBIT THE STATES FROM USING

# THE GROWTH OF FEDERAL POWER
## MCCULLOCH V. MARYLAND (1819)

### BACKGROUND

In 1791, Congress chartered a national bank, the First Bank of the United States, amid great controversy. Secretary of State Thomas Jefferson opposed the bank because the authority to create it was not among the powers specifically enumerated by the Constitution. In contrast, Secretary of the Treasury Alexander Hamilton supported the bank and the power of Congress to establish it. He believed that the action of Congress was justified as an exercise of authority reasonably implied by the delegated powers. Despite the controversy, no legal challenge to the bank arose, and it operated until its charter expired in 1811.

### CASE

Congress chartered the Second Bank of the United States in 1816. It, too, became the object of controversy, particularly in the West and South. Critics accused the bank of corruption and inefficiency. The most serious charge was that the bank was responsible for an economic downturn that ruined thousands of investors. Several states responded to the public outcry against the bank by adopting restrictions on it or levying heavy taxes against it. Maryland, for example, required payment of an annual tax of $15,000 on the bank's Baltimore branch, which, in those days, was a sum large enough to drive the bank out of business in the state. When James W. McCulloch, the bank's cashier, refused to pay the tax, Maryland sued. The case presented two important constitutional issues: 1) Does the national government have authority to charter a bank?; and 2) Does a state have the power to tax an arm of the national government?

### DECISION

Chief Justice John Marshall wrote the unanimous opinion of the U.S. Supreme Court, answering both questions. First, the Court upheld the authority of Congress to charter a bank on the basis of the doctrine of implied powers. Marshall noted that although the Constitution does not specifically grant Congress the power to incorporate a bank, the Constitution does say that Congress may lay and collect taxes, borrow money, and raise and support armies. What if, Marshall asked, tax money collected in the North is needed in the South to support an army? The creation of a national bank to transport that money would be a "necessary and proper" step to that end. The power to charter the bank, Marshall held, was implied by the Necessary and Proper Clause.[5] Second, the Court ruled that Maryland's tax was unconstitutional. The power to tax, said Marshall, is the power to destroy because a high tax can drive the object of the taxation out of existence. If Maryland or any state has the authority to tax an arm of the national government, it could effectively shut it down and that would be contrary to the nature of the federal union as stated in the National Supremacy Clause.

### IMPLICATIONS

The Supreme Court's decision in *McCulloch v. Maryland* supported the position of those who favored national government supremacy. By giving broad scope to the doctrine of implied powers, the Court provided the national government with a vast source of power. By stressing the importance of the National Supremacy Clause, the Court denied states the right to interfere in the constitutional operations of the national government.

The Supreme Court has not always been as receptive to the exercise of federal power as it was in *McCulloch v. Maryland*. In 1857, a few years before the outbreak of the Civil War, the infamous *Dred Scott* decision held that the national government lacked authority to regulate slavery in the territories.[6] Similarly, in the early 1930s, the Supreme Court limited the power of the national government to respond to the Great Depression by striking down much of the **New Deal**, the legislative package of reform measures proposed by President Franklin Roosevelt for dealing with the economic crisis.

> The Supreme Court's decisions in *Dred Scott* and its anti–New Deal rulings were all eventually reversed.

The Supreme Court's decisions in *Dred Scott* and its anti–New Deal rulings were all eventually reversed. Congress and the states overturned the *Dred Scott* decision by ratifying the Thirteenth, Fourteenth, and Fifteenth Amendments. The Supreme Court reversed itself in the late 1930s, eventually holding New Deal legislation constitutional. For half a century thereafter, the Supreme Court found few constitutional limitations on the exercise of federal power.

In recent years, however, the Supreme Court has issued a series of states' rights rulings. In 1995, the Supreme Court ruled that Congress had overstepped its authority when it enacted the Gun-Free School Zones Act of 1990, banning firearms within 1,000 feet of a school. The Court found the act unconstitutional, ruling that Congress can regulate only the economic activity that "substantially affects" interstate commerce, and that the possession of a firearm in the

**New Deal** a legislative package of reform measures proposed by President Franklin Roosevelt for dealing with the Great Depression.

# Taking Sides

# Federalism and the States

**What level of government is best equipped to determine and enforce individual rights and obligations?**

**Is Madison correct in his belief that the authority of both the federal and state governments should be allowed to fluctuate in response to historical events?**

**Overview:** The doctrine of federalism was meant to be a flexible mechanism within which to address the needs and desires of the American people. James Madison contends in the *Federalist Papers* that, over time, the American people will themselves determine which level of government should have primary law and policy-making authority, and that this authority will alternate between the federal and state governments in response to historical events.

Over the past few years, the proper role of both federal and state governments in determining social policy has been front and center in the domestic policy debates surrounding marriage rights, though with an unusual turn of events. Many social conservatives, typically linked to a limited-government philosophy which holds that the states should have significant authority over individual citizens, now argue for a constitutional amendment to define marriage rights. Social liberals, who have long held that the federal government has the primary role in protecting reproductive rights, now make the argument that it is up to the states to determine marriage rights. What gives?

Neither side is being hypocritical; they are simply pursuing political strategies within the framework of the Constitution that promote their conception of American life. The question being posed, however, raises a fundamental constitutional issue: Who determines the rights of the people? Is it the federal government—particularly the judiciary—or the state governments who have the Tenth Amendment authority to inform the American people of their rights?

## supporting an increased policymaking role for the states

**state governments are closer to the people and are better suited to represent their needs.** For example, the people of the state of California have determined that marriage is defined by the union of a man and a woman, whereas the states of Massachusetts and Connecticut have held that homosexuals cannot be denied marriage licenses.

**the founders were correct in their assessment that the states could be "laboratories" in which there will be policy innovation.** Take, for instance, global warming policy. The state of California enacted legislation in 2006 that mixes innovative market and regulatory mechanisms that may be copied by other states to help reduce carbon discharge.

**the Tenth Amendment gives the states the authority to determine the specific rights of their citizens.** The recent decisions of the Supreme Court that have restored the right of the states to govern individual citizens are simply the return to proper constitutional principles.

## against an increased policymaking role for the states

**the states have demonstrated that they are incapable of enforcing significant policy.** For example, the state of Louisiana demonstrated it could not effectively undertake disaster preparedness in the aftermath of Hurricane Katrina. Later policy analysis showed that most states lack the means to handle significant disasters.

**some state governments, due to their small size, do not have the means to adequately address the policy needs of their citizens, and this creates *de facto* inequality that may violate the Fourteenth Amendment.** For example, the state of Texas on its own has the world's eighth-largest economy and is thus better positioned to address the needs of its citizens than Arkansas, one of the poorest states in the country.

**changes in technology and social mores make it imperative that the federal government increase its regulatory control.** For example, the American founders could not foresee such technological and communications innovation as the computer and the Internet. Only an institution with the resources of the federal government can regulate the use and content of the Internet equitably and fairly.

vicinity of a school does not meet that criterion.[7] In 1997, the Supreme Court overturned a provision in the **Brady Act**, a federal gun control law that requires a background check on an unlicensed purchaser of a firearm. The Court ruled unconstitutional a provision in the bill that required local law enforcement agencies to conduct background checks on potential gun purchasers. The Court said that the national government did not have the authority to force state governments to carry out its regulatory policies.[8] In 2000, the Supreme Court threw out a provision in the federal Violence Against Women Act that gave the victims of sexual assault the right to sue their attackers for damages. Congress based the measure on its constitutional power to regulate interstate commerce, but the Court ruled that violent crime is insufficiently connected to interstate commerce to justify Congress taking action.[9]

**Brady Act** a federal gun control law that requires a background check on an unlicensed purchaser of a firearm in order to determine whether the individual can legally own a weapon.

**Congress took** advantage of the Supreme Court's broad interpretation of the doctrine of implied powers to exercise authority in a wide range of policy areas. In particular, Congress made frequent use of the Commerce Clause to justify legislation. The Commerce Clause is the constitutional provision giving Congress authority to "regulate commerce ... among the several states." Congress used the Commerce Clause as a basis for legislation dealing with such diverse subjects as child labor, agricultural price supports, and racial discrimination in public places. In each instance, Congress argued that the particular activity it sought to regulate was part of interstate commerce, which Congress is empowered to regulate, and in each instance, the Supreme Court eventually accepted the argument.

## Under the Umbrella of the Commerce Clause

# Supreme Court Decisions:
# National Supremacy vs. States' Rights

■ Decisions for National Supremacy
■ Decisions for States' Rights

**1819 | *McCulloch v. Maryland*** Determined that Maryland had no power to interfere with the Second Bank of the United States.

**1958 | *Ableman v. Booth*** Held that state courts cannot issue rulings that contradict the decisions of federal courts.

**1997 | *Printz v. United States*** Ruled unconstitutional provision of the Brady Handgun Violence Prevention Act that would compel local officers to conduct background checks.

**2005 | *Gonzales v. Raich*** Allowed that Congress may ban the use or possession of marijuana, even in states that permit its use for medicinal purposes.

| 1820 | 1930 | 1940 | 1950 | 1960 | 1990 | 2000 | 2010 |

**1824 | *Gibbons v. Ogden*** Held that the power to regulate interstate navigation was granted to Congress by the Commerce Clause.

**1857 | *Dred Scott v. Sanford*** Declared that Congress had no authority to abolish slavery in federal territories.

**1932 | *Worcester v. Georgia*** Ruled that Native Americans were entitled to federal protection from state governments' actions that would infringe on their sovereignty.

**2000 | *U.S. v. Morrison*** Struck down parts of the Violence Against Women Act as unconstitutional because they exceeded congressional power.

**2006 | *Gonzales v. Oregon*** Ruled that the Federal Justice Department cannot block physician-assisted suicides, as permitted by an Oregon law.

# federal grant
## PROGRAMS

a **federal grant program** is a program through which the national government gives money to state and local governments to spend in accordance with set standards and conditions. NCLB is an example of a federal program that deals with public education. Other federal programs address such policy areas as transportation, childhood nutrition, healthcare, public housing, vocational education, airport construction, hazardous waste disposal, job training, law enforcement, scientific research, neighborhood preservation, mental health, and substance abuse prevention and treatment.

## functions of
## FEDERAL GRANTS

health 232.3
income security 94.9
education/employment 57.2
transportation 56.1
community and regional development 17.1
environment 5.9
administration of justice 4.2
general government 4.2
other 3.3
agriculture 0.9
total: $462 Billion

The national government provides state and local governments with more than $450 billion in grant funding. Medicaid is the largest federal grant program, accounting for more than 43 percent of federal grant funding.
www.gpoaccess.gov/usbudget/fy09/bis.html

## takeaction
### FEDERAL PROGRAMS AND YOU >>

Federal grants and loans are important for students and the institutions they attend. Many students depend on federal financial aid to complete their degrees. Furthermore, federal grant and loan programs effectively subsidize higher education by making it possible for students to go to college. Institutions that lose their accreditation must often close their doors because they forfeit their ability to award federal financial aid to their students.

Federal financial assistance to students comes in the form of grants and loans. Students need not repay grant money, but loans must be repaid. Pell Grants provide federal financial assistance to students based on their financial need. The amount of money that students can receive depends on the cost of their education and their available financial resources. Federal Family Education Loans (FFEL) and the Stafford Loan Program enable students to borrow money to attend college. Depending on their financial need, students may be eligible for subsidized federal loans, which do not begin assessing interest until recipients begin repayment.

Your assignment is to complete the paperwork to apply for federal financial aid. Visit your college's financial aid office or go to its website to obtain the appropriate documents. You may wish to attend a financial aid seminar to learn what aid is available and whether you are eligible. Complete the paperwork and submit the original or a copy to your instructor to document that you have completed the assignment.

### HOW YOU'RE FOOTING THE BILL:
### UNDERGRADUATE FINANCIAL AID

FEDERAL LOANS ($39.1)
INSTITUTIONAL GRANTS ($20.6)
PELL GRANTS ($12.9)
STATE GRANTS ($7.5)
PRIVATE & EMPLOYER GRANTS ($7.3)
EDUCATION TAX CREDITS & DEDUCTIONS ($5.1)
FEDERAL GRANT PROGRAMS OTHER THAN PELL ($3.6)

Undergraduate student aid (in billions) in 2007.

## Program Adoption

Congress and the president adopt federal programs through the legislative process. Both houses of Congress must agree to establish a program and the president must either sign the legislation or allow it to become law without signature. If the president vetoes the measure, it can become law only if Congress votes to override the veto by a two-thirds margin in each house. Congress passed the No Child Left Behind Act in late 2001 and President Bush signed it into law in early 2002.

**federal grant program** a program through which the national government gives money to state and local governments to spend in accordance with set standards and conditions.

# DEPARTMENT OF EDUCATION BUDGET

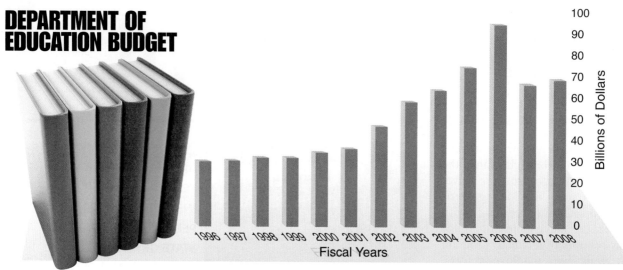

Source: Office of Management and Budget

Federal programs must be authorized and funds appropriated for their operation. The **authorization process** is the procedure through which Congress legislatively establishes a program, defines its general purpose, devises procedures for its operation, specifies an agency to implement the program, and indicates an approximate level of funding for the program but does not actually provide money. Although Congress authorizes some federal programs on a permanent basis, it stipulates that other programs must be re-authorized periodically. NCLB is the re-authorizing legislation for the Elementary and Secondary Education Act (ESEA) of 1965, which was the authorization legislation for most federal education programs.

The **appropriations process** is the procedure through which Congress legislatively allocates money for a particular purpose. The appropriations process takes place annually. Federal programs do not function unless Congress authorizes them *and* appropriates money for their operation. Without money, programs go out of business or, if they are new programs, never begin functioning. Even if opponents of a federal program cannot prevent its authorization, they can accomplish the same goal by cutting or eliminating the program's funding.

## Types of Federal Programs

Federal programs come in a variety of forms.

**Categorical and Block Grants.** A **categorical grant program** is a federal grant program that provides funds to state and local governments for a narrowly defined purpose, such as removing asbestos from school buildings or acquiring land for outdoor recreation. In this type of program, Congress allows

**FEDERAL PROGRAMS DO NOT FUNCTION UNLESS CONGRESS AUTHORIZES THEM AND APPROPRIATES MONEY FOR THEIR OPERATION**

state and local officials little discretion as to how the money is spent. Categorical grants comprise more than 90 percent of all federal grants and provide nearly 90 percent of federal grant money to state and local governments.[10] A **block grant program** is a federal grant program that provides money for a program in a broad, general policy

**authorization process** the procedure through which Congress legislatively establishes and defines a program, but does not actually provide funding for it.

**appropriations process** the procedure through which Congress legislatively allocates money for a particular purpose.

**categorical grant program** a federal grant program that provides funds to state and local governments for a fairly narrow, specific purpose.

**block grant program** a federal grant program that provides money for a program in a broad, general policy area.

area, such as childcare or job training. State and local governments have more discretion in spending block grant funds than they have in spending categorical grant money.

Officials at different levels of government hold contrasting views about categorical and block grants. Most state officeholders favor block grants because they allow states more discretion in implementation. In contrast, members of Congress usually prefer categorical grants because they enable Congress

# Education Policy and Federalism in Germany

Encouraged by the Allied powers, Germany created a federal system after World War II. Having fought two world wars against Germany, the allies wanted the Germans to create a political system that would disperse power among the national government and a series of states, rather than concentrate it in a central government. The German federal system divides power between a national government and 16 states called *länder*.[11]

Although the German Constitution grants the *länder* exclusive jurisdiction over education policy, the German public supports a uniform national approach to education. Unlike the American states, the *länder* are more accurately described as administrative units rather than historically or culturally distinct regions. Public opinion favors centralized education policymaking with a uniform national policy because German society is culturally homogeneous, and the public wants the schools to promote national unity. The German public also believes that a consistent national educational policy promotes academic excellence, whereas educational diversity produces mediocrity.

The *länder* use the Standing Conference of Ministers of Culture (KMK) to circumvent the constitutionally required decentralization of educational policy. The KMK has negotiated an agreement to standardize the curriculum, establish uniform educational assessment criteria, and coordinate the timing and duration of the school year among the *länder*. Consequently, Germany has a uniform national education policy despite the constitutional requirement of decentralization.[12]

## Questions

1. Would the German public favor or oppose an educational initiative such as No Child Left Behind? Why or why not?

2. Why do Americans, unlike the Germans, resist a national set of educational policies?

3. Do you believe states should be able to set their own education policies or should education policy be determined at the national level?

Students in German schools follow a national curriculum.

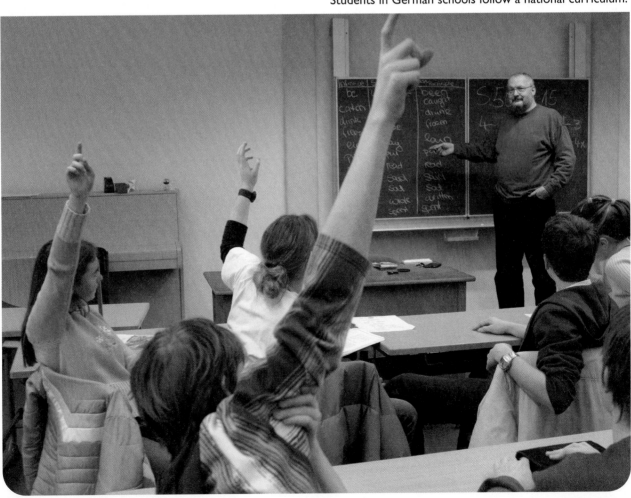

to exercise more control over implementation. Members of the U.S. House, in particular, like categorical grants because they entail special projects that can be targeted to individual congressional districts.[13]

**Project and Formula Grants.** Federal grants differ in the criteria by which funding is awarded. A **project grant program** requires state and local governments to compete for available federal money. State and local governments make detailed grant applications which federal agencies evaluate to make funding decisions. A **formula grant program** awards funding on the basis of a formula established by Congress. In contrast to project grants, formula grants provide money for every state and/or locality that qualifies under the formula. Most formulas are based on state population with modifications designed to focus on areas of greater need and to ensure that every state receive at least a minimal amount of money.[14] Formula grants outnumber project grants by a four-to-one ratio. Most federal money is awarded through formula grants as well.[15]

**think**

**If you were a member of Congress, would you prefer block grants or categorical grants?**

## Grant Conditions

Federal grants usually come with conditions. A **matching funds requirement** is the legislative provision that the national government will provide grant money for a particular activity only on condition that the state or local government supplies a certain percentage of the total money required for the project or program. For example, the federal government covers only 75 percent of the cost of highway construction projects, requiring states to provide a 25 percent match. About half of all federal grant programs require funding participation by the recipient.[16]

## federal GRANTS

| | Purpose | Discretion given to state and local governments | Example |
|---|---|---|---|
| **Categorical Grant** | Narrowly defined purpose | Very little flexibility | Food Stamp Program |
| **Block Grant** | For a broad, general policy area | Some flexibility | Community Development Program |
| | **How is money allocated?** | | **Example** |
| **Project Grant** | • State and local governments compete for available federal money<br>• Doesn't provide money for every state/locality that qualifies | | National Sciences Foundation grants for biological sciences |
| **Formula Grant** | • Funding awarded based on formula established by Congress to focus on areas of greater need<br>• Provides money for every state/locality that qualifies | | School Lunch Program, Unemployment Insurance, Temporary Assistance for Needy Families (TANF) |

# Binge Drinking

## COLLEGE PRESIDENTS WANT DRINKING AGE LOWERED TO 18

**By Jennifer Maloney**
**AUGUST 19, 2008**

COLLEGE PRESIDENTS from more than 100 schools across the country are calling on lawmakers to do something about binge drinking: Consider lowering the drinking age from 21 to 18.

"Twenty-one is not working," says the group's statement, signed by presidents from prominent colleges such as Dartmouth, Duke and Syracuse. "A culture of dangerous, clandestine 'binge drinking'–often conducted off-campus–has developed."

Even before the presidents begin the public phase of their efforts, which might include newspaper ads in the coming weeks, they face sharp criticism.

Mothers Against Drunk Driving says lowering the drinking age would lead to more fatal car crashes. It accuses the presidents of misrepresenting research and looking for an easy way out of an inconvenient problem, and urges parents to think carefully about safety at colleges whose presidents have signed on.

The current law, Duke University president Richard Brodhead said, "pushes drinking into hiding, heightening its risks, including risks from drunken driving, and it prevents us from addressing drinking with students as an issue of responsible choice."

The two sides agree alcohol abuse by college students is a huge problem, but disagree on whether raising the legal drinking age to 21 has saved lives.

In 1984, Congress voted to penalize any state that set its legal drinking age lower than 21 by rescinding 10 percent of that state's federal highway funding. Here are some pros and cons of lowering the drinking age, according to organizations that have studied the issue.

### PROS

The United States has the oldest drinking age in the world. Most nations allow alcohol consumption at 16 or 18, and some have no minimum drinking age at all.

A lower drinking age could lead to less binge drinking, experts say, since 18- to 20-year-olds won't have to imbibe surreptitiously.

At 18, Americans can marry, serve in the military, vote and enter into legally binding contracts.

### CONS

Safer roads. Laws setting the drinking age at 21 cut traffic fatalities involving drivers age 18–20 by 13 percent, according to a National Highway Traffic Safety Administration study.

Since states' laws differ on the drinking age, the result could be 18- to 20-year-olds traveling across state lines to buy or consume alcohol with sometimes disastrous results.

Adolescents' brains, some studies say, are still developing past the age of 18 and significant alcohol use can interfere in that process.

## ↗ CRITICAL THINKING QUESTIONS:

- Why do you think college presidents rather than college students are taking the lead on this issue?
- From your personal experience, does the 21-year minimum legal drinking age work to reduce drunken driving by young adults?
- Do you think that state legislatures would even consider reducing the minimum legal drinking age until Congress repeals the legislation that penalizes (with a loss of highway funding) states which have a lower-than-21 drinking age?

>> END

Matching funds requirements sometimes force states and localities to devote ever-growing sums of money to particular programs. Consider the impact on state budgets of **Medicaid**, a federal program designed to provide health insurance coverage to low-income persons, people with disabilities, and elderly people who are impoverished. The federal government and the states split the cost of Medicaid, with the federal government pick-

Congress also imposes mandates on recipients of federal funds. A **federal mandate** is a legal requirement placed on a state or local government by the national government requiring certain policy actions. Some mandates apply to grants recipients in general. These include provisions in the area of equal rights, equal access for the disabled, environmental protection, historic preservation, and union wage rates for contractors' person-

Grant conditions and federal mandates impose substantial costs on state and local governments. The National Conference on State Legislatures estimates the annual cost of federal mandates to states at $30 billion.[19] The most expensive federal programs for states and localities are federally mandated special education programs, NCLB, and prescription drug costs for people eligible for both Medicare and Medicaid.[20]

ing up 50 to 80 percent of the cost, depending on a state's wealth. Healthcare costs, especially the cost of prescription drugs, are rapidly rising. Medicaid is the most rapidly growing item in most state budgets, accounting for 13 percent of state general fund expenditures.[17]

nel. Individual programs often have particular strings attached as well. In order to receive federal law enforcement grants, for example, states must collect data on sex offenders, include DNA samples, and prepare a statewide sex offender registry database.[18]

**federal mandate** a legal requirement placed on a state or local government by the national government requiring certain policy actions.

the THINKSPOT
www.thethinkspot.com

## CONCLUSION
# federalism
# & PUBLIC POLICY

the federal system is a fundamental part of the legal/constitutional environment for policymaking, affecting every stage of the policy process.

## Agenda Building

The United States does not have a single government but rather thousands of interconnected governments. Each level of government has its own policy agenda and procedures for policy adoption.

State and local governments have adopted legislation to address some policy issues because the federal government has failed to act. Frustrated with a lack of federal action on illegal immigration, for example, many states have adopted measures designed to address the issue. Several states have passed legislation to prevent illegal immigrants from obtaining driver's licenses.[21]

## Policy Formulation and Adoption

The federal system affects policy formulation. To a degree, each state is a policy laboratory. Both the federal government and other states draw from the experiences of particular states in formulating their own policies. For example, policymakers across the nation are closely watching the implementation of a healthcare program in Massachusetts aimed at providing universal health insurance coverage. The government subsidizes the cost of health insurance for lower-income people.[22] If the Massachusetts plan proves successful, it could be the basis of a national program.

The federal system influences policy adoption. Most policy issues in the United States are addressed by policies adopted by more than one unit and level of government. The national government, state governments, and local governments all adopt policies concerning issues such as education, healthcare,

> **Most policy issues in the United States are addressed by policies adopted by more than one unit and level of government.**

the environment, resource development, and law enforcement.

The national government affects state and local policy adoption through mandates and preemption. Federal mandates require states and localities to take certain actions. The National Voter Registration Act (also known as the Motor Voter Act) forces state governments to make it easier for people to register to vote. The Asbestos Hazard Emergency Response Act requires state and local governments to remove asbestos from all public buildings.

The federal government prevents state and local governments from making policy in some policy areas. An act of Congress adopting regulatory policies that overrule state policies in a particular regulatory area is known as **federal preemption of state authority.** Since 1965, Congress and the president have adopted more than 350 laws preempting state regulation, including

**federal preemption of state authority** an act of Congress adopting regulatory policies that overrule state policies in a particular regulatory area.

preemptions of state policies dealing with cellular phone rates, nuclear power safety, nutrition labeling, and private pension plans.[23] States may not regulate airlines, bus and trucking companies, mutual funds, or the telecommunications industry. For example, federal law prevents cities and other units of local government from banning the construction of cell towers even though many local residents would like to keep the towers out of their neighborhoods because they are unsightly and negatively affect property values.[24]

## Policy Implementation and Evaluation

Federalism affects policy implementation. Many of the policies adopted by the national government require implementation by state and local officials. NCLB is a federal education program that must be implemented by state and local governments. Federal regulations also affect the implementation of public policies adopted at the state level.

Finally, the federal system influences policy evaluation. Public officials at all levels of government evaluate policy and give feedback. State and local officials frequently communicate their evaluations of federal programs to members of Congress and senators from their states. Federal officials often evaluate the effectiveness of federal programs by assessing their implementation at the state and local level. Congress uses feedback from evaluation reports to redesign federal programs.

# TEST yourself

1. Which of the following is the foremost goal of the No Child Left Behind Act (NCLB)?
   A. To ensure that students with disabilities have access to educational opportunities
   B. To ensure that all public schools are racially integrated
   C. To make public school systems accountable for the progress of all students
   D. To provide free or reduced rate meals for school children from low-income families

2. A political system that divides power between a central government with authority over the whole nation and a series of state governments is known as which of the following?
   A. Federal system of government
   B. Confederation
   C. Unitary government
   D. Republic

3. Article I, Section 8 of the U.S. Constitution declares that Congress has the authority to coin money. Coining money is an example of which of the following?
   A. Delegated powers
   B. Implied powers
   C. Checks and balances
   D. Concurrent powers

4. Which of the following is true about Congress?
   A. The Constitution vests legislative power in Congress.
   B. Congress has the power of the purse.
   C. The Constitution delegates certain powers to Congress in Article I, Section 8.
   D. All of the above

5. Which of the following statements is accurate about the powers of Congress?
   A. Congress can exercise any power it wishes to exercise because it is a sovereign body.
   B. Congress can exercise any power except those powers prohibited by the U.S. Constitution.
   C. Congress can exercise only those powers delegated to it by the U.S. Constitution or implied through the application of the Necessary and Proper Clause.
   D. Congress can exercise only those powers given to it in the Bill of Rights.

6. In Article I, Section 8, the Constitution grants Congress authority to "regulate commerce among the several states." Congress passes legislation establishing regulations for interstate trucking, including safety standards for trucks and drivers. Which of the following constitutional provisions or principles gives Congress the authority to set standards for trucks and truck drivers?
   A. National Supremacy Clause
   B. Implied powers
   C. Concurrent powers
   D. Equal Protection Clause

7. The Elastic Clause is another name for which of the following constitutional provisions?
   A. National Supremacy Clause
   B. Equal Protection Clause
   C. Necessary and Proper Clause
   D. Commerce Clause

8. The Constitution delegates which of the following powers to the president?
   A. The power to regulate commerce among the states
   B. The power to command the armed forces
   C. The power to declare war
   D. All of the above

9. Suppose Congress passes a law which conflicts with the state constitution of Georgia. Which takes precedence—the U.S. law or the Georgia Constitution?
   A. The Georgia Constitution, because of the Tenth Amendment
   B. The Georgia Constitution, because all constitutions take precedence over all laws
   C. The U.S. law, because of the delegated powers
   D. The U.S. law, because of the National Supremacy Clause

10. A person wanted for a crime in New York flees to Florida where he is arrested. The procedure for returning the accused person to New York to face criminal charges is known as which of the following?
    A. Full Faith and Credit
    B. Privileges and Immunities
    C. Extradition
    D. Delegated powers

**11** The Tenth Amendment is the constitutional basis for which of the following?

A. Reserved powers

B. Delegated powers

C. Implied powers

D. Concurrent powers

**12** Both state governments and the national government have the constitutional authority to tax and spend. Therefore, the power to tax and spend is an example of which of the following?

A. Reserved powers

B. Delegated powers

C. Implied powers

D. Concurrent powers

**13** Which of the following statements would be most likely to come from an advocate of a strong national government as opposed to a supporter of states' rights?

A. National control makes for better public policies.

B. The Constitution is a compact among the states and the powers of the national government should be narrowly interpreted.

C. The powers of the national government should be closely limited to the delegated powers.

D. All of the above

**14** Would states' rights advocates favor or oppose the NCLB?

A. They would favor the law because it provides federal money to support state education programs.

B. They would favor the law because a Republican president was behind the adoption of the measure.

C. They would oppose the law because it increased federal involvement in education policy, which is traditionally an area of state responsibility.

D. They would oppose the law because it didn't provide enough money to support public education.

**15** Which of the following was part of the Supreme Court's ruling in *McCulloch v. Maryland*?

A. The Supreme Court ruled that Congress lacked the constitutional authority to charter a bank.

B. The Supreme Court ruled that the powers of Congress were limited to the delegated powers.

C. The Supreme Court upheld the Maryland tax on the bank.

D. None of the above

**16** A federal grant program that provides funds to state and local governments for a fairly narrow, specific purpose is known as which of the following?

A. Block grant

B. Formula grant

C. Categorical grant

D. Program grant

**17** A federal grant program that provides money for a program in a broad, general policy area, such as childcare or job training, is known as which of the following?

A. Block grant

B. Formula grant

C. Categorical grant

D. Program grant

**18** A grant program that requires state and local governments to compete for available federal money is known as which of the following?

A. Block grant

B. Formula grant

C. Categorical grant

D. Project grant

**19** A grant program that awards funding on the basis of a formula established by Congress is known as which of the following?

A. Block grant

B. Formula grant

C. Categorical grant

D. Program grant

**20** NCLB requires that states meet certain goals in order to continue receiving federal funds. This requirement is an example of which of the following?

A. Federal mandate

B. Matching funds requirement

C. Federal preemption of state authority

D. Project grant

---

KNOW *the* **score**

18–20 correct: Congratulations! You are well informed!

15–17 correct: Your political knowledge is a bit low—be sure to review the key terms and visit TheThinkSpot.

<14 correct: Reread the chapter more thoroughly.

---

1. C; 2. A; 3. A; 4. D; 5. C; 6. B; 7. C; 8. B; 9. D; 10. C; 11. A; 12. D; 13. A; 14. C; 15. D; 16. C; 17. A; 18. D; 19. B; 20. A

**4 PUBLIC**

Same-sex couples have been able to marry legally in Massachusetts since May 2004. Gay marriage resulted from a ruling by the Massachusetts Supreme Judicial Court (SJC) holding that the state lacked a rational basis for denying couples a marriage license simply because they wanted to marry a person of the same gender.

The opponents of gay marriage acted swiftly. In Massachusetts, an effort was begun to amend the state constitution to overturn the ruling. Twenty-five states adopted amendments to their state constitutions to prohibit same-sex marriage and six other states enacted legislative bans. On the national level, some members of Congress proposed an amendment to the U.S. Constitution to limit marriage to opposite sex couples. President George W. Bush endorsed the effort and stressed the issue during his 2004 reelection campaign.

By 2010, however, the momentum had changed. Both the attempt to amend the Massachusetts Constitution and the proposed amendment to the U.S. Constitution were apparently dead. Several states, including Iowa, New Hampshire, Vermont, and Connecticut, joined Massachusetts in granting same-sex couples marriage rights. Thirteen other states enacted civil union or domestic partnership laws giving same-sex couples the same legal rights as married couples.

The changing momentum on gay marriage both reflected and drove changes in **public opinion**. Between 2004 and 2009, support for gay marriage increased from 22 percent to 33 percent while opposition fell from 40 percent to 28 percent.[1] The growing support for gay marriage made it easier for public officials to resist efforts to ban same-sex unions and, in some states, support gay marriage. Meanwhile, the implementation of gay marriage in Massachusetts helped change public opinion because none of the calamities predicted by marriage opponents occurred.

# OPINION

"I DO" SUPPORT THE FREEDOM TO MARRY
Equality California | eqca.org

## ESSENTIALS...

**public opinion** combined personal opinions of adults toward issues of relevance to government.

# political SOCIALIZATION

the process through which individuals acquire political knowledge, attitudes, and beliefs is called **political socialization**. Socialization is a learning process, but it does not always take place in a classroom. Informal learning, filling out an income tax return, serving on a jury, and standing for the National Anthem also provide opportunities for political socialization.

## Process of Socialization

Grade-school students recognize terms such as *Congress*, *political party*, and *democracy*, but they do not understand their meanings. Many youngsters can name the political party their family supports, but they are unable to distinguish between the two major parties on issues. Almost all young children have a positive attitude toward government and its symbols. Most can distinguish the American flag from other flags, for example, and say they like it best.

In adolescence, young people begin to separate individuals from institutions. They understand, for example, that one can criticize the president while supporting the presidency. Adolescents are aware of processes such as voting and lawmaking, and their general understanding of these processes is more sophisticated.

Attitudes begin to diverge in the adolescent years. For example, many African American children grow less trustful of authority figures, especially police officers.[2] Political events can also drive adolescent socialization. For example, young people gain knowledge and develop party attachments during a presidential campaign. The more intense the po-

litical event, the more enduring the political views it creates. The Civil War and the Great Depression had a lifelong impact on generations of Americans.[3]

Political socialization continues in adulthood. Attitudes and basic political knowledge crystallize during early adulthood and tend to persist throughout life.[4] Nonetheless, as adults go to work, start families, and retire, they may change their views on specific political issues.

## Agents of Socialization

**Agents of socialization** contribute to political socialization by shaping formal and informal learning.

**political socialization** the process whereby individuals acquire political knowledge, attitudes, and beliefs.
**agents of socialization** those factors that contribute to political socialization by shaping formal and informal learning.

**Family.** Children acquire attitudes toward politics from their families. Voters, for example, are usually the children of voters.[5] Children of politically knowledgeable parents are themselves more likely to be well-informed about government and politics.[6]

Families influence at least the initial development of political party affiliation. As parents talk with one another and with their children, they are unconsciously constructing a "family identity" that may include party identification.[7] A study of fourth graders found that 60 percent of the youngsters identified with a party even though they had virtually no knowledge of party history, issues, or candidates.

Political similarities between parents and children diminish over time. Young adults frequently change their political and party affiliation in response to new socializing experiences. By the age of 25, young adults often adjust their political party identification to place it in line with the party they prefer on the issues about which they care.[8]

**School.** Civics classes enhance student knowledge of American government and politics. Coursework may lead students to watch news programs or read about current events online. Students may ask their parents more questions about political affairs.[9] Furthermore, community volunteers, fulfilling a high-school course requirement, may develop a lifetime habit of participation in community organizations and voting.[10]

Schools teach patriotism. In the classroom, students pledge allegiance to the flag, sing patriotic songs, commemorate national holidays, and study the lives of national heroes. Schools may provide ex-

**think**
Should schools teach youngsters to be patriotic Americans?

tracurricular activities, including student government organizations. Young people who learn participatory skills in school typically become participatory adults.[11]

Schools teach young people how to work within a power structure. Youngsters inevitably develop attitudes about authority and their roles as participants in a system. Some scholars believe that a primary focus of schools on compliance with rules hinders the development of political participation skills. This phenomenon is particularly true of schools in low-income areas.[12]

College students differ politically from high-school graduates. College life does appear to influence political attitudes as students are exposed to a variety of new ideas and people. As a result, they are less likely than non-college graduates to share their family's political views. However, college-bound youngsters already tended to vary from non-college peers even before they entered college.

**Religious Institutions.** People who are active in religious organizations are more likely to be politically engaged as well.[13] This association between religious and political activism is particularly important for African Americans.[14] Historically, the black church has been an important training ground for political leadership.

People tend to join religious organizations that promote their own political beliefs, but these can also influence political views.[15] This is particularly true for religious groups demanding an intense commitment of faith and a belief in religion as a source of truth. Members who accept the religious organization as the authoritative interpreter of the word of God often respect the political pronouncements of religious leaders as well.[16]

## What America Believes

- Religion very important
- Attended church/synagogue in the past week

**62%** **43%** — U.S.
**28%** **26%** — Canada
**17%** **17%** — Great Britain

Americans are more religious than people in most industrial nations. More than 60 percent of Americans tell survey researchers that religion is very important in their lives, and nearly two-thirds belong to a church, synagogue, or other religious body.

Lydia Saad, "Religion Is Very Important to Majority of Americans," December 5, 2003, available at www.gallup.com.

**think** Should churches and other religious institutions take positions on political issues and candidates?

**Peer Groups.** Friends and coworkers also shape political attitudes and beliefs. Those who know gays or lesbians are more supportive of gay rights.[17] Studies show that discussions among friends are more important than the media in influencing voter decisions.[18] When adults change jobs or neighborhoods, new peer groups may change their political views as well.[19]

People are more likely to share the values of a group that is important to them. Nonetheless, people may choose to remain in a group even when they disagree with its values. A study of conservative Christian churches found that nearly 40 percent of women members held feminist views contrary to those of their church. The feminist women remained in the church because they perceived little connection between their religious and political views.[20]

**Media.** Political participation is closely associated with media usage, especially newspaper and news-magazine readership. Nearly everyone who votes reads a newspaper. Young people who use media frequently understand American government and are more supportive of American values, such as free speech.[21]

The media, especially television, have been shown to determine the importance Americans attach to issues. Television news stories influence Americans' priorities.[22] Media reports also shape public opinion of a president. The more media focus on a policy issue, the more the public incorporates its knowledge of that issue into its overall judgment of a president.[23]

## Can Political Attitudes Be Genetically Transmitted?

Researchers compared the political attitudes of monozygotic (identical) and dizygotic (non-identical) twins in the United States and Australia. They found a genetic basis for the way individuals respond to environmental conditions. Political similarities between parents and children, then, may have as much to do with genetics as with socialization. The researchers suggest that the ideological division in American politics may have a genetic basis. They identify two distinct ideological orientations. People with an "absolutist" orientation are suspicious of immigrants, yearn for strong leadership and national

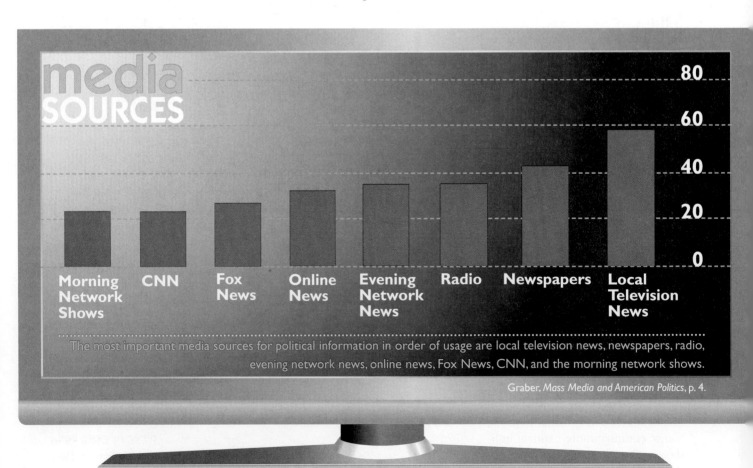

media SOURCES

Morning Network Shows | CNN | Fox News | Online News | Evening Network News | Radio | Newspapers | Local Television News

The most important media sources for political information in order of usage are local television news, newspapers, radio, evening network news, online news, Fox News, CNN, and the morning network shows.

Graber, *Mass Media and American Politics*, p. 4.

unity, and seek an unbending moral code. They favor punishment for those who violate society's moral code, tolerate economic inequality, and hold a pessimistic view of human nature. In contrast, people with a "contextualist" orientation are tolerant of immigrants and seek a context-dependent approach to proper social behavior. They dislike predetermined punishments, distrust strong leaders, disapprove of economic inequality, and hold an optimistic view of human nature.[24]

# measuring
## PUBLIC OPINION

**S**urvey research, the measurement of public opinion, is a familiar part of the American scene. Businesses use market surveys to assess public tastes for their products and services. Political campaigns employ polls to plan strategy. Public officials use surveys to assess public understanding of problems and issues.[25] The media use opinion surveys to gauge public reaction to political events and assess the popularity of officeholders and candidates.

## Sampling

In survey research, a **universe** is the population researchers wish to study. It may consist of all adult Americans, or Californians, or likely voters. Survey research enables scholars to examine the characteristics of a large group.

A **sample** is a subset, or smaller part of a universe. It must be chosen carefully to reflect its universe. A sample will allow for a **margin of error** (or **sample error**), a statistical term that refers to the accuracy of a survey. The margin of error's size depends on the size of the sample. The table to the right lists the margins of error for various sample sizes for a large universe. The margin of error decreases as the sample size increases and vice versa. The margin of error for samples of under 100 is so large as to make the survey meaningless. Researchers can reduce the margin of error by increasing the sample size. However, they can never eliminate error unless they survey every member of the universe. In practice, most professional survey research firms aim for a margin of error of plus or minus 3 to 4 percentage points.

The margin of error for a sample of 1,065 persons out of a universe of 500,000 or more is plus or minus 3 percentage points, 95 percent of the time. For example, suppose that we know that 10 percent of all adults are left-handed. Sampling theory tells us that, 95 percent of the time, a randomly selected sample of 1,065 people will include 7, 8, 9, 10, 11, 12, or 13 percent left-handers, that is, plus or minus 3 percentage points from 10, or the true proportion of left-handed people in this universe. Five percent of the randomly selected samples of 1,065 persons will produce an error that is greater than 3 percentage points. In other words, 5 samples out of 100 will contain a proportion of left-handed people less than 7 percent or more than 13 percent.

Survey research is not exact. Suppose one survey shows that Candidate X is leading Candidate Y by a 48 percent to 46 percent margin, while another survey indicates that Candidate Y is leading by 49 percent to 45 percent. The margin of error in each

## MARGINS OF ERROR for a Universe Greater than 500,000

| margin of error | sample size |
|---|---|
| +/– 4% | 600 |
| +/– 3% | 1,065 |
| +/– 2% | 2,390 |
| +/– 1% | 9,425 |

survey is a plus or minus 4 percentage points. Statistically, the surveys show the same result—support for the two candidates is within the margin of error. Neither candidate is actually ahead.

Statistical chance dictates that 5 percent of samples taken will have a margin greater than the margin of error. For example, even if two candidates are actually tied in voter support, an occasional sample will show one or the other with a lead greater than the margin of error. Over the course of an election campaign, surveys may show a good deal of small voter movement between candidates, or an occasional major shift in public support even though no actual change in voter support for the two candidates has taken place.

For accuracy, a sample must be representative of its universe. If researchers are interested in the views of all Americans, a sample of a thousand people from Atlanta, a thousand women, or a thousand callers to a radio talk show would not likely be representative. An unrepresentative sample is a **biased sample,** that is, a sample that tends to produce results that do not reflect the true characteristics of the universe because it is unrepresentative of the universe. Internet polls are unreliable because the sample consists of people who choose to participate, sometimes more than once.

A biased sample led to one of the most famous polling mistakes in history. Beginning in 1916, *Literary Digest* conducted presidential polls

"SURVEYS CONDUCTED BEFORE LOW TURNOUT ELECTIONS ARE FREQUENTLY INACCURATE BECAUSE POLLSTERS ARE UNABLE TO SEPARATE ACTUAL VOTERS AND NONVOTERS"

every four years. In 1936, the magazine mailed 10 million ballots to names taken from telephone directories and automobile registration lists. About two million people responded, and *Literary Digest* predicted that Republican Alf Landon would defeat Democrat Franklin Roosevelt. In fact, Roosevelt was reelected by the largest landslide in American history!

What went wrong? *Literary Digest*'s sample did not represent the universe of voters. At the height of the Great Depression, the people with telephones and automobiles

were middle- and upper-income, usually Republican, voters. Poor and working-class people could not afford cars and telephones, but they could vote, and they voted for Roosevelt.

The ideal approach is to employ a **random sample**. A random sample gives each member of a universe an equal likelihood of being included; it is unbiased. Researchers could select a random sample by picking names from a student list, for example, if the universe were students of a particular college. It is not always this easy. A random sample of voters in an upcoming election is difficult because no master list exists. Identifying likely voters is especially challenging because people don't like to admit they may not vote. Surveys conducted before low-turnout elections are frequently inaccurate because pollsters are unable to separate actual voters from nonvoters.

National survey research firms generate samples starting from a list

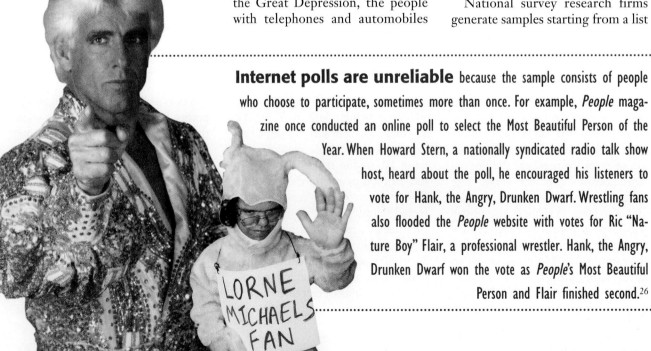

**Internet polls are unreliable** because the sample consists of people who choose to participate, sometimes more than once. For example, *People* magazine once conducted an online poll to select the Most Beautiful Person of the Year. When Howard Stern, a nationally syndicated radio talk show host, heard about the poll, he encouraged his listeners to vote for Hank, the Angry, Drunken Dwarf. Wrestling fans also flooded the *People* website with votes for Ric "Nature Boy" Flair, a professional wrestler. Hank, the Angry, Drunken Dwarf won the vote as *People*'s Most Beautiful Person and Flair finished second.[26]

LORNE MICHAELS FAN

of all telephone exchanges in the United States and an estimate of the number of households served by each exchange. A computer creates a master list of telephone numbers and then selects a random sample from its list. The computer creates a list of possible numbers rather than using actual telephone numbers so that unlisted telephone numbers will be as likely to be included as listed numbers. To correct for the possible bias of including only people who are usually home and answer their telephones, polling firms call back repeatedly at different times over several days. Once someone answers, the researchers do not necessarily interview that person. They ask for all the adults in the household and then randomly select a name.

Many people refuse to participate in opinion polls. The response rate for major national surveys is less than 30 to 40 percent. It is even less for snapshot polls taken overnight. Cell phones are another problem for survey researchers. Because wireless carriers charge users by the minute, cell phone users are less likely to participate than people using landlines.[27] Scholars are concerned that low response rates may make surveys inaccurate. Researchers attempt to compensate for differing response rates by adding men, young adults, and other demographic groups, which would otherwise be underrepresented in the sample.[28]

Measuring public opinion on controversial issues is especially difficult. Respondents may not answer questions honestly when they have to do with race, for example, because they do not want to appear prejudiced. Researchers have found voter preferences in contests between African American and white candidates typically overestimate the vote for the African American candidate because white voters may misreport their candidate preferences.[29]

## Question Wording

Question wording can affect survey responses because it provides a frame of reference for a question.[30] For example, a majority of Americans say that they oppose gay marriage, yet the nation is evenly divided on whether homosexual couples should be allowed "to legally form civil unions, giving them some of the legal rights of married couples." If the wording mentions "healthcare benefits and Social Security survivor benefits," approval rises to more than 60 percent.[31] Many Americans react negatively to

As an increasing number of young people opt out of landlines, survey researchers must find ways to ensure this demographic group is not underrepresented.

the use of the word *marriage* because it has a religious frame of reference. In contrast, questions that mention healthcare and Social Security benefits frame the issue in a legal rather than a religious context.

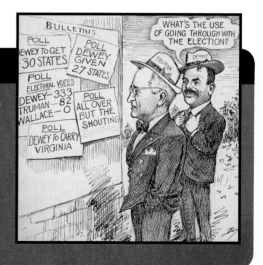

## Gay Marriage and Public Opinion

**BY KARLYN BOWMAN,** *Forbes.com*

**APRIL 27, 2009**

IN RECENT WEEKS, there has been flurry of activity on the same sex marriage front. Iowa (in a ruling by that state's Supreme Court) and Vermont (by a vote of the legislature) have legalized gay marriage. Other states are also in line to do so. Legislatures and courts have moved on the issue, but has public opinion?

Answers to survey questions about homosexuality show greater acceptance. For example, should homosexuality be legal? Forty-three percent gave that response to Gallup in 1977; 55% did in 2008. Should homosexuality be considered an acceptable alternative life style? Again from Gallup, 34% agreed in 1982, 57% do today. Should homosexuals have equal rights in terms of job opportunities? Fifty-five percent said yes in 1977, 89% in 2008. And what about gays in the military? Two-thirds support it, up about 10 percentage points from a decade ago.

Beyond that, two-thirds or more now say that inheritances, Social Security benefits, health insurance and hospital visitation should be available to gay and lesbian partners.

Most polls about civil unions date to the beginning of this decade. In February 2000, a Princeton Survey Research Associates/ *Newsweek* poll found that 47% of respondents said there should be legally sanctioned gay and lesbian unions or partnerships. In December of last year, 55% gave that response.

What accounts for the growing acceptance? Six in 10 people polled told Gallup last year that a friend, family or co-worker had told them he or she was gay—and familiarity fosters acceptance. We have also seen dramatic changes in views about the nature of homosexuality. Twelve percent said it was something you are born with in 1977; now 39% believe that is the case.

Finally, as older generations are replaced by younger ones, attitudes on this issue nationally have shifted in the liberal direction. Interestingly, young people are more likely than people in other age groups to see homosexuality as a lifestyle choice and not something people are born with, but, at the same time, they are also more likely to believe it cannot be changed.

But while Americans' opinions on gay marriage have become more liberal, courts and legislatures remain ahead of them. Majorities continue to oppose it. In 1988, in answer to NORC's question, only 12% agreed with the statement: "Homosexual couples should have the right to marry one another." In 2008, responding to Gallup and *Newsweek* polls, around 40% said they should have the right—but around 55% were opposed. In the *Newsweek* poll, 51% of 18- to 34-year-olds supported gay marriage; 22% of those 65 or older did.

### ↗ CRITICAL THINKING QUESTIONS:

- Why does knowing someone who is gay lead to greater acceptance of gay marriage?
- Why do you think younger people are more accepting of gay marriage than are older adults?
- In 20 years, would you expect that gay marriage would be allowed in a majority of states? Why or why not?

>> END

**think**

Should public officials use opinion surveys to determine what policies are most popular and then adopt those policies?

## Question Sequencing

The order of survey questions may also affect a survey's results. Question order can shape the context of responses. For example, asking about presidential job performance after questions about a particular government policy may affect a president's popularity if that policy is perceived as successful or unsuccessful. Professional researchers try to control this effect by rotating the order in which questions are asked.[32]

## Attitudes, Non-Attitudes, and Phantom Opinions

Professional pollsters offer respondents an opportunity to confess that they have not heard of an issue or do not have an opinion. Some survey researchers also ask respondents to indicate the intensity with which they hold their views and take that intensity into account in interpreting survey results.

Phantom opinions are made-up responses from respondents who do not want to appear uninformed.[33] A survey sponsored by the *Washington Post* asked a national sample of Americans this question: "Some people say the 1975 Public Affairs Act should be repealed. Do you agree or disagree that it should be repealed?" The survey found that 24 percent of the sample agreed, while 19 percent said that it should not be repealed. The other 57 percent had no opinion. Ironically, the people with no opinion were the best informed. The Public Affairs Act did not exist. Survey researchers made it up in order to test how many respondents would express an opinion on an issue about which they could obviously have no knowledge.[34]

## Interviewer-Respondent Interaction

The race or gender of an interviewer can affect survey results. For example, a survey measuring racial attitudes found black respondents were much more likely to say that white people could be trusted when the interviewer was white than when asked the same question by an African American.[35] Similarly, women are more likely to give pro-choice responses to questions about abortion to female interviewers than they are to male interviewers.[36]

## Timing

Even the most carefully conducted survey is only a snapshot of public opinion on the day of the poll. In March 1991, for example, following the American victory in the first Gulf War, the Gallup Poll showed that the approval rating of the first President Bush was 89 percent. Political observers predicted the president would win reelection easily. By August 1992, however, Bush's popularity rating had fallen below 35 percent, and three months later, he was defeated. [37]

# FRAMING THE QUESTION

**survey questions**

**...and the problems with these survey questions:**

**1** If you are now covered by Medicare, or if you soon will be, would you be willing to pay higher premiums, deductibles, or income tax surcharges for the following?
a) Catastrophic hospital coverage
b) Catastrophic nursing home coverage
c) Both
d) Neither

It forces respondents to choose among an unrealistically limited set of options. Some people might be willing to pay higher premiums and deductibles but not income tax surcharges or vice versa. How would they respond to the question?

**2** Do you believe abortion should be legal?
a) Yes
b) No
c) No opinion

Many people believe that abortion should be legal under certain circumstances but illegal under others. The question, with its oversimplified answer alternatives, would force these people to misstate their views.

**3** Should scientists and doctors be allowed to pursue stem cell research for the treatment of Alzheimer's, Parkinson's, diabetes, spinal cord injuries, and other tragic conditions?
a) Yes
b) No
c) Not sure

A biased question is a survey question that produces results tilted to one side or another. The question is biased because it misstates the issue. The policy debate over stem cell research is not over whether scientists should be allowed to conduct research but whether federal funds should support it. Furthermore, the question is biased because it ignores the concerns of stem cell research opponents while calling attention to the "tragic conditions" that stem cell research might be able to help.

# political
## KNOWLEDGE

political scientist W. Russell Neuman divides the public into three groups based on their knowledge and interest in government and politics. At one end of the spectrum, a large group of people, about a fifth of the population, is indifferent to politics; they have no opinions. At the other end are political junkies, a small group, probably less than 5 percent of the population, who are very interested and informed. The great majority of Americans fits in the middle category. They follow politics halfheartedly. They have opinions on some issues, but their views on many issues are vague and incomplete.[38]

Some groups of Americans are more knowledgeable than others. Men know more about politics than women. Whites are better informed than African Americans. Wealthy people are more knowledgeable than the poor. Republicans know more than Democrats. Well-educated people are better informed than people with less formal schooling.[39]

Knowledgeable Americans vote and cast an informed ballot. In 1994, 70 percent of well-informed survey respondents reported voting in that year's congressional elections. Only 25 percent of less knowledgeable respondents voted. Furthermore, knowledgeable respondents voted for candidates whose views on issues coincided with their own. In contrast, there was almost no relationship between the political issues that low-knowledge voters said mattered to them and the issue positions of the candidates for whom they voted.[40]

Some observers believe political ignorance has led to a "dumbing down" of campaigns, and to negative advertising in particular. Political scientist Samuel Popkin says that candidates now conduct two campaigns: one at informed voters, stressing issues and policy positions, the other directed at less well-informed voters, attacking the character of their opponents.[41]

## Support for Democratic Principles

Survey data on gay and lesbian rights raise questions about public support for basic democratic principles of majority rule and minority rights.

# what didn't?
## AMERICA KNOW?

| | Knew it | Blew it |
|---|---|---|
| 1. Who delivered the Gettysburg Address? | 67% | 33% |
| 2. Who was the first president of the U.S.? | 92% | 8% |
| 3. What is the name of the National Anthem? | 58% | 42% |
| 4. Two of the three branches of the U.S. government are called the executive and the legislative branches. What is the third branch called? | 59% | 41% |
| 5. How many U.S. senators are there from each state? | 34% | 66% |
| 6. In what document are these words found? "We hold these truths to be self-evident, that all men are created equal." | 34% | 64% |
| 7. Who wrote the "Letter from Birmingham Jail"? | 33% | 67% |
| 8. What are the first 10 amendments of the U.S. Constitution called? | 47% | 53% |
| 9. Who is the current vice president of the U.S.? | 69% | 31% |
| 10. Who is the current chief justice of the U.S. Supreme Court? | 17% | 83% |

Although some Americans are quite knowledgeable about public affairs, a majority of the nation's adults cannot accurately name their own representative in Congress or even one of the U.S. senators from their state. Most Americans are unable to identify the Bill of Rights. Less than a fifth can name the current Chief Justice of the United States.

George H. Gallup, Jr., "How Many Americans Know U.S. History? Part I," October 21, 2003, available at www.gallup.com.

1. Abraham Lincoln 2. George Washington 3. The Star-Spangled Banner 4. Judicial 5. Two 6. Declaration of Independence 7. Martin Luther King, Jr. 8. The Bill of Rights 9. Joe Biden 10. John G. Roberts

Americans believe that "homosexuals should . . . have equal rights in terms of job opportunities" by a substantial 87 percent to 11 percent margin. However, the survey found that 43 percent oppose hiring gays and lesbians as elementary school teachers and 47 percent oppose homosexuals in the clergy.[42]

Do Americans support the democratic principles of majority rule and minority rights? Political scientists have studied this question for decades. During the 1950s, Professor Samuel Stouffer conducted a study to evaluate public opinion toward individual rights. He found a high level of intolerance toward persons with unpopular views. For example, only 27 percent of the persons interviewed would permit "an admitted communist" to make a speech.[43]

In 1960, political scientists James W. Prothro and C. W. Grigg published what has become a classic study of political tolerance. Survey respondents overwhelmingly endorsed the election of public officials by majority vote and stated that people with minority opinions should have the right to express their views. In more specific questions, however, researchers found dramatically less support for minority rights. Respondents said that a communist should not be allowed to take office. Others stated that atheists should not be allowed to speak publicly against religion.[44] Later research has confirmed that Americans are more likely to endorse democratic principles in the

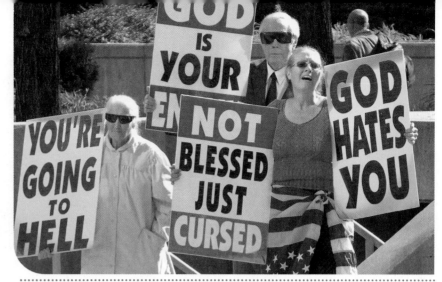

Americans favor civil liberties for groups they like; they oppose civil liberties for groups they dislike. Many Americans dislike Reverend Fred Phelps and the members of his Westboro Baptist Church who picket the funerals of military personnel killed in Iraq and Afghanistan. Phelps and his followers believe that the war is God's punishment for the nation's tolerance of homosexuality.

abstract. One study found that a majority of Americans opposed many of the specific guarantees of individual rights found in the Bill of Rights.[45]

A number of studies conducted in the 1970s concluded that Americans were more tolerant of political diversity. Using questions almost identical to Stouffer's of two decades before, researchers found significantly more Americans willing to tolerate atheists, socialists, and communists. Some concluded that this trend reflected the views of a younger, more urban, and better-educated population.[46]

More recent research contradicts this conclusion. Attitudes toward socialists, communists, and atheists have become more tolerant, but

many Americans express intolerant attitudes toward racists and persons advocating military rule. Americans are apparently no more tolerant of persons with unpopular views today than they were in the 1950s. The targets of intolerance have changed, and there are fewer unpopular groups than 50 years ago.[47]

**Civil liberties** are the protections of the individual from the unrestricted power of government. People may respond to questions about civil liberties based on their perception of a particular group's threat. In the 1950s, many Americans favored limiting free speech for communists. Americans today feel less threatened by communists than by racist groups such as the Ku Klux Klan. When answering survey questions, they express more tolerance for communists than for members of the Klan.[48] In sum, Americans favor civil liberties for groups they like; they oppose them for groups they dislike.

This seeming indifference of many Americans to civil liberties disturbs observers. Tolerance for people of other races, ethnicities, religions, and political beliefs is an

**civil liberties** the protection of the individual from the unrestricted power of government.

# American opinion polls

1824 | The first American poll says Andrew Jackson will defeat John Quincy Adams for the presidency. (He doesn't!)

1932 | George Gallup conducts his first opinion surveys.

1948 | All major opinion polls (including the Gallup Poll) predict that New York Governor Thomas Dewey will defeat Harry Truman. (He doesn't!)

| 1820 | 1830 | 1910 | 1920 | 1930 | 1940 | 1950 |

1916 | The *Literary Digest* prints the first of its presidential polls. Its predictions prove accurate.

1936 | The *Literary Digest* gets it wrong when FDR defeats Landon for reelection.

important underpinning of democracy.[49] Many political theorists believe that a free society requires a high degree of popular support for civil liberties. How, then, can we explain the stability of our democracy when research has often found a lack of support for the fundamental principles of democracy?

Political scientists identify three factors accounting for the preservation of political freedom in the United States. First, the Constitution protects individual rights.[50] These legal guarantees provide an important foundation for individual rights. Second, Americans do not agree on their feared target groups. Some people worry about communists, but others want to silence members of the Klan. Since Americans cannot agree on target groups, they are unable to unite behind undemocratic public policies. Finally, a number of political scientists believe that the attitudes of the general public about civil liberties issues are not nearly as important as the views of **political elites**, the people who exercise a major influence on the policymaking process. Support for democratic principles is stronger among people who are politically active and well-informed than it is among individuals who are politically uninvolved. Democracy endures because those who make policy—political elites—understand and support the principles of majority rule and minority rights.[51]

## Political Trust and Political Legitimacy

**Political legitimacy** is the popular acceptance of a government and its officials as rightful authorities in the exercise of power. Democracy de-

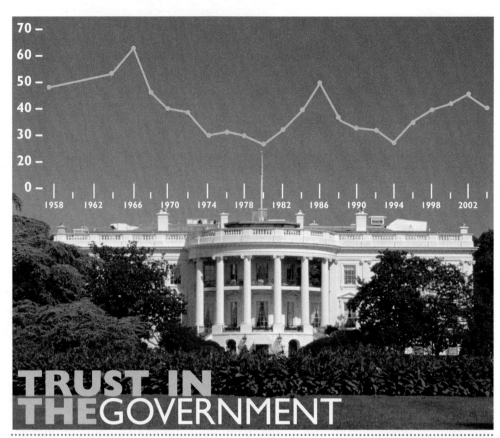

# TRUST IN THE GOVERNMENT

Political scientists average the answers to various questions to create a Trust Index. The index fell during the 1960s and 1970s, rose in the 1980s, fell again in the 1990s, increased dramatically after the terrorist attacks on September 11, 2001, and then dropped yet again.

"The NES Guide to Public Opinion and Electoral Behavior," available at www.electionstudies.org

pends on the voluntary cooperation of its citizens. People pay taxes and obey laws because they accept the authority of the government. They seek political change through the electoral process and peacefully accept the outcomes of election contests. If a significant proportion of the population loses trust in the political system, the quality of democracy declines. Tax evasion and disrespect for the rule of law increase. The potential for a revolutionary change in the political order may develop.

Political scientists attempt to measure the level of political trust in society through a set of questions developed by the Center for Political Studies (CPS), a social science research unit at the University of Michigan. The questions probe the degree to which citizens believe that government leaders are honest and competent.

**political elites** the people who exercise a major influence on the policymaking process.

**political legitimacy** the popular acceptance of a government and its officials as rightful authorities in the exercise of power.

Political scientists disagree on interpreting the data. Some believe that the figures show Americans have lost confidence in their government. Other political scientists argue that public support for American democracy remains solid. They believe that the survey questions may be poorly worded; they actually measure public approval (or disapproval) of current government officials rather than support for the political system.[52]

# Civil Unions in Denmark

In 1989, Denmark became the first country in the world to grant legal recognition to same-sex relationships. The Danish arrangement, which is a form of **civil union**, is known as registered partnership. Since Denmark adopted registered partnerships, five nations (Belgium, Spain, Canada, South Africa, and the Netherlands) have approved same-sex marriage. More than a dozen other countries allow civil unions or registered partnerships, including France, Germany, and the United Kingdom.

The debate over the Danish Registered Partnership Act resembled the current debate over gay marriage in the United States. The proponents of the legislation spoke of the importance of the nation treating all couples equally under the law. They argued that legal recognition of gay unions would promote the development of stable relationships. By discouraging sexual promiscuity, registered partnership would reduce the spread of AIDS and other sexually transmitted diseases. In contrast, opponents of the measure warned that government recognition of same-sex partnerships would weaken support for traditional marriage. The government should protect traditional marriage, they said, by reserving it for traditional couples.

The Danish Registered Partnership Act passed the Danish parliament by a vote of 71 to 47. "Two people of the same sex may have their partnership registered," the law declared. Whenever the word "marriage" or the word "spouse" appears in Danish law, it is construed to include registered partners. For all intents and purposes, then, registered partners are married in the eyes of Danish law.

Nearly 6,000 Danes were classified as registered partners in 2005 compared with more than 2 million married people. Although the number of registered partners has been rising, most gay men and lesbians are not involved in partnerships. About a sixth of same-sex couples are raising children.

Registered partnerships have apparently had no appreciable effect on the marriage rate in Denmark. The long-term trend in countries throughout the region, a trend that predates registered partnerships and same-sex marriage, has been toward lower marriage rates, higher divorce rates, and higher birthrates outside of marriage. In Denmark, the marriage rate was higher in 2000 than it was in 1989 when the registered partnership act was adopted. The divorce rate was roughly the same.

## Questions

1. Are registered partnerships (or civil unions) second-class marriages or are they an acceptable compromise between the proponents and opponents of same-sex marriage?

2. Would you expect the adoption of same-sex marriage throughout the United States to have an impact on traditional marriage rates? Why or why not?

3. Why do you think most gay men and lesbians in Denmark are not involved in registered partnerships?

**civil union** a legal partnership between two men or two women that gives the couple all the benefits, protections, and responsibilities under law that are granted to spouses in a traditional marriage.

# Political Efficacy

**Political efficacy** is the extent to which individuals believe they can influence the policymaking process. Political efficacy is related to participation. People who believe that they can affect government policies are more inclined to participate politically than those who do not.

**Internal political efficacy** is the assessment by an individual of his or her personal ability to influence the policymaking process. The concept addresses knowledge of the political system and ability to communicate with political decision-makers. Scholars measure internal political efficacy by asking this agree/disagree question: "Sometimes politics and government seem so complicated that a person like me can't really understand what's going on." Agreement with the statement indicates a low level of internal political efficacy. In 2000, 60 percent agreed with the statement compared with 32 percent who disagreed.[53] Internal political efficacy rose during the 1980s and 1990s, when voting turnout was in decline. So it appears that the concept is not related to voter participation. Low levels of internal political efficacy may explain why many Americans do not participate politically in other ways, but they apparently do not account for changes in voter participation rates.

**External political efficacy** refers to the assessment of an individual of the responsiveness of government to his or her concerns. This concept deals with an individual's evaluation of the willingness of government officials to respond to the views of ordinary citizens. Political scientists have created a Government Responsiveness Index based on responses to questions such as the following: "Over the years, how much attention do you feel the government pays to what the people think when it decides what to do?" The index generally declined from the mid-1960s through the early 1980s, but it has subsequently increased.[54] Scholars believe that external political efficacy is associated with voter participation.[55]

**political efficacy** the extent to which individuals believe they can influence the policymaking process.

**internal political efficacy** the assessment by an individual of his or her personal ability to influence the policymaking process.

**external political efficacy** the assessment of an individual of the responsiveness of government to his or her concerns.

# takeaction

## FAMILY POLITICS >>

Political scientists believe that families play an important role in the socialization process. Politically active families typically raise children who become politically active adults. Families also pass along their party identification to their offspring, at least initially. Young adults may eventually change their party allegiance to join the party that more closely matches their adult policy preferences.

How did your family impact your political socialization, particularly your level of political involvement and your party identification? Your instructor is going to conduct a class discussion on this topic during an upcoming class session. Prepare to join in the discussion by taking the following steps:

1. Jot down some information about your own level of political involvement and party affiliation. Are you registered to vote? Are you a regular voter? Have you ever joined a political group or participated in a political campaign? How closely do you follow current events? Do you consider yourself a Republican, Democrat, an independent, or a supporter of another political party? Have you always had the same party affiliation?

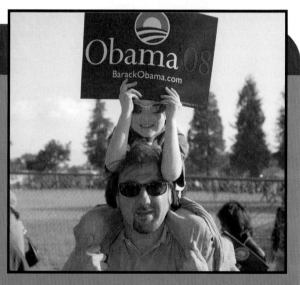

2. Record your recollections of your family's political involvement and party loyalties. Were your parents or the adults who raised you politically active? What was their political party allegiance?

3. Speak with your parents or other members of your family to verify the accuracy of your recollections. Do their memories match your recollections?

4. Finally, consider the role your family played in your personal political socialization and be prepared to discuss the topic in class.

# political PHILOSOPHY

In American politics, the terms *liberalism* and *conservatism* are used to describe political philosophy. **Liberalism** is a political philosophy that favors the use of government power to foster development of the individual and promote the welfare of society. Liberals believe that the government can (and should) advance social progress by promoting political equality, social justice, and economic prosperity. Liberals usually favor government regulation and government spending for social programs. Liberals value social and cultural diversity, and defend the right of individual adult choice on issues such as access to abortion. **Conservatism,** on the other hand, is the political philosophy that government power undermines individual development and diminishes society. Conservatives argue that government regulations and social programs generally harm rather than help. Charities, private businesses, and individuals can solve problems if the government leaves them alone. Conservatives also believe that the government should defend the traditional values of society.

The terms *right* and *left* are also used to describe political ideology. The **political right** refers to conservatism, the **political left** to liberalism. Similarly, **right wing** means conservative; **left wing** means liberal.

Liberals and conservatives approach the problems of the nation differently. Liberals advocate government action to assist disadvantaged groups. They generally support programs such as Social Security, Medicare, and affirmative action programs. In contrast, conservatives argue that government, especially the national government, is too inefficient to solve the nation's social problems. They believe that government should reduce spending on social programs and cut taxes to promote economic growth, which, the conservatives argue, will benefit everyone.

Liberals support government regulation of business. They support environmental-protection laws, consumer-protection regulations, and occupational safety and health standards. Liberals are more likely than conservatives to endorse trade restrictions on foreign companies. Conservatives fear that government reg-

Few issues in the United States are as divisive as the issue of abortion.

ulations will disrupt the market economy. They believe regulations drive up the cost of doing business, increase prices and lower wages.

Consider the issue of the environment. Liberals advocate regulation to ensure clean air and water. They favor government responses to the threat of **global warming,** the gradual warming of the Earth's atmosphere caused by burning fossil fuels and industrial pollutants. In contrast, conservatives want to move slowly on environmental issues to avoid harming economic growth. They prefer market-oriented solutions rather than government mandates.

On social issues, conservatives and liberals trade positions on the role of government. Conservatives favor government intervention, while liberals prefer less government involvement. Conservatives define social issues in terms of their traditional family values. Conservatives generally support rigorous enforcement of pornography laws, the adoption of a constitutional

> **THE TERMS LEFT AND RIGHT** COME FROM THE 1789 MEETING OF THE ESTATES GENERAL, THE PARLIAMENT OF PRE-REVOLUTIONARY FRANCE. THE DELEGATES MET IN A HALL AT THE PALACE OF VERSAILLES. THE SEATS ON THE LEFT OF THE HALL WERE RESERVED FOR THE COMMONERS WHO WANTED POLITICAL CHANGE AND REFORM. THE SEATS ON THE RIGHT OF THE HALL WERE USED BY THE NOBILITY, WHO RESISTED CHANGE. THE TERMS LEFT AND RIGHT CAME TO MEAN THE POLITICAL POSITIONS TAKEN BY THE TWO GROUPS.

amendment against abortion, and the enactment of an amendment permitting school prayer. Conservatives oppose assisted suicide, most stem cell research, and the legalization of same-sex marriage. Liberals prefer that government stay out of these questions except to protect the rights of the individual.

Ironically, both liberals and conservatives criticize government. Liberals say that the government does not act strongly enough to help disadvantaged groups gain economic and political power and that government favors the interests of the rich and powerful. Conservatives, on the other hand, criticize government for interfering with the efficient working of the free enterprise system. Conservatives believe that government economic intervention hurts everyone.

The usefulness of the terms *liberalism* and *conservatism* is limited. Real-life differences between liberals and conservatives are often matters of degree rather than dramatic contrast. In addition, a number of issues do not fit neatly into liberal/conservative divisions. Finally, few Americans are consistently liberal or conservative. Most Americans hold conservative views on some issues, liberal opinions on others.

## Are Americans Liberal or Conservative?

Public opinion surveys typically find more self-identified conservatives than liberals. Nonetheless, studies have found that many Americans cannot accurately define liberalism or conservatism. Furthermore, research shows that relatively few people structure their thinking along liberal-conservative lines.[56]

A different way to assess political philosophy is to inquire about the

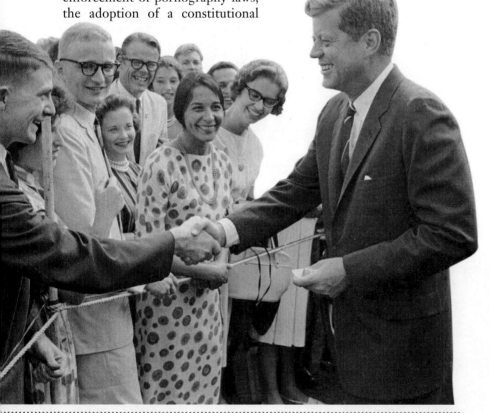

Liberals believe in the efficacy of government action to solve social problems. President John F. Kennedy phrased the concept in the following terms: "If a free society cannot help the many who are poor, it cannot save the few who are rich."

**global warming** the gradual warming of the Earth's atmosphere caused by burning fossil fuels and industrial pollutants.

| EXTREMELY LIBERAL | LIBERAL | SLIGHTLY LIBERAL | MODERATE/MIDDLE OF THE ROAD | SLIGHTLY CONSERVATIVE | CONSERVATIVE | EXTREMELY CONSERVATIVE |
| --- | --- | --- | --- | --- | --- | --- |
| 2 | 9 | 12 | 26 | 13 | 16 | 3 |

**ARE AMERICANS LIBERAL OR CONSERVATIVE?**

DON'T KNOW — 20

According to the National Election Studies (NES), 23 percent of Americans described themselves as slightly liberal, liberal, or extremely liberal in 2004, compared with 32 percent who said they were slightly conservative, conservative, or extremely conservative. Meanwhile, 26 percent described themselves as moderate or middle of the road.

"The NES Guide to Public Opinion and Electoral Behavior," available at www.umich.edu/~nes.

role of government. When asked to choose between "more government services and more spending" or "fewer services to reduce spending," survey respondents favored the former 43 percent to 20 percent, with the rest either in the middle or declaring they don't know.[57]

Surveys show that few Americans favor decreasing or ending federal government involvement in consumer protection, medical research, financing college education, or job training for low-income people.[58]

Survey researchers Albert H. and Susan Davis Cantril's Cantril Index shows that many Americans have mixed feelings about government, but more people support an active government than oppose it. The Cantrils classify 39 percent of adult Americans as steady supporters of government compared to 10 percent who are steady critics. They classify 12 percent of their sample as ambivalent supporters of government and 20 percent as ambivalent critics. Eleven percent of the sample could not be classified.[59]

## Opinion Differences Among Groups

Surveys show that political attitudes vary based on factors such as social class, race, and gender. For example, support for gay and lesbian rights is strongest among women, younger adults, people who live on either coast, college graduates, higher-income groups, people who live in urban and suburban areas, Democrats and independents, self-identified liberals, and Catholics. Opposition is greatest among men, older adults, Southerners, people with relatively little formal education, lower-income groups, self-identified conservatives, Republicans, and Protestants.[60]

**Social Class.** On social welfare issues, lower-income people tend to be more liberal than middle- and upper-income Americans. In contrast, lower-income individuals are often more conservative than other income groups on such non-economic issues as women's rights and the rights of defendants. Lower-income whites are also less support-ive of civil rights for African Americans than are middle-income whites.

**Isolationism** is the view that the United States should stay away from the affairs of other nations. Lower-income individuals are more isolationist but also more supportive of using military force to deal with other nations. Working-class people often oppose free trade, fearing the loss of jobs to international competition. Middle- and upper-income people are less isolationist, favoring free trade, foreign aid, and negotiated settlements of disputes.[61]

**Race & Ethnicity.** African Americans and Latinos favor activist government. Members of both minority groups typically support affirmative action, a program designed to ensure equal opportunities in employment and college admissions for racial minorities and women. African Americans, in particular, perceive widespread racial discrimination in

**isolationism** the view that the United States should stay out of the affairs of other nations.

society and believe that it is the major reason that many African Americans have trouble finding good jobs and adequate housing. They want government to play an active role in the quest for racial equality.

Many whites believe that African Americans have already achieved equality. (In fact, African Americans continue to lag behind whites in employment, income, education, and access to healthcare.) Whites who believe that African Americans are as well off as white Americans are opposed to government programs designed to assist blacks to improve their status.[62]

Although African Americans and Latinos are less likely to support the death penalty than whites, they are more likely to hold conservative views on the issues of abortion and gay marriage. African American and Latino conservatism on these issues reflects relatively high rates of

church attendance for both minority groups.[63]

**Religion.** The **religious left** refers to those who hold liberal views because of their religious beliefs, whereas the phrase **religious right** refers to those who hold conservative views because of their religious beliefs. Both groups feel motivated by their religious beliefs to participate in politics. Most members of the religious left are associated with mainline Protestant Christian churches, such as the Presbyterians, Episcopalians, and Church of Christ (Disciples), or with the Jewish faith. It also includes Buddhists and many people who declare that they are "spiritual" but not associated with organized religion.[64] Christian conservatives tend to be associated with white evangelical Protestant churches, such as Assemblies of God and the Southern Baptist Convention.[65]

**religious left** those who hold liberal views because of their religious beliefs.

**religious right** those who hold conservative views because of their religious beliefs.

Not all religious groups are left or right. Roman Catholics, for example, oppose abortion and gay marriage, positions associated with the religious right, but also oppose the death penalty, support civil rights and immigrant rights, and favor government efforts to end poverty.

In contemporary American politics, the religious right has more influence than the religious left. Whereas most mainline Protestant churches have been losing members for years, conservative evangelical churches are growing. Furthermore, church attendance is higher among conservative evangelicals.[66]

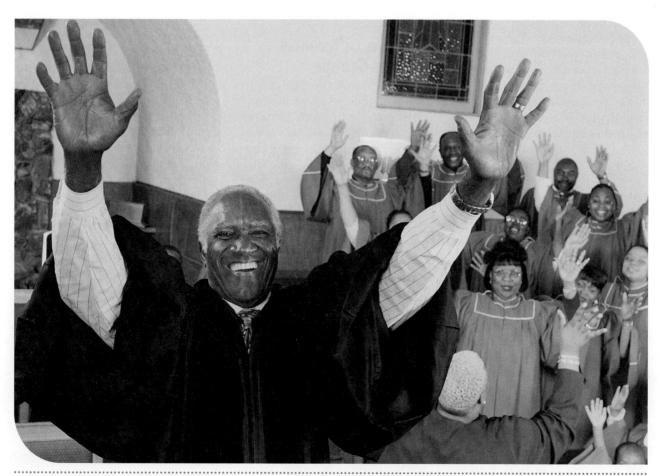

African Americans are relatively conservative on the issues of abortion and gay and lesbian rights, reflecting their high rates of church attendance.

# Media and Public Opinion

**Should the media report the results of their own polls as news? Isn't this the same as "creating" news rather than reporting it?**

**Should government officials be responsive to public opinion polling?**

**Overview:** The First Amendment was ratified in order to protect free (political) speech, freedom of the press, the right to petition the government for redress of grievances (the right to directly approach and criticize the government), and the right to peaceably assemble. These freedoms are essential if citizens are to engage in the open debate and national discussion necessary for self-rule and democratic politics.

The founders were not blind to the fact that a free and open press (for our purposes, we will use the term "media") would be partisan, at times wrong, and would attempt to mobilize and change public opinion. Contentious and acrimonious public debate is considered to be part of the essence of political freedom. Those at the time of the American founding, however, could not foresee the incredible change in technology and society that today causes citizens to suffer from "information overload." We seek sources of information that can be consumed quickly, accurately, and at little cost.

Historically, the news media has prided itself on providing unbiased and relevant information through which Americans can make informed decisions. Part of this information has been the reporting of political polling, especially in political campaign seasons. A new trend, is developing, though, which has political and media analysts concerned with the quality and bias in reporting public opinion polling data. From Fox News to the *New York Times*, there is concern that editorial positions are being authenticated by self-selected polls which are then reported as "news" in attempts to sway public opinion based on demonstrably false journalism. How is the average, busy citizen to get his or her information? Does this new practice harm the credibility of a necessary, informal political institution?

## supporting the use of polling data as news

**public opinion polls are a legitimate source of news.** In order to make informed decisions, citizens must have access to the same polling data that inform the political and policymaking class.

**public opinion polling provides the American people an insight into the politics of the day.** Reporting polling data allows individuals to know what their fellow citizens think and desire, where they are in the ideological spectrum, and whether government is adequately addressing these issues.

**public opinion polling organizations make their data available on the Internet.** Today, most polling organizations make their questions and data available online. This allows citizens to fact-check research and draw conclusions for themselves.

## against the use of polling data as news

**polling data may be misrepresented to support a media outlet's editorial position.** For example, in March 2007, an ABC/BBC poll reported findings on how Iraqis viewed the war in Iraq. In this poll they neglected to mention an oversampling of Sunni Arabs, and this dramatically skewed the poll's result.

**polling samples may be skewed to provide a predetermined outcome.** Sometimes poll samples determine the outcome of a poll. A case in point would be a poll commissioned by the *Los Angeles Times* in which the sample was heavily skewed toward one political party, with the effective poll result favoring the candidate of that oversampled party.

**public opinion polling assumes American democratic government should be responsive to public opinion.** The founders designed the constitutional institutions and principles to "slow down" and moderate the effects of public opinion on political institutions with a view to the idea that majority opinion can be unjust. Take, for example, the discriminatory, legal doctrine of "separate but equal."

Because of the growth of conservative Christian churches, active church participation is now associated with political conservatism. At least among whites, the more actively involved people are with religious organizations, the more likely they are to hold conservative political views. For African Americans, the church is a basis for liberal activism on economic issues. Nonetheless, African American churchgoers hold more conservative views on social issues, such as abortion and gay and lesbian rights, than do African Americans who do not participate in a church.[67]

**Generation.** Younger Americans are more tolerant of ethnic, racial, and social diversity than older adults. People below the age of 30 are more sympathetic to affirmative action and are more likely to favor gay and lesbian rights.[68]

## YOUNGER AMERICANS are more *tolerant* of ethnic, racial, and social diversity than OLDER ADULTS

Studies find no evidence that people grow more conservative with age. Instead, age-related differences in political views reflect the impact of socializing events common to a generation.[69] Younger Americans may also be more tolerant because they are better educated than previous generations.[70]

**Region.** In general, people from the East and West coasts are more liberal than people from the South, Midwest, or Rocky Mountain regions. Most regional differences can be explained by class, race, and religion, but some genuine regional variations based on unique cultural and historical factors may also play a role.

**Gender.** The phrase **gender gap** refers to differences in party identification and political attitudes between men and women. Women are more likely to vote for Democratic candidates and to favor government programs to provide healthcare and education, and to protect the environment. Women are less likely than men to favor increased defense spending and to support the wars in Afghanistan and Iraq.[71] They hold similar views on the issues of abortion rights, women's equality, and gay marriage.[72]

**gender gap** differences in party identification and political attitudes between men and women.

# public opinion
## & PUBLIC POLICY

**p**ublic opinion affects every stage of the policymaking process.

### Agenda Building
Candidates and officeholders tend to focus on the issues that interest voters. If polls show that voters are concerned about healthcare, then politicians discuss healthcare. If polls indicate that immigration is a major concern, politicians talk about immigration. Some issues become part of the policy agenda because of the actions of interest groups or public officials. Nonetheless, government officials are unlikely to ignore any issue that is important to a large part of the general public.

### Policy Formulation and Adoption
Years ago, political scientist V.O. Key, Jr., introduced the concept of latent opinion to explain the relationship between public opinion and policy formulation and adoption. **Latent opinion** is not what voters think about an issue today, but what public opinion would be by election time if a political opponent made a public official's position on the issue the target of an attack.[73] Elected officials make thousands of policy decisions, and public officials consider public opinion during policy formulation and adoption because they recognize that a future

**"PUBLIC OPINION AFFECTS EVERY STAGE OF THE POLICYMAKING PROCESS."**

political opponent could raise the issue during an election campaign.

Contemporary political scientist James A. Stimson introduced the concept of a **zone of acquiescence,** which is the range of policy options acceptable to the public on a particular issue. Stimson says that some policy options are either too conservative or too liberal to be acceptable to a majority of the public. The zone of acquiescence encompasses policy options that lie between the two extremes. The size of the zone varies from issue to issue and may change if public opinion grows more conservative or more liberal. Policymakers tend to choose policy options within the zone of acquiescence; otherwise they risk electoral defeat.[74]

The zone of acquiescence highlights important points about the relationship between public opinion and public policy. First, public opinion affects policy by limiting options. On most issues, the zone of acquiescence is broad enough to include a number of options from which public officials may choose. Public opinion sets this range of acceptable alternatives, but it does not determine which options are selected. Other factors, including the influence of interest groups and political parties, come into play.

Second, the zone of acquiescence does not imply that policies selected will not arouse controversy. The zone of acquiescence is based on majority preferences, but may alarm minorities. Although abortion is legal in the U.S., for example, it remains controversial for many Americans.

Third, the zone of acquiescence is affected by the policymaker's constituency. A **constituency** is the district from which an officeholder is elected. **Constituents** are the people an officeholder represents. A member of Congress elected from a district with a majority of African American constituents, for example, faces a more liberal zone of acquiescence on economic issues than does one whose constituents are mostly upper-income whites. The president, meanwhile, must deal with a nationwide constituency.

Fourth, the zone of acquiescence for a particular issue changes as public opinion changes. During the 1980s, as public opinion grew more conservative on law and order issues such as the death penalty, so too did the range of acceptable policy options available to officials. Today, although the issue remains controversial, most Americans now favor either gay marriage or civil unions. Consequently, these options are now included in a range of acceptable policy options, especially in large urban areas in the Northeast and on the West Coast where people are more likely to hold liberal views on the issue.[75]

## Policy Implementation and Evaluation

Policymakers consider public opinion, at least indirectly, in policy implementation. Officials enforce

**latent opinion** what public opinion would be at election time if a political opponent made a public official's position on the issue the target of a campaign attack.

**zone of acquiescence** the range of policy options acceptable to the public on a particular issue.

**constituency** the district from which an officeholder is elected.

**constituents** the people an officeholder represents.

policies that enjoy broad public support. As public sentiment has mounted against drunk driving, officials have adopted tougher DWI laws, and enforced them more aggressively. In contrast, the Supreme Court's decision against state-sponsored prayer in schools enjoys relatively little public support. Many school officials ignore violations until parents complain.

Finally, public opinion influences evaluation. Public officials are more likely to scrutinize policies that have proved unpopular or lack strong public support. Congress and the press are more likely to investigate a program that is perceived as ineffective or that is unpopular with the public, as well.

the THINKSPOT
www.thethinkspot.com

# TEST yourself

1. The process whereby individuals acquire political attitudes, knowledge, and beliefs is known as which of the following?
   A. Political efficacy
   B. Political socialization
   C. Political trust
   D. Political science

2. Which of the following statements about the socialization process is NOT true?
   A. Political socialization ends when individuals reach their early 20s.
   B. Young children typically identify with the same political party as their parents.
   C. Schools historically have taught the children of immigrants to be patriotic Americans.
   D. Personal involvement in religious organizations is associated be political participation.

3. Which of the following agents of socialization plays an important role in shaping the party identification of youngsters?
   A. Family          B. School
   C. Peers           D. Media

4. The universe for a study designed to measure the attitudes of college students would be which of the following?
   A. The individuals who are interviewed for the study
   B. All college-age adults
   C. All college students
   D. All Americans

5. How often will a professionally administered survey differ from the universe by more than 3 percentage points merely on the basis of chance?
   A. Never. If the sample is truly random, it will never differ by more than the margin of error.
   B. One time in 20. Even a perfectly drawn sample will by chance be outside the margin of error 5 percent of the time.
   C. 3 percent of the time. The margin of error indicates the error factor built into a survey.
   D. One time in five. A well-conducted survey will be wrong 20 percent of the time.

6. A public opinion poll taken a month before the election has a margin of error of 3 percentage points. The poll shows Candidate A ahead of Candidate B 46 percent to 44 percent, with the rest undecided. What is the best analysis of the result of the poll?
   A. Candidate A is ahead by at least 2 percentage points but may actually be ahead by 5 percentage points.
   B. Candidate A is ahead but it is impossible to know by how much.

C. Candidate B is actually ahead because Candidate A did not reach the 50 percent support level.
D. The candidates are in a statistical tie because the difference in their support is within the margin of error.

7. A major Internet provider regularly conducts online polls. Sometimes tens of thousands of people participate. Would the results of these polls be accurate?
   A. Yes. Everyone has a chance to participate.
   B. No. The sample size is too small.
   C. No. The sample size is too large.
   D. Probably not. It is unlikely that the sample is a representative sample of the universe.

8. A survey conducted October 1 shows Candidate A with 55 percent support and Candidate B with 40 percent. What is the best evaluation of the survey?
   A. Candidate A is ahead today but surveys can't predict the future.
   B. Neither candidate is ahead because the survey is within the margin of error.
   C. Candidate A will win by a 15-percentage-point margin.
   D. Candidate A will win by a margin of 11 to 19 percentage points.

9. Which of the following statements is NOT true about political knowledge?
   A. Only a minority of Americans is especially knowledgeable about politics and government.
   B. Knowledgeable Americans are more likely to vote than people who lack political information.
   C. Young people are more knowledgeable about politics and government than are older adults.
   D. Well-informed voters are more likely to support candidates whose views on issues of importance to them coincide with their own than are voters who are poorly informed.

10. An opinion survey includes this question: "Professor ABC at State University has written that the United States deserved the 9/11 attacks because it supports Israel and undemocratic Arab governments. Should the professor be fired?" What would you expect the survey to show?
    A. A majority would oppose firing the professor because most Americans support freedom of speech.
    B. A majority would support firing the professor because most Americans oppose freedom of speech.
    C. A majority would support firing the professor because they are outraged by his position on 9/11 and aren't considering the civil liberties issue.
    D. A majority would oppose firing the professor because they agree with his point of view.

11. Which of the following groups would you expect to express the highest level of support for civil liberties?
    A. Low-income people
    B. Political elites
    C. People who seldom, if ever, vote
    D. Recent immigrants

12. The popular acceptance of a government and its officials as rightful authorities in the exercise of power is a good definition of which of the following?
    A. Political efficacy      B. Political tolerance
    C. Political legitimacy    D. Opinion leaders

13. Which of the following would be a likely result of a low level of political legitimacy in a society?
    A. Election turnout would be high.
    B. Most people would voluntarily obey laws and regulations.
    C. People wanting political change would turn to the electoral system rather than violence to bring about change.
    D. None of the above

14. Latent opinion becomes important only if:
    A. A voter understands how the government works.
    B. A voter thinks that government is not interested in his or her views.
    C. Men and women agree on a political position.
    D. A political opponent makes an issue of a politician's position.

15. Which of the following statements reflects a high level of internal political efficacy?
    A. "I don't believe that government officials care what I think."
    B. "I have a good understanding of how the government works."
    C. "I think that most of the people running the government are crooks."
    D. "Sometimes politics and government seem so complicated that a person like me can't understand it."

16. The assessment of an individual of the responsiveness of government to his or her concerns is a definition of which of the following?
    A. Political trust
    B. External political efficacy
    C. Internal political efficacy
    D. Political legitimacy

17. Which of the following positions would be most likely to be taken by a conservative?
    A. "Government has a responsibility to ensure that all Americans have access to affordable healthcare."
    B. "Government should act aggressively to adopt regulations to slow global warming."
    C. "Government has a responsibility to protect the unborn by limiting access to abortion."
    D. "Government should address the problem of homelessness by providing more public housing."

18. Which of the following statements reflects a liberal ideology?
    A. The government that governs least is best.
    B. Government regulations often do more harm than good.
    C. The government has no business telling women that they must carry a fetus to term.
    D. All of the above

19. Which of the following statements about the gender gap is correct?
    A. Woman are more likely than men to vote Republican.
    B. Woman are more likely than men to be pro-choice.
    C. Woman are more likely than men to favor American military intervention abroad.
    D. Women are more likely than men to favor government programs to provide healthcare and education.

20. How would Professor James Stimson explain the relationship between public opinion and the policymaking process?
    A. Elected officials can adopt any policy because most Americans are too uninformed to know or care.
    B. Policymakers must follow public opinion closely or risk being voted out of office.
    C. Public opinion sets limits on policymakers, but within those limits policymakers are free to act.
    D. If selected policies turn out badly, voters punish the officials who adopted them by voting them out of office.

KNOW *the* **score**

18–20 correct: Congratulations! You are well informed!

15–17 correct: Your political knowledge is a bit low—be sure to review the key terms and visit TheThinkSpot.

<14 correct: Reread the chapter more thoroughly.

1. B; 2. A; 3. A; 4. C; 5. B; 6. D; 7. D; 8. A; 9. C; 10. C; 11. B; 12. C; 13. D; 14. D; 15. B; 16. B; 17. C; 18. C; 19. D; 20. C

test yourself  99

# 5 POLITICAL

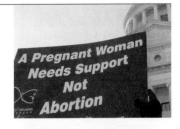

**M**ore people voted in 2008 than in any previous American presidential election. The political year began in January in New Hampshire. More than 530,000 New Hampshire residents cast ballots in the 2008 presidential primary, a 34 percent increase over the previous record, which was set in 2000. As the election year progressed, one state after another set turnout records. Primary election participation increased by 47 percent in Missouri; it was up by 69 percent in New Jersey.[1]

The election year concluded with the November general election, when more than 131 million Americans cast ballots for president, the largest election turnout in American history in terms of the total vote. Participation increased on a percentage basis as well, with an estimated 61.6 percent of the voting eligible population casting ballots, the largest election turnout since 1968. After a period of declining voter turnout, 2008 marked the third consecutive presidential election in which voter participation rates rose. Voter turnout increased from 51.7 percent of the voting eligible population in 1996 to 54.2 percent in 2000 and 60.3 percent in 2004 before increasing by another 1.3 percentage points in 2008.[2]

Voter turnout in the 2008 presidential election introduces this chapter on political participation. The chapter discusses voting and other forms of political participation in the United States, including participation rates and the impact of political participation on the policymaking process.

# PARTICIPATION

# ESSENTIALS...

*after studying Chapter 5, students should be able to answer the following questions:*

> What are the methods individuals use to participate in the policy process, and why are some methods used more frequently than others?

> What are the most important factors influencing individual participation in the policy process?

> What is the relationship between level of participation and income, age, race/ethnicity, and gender?

> What are the trends in voter turnout in presidential elections since the 1960s? Why have participation rates increased in recent elections?

> Why are voter participation rates in the United States lower than participation rates in most other democracies?

> How do the political and policy preferences of those people who participate in politics compare with the preferences of adult Americans in general?

> What is the role of participation in the policymaking process?

# forms of
## PARTICIPATION

**political participation** is an activity that has the intent or effect of influencing government action. Voting is the most common form of political participation. More than three-fourths of the respondents to the American National Election Studies (ANES) reported casting ballots for president in 2004. (*Reported* turnout typically exceeds *actual* turnout because people do not want to admit to an interviewer that they neglected to vote.)[3]

Election turnout is closely related to the level of interest in a particular contest.[4] Presidential races typically attract more voters on a percentage basis than other types of elections because of their high-profile nature. In contrast, voter turnout for congressional elections held in non-presidential (midterm) election years seldom exceeds 45 percent of the voting eligible population. The voter participation rate in the 2006 midterm election was 40 percent. Even though that was the highest midterm election turnout since 1970, the figure was substantially less than the turnout in the presidential election years of 2004 and 2008.[5]

Voting is not the only way people participate in election contests. Voters who want to do more for a candidate or political party contribute money, prepare campaign mailers, telephone potential voters, put up yard signs, and work the polls on Election Day. Political participation is not only about elections. At any time, people may attempt to influence the policy process by writing, phoning, or e-mailing public officials. Surveys show that about a third of Americans have contacted public officials, usually at the state or local level.[6] See figure on the following page.

Americans also try to influence the policy process by joining or supporting interest groups, such as Mothers Against Drunk Driving (MADD) or the National Rifle Association (NRA). Some Americans participate through unconventional political acts, such as protest demonstrations, sit-ins, or violence.

**political participation** an activity that has the intent or effect of influencing government action.

Police arresting a protester at the Republican National Convention in Minneapolis in 2008.

# POLITICAL PARTICIPATION

78% VOTED

48% TRIED TO INFLUENCE OTHERS TO VOTE

21% DISPLAYED BUTTONS OR BUMPER STICKERS

13% CONTRIBUTED MONEY TO CANDIDATES OR A PARTY

8% ATTENDED A POLITICAL MEETING

3% WORKED FOR A CANDIDATE OR PARTY

Although voting is the most common form of political participation, it is not the only way that citizens participate in the policymaking process.

http://www.electionstudies.org/nesguide/gd-index.htm#

# explaining
## PARTICIPATION

the most important factors influencing individual participation are personal resources, psychological engagement, voter mobilization, and community involvement.[7]

## Personal Resources

The personal resources most closely associated with political participation are time, money, and civic skills, such as communication skills and organizational ability. Each form of political activity requires a different configuration of resources. People who want to contribute money to candidates and political parties must have financial resources. Individuals who work in campaigns or participate in political groups and activities must have both time and civic skills.[8] Participation rates are higher for activities that require relatively little time, few skills, and little or no expense. Voting is the most common form of political participation because it re-

quires a relatively small amount of time and no expense. In contrast, relatively few people work in political campaigns or give money to candidates because those activities require significant amounts of time, civic skills, and money.

## Psychological Engagement

People take part in the policymaking process when they are knowledgeable, interested, and have a strong sense of political efficacy. Individuals who believe that a particular government policy affects their personal welfare are more likely to participate.[9] For example, lower-income Social Security recipients are more likely to participate on that issue than are upper-income recipients, probably because they are more dependent financially on their Social Security checks.[10] In contrast, people who

**political efficacy** the extent to which individuals believe they can influence the policymaking process.

**voter mobilization** the process of motivating citizens to vote.

are uninformed or disinterested in politics are also usually uninvolved. Participation also depends on a sense of **political efficacy**, which is the extent to which individuals believe that they can influence the policymaking process.[11]

## Voter Mobilization

Political participation depends on **voter mobilization**, the process of motivating citizens to vote. The likelihood that individuals will vote, participate in an election campaign, join a political group, or engage in some other form of political participation increases if those individuals are asked to participate.[13] Political parties encourage people to vote

"3.95 million individuals gave money to Obama's presidential campaign."[12]

**think**

Under what circumstances, if any, would you consider joining a protest demonstration?

and volunteer for campaigns. Interest groups educate citizens about political issues and urge their involvement in the policy process. Face-to-face contacts significantly increase the likelihood that individuals will go to the polls, especially if the contacts take place near Election Day.[14] In contrast, direct mail and telephone calls are less effective at increasing turnout.[15]

## Community Involvement

Finally, people participate politically because of their involvement in their communities. Individuals who have close community ties, such as home ownership and membership in community organizations, are more likely to participate. They regard voting and other forms of political participation as their civic duty because they can see the connection between participation and the quality of life in their community.[16]

# patterns of PARTICIPATION

**P**articipation rates vary among individuals based on such factors as income, age, race/ethnicity, and gender.

## Income

Affluence and activity go together for every form of political participation. The higher the family income, the more likely a person is to vote. According to the U.S. Census Bureau, the reported rate of voter turnout in 2008 for people in families earning more than $150,000 a year was 82 percent. For families earning less than $10,000, the turnout was 49 percent.[17] The gap between high- and low-income groups is even higher for other types of participation. People who are well-off financially are more likely than low-income people to give money to candidates and parties, join organizations, contact public officials, and engage in political protests.[18] (See figure on the following page.)

Participation rates and income are associated because resources and psychological attachment rise with income. Obviously, people in higher income groups have more money to contribute to political causes. Because income and education are closely related, more affluent citizens are better informed about government and politics than are less wealthy individuals. They have better communication and organizational skills, as well.

## Age

The figure below shows reported voter participation rates by age group in the 2008 presidential election. Voter turnout is lowest for the youngest group. Younger adults have fewer resources and are less interested in the policy process than older adults. As adults mature, their incomes increase and their skills develop. Older adults establish roots in their communities that increase their interest and awareness of the political process. Consequently, participation increases with each successive age group, with the peak voting years coming between 65 and 74 years of age. After age 75, voter participation begins to decline because illness and infirmity force the elderly to reduce their involvement in the policy process.

**voting turnout by age group**

| | |
|---|---|
| 18–24 | 49% |
| 25–44 | 60% |
| 45–64 | 69% |
| 65–74 | 72% |
| 75+ | 68% |

**be powerful. be heard.**

Hip-hop personality Russell Simmons urges high school students to register to vote at a rally in New Jersey.

# COMPARING PARTICIPATION RATES OF
# HIGH-INCOME AND LOW-INCOME INDIVIDUALS

http://www.apsanet.org/imgtest/taskforcereport.pdf

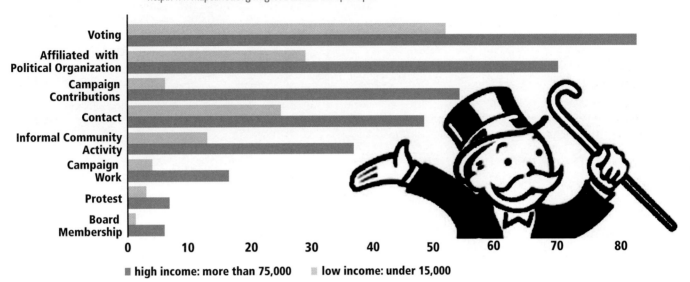

- Voting
- Affiliated with Political Organization
- Campaign Contributions
- Contact
- Informal Community Activity
- Campaign Work
- Protest
- Board Membership

0   10   20   30   40   50   60   70   80

■ high income: more than 75,000   ■ low income: under 15,000

## Race/Ethnicity

Participation varies among racial and ethnic groups. The voter turnout in 2008 was 66 percent for whites, 65 percent for African Americans, 48 percent for Asian Americans, and 50 percent for Hispanic Americans.[19] (See figure below.) African Americans are more likely to engage in protests and participate in political campaigns than whites, but they are less likely to contribute campaign money than whites. Participation rates for Lati-

nos are lower than for other groups across the full range of political activities.[20]

Many members of racial/ethnic minority groups are ineligible to vote. Only 2 percent of whites 18 years of age or older were unable to register and vote in 2008 because they were not citizens. The percentage of non-citizens among African Americans was 6 percent. It was 32 percent for Asian Americans and 37 percent for Latinos.[21] Meanwhile, 5.3 million Americans are disqualified from voting because they are incarcerated or have prior criminal convictions. Eleven states

permanently disenfranchise individuals convicted of serious crimes. The policy of denying voting rights to criminal offenders disproportionately affects minority Americans, particularly African American males, 14 percent of whom are disenfranchised because of criminal convictions.[22]

Racial/ethnic patterns of participation also reflect the importance of recruitment to political participation. Participation rates for African Americans exceed expectations because of the effectiveness of organizations, such as churches and political groups, that stimulate participation in the African American community.[23]

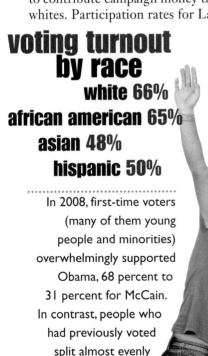

# voting turnout by race
## white 66%
## african american 65%
## asian 48%
## hispanic 50%

In 2008, first-time voters (many of them young people and minorities) overwhelmingly supported Obama, 68 percent to 31 percent for McCain. In contrast, people who had previously voted split almost evenly between the two candidates.

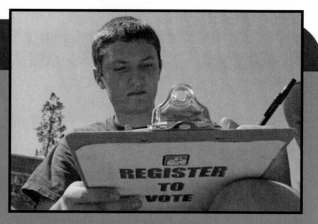

## takeaction
### REGISTERING TO VOTE

Voting is a two-step process. Before Americans can vote, they must register. To register, citizens provide voter registration officials with their name and address, and an assertion that they meet the legal requirements to vote. Registration is important because most people who register do subsequently vote.

Your assignment is to learn how the voter registration process works in your state. You can obtain voter registration information from an office of county government, driver's license bureau, welfare office, and some public libraries. Complete the voter registration card and submit it to your instructor to document that you have done the assignment. If you are not eligible to vote (you might not yet be 18 or an American citizen) write the word VOID on the card. If you are already a registered voter or do not wish to register at this time, write DO NOT PROCESS on the card so that your instructor will not forward the document to the voter registration office. Otherwise, this is your opportunity to register to vote. You may even want to obtain extra voter registration cards to share with friends and family members.

## Gender

Women are more likely to vote than men, but men are more likely to engage in other forms of political participation. In 2008, 66 percent of women reported that they voted compared with 62 percent of men.[24] Substantially more men than women are disqualified from voting because of criminal convictions.

Women are just as likely as men to participate in election campaigns, but they are less likely to contribute money to political campaigns, contact public officials, or join political organizations.[25]

These data reflect differences in resources and psychological engagement between men and women. Women on average have lower average incomes than men. As you have read, income is closely associated with forms of participation other than voting. Furthermore, surveys indicate that men are more informed about and interested in politics and government than women, even when they have the same level of education.[26]

# trends in
# VOTER TURNOUT

**p**olitical scientists who study election participation measure voter turnout relative to the size of the **voting eligible population (VEP)**, the number of U.S. residents who are legally qualified to vote. The VEP differs from the **voting age population (VAP)**, which is the number of U.S. residents who are 18 years of age or older, because it excludes individuals who are ineligible to cast a ballot. In contrast to the VAP, the VEP does not include non-citizens, convicted criminals (depending on state law), and people who are mentally incapacitated.

The 2004 and 2008 presidential elections suggest that the United States is experiencing a voting revival. After years of declining or flat electoral participation rates, voter turnout has surged to a level not seen in nearly 40 years. The increase reflected the result of massive voter mobilization efforts coupled with high public interest in the

**voting eligible population (VEP)** the number of U.S. residents who are legally qualified to vote.
**voting age population (VAP)** the number of U.S. residents who are 18 years of age or older.

election. The two major political parties, supported by their interest group allies, organized sophisti-

**Should people with prior criminal convictions be permanently disqualified from voting?**

cated get-out-the-vote (GOTV) campaigns in 2004 and 2008, focusing on the **battleground states**, which are swing states in which the relative strength of the two major party presidential candidates is close enough so that either candidate could conceivably carry the state. Campaign volunteers and paid organizers telephoned, mailed, e-mailed, or visited millions of potential voters, encouraging them to go to the polls. Exposure to intense campaign activity increases political engagement, especially among low-income voters, a group with typically low voter turnout rates.[27] In the meantime, hot-button issues such as the war in Iraq, the war on terror, gay marriage, healthcare reform, taxes, high gas prices, and the economy energized citizens to go to the polls. According to the ANES, 40 percent of Americans said they were "very much interested" in the 2004 presidential campaign, the highest level of interest in the history of the poll and 14 percentage points higher than the level of interest expressed in 2000.[28] Interest in the 2008 election may have been even higher.

**battleground states** swing states in which the relative strength of the two major-party presidential candidates is close enough so that either candidate could conceivably carry the state.

More than 62 percent of the VEP cast ballots in the 1964 presidential election, capping a steady 36-year rise in voter turnout. For the next 30 years, voter participation rates declined, reaching to a 70-year low in 1996 at 51.7 percent. Election turnout subsequently rebounded to 54.2 percent in 2000, 60.3 percent in 2004, and 61.6 percent in 2008.

# participation rates in
## COMPARATIVE PERSPECTIVE

Voting turnout in the United States is relatively low compared to other industrialized democracies. According to data collected by the International Institute for Democracy and Electoral Assistance, the United States lags behind most other countries in the world in electoral participation in national legislative elections.[29]

More than a fourth of the potential electorate in the United States is not registered to vote.[30] Political scientists identify three factors that result in the relatively lower American voter turnout rate. First, American election procedures are more cumbersome than they are in most

**Does it really matter that many Americans do not vote?**

**separation of powers** the division of political power among executive, legislative, and judicial branches of government.

other democracies. Before Americans can vote in most states, they must register, usually no later than 30 days before an election. In most other democracies, the government takes the initiative to register eligible voters. American elections traditionally take place on Tuesday, whereas other countries declare a national holiday so citizens can vote without missing work. The United States also holds more frequent elections and elects larger numbers of public officials. Many Americans stay home, confused by the length and complexity of the ballot.[31]

Second, voter participation rates

in the United States are lower because American political parties are weaker than those of other democracies. Strong political parties increase voter turnout by educating citizens about candidates and issues, stimulating interest in elections, and mobilizing citizens to vote. Political scientist G. Bingham Powell Jr. estimates that if American political parties were more centralized and had stronger ties to other social organizations, such as labor unions, religious bodies, and ethnic groups, then voter participa-

**"I was just too busy."**

*The #1 reason Americans give for not voting is that they couldn't find the time.*

tion would rise by as much as 10 percent.[32]

Finally, many American voters stay home because they do not perceive that elections have much impact on policy. Winning candidates may not be able to keep promises because of **separation of powers**, the division of political authority among the executive, legislative, and judicial branches of government. During the 2006 election campaign, for example, Democratic congressional candidates called for the withdrawal of American troops from Iraq. Even though the Democrats captured majorities in both the House and Senate, they could not keep this promise. Their majority was too slim to pass proposals to bring home the troops, or to override President George W. Bush's veto.

# COMPARING VOTING RATES

Mexico 59% | UK 61% | US 62% | Canada 65% | Germany 78% | Sweden 82% | Italy 84% | Denmark 87% | Belgium 91% | Australia 95%

Voting turnout in most recent national election.

# Compulsory Voting in Australia

Compulsory voting is the legal requirement that citizens participate in national elections. It is a low-cost, efficient remedy to the problem of low turnout. Voter participation rates are almost 20 percent higher in nations with compulsory voting than they are in other democracies.[33] Almost everyone votes in Australia, a nation that has had compulsory voting since 1924. For example, voter turnout was 95 percent in the 2007 national election.[34]

The Australian Election Commission (AEC) enforces the nation's compulsory voting law. The AEC sends a "please explain" letter to people who fail to vote in a particular election. Election no-shows can either pay a fine or offer an explanation. If the AEC decides that the explanation is valid, it can waive the fine. The courts settle disputes between the AEC and individual non-voters over the validity of excuses. The proportion of Australians fined for failing to vote never exceeds 1 percent of the electorate.[35]

Political scientists believe that compulsory voting strengthens political parties. Because parties do not have to devote resources to turning out the vote, they can focus on persuasion and conversion. Compulsory voting builds party loyalty. Survey research in Australia finds that most Australian voters express firm and longstanding commitments to a party. You have read that lower-income people are less likely to vote than middle-income citizens. So, compulsory voting also benefits political parties representing the working-class interests more than those representing middle- and upper-income voters because lower-income people are less likely to vote than middle-income citizens.

## Questions

1. Does the problem of non-voting need a legal remedy?

2. Do you think compulsory voting in the United States would increase turnout substantially?

3. Do you think that the United States will ever adopt compulsory voting? Why or why not?

**compulsory voting** the legal requirement that citizens participate in national elections.

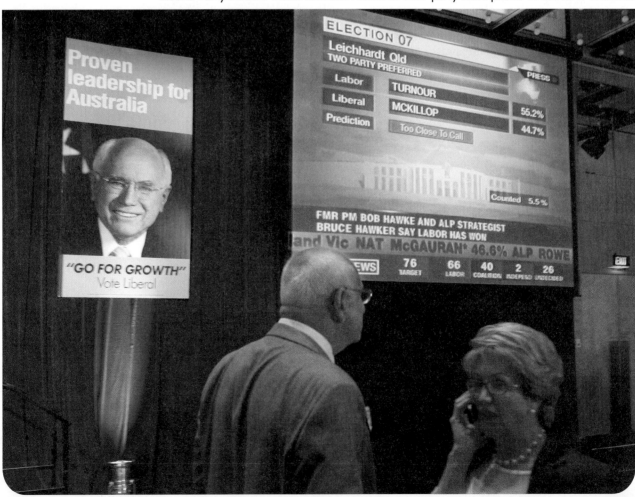

Liberal Party leaders watch election results as their party loses power in the 2007 election.

# participation
## BIAS

**i**s participation biased in favor of some groups and against others? Conventional political wisdom holds that low election turnout helps the Republicans, whereas Democrats benefit from a large turnout. Studies indicate that non-voters are more likely to be young people, the unemployed, laborers, lower-income persons, individuals with relatively little formal education, people who are not married, Latinos, and people who seldom attend religious services.[36] Surveys show that these groups of people also tend to vote for Democratic candidates more frequently than Republicans. So Democrats often favor reforming registration laws and other voting procedures to enhance voter turnout. For the same reason, Republican officials generally oppose election law reform. Nonetheless, the 2004 election demonstrated that higher voter turnout does not necessarily benefit the Democratic Party. The Kerry campaign increased the Democratic vote by 16 percent over Al Gore's showing in 2000, but that was not enough because the Republican presidential vote grew by 23 percent.[37]

Research does, however, show a bias in political attitudes. Political activists are more conservative than the population as a whole on economic issues. People who partici-

## RESEARCH DOES SHOW A BIAS IN POLITICAL ATTITUDES

pate in the policy process are less likely to support government spending for public services, government help for minority groups,

and programs to assist the poor. Individual campaign contributors tend to be more conservative and more Republican than the electorate as a whole.[38] To the extent that elected officials respond to the demands of voters, public policies will be consistent with the interests of middle- and upper-income groups rather than the working class.

Interest group and political party activities contribute to the participation bias as well. In the nineteenth and early twentieth centuries, the nation's most important interest groups were large membership organizations that drew people from all strata of society, rich and poor alike. These groups advocated government policies that benefited people across class lines, such as Social Se-

Protestors outside the Arkansas State Capitol at the 30th Annual March for Life rally in 2008.

A Pregnant Woman Needs Support Not Abortion

1-800-395-Help
...oMoreAwareness.org

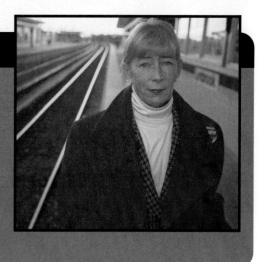

curity, Medicare, public schools, and programs for war veterans. Since the middle of the twentieth century, large membership organizations, such as labor unions, have declined, whereas professionally managed advocacy groups composed mainly of middle- and upper-middle-class professionals have proliferated. These groups push middle-class agendas.[39] Political parties contribute to the imbalance in participation rates as well by targeting their campaigns at people with voting histories. With rare exceptions, political campaigns focus on turning out their core supporters rather than trying to expand the electorate.[40]

# CONCLUSION
# political participation
# & PUBLIC POLICY

the nature of America's constitutional system of government makes it difficult to identify the connection between individual participation and public policy. In most cases, citizens do not make policy directly as they would in a **direct democracy**. The United States is a **representative democracy;** citizens elect representatives to make policy on their behalf. Furthermore, federalism, the bicameral Congress, and the separation of powers with checks and balances ensure that most public policies reflect the interaction of numerous public officials, both elected and appointed, at different levels and in different branches of government. Establishing a linkage between a particular policy and one person's vote, campaign contribution, letter to a representative, or protest would be difficult. Nonetheless, individual participation plays a role in the nation's policy process.

## Agenda Building
Individuals can have an impact on the national policy agenda. The modern campaign to ratify the Twenty-seventh Amendment to the U.S. Constitution was begun by one individual. The amendment requires that a congressional pay raise not take effect until after the next election. It was first proposed in 1789 but failed to be ratified by the required number of states. The amendment was presumed dead until 1982, when an aide to a state legislator in Texas began a campaign for its ratification. Ten years later, enough states had ratified the amendment for it to become part of the Constitution.

## Policy Formulation and Adoption
Most of the nation's elected officials are self-starters in the sense that they decide to seek office. Individual citizens who choose to run for office can often have a great effect on policy formulation and adoption.

> **direct democracy** a political system in which the citizens vote directly on matters of public concern.
>
> **representative democracy** a political system in which citizens elect representatives to make policy decisions on their behalf.

The Department of Transportation hires local contractors to build highways, bridges, and other highway construction projects.

The chances for individuals to influence policy formulation and adoption are greatest at the local level. Relatively few individuals can win election or appointment to a major state or national office, but thousands of people have the opportunity to serve in an elected office at the local level—on school boards, city councils, or local utility boards. Furthermore, individual voices on issues of concern can be heard more readily at the local level than on the national level.

## Policy Implementation and Evaluation

Individuals can affect policy implementation. For example, the owners of Adarand Constructors, a Colorado construction company, decided to file suit against the federal Department of Transportation (DOT) over the procedures followed by the agency in the construction of federal highway projects. The lawsuit challenged the DOT practice of favoring firms owned by individuals who are "black, Hispanic, Asian Pacific, Subcontinent Asian, and Native American." The U.S. Supreme Court eventually ruled against the DOT, declaring that the agency could grant a minority preference only in those circumstances when it could show a clear history of discrimination against minority contractors.[41] The DOT had to abandon its practice of granting preference to minority contractors. Finally, individuals can participate in policy evaluation. Citizens can express their views on government policies by contacting their elected officials. Members of Congress (or at least members of their staff) read the mail. A clearly written, thoughtful letter or e-mail message can have an impact. Individuals can also participate informally in policy evaluation by writing letters to the editor of their local newspaper or by calling a radio talk program.

the
THINKSPOT
www.thethinkspot.com

# Electronic Voting: Helpful or Harmful?

**What can be done to ensure all votes are cast and counted fairly? Are electronic voting machines as resistant to tampering as their adherents claim?**

**Are there more efficient ways to ensure that elections are truly legitimate? Is there a better way to ensure elections are "transparent," with the results made public for all to scrutinize?**

**Overview:** For most of American history, Americans have been only intermittently concerned with voter fraud. However, with the contested presidential election of 2000, in which President George W. Bush attained office through a decision handed down by the U.S. Supreme Court, many Americans began to focus their attention on the electoral process—particularly on the act of voting. Indeed, the Florida vote demonstrated that voting irregularities are not as infrequent as most Americans believe and that every vote counts (this is not as rare as most Americans think; in the 1960

presidential election, for example, President John F. Kennedy was awarded 49.7 percent of the popular vote to Richard Nixon's 49.5 percent—roughly a difference of 100,000 votes out of 68 million votes cast). In fact, there have been numerous reports of voting fraud in the 2004 and 2006 elections.

The Florida vote revealed that many voters rely on old, outdated, and often defective machines. With advances in technology, states have begun to explore the mass use of

computerized and electronic voting machines. This new technology, however, poses new problems and new potential for abuse—how is a voter to know that his or her vote has truly been cast? Aren't databases and electronic storage systems subject to electoral and technical exploitation as well? Or should Americans continue to accept the unpleasant fact there will always be those few who will subvert the electoral process for political gain?

## supporting electronic voting

**electronic voting machines will lower the rate of "spoiled ballots."** There will be no "hanging chads" or "pregnant ballots"; poorly punched ballots are often unrecorded, and electronic voting can eliminate this particular voting error.

**electronic voting devices are accessible to the disabled and elderly.** Electronic voting will allow voters to more easily see and understand the ballot selections, and will allow many disabled to vote in privacy.

**electronic voting machines can be programmed in many languages.** This makes voting easier for those who do not speak English well, and is of particular benefit to newly naturalized American citizens.

## against electronic voting

**computer scientists have yet to develop tamper-free software.** Johns Hopkins University researchers have found that it is almost impossible to know if software has been tampered with to alter voting results.

**there may be problems with the transmission of vote results.** Though it is not necessary to transmit ballot results through the Internet, most phone lines are increasingly connected to the Internet, thus increasing the chances of a hacker accessing and altering vote tallies.

**as of 2006, electronic voting machines do not provide an independent record of individual ballots.** Neither voters nor election officials have a hard copy of individual ballots to count in case of a malfunction or suspected fraud.

# TEST yourself

1. Which of the following is the most common form of political participation?
   A. Contributing money to candidates
   B. Joining an interest group
   C. Contacting an elected official
   D. Voting

2. In which of the following elections would you expect the highest turnout when measured as a proportion of the total of eligible voters?
   A. Local election for mayor
   B. Election for governor
   C. Election for senator
   D. Presidential election

3. Which of the following is a form of political participation?
   A. Writing a letter to a local official about a problem.
   B. Giving money to a candidate for a school board election.
   C. Putting up a yard sign to support a candidate for the state legislature.
   D. All of the above.

4. Which of the following is the best explanation for why more people vote than volunteer to work in a political campaign?
   A. Voting requires less time and effort than volunteer work.
   B. Voting has a greater impact on the outcome of an election than volunteer work.
   C. Most political campaigns don't want volunteer help because they prefer to rely on professional campaign consultants.
   D. None of the above.

5. The process of motivating people to vote is known as which of the following?
   A. Political efficacy
   B. Political participation
   C. Voter mobilization
   D. Straight-ticket voting

6. Which of the following play(s) a positive role in voter mobilization?
   A. Political parties
   B. Interest groups
   C. Individual contacts
   D. All of the above

7. Would you expect the voter turnout rate to be higher for people earning $80,000 a year or those making $30,000 a year?
   A. Turnout would be greater for the higher-income group.
   B. Turnout would be greater for the lower-income group.
   C. Turnout would be the same for both groups.
   D. Turnout would be greater for the higher-income group in all elections but presidential elections, where the turnout rate would be the same.

8. What is the relationship between age and political participation?
   A. Participation rates fall as people age.
   B. Participation rates increase as people age.
   C. Participation rates increase as people age until individuals reach old age and then participation rates turn downward.
   D. Participation increases through middle age and then gradually declines throughout the last half of the individual lifespan.

9. For which of the following age groups would you expect the voting participation rate to be the lowest?
   A. People in their 20s
   B. People in their 30s
   C. People in their 40s
   D. People in their 50s

10. Suppose the Constitution were amended to give 17-year-olds the right to vote. What impact would that action likely have on voter turnout as a proportion of the voting age population?
    A. It would increase voter turnout because more people would be eligible to vote.
    B. It would decrease voter turnout because the voting age population would be enlarged to include individuals relatively unlikely to vote.
    C. It would increase voter turnout because the voting age population would be enlarged to include individuals who are likely to vote.
    D. Voter turnout would be unchanged because 17-year-olds are just as likely to vote as anyone else.

11. Which of the following statements about voter turnout by different groups is correct?
    A. Voter turnout among Latinos is usually greater than turnout among African Americans.
    B. Voter turnout among young people is usually greater than turnout among adults.
    C. Voter turnout among low-income persons is usually greater than turnout among high-income persons.
    D. Voter turnout among women is usually greater than turnout among men.

**12** Which of the following groups is the least represented in all areas of political participation compared with the other groups?

A. Latinos

B. Whites

C. African Americans

D. The groups participate at roughly the same rate.

**13** Which of the following statements accurately explains why Latino voter participation rates are lower than they are for other groups?

A. As a group, Latinos are not as well-educated as whites and Asian Americans.

B. As a group, Latinos earn lower incomes than whites and Asians.

C. A higher percentage of Latinos are not citizens compared to other racial/ethnic groups.

D. All of the above.

**14** Which of the following groups is most seriously affected by state laws that disqualify individuals with serious criminal offenses from voting?

A. White women

B. Latino males

C. African American males

D. White males

**15** Compared with men, women are more likely to do which of the following?

A. Vote

B. Give money to candidates

C. Join a political group

D. There are no differences in participation rates between men and women.

**16** Why is the voting age population (VAP) an imperfect database to measure voter participation?

A. The census has a fairly accurate count of the population, but measures of the population by age group are imprecise.

B. Voter turnout numbers are often inaccurate.

C. The VAP includes large numbers of people who are not eligible to vote, including non-citizens and people who are incarcerated.

D. All of the above.

**17** Which of the following statements best describes recent trends in voter turnout?

A. Voter turnout in presidential elections has increased in each of the last three presidential elections.

B. Voter turnout in presidential elections has been falling consistently since the early 1960s.

C. Voter turnout in presidential elections has been rising consistently since the early 1960s.

D. Voter turnout in presidential elections has fallen in each of the last three presidential elections.

**18** How does voter turnout in the United States compare with turnout in other Western democracies?

A. Turnout in the United States is relatively low.

B. Turnout in the United States is relatively high.

C. Turnout in the United States is average.

D. Turnout in the United States is relatively high for national elections, but low for state elections.

**19** Which of the following statements about compulsory voting in Australia is true?

A. People who do not vote in Australia can go to jail for as long as a year.

B. Voter turnout in Australia is much higher than it is in the United States.

C. Political scientists believe that compulsory voting in Australia harms working class parties because it weakens the advantage labor unions enjoy in turning out their vote.

D. None of the above.

**20** Which of the following statements about political participation is true?

A. Democrats always benefit from high voter turnout.

B. Political activists are more liberal than the population as a whole on economic issues.

C. Interest groups and political parties typically promote the interests of the working class.

D. None of the above.

---

KNOW *the* **score**

18–20 correct: Congratulations! You are well informed!

15–17 correct: Your political knowledge is a bit low—be sure to review the key terms and visit TheThinkSpot.

<14 correct: Reread the chapter more thoroughly.

---

1.D; 2.D; 3.D; 4.A; 5.C; 6.D; 7.A; 8.C; 9.A; 10.B; 11.D; 12.A; 13.D; 14.C; 15.A; 16.C; 17.A; 18.A; 19.B; 20.D

# 6 THE

Technology is transforming American politics. Almost every candidate for office has a basic webpage with pictures, a biography, issue positions, and a fundraising link that accepts major credit cards. Technologically sophisticated candidates and officeholders utilize the full array of social media, including Facebook, MySpace, YouTube, and Twitter.

No politician uses technology more effectively than Barack Obama. In 2008, the Obama campaign created an e-mail list of more than 13 million addresses. The most popular Obama Facebook page had 6.4 million supporters. Obama used his online network to deliver campaign messages, organize volunteers, and raise money. The Obama campaign broke all fundraising records by raising more than half a billion dollars from three million online donors.[1] After becoming president, Obama used his online network to organize support for his legislative initiatives and appointments. In 2009, for example, the White House used its e-mail list to mobilize support for Sonia Sotomayor, the president's nominee to serve on the U.S. Supreme Court. Vice President Joe Biden e-mailed Obama supporters, asking them to sign an online petition in support of Sotomayor. Visitors to Obama's webpage could e-mail their senators about the nomination without leaving the site.[2]

Technology enables candidates and officeholders to communicate directly with their supporters without having to go through a news media filter. During the 2008 presidential campaign, for example, Obama announced his choice of a vice presidential running mate by text messaging supporters rather than holding a press conference. Social media in particular have the ability to engage campaign supporters because they are immediate, targeted, and interactive. Political consultant Matt Glazer says that the value of the social media is to turn casual supporters into informed supporters, and informed supporters into donors and volunteers.[3]

# MEDIA

# the media
## LANDSCAPE

## ESSENTIALS...

*after studying Chapter 6, students should be able to answer the following questions:*

> How would you describe the media landscape in the United States, and what has been the impact of YouTube and other new communication technologies on the policymaking environment?

> How does media consolidation affect news coverage? How do candidates and officeholders attempt to manipulate news coverage?

> Are the news media biased?

> What is the role of the media in the policymaking process?

In contrast to much of the world, there is little direct government ownership of media outlets in the United States. The federal government operates the Armed Forces Radio and Television Service, which provides news and entertainment to members of the U.S. Armed Forces worldwide. Many local entities, including cities, schools, and colleges, operate cable television stations. City governments may use their cable television channels to air city council meetings and other public service programming. Universities and colleges sometimes operate radio stations.

The Public Broadcasting Service (PBS) and National Public Radio (NPR) are private non-profit media services with public and private financial support. PBS is a non-profit private corporation that is owned jointly by hundreds of member television stations throughout the United States; NPR is a non-profit membership organization of radio stations. The Corporation for Public Broadcasting is a government agency chartered and funded by the U.S. government to promote public broadcasting. It provides some funding for both PBS and NPR. Public radio and television stations also benefit from corporate donations and financial contributions from the general public. PBS and NPR regularly interrupt their programming to ask their viewers and listeners to pledge their financial support.

Private businesses, often large corporations, own and operate most media outlets in the United States. Most **print media** (newspapers and

**print media** newspapers and magazines.

# THE TWITTER REVOLUTION

**Throughout June 2009,** millions of demonstrators took to the streets in Iran to protest the presidential election results, which reported a decisive victory for the incumbent, Ahmadinejad, despite a widespread belief that he had actually lost to Mousavi, his principle challenger.

Attempting to censor the information disseminated abroad and prevent protestors from organizing, the Iranian government denied journalists access, shut down websites, and blocked cell-phone reception. To get around this, Iranians and their supporters around the world mobilized and communicated via Twitter, a free social networking and micro-blogging service. Through 140-character "Tweets," users posted on-the-ground accounts of events in real time. The traditional news media reported extensively on the information in these Tweets, and Twitter proved to be a powerful tool for spreading information both within Iran and abroad.

Yet while some praise this democratization of news dissemination, others worry about the lack of safeguards to ensure accuracy or verify sources. Users inadvertently spread erroneous rumors, and some reported that the government was covertly spreading misinformation.

magazines) and **broadcast media** (television, radio, and the Internet) outlets are part of large chains. Consolidation is an important trend in media ownership. The ten largest newspaper groups control a majority of newspaper circulation in the nation. Most television stations belong to national networks, such as CBS, NBC, ABC, Fox, WB, or UPN. Clear Channel Communication and Cumulus Media own hundreds of radio stations, including many in the same city.[4] Cross-media ownership is common as well, in which one corporation owns several types of media. The Tribune Company, for example, owns the *Chicago Tribune* newspaper as well as several radio and television stations in the Chicago area and dozens of other newspapers, television stations, and radio stations around the country.[5]

The media landscape is changing. In terms of circulation and ratings, many mainstream media outlets, especially newspapers, newsmagazines, and the network evening news, have been in decline for years. Between 2001 and 2007, daily newspaper circulation fell by 8 percent; Sunday newspaper circulation dropped by 11

## SOME OF WHAT NEWS CORPORATION OWNS:

**NEWSPAPERS:** MORE THAN 175 NEWSPAPERS WORLDWIDE

**PROGRAMMING & PRODUCTION:** FOX TELEVISION

**BOOKS:** HARPERCOLLINS

**MAGAZINES:** NEWS AMERICA MARKETING GROUP

**SATELLITE:** SKY NEWS

**FILM:** FOX STUDIOS

**INTERNET:** INTERMIX

**MISC:** RECORDS, DIGITAL TECHNOLOGY, SPORTS TEAMS

CEO: Rupert Murdoch
Number of Employees: 44,000

viewers a year.[6] (See figure on the following page.)

Whereas traditional media sources are in decline, the **new media**, a term describing alternative media sources, such as the Internet, cable television, and satellite radio, are in

# young people in particular are turning away from traditional media sources in favor of the new media

percent. Circulation for the "big three" newsmagazines (*Time*, *Newsweek*, and *U.S. News*) is falling. Ratings for the network evening news and morning news shows are in a long decline as well. Over the past 25 years, the combined audience for the network evening news has fallen on average by a million

ascendance. Young people in particular are turning away from traditional media sources in favor of the new media.[7] In 1992, newspapers and television network news were the most important reported media sources for news about that year's presidential campaign. By 2004, however, the most important re-

ported sources of information about the presidential contest were newspapers, cable television, network television, radio, and the Internet.[8] Fox News, CNN, and MSNBC offer news coverage around the clock. Radio talk shows offer news and opinion much of the day. In the meantime, anyone with a computer can create a website or write a **weblog or blog**, an online personal journal or newsletter that is regularly updated. Although online news

**broadcast media** television, radio, and the Internet.

**new media** a term used to refer to alternative media sources, such as the Internet, cable television, and satellite radio.

**weblog or blog** an online personal journal or newsletter that is regularly updated.

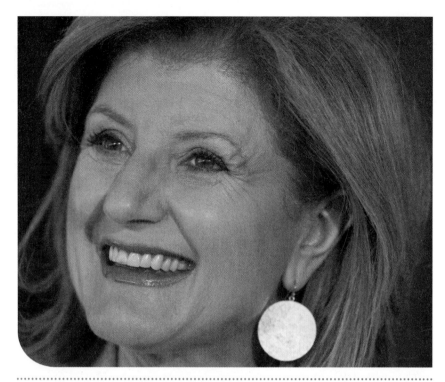

sources vary considerably in quality and credibility, some have become important sources of information. The Matt Drudge website, the *Drudge Report*, was the first media source to break the news about the relationship between White House intern Monica Lewinsky and President Bill Clinton. Blogs in particular are important opinion outlets. In fact, liberal bloggers have become such an important source of opinion leadership in the Democratic Party that presidential candidates have hired some of them to write blogs for their campaign websites.

Candidates and elected officials have adapted to the new media en-

Arianna Huffington's blog, the Huffington Post, is a popular online destination for people seeking news and opinion from a liberal perspective.

vironment by using the Internet for communication and fundraising. Between 1996 and 2004, the percentage of major party candidates for Congress with campaign web-

sites increased from 22 percent to 81 percent.[9] Although every major presidential candidate has an online presence in 2008, Barack Obama used the Internet more effectively than any of his opponents, raising millions of dollars online.

Network evening news viewership has been steadily declining for years, as more people turn to alternative sources of news.

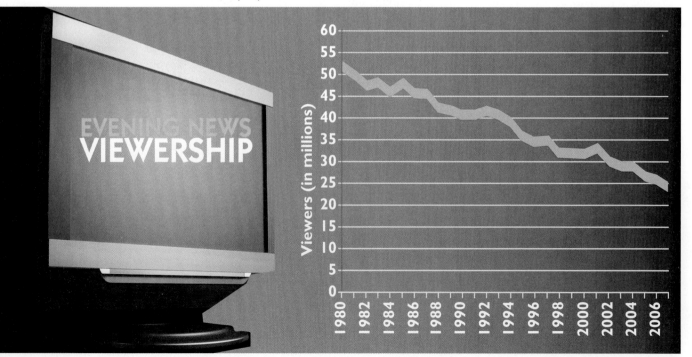

EVENING NEWS **VIEWERSHIP**

Viewers (in millions)

Source: Nielsen Media Research

# Government Control of the Media in Cuba

The government tightly controls the media in Cuba. The Cuban government owns the electronic media and controls its content. Foreign news agencies are forced to hire local journalists through government offices if they wish to cover news stories in Cuba. Independent journalists are subject to harassment, detention, and physical attacks. Journalists found guilty of publishing anti-government propaganda or of insulting government officials can be sentenced to long prison terms. According to Reporters Without Borders, an international non-profit organization that advocates freedom of the press, two dozen journalists were held in Cuban prisons in poor conditions in 2008.[10]

The Cuban government attempts to control Internet access by banning private Internet connections. As a result, less than 2 percent of the Cuban population has Internet access. People who want to surf the web or check their e-mail must go to Internet cafés, universities, or other public sites where their activities can be closely monitored. The computers in Internet cafes and hotels have software installed to alert police whenever it spots "subversive" words. Cuban residents who write articles critical of the Cuban government for foreign websites are subject to 20-year prison terms.[11]

The U.S. government attempts to break the Cuban government's monopoly on information with Radio Martí, which broadcasts on shortwave and medium-wave transmitters from Miami, Florida. Miami's most popular Spanish-language AM radio station, powerful enough to be heard throughout Cuba, also carries an hour of news from Radio Martí each night at midnight. The Cuban government jams the shortwave and medium-wave Radio Martí broadcasts throughout the island, and the AM radio station in Havana, so their effectiveness is questionable.

## Questions to Consider

1. Can a country be a democracy without a free press? Why or why not?

2. Is it ever appropriate for a government to manage the news media?

3. Should the United States continue to fund Radio Martí?

Young Cubans cheer for a protest singer against Cuban police methods at a rally.

# covering
## THE NEWS

**a** major goal of news media outlets is to attract as large an audience as possible. Newspaper advertising rates depend on readership. Arbitron ratings of listeners determine advertising rates for radio stations; Nielsen ratings count television viewers. Online advertising rates depend on website traffic. Even non-profit media outlets such as PBS and NPR want to attract large audience support for their programming, in hopes of having more successful pledge drives.

Media outlets take different approaches to building an audience. Television networks, big city newspapers, and newsmagazines aim to attract as large an audience as possible. They cover mainstream news from a middle-of-the-road perspective with an eye to entertainment value by highlighting dramatic events and celebrities. Stories about Britney Spears get more coverage than in-depth analyses of budget policy. Re-

ports on crime, traffic accidents, and severe weather dominate local news to the near exclusion of serious coverage of local policy issues. In contrast, other media outlets try to build a niche audience by targeting audiences based on political philosophy, issue focus, or religious values. Political activists can find a set of websites, blogs, radio talk shows, magazines, and television shows that reinforce their point of view.

Media consolidation affects news coverage. Because of chain ownership, newspaper stories written for the *New York Times* or *Washington Post* may appear in identical form in local newspapers around the nation. In any given week, all three major newsmagazines may feature the same cover story. Meanwhile, local radio and television stations rely on network news feeds for national news. As a result, news outlets around the country tend to focus on the same handful of national stories

each day, often told from the same perspective and sometimes in the same words. Because of staff reductions, local media outlets focus on national election coverage rather than state and local contests.[12]

Campaign organizations attempt to manage news coverage to present their candidates in the most positive light. Indeed, the presidential campaigns of Reagan in 1980 and 1984 and George H. W. Bush in 1988 were the prototype of campaign control of news media coverage. The Reagan-Bush strategy, which most campaigns now attempt to copy, was based on several principles. First, campaign managers choose a single theme to emphasize each campaign day, such as crime, the environment, or defense. If the candidate and the members of the candidate's team address the same issue and only that issue, the news media will be

## POLITICS & THE INTERNET

**1991 | High Performance Computing and Communication Act of 1991 (sponsored by then Senator Al Gore) leads to the information superhighway.**

**1996 | equal numbers of voters report getting information from websites and from periodicals.**

**1999 | Sean Fanning creates NAPSTER; the Blackberry is introduced.**

| 1900 | 1991 | 1992 | 1993 | 1994 | 1995 | 1996 | 1997 | 1998 | 1999 |

**1991 | World Wide Web (WWW) begins.**

**1992 | "Surfing the net" is coined.**

## DRUDGE REPORT

**1998 | the online *Drudge Report* breaks the news of President Bill Clinton's affair with intern Monica Lewinsky.**

## Politics more popular than than "American Idol"? It was in 2008.

| | |
|---|---|
| World Series | 18.8 million viewers |
| American Idol | 24 million viewers |
| Obama Infomercial | 33.6 million viewers |
| Sarah Palin Convention Speech | 37.2 million viewers |
| Obama Convention Speech | 38.4 million viewers |
| McCain Convention Speech | 38.9 million viewers |
| First Presidential Debate | 52.4 million viewers |
| Third Presidential Debate | 56.5 million viewers |
| Second Presidential Debate | 63.2 million viewers |
| Vice Presidential Debate | 69.6 million viewers |

The major events of the 2008 presidential campaign consistently received better television ratings than entertainment programs. Even Barack Obama's infomercial, which was a paid 30-minute campaign commercial run a week before the election, had better ratings than the last game of the baseball World Series and the finale of "American Idol."

more likely to focus on that issue in their daily campaign reports.

Second, the campaign selects an eye-catching visual backdrop for its candidate that reemphasizes the theme of the day, such as the Statue of Liberty, a retirement home, or a military base. In 1988, George H. W. Bush even staged a campaign event in a factory that made American flags. Campaign organizers try to ensure that everyone in the audience is friendly so that television images convey the impression of popular support. When President George W. Bush ran for reelection in 2004, he typically appeared at invitation-only rallies to ensure that news reports would be filled with pictures of smiling faces and cheering crowds.

Finally, campaign managers carefully brief the candidate to stick with the campaign script. Each speech includes one or two carefully worded phrases that can be used as

**2007 | Microsoft is fined $1.3 billion by EU for violating EU free competition rules**

**2001 | MoveOn.org is founded as a news source and fundraiser for liberal causes.**

**2003 | Howard Dean's campaign depends on online giving, bypassing traditional fundraising activities.**

2000 2001 2002 2003 2004 2005 2006 2007 2008

**2000 | Dot.com bubble bursts.**

**2002 | 58.5% of U.S. population uses the Internet regularly.**

**2005 | YouTube is launched.**

**2008 | Obama's website collects $500 million in political contributions during the 2008 campaign.**

## WIKIPEDIA
*The Free Encyclopedia*

# Media 6.0 vs. the Typewriter

**Does regulation of the Internet media infringe upon Americans' press, speech, and grievance rights? Why or why not?**

**Does the traditional media itself need a "watchdog," and can the Internet media perform this function to ensure accountability on the part of the press?**

**Overview:** When a gunman opened fire on Virginia Tech's campus in April, 2007, many Americans went straight to their computers for information about the event. From the campus and community, witnesses and victims began sharing cellphone photos and videos, text messages, and e-mails with authorities, friends, and loved ones. This information and the resulting commentary became immediately available on websites like Wikipedia, which reported an average of four visits a second for the first two days after the shooting, dramatically diminishing the authority of traditional media to frame the story.

In addition to the traditional press, politicians are being held accountable and subjected to scrutiny by the In-

ternet media. For example, in the 2004 presidential contest, John Kerry had to address incorrect or false statements he made on the Senate floor in 1986, statements dredged up through Internet research and posted on political blogs. How have elected politicians and traditional media responded to this new reality? By calling for regulation of Internet political speech and media, of course!

Such media luminaries as the *New York Times* editorial page have called for subjecting the Internet media to the same restrictions and standards as the traditional press. Many Internet commentators consider this an attempt to "rein in" or staunch the growing audience and influence

of the new nontraditional media by having government action regulate the increasing crowd of "citizen journalists" who are simply exercising First Amendment rights. The *Times* and others argue that untrained journalists are not capable of providing superior quality and content, but the media marketplace seems to be telling a different story.

Legislation has been introduced to make Internet communication subject to the Bipartisan Campaign Reform Act (BCRA)'s "promote, attack, support, or oppose" rule in which any of those activities can be interpreted as "campaign" speech, and thus become subject to federal regulation.

## supporting new media regulation

**there is no editorial oversight.** A primary reason for the quality enjoyed by traditional news establishments is that there are experienced, educated, and expert editors and producers who can discern whether a source is trustworthy and valid. Untrained journalists typically do not have the requisite experience or education to make that call.

**it is difficult for news consumers to determine advocacy from reporting.** Many Internet media sites not only report news, but engage in political support as well. It is difficult for the average news consumer to separate news from advocacy, so these sites should be subject to the same restrictions and guidelines as traditional media.

**no First Amendment right is absolute.** Acrimonious debate and false or misreporting of events harm the quality of the American polity's discourse and knowledge, and government regulation is a proper solution to assuring a well-informed and engaged citizenry.

## against new media regulation

**a free press is considered a bulwark against governmental corruption and tyranny.** All citizens have the right to investigate government corruption or waste and publish their findings. A free press can force government accountability and pressure government and elected officials to act in the public interest.

**the new Internet media acts as a watchdog over the traditional press.** The Internet media has exposed misreporting by the *New York Times*, CBS News, and the *Los Angeles Times*, among others, and the Internet media are forcing accountability on both journalists and editors/producers alike.

**Americans have the First Amendment right for the redress of grievances.** Not only does the Internet allow Americans to expose political corruption, but it also allows Americans to opine and discuss government and politics without the filter of editors and producers.

President George W. Bush greets military pilots after landing on their aircraft carrier in 2003. He then used the carrier as a stage from which to deliver a speech proclaiming an end to combat operations in Iraq.

sound bites on the evening news. A **sound bite** is a short phrase taken from a candidate's speech by the news media for use on newscasts. Candidates who lack discipline or who are prone to gaffes distract from their own message.

Once in office, elected officials establish sophisticated communications operations to manage the news. President George W. Bush's communications operation had 63 full-time employees organized among offices of communication, media affairs, speechwriting, global communications, press, and pho-tography. Other communication employees worked in the offices of the vice president, first lady, and the National Security Council. Altogether, the Bush administration employed more than 300 people full-time to manage and support its communications operation.[13]

The Bush administration's communications strategy attempted to tie policy, politics, and communications together. Professor Bruce Miroff says that the Bush administration depicted the war in Iraq as if it were a professional wrestling match in

## "Brownie, You're doing a heck of a job."

which the audience (the American people) watches the good guy (President Bush) overpower the bad guy (Saddam Hussein). President Bush declared victory on May 1, 2003 after landing a jet on the deck of the aircraft carrier *Abraham Lincoln*. Bush, dressed in a green flight suit, used the aircraft carrier as a stage to announce that combat operations in Iraq were over. A large banner over the president's head read "Mission Accomplished."[14]

**sound bite** a short phrase taken from a candidate's speech by the news media for use on newscasts.

Katrina flood survivors paint a plea for help on their roof in September 2005. The power and proliferation of these images proved a communications catastrophe for the Bush administration.

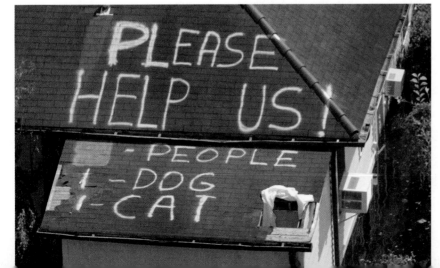

Candidates and officeholders do not always succeed in managing the media. Ask former Virginia Senator George Allen, who was a heavy favorite to win reelection to the U.S. Senate in 2006 until he interrupted a campaign rally to introduce a native-born American college student of Indian descent as "Macaca." The incident became Allen's undoing after opponents posted a tape of Allen making the remark on YouTube. Although Allen tried to explain that he called the student Macaca because of his Mohawk-style haircut, bloggers pointed out that Macaca is considered a racial slur. The controversy dominated the media for weeks.

Events can also overwhelm an officeholder's communications strategy. Hurricane Katrina, for example, was a communications catastrophe for the George W. Bush administration. Rather than interrupt his vacation, President Bush left Secretary of Homeland Security Michael Chertoff in charge. Television viewers saw thousands of people stranded on roofs and huddled in the New Orleans Superdome, but Chertoff declared his pleasure at the federal response to the disaster. President Bush finally arrived several days after the hurricane, and his rhetoric seemed out of touch with reality in New Orleans. "Brownie," he said to Federal Emergency Management Administration (FEMA) Director Michael Brown, "you're doing a heck of a job."[15]

# media BIASES

**think** — What role should the media play in the dissemination of news, and how important is media objectivity?

**O**bjective journalism is a style of news reporting that focuses on facts rather than opinion, and presents all sides of controversial issues. Major newspapers, broadcast television news, and the major cable news networks pride themselves on their commitment to objective journalism.

The trademark slogan for the Fox News Channel is "fair and balanced." Even though newspapers endorse candidates on their editorial pages, the ideal of objective journalism is that candidate endorsements have no impact on the content or tone of news coverage.

Nonetheless, many political activists believe that the press is biased. Conservatives accuse the media of a liberal bias. For evidence, they cite a survey showing that 44 percent of news journalists identified with the Democratic Party compared with only 16 percent who said they were Republicans. (Another 34 percent were independent.)[16] Conservatives believe that the media slant the news in favor of liberal policy perspectives while ignoring conservative points of view. At the same time, many liberals believe that the media have a conservative bias. Conservative commentators, such as Rush Limbaugh, dominate talk radio and most newspaper editorial endorsements typically go to Republicans. Liberals dismiss talk of a Democratic bias among reporters because the newspapers, television networks, and

> " WE KNOW THAT POLLS ARE JUST A COLLECTION OF STATISTICS THAT REFLECT WHAT PEOPLE ARE THINKING IN 'REALITY.' AND REALITY HAS A WELL-KNOWN LIBERAL BIAS. "
> Stephen Colbert

newsmagazines for which journalists work are large corporations, owned and operated in most cases by conservative Republicans. Management sets editorial policy, they say, not reporters.

Research suggests that media sources may indeed play favorites.

**objective journalism** a style of news reporting that focuses on facts rather than opinion, and presents all sides of controversial issues.

Stephen Colbert, popular host of the mock-news show, *The Colbert Report*. Colbert coined the term "truthiness," which he uses to describe things that a person claims to know intuitively or "from the gut" without regard to evidence, logic, intellectual examination, or facts.

The network evening news treats Democratic candidates more favorably than it does Republicans. The Democratic candidate for president has enjoyed more favorable coverage on the network evening news than the Republican candidate in three of the last five presidential elections. Coverage was balanced in the other two elections. In 2004, for example, 57 percent of the network news reports on Democratic presidential candidate John Kerry were positive, compared with 37 percent of the news reports on President George W. Bush. Nonetheless, scholars have no evidence that news coverage affects election outcomes. Kerry lost the election despite receiving more favorable network news coverage than Bush. Furthermore, citizens have more news sources available to them than the network news, including newspapers, radio, Internet websites, and cable television. Fox News coverage of the 2004 presidential election was decidedly Bush-friendly. Fifty-three percent of Fox News stories on the president were positive compared with

# ARE THE MEDIA BIASED?

A GREAT DEAL **31%**

A FAIR AMOUNT **31%**

NOT TOO MUCH **25%**

NOT AT ALL **9%**

DON'T KNOW/REFUSED **4%**

To what extent do you see political bias in news coverage? Pew Research Center for the People & the Press Political Communications Survey, Dec. 2007, http://people-press.org/questions/?qid=1697968&pid=51&ccid=51#top.

only 21 percent of the Kerry stories.[17] In practice, news consumers often choose media outlets that reflect their particular biases. The CNN and Fox cable news audiences perceive political reality differently. Conservative Republicans watch Fox, while liberal Democrats tune in to CNN.[18] (See figure on the following page.)

Political science research has also identified media biases that are not based on party affiliation or political ideology. Research on Senate races, for example, has found that newspapers tend to slant the information on their news pages to favor the candidate endorsed by the paper on

its editorial page, regardless of that candidate's party affiliation.[19] Furthermore, studies show that the press is biased against presidential incumbents, without regard for party and ideology. An **incumbent** is a current officeholder. All recent presidents, Democrats and Republicans alike, received more negative press coverage than did their opponents when they ran for reelection.[20]

The press has grown increasingly negative. Since the 1960s, bad news has increased by a factor of three and is now the dominant theme of national political news coverage. Thirty years ago, press coverage of public affairs emphasized the words of newsmakers and stressed the positive. The press grew more critical during the 1970s as journalists began to counter the statements of government officials rather than just report them. By the late 1970s, the focus of the Washington, D.C.

**incumbent** current officeholder.

# takeaction

## FAVORITE NEWS AND INFORMATION LINKS >>

Do you have a favorite set of online sources of information and opinion? Your assignment is to create an annotated inventory of online sites. For each entry, indicate the name of the site, give its URL, describe it, and explain why you have selected it. Select at least one site in each of the following categories:

- National news source that emphasizes objective journalism;
- State and local news source that emphasizes objective journalism;

- Political commentary, combining news and opinion;
- Issue-oriented website that focuses on a particular issue, either objectively or subjectively;
- Educational or professional website related to your college major or career goals; and
- Personal-interest website that deals with a hobby, sports team, or entertainment that you enjoy.

## YOU ARE WHAT YOU WATCH

ABC
Fox

Percent

80
70
60
50
40
30
20
10
0

Positive evaluations
of Kerry
(9/7–11/01/04)

Positive evaluations
of Bush
(9/7–11/01/04)

Republican's news
source

Democrat's news
source

People tend to seek out viewpoints that reinforce their own. More
Republicans prefer news from Fox, and more Democrats seem to prefer ABC.

press corps was **attack journalism**, which is an approach to news reporting in which journalists take an adversarial attitude toward candidates and elected officials. Reporters decided to examine the actions of newsmakers critically, countering the statements of public officials with the responses of their critics and adversaries.[21] As a result, campaign coverage has grown negative. In 1960, 75 percent of press references to both major party presidential candidates (Richard Nixon and John Kennedy) were positive. In contrast, only 40 percent of references to the major party presidential candidates in 1992 (George H. W. Bush and Bill Clinton) were positive.[22]

**attack journalism** an approach to news reporting in which journalists take an adversarial attitude toward candidates and elected officials.

## CONCLUSION
# the media
# & PUBLIC POLICY

the media play an important role in the policymaking process, especially during the agenda building and policy evaluation stages.

### Agenda Building

Political scientists say that the press plays a **signaling role,** the accepted responsibility of the media to alert the public to important developments as they happen. The media may be unable to tell people what to think, but they generally succeed in telling people what to think about. In early 2007, the *Washington Post*

published a series of stories about the poor quality of care injured service personnel had been receiving at Walter Reed Army Medical Center in Washington, D.C. Other media outlets quickly picked up on the coverage and the issue of medical care for Iraq War veterans soon rose to the forefront of the policy agenda. Several congressional committees held hearings on the issue, the Bush administration called for an investigation, and the secretary of defense removed the military commanders in charge of veterans' care at Walter Reed.

**signaling role** a term that refers to the accepted responsibility of the media to alert the public to important developments as they happen.

### Policy Formulation and Adoption

The media play an indirect role in policy formulation and adoption. The media influence policy adoption through **framing,** which is the process by which a communication source, such as a news organization, defines and constructs a political issue or public controversy. The way the media present an issue helps define the approaches that policymakers will take to its resolution. The vivid images of flooded homes and people seeking shelter in the New Orleans Superdome and the accounts of bureaucratic bungling ensured that policymakers would regard Hurricane Katrina as not just a natural disaster, but also the failure of the government to respond effectively to a crisis. The media do not adopt policies, but they do publicize policy adoption by reporting on acts of Congress, Supreme Court decisions, and presidential actions. The press also provides political leaders with a means to communicate with the public, to explain government policies, and ask for support.

Two wounded veterans flank a wounded soldier's wife in 2007, as she testifies at a congressional hearing. They are describing shocking conditions at the Walter Reed Army Medical Center in Washington, D.C.

## Policy Implementation and Evaluation

The media have a larger role in policy evaluation than policy implementation. Other than carrying out FCC rules, the media do not implement public policies. They are, however, important participants in policy evaluation, offering both empirical and normative policy analyses. An **empirical analysis** is a method of study that relies on experience and scientific observation, whereas a **normative analysis** is a method of study that is based on certain values. The media are an important source of empirical policy evaluation. In recent years, media outlets have issued a broad

range of empirical analyses of government programs and activities, including investigative reports on the conduct of the war in Iraq, the implementation of the Medicare prescription drug program, and the effectiveness of airport luggage screening. The media also publicize empirical reports completed by government agencies and independent groups. In addition to empirical evaluation of policy, the media offer a broad spectrum of normative policy evaluations, ranging from newspaper editorials to radio talk show commentaries and blog postings. Media policy evaluations

often set the agenda for policy modifications and the adoption of new policies.

**framing** the process by which a communication source, such as a news organization, defines and constructs a political issue or public controversy.

**empirical analysis** a method of study that relies on experience and scientific observation.

**normative analysis** a method of study that is based on certain values.

the **THINK**SPOT
www.thethinkspot.com

# TEST yourself

**1** Which of the following media outlets is owned by the U.S. government?
A. The *New York Times*
B. CBS Evening News
C. National Public Radio
D. None of the above

**2** Which of the following is a set of radio stations?
A. NPR
B. PBS
C. Corporation for Public Broadcasting
D. None of the above

**3** Which of the following is a set of television stations?
A. NPR
B. PBS
C. Corporation for Public Broadcasting
D. None of the above

**4** Clear Channel Communication is most closely associated with which of the following?
A. Newspapers
B. Internet
C. Radio stations
D. Cable television

**5** Cross-media ownership refers to which of the following?
A. A corporation owning several different types of media outlets
B. A corporation owning a chain of television stations in more than one city
C. A corporation owning multiple radio stations in the same city
D. A newspaper jointly owned by several corporations

**6** Which of the following have been suffering from a loss of viewers or readers?
A. Daily newspapers
B. Network evening news shows
C. Newsmagazines
D. All of the above

**7** Which of the following would be characterized as new media?
A. The *Washington Post*
B. CBS television
C. The *Chicago Tribune*
D. None of the above

**8** Matt Drudge is most closely associated with which of the following?
A. An Internet website
B. CNN
C. The *New York Times*
D. *Time* magazine

**9** Which of the following media outlets is more important to the Democratic Party than it is to the Republican Party?
A. Talk radio
B. Fox News
C. Internet blogs
D. All of the above

**10** A blog would be characterized as which of the following?
A. Print media
B. Attack journalism
C. New media
D. All of the above

**11** Which of the following can best be defined as an online personal journal?
A. A blog
B. A sound bite
C. Print media
D. Talk radio

**12** Arbitron ratings are the basis for setting advertising rates for which of the following media outlets?
A. Radio
B. Television
C. Newspapers
D. Internet

**13** Nielsen ratings are the basis for setting advertising rates for which of the following media outlets?

A. Radio

B. Television

C. Newspapers

D. Internet

**14** "Read my lips: No new taxes." This is an example of which of the following?

A. Objective journalism

B. Attack journalism

C. Equal-time rule

D. A sound bite

**15** A news editor directs her staff to focus on the facts of the news and avoid interjecting bias or opinion into reporting. The news editor is advocating which of the following?

A. Attack journalism

B. Using sound bites

C. The liberal agenda

D. Objective journalism

**16** Rush Limbaugh is most closely associated with which of the following?

A. Talk radio

B. An Internet blog

C. Fox News

D. The *Washington Post*

**17** Which of the following pairs do *not* go together?

A. Rush Limbaugh and conservative Republican listeners

B. Fox News and liberal Democrats

C. The *Huffington Post* Internet website and the new media

D. The *New York Times* and print media

**18** Which of the following has research on bias in the network evening news discovered?

A. The network evening news treats Democratic candidates more favorably than it does Republicans.

B. The network evening news treats Republican candidates more favorably than it does Democrats.

C. The network evening news treats all candidates equally.

D. The network evening news typically favors incumbent presidents running for reelection regardless of political party.

**19** The media have the greatest impact in which of the following stages of the policymaking process?

A. Agenda setting

B. Policy formulation

C. Policy adoption

D. Policy implementation

**20** Which of the following is best described as a normative analysis?

A. The U.S. Census Bureau estimates that more than 11 million people are in the country illegally.

B. The General Accountability Office publishes a study on the economic impact of undocumented workers on the American economy.

C. A religious leader writes a blog urging the government to show compassion to people who have lived illegally in the United States for years.

D. All of the above.

KNOW *the* **score**

18–20 correct: Congratulations! You are well informed!

15–17 correct: Your political knowledge is a bit low—be sure to review the key terms and visit TheThinkSpot.

<14 correct: Reread the chapter more thoroughly.

1. D; 2. A; 3. B; 4. C; 5. A; 6. D; 7. D; 8. A; 9. C; 10. C; 11. A; 12. A; 13. B; 14. D; 15. D; 16. A; 17. B; 18. A; 19. A; 20. C

**7 INTEREST**

T he National Rifle Association (NRA) is one of the most successful interest groups in American politics. The NRA defends the rights of gun owners and opposes gun control. It has largely managed to define the gun debate as the right to own, sell, and carry a weapon. Congress has not seriously considered passing gun control legislation in more than a decade. In fact, Congress failed in 2004 even to reauthorize the federal Assault Weapons Ban.

Ironically, the NRA is successful despite public opinion. Many Americans favor strict gun control regulations. A Gallup poll taken in 2008 found that 73 percent of respondents believe that the Second Amendment grants individuals the right to own a firearm, but the same survey showed that 49 percent of Americans believe that gun control regulations should be made "more strict," compared with 11 percent who think they should be made "less strict." Another 38 percent of respondents favor keeping gun control laws as they are.[1]

The role of the NRA in American politics introduces this chapter on interest groups. The chapter begins by identifying various types of interests groups in American politics, discussing their political goals, and assessing their relative strength. The chapter examines the tactics interest groups employ to achieve their goals and discusses the factors that affect the relative strength of groups. Finally, the chapter considers the role of interest groups in the policymaking process.

# GROUPS

ESSENTIALS...

*after studying Chapter 7, students should be able to answer the following questions:*

> What types of interest groups are active in American politics and what are their political goals?

> What methods do interest groups use to influence the outcomes of elections?

> How do the campaign contribution strategies of business PACs differ from those of labor-oriented PACs? What are insider and outsider approaches to lobbying?

> What is the role of interest groups in the policymaking process, and what factors have an impact on their effectiveness?

# types of
# INTEREST GROUPS

**a**n **interest group** is an organization of people who join together voluntarily on the basis of some shared interest for the purpose of influencing policy. Motivations for why people join interest groups vary, some of the most important being the causes people feel passionate about and the benefits they derive from membership. For example, the **free-rider barrier** to group membership is the concept that individuals will have little incentive to join and contribute to a group if benefits go to members and nonmembers alike. Groups attempt to compensate for the free-rider barrier by offering selective benefits that go only to group members. These benefits generally fall into three categories: material benefits, solidarity benefits, and purposive benefits. For example, NRA members enjoy tangible material benefits such as firearms training classes, gun-loss insurance, and discounts on travel. They enjoy social, solidarity benefits, like the connections they create while participating in clinics, tournaments, and associations. And they receive purposive benefits in that many feel passionately that they have a constitutional right to keep and bear arms and that their membership furthers the protection of that right.

## Business Groups

Business groups are the most numerous, and probably the most potent, of America's interest groups. Business interests attempt to influence public policy both as individual firms and through a variety of front

organizations. General Motors, Philip Morris, Microsoft Corp., Halliburton, and other large firms are major players in national politics, aggressively promoting their interests with government officials. Exxon Mobil Corporation and other energy companies, for example, favor the relaxation of federal environmental standards to enhance energy production. They also support legislation designed to open the Arctic National Wildlife Refuge (ANWR) to oil and gas production.

Business interests join together across industry lines to promote

## BUSINESS GROUPS ARE THE MOST NUMEROUS OF AMERICA'S INTEREST GROUPS

**interest group** an organization of people who join together voluntarily on the basis of some interest they share for the purpose of influencing policy.

**free-rider barrier** the concept that individuals will have little incentive to join and contribute to a group if benefits go to members and nonmembers alike.

**think**

Why might businesses and labor unions oppose each other over legislation?

pro-business public policies. The **Chamber of Commerce** is a business federation representing the interests of more than three million businesses of all sizes, sectors, and regions.[2] It has a national organization with headquarters in Washington, D.C., state organizations in every state, and chapters in thousands of cities throughout the nation.

Business groups also work through **trade associations**, organizations representing the interests of firms and professionals in the same general field. Large financial institutions, such as Bank of America and JPMorgan Chase, belong to the American Bankers Association. Business groups may also create front organizations to promote particular issue positions. Wal-Mart, Intel Corporation, GlaxoSmithKline, and other firms fund an organization called the Class Action Fairness Coalition to support legislation designed to make it more difficult to file class action lawsuits.

Business groups are well-positioned to influence policy. They are numerous, dispersed throughout the country, organized, and well-funded. Small business owners and corporate executives are prominent figures in communities around the nation. They often know their member of Congress personally and understand how to articulate their views effectively to policymakers. Furthermore, business groups have funds to contribute to political causes. During the 2008 presidential election cycle, business interests gave $1.8 billion to political campaigns, substantially more than the $68 million contributed by organized labor.[3]

## Labor Unions

Organized labor is an important political force in America although it is not as powerful as it once was. More than a fourth of the civilian labor force belonged to a union in 1970 compared with only 12.1 percent in 2007.[4] Manufacturing industries, such as automobile assembly and steel production, in which unions have historically had their best organizing successes, now employ significantly fewer workers than they did 40 years ago. More than 20 states have adopted **right-to-work laws**, statutes that prohibit union membership as a condition of

**Chamber of Commerce** a business federation representing the interests of businesses of all sizes, sectors, and regions.

**trade associations** organizations representing the interests of firms and professionals in the same general field.

**right-to-work laws** statutes that prohibit union membership as a condition of employment.

A wide variety of interest groups make up the American electorate.

employment.[6] Furthermore, many employers aggressively resist unionization. For example, Wal-Mart, the nation's largest employer, has successfully fought off efforts to unionize its workforce. Not one of Wal-Mart's 3,500 American stores is unionized.[7]

The largest union group in the nation is the American Federation of Labor-Congress of Industrial Organizations (AFL-CIO). It is composed of 56 separate unions with a combined membership of 10.5 million.

Organized labor is strongest in the **Frostbelt** (the Northeast and Midwest), weakest in the **Sunbelt** (the South and West). Unions are powerful in the large, industrialized states of the Northeast and Midwest. In Michigan, for example, the United Auto Workers (UAW) may be the state's single most potent political force. In contrast, labor is not as well organized or as politically influential in the Sunbelt, the nation's fastest growing area. In many Sunbelt states, organized labor is hurt by anti-union laws and by a diverse and divided work force, many of whose members are hostile to organized labor.

Organized labor endorses public policies that promote workplace health and safety, supports efforts to build union membership, and favors attempts to improve the quality of life for working-class Americans. Unions believe that the federal government should aggressively enforce laws affecting workplace health and safety. They support government policies requiring the use of union labor and union wage scales on construction projects built with federal funds. They favor increasing the federal **minimum wage,** the lowest hourly wage that an employer can legally pay covered workers. Unions endorse efforts to strengthen the private pension system and Social Security.

## Professional Associations

Doctors, lawyers, real estate agents, and other professionals form associations to advance their interests. Professional associations are influential because of the relatively high socioeconomic status of their membership. Professionals have the resources to make their voices heard, and they enjoy an added advantage because many elected officials come from the ranks of their professions, especially the legal profession.

Professional associations are concerned with public policies that affect their members. The American Medical Association (AMA), an interest group representing the concerns of physicians, would like government to limit the amount of money judges and juries can award in medical malpractice lawsuits. The American Bar Association (ABA), a lawyers' group, opposes the AMA on the issue. Professional associations sometimes take stands on policy issues outside the immediate concerns of their membership, such as tax policy, defense spending, and women's rights.

**Frostbelt** the northeastern and midwestern regions of the United States.
**Sunbelt** the southern and western regions of the United States.
**minimum wage** the lowest hourly wage that an employer can legally pay covered workers.

## Racial and Ethnic Minority Rights Groups

African Americans, Latinos, Asian Americans, Native Americans, and other racial and ethnic minority groups have created interest groups to promote their political causes. The National Association for the Advancement of Colored People (NAACP) is an interest group organized to represent the concerns of African Americans. The League of United Latin American Citizens (LULAC) is a Latino interest group. The American Indian Movement (AIM) is a group representing the views of Native Americans. Organizations that represent the interests of racial and ethnic minorities are an important political force in most big cities and in states where minority populations are large enough to translate into political power. In addition, minorities, especially African Americans and Latinos, play an important role in national politics.

Racial and ethnic minority groups share the goals of equality before the law, representation in elective and appointive office, freedom from discrimination, and economic advancement. Minority groups are interested in the enforcement of laws against discrimination; the election and appointment of minorities to federal, state, and local offices; and the extension of government programs to fight poverty. Racial and ethnic minority groups generally support **affirmative action** programs designed to ensure equal opportunities in employment and college admissions for racial minorities and women. Minorities support the enforcement of the **Voting Rights Act (VRA)**, a federal law designed to protect the voting rights of racial and ethnic minorities. In addition, LULAC and other Latino-rights organizations favor immigration reforms that would allow long-standing undocumented workers to work in the United States legally and eventually to become citizens.

### Religious Groups

Throughout American history, religious organizations have been actively involved in the policy process. Today, the most active religiously oriented political groups are associated with the **religious right,** which

*Latino-rights organizations favor immigration reforms*

**affirmative action** steps taken by colleges, universities, and private employers to remedy the effects of past discrimination.

**Voting Rights Act (VRA)** a federal law designed to protect the voting rights of racial and ethnic minorities.

**religious right** individuals who hold conservative views because of their religious beliefs.

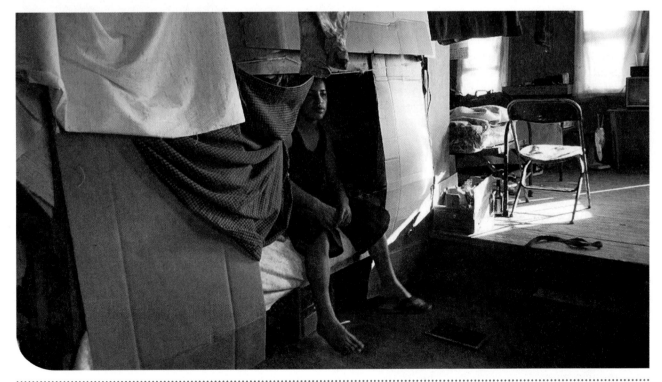

A young Mexican migrant worker in Pennsylvania shares his room with others. Each man's bed is closed off by pieces of cardboard.

"Our commitment to Jesus Christ compels us to solve the global warming crisis."

Jim Wallis, the leader of the Christian left Sojourners, has regularly spoken out on poverty, the environment, and other social justice issues.

April 22, 2008, Earth Day speech, George Washington University

is a term that refers to individuals who hold conservative views because of their religious beliefs. Focus on the Family, Family Research Council, and other conservative religious organizations are concerned with such causes as abortion, same-sex marriage, and prayer in school. Since the 2004 presidential election, religious liberals have begun organizing to counter the influence of the religious right. This **religious left,** people who hold liberal views because of their religious beliefs, has established a number of organizations and created websites. Issues important to the religious left include opposition to the war in Iraq and the adoption of government programs to fight poverty and protect the environment.[8]

Conservative Christian organizations have been more successful at

the ballot box than they have been in building influence in Washington, DC, because many Christian conservatives are uncomfortable with the policy compromises necessary to move legislation through Congress.[9]

Conservative Christian groups benefit from a core of highly committed supporters who can be mobilized to go to the polls and to contact members of Congress over issues, such as abortion and gay marriage. In 2004, for example, Christian conservatives turned out in large numbers in states that held referenda on the issue of gay marriage.[10] Most Christian conservative voters also supported the reelection of President Bush. Nonetheless, many conservative Christian activists are frustrated by the inability of Congress and the president to outlaw abortion and prohibit gay marriage through constitutional amendment.

"If neither of the two major political parties nominates an individual who pledges himself or herself to the sanctity of human life, we will join others in voting for a minor party candidate."

## Citizen, Advocacy, and Cause Groups

Citizen groups are organizations that support government policies they believe will benefit the public at large. For example, Common Cause, which calls itself "the citizen lobby," is a group that works for campaign finance reform and other good government causes. Other citizen groups include the Sierra Club, an environmental organization, and the American Civil Liberties Union (ACLU), a group defending the rights of individuals as outlined in the U.S. Constitution.

**Advocacy groups** are organizations that seek benefits for people who are in some way incapacitated or otherwise unable to represent their own interests. The Children's Defense Fund, for example, promotes the welfare of children. The Coalition for the Homeless is an organization that works on behalf of

homeless persons. Other examples of advocacy groups include the Alzheimer's Association and the American Cancer Society.

James Dobson, the head of the Christian right Focus on the Family, strongly opposes same-sex marriage and abortion, among other issues. Dobson endorsed John McCain after McCain selected Sarah Palin as his running mate.

(New York Times, Op-Ed, October 4, 2007)

**religious left** individuals who hold liberal views because of their religious beliefs.

**citizen groups** organizations created to support government policies that they believe will benefit the public at large.

**advocacy groups** organizations created to seek benefits on behalf of groups of persons who are in some way incapacitated or otherwise unable to represent their own interests.

# Church and State in Mexico

Mexico is an overwhelmingly Catholic country. In 2000, 85 percent of the population told surveyors that they were Roman Catholic, compared with 4 percent who claimed to be Protestant, 4 percent who identified with another religion, and 6 percent who declared that they had no religious affiliation. Furthermore, most Mexicans are practicing Catholics. More than 40 percent of Mexican Catholics attend church on a weekly basis; another 20 percent attend at least once a month.[11]

Nonetheless, Mexico has a strong history of **anti-clericalism**, opposing the institutional power of religion, and the involvement of the church in any aspect of public or political life. Even though individual citizens enjoyed the right to worship as they pleased, the government restricted the power of the Catholic Church for years. The Mexican Constitution of 1917 established state superiority over religion, limited the role of the church in education, and deprived clergy of the right to vote.

Public education incorporated anti-church rhetoric in student lessons.[12]

The Mexican government suppressed the church in order to keep it from becoming a threat to state authority. Until recently, the Mexican government was semi-democratic at best. Although Mexico held regular elections, one political party, the Institutional Revolutionary Party (PRI), always won because it manipulated election laws and rigged the vote count to ensure the success of its candidates. Undemocratic governments attempt to restrict all sources of opposition. Government officials in Mexico regarded the Roman Catholic Church as a potential threat to their control because the overwhelming majority of Mexicans were practicing Catholics.

As Mexico has become more democratic, the government has eased restrictions on the church, and its political involvement has grown. Clergy now enjoy the right to vote and speak out on political issues. As a result, the church

has become an important interest group in Mexican politics.[13] It has addressed a number of political issues including the distribution of wealth, illicit drugs, and democratization. In particular, the church has criticized the government for not doing more to help the poor.[14]

## Questions

1. Should churches take positions on political issues?

2. Do religious organizations play the role of interest groups in American politics?

3. Are interest groups essential to democratic development?

**anti-clericalism** a movement that opposes the institutional power of religion, and the involvement of the church in all aspects of public and political life.

Many Mexicans are deeply religious. Here, men and boys carry crosses on Good Friday in a working-class neighborhood of Mexico City.

MORE THAN 100 COLLEGE presidents have called on lawmakers to consider lowering the minimum legal drinking age from 21 to 18. They believe college students will drink anyway, but that they do so in excess because of age restrictions.

MADD officials say that alcohol-related fatal car accidents have fallen 60 percent since the drinking age was raised in 1984 to 21 and that lowering the drinking age would reverse this trend.

**Cause groups** are organizations whose members care intensely about a single issue or a small group of related issues. The National Right to Life Committee is an organization opposed to abortion, whereas NARAL Pro-Choice America favors abortion rights. The Club for Growth is a cause group that favors a low-tax and limited government agenda. The AARP (formerly known as the American Association of Retired Persons) represents the concerns of older Americans. Other cause groups include the NRA, the National Organization for Women (NOW), a group promoting women's rights, and the Human Rights Campaign (HRC), an organization supporting gay and lesbian rights.

Citizen, advocacy, and cause groups have achieved some victories in American politics. Many of these groups are expert at attracting media attention to their issues by releasing research reports or conducting high-profile public demonstrations. Earth Day, for example, is an annual event designed to call attention to environmental concerns. The National Right to Life Committee holds a demonstration in Washington, D.C. every year on the anniversary of *Roe v. Wade*, the Supreme Court ruling that a woman's constitutional right to privacy includes the right to abortion during the first two trimesters of a pregnancy.

Many public policies reflect the policy values of citizen, advocacy, and cause groups. The Endangered Species Act, the Clean Air Act, and other pieces of environmental legislation testify to the effectiveness of the Sierra Club and other environmental organizations. Mothers Against Drunk Driving (MADD), an interest group supporting the reform of laws dealing with drunk driving, motivated a successful effort to stiffen the nation's DWI laws.

Although the policy impact of citizen, advocacy, and cause groups has been significant, the policy influence of these groups seldom extends beyond their special issues. The powerful NRA is effective only on gun issues. Environmental groups are not influential beyond environmental issues. Abortion groups address only abortion-related issues.

**cause groups** organizations whose members care intensely about a single issue or small group of related issues.

# interest group
## TACTICS

Interest groups employ a variety of tactics to achieve their goals.

## Electioneering

Many interest groups seek policy influence by participating in the electoral process. A number of groups try to affect election outcomes by targeting enemies and endorsing friends. Each congressional election year, Friends of the Earth, an environmental group, targets a "Dirty Dozen," 12 members of Congress who voted consistently against the group's positions on environmental legislation. The group hopes that environmentally conscious citizens will vote against the representatives on the list. Other groups endorse candidates friendly to their causes. During the 2008 presidential campaign, the AFL-CIO and NARAL Pro-Choice America endorsed Democrat Barack Obama, while the NRA and the National Right to Life Committee threw their support behind Republican John McCain.

Some interest groups focus on educating their members and sup-

**CONGRESSIONAL VOTING SCORECARDS** rate U.S. senators and representatives on their voting records, measured in terms related to the political views of the group issuing the scorecard.

Note that NARAL Pro-Choice America, a group concerned with a limited range of issues, uses a narrower set of votes than does the Eagle Forum, a conservative action group with a broader political agenda. http://www.votesmart.org/ issue_rating.php

**MITCH MCCONNELL: REPUBLICAN KY, U.S. SENATE**
NARAL Pro-Choice America Rating: 0
Eagle Forum Rating: 88

**JOE BARTON: REPUBLICAN TX, U.S. HOUSE**
NARAL Pro-Choice America Rating: 0
Eagle Forum Rating: 88

**LAMAR ALEXANDER: REPUBLICAN TN, U.S. SENATE**
NARAL Pro-Choice America Rating: 0
Eagle Forum Rating: 88

**NANCY PELOSI: DEMOCRAT CA, U.S. HOUSE**
NARAL Pro-Choice America Rating: 100
Eagle Forum Rating: 0

**HARRY REID: DEMOCRAT NV, U.S. SENATE**
NARAL Pro-Choice America Rating: 100
Eagle Forum Rating: 5

**JOHN KERRY: DEMOCRAT MA, U.S. SENATE**
NARAL Pro-Choice America Rating: 100
Eagle Forum Rating: 12

porters about the candidates. The AFL-CIO uses newsletters, phone banks, and rallies to encourage union members to support endorsed candidates. Many interest groups keep scorecards, showing how members of Congress voted on issues important to the group and assigning scores to senators and representatives indicating whether they are friend or foe.

Some groups participate in the electoral process financially. Federal law requires that interest groups contributing money directly to candidates must make their contributions through a **political action committee (PAC)**, an organization that raises and distributes money in election campaigns. During the 2007–2008 election cycle, the biggest spenders were PACs associated with the Service Employees Inter-

national Union ($64 million), Act-Blue ($53 million), MoveOn.org ($36 million), and EMILY's List ($34 million).[15] EMILY's List is a PAC working for the election of pro-choice Democratic women to office. (EMILY is the acronym for Early Money Is Like Yeast, not a woman's name.) MoveOn.org is an advocacy group that raises money for Democratic candidates. ActBlue is a liberal advocacy group.

Interest groups follow different campaign-funding strategies. Labor unions work to increase the number of members of Congress (usually Democrats) sympathetic to their point of view. Although most labor money goes to incumbent members of Congress, unions are willing to fund challengers and candidates for open seats if they stand a reasonable chance of winning. During the 2007–2008

election cycle, 33 percent of labor PAC donations went to challengers and candidates for open seats.[16]

Many cause groups are interested primarily in increasing the number of elected officials who share their views. Although some cause groups work to elect friends and defeat enemies regardless of party, most groups are closely associated with one political party or the other. The bulk of NRA support goes to Republican Party candidates, for example, whereas most of the candidates backed by NOW are Democrats.

Business groups have broad policy interests, so they are more pragmatic than organized labor or most cause and advocacy groups. Business interests recognize that a public official may oppose them on one issue but support them on another issue. Business PACs contribute money to candidates to obtain **access,** the opportunity to commu-

How do you think political action committees affect democracy? Do they make elections more democratic or less so?

**political action committee (PAC)** an organization created to raise and distribute money in election campaigns.

nicate directly with legislators and other government officials in hopes of influencing the details of policy. Many business-oriented PACs follow the **Friendly Incumbent Rule**,

> most PAC money goes to incumbents, especially in races for the House, because they win more often than challengers

which is a policy whereby an interest group will back any incumbent who is generally supportive of the group's policy preferences, regardless of the party or policy views of the challenger. In 2007–2008, 90 percent of corporate PAC money went to incumbents, with most of the rest going to candidates for open seats. Because business-oriented groups favor incumbents, they tend to divide their contributions between the two political parties, despite the traditional alliance between business interests and the Republican Party.

Interest groups tend to support incumbents. They would rather give to a strong candidate who is only somewhat supportive of their cause than throw their money away on an almost certain loser who completely supports the group's goals. Most PAC money goes to incumbents, especially in races for the House, because they win more often than challengers.

The figure on p. 144 shows the distribution of PAC contributions for seats in the House during the 2007–2008 election period. PACs gave nearly $332 million to incumbents compared with $49 million to challengers and $32 million to candidates for open seats.

Some interest groups participate in elections through **527 committees**, organizations created by individuals and groups to influence elections by raising and spending money that candidates and political parties cannot legally raise and spend. Federal law limits the amount of money individuals and groups can legally give to candidates and parties, but it does not apply to 527 committees. Groups can contribute as much money as they like to a 527 committee, which can then use the money for voter mobilization and "issue advocacy." Al-

though the law prevents 527 committees from running advertisements either for or against particular candidates, it allows issue advertisements that are typically designed to influence voter opinion on the candidates without explicitly telling people how to cast their votes.

**access** the opportunity to communicate directly with legislators and other government officials in hopes of influencing the details of policy.

**Friendly Incumbent Rule** a policy whereby an interest group will back any incumbent who is generally supportive of the group's policy preferences, without regard for the party or policy views of the challenger.

**527 committees** organizations created by individuals and groups to influence the outcomes of elections by raising and spending money that candidates and political parties cannot legally raise.

| INTEREST GROUP | Total Expenditures |
|---|---|
| Service Employees International Union | $64 million |
| ActBlue | $53 million |
| MoveOn.org | $36 million |
| EMILY's List | $34 million |
| American Fedn of St/Cnty/Munic Employees | $30 million |
| Friends of [presidential candidate] Fred Thompson | $24 million |
| American Federation of Teachers | $19 million |
| National Assn of Realtors | $17 million |
| Intl Brotherhood of Electrical Workers | $17 million |
| National Rifle Association | $16 million |
| Teamsters Union | $15 million |
| United Auto Workers | $13 million |
| Laborers Union | $12 million |
| National Education Association | $9 million |
| Plumbers/Pipefitters Union | $9 million |

**TOP 15 INTEREST GROUP BY TOTAL EXPENDITURES 2007–2008**

Center for Responsive Politics; http://www.opensecrets.org/lobby/index.php

## Lobbying

**Lobbying** is the attempt to influence a policy decision by communicating information through a representative of an interest group to a government official. Groups lobby both the legislative and executive branches of government, attempting to influence every stage of the policy process. The number of Washington, D.C. lobbyists, including support staffs, is estimated at more than 250,000.[17] Some interest groups have full-time lobbyists on their professional staffs, whereas other groups hire Washington law firms or consulting agencies to lobby on their behalf. More than 150 former members of Congress are lobbyists.[18]

Information is the key to lobbying. Successful lobbyists provide members of Congress with accurate facts and figures. Although lobbyists offer their own interpretation of data and voice arguments to support their group's particular policy preferences, they do not lie because they know that their effectiveness depends on their credibility. In fact, lobbyists are an important information source for government officials.[19]

The most successful lobbying efforts of Congress are those supported by campaign contributions and buttressed by pressure from people living in a representative's district or a senator's home state.[20] Interest groups lay the groundwork for effective lobbying by giving money to political campaigns. Lobbyists sometimes serve as campaign treasurers for members seeking re-election. Major trade associations have purchased Capitol Hill townhouses for fundraisers so that members of Congress can attend events and go quickly back to the Capitol to cast votes.[21] Although campaign contributions do not necessarily buy votes, they do generally guarantee access to decision-makers. While Congress is in session, well-organized groups support their lobbyists in Washington by encouraging group members in the home districts of key legislators to contact their representatives.

Interest groups use different approaches to influencing policy. Most labor unions and business groups employ what might be called an insider's approach to achieving influence. These groups have a long-range interest in several policy areas. They give PAC contributions to gain access for their lobbyists who then work to get to know the public officials on a personal basis. Whatever pressure these groups bring to bear on pub-

**lobbying** the communication of information by a representative of an interest group to a government official for the purpose of influencing a policy decision.

total lobbying spending

2008

2007

2005

2003

1999    2001

In 2008, interest groups reported spending more than $3.3 billion for lobbying expenses.

Center for Responsive Politics; http://www.opensecrets.org/ lobby/ index.php

**HEY BIG spender!**

**TOP 10 SPENDERS IN 2008 ON LOBBYING ACTIVITIES**

| Lobbying Client | Total |
| --- | --- |
| U.S. Chamber of Commerce | $91,725,000 |
| Exxon Mobil | $29,000,000 |
| AARP | $27,900,000 |
| PG&E Corp | $27,250,000 |
| Northrop Grumman | $20,743,252 |
| American Medical Assn | $20,555,000 |
| Pharmaceutical Rsrch & Mfrs of America | $20,220,000 |
| American Hospital Assn | $20,102,684 |
| Koch Industries | $20,023,000 |
| General Electric | $19,379,000 |

Center for Responsive Politics, http://www.opensecrets.org/lobby/top.php?showYear=2008&indexType=s

lic officials is subtle and unspoken. They believe threats are counterproductive and harmful to the construction of a long-term relationship between the interest group and the officeholder. Groups taking an insider's approach are usually able to take the outcome of elections in stride because they cultivate relationships with members of both political parties.

Lobbyists using the insider approach do not expect to affect the way members of Congress vote on final passage of high-visibility legislation. Instead, their goal is to influence the details of legislation to include loopholes that benefit the interest group they represent. For example, recent legislation increasing the minimum wage included a provision that "clarifies that foreign trade income of an FSC and export trade income of an ETC do not constitute passive income for purposes of the PFIC definition." That particular phrase was worth $22 million in tax savings for Hercules, Inc., a chemical manufacturer.[22]

In contrast, other groups, whose policy goals are more narrowly focused, follow an outsider's approach to influencing policy. The NRA, National Right to Life Committee, and some other cause groups focus on a relatively small set of high-profile issues. Members of Congress either support them or oppose them on

their pet issues. Groups using an outsider's strategy are more heavy-handed in dealing with public officials than are interest groups with a broader range of policy concerns. Groups taking an outside approach are less willing to compromise

**DISTRIBUTION OF PAC $ IN MILLIONS.**

**INCUMBENTS** $331.6 (80%)
**CHALLENGERS** $48.8 (12%)
**OPEN SEATS** $32.4 (8%)

2007–2008 election period
www.fec.gov/press/press2009/20090415PAC/documents/2contrib2008.pdf

on policy issues than are insider groups, and more likely to threaten (and attempt to carry out) political reprisals against officeholders who oppose them.

## Creating Public Pressure

Some interest groups attempt to achieve their goals by generating public support for their policy positions and focusing it on government officials. Groups launch public relations campaigns to convince the general public that their particular point of view embodies the public interest. The NRA, for example, purchased a series of magazine advertisements designed to improve the public image of the group. The

advertisements featured hunters, police officers, and business people with the caption, "I am the NRA." Some tobacco companies have conducted high-profile media campaigns against underage smoking to counter criticism that tobacco advertisers have targeted youngsters.

The most sophisticated public relations campaigns are aimed at orchestrating citizen pressure on members of Congress and other public officials. The AFL-CIO ran radio and television advertisements in selected congressional districts attacking Republican members of the House for preventing legislation to raise the minimum wage from coming to a vote. More than 20 Republican House members broke with their party leadership and voted to increase the minimum wage. Their votes proved the difference. The legislation passed the House and eventually became law.[23]

## Protest Demonstrations

Groups that cannot afford public relations experts and advertising costs pursue their goals by means of protest demonstrations. Civil rights organizations used this technique in the 1960s. Today, it is employed by groups pursuing a variety of goals, ranging from organizations opposed to construction of a nuclear power plant to anti-pornography crusaders picketing convenience stores that

# Interest Groups and Politics

**Should interest groups be allowed to participate in the political process? If not, why not? If so, should they be regulated?**

**Is interest group activity harmful to the democratic process? If not, why not? If so, why do they have constitutional protection?**

**Overview:** The First Amendment to the Constitution guarantees Americans the right to form political associations to influence government, policy, and elected officials, and also to express concerns and fears about the direction and activity of government and elected representatives. A problem arises when it seems as if law is being made by those groups or interests who have the financial resources to influence lawmakers. This contravenes American democratic theory.

In 2002, the Bipartisan Campaign Reform Act (BCRA) was passed in an attempt to clean up election campaigns. It took soft money—unlimited funds given to the political parties by groups and interests for electoral purposes—out of the election process. The idea was to lessen the effect of money on American campaigns and elections, and thus lessen the influence of groups and interests on the political process. One unintended consequence was the rise of 527 groups—groups named for a provision in federal law that grants tax-exempt status to any group "operated primarily for the purpose" of exercising influence over elections and appointments to elective or public office. These groups are permitted to advertise, print literature and books, and conduct get-out-the-vote drives. They cannot directly or explicitly support a candidate for office, but because they are created primarily to advocate partisan causes, there is implicit support for a particular candidate or party. This can subvert the spirit of the reform.

527s are understood to further national political discussion by highlighting issues that might be ignored by the campaigns or national media. But do they really improve the health of American democracy? Do they represent the interests of the American people?

## supporting the use of interest group 527s

**it is the heart of democratic politics to allow interest groups to have a political voice.** The First Amendment gives Americans the freedom to associate, and to speak and to publish political ideas and opinions. Interest group political activity forces issues out for public consumption.

**527s will "level the political playing field" for various and competing interests.** 527 groups can be created by ordinary, like-minded citizens to further their particular interest or issue, thus allowing citizens to pool their efforts and resources to address political issues.

**527s will help limit political corruption by severing the tie between politicians and groups seeking access.** Campaign finance reform was in part designed to stop officeholders from seeking, and interest groups from giving soft money to political parties. 527s allow independent interests to engage in political activity without seeking access to officeholders.

## against the use of interest group 527s

**candidates will lose control of their campaigns.** Well-funded or publicized 527 groups can change the terms of political debate. For example, the 527 group Swift Boat Veterans for Truth was effectively able to promote its anti-John Kerry message, which forced a public debate on the candidate's past rather than on the campaign's platform.

**campaigns will become increasingly shrill and negative.** The Cato Institute reports that negative political ads work and that, due to the partisan nature of 527 groups, there is a fear that an already acrimonious political climate will become even more so.

**interest groups will have increased political power at the expense of elected representatives.** Allowing interest groups unlimited funding for political activity may give them a disproportionate voice in public policy debates. These groups may have the funding to wage media campaigns where elected officials may not, and this can drown out an official's position.

Members of PETA (People for the Ethical Treatment of Animals) offer free gas and sandwiches to people who pledge to try vegetarianism.

sell *Playboy* magazine. In general, protest demonstrations are a tactic used by groups unable to achieve their goals through other means. Sometimes the protest catches the attention of the general public, which brings pressure to bear on behalf of the protesting group. In most cases, though, protests have only a marginal impact on public policy.

## Litigation

A number of interest groups specialize in the use of litigation (i.e., lawsuits) to achieve their goals. The American Civil Liberties Union (ACLU) provides legal assistance to individuals and groups in controversies involving individual rights and liberties, including disputes over freedom of religion, free speech, and the death penalty. The American Center for Law and Justice and the Liberty Counsel are organizations that litigate in support of conservative Christian goals, such as opposition to abortion rights and gay marriage. Other interest groups use litigation as one of several approaches to achieving their policy goals. In 2008, the NRA won a major legal victory when the U.S. Supreme Court held for the first time that the Second Amendment protects an individual's right to possess a firearm.[24]

## Political Violence

Some groups employ unconventional methods to achieve their goals. The Animal Liberation Front, Stop Animal Exploitation Now, and some other animal rights groups take aggressive action to oppose animal research. Although most animal rights demonstrations are peaceful and legal, some opponents of animal research resort to violence. Protestors have broken into university laboratories, released lab animals, and destroyed property. Some researchers have been threatened with physical assault and death, and had their homes vandalized.[25]

## **take**action

### POLITICS AT THE MOVIES >>

Some filmmakers aim not just to entertain but also to convey political messages. View a film with political themes and answer the following questions:

1. What is the title of the film and when was it released?
2. What is the film about? Write a paragraph in which you summarize the storyline of the movie in your own words. Do not copy word-for-word from a review or film synopsis.
3. What political issue or issues does the film address?
4. What point of view does the film express?
5. Do you agree or disagree with the political views presented in the film? Why or why not?

Select one of the following films with political themes: *Absence of Malice, All the King's Men, American History X, An Inconvenient Truth, Apocalypse Now, Bobby, Boys Don't Cry,*

*Charlie Wilson's War, China Syndrome, Citizen Kane, Do the Right Thing, Dr. Strangelove, Fahrenheit 451, Fahrenheit 9/11, Frost/Nixon, Goodnight and Good Luck, Inherit the Wind, JFK, Man of the Year, Milk, Mississippi Burning, Mr. Smith Goes to Washington, Manchurian Candidate, Network, No End in Sight, Nothing but the Truth, Once Were Warriors, Philadelphia, Platoon, Primary Colors, Recount, Sicko, Syriana, Thank you for Smoking, W., or Wag the Dog.*

# the strength
## OF INTEREST GROUPS

**t**he policymaking influence of interest groups depends on several factors:

### Alliances with Political Parties

In American politics, some interest groups have loose, informal alliances with political parties. Labor unions, African American rights groups, women's organizations, environmentalists, gun-control groups, abortion-rights organizations, and gay and lesbian rights groups are generally aligned with the Democratic Party. Business groups, the NRA, National Right to Life Committee, anti-tax organizations, and conservative Christian organizations are tied to the Republican Party. Interest groups have more policymaking influence when the party with which they are allied is successful than when it is out of office.

### Alliances with Members of Congress and Executive Branch Officials

The policymaking influence of interest groups depends on their ability to cultivate relationships with key officials in the legislative and executive branches of government, regardless of which party controls Congress or the White House. Business groups compensate for Democratic control of Congress by establishing ties with committee and subcommittee chairs through campaign contributions and effective lobbying. Frequently, business lobbyists succeed in softening the impact of regulatory legislation on their particular industry.

### Public Opinion

Public opinion affects the ability of interest groups to achieve their policy goals. Interest groups are most successful when their policy goals enjoy strong public support.

### Unity among Groups Representing the Same Cause

Interest groups have more influence when organizations representing the same or similar interests or points of view share goals and speak with one voice.

### Opposition from Other Groups

A group's policy influence depends on the extent of opposition from other groups. Interest groups are most successful on issues in which there is no conflict among groups.[26] Doctors' groups and lawyers' associations, for example, butt heads over the issue of medical malpractice insurance reform. Environmental and business groups often oppose one another on environmental issues. On many issues, public officials can choose which interests to court, playing one group off against another.

## CONCLUSION
# interest groups
## & PUBLIC POLICY

**i**nterest groups are an important part of the policymaking process in a democracy. Interest groups moderate the interaction between ordinary citizens and government officials. They educate citizens about political issues, mobilize supporters to go to the polls, make policy demands on the government, and attempt to hold elected officials accountable for their actions. Democracy is strongest in societies with large number of competing interest groups because they help prevent the concentration of power.[27]

### Agenda Building

Interest groups are prominent participants in the process that determines the issues that are part of the nation's policy agenda. Much of American politics involves battles between groups on different sides of an issue trying to sell their perspective on the issue to the general public and to government decision-makers. Whereas public health groups address the issue of government regulation of tobacco from a health perspective, tobacco companies attempt to frame the issue in terms of economics or government regulation. Tobacco interests partner with restaurant associations to oppose state and local efforts to prohibit smoking in restaurants and other public places, arguing that the restriction would hurt business. The added advantage of this strategy for the tobacco industry is that it allows a group with a more favorable public image than tobacco companies to take the public relations lead on the issue.

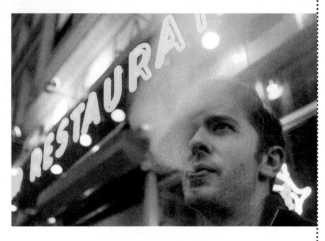

Interest groups contribute to the polarization of American politics because groups tend to represent issue extremes rather than more moderate policy options. For example, people who believe that abortion should be legal but restricted represent the majority, but their voices are not heard. People who believe that abortion should be legal but greatly restricted have no group to speak for them even though they represent the majority.[28] Polls show that only a minority of Americans believe that abortion should be illegal in all circumstances (18 percent) or legal in all circumstances (26 percent).[29]

## Policy Formulation and Adoption

Interest groups play a major role in policy formulation. Groups are seldom satisfied with putting their particular issue on the policy agenda. They also want government to address the issue from their perspective. The oil and gas industry favors energy policies that focus on expanding production. In contrast, environmentalists push for an energy policy that emphasizes conservation and the development of alternative fuels. Sometimes government policies reflect the triumph of one set of interest groups over another. More frequently, public policies are the result of compromise among competing interests over the details of policy.

Interest groups do not adopt policies directly because adoption is the responsibility of members of Congress, the president, and other government officials. Nonetheless, interest groups try to affect policy adoption. By contributing money to candidates and making endorsements, groups attempt to influence the selection of officeholders. After the election is over, groups lobby for and against the adoption of particular policies. Americans for Tax Reform, a cause group, asks candidates and officeholders to sign a "Taxpayer Protection Pledge," a written promise to oppose any and all efforts to increase taxes. The list of elected officials who have signed the pledge includes 193 members of the House, 41 senators, 8 governors, and more than 1,200 state legislators.[30]

## Policy Implementation and Evaluation

Interest groups work to influence policy implementation. Groups that have been successful during the policy formulation and adoption stages try to ensure that the policies are implemented favorably, whereas groups who lost at earlier stages work to minimize the impact of a policy.

Finally, interest groups attempt to put their interpretation onto a policy's evaluation in hopes that government officials will change it to reflect their perspective. Environmental organizations blame the nation's energy policy for global warming and rising gasoline prices, arguing that the nation needs to focus on conservation and the development of alternative fuels. In contrast, the oil and gas industry insists that the solution to high gasoline prices is more energy development, both in the ANWR and offshore.

the THINKSPOT
www.thethinkspot.com

# More Guns, Safer Campus?

**By PAT DOYLE,** *Minneapolis-St. Paul Star Tribune*

**APRIL 16, 2008**

A year after a deranged gunman killed 32 students and faculty at Virginia Tech, a debate over thwarting future attacks continues in Minnesota, where a legislator advocates allowing students to carry concealed weapons for protection on campus.

The proposal by Rep. Tony Cornish, R-Good Thunder, faces an uphill climb but reflects a national movement among gun advocates and some students to overturn prohibitions on students carrying weapons at college.

Contradicting the prevailing view and policies of Minnesota universities, the gun supporters argue that trained, armed students would prevent or minimize violence on campus.

Alex Tripp, a student at Minnesota State University, Mankato, who is active in the effort to allow students to carry guns, cited the shootings at Virginia Tech and Northern Illinois University in a recent letter to Cornish urging a change in state law.

"Before last year's shootings I never was scared on campus," Tripp wrote. "After these two shootings, I am scared. Very scared."

But opponents of the measure say there is no evidence that allowing students to carry concealed weapons would improve campus safety.

"It would raise more risks," said Heather Martens, president of Citizens for a Safer Minnesota, adding that firearms would introduce a new danger to college drinking and suicide attempts. She said the 2003 state law allowing adults to carry concealed weapons in most places didn't improve public safety, so "why would it improve public safety on campuses?"

Martens was among two dozen people attending a rally outside the Capitol Wednesday to urge tougher background checks for gun purchasers, saying the Virginia violence might have been prevented with better regulations.

University general counsel Mark Rotenberg said rare episodes of violence at American universities don't justify allowing guns on campus for protection.

"There are spectacular examples . . . of violence on university campuses, but the facts are that this university and most university campuses are among the very safest places in the urban area," he said.

Rep. Michael Paymar, DFL-St. Paul, who opposes Cornish's campus gun bill, warned that it could advance as part of broader legislation. Paymar has proposed a bill calling for better background checks that has stalled in the Legislature. At the rally, he blamed the inaction on his own bill on lobbying by the National Rifle Association, which "has put the fear of God in legislators."

Tripp, a 21-year-old junior, is a member of Students for Concealed Carry on Campus, which claims 25,000 members nationwide. He does not recall a serious incident at Mankato State, but said, "You never know when something like this could happen, and we don't think we should be left defenseless."

## ↗ QUESTIONS:

- Do you favor allowing students, faculty, and staff to carry a concealed weapon on campus legally? Why or why not?
- What interest groups would you expect to line up on either side of the issue?
- If the legislature in your state were considering a measure to allow guns on campus, what steps could you and your classmates take to support (or oppose) the bill?

**>> END**

# TEST yourself

1. Which of the following organizations is a business federation representing the interests of businesses of all sizes, sectors, and regions?
   A. National Federation of Independent Businesses
   B. AFL-CIO
   C. U.S. Chamber of Commerce
   D. NAACP

2. Which of the following organizations would be most likely to favor the repeal of state right-to-work laws?
   A. U.S. Chamber of Commerce
   B. AFL-CIO
   C. Club for Growth
   D. LULAC

3. Which of the following statements is true about organized labor?
   A. The percentage of the workforce that belongs to labor unions has been in decline for years.
   B. Wal-Mart, the nation's largest employer, has successfully resisted unionization efforts.
   C. Organized labor is stronger in the Frostbelt and weaker in the Sunbelt.
   D. All of the above.

4. Which of the following organizations would be most likely to favor increasing the minimum wage?
   A. U.S. Chamber of Commerce
   B. American Farm Bureau
   C. AFL-CIO
   D. AARP

5. Which of the following organizations would be most likely to favor affirmative action in college and university admissions?
   A. NAACP
   B. AFL-CIO
   C. AARP
   D. Sierra Club

6. Which of the following pairs of organizations would be most likely to be on the opposite sides of the issue of abortion?
   A. Right to Life and NARAL Pro-Choice America
   B. U. S. Chamber of Commerce and the AFL-CIO
   C. Club for Growth and the NRA
   D. Sierra Club and NOW

7. Which of the following organizations would be most likely to celebrate Earth Day?
   A. Sierra Club
   B. Human Rights Campaign
   C. NARAL Pro-Choice America
   D. Common Cause

8. Which of the following organizations would be most likely to endorse a Democratic candidate for president in the next election?
   A. Right to Life
   B. U.S. Chamber of Commerce
   C. NRA
   D. NARAL Pro-Choice America

9. What are political action committees (PACs)?
   A. They are organizations representing the interests of firms and professionals in the same general field.
   B. They are organizations whose members care intensely about a single issue or small group of related issues.
   C. They are organizations created to raise and distribute money in election campaigns.
   D. They are organizations created to seek benefits on behalf of groups of persons who are in some way incapacitated or otherwise unable to represent their own interests.

10. PACs associated with which of the following types of interest groups raise the most money?
    A. Business groups
    B. Labor groups
    C. Racial/ethnic groups
    D. Agricultural groups

11. PACs associated with which of the following tend to give most of their campaign contributions to incumbent members of Congress of both political parties?
    A. Business groups
    B. Labor unions
    C. NRA
    D. Cause groups

12. Which of the following candidates would you expect to benefit the most from PAC contributions?
    A. A Republican challenger
    B. A Democratic challenger
    C. A candidate from either party running for an open seat
    D. An incumbent from either party running for reelection

**13** A PAC representing Interest Group A contributed to Congressman B's reelection campaign even though the congressman sides with the interest group's issue positions only about 60 percent of the time. The PAC is acting in accordance with which of the following principles?

A. Friendly Incumbent Rule

B. Common Cause

C. Club for Growth

D. Affirmative action

**14** An organization created by individuals and groups to influence the outcomes of elections by raising and spending money that candidates and political parties cannot legally raise is known by which of the following names?

A. Political action committee

B. Interest group

C. Political party

D. 527 committee

**15** Which of the following statements about lobbying and lobbyists is true?

A. Groups lobby the legislative branch of government but not the executive branch.

B. Interest group lobbyists frequently focus on the details of legislation rather than votes on final passage.

C. Former members of Congress are prohibited by law from becoming lobbyists.

D. None of the above.

**16** What is the best assessment of the relationship between campaign contributions and interest group lobbying?

A. Money buys votes. Members of Congress vote for the causes supported by the groups that give them the most money.

B. Money buys access. Members of Congress are willing to meet with lobbyists representing groups that provide them with campaign contributions.

C. Money and lobbying are unrelated. Members of Congress are open to consider all views regardless of political contributions.

D. Because of campaign finance regulations, interest groups are prohibited from contributing money to help members of Congress run for reelection.

**17** Which of the following statements is true about the use of protest demonstrations as a political strategy?

A. Protest demonstrations are a tactic used by groups unable to achieve their goals through other means.

B. Business and trade groups are more likely to use protest demonstrations than are other organizations.

C. Protests are among the more effective approaches interest groups have for achieving their goals.

D. All of the above.

**18** Which of the following organizations specializes in the use of litigation to achieve its goals?

A. Chamber of Commerce

B. American Bar Association

C. ACLU

D. Club for Growth

**19** Which of the following types of interest groups is typically allied with the Republican Party?

A. Organized labor

B. Environmental organizations

C. African American rights groups

D. Anti-tax groups

**20** Which of the following types of interest groups is typically allied with the Democratic Party?

A. Business groups

B. Abortion rights organizations

C. Conservative Christian organizations

D. None of the above

KNOW *the* **score**

18–20 correct: Congratulations! You are well informed!

15–17 correct: Your political knowledge is a bit low—be sure to review the key terms and visit TheThinkSpot.

<14 correct: Reread the chapter more thoroughly.

1. C; 2. B; 3. D; 4. C; 5. A; 6. A; 7. A; 8. D; 9. C; 10. A; 11. A; 12. D; 13. A; 14. D; 15. B; 16. B; 17. A; 18. C; 19. D; 20. B

**8 POLITICAL**

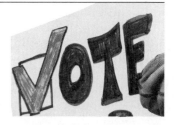

The Democratic Party won the 2008 election, capturing the presidency for the first time in three elections and strengthening its hold on Congress. In the race for the White House, Democratic presidential candidate Barack Obama defeated Republican John McCain. Obama carried 28 states and the District of Columbia with a total of 365 electoral votes, while McCain took 22 states with 173 electoral votes. Obama also claimed a majority of the popular vote, 53 percent to 46 percent for his Republican opponent. Obama's share of the popular vote was the largest for any Democrat running for president since Lyndon Johnson in 1964.

Democrats did well in other races as well. While Obama was winning the White House, the Democratic Party expanded its majorities in Congress, picking up 8 seats in the Senate and 21 seats in the House. When the new Senate convened in 2009, it contained 59 Democrats and 41 Republicans. The new House included 257 Democrats and 178 Republicans. At the state level, Democrats held the governorships of 29 states compared with 21 state governors who were Republican. In 27 states, Democrats held majorities in both legislative chambers compared with 14 states in which the Republican Party enjoyed full control. The legislatures in eight states were split; the Nebraska legislature is nonpartisan, which means that candidates run for seats without party labels.

# PARTIES

# ESSENTIALS...

# the party
## SYSTEM

**a** **political party** is a group of individuals who join together to seek government office in order to make public policy. A party differs from an interest group in its effort to win control of the machinery of government. Both parties and interest groups participate in election campaigns, but only parties actually run candidates for office. Candidates for Congress run as Democrats or Republicans, not as representatives of labor unions or corporations.

The number of political parties varies from country to country. The United States has a **two-party system**, which is the division of voter loyalties between two major political parties, resulting in the near exclusion of minor parties from seriously competing for a share of political power. After the 2008 election, 98 of 100 U.S. senators were elected as either Democrats or Republicans. (Bernie Sanders of Vermont and Joe Liebermann of Connecticut won elections as independents, but both caucus with the Democrats and are counted as Democrats for the purpose of committee assignments. Liebermann calls himself an "independent Democrat.") The two major parties held all 435 seats in the U.S. House and all 50 offices of state governor.

A **third party** is a minor party in a two-party system. Third-party candidates and independents may compete for office in a two-party system, but usually with a notable lack of success. The roster of third parties in the United States includes Green, Reform, Libertarian, Natural Law, Official Constitution,

Workers World, Socialist, and Socialist Equality parties. The Green and the Libertarians are the most successful, winning a handful of local races.

Why does the United States have a two-party system rather than a system with three or more major

> **think**
>
> **Would you vote for a third-party candidate that you liked even if you thought that he or she had no real chance of winning the election?**

political parties as in many other democracies? Political scientists offer two sets of explanations—the electoral system and the absence of deep-seated political divisions in American society. Maurice Duverger, a French political scientist, wrote in the 1950s that a **plurality election system**, which is a method for choosing public officials by awarding office to the candidate with the most votes, favors a two-party system.[1] Candidates for executive and legislative office in the

**political party** a group of individuals who join together to seek government office in order to make public policy.

**two-party system** the division of voter loyalties between two major political parties.

**third party** a minor party in a two-party system.

**plurality election system** a method for choosing public officials that awards office to the candidate with the most votes; it favors a two-party system.

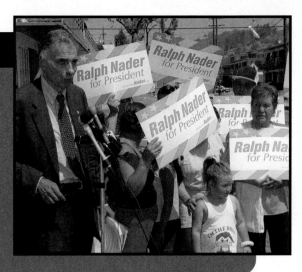

United States run from geographic areas and the candidate with more votes wins the office. Candidates who finish second or third win nothing, no matter how close the race. The **Electoral College**, established in the Constitution for indirect election of the president and vice president, is especially inhospitable to third-party candidates because it awards electoral votes, the only votes that really count, to candidates who win the most popular votes in a state. In 1992, for example, Reform Party candidate Ross Perot won no electoral votes, despite taking 19 percent of the popular vote, because he carried no states. The dilemma for minor parties in the United States is that if they do not quickly develop enough popular support to win elections, the voters will not take them seriously. If voters believe that a party and its candidates are unlikely to win, they often decide to choose between the major party candidates because they do not want to throw away their votes.[2]

Scholars also believe that a nation's party system reflects the fundamental social and political divisions of society. The more intense the divisions, the more likely it is that the nation will have a multiparty system. The United States has a two-party system, they say, because Americans are relatively united. Americans may disagree about the role of government in society, but they generally share the basic values of capitalism and democracy. People with opposing views on some issues can unite under the same party banner because they agree on other issues.

**Electoral College** the system established in the Constitution for indirect election of the president and vice president.

# 1992 Popular Vote vs. Electoral Vote

**BILL CLINTON**
**DEMOCRAT**
Home State: Arkansas
Electoral Vote: 370
States Carried: 32+D.C.
Popular Vote: 44,909,806
Percentage: 43.0%

**GEORGE H.W. BUSH**
**REPUBLICAN**
Home State: Texas
Electoral Vote: 168
States Carried: 18
Popular Vote: 39,104,500
Percentage: 37.7%

**ROSS PEROT**
**INDEPENDENT**
Home State: Texas
Electoral Vote: 0
States Carried: 0
Popular Vote: 19,217,213
Percentage: 18.9%

The National Archives and Records Administration

Israel has a **multiparty system,** which is the division of voter loyalties among three or more major political parties. The Knesset, the lower house of the Israeli national legislature, included 12 parties after the 2009 elections. Kadima, the largest party in the Knesset, held 28 of 120 seats. In order to achieve a majority in the Knesset, Kadima had to form a coalition with several smaller parties.

Israel has **proportional representation (PR)**, which is an election system that awards legislative seats to each party approximately equal to its popular voting strength. As long as a party receives at least 2 percent of the total vote, the minimum threshold for gaining representation, the party wins seats in the Knesset in proportion to its share of the vote. In 2009, for example, Kadima won 23 percent of the seats in the Knesset based on 22 percent of the popular vote. Proportional representation is related to multiparty systems because voters know that their votes will count. Unless a party has almost no popular support, each vote it receives will enable it to increase its representation in the Knesset.

Voters in Israel cast their ballots for the party rather than individual candidates by choosing a letter symbol. Before the election, each party prepares a list of candidates for the Knesset and ranks them in order, placing party leaders at the top. If the party wins five seats, the first five candidates on the list become members of the Knesset. If it wins ten seats, the first ten candidates are elected. Candidates are chosen to represent their party in the Knesset rather than individual geographic districts as in the United States.[3]

Democracies with multiparty systems are countries with intense social and political divisions. People who disagree fundamentally about the nature of society and the role of government are less likely to form broad-based coalition parties such as those that exist in the United States. Instead, they create smaller, more narrowly based parties. Societies that are deeply divided are likely to have several political parties.

Many political scientists believe that electoral laws and a nation's social structure interact. Nations with deep social and political divisions create electoral systems based on proportional representation in order to allow the democratic expression of those divisions at the ballot box. In contrast, countries with fewer divisions establish election procedures that favor a two-party system.[4]

## Questions

1. If the United States were to adopt proportional representation, do you think that a multiparty system would soon develop? Why or why not?

2. If Israel were to adopt a plurality election system, do you think a two-party system would eventually emerge in that country? Why or why not?

3. What are the advantages and disadvantages of each type of party system?

**multiparty system** the division of voter loyalties among three or more major political parties.

**proportional representation (PR)** an election system that awards legislative seats to each party approximately equal to its popular voting strength.

## 2009 ISRAELI NATIONAL ELECTION

| PARTY | # VOTES | # SEATS |
|---|---|---|
| Kadima | 758,032 | 28 |
| Likud | 729,054 | 27 |
| Yisrael Beiteinu | 394,577 | 15 |
| Labor Party | 334,900 | 13 |
| Shas | 286,300 | 11 |
| United Torah Judaism | 147,954 | 5 |
| United Arab List-Ta 'al | 113,954 | 4 |
| National Union | 112,570 | 4 |
| Hadash | 112,130 | 4 |
| New Movement-Meretz | 99,611 | 3 |
| The Jewish Home | 96,765 | 3 |
| Balad | 83,739 | 3 |

This menorah sculpture outside of the Knesset building is a symbol of Israel's statehood and sovereignty.

http://www.knesset.gov.il/elections17/eng/Results/main_results_eng.asp

# party
## ORGANIZATION

the organization of political parties in the United States reflects the federal system, with organizations at both the state and national levels of government. At the state level, the Democratic and Republican party organizations are led by executive party committees, which are elected by party activists who participate in local party meetings, district conventions, and state party conventions. The executive committee usually elects the state party chair.

A national committee and a national chair lead the national party organizations. The national committee consists of a committeeman and committeewoman chosen by the party organizations of each state and the District of Columbia. The national committee elects the national committee chair. When the party controls the White House, the president usually handpicks the national chairperson.

The Democratic National Committee (DNC) and Republican National Committee (RNC) work to increase the number of party officeholders. Each party tries to recruit a strong list of candidates for the next election. Although the national party organizations do not control nominations, they can encourage potential candidates to run. They also provide candidates with technical assistance and campaign advice. The DNC and RNC support their candidates with polling data, issue research, media assistance, and advice on campaign strategy. Both national parties offer campaign seminars, teaching inexperienced candidates how to do everything from raising money to dealing with the media. The most important service the national party organizations provide for their candidates is money.

The Republicans have historically enjoyed a significant fundraising advantage over the Democrats because of the socioeconomic status of their support base and because of their fundraising expertise. People who identify with the Republican Party have more money than those who consider themselves Democrats. Moreover, the Republicans have also benefited from a more efficient fundraising operation, especially direct mail. However, the Democrats have closed the fundraising gap, primarily because they have taken better advantage of the Internet than their Republican opponents.[5] In 2008, the Democratic and Republican national campaign organizations raised more than $900 million each to support their candidates with the Democra-

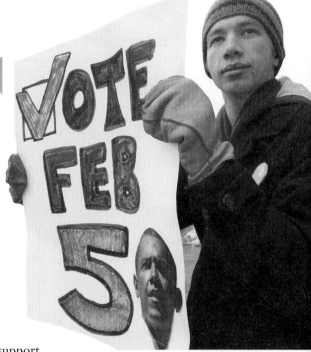

A volunteer for Obama reminds voters to go to the polls on Super Tuesday, February 5, 2008.

tic Party enjoying a small fundraising advantage.

Political parties take a different approach to campaign finance than do interest groups. Most interest groups contribute primarily to incumbent officeholders because they want to develop positive relationships with influential members of Congress. Their goal is **access**, the opportunity to communicate directly with legislators and other government officials in hopes of influencing the details of policy. In contrast, the goal of political parties is to control the government itself. Consequently, they contribute most of their money to candidates in competitive races, whether incumbents or challengers.[6]

**access** the opportunity to communicate directly with legislators and other government officials in hopes of influencing the details of policy.

The Republican and Democratic parties raised more than $3.1 billion for the 2008 election. As a comparison, the gross domestic product (the total value of all goods and services produced) of Greenland in 2007 was $1.7 billion.

# the party balance
## DEMOCRATS, REPUBLICANS, AND INDEPENDENTS

Political scientists measure party identification by asking survey respondents if they consider themselves to be Democrats, Republicans, or independents. In 2008, Democrats outnumbered Republicans by 36 percent to 27 percent, with another 36 percent declaring that they were independents. The figures represented a slight gain in party identification for the Democratic Party since 2004 but a sizable decline for the **Grand Old Party (GOP)**, a nickname for the Republican Party. In 2004, the two parties were on nearly equal footing among the electorate.

The Democratic Party has made electoral gains since 2004, not just because the proportion of Republican Party identities has declined, but also because independents are more likely to vote Democratic. In 2004, independents divided almost equally among independents who leaned Democratic, independents who leaned Republican, and true independents. The ratio of Democrats and Democratic-leaning independents to Republicans and Republican-leaning independents was close, 47 percent to 44 percent. (The Republican Party won the 2004 election because Democratic turnout was less than Republican turnout.) In contrast, independents leaning Democratic outnumbered

independents who leaned Republican by a three-to-two margin in 2008. The combination of Democrats and Democratic-leaning independents represented 51 percent of the electorate compared with 37 percent Republican and Republican-leaning independents.[7]

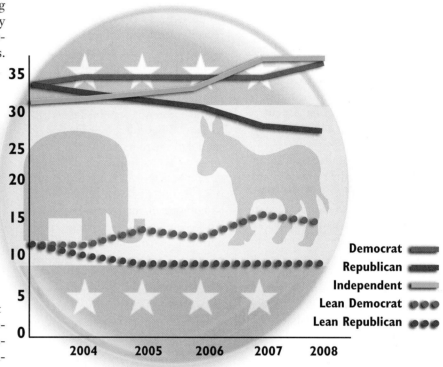

**Democrat** ▬▬
**Republican** ▬▬
**Independent** ▭
**Lean Democrat** ●●●
**Lean Republican** ●●●

2004    2005    2006    2007    2008

The Democratic Party has made electoral gains since 2004 not just because the proportion of Republican Party identifiers has declined, but also because independents are more likely to vote Democratic.

http://pewresearch.org/pubs/773/fewer-voters-identify-as-republicans

**Why might a voter choose not to identify with a particular party?**

**Grand Old Party (GOP)** Nickname of the Republican Party.

> **"We in America do not have government by the majority. We have government by the majority who participate."**
> Thomas Jefferson

# Are Party Conventions Irrelevant?

**Are party conventions an anachronism? Are there better means to nominate presidential candidates and develop party platforms?**

**Do conventions, in fact, help focus voters on the candidates and the issues of election campaigns? Do they serve a purpose in mobilizing the American public for a general election?**

**Overview:** For the greater part of American political history, the primary vehicle for nominating presidential candidates was the party convention. After the first convention was held in 1831, conventions became political forums in which parties not only nominated presidential candidates, but also in which policy and issues were debated by the party faithfuls (that is, delegates selected by their local and state party organizations) to provide both a nominee and platform to offer the American people at election time.

Historically, conventions provided high political drama and a medium through which contentious social and political issues were debated. For example, the Democratic Convention of 1968 was overshadowed by social unrest, the Vietnam War, violence, and protesters, with the result, in part, being a call for reform of the party nominating and convention processes.

With the era of television and reform, the conventions have become ratifying conventions in which the parties present to the country their respective nominees chosen months before the actual convention. Politics and debate have been relegated behind closed doors, so as to offer voters the illusion of party unity. This gives television coverage the quality of an infomercial or advertising. As viewership of conventions has declined, so has network coverage, which again gives the impression that conventions are nothing more than slick, political advertising—why cover something devoid of substance? But is this, in fact, true? Do conventions serve a valid and important purpose? What about the development of the party platform or introduction of a party's nominee, for instance? Are conventions, in fact, irrelevant?

## supporting — the increasing irrelevance of party conventions

**voters are increasingly disaffected with the current party nomination and convention process.** Harvard's John F. Kennedy School of Government's Vanishing Voter Project shows that voters increasingly complain of progressively longer campaign seasons. Voters may now be looking at conventions as a way to rein in this problem.

**party conventions are now devoid of substance.** In the past, party conventions were used to select presidential nominees, air policy disputes, and debate contentious issues. Now, the nominee is known months in advance and intraparty squabbles are held behind closed doors so as to foster the illusion of party unity.

**polling data shows declining public interest in party conventions.** On the media aspect of conventions, there is growing consensus that conventions are nothing more than infomercials in which the parties act as political advertising agencies.

## against — the increasing irrelevance of party conventions

**party conventions give party activists a chance to influence the party platform.** A party convention gives party members a forum in which to present their concerns and to aid in writing the party platform.

**the essence of a convention happens away from the convention floor.** During a convention, there are hundreds of meetings and events that allow party members to exchange ideas, plot strategy, and network—thereby energizing activists for the campaign's final months.

**conventions introduce most Americans to a party's candidate.** Research shows that the vast majority of Americans do not follow politics or presidential campaigns until the late-summer and autumn of a general election year. Conventions give the parties a chance to present their nominee and policy positions in a favorable light and for an extended length of time before the campaign season begins in earnest.

# voting
## PATTERNS

**V**oting patterns reflect differences in income, race and ethnicity, education, gender, age, family and lifestyle status, region, ideology, and religion.

### Income

Economic status is one of the most enduring bases for voting divisions in America. Since the 1930s, Republican candidates have typically done better among upper-income voters, whereas Democrats have scored their highest vote percentages among lower-income groups. In 2008, **exit polls**, which are surveys based on random samples of voters leaving the polling place, found that Obama outpolled McCain among voters with family incomes less than $50,000 a year by 60 percent to 38 percent. The two candidates evenly split the votes of people in families with annual incomes greater than $50,000.[8]

### Race and Ethnicity

Voting patterns reflect the nation's racial divisions. White voters lean Republican. In 2008, whites backed McCain 55 percent to 45 percent for Obama. In contrast, minority voters support the Democrats. In 2008, African Americans supported Obama over McCain by a lopsided 95 percent to 4 percent. Asian Americans gave Obama 61 percent of their votes compared with 35 percent who supported McCain. Democratic candidates also enjoy strong support from most Latinos. In 2008, Obama won the Latino vote 66 percent to 32 percent for McCain.[9] Latino voters were especially important for Obama because they apparently provided his margin of victory in Colorado, Florida, Nevada, and New Mexico, four hotly contested states that George W. Bush won in 2004.[10] Not all groups of Latinos share the same perspective on party affiliation. Whereas Mexican Americans and Puerto Ricans typically vote Democratic, most Cuban Americans support the GOP because of the Republican Party's strong anti-Castro position.[11]

"They will not only try to attack you if you try to point out what's going on in white America—U.S. of KKK…"

### Education

The Democratic Party is strongest with voters at either end of the education ladder. In 2008, Obama led McCain by 63 percent to 35 percent among voters who had not graduated from high school. Obama won the votes of high school graduates as well by a more modest 52 percent compared to 46 percent for his Republican opponent. The two parties evenly split the votes of college graduates. Among voters with postgraduate degrees, however, Obama led his Republican opponents by 58 percent to 40 percent.[12] For the most part, the relationship between education and party support reflects differences in income. As people move up the education ladder, they also move up the income ladder. Individuals in higher income brackets are more likely to vote Republican than are lower income voters. The pattern holds true

**exit polls** surveys based on random samples of voters leaving the polling place.

"The profound mistake of Reverend Wright's sermons is… that he spoke as if… no progress has been made;… [W]hat is called for is nothing more, and nothing less, than what all the world's great religions demand—that we do unto others as we would have them do unto us."

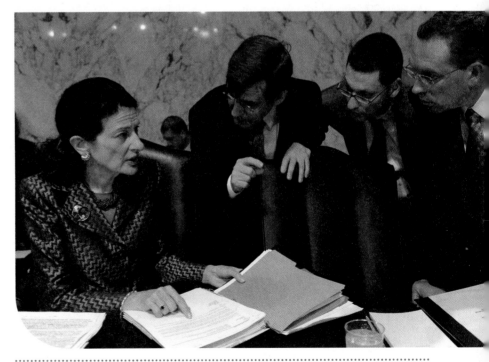
through college but not into graduate and professional school. People who have postgraduate college degrees tend to vote Democratic because many of them hold liberal positions on social issues such as abortion rights, environmental protection, gay and lesbian rights, the war in Iraq, and affirmative action.

## Gender

For more than 40 years, American voters have divided along gender lines, producing a gender gap, the differences in party identification and political attitudes between men and women. The **gender gap** has emerged in American politics because men have moved away from the Democratic Party. In 1952, a majority of both men and women

**gender gap** differences in party identification and political attitudes between men and women.

Republican Senator Olympia Snowe of Maine is one of a small number of moderate Republicans in Congress. In 2009, she negotiated with Democrats over the details of healthcare reform legislation.

identified with the Democratic Party. Since then, the percentage of women identifying with the Democrats has risen while the proportion of men has declined. The gender gap was greatest in the 1996 presidential election, at 14 percentage points. Since then, the gap has somewhat narrowed. In 2008, half of male voters supported Obama compared with 56 percent of women voters.[13]

## Age

Polling data reveal that younger voters have been moving toward the Democratic Party. In fact, Obama won because of his support from younger voters. He outpolled McCain among voters under the age of 30 by 66 percent to 32 percent. Obama won the 30-to-44 age bracket as well, but by a closer margin of 52 percent to 46 percent. The two candidates split the votes of people age 45 to 64. McCain won a majority of voters over the age of 65, 53 percent to 45 percent for Obama.[14]

## Family and Lifestyle Status

People who are members of traditional families tend to vote Republican. In 2008, married voters supported McCain by 51 percent to 47 percent for Obama. In contrast, Obama led his Republican opponent among single people by 65 percent to 33 percent. Voters who identified as gay, lesbian, or bisexual supported Obama by 70 percent to 27 percent for McCain.[15]

## Region

Regional voting patterns have changed. Today, Democrats run best in the Northeast and on the West Coast. The GOP is strongest in the South, the Great Plains, and the Rocky Mountain West. The Midwest has become a

## 2008

"*Obama outpolled McCain among voters* under the age *of 30 by 66% to 32%*"

battleground region between the two parties. In 2008, Obama was strongest in the Northeast, winning 59 percent of the vote and carrying every state in the region. McCain ran best in the South, outpolling Obama 53 percent to 46 percent, and winning every southern state except Florida, North Carolina, and Virginia.[16]

## Political Ideology

The Democratic and Republican parties are ideologically polarized.

Conservatives are aligned with the GOP; liberals vote Democratic. In 2008, liberals supported Obama over McCain by a substantial 88

percent to 10 percent. In contrast, conservatives backed McCain by an impressive 78 percent to 20 percent. Moderates tend to be swing voters. Obama captured the votes of moderates, 60 percent, compared to 39 percent for McCain.[17]

The political parties were once more ideologically diverse than they are today. Many conservatives identified with the Democratic Party, especially in the South, whereas the Republican Party had a liberal wing based principally in the Northeast. Important legislation frequently passed Congress with the support of bipartisan coalitions. For example, the Civil Rights Act of 1964 passed Congress because moderate and liberal Republicans joined liberal Democrats to overcome the opposition of southern Democrats.

The political parties are more ideologically distinct today because their coalitions of supporters have changed. The move of Southern white conservatives from the Democratic Party to the GOP has made the Democrats more liberal and the Republicans more conservative. The Democratic Party has adopted liberal positions on a range of social issues in order to appeal to middle-class voters concerned with abortion rights, the environment, and gay and lesbian rights. The Republican Party, meanwhile, has taken conservative positions on social issues to bolster its support among conservative Christians.[18]

## Religion

Religion and party support are closely related. During the last party era, voting patterns reflected religious affiliation. Protestants generally supported the Republican Party, Catholics leaned to the Democratic Party, and Jews were strongly Democratic. Today, party divisions based on religion have grown more complex. Although most Jews still vote for Democrats, Catholics have become a swing group. Conservative white evangelical Protestants (including Southern Baptists, Pentecostals, and members of the Assemblies of God) are firmly Republican, as are members of the Church of Jesus Christ of Latter-day Saints (the Mormons). Latinos as a whole typically support the Democrats, but the GOP is stronger among Latino evangelicals than among Latino Catholics, who remain firmly Democratic.[19] White members of mainline Protestant denominations (including Methodists, Episcopalians, and Presbyterians) lean Republican as well, but less so than do evangelicals. Most African Americans are Democrats, regardless of their religious preferences.[20] In 2008, Jews supported Obama over McCain by 78 percent to 21 percent. Catholics backed Obama as well, but the margin was more narrow: 54 percent to 45 percent. Protestants voted for McCain by 54 percent, compared to 45 percent for Obama.[21]

In the current party system, voting patterns are also based on frequency of attendance at religious services. White Protestants and Catholics who attend worship services regularly are more likely to vote Republican than are people in the same group who attend services less frequently.[22] In 2008, McCain led among voters who said that they attended religious services more than once a week by 55 percent to 43 percent for Obama. In contrast, voters who declared that they seldom attended religious services voted for Obama by 59 percent to 40 percent. People who never attended services backed the Democrat by 67 percent to 30 percent.[23]

## Place of Residence

Voting patterns reflect place of residence. Generally, Democrats win urban areas, Republicans carry rural areas, and the suburbs are a battleground between the two parties. In 2008, Obama outpolled McCain in large urban areas by 63 percent to 35 percent, whereas the Republican candidate won rural areas by 53 percent to 45 percent. The vote in the suburbs was 50 percent for Obama to 48 percent for McCain.[24]

## Issue Orientation

Since 1960, the parties have grown further apart philosophically, with the Democrats generally taking liberal positions and the Republicans expressing conservative views. **Liberalism** is the political philosophy that favors the use of government power to foster the development of the individual and promote the welfare of society. Democrats believe that a strong government is needed to provide essential services and to remedy social inequalities. Democrats make an exception to their endorsement of strong government when it comes to cultural issues, such as abortion and homosexuality. They believe that government should leave decisions on those sorts of issues to the individual. In contrast, the Republican Party embraces **conservatism,** which is the political philosophy that government power undermines the development of the individual and diminishes society as a whole. Republicans believe that a strong government interferes with business and threatens individual freedom. The exception to this approach for Republicans is that they believe that government should enforce traditional values on issues such as abortion.

A **party platform** is a statement of party

principles and issue positions. The 2008 Democratic and Republican Party platforms, which are excerpted in the table on the following page, show clear philosophical differences between the parties on many issues. By no means, however, do the parties take opposite sides on all issues. Some differences are nuanced. Consider gun control. Both parties endorse a right of gun ownership, but they disagree on the efficacy of gun regulation. The Democrats endorse "reasonable regulation," while the Republicans declare that gun control penalizes the law-abiding without having an impact on crime. Finally, the two parties take similar positions on some issues. Both the Democratic and the Republican platforms declare support for Israel.

> **liberalism** the political philosophy that favors the use of government power to foster the development of the individual and promote the welfare of society.
>
> **conservatism** the political philosophy that government power undermines the development of the individual and diminishes society as a whole.
>
> **party platform** a statement of party principles and issue positions.

> White Protestants and Catholics who attend worship services regularly are more likely to vote Republican than are people in the same group who attend services less frequently.

# 2008 Party Platforms

|  | **Democratic Position** | **Republican Position** |
|---|---|---|
| **Healthcare** | Declares that every American should be guaranteed affordable, comprehensive healthcare, which should be a shared responsibility between employers, workers, insurers, providers, and government. | Supports health savings accounts that provide tax breaks to individuals who save money to pay for their own health insurance coverage. |
| **Social Security** | Opposes Social Security privatization and increasing the retirement age. Promises to raise revenue to support the program by applying the Social Security payroll tax on incomes over $250,000 a year. | Promises that anyone now receiving Social Security benefits will not have their benefits cut or their taxes increased. Calls for partial privatization through the creation of personal investment accounts. |
| **Iraq and Afghanistan** | Promises to bring the war in Iraq to a responsible end. Declares that the war in Afghanistan and the fight against the Taliban should be the nation's top military priority. | Says that the waging of war—and the achieving of peace—should never be micromanaged in a party platform. Calls for increasing troop strength in Afghanistan. |
| **Israel** | Declares that under all circumstances, the United States must ensure that Israel enjoys a qualitative edge for its national security and its right to self-defense. | Declares support for Israel and pledges that the United States will ensure that Israel enjoy a qualitative edge in defense technologies over any potential adversaries. |
| **Energy** | Says that the government should provide incentives to increase domestic production of clean and renewable energy. Declares that the United States must reduce oil consumption by 35 percent by 2030 and calls for more fuel-efficient automobiles. | Advocates the use of free market incentives to promote energy conservation. Calls for drilling in the Arctic National Wildlife Refuge (ANWR), on federal lands in the western United States, and offshore. Supports the construction of new nuclear power plants as well as alternative sources of energy. |
| **Tax policy** | Says that families earning more than $250,000 a year will have to give back some of the tax cuts granted them during the Bush administration. Promises to increase the Earned Income Tax Credit (EITC) with the goal of cutting the poverty rate in half in ten years. | Favors making the tax cuts enacted during the early years of the Bush administration permanent. Proposes a major reduction in the corporate income tax rate. |
| **Immigration reform** | Calls for securing the nation's borders. Endorses immigration reform that will allow undocumented immigrants the opportunity to become citizens. | Declares that border security is essential to national security. Opposes amnesty. Supports English as the official language of the nation. |
| **Gun control** | Promises to preserve the right to own and use firearms, while recognizing the need for reasonable regulation. | Strongly supports the individual right to own and bear arms. Declares that gun control only penalizes law-abiding citizens and is ineffective at preventing crime. |
| **Affirmative action** | Supports affirmative action to redress discrimination and achieve diversity in federal contracting and higher education. | Opposes discrimination while rejecting all preferences, quotas, and set-asides based on skin color, ethnicity, or gender. |
| **Abortion** | Strongly and unequivocally supports Roe v. Wade and a woman's right to choose a safe and legal abortion, regardless of ability to pay. | Favors a constitutional amendment to prohibit abortion. |
| **Gay and lesbian rights** | Endorses federal legislation to prohibit job discrimination based on sexual orientation. Supports equal responsibility, benefits, and protections for same-sex couples. Declares that all men and women should be allowed to serve in the military without regard for sexual orientation. | Endorses a constitutional amendment to define marriage as between one man and one woman. Opposes legal recognition of same-sex relationships or granting benefits to same-sex couples. |

# divided GOVERNMENT

**divided government** the phenomenon of one political party controlling the legislative branch of government while the other holds the executive branch.

**d**ivided government refers to the phenomenon of one political party controlling the legislative branch of government while the other holds the executive branch. Consider the information shown in the figure on p. 165. During the 24-year period between 1969 and 1993, the Democratic Party controlled both the presidency and Congress for only six years. During the rest of the period, the Republican Party held the White House and the Democrats controlled at least one house of Congress. Political scientists explained divided government by declaring that the Republican Party enjoyed an advantage in presidential elections, whereas the Democrats had become the party of Congress, especially the House of Representatives. The 1992 and 1994 elections turned this explanation on its head

**BETWEEN 1952 AND 2008, 12 ELECTIONS RESULTED IN UNIFIED GOVERNMENT WHILE 17 ELECTIONS PRODUCED DIVIDED GOVERNMENT.**

when Democrat Bill Clinton broke the Republican lock on the White House (in 1992) and the GOP captured control of both houses of Congress (in 1994). Consequently, political scientists began to look for explanations of divided government in general.

Historical research shows that divided government is not unique to the late twentieth century, although it has become more frequent. The first instances of divided government occurred before the Civil War. In the nineteenth century, 16 of 50 elections produced divided government, with different parties controlling the White House and at least one chamber of Congress.[25] Between 1900 and 1952, 22 elections produced unified government; 4 resulted in divided government. Divided government has now become commonplace. Between 1952 and 2008, 12 elections resulted in unified government while 17 elections produced divided government.[26] Divided government is common at the state level as well.

The Constitution sets the stage for divided government. In a parliamentary system, the national legislature chooses the chief executive (often called a prime minister) by majority vote. Consequently, the party or coalition of parties that controls the legislature also controls the executive. In contrast, the United States has **separation of powers**, which is the division of political power among executive, legislative, and judicial branches of government. Members of Congress and the president are elected independently from each other. They have different constituencies, serve terms of different length, and stand for election at different times. In particular, midterm elections are more likely to produce divided government than presidential election years. With relatively few exceptions, the president's party loses seats in the House in a midterm election. On nine occasions since 1894, midterm elections have produced divided government or added a second chamber to opposition

control.[27] In 2006, for example, the Democratic Party won control of Congress, producing divided government after a period of unified Republican control. The 2008 election ended divided government because Democrats won control of both the White House and Congress.

Elections for president, Congress, and the Senate usually feature different issues. Whereas candidates for president stress national issues involving foreign policy, defense, and the strength of the nation's economy, candidates for the House of Representatives focus on local issues, such as cleaning up an area waterway or the proposed closure of a regional military base. Local voters may choose the presidential can-

**separation of powers** the division of political power among executive, legislative, and judicial branches of government.

# PARTY CONTROLLING
## EXECUTIVE AND
## LEGISLATIVE BRANCHES

- United under Democratic Party
- United under Republican Party
- Divided Government

**8 years | Divided** Republican President, Democratic Congress

**6 years | Divided** Republican President, Democratic House, Republican Senate

**2 years | United** Democratic President, Democratic Congress

**2 years | Divided** Republican President, Republican House, Democratic Senate[28]

**2 years | Divided** Republican President, Democratic Congress

| 1969–77 | 1977–81 | 1981–87 | 1987–93 | 1993–95 | 1995–01 | 2001–03 | 2003–07 | 2007–09 | 2009– |

**4 years | United** Democratic President, Democratic Congress

**6 years | Divided** Republican President, Democratic Congress

**6 years | Divided** Democratic President, Republican Congress

**4 years | United** Republican President, Republican Congress

**United** Democratic President, Democratic Congress

Divided government is not unique to the late twentieth century, but it has become more frequent.

## MIDTERM ELECTIONS
## *CHANGING HORSES*
### GAINS/LOSSES FOR THE PRESIDENT'S PARTY:

**1962** -4 (John F. Kennedy – D)

**1966** -47 (Lyndon Johnson – D)

**1970** -12 (Richard Nixon – R)

**1974** -48 (Gerald Ford – R)

**1978** -15 (Jimmy Carter – D)

**1982** -26 (Ronald Reagan – R)

**1986** -5 (Ronald Reagan – R)

**1990** -8 (George H. W. Bush – R)

**1994** -52 (Bill Clinton – D)

**1998** +5 (Bill Clinton – D)

**2002** +5 (George W. Bush – R)

**2006** -30 (George W. Bush – R)

didate who they believe will work the hardest to cut taxes while voting for the candidate for Congress who promises to support increased federal spending in the region.[29]

At any given time, Party A may have an advantage on national issues while Party B is perceived by voters as being stronger on local issues. During the 1980s, presidential elections focused on defense, tax rates, and cultural values–issues that favored the Republicans. In contrast, races for Congress focused on more specific policy concerns, such as protecting Social Security, helping farmers or unemployed workers, and promoting local economic development. These were issues that gave Democrats the advantage.[30] Divided government reflects the divided issue preferences of

Americans. Voters want low inflation, a less obtrusive government, and low taxes—positions associated with the GOP. Voters also want the government to ensure a safe environment, promote education, and protect the integrity of the Social Security and Medicare programs—issues that favor the Democratic Party.[31]

Political scientists disagree as to whether divided government is the result of conscious voter choice. Some scholars doubt that the voters choose divided government. Their research shows that few voters literally decide to vote for a Democrat for president and a Republican for Congress, or vice versa, in hopes of producing divided government.[32] In contrast, other research indicates that even though the proportion of voters who split their ticket in order to balance the House with a president of the other party is small, the number is large enough to affect election outcomes.[33]

## CONCLUSION
# political parties
## & PUBLIC POLICY

**P**olitical parties are similar to interest groups in that both connect individuals and groups to the government. The concept of democracy is that government policies reflect the policy preferences of citizens. In large, complex societies such as the United States, political parties are a means whereby individuals and groups can make their policy preferences known to government decision-makers and then hold those officials accountable for the adoption and successful implementation of those policy preferences.

### Agenda Building
Political parties help set the policy agenda. Individuals and groups

work through political parties to identify problems and raise issues for government action. In recent years, for example, religious conservatives have worked within the Republican Party to call attention to what they see as the moral decay of American society. The GOP has articulated their concerns in its party platform, and Republican candidates and elected officials have raised moral issues during election campaigns and while in office. Similarly, the Democratic Party has been a vehicle to advance the cause of groups and individuals concerned with safeguarding the environment, advancing the cause of minority rights, and protecting abortion rights.

### Policy Formulation and Adoption
Political parties play an important role in policy formulation and adoption. Parties not only raise issues, but they also develop policy solutions to address the problems they identify. For example, the 2000 Republican Party platform included an outline of a tax cut proposal that eventually became the Economic Growth and Tax Reconciliation Act, which became law in 2001 after Republicans captured the White House and won control of both houses of Congress. In Congress, Democrats and Republicans meet in separate groups to formulate policy proposals and plan strategy for their adoption. The passage of the Eco-

nomic Growth and Tax Reconciliation Act in 2001 represented a victory for Republicans in Congress over the organized opposition of the congressional Democrats.

Although political parties do not directly adopt policies, they facilitate policy adoption by bridging the separation of powers between the legislative and executive branches. The president works with fellow party members in Congress to pass legislation they support or to defeat legislation favored by the other party. President George W. Bush worked closely with Republican congressional leaders in Congress to pass his tax cut proposal, making compromises when necessary to ensure majority support. In the end, the measure won unanimous Republican support and the votes of a few Democrats, mostly members of Congress from states and districts that voted for Bush in the 2000 presidential election.

Political parties play an especially important role in America's separation of powers system because they reduce the number of political actors necessary to achieve policy compromises. Without political parties, congressional leaders would have to negotiate with dozens, perhaps hundreds, of members of the House and Senate in order to build majority support for policy proposals. In practice, the party leadership in each chamber, along with the White House, negotiates policy compromises on the final version of major legislation.[34]

## Policy Implementation and Evaluation

Political parties participate indirectly in policy implementation. Presidential appointees are responsible for administering the agencies and departments of the executive branch of government. Most of the men and

In 2008, the Republican Party's energy platform called for more domestic energy production, including offshore and in the Arctic National Wildlife Refuge (ANWR).

women whom presidents select as department heads and agency administrators are fellow party members. Appointed executive-branch officials typically bring their partisan perspectives with them to the task of policy implementation. For example, Democratic presidents typically appoint administrators who have a background in environmental activism to head the Environmental Protection Agency (EPA). They are committed to aggressively enforcing the nation's environmental laws. They approach enforcement from the perspective of working with business and industry to achieve voluntary compliance with the law whenever possible.

Political parties play a key role in policy evaluation. Every democracy in the world has at least two political parties. The political party or party coalition holding the reins of government in a democracy is the **governing party**. It plays the most

important role in policy adoption and implementation. The political party out of power in a democracy is the **opposition party**. The opposition party criticizes the policies of the governing party and offers alternatives. The opposition party ensures that citizens receive more information about government policies and programs than the official statements of government leaders. The opposition party has an incentive to highlight failures and seek out inefficiency and corruption. The opposition also presents alternative policies and offers its leaders to the voters at the next election. Opposition parties help make democracy work by providing information to citizens and offering voters alternative policies and alternative sets of leaders to those put forward by the governing party.

**governing party** the political party or party coalition holding the reins of government in a democracy.

**opposition party** the political party out of power in a democracy.

EVERY DEMOCRACY IN THE WORLD HAS AT LEAST TWO POLITICAL PARTIES

# TEST *yourself*

**1** Which of the following terms is best defined as a group of individuals who join together to seek government office in order to make public policy?

A. Interest group

B. Political action committee

C. Issue network

D. Political party

**2** The Green, Reform, and Libertarian parties are examples of which of the following?

A. Interest groups

B. Party eras

C. Third parties

D. Political action committees

**3** Which of the following is not a reason why the United States has a two-party system rather than a multiparty system?

A. The plurality election system awards office to the candidate with the most votes, leaving candidates who finished a strong second or third with nothing.

B. The Electoral College awards electoral votes only to candidates who win the most votes in each state.

C. The United States is not deeply divided along social and political lines.

D. Federal law limits the number of parties on the ballot to two.

**4** An election system that awards office to the candidate with the most votes is known by which of the following terms?

A. Proportional representation

B. Party realignment

C. Plurality election system

D. Two-party system

**5** Which of the following statements is true about Israel but is not true about the United States?

A. If a political party gets 10 percent of the vote, it will get 10 percent of the seats in the national legislature.

B. Candidates for the national legislature run from geographical areas called districts.

C. Nearly all of the members of the national legislature are members of one of two major political parties.

D. Voters may be reluctant to vote for a smaller party because they do not want to "throw their vote away" on a party that has no chance to gain representation.

**6** Which of the following statements is true about political parties and elections in Israel?

A. Candidates are chosen in primaries to run from districts.

B. Voters cast their ballots primarily for political parties rather than for individual candidates.

C. Israel has a two-party system similar to the party system in the United States.

D. All of the above

**7** Which of the following statements is true about party fundraising?

A. The Democratic Party has historically raised more money than the Republican Party.

B. The Republican Party closed the fundraising gap with the Democrats in 2006 and especially 2008.

C. The Republican Party has caught up with the Democrats because of Internet fundraising.

D. None of the above

**8** The Grand Old Party (GOP) refers to which of the following?

A. Libertarian Party

B. Green Party

C. Democratic Party

D. Republican Party

**9** Which of the following statements about party identification is accurate?

A. Since 2004, the proportion of Democrats in the population has increased by at least 5 percentage points.

B. Since 2004, the proportion of independents in the population has decreased by at least 5 percentage points.

C. Since 2004, the proportion of Republicans in the population has decreased by at least 5 percentage points.

D. None of the above

**10** Which of the following statements about independents is accurate?

A. Most independents are men.

B. As a group, independents are more religious than are Democrats and Republicans.

C. Most independents are so disinterested in politics that they are not registered to vote.

D. None of the above

**11** Among which of the following income groups would you expect the Republican candidate for president to do best in the next presidential election?

A. People making less than $30,000 a year

B. People making between $30,000 and $60,000 a year

C. People making between $100,000 and $150,000 a year

D. People making more than $200,000 a year

**12** Which of the following groups would be *least* likely to give a majority of its votes to the Democratic candidate for president in the next election?

A. Asian Americans

B. African Americans

C. Whites

D. Latinos

13 Which of the following statements is true about members of the groups that support each of the two major political parties?
A. Men are more likely than women to vote Democratic.
B. The more education one has, the more likely that person is to vote Republican.
C. White voters are more likely than non-white voters to support Republican candidates.
D. None of the above

14 Which of the following statements is true about voter preferences?
A. Gay and lesbian voters tend to vote Republican.
B. Married voters tend to vote Democratic.
C. Women are more likely to vote Republican than are men.
D. None of the above

15 The Republican Party is strongest in which of the following regions?
A. South
B. West Coast
C. Midwest
D. Northeast

16 Which of the following groups tends to vote Democratic?
A. People who call themselves conservative
B. Gays and lesbians
C. People living in small towns and rural areas
D. Men

17 Which of the following groups tend to vote Republican?
A. People who attend religious services on a weekly basis
B. Women
C. People living in inner-city areas
D. Jews

18 Which of the following groups would be the most supportive of Democratic candidates?
A. Catholics
B. White evangelical Protestants
C. Jews
D. Members of mainline Protestant denominations

19 Political Party A controls both houses of Congress while Political Party B holds the presidency. This situation is an example of which of the following?
A. Divided government
B. Responsible parties
C. Proportional representation
D. Realignment

KNOW *the* **score**
18–19 correct: Congratulations! You are well informed!
15–17 correct: Your political knowledge is a bit low—be sure to review the key terms and visit TheThinkSpot.
<14 correct: Reread the chapter more thoroughly.

1. D; 2. C; 3. D; 4. C; 5. A; 6. C; 7. D; 8. D; 9. C; 10. A; 11. D; 12. C; 13. C; 14. D; 15. A; 16. B; 17. A; 18. C; 19. A

**9 CAMPAIGNS**

The race for the 2008 Democratic presidential nomination was historic. Although several well-known party leaders launched presidential bids, the field soon narrowed to two contenders attempting to make history—Illinois Senator Barack Obama and New York Senator Hillary Clinton. The son of a white woman from Kansas and a black immigrant from Kenya, Obama hoped to become America's first African American president. Clinton, the wife of former President Bill Clinton, would be the nation's first female president.

Clinton was the early favorite. She was better known than Obama, a self-described "skinny guy with a funny name and an improbable life story." Many Democratic voters were favorably disposed toward Clinton because they fondly remembered her husband's administration. Nonetheless, Obama had advantages. He was a fresh face, a Washington outsider, and that image proved helpful at a time when polls showed that most Americans believed the nation was on the wrong track. Obama also benefited from having opposed the war in Iraq from the beginning, a position important to many Democratic primary voters.

The contest between Obama and Clinton was notable for both its duration and closeness. In 2000 and 2004, the Democratic Party had identified its nominee before the end of March. With the 2008 primary schedule more frontloaded than ever before, most observers expected that one candidate would have the nomination wrapped up no later than the end of February. Nonetheless, neither Obama nor Clinton was able to pull away from the other until early June, when Obama finally captured enough delegates to claim the nomination. The margin of victory was narrow—fewer than 200 of the more than 4,000 total delegates separated the two candidates.

# AND ELECTIONS

# ESSENTIALS...

*after studying Chapter 9, students should be able to answer the following questions:*

> What are the various types of elections held in the United States?

> How do "one, person, one vote" and the Voting Rights Act (VRA) affect representation, the redistricting process, and public policy?

> What are the goals of an election campaign, and what approaches do candidates take to achieve those goals? What is the role of money in election campaigns?

> How do elections for the U.S. House and U.S. Senate differ?

> How does the presidential nomination process work?

> What were the key stages in the 2008 presidential nomination process?

> What role does the Electoral College system play in presidential elections?

> What roles do base voters and swing voters play in an election? How do party identification, issues, campaigns, and retrospective and prospective voting affect voter choice?

> What is the role of elections in the policymaking process?

# types of ELECTIONS

**a**mericans have the opportunity to cast ballots in several types of elections. A **general election** is an election to fill state and national offices in November of even-numbered years. Voters choose among Democratic and Republican candidates, and sometimes third-party candidates and independent candidates not affiliated with any political party. General election voters may cast a split ticket or a straight ticket ballot. A **split ticket ballot** involves voters casting their ballots for candidates of two or more political parties. In contrast, a **straight ticket ballot** refers to voters selecting the entire slate of candidates from one party only.

Most general elections are plurality elections. In every state but Georgia, the candidate with the most votes wins the general election, regardless of whether the candidate has a majority of ballots cast. Georgia requires a **runoff**, a later election between the two candidates receiving the most votes when no candidate has won a majority in the initial general election.

In most states, major parties choose their general election candidates in primary elections, which are scheduled

a month or more before the November general election. A **primary election** is an election held to determine a party's nominees for the general election ballot. Democrats compete against other Democrats;

**general election** an election to fill state and national offices held in November of even-numbered years.

**split ticket ballot** voters casting their ballots for the candidates of two or more political parties.

**straight ticket ballot** voters selecting the entire slate of candidates of one party only.

**runoff** an election between the two candidates receiving the most votes when no candidate got a majority in an initial election.

**primary election** an election held to determine a party's nominees for the general election ballot.

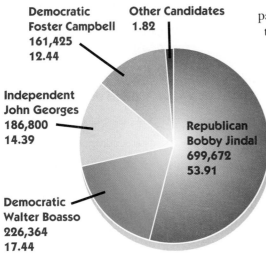

Democratic Foster Campbell
161,425
12.44

Other Candidates
1.82

Independent John Georges
186,800
14.39

Republican Bobby Jindal
699,672
53.91

Democratic Walter Boasso
226,364
17.44

Vote totals and percentages in the 2007 Louisiana gubernatorial election. On the day of the election, all candidates of all parties compete in an open, blanket primary.

Republicans compete against Republicans. In a number of states, a candidate must achieve a certain threshold level of support at a state party convention in order to qualify for the primary ballot. The candidate with the most votes wins the primary election in most states, regardless of whether the candidate has a majority. Some states, including most southern states, require a runoff between the top two primary election candidates if no one receives a majority in the first vote.

Some states conduct closed primaries; other states hold open primaries. A **closed primary** is an election system that limits primary election participation to registered

party members. Only registered Republicans can compete in the GOP primary; participants in the Democratic primary must be registered Democrats. In contrast, an **open primary** is an election system that allows voters to pick the party primary of their choice without regard to their party affiliation.

Louisiana selects state and local officials by means of a **blanket primary**, a primary election system that allows voters to select candidates without regard for party af-

filiation. If no candidate receives a majority in the primary, the two leading candidates face each other in the general election, regardless of party affiliation.

**closed primary** an election system that limits primary election participation to registered party members.

**open primary** an election system that allows voters to pick the party primary of their choice without regard to their party affiliation.

**blanket primary** a primary election system that allows voters to select candidates without regard for party affiliation.

In 2007, Bobby Jindal, an American of Indian descent, became Louisiana's first minority governor. Because Jindal received more than 50 percent of the popular vote, no runoff was necessary.

# election
## DISTRICTS AND REDISTRICTING

**a**merican voters select public officials in a combination of at-large and district elections. In an **at-large election,** citizens of an entire political subdivision, such as a state, vote to select officeholders. U.S. senators, state governors, and other state executive-

branch officials are elected at-large in statewide elections. States, such as Alaska, Delaware, and Wyoming, that have only one representative in the U.S. House of Representatives choose their member of Congress in statewide at-large elections as well.

**at-large election** a method for choosing public officials in which the citizens of an entire political subdivision, such as a state, vote to select officeholders.

In a **district election,** a political subdivision, such as a state, is divided into geographic areas called districts, and each district elects one official. States with more than one U.S. representative choose their members of Congress from districts. Michigan, for example, has 15 U.S. congressional districts, each of which elects one representative. The members of state legislatures are also chosen in district elections.

## Reapportionment

Legislative district boundaries must be redrawn every ten years after the national census is taken. Census data are used for apportioning the 435 seats of the U.S. House of Representatives among the states. **Apportionment** is the allocation of legislative seats among the states. States that have grown rapidly since the last census gain seats in the House, whereas states that lost population or grew relatively slowly lose representation. After the 2000 Census, nine states lost one or more seats in the House; eight states gained one or more seats. New York had to shuffle district boundaries to reduce the number of its congressional districts from 31 to 29. In contrast, Florida increased its House districts from 23 to 25.

Legislative districts must also be redrawn when there is population movement within a state. **Redistricting** is the process through which the boundaries of legislative districts are redrawn to reflect population movement. During the first half of the twentieth century, a number of states failed to redistrict despite dramatic population movement from rural to urban areas. As a result, the population size of legislative districts varied dramatically. In Illinois in the early 1960s, one U.S. congressional district in Chicago had a population of 914,053, while another district in rural southern Illinois contained only 112,116 people.[1]

The U.S. Supreme Court dealt with the issue of legislative reapportionment in a series of cases, the most important of which were *Baker v. Carr* (1962) and *Wesberry v. Sanders* (1964).[2] **Reapportionment** is the reallocation of legislative seats. In these and other cases, the Supreme Court established the doctrine of **one person, one vote,** which is the judicial ruling that the Equal Protection Clause of the Fourteenth Amendment to the U.S. Constitution requires that legislative districts be apportioned on the basis of population. The Supreme Court

has also stipulated that legislative district boundaries be drawn to ensure nearly equal population size.

**district election** a method for choosing public officials that divides a political subdivision, such as a state, into geographic areas called districts; each district elects one official.

**apportionment** the allocation of legislative seats among the states.

**redistricting** the process through which the boundaries of legislative districts are redrawn to reflect population movement.

**reapportionment** the reallocation of legislative seats.

**one person, one vote** the judicial ruling that the Equal Protection Clause of the Fourteenth Amendment to the U.S. Constitution requires that legislative districts be apportioned on the basis of population.

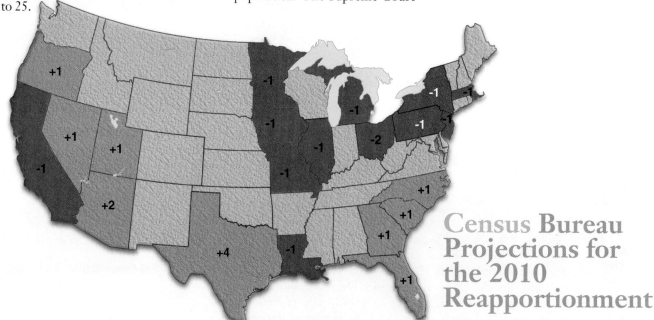

+1  -1  -1  -1
+1  -1  -1  -1
-1  -1  -2  -1
+2  -1  +1
+4  -1  +1
+1
+1

## Census Bureau Projections for the 2010 Reapportionment

The Census Bureau projects once again that states in the Sunbelt (the South and Southwest) will gain seats in the U.S. House after the 2010 Census. Most of the states losing seats will be located in the Frostbelt (the Northeast and Midwest).

http://www.nationaljournal.com/njonline/no_20081222_1323.php

## Voting Rights Act (VRA)

The **Voting Rights Act (VRA)** is a federal law designed to protect the voting rights of racial and ethnic minorities. The VRA makes it illegal for state or local governments to enact or enforce election rules and procedures that diminish the voting power of racial, ethnic, or language minority groups. In the late 1980s and early 1990s, the Justice Department declared that if a district *could* be drawn that would likely elect an African American or Latino candidate then it *must* be drawn. State legislatures would have to create the maximum possible number of **majority-minority districts,** which are legislative districts with populations that are more than 50 percent minority.[3]

Why would a Republican administration choose to implement the VRA to increase African American and Latino representation in Congress and state legislatures? After all, most minority lawmakers are Democrats. The reason was simple: The policy also helped the Republican Party to gain seats.[4] In order to construct majority African American and Latino districts, state legislatures redrew district lines to shift minority voters away from adjacent districts into new majority-minority districts. Because most African American and Latino voters are Democrats, the redistricting reduced Democratic voting strength in surrounding districts, threatening the political survival of some white Democratic members of Congress. Nationwide, the creation of majority-minority districts after the 1990 Census helped white Republicans pick up about ten seats in Congress, defeating white Democrats who were stripped of some of their minority voter support.[5]

In the mid-1990s, the U.S. Supreme Court overruled the Justice Department's interpretation of the VRA. The Court responded to legal challenges filed against majority-minority districts created in Louisiana, Georgia, and other southern states by ruling that state

**AFTER REPUBLICANS WON CONTROL** of the Texas legislature in the 2002 election, Republican Governor Rick Perry called a special session of the legislature to redraw the state's congressional district boundaries in hopes of increasing the number of Republicans in the Texas congressional delegation from 10 to as many as 17. The 11 Democratic members of the state senate initially thwarted the Republican scheme by flying to Albuquerque, New Mexico, in order to ensure that the 31-member state senate would lack the two-thirds quorum needed to conduct official business. The strategy worked for two 30-day special sessions, but with Perry preparing to call a third session, the Democrats broke ranks when one Democratic senator went home. Although the other Democrats were furious with their colleague, they had no choice but to end their boycott and return to Texas. The Texas Democrats in the picture below are smiling, but that is probably because they are glad to be home after more than a month in a hotel in Albuquerque. After all, they lost the political war. The legislature passed House Majority Leader Tom DeLay's redistricting plan and Republicans picked up five Texas congressional seats in the 2004 election.

TEXAS DEMOCRATS RETURNING FROM NEW MEXICO

governments cannot use race as the predominant, overriding factor in drawing district lines without a compelling reason. The Court has held that states are free to redistrict as long as the districts they draw do not diminish the political influence of minorities. The VRA does not require states to create additional majority-minority districts in order to increase minority representation.[6] Furthermore, the Court ruled in 2003 that states have the leeway to create "coalitional districts" in which minority voters do not form a numerical majority, but are numerous enough so that coalitional voting will give a minority candidate a realistic opportunity to be elected.[7]

> **Voting Rights Act (VRA)** a federal law designed to protect the voting rights of racial and ethnic minorities.
>
> **majority-minority district** legislative districts whose population is more than 50 percent African American and Latino.

## Gerrymandering

Redistricting can be used to advance the interests of one political party or a particular individual. In fact, the practice is so common that there is a word for it, **gerrymandering**, the drawing of legislative district lines for political advantage. The term dates from early nineteenth-century Massachusetts when Governor Elbridge Gerry engineered the creation of a district so complicated that observers said it resembled a salamander, hence the term Gerry-*mander*.

Political science research shows that gerrymandering can have an important, but not overwhelming, effect on election outcomes. A political party with complete control of the redistricting process can put itself in a position to increase its representation in the U.S. House by about 6 percent. It can also protect between 17 and 25 percent of its incumbents from significant challenges from the other party.[8] After the 2000 redistricting, the number of congressional districts that were competitive between the two major political parties declined significantly.[9] Nonetheless, the impact of gerrymandering is short-lived, disappearing after two or three elections.[10]

**gerrymandering** the drawing of legislative district lines for political advantage.

# election CAMPAIGNS

**a** n **election campaign** is an attempt to get information to voters that will persuade them to elect a candidate or not to elect an opponent.

## The Role of Money
Money is the most controversial feature of American electoral politics.

**The Cost of Campaigns** Election campaigns cost money. In 2008, Obama and McCain together raised and spent more than $1 billion in their race for the White House, with Obama bringing in more than twice the money of his Republican opponent. Races for Congress are expensive as well. Winning a seat in the U.S. House typically takes more than $1 million. The cost of a successful Senate race varies, depending on the size of the state. The average race costs around $6 million.

The candidate with the most money usually wins, but not always. In 2008, the better-funded candidate won more than 90 percent of the races for the U.S. House and U.S. Senate. Nonetheless, since 2000, the five best-funded U.S. Senate candidates were Democrat Hillary Clinton of New York ($45 million), Democrat Blair Hull of Illinois ($29 million), Republican Rick Santorum of Pennsylvania ($28 million), Republican Arlen Specter of Pennsylvania ($23 million), and Republican Norm Coleman of Minnesota ($19 million).[11] Of the five, only two, Clinton, who is now Secretary of State, and Specter, who is now a Democrat, won their races; the other three lost.

In 2008, Obama and McCain raised and spent more than $1 billion in their race for the White House, with Obama raising almost twice as much as his Republican opponent.

**The Campaign Budget** The largest item in most campaign budgets is advertising, particularly on television. The cost of advertising time varies greatly, depending on the market and the medium. Television, especially network television during primetime, is the most expensive. Cable television, radio, and newspapers are less costly. Advertising in larger markets, such as New York

**election campaign** an attempt to get information to voters that will persuade them to elect a candidate or not elect an opponent.

City or Los Angeles, is substantially more expensive than advertising in smaller markets, such as Baton Rouge, Louisiana, or Albuquerque, New Mexico. Running a serious political campaign in a populous state with several major media markets is many times more costly than running a campaign in a less populous state without a major media market.

Political campaigns have expenses other than advertising. Campaigns have offices with telephone banks, computers, fax machines, furniture, supplies, and utility costs. Campaigns hire consultants and employ professionals for fundraising, event coordination, media relations, Internet connection, and volunteer coordination. In 2000, the Bush presidential campaign rented 34 offices and employed a full-time staff of 175.[12] Candidates for president or statewide office also spend a good deal of money for travel. Fundraising itself is a campaign expense. In 2004, the Bush campaign spent $50 million on fundraising, $1 for every $4.87 raised.[13]

**Sources of Campaign Money** Wealthy individuals sometimes finance their own election campaigns. In 2008, Jared D. Polis of Colorado ($6 million), Sandy Treadwell of New York ($6 million), and Doug Ose of California ($4 million) headed a list of seven candidates for the U.S. House or U.S. Senate who invested at least $2 million of personal funds in their own election campaigns. Polis and one of the other big spenders won; the other five lost.[14] Self-financing is usually a sign of weakness because candidates with enough support to win office can raise money for their campaigns.

Candidates who are not wealthy enough to bankroll their own campaigns (or who choose to hold onto their money) must rely on others to finance their election efforts. Individual campaign contributors are the most important overall source of campaign cash, accounting for 60 percent of total receipts for U.S. House and Senate candidates, and more than 90 percent of the money raised by the two major-party presidential candidates in 2008, not counting federal funds.[15] Candidates raise money from individuals through direct solicitations, usually on the telephone or at fundraising dinners or receptions, by means of direct mail, and over the Internet. Candidates spend hours on the phone calling wealthy supporters asking for the maximum contribution under federal law, which in 2008 was $2,300 per individual contributor.

George W. Bush developed a sophisticated system for raising money from individuals that netted millions of dollars for his two presidential campaigns. In 2000, more than 500 Bush supporters called Pioneers (mostly wealthy energy company officials, lobbyists, and corporate executives) raised $100,000 each in individual contributions up to $1,000, which was then the maximum amount an individual could give.[16] Each of the Pioneers tapped at least 100 people for contributions and earmarked their contribution checks

The largest item in most campaign budgets is advertising, particularly on television.

with a special identification code in order to get credit. The Bush campaign rewarded Pioneers with special receptions and individual meetings with the candidate. Subsequently, President Bush appointed at least 19 of the Pioneers as ambassadors to other countries.[17] In 2004,

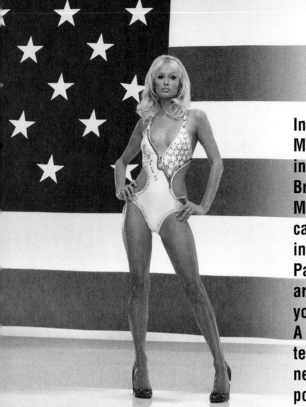

# "I'm John McCain, and I approve this message."

In 2008, an early controversial campaign ad from the McCain camp called Barack Obama "the biggest celebrity in the world" and flashed images of him after images of Britney Spears and Paris Hilton. In response to criticism, McCain campaign manager Rick Davis said, "It's not our campaign that is trying to make him into an international celebrity. It's his... Paris Hilton and Britney Spears... are international celebrities, so, you know, apples to apples." A Spears publicist's response was terse: "Why would we want to get Britney Spears involved in presidential politics?"

with the contribution limit raised to $2,000 a person, the Bush campaign created a second category of fundraisers called Rangers, who agreed to raise at least $200,000 for the president's reelection.

Direct mail is another important fundraising tool. Typically, Candidate A sends a long, detailed letter to supporters warning of dire consequences if the other candidate wins the election. The only way to prevent the calamity and save the country, the letter declares, is to contribute money to Candidate A by writing a check today and inserting it in the return envelop included in the mailing. Direct mail is an expensive fundraising tool because it takes time and money to develop an address list of people who are likely to respond positively to appeals for campaign money. Mailing expenses are costly as well. Nonetheless, direct mail can be effective. For years, the Republican Party held a fundraising advantage over the Democrats because it had a more sophisticated direct mail operation.

The Internet is the latest innovation in campaign fundraising. Campaigns create a sharp-looking website designed to attract the attention of supporters who can donate online with a credit card and a few mouse clicks. The advantage of Internet fundraising is that it is relatively inexpensive, especially compared to direct mail. Campaigns can send e-mails again and again to supporters, giving them campaign updates and asking for funds at virtually no expense.[18]

**think** Do you think campaigns are too expensive, or is spending the necessary means to increase voter knowledge?

Interest groups give money directly to candidates through political action committees (PACs), organizations created to raise and distribute money in election campaigns. PACs are an important source of funds in races for the U.S. House, accounting for more than a third of the total money raised by House candidates. In contrast,

PACs gave relatively little money directly to Senate or presidential candidates.[19] Federal law limits the amount of money a PAC can give a candidate for federal office to $5,000 for each election.

The role of political parties in campaign fundraising has changed because of the adoption of the **Bipartisan Campaign Reform Act (BCRA)** of 2002, which is a campaign finance reform law designed to limit the political influence of big money campaign contributors. The BCRA, which is also know as "McCain-Feingold" after its two Senate sponsors, Senator John McCain and Senator Russ Feingold, prohibited political parties from raising **soft money,** funds raised by political parties that are not

**Bipartisan Campaign Reform Act (BCRA)** a campaign finance reform law designed to limit the political influence of "big money" campaign contributors.

**soft money** the name given to funds that are raised by political parties that are not subject to federal campaign finance regulations.

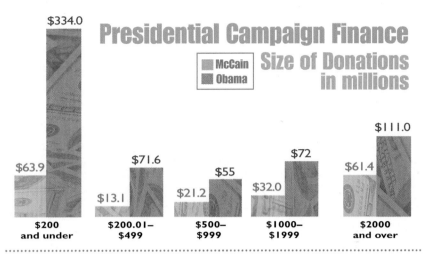

## Presidential Campaign Finance

**Size of Donations in millions**

■ McCain
■ Obama

| | $200 and under | $200.01–$499 | $500–$999 | $1000–$1999 | $2000 and over |
|---|---|---|---|---|---|
| McCain | $63.9 | $13.1 | $21.2 | $32.0 | $61.4 |
| Obama | $334.0 | $71.6 | $55 | $72 | $111.0 |

Over half of the money Barack Obama raised in the 2008 campaign came through donations of $200 or less.

subject to federal campaign finance regulations. Before the adoption of the BCRA, parties raised hundreds of millions of dollars in unregulated, large contributions from individuals, corporations, and unions. The BCRA prohibited parties from raising soft money beginning with the 2004 election, forcing them to rely on **hard money,** funds raised subject to federal campaign contribution and expenditure limitations.[20]

Much of the millions of dollars in soft money contributions that once went to political parties now goes to 527 committees. These are organizations created by individuals and groups to influence the outcomes of elections by raising and spending money that candidates and political parties cannot legally raise. As long as 527 committees operate independently of political campaigns and stop short of explicitly calling for a candidate's election or defeat, they can raise and spend unlimited amounts of unregulated soft money. In the 2004 presidential campaign, 527 committees raised and spent millions of dollars to support one side or the other. For example, the Swift Boat Veterans for Truth was a 527 committee that undermined Kerry's status as a decorated war hero with advertisements attacking Kerry's service in Vietnam. As long as 527 committees do not explicitly coordinate their work with either political party or presidential campaign, the BCRA does not apply to them.[21]

## Campaign Organization and Strategy

Big-time campaigns are long, drawn-out affairs. Challengers begin planning and organizing their campaigns years before the election. Incumbents, meanwhile, never really stop campaigning. Many observers believe that American politics now features constant election campaigns because newly elected officeholders start work on their reelection the day they take the oath of office.

Candidates spend the early months of the race raising money, building an organization, seeking group endorsements, and planning

strategy. One of the first tasks of a campaign is to prepare the candidate. This often means outfitting the candidate with a new wardrobe, a new hairstyle, and a slimmer waistline. Some critics of George W. Bush believe that he purchased his ranch in Crawford, Texas, in 1999 because it would provide an attractive backdrop for television reports on the candidate during the 2000 presidential election campaign. It would also help him project an image as a regular guy rather than the privileged son of a famous

**hard money** funds that are raised subject to federal campaign contribution and expenditure limitations.

**THE COST** of getting a candidate's image right routinely draws negative press. During the 2004 campaign, John Edwards made headlines by having his hair cut by star stylist Joseph Torrenueva. The cost? Anywhere from $300 to $1,250 per cut. The news further damaged Edwards's image, which had already been hurt by a YouTube clip showing Edwards primping for a campaign appearance to the tune of West Side Story's "I Feel Pretty."

During the 2008 campaign, Sarah Palin was ridiculed because the Republican Party spent $150,000 on her makeup, hair, and wardrobe. Sneering detractors labeled the Alaska governor "Caribou Barbie."

# The Internet and Campaign Revolution

## How has the Internet changed political campaigns?

## Does the Internet make political campaigns more, or less, democratic?

**Overview:** American campaigns and elections have changed with the simultaneous changes in technology and communications media. With each development, from print and the telegraph through radio and television, candidates have employed the new technology to reach more and more voters.

It is generally recognized that Howard Dean's presidential campaign laid the groundwork for future political campaigns. Through an innovative use of the Internet, he was able to raise over $40 million from small donors and supporters prior to the Iowa caucuses—an unprecedented feat from a relatively unknown challenger. Additionally, Dean started blogs so that supporters could communicate with each other and discuss strategy and policy with the campaign. He also pioneered the use of the Internet for campaign mobilization called meetups. Meetup software enables supporters to organize (on their own) rallies and meetings to discuss strategy and policy, and to organize grassroots activity such as get-out-the-vote drives (GOTVs). This saves campaigns valuable time and money, as supporters and volunteers have the tools to organize at the grassroots level and disseminate information on their own.

The Internet is now considered the fastest and, increasingly, the most influential means of political communication. All of the candidates in the 2008 presidential campaigns made extensive use of the Internet to reach out to donors, organize local events, rally volunteers, and keep supporters abreast of developments and issues.

Though in its infancy, the Internet will shape campaigns and politics—until the next technological innovation comes along.

## supporting — using the Internet for campaigns

**the Internet is a low-cost means for grassroots campaign organization and activity.** The Internet allows for discussion forums, meetups, blogs, and real-time direction among the candidate, campaign staff, volunteers, and supporters. This broadens grassroots involvement and activity.

**the Internet allows for alternative access to campaign news and information.** Blogs give supporters real-time campaign information and political analysis as well as updated campaign strategy and information.

**the Internet provides campaign news and information not found in traditional media outlets.** The Pew Internet and American Life study indicates that Americans are more and more frequently turning to the Internet for political information, citing that they cannot find the information they want in traditional media outlets.

## against — using the Internet for campaigns

**currently, politically active Internet users do not reflect population demographics.** For example, the Dean campaign was able to recruit more than 500,000 supporters over the Internet. They were scattered around the 50 states and were unable to cast votes in the Iowa caucuses or New Hampshire primary.

**the Internet can foster an illusion of support.** By communicating primarily and almost exclusively through Dean's blogs and MoveOn.org, Dean supporters were unaware of other political currents and thus insulated themselves from criticism and debate.

**the promise that the Internet will democratize campaign politics has yet to be realized.** The current reality is that campaign information and activity is cleared through a campaign's central organization, which carefully controls and scripts the activities at each Internet event.

family and a graduate of Harvard and Yale.

An important goal for many campaigns is to improve the candidate's name recognition, especially if the

*the housing bubble caused it.*

candidate is not an incumbent. Citizens generally will not vote for someone with whom they are unfamiliar. Races for less visible offices may never move beyond the name-recognition stage. It helps if voters are already familiar with the candidate. Tom Osborne easily won a seat in Congress from Nebraska after retiring from a long and successful career as the head football coach at the University of Nebraska.

Besides building name recognition, campaigns attempt to create a favorable image of the candidate. Candidates air campaign advertisements that stress their qualifications for the office and associate the candidate with popular themes and images. In 2008, for example, Senator McCain

new in American politics. Thomas Jefferson's enemies denounced him as the anti-Christ. Opponents accused President Grover Cleveland of beating his wife and fathering an illegitimate child. Critics attacked Theodore Roosevelt as a drunkard and a drug addict. In 1950, George Smathers defeated Senator Claude Pepper in Florida by calling Pepper "a shameless EXTROVERT" who has "a sister who was once a THES-

BURNING DOWN the house
Foreclosures Started Piling Up...

▶ ─────────●──────────── 03:30 / 10:51 ◀))) ▢ ⬆

*This YouTube still is from "Burning Down the House: What Caused Our Economic Crisis?" which attempted to tie the 2008 U.S. financial meltdown to prominent Democrats, including Barack Obama. The advantage? Creation cost was low, airtime was high (10 minutes, 52 seconds), no one paid for TV airtime, and approving viewers could forward links to all their friends. By Election Day, it had been viewed nearly two million times.*

used his personal history as a prisoner of war in Vietnam as evidence that he was strong enough to be an effective commander in chief. Obama's image as an energetic, relatively young man helped reinforce his message of change and reform.

Campaigns try to create an unfavorable impression of the opponent. Negative campaigning is nothing

PIAN."[22] (If your dictionary is not handy, an extrovert is someone who is outgoing and a thespian is an actor.)

Research is mixed on the effectiveness of negative campaigning. Sometimes it works, but sometimes it backfires. In general, negative campaigning is a more effective strategy for challengers than it is for

incumbents, who are more successful with a positive campaign. Nonetheless, incumbents are often able to effectively counter a challenger's attacks. Political scientists find no evidence that personal attacks or attacks that distort the record are effective.[23]

Early in a campaign, candidates work to build name identification and establish their credibility by producing a message that is primarily positive. As the election approaches, candidates who trail in the polls often decide that positive advertising alone will not close the gap with their opponents, so they go on the attack in hopes of undermining their opponent's support.[24] Incumbents sometimes launch attack ad campaigns against their challengers early in the election season in hopes of creating a negative image for the challenger before the challenger has a chance to establish a positive identification. Candidates who suffer attack are likely to respond in kind because they know that voters presume that an unanswered attack is true.[25]

Election campaigns for major offices are fought on the ground and

*people deserve to know.*

in the air. Campaign professionals use the term **ground war** to refer to campaign activities featuring direct contact, such as door-to-door canvassing and personal telephone contacts, between campaign workers and citizens. In 2008, the Obama and McCain campaigns

**ground war** campaign activities featuring direct contact between campaign workers and citizens, such as door-to-door canvassing and personal telephone contacts.

deployed small armies of volunteers and paid campaign workers to register voters and get out the vote. Both parties concentrated their efforts on the **battleground states**, the swing states in which the relative strength of the two major-party presidential candidates is close enough that either candidate could conceivably carry the state. The **air war** refers to campaign activities that involve the media, including television, radio, and the Internet. In 2008, campaign professionals focused their television advertising on network shows and cable channels that data analyses showed were popular with people most likely to support the candidates of their party.

**battleground states** swing states in which the relative strength of the two major-party presidential candidates is close enough so that either candidate could conceivably carry the state.

**air war** campaign activities that involve the media, including television, radio, and the Internet.

# congressional
## ELECTIONS

in America's representative democracy, citizens elect the Congress. Voters choose members of the House to serve two-year terms. Senators run statewide for six-year terms. Because Senate terms are staggered, voters elect one-third of the Senate every two years.

### House Elections

The most striking feature of elections for the U.S. House of Representatives is that most incumbents are reelected. In 2008, only 25 incumbents were defeated for reelection—4 in a primary election and 19 in the general election—for a success rate of 94 percent for those members seeking reelection. Since 1986, more than 95 percent of incumbent representatives seeking reelection have won. Furthermore, many races are not close. In 2008, only 51 House races were decided by a margin of 10 percentage points or less.[27]

Incumbency affords sitting members of Congress a number of electoral advantages. Most incumbent House members are much better known than challengers and they are almost always better funded. In 2008, the average House incumbent raised $1.4 million compared with less than $400,000 for the average challenger.[28] Another reason for the high reelection rate for incumbents is that many congressional districts are safe for one party or the other. Incumbents in districts that are safe for their party may face serious challengers in the party primary, but they will probably not be unseated in a general election.

Historically, the political party holding the White House loses seats in the House of Representatives in midterm elections. Between 1920 and 1980, the president's party lost ground in the House in 15 of 16 midterm elections, dropping an average of 35 seats. The phenomenon was so pronounced and appeared so regularly that political scientists de-

> In 2008, only 51 House races were decided by a margin of 10 percentage points or less.

"Let's try voting for the greater of the two evils this time and see what happens."

veloped theories to explain it. One set of theories focused on the withdrawal of coattails. The **coattail effect** is a political phenomenon in which a strong candidate for one office gives a boost to fellow party members on the same ballot seeking other offices. Coattails are particularly important in election contests in which voters have relatively little information about either candidate, such as open-seat races for the U.S. House. In presidential election years, some of the people who turn out to cast their ballots for a popular presidential candidate either vote a straight ticket or support candidates from the same party as their presidential choice even though they have no real candidate preference. Two years later, without a presidential race on the ballot, many of the congressional candidates who benefited from the coattail effect lose without it. A second set of theories attempts to explain the tendency of the president's party

to lose House seats in the midterm on the basis of ideological balancing. Moderate voters support the opposition party in order to restrain the president from pushing policies that they perceive to be ideologically extreme. Some voters may also use their vote at midterm to punish the president's party for poor performance, especially the performance of the economy.[29]

## Senate Elections

Senate races are more competitive than House elections. Incumbency is a factor in Senate contests, but it is not the overwhelming advantage that it is in House races. Furthermore, Senate races are typically closer than House contests, even when the incumbent wins. In 2008, 8 of 35 Senate races were decided by 10 percentage points or less.

Political scientists identify a number of differences between Senate and House races that account for the relatively greater vulnerability of

Senate incumbents. First, Senate constituencies are more diverse than most House constituencies and, hence, more competitive. Second, incumbent senators generally face stronger challengers than House incumbents. A seat in the Senate is an important-enough prize to attract the candidacies of governors, big-city mayors, members of the House, and well-known figures such as astronauts, war heroes, sports stars, and show business celebrities. Finally, research has found that voters tend to perceive Senate races as national election contests. As a result, national issues often play a prominent role in Senate campaigns and national trends frequently affect Senate election outcomes.

**coattail effect** a political phenomenon in which a strong candidate for one office gives a boost to fellow party members on the same ballot seeking other offices.

# takeaction

## IN-PERSON POLITICS >>

Although this is the age of television campaigns and Internet websites, volunteers still have a place in election campaigns. They mail campaign literature to registered voters, telephone supporters to encourage them to vote, and drive citizens to the polls on Election Day. Whereas volunteers augment the work of campaign professionals in races for major office, they are often the backbone of campaigns for local office.

Your assignment is to research campaign activity by volunteering for the candidate of your choice. Contact the local political party organizations to identify local campaigns that are seeking volunteers. Your instructor may be able to assist you in making contact with a campaign as well. To verify your volunteer work, bring your instructor a signed note from the campaign office manager on letterhead stationery indicating the time you spent on the campaign. Also, prepare a written report discussing your volunteer work and your impressions of the campaign. It should cover the following points:

• Identify the candidate and the office the candidate seeks, noting whether the candidate is the incumbent.

• Identify the location and describe the physical layout of the campaign office.

• Describe the other people working in the campaign as to age, gender, race, and ethnicity.

• List the task you completed for the campaign, explaining why you believe your work was important to the campaign's success.

• Assess whether the campaign office was well-organized or disorganized.

• Describe your impression of the experience, discussing whether you had a good time and if you ever plan to volunteer to work for a campaign again.

Eight Democratic hopefuls began the presidential primary race in 2007. The race quickly narrowed to Senators Obama and Clinton.

# presidential
## ELECTIONS

the presidential election process consists of two distinct phases with different rules, requiring candidates to wage two separate campaigns. The first phase is the contest for the nomination. Candidates compete for their party's nomination, which is awarded at a national party convention by majority vote of the delegates in attendance. The second phase is the general election contest. The two major party candidates, along with third-party candidates and independents, compete to win an Electoral College majority in the November general election.

## The Presidential Nomination Phase

In the first phase of the presidential-election process, candidates compete for their political party's nomination. In the summer of a presidential election year, the two major parties hold national conventions to which the party organizations in each state, the District of Columbia, and the various territories send delegates. The Democratic Party traditionally invites more delegates to its convention than does the GOP. In 2008, 4,049 delegates attended the Democratic National Convention in Den-

ver, whereas 2,380 delegates attended the Republican National Convention in Minneapolis.

The size of each state's convention delegation varies, depending on a formula set by the party that includes both the state's population and the success of the party in the state. In 2008, for example, California, the nation's largest state, sent 363 delegates to the Democratic convention and 161 delegates to the Republican convention. Arkansas, a relatively small state, sent 35 delegates to the Democratic convention, 31 to the GOP meeting.

By majority vote of the delegates, the convention selects the presidential and vice-presidential nominees to run on the party's ticket in the November general election. Until the conventions have done their work, the real contest is not between Democrats and Republicans, but among Democrats for the Democratic presidential nomination and among Republicans for their party's nomination. Because the convention delegates make the actual selection, candidates focus on the delegate-selection process in each state, hoping to get their supporters selected as delegates to the national conven-

tion. In 2008, Clinton, Obama, and former North Carolina Senator John Edwards were the leading candidates for the Democratic nomination. McCain, former Massachusetts Governor Mitt Romney, former Arkansas Governor Mike Huckabee, and former New York City Mayor Rudy Giuliani contended for the GOP nomination.

**The Delegate-Selection Process** The process of selecting delegates to the national party conventions varies from state to state. Most delegates are chosen in presidential preference primaries. A **presidential preference primary** is an election in which party voters cast ballots for the presidential candidate they favor and, in so doing, help determine the number of national convention delegates that candidate will receive. Democratic voters select among Democratic candidates; Republican voters choose among GOP presidential contenders.

# Legislative Elections in Brazil

Brazil elects the members of its national legislature using a system in which each state is an at-large, multi-member district. The size of a state's legislative delegation varies from 8 to 70 members, depending on its population. Political parties can nominate as many candidates as there are seats at stake, but only the names of the parties appear on the ballot. Voters can cast their ballots either for a party or for a particular candidate by writing in the candidate's name or number. The total number of votes a party receives is the sum of its party votes and the votes cast for its individual candidates.

The number of seats a party wins is based on **proportional representation (PR)**, which is an election system that awards legislative seats to each party approximately equal to its popular voting strength. If the combined votes for a party and its candidates total 25 percent of the votes cast in the state, then the party wins 25 percent of the seats at stake. The candidates on the party slate with the most individual votes actually claim the seats. If a party has enough combined party and candidate votes to win five seats, for example, the five individual candidates on its party list who received the most votes are the individuals chosen to serve in the national legislature.[30]

The Brazilian electoral system provides for competition not just among political parties but also among candidates in the same party. In practice, legislative candidates focus on building their personal vote totals, often by campaigning in a geographical stronghold or targeting a particular group of voters, such as industrial workers, ethnic minorities, or members of Protestant Christian churches (who are a minority in Catholic Brazil). The electoral system affects policymaking because legislators worried about winning reelection focus their energy on **pork barrel spending**, which are expenditures to fund local projects that are not critically important from a national perspective. Political scientists also believe that the system increases the power of Brazil's president, who trades support on local projects for legislative votes on national issues.[31]

## Questions

1. How does the Brazilian legislative electoral system differ from the American system?

2. Is the Brazilian system democratic? Why or why not?

3. Do you think Brazilian legislators focus more on pork barrel spending than do the members of the U. S. Congress? Why or why not?

**proportional representation (PR)** an election system that awards legislative seats to each party approximately equal to its popular voting strength.

**pork barrel spending** expenditures to fund local projects that are not critically important from a national perspective.

People pass by a poster of Brazil's President Luiz Inacio Lula da Silva in Rio de Janeiro, Brazil.

**think**

**Should superdelegates play a role in choosing a party's presidential nominee?**

Presidential primary election campaigns are similar to other election campaigns except that the candidates must appeal to a different voter pool. Primary elections typically attract fewer voters than the general election. In 2008, 530,000 voters participated in the New Hampshire presidential preference primary compared with 700,000 who turned out for the November general election in that state.[32] Primary election voters differ from general election voters in that primary voters identify strongly with the party in whose primary they vote. In contrast, the electorate for the general election includes a larger proportion of independents and people who identify weakly with a party.

| California Democratic Primary | Percentage of Votes | Percentage of Delegates Awarded |
|---|---|---|
| | Clinton (52%) | 55% |
| | Obama (42%) | 45% |
| | Others (6%) | 0% |

The Democratic Party allocates state convention delegates proportionally.

| Florida Republican Primary | Percentage of Votes | Percentage of Delegates Awarded |
|---|---|---|
| | McCain (36%) | 100% |
| | Romney (31%) | 0% |
| | Giuliani (15%) | 0% |
| | Huckabee (13%) | 0% |
| | Others (5%) | 0% |

The Republican Party awards convention delegates on a winner-take-all basis.

The nature of the primary electorate affects the approaches candidates must take to winning the

## In 2008, 350,000 people took part in the Iowa caucus compared with 1.5 million who voted in the general election.

nomination. People who identify strongly with the GOP are more conservative than voters as a group, whereas people who identify strongly with the Democratic Party are more liberal.[33] Consequently, Republican presidential contenders usually stress conservative themes during the nomination phase, whereas Democratic candidates emphasize liberal positions. Primary voters do not just consider policy preferences in choosing among candidates; they also evaluate each candidate's chances of winning the November general election.[34] The most liberal Democratic candidate and the most conservative Republican candidate may not win the nomination if large numbers of their party's primary voters believe they would not be strong candidates in the general election.

States that do not conduct presidential preference primaries use the caucus method to choose national convention delegates. The **caucus method of delegate selection** is a procedure for choosing national party convention delegates that involves party voters participating in a series of precinct and district or county political meetings. The process begins with party members attending local precinct meetings or caucuses that elect delegates to district or county meetings. The district/county meetings in turn select delegates for the state party convention. Finally, the state convention chooses national-convention delegates.

Candidates use a different strategy for competing in caucus states than they employ in states with primary elections. Because caucus meetings require more time and effort than simply voting in a primary, the number of people who participate in them is generally fewer than primary participants and far fewer than the number of people who turn out for general elections. In 2008, for example, 350,000 people took part in the Iowa caucus compared with 1.5 million who voted in the general election.[35]

Most caucus participants are party activists who tend to be more liberal (in the Democratic Party) or more conservative (in the Republican Party) than party voters or the electorate as a whole. Furthermore, a fairly high percentage of party activists who participate in caucuses are "true believers," who are more interested in imposing their policy preferences on the public agenda than in electing their party's candidates to office.[36] Consequently, in each party, ideologically extreme candidates (i.e., strong conservatives in the GOP, strong liberals in the Democratic Party) do better in caucus states than in primary states.[37]

Candidates who do well in presidential preference primaries and

**caucus method of delegate selection**

a procedure for choosing national party convention delegates that involves party voters participating in a series of precinct and district or county political meetings.

caucuses win delegates pledged to support their nomination at the national convention. The Democratic Party awards delegates in rough proportion to a candidate's level of support as long as the candidate surpasses a 15-percent threshold. The top figure on p. 186 compares the 2008 Democratic primary vote in California with the distribution of delegates. As the figure shows, Clinton won the primary with 52 percent of the vote to Obama's 42 percent. Edwards and several other candidates split the remaining 6 percent of the ballots. The figure also graphs the distribution of delegates in California, with Clinton getting 55 percent of the 370 delegates at stake compared with 45 percent of the delegates going to Obama. The other candidates failed to earn delegates because none of them surpassed the minimum vote threshold.

Republican Party rules award delegates on a winner-take-all basis. The bottom figure on p. 186 graphs the 2008 Republican primary vote and delegate distribution in Florida. As the figure indicates, McCain won the Florida primary with a little more than a third of the vote. Three other candidates—Romney, Giuliani, and Huckabee—each earned a significant number of votes. Nonetheless, as the figure shows, McCain won all of Florida's 57 delegates because of the Republican Party's winner-take-all allocation of delegates.

In addition to delegates selected through presidential preference primaries and caucuses, the national Democratic Party convention includes several hundred Democratic officeholders and party officials who are called **superdelegates**. The 2008 Democratic National Convention included 796 superdelegates, 19 percent of the total. Superdelegates are chosen on the basis of the offices they hold rather than their support for a particular candidate. In contrast to delegates selected through presidential preference primary elections and caucuses, superdelegates are officially

uncommitted, pledged to support no candidate. The superdelegate system ensures that Democratic officeholders and party leaders can attend the convention as delegates, regardless of their candidate preferences. The system also bolsters the position of insider candidates who enjoy the support of party leaders. In 2008, superdelegates found themselves in a position to name a presidential nominee because the closeness of the Obama-Clinton race prevented either candidate from winning a majority of pledged delegates. Most superdelegates chose to go with Obama because he was the candidate who won the most pledged delegates.

**superdelegates** Democratic Party officials and officeholders selected to attend the national party convention on the basis of the offices they hold.

**THE IOWA CAUCUS** draws participation from both parties, but the rules differ. Republicans caucus to cast secret ballots after listening to speeches about each candidate. Delegates from each caucus go on to county conventions. County-level meetings choose delegates to the Iowa Republican State Convention. The state convention is not bound by a previous caucus results when it makes its final selection.

The Democratic caucus system is more complicated. Each precinct allocates delegate seats in proportion to the votes in precinct caucuses. Supporters gather in a designated area of the caucus room. There may also be an area reserved for undecided voters. Then there is a 30-minute period in which attendees try to convince others, particularly the undecided, to support the candidate of their choice.

Debate is halted, and each candidate's supporters are counted. Candidates who fail to get a specified percentage of the vote are eliminated. Then another 30-minute period is called so attendees can reorganize around the remaining candidates. In a caucus, a voter's second choice can be as important as his or her first choice.

The voting closes after a head count of each group is made. Each candidate's supporters choose delegates to a county convention. These delegates choose representatives for the state convention, where the state delegates to the Democratic National Convention are chosen. Delegates are permitted to change their support after the first ballot—but in practice, this rarely happens at the later conventions.

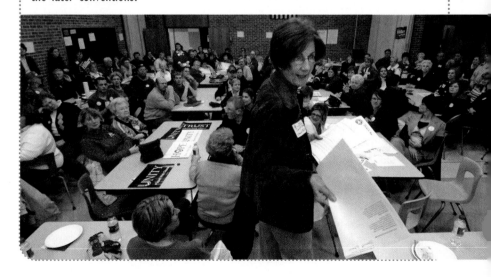

# the road to
## THE NOMINATION

In 2008, the presidential nomination process had six stages.

## Pre-Primary Positioning Stage

The men and women who want to be president begin the process of seeking their party's nomination more than a year before any votes are cast. They assemble campaign teams, collect endorsements, establish campaign organizations in key primary and caucus states, build name recognition among party voters and activists, and raise money. Because the nomination process is frontloaded, candidates need to have millions of dollars on hand in order to conduct campaigns in dozens of states in the space of just a couple of months. Furthermore, media attention mirrors fundraising success. Obama was able to compete against Clinton and eventually to win the nomination because of his remarkable fundraising operation.

Federal campaign finance laws allow for partial federal funding of presidential campaigns during the nomination stage. In order to qualify for federal matching funds, candidates must prove they are serious contenders by raising at least $5,000 in each of 20 states in individual contributions of $250 or less. Once a candidate qualifies for federal funding, the government will match individual contributions dollar for dollar up to $250. Candidates who accept the money must agree to an overall pre-convention spending ceiling and state-by-state limits that vary, based on the population of a state. Candidates who reject federal funding are free to raise and spend as much money as they can.

Most serious presidential candidates no longer participate in the federal funding system because they are unwilling to accept the spending and fundraising limits. In 2004, candidates who took federal matching funds were limited to $51 million during the nomination period, including federal funds. In contrast, Kerry and Bush, both of whom rejected federal financing, raised and spent more than $200 million apiece on their campaigns. In 2008, Obama and Clinton, both of whom rejected federal funds, collected well over $250 million in campaign contributions for the nomination fight.[38]

## Iowa and New Hampshire: Narrowing the Field

The first caucus (in Iowa) and the first primary (in New Hampshire) help define the candidate field by establishing some candidates as frontrunners and eliminating others as serious contenders. Candidates who do well in Iowa and New Hampshire gain name recognition and momentum that can be used to raise money and win votes in later contests, whereas candidates who do poorly are doomed to failure, with neither media attention nor an ability to raise campaign money. The eventual nominee almost always finishes in the top three in Iowa and the top two in New Hampshire.

The strategy of the Obama campaign was to finish ahead of Clinton in Iowa. The Clinton campaign initially had misgivings about even competing in Iowa, but when a memo surfaced suggesting that she skip Iowa, Senator Clinton declared that she was going all-out to win the Iowa Caucus. That was a mistake. Obama outspent Clinton in Iowa, held more campaign events in the state, and had a better organization. Obama was a political phenomenon, attracting tens of thousands of people to his campaign events. At each speech or rally, his organizers gathered thousands of names, telephone numbers, and e-mail addresses, and then used the information to create a grassroots campaign organization and to raise money. Obama won the Iowa Caucus; Clinton finished third, just behind former senator and vice-presidential candidate John Edwards.[39]

Obama hoped to become the clear frontrunner for the nomination by winning the New Hampshire primary, held in early January, just a few days after the Iowa Caucus. Riding a wave of favorable publicity generated by his Iowa Caucus win, Obama moved up in the polls in New Hampshire and seemed poised to deliver another blow to the Clinton campaign.[40] Nonetheless, Clinton won a narrow victory in New Hampshire by capturing a large majority of white, working-class women voters.

## Super Tuesday

Over the years, state legislatures around the country have moved their nomination contests to early in the year in hopes that their states would have more influence in the nomination process. In 2008, 24 states scheduled primaries or caucuses on February 5, including the big states of California, New York, Illinois, and New Jersey. Candidates with money, organization, and name recognition benefit from the frontloaded nomination process because they have the resources to compete in dozens of states within a matter of a few days. Super Tuesday often settles the nomination contest, at least for the Republicans, because of the party's winner-take-all delegate rule. Senator McCain became the inevitable Republican nominee because he won the most votes and, consequently, all of the delegates at stake in California, New York, New Jersey, and Illinois. The other major contenders soon dropped out of the race.

The Democratic nomination can take longer to settle because the Democratic Party awards delegates on a proportional basis. In 2008, Clinton and Obama split the Super Tuesday contests. Even though Clinton won New York, California, and New Jersey, she earned only a few more delegates than her opponent in each state because the vote was relatively close and the party's proportional rule ensured a near equal division of delegates between the two candidates.

## The Post–Super Tuesday Contests

Obama emerged from Super Tuesday better positioned to win the nomination than Clinton. The Clinton campaign assumed that she would effectively capture the nomination on Super Tuesday, whereas the Obama organization prepared for the nomination fight to continue well beyond the Super Tuesday voting. Obama organized each of the states holding caucuses and primaries in the days and weeks immediately following Super Tuesday, but Clinton did not. Obama also took the fundraising lead. Between February 5 and March 5, Obama won 11 consecutive contests, building a delegate lead of more than 150. Clinton recovered to win primaries in Texas, Ohio, Pennsylvania, and other states, but Obama won contests as well, and she failed to close the gap. When the last primaries were held in early

June, Obama had a clear delegate lead. Enough superdelegates announced their support to give him the nomination.

## The Transition

Once the frontrunner has enough delegates to ensure nomination, party leaders urge the remaining candidates to drop out, in the name of party unity. In the meantime, the campaign of the eventual nominee begins to stress themes geared toward general election voters rather than the voters who participate in primaries and caucuses. In 2008, the transition began for McCain shortly after Super Tuesday, whereas Obama had to wait until he wrapped up his nomination in early June.

## The National Party Conventions

The official role of a convention is to adopt a **party platform**, which is a statement of party principles and issue positions, and to nominate a presidential and a vice-presidential candidate. Traditional wisdom holds that platforms are meaningless documents, but research shows that administrations fulfill about 70 percent of their platform promises.[41]

The most important business of a convention is the official selection of the presidential nominee, ratifying the choice made during the primary season. Traditionally, the nomination takes place during primetime on the third evening of the convention. Festivities begin as speakers place the names of prospective nominees before the convention and their supporters respond with exuberant (and planned) demonstrations. Eventually, the time comes to call the roll of the states and the delegates vote. A majority of the delegates must agree on a nominee. At every convention for more than 60 years, the

delegates have selected a winner on the first ballot.

The final official business of the convention is to pick a vice-presidential candidate. The presidential candidate usually makes the choice weeks before the convention meets and the delegates ratify it. Above all else, presidential nominees look for running mates who will help them win in November. Historically, presidential candidates have tried to **balance the ticket**, which is an attempt to select a vice-presidential candidate who will appeal to different groups than the presidential

Obama selected Biden to counter McCain's experience and foreign policy strength, while McCain chose Palin to counter Obama's youth and appeal to women and minority voters.

nominee. Also, it is helpful if the vice-presidential candidate comes from a populous state, such as California, Texas, New York, or Florida.

Both Obama and McCain used their vice-presidential selections to shore up perceived weaknesses. Obama chose Senator Joe Biden of Delaware, a 35-year veteran of the U.S. Senate and chair of the Senate Foreign Relations Committee. Obama wanted Biden to balance his

own relative lack of experience, especially in foreign and defense policymaking. Obama may have also hoped that Biden, a Roman Catholic who was born in Pennsylvania, would attract white working-class voters in the Midwest and Catholic voters nationwide. McCain, meanwhile, surprised almost everyone by choosing Alaska's 44-year-old governor, Sarah Palin. McCain hoped to energize the conservative base of his party because Palin is an outspoken opponent of abortion and gay marriage. He may have also hoped to attract the support of some women who were disappointed that Hillary Clinton had not won.

Biden probably did more to help Obama than did Palin to assist McCain. Except for occasional verbal missteps, Biden avoided controversy while campaigning vigorously for the ticket. **Exit polls**, surveys based on random samples of voters leaving the polling place, found that two-thirds of the electorate believed that Biden would be qualified to be president. Palin excited the conservative base of the Republican Party, attracting large crowds at campaign events and mobilizing volunteers to work for the ticket, but her lack of experience and shaky interview performances left many observers questioning her fitness. According to the exit polls, 60 percent of the electorate said she was not qualified to be president.[42]

**party platform** a statement of party principles and issue positions.
**balance the ticket** an attempt to select a vice-presidential candidate who will appeal to different groups of voters than the presidential nominee.
**exit polls** surveys based on random samples of voters leaving the polling place.

# general
## ELECTION PHASE

**a**fter the party conventions, the presidential election process enters its second and decisive phase. The field of presidential candidates has narrowed to one Democrat, one Republican, and several other candidates running on third-party tickets or as independents. The rules of the political game have changed as well, as each campaign considers what it must do to win an Electoral College majority.

## The Electoral College

The **Electoral College** is the system established in the Constitution for the indirect election of the president and vice president. Under the Electoral College system, each state is entitled to as many electoral votes as the sum of its representatives in the U.S. House and Senate. Florida, for example, with 25 representatives and 2 senators, has 27 electoral votes; California, with 53 representatives and 2 senators, has 55. Altogether, the number of electoral votes is 538, based on 435 members of the House, 100 senators, and three electors for the District of Columbia. It takes a majority, 270 electoral votes, to elect a president.

**Electors** are individuals officially selected in each state to cast that state's electoral votes. Each state selects as many electors as it has electoral votes. The Framers of the Constitution anticipated that the members of the Electoral College would be experienced state leaders who would exercise good judgment in the selection of a president and vice president. In practice, however, the electors have been people chosen by party leaders to cast the state's electoral ballots for their party's nominees for president and vice president if their party's ticket carries the state. Electors are usually long-time

party activists selected as a reward for their service to the party. (The U.S. Constitution prohibits members of Congress from serving as electors.) Instead of exercising their own judgment to choose candidates for president and vice president, electors almost always cast their votes for their party's candidates.

The Constitution empowers the states to determine the manner of selecting their electors. Every state but Maine and Nebraska uses a winner-take-all election system. The entire slate of electors backing the winning presidential candidate earns the right to serve as the official set of electors, regardless of the margin of victory or whether the candidate won a majority of the state's vote. The states of Maine and Nebraska award electors based on

the total statewide vote *and* the vote in each congressional district. In 2008, Obama and McCain split Nebraska's five electoral votes 4—1. Obama earned one electoral vote because he had the most votes in the state's Second Congressional District. McCain took Nebraska's other four electoral votes by winning the First and Third Congressional Districts and having the most votes statewide.

**Electoral College** the system established in the Constitution for indirect election of the president and vice president.

**electors** individuals selected in each state to officially cast that state's electoral votes.

## Comparing two States with Equal Electoral Votes

**ELECTORAL VOTES: 3**

**ALASKA**
Land area: 663,267 square miles
Population: 683,478
Population density: 1.03 people per square mile

**DELAWARE**
Land area: 2,490 square miles
Population: 864,764
Population density: 442.6 people per square mile

When voters choose among candidates in November, they are actually casting their ballots for electors pledged to support particular presidential and vice-presidential candidates. In 32 states, the names of the electors do not even appear on the ballot. A California voter casting a ballot for Obama in 2008 was really voting for a slate of 55 electors pledged to vote for the Obama-Biden ticket for president and vice president. A McCain voter in California cast a ballot for a different set of 55 electors, a slate pledged to back the McCain-Palin ticket.

The Electoral College meets to vote for presidential candidates more than a month after the popular vote. In December, the electors selected on Election Day in November gather in their state's capital city to officially mark their ballots for president and vice president. The electors chosen by the voters of Georgia, for example, meet in Atlanta, that state's capital city. New York's electors gather in Albany, that state's capital. In January, Congress convenes in joint session (both chambers meeting together), opens the ballots, and announces the official outcome.

If no candidate receives a majority of electoral votes, Congress picks the president and vice president. The Constitution states that the House chooses the president from among the three presidential candidates with the most electoral votes. Each state delegation has one vote, and a majority (26 states) is needed for election. In the meantime, the Senate names the vice president from the top two vice-presidential candidates. Each senator has one vote and a majority is required for election.

The 2000 presidential election made the Electoral College the center of controversy. Al Gore won the popular vote because he piled up huge margins of victory in California and New York, whereas George W. Bush won other states by smaller margins. Gore carried California and New York, the two largest states he won, by a combined victory margin of 2.9 million votes. In contrast, Bush won Texas and Florida, the two states with the most electoral votes in his column, by a combined margin of only 1.4 million votes. Bush also benefited from the federalism bonus that awards every state three electoral votes (because of its two senators and one representative) regardless of size. Because Bush carried 11 of 18 smaller states, he won more electoral votes than he would have received on the basis of population alone.[43]

The critics of the Electoral College warn that the electors may vote for persons other than their party's presidential and vice-presidential candidates. Fewer than half the states legally require the electors to cast their ballots for their party's nominees. In 2004, for example, one Democratic elector from Minnesota cast an official presidential ballot for vice-presidential candidate John Edwards instead of John Kerry, apparently by accident because none of the state's ten electors

> Fewer than half the states legally require the electors to cast their ballots for their party's nominees

owned up to the action. The 2000 election was so close that two Bush electors could have changed the outcome had they switched their votes from Bush to Gore. Nonetheless, academic observers downplay the seriousness of this problem because most electoral vote margins are large enough that dozens of electors would have to change their votes to affect an election's outcome. Moreover, electors rarely prove unfaithful. Since 1789, only 10 out of nearly 22,000 electors have voted "against instructions."[45] None affected the outcome of an election.

Another criticism of the Electoral College is that Congress could end up picking the president and vice president. Although this procedure is set out in the Constitution, many Americans might be disturbed by the prospect of a chief executive

## btw...

Bush is not the only person to be elected president despite losing the national popular vote. In 1876, Samuel Tilden lost to Rutherford B. Hayes even though he received more popular votes than did his opponent. Similarly, Grover Cleveland won the popular vote in 1888 but lost the Electoral College—and the presidency—to Benjamin Harrison. The chances of a "wrong winner" electoral vote outcome are about one in three when the popular vote margin is 500,000 votes or fewer.[44] Nonetheless, election outcomes this close are rare. Only two other presidential races in the twentieth century had popular vote margins of fewer than 500,000 votes—the Kennedy-Nixon election in 1960 and the Nixon-Humphrey contest in 1968.

chosen through behind-the-scenes maneuvering. It might also weaken the office of the presidency by making the incumbent dependent on congressional selection.[46] In 1824, the last time Congress named the president, the selection of John Quincy Adams over Andrew Jackson was marred by dark rumors of a backroom deal. In recent years, the closest the nation has come to see-

president by ensuring that even fairly close presidential elections produce a clear winner. Even though Bill Clinton took only 43 percent of the popular vote in 1992, he won 69 percent of the electoral vote. The Electoral College turned a badly divided popular vote, split 43 percent for Clinton to 38 percent for Bush to 19 percent for Perot, into a one-sided Electoral

sometimes undermines the political legitimacy of a president. The outcome of the national Electoral College vote in 2000 depended on the result of the popular vote in Florida, which was too close to call. For more than a month, county canvassing boards, state officials, the Florida legislature, Florida judges, the Florida Supreme Court, and the U.S. Supreme Court struggled over ballot-counting issues. The outcome of the Florida vote ultimately hinged on the decision whether and how to count more than 40,000 ballots voting machines had failed to count. Many observers believed that a hand count of 40,000 additional ballots would give the election to Gore because most of the ballots were from counties that voted heavily for him. After a district court judge in Florida ruled against a hand count, the Florida Supreme Court, all of whose members were Democrats, voted 4—3 to order a hand count. Within less than a day, the U.S. Supreme Court voted 5—4 to halt the count. The five justices in the majority were all appointees of President Reagan or President George H. W. Bush, the father of the presidential candidate who benefited from the decision. Many observers believed that the involvement of the courts in the election outcome would undermine the legitimacy of the new president, regardless of the outcome of the dispute. Had Gore won because the Florida Supreme Court ordered a hand recount, Republicans would have charged that his victory was tainted by the intervention of a partisan court. As it were, many Democrats argued that Bush's election was illegitimate because of the intervention of a narrow partisan majority on the U.S. Supreme Court.

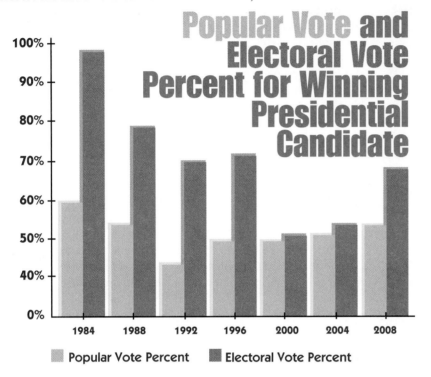

**Popular Vote and Electoral Vote Percent for Winning Presidential Candidate**

- ▮ Popular Vote Percent
- ▮ Electoral Vote Percent

ing an election go to Congress was in 1968, when independent candidate George Wallace won 46 electoral votes. Despite winning 19 percent of the popular vote in 1992 and 8.5 percent in 1996, Ross Perot won no electoral votes because he failed to carry any states.

The strength of the Electoral College is that it conveys political legitimacy to the winner in closely fought presidential elections. **Political legitimacy** is the popular acceptance of a government and its officials as rightful authorities in the exercise of power. If citizens and other public officials believe that a president lacks political legitimacy, the president will have difficulty exercising authority. The proponents of the Electoral College argue that it enhances the legitimacy of the

College victory. The morning after the election some newspapers even used the word *landslide* to describe Clinton's victory. The figure above compares the popular vote with the electoral vote percentage for the winning presidential candidate from 1984 through 2008. In every election, the winning candidate's electoral vote percentage was greater than the popular vote percentage, even in the 2000 election, when the Electoral College turned a popular vote loser into an Electoral College winner. The defenders of the Electoral College believe that it is beneficial because it gives the winning presidential candidate the appearance of the majority support necessary to be an effective president.

Nonetheless, the 2000 election showed that the Electoral College

In the aftermath of the 2000 election, some members of Congress proposed constitutional amendments

**political legitimacy** the popular acceptance of a government and its officials as rightful authorities in the exercise of power.

## FLORIDA RECOUNT

**271 to 266:** Electoral votes Bush ultimately won to Gore's final count

**25:** Electoral votes at stake in Florida

**537:** Votes that Bush officially exceeded Gore by in Florida, after all court cases

**40,000:** Ballots in selected counties where Gore supporters hoped to see manual recounts to determine voter intent

**4–3:** Florida Supreme Court jurors in favor of the recount versus those opposed

**5–4:** U.S. Supreme Court justices who voted to halt the recount versus those opposed

candidate with the most votes nationwide wins. They also think direct election would increase turnout because every vote would count equally regardless of the state in which it was cast.[47]

Nonetheless, direct election of the president has its detractors. Some critics complain that candidates would make fewer public appearances, concentrating even more on television than they do now. Other opponents fear that a proliferation of independent and minor-party candidates would undermine the legitimacy of the eventual winner. Once again, consider the 1992 presidential election. Had Clinton won the presidency based on 43 percent of the popular vote instead of 69 percent of the electoral vote, would his administration have enjoyed the same level of political legitimacy as it did with his solid Electoral College victory?

## The Fall Campaign

The goal of the general election campaign is to win 270 electoral votes. Each campaign targets states based on their electoral votes and the perception of the closeness of the race in the state and allocates campaign resources accordingly.[48] States with few electoral votes receive little attention from the candidates, whereas California, Texas, New York, Florida, and other large states are preeminently im-

portant. In recent presidential elections, Texas, California, and New York have seen relatively little campaign activity because they have not been politically competitive. The Republicans have dominated presidential races in Texas, whereas the Democrats have had a lock on California and New York. In contrast, Florida, Ohio, Pennsylvania, and Michigan have been battleground states.

Campaign funding rules are different for the general election period than they are during the primary season. Once the major party nominees are chosen, they are eligible for complete funding for the general-election campaign ($84.1 million in 2008). Candidates who accept the money may neither raise nor spend additional funds. In 2008, McCain accepted public financing, but Obama refused it because he thought he would be able to raise and spend more money than federal funding would have provided; he was right. Obama raised several hundred million dollars for the general election campaign, giving him a substantial financial advantage over McCain.

The presidential and vice-presidential debates are often the most publicized events of the fall campaign. Debates affect people's views of the candidates both because of the presentations made by the candidates themselves and because of media analyses.[49] Nonetheless, research shows that debates typically have little impact on election outcomes. The debate between John Kennedy and Richard Nixon is widely regarded as the turning point of the 1960 presidential race, but only because of the closeness of that contest.

Most campaign events, not just debates, have relatively little impact on the election outcomes because relatively few voters are open to persuasion. In 2004, more than 60 percent of the electorate decided how to vote before the national party conventions.[50] In 2008, 60 percent of the electorate decided how to vote

to abolish the Electoral College and replace it with direct popular election. The advocates of direct election point out that their system is simpler than the Electoral College and more democratic because it ensures that the

> In 2008, 60 percent of the electorate decided how to vote before the national party conventions. Only 10 percent of the 2008 electorate made their voting choice within a week of election day.

before the national party conventions. Only 10 percent of the 2008 electorate made their voting choice within a week of election day.[51]

The electorate includes both base voters and swing voters. **Base voters** are rock-solid Republicans or hardcore Democrats, firmly committed to voting for their party's nominee. In contrast, **swing voters** are citizens who could vote either way. Base voters typically outnumber swing voters by a large margin. In 2004, polling indicated that 42 percent of voters were the Democratic base; 45 percent were the Republican base. Only 13 percent could be classified as swing voters.[52] The base vote decides most elections. Bush won the 2004 election because his party had the larger base that year, and the Republicans did a better job than the Democrats at turning out their base. Swing voters make a difference only when the base vote for each party is nearly equal in size and one candidate or the other attracts a substantial majority of the swing vote. Political scientist William G. Mayer calculates that the swing vote was critical to the outcome of the close elections of 1976, 1980, 1992, and 2000, but other recent elections were decided by the base.[53] In 2008, voters identifying with the Democratic Party outnumbered Republican Party identifiers 39 percent to 32 percent, giving Obama a distinct advantage. Obama also capture 52 percent of independents, which represented 29 percent of the electorate.[54]

## Blue States, Red States, and the 2008 Election

Some political observers believe that the United States is deeply and closely divided along regional lines into Republican **red states** and Democratic **blue states,** so named because of the colors used on the Electoral College map to show states that went Republican (red) or Democratic (blue). In this view, red states are pro-gun, pro-life, anti-gay Christian conservative strongholds opposed to government regulation and high taxes, whereas blue states are secular liberal bastions that favor gun control, abortion rights, gay rights, and well-funded government programs aimed at alleviating societal problems.

President Bush won reelection by carrying every state in the South, every state in the Great Plains, and every state in the Rocky Mountain. Kerry won the Northeast and every state on the West Coast except Alaska. The two candidates split the Midwest. The 2004 electoral vote division closely resembled the 2000 election. The only states that flipped from one party to the other were New Mexico and Iowa, which went for Gore in 2000 but Bush in 2004, and New Hampshire, which switched from Bush in 2000 to Kerry in 2004.

In 2008, Obama broke out of the blue state–red state stalemate by winning a number of formerly red states. In addition to holding on to every state that Kerry took in 2004, Obama expanded his base in the Northeast by winning New Hampshire. He shored up his position in the Midwest, taking Ohio, Indiana, and Iowa. Obama made inroads in the South, the reddest region in the nation, winning Virginia, North Carolina, and Florida. Finally, he carved out a section of the Southwest, taking Colorado, New Mexico, and Nevada.

**base voters** rock-solid Republicans or hardcore Democrats, firmly committed to voting for their party's nominee.

**swing voters** citizens who could vote for either party in an election.

Vice President Richard Nixon and Senator John Kennedy met in the first televised presidential debate in 1960.

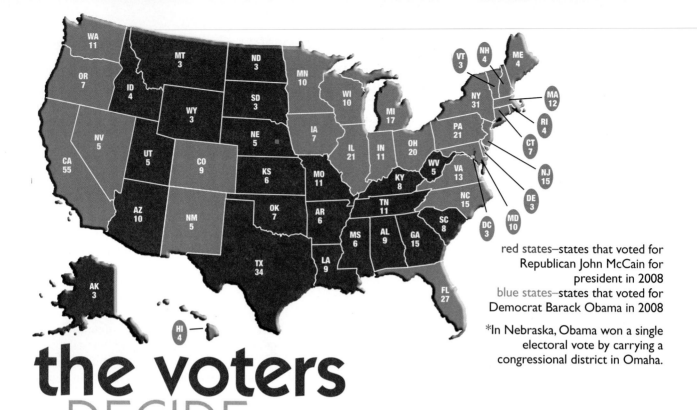

red states—states that voted for Republican John McCain for president in 2008
blue states—states that voted for Democrat Barack Obama in 2008

*In Nebraska, Obama won a single electoral vote by carrying a congressional district in Omaha.

# the voters DECIDE

**W**hy do voters decide as they do? Political scientists identify a number of factors influencing voter choice.

## Party Identification

Voter choice is closely related to political party identification.[55] Democrats vote for Democratic candidates; Republicans back Republicans. On average, 75 percent of voters cast their ballots for the candidate of the party with which they identify. In 2008, 89 percent of Republicans voted for McCain while 89 percent of Democrats backed Obama.[56] Keep in mind, however, that party identification is a complex phenomenon. People identify with one party or the other because they agree with its issue positions, have confidence in its leaders, or feel comfortable with groups associated with the party. When citizens decide to vote for Candidate A because Candidate A is a Democrat (or Republican), their choice is more than blind allegiance to a party label, it is also a response to the perceived issue positions and image of the party.

## Issues

Issues are almost as important as party identification in explaining voter preferences, especially for better informed voters.[57] Informed voters select candidates based on ideology and the issue positions of the candidates. Intense campaigns make it easier for citizens to obtain information, increasing the level of issue voting. Less well-informed voters fall back on party identification. Poorly informed voters and people who are ambivalent on parties and issues base their voting decisions on other factors, such as their judgment about the state of the economy.[58]

## Campaigns

Campaigns educate voters about candidates and issues.[59] Candidates who choose not to conduct a campaign or who lack the necessary funding to get their message across almost never win. Challengers for congressional seats who have less than a quarter million dollars to spend have less than a 1-percent chance of winning.[60]

Research shows that campaign tactics vary in effectiveness. Campaign advertising affects voters in concert with their party identification, making Democrats more likely to vote Democratic, and Republicans more likely to support GOP candidates. The issues that work best for the Democrats are education, childcare, and healthcare. In contrast, Republicans benefit when they can shift the issue focus to taxes, morality, economic growth, and foreign policy.[61]

Political scientists believe that election campaigns affect election outcomes, but they are not as important as the state of the economy and the political context in which the race is run. The three most important underlying factors affecting the outcome of a presidential race are the following: 1) the incumbent president's approval rating in the months before the election; 2) the growth rate of the economy in the quarter prior to the election; and 3) the length of time the president's party has held the White House.[62] All three of these factors worked against

**What are the most important qualities a candidate for president should have in order to get your vote?**

McCain in the 2008 presidential campaign. He was a Republican trying to keep his party's hold on the White House for the third election in a row despite incumbent President Bush's low approval rating and a serious economic downturn. In 2008, 71 percent of the voters told pollsters that they disapproved of the way Bush was handling his job, and two-thirds of them cast their ballots for Obama. Half the electorate described the economy as "poor" or "not so good"; 54 percent of them voted for Obama compared with 44 percent for McCain.[63]

## Retrospective and Prospective Voting

Citizens make voting decisions based on their evaluations of the past and expectations for the future.

**Retrospective voting** is the concept that voters choose candidates based on their perception of an incumbent candidate's past performance in office or the performance of the incumbent party. If voters perceive that things are going well, incumbent officeholders and their party usually get the credit. They get the blame, though, if voters think the situation is poor. The economy is the most important factor affecting retrospective voter, but war and peace matter as well.[64] In 2008, 75 percent of the electorate told survey researches that the country was "seriously off on the wrong track"; 62 percent of them voted for Obama.[65]

Voter evaluations of candidates have a prospective component as well. **Prospective voting** is the concept that voters evaluate the incumbent officeholder and the incumbent's party based on their expectations of future developments. One study finds that voter expectations of economic performance have a strong influence on voter choice.[66] Another study shows that voters reward or punish the president based on their view of the nation's economic prospects rather than the current standard of living.[67]

**retrospective voting** the concept that voters choose candidates based on their perception of an incumbent candidate's past performance in office or the performance of the incumbent party.

**prospective voting** the concept that voters evaluate the incumbent officeholder and the incumbent's party based on their expectations of future developments.

After setting a record high in October 2007, the Dow Jones Industrial Average, which is a standard measure of stock prices, lost nearly half its value by November 2008.

# CONCLUSION
# elections
# & PUBLIC POLICY

**e**lections play a significant role in the policymaking process.

## Agenda Building

Election campaigns focus public attention on issues and shape the policy agenda. Challengers identify issues that incumbents have rejected in hopes of convincing voters to turn the incumbent officials out of office. When challengers are successful, they have an incentive to address the issues they raised in the campaign or risk being accused of failing to deliver in the next election. Even when incumbents win reelection, they are likely to respond to the most popular issues raised by their challengers to prevent them from being used against them in future contests.[68]

**electoral mandate** the expression of popular support for a particular policy demonstrated through the electoral process.

## Policy Formulation and Adoption

Political commentators sometimes use the concept of electoral mandate to discuss the relationship between elections and public policy. An **electoral mandate** is the expression of popular support for a particular policy demonstrated through the electoral process. The concept of electoral mandate reflects the democratic ideal that elections enable citizens to shape the course of public policy by selecting candidates who endorse policies the voters favor. In theory, candidates and parties offer competing sets of policy proposals. The voters choose the set of policies they prefer, and the newly elected officials then proceed to enact the set of policies on which they campaigned. In other words, they have a mandate to carry out their policy proposals.

In the U.S., the relationship between elections and specific public policies is indirect at best. Election constituencies overlap. Whereas the president is chosen nationally through the Electoral College, senators and governors are elected in statewide elections. Members of the U.S. House and state legisla-

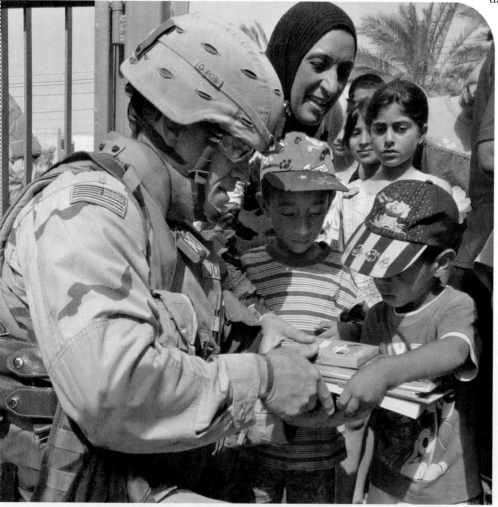

As conditions in Iraq improved throughout 2008, the war diminished in importance as an election issue.

tures are chosen from districts. One group of voters, desiring one set of policy outcomes, selects the president while other groups of voters, preferring other policy outcomes, elect members of the Congress.

Elections are fought over many issues. The war in Iraq, the war on terror, healthcare reform, taxes, global warming, gasoline prices, the federal budget deficit, and abortion all played a role in the 2008 presidential election contest between Obama and McCain. Races for Congress and the U.S. Senate featured those issues and others as well. Without a single dominant issue or a group of dominant issues, the election outcome cannot reflect clear policy preferences on the part of the electorate. Nonetheless, winning candidates often declare a mandate, claiming that their election signifies popular support of their policies. After President George W. Bush won reelection, he declared that his victory gave him the political capital he needed to push for Social Security reform.

Political scientists identify three ways in which elections influence policy. First, elections change the composition of the government. Elections do not make policy, but they select the people who do. Democrats and Republicans differ about the role of government. Furthermore, contrary to popular belief, research shows that candidates keep their campaign promises most of the time.[69] Second, policymakers calculate the electoral implications of policy positions and act accordingly. Public officials, concerned about their reelection and the future electoral prospects of their party, take policy actions with an eye on the next election. In short, elections make policy responsive to voters either through changing the occupants of government or by influencing officeholders to modify their policies to conform to the preferences of the electorate.[70] Finally, unexpected election results shock the political system, giving the impression of a mandate (whether voters intended one or not). The perception of a mandate is critical to overcoming the institutional barriers to policy change.[71]

**elections enable citizens to shape the course of public policy**

## Policy Implementation and Evaluation

Elections have an indirect influence on policy implementation. Public officials may interpret an election outcome as an indication that the voters want the government to implement a policy more or less aggressively. When the Republican Party lost seats in the House in the 1998 midterm election, many observers judged the outcome as an indication that the voters were unenthusiastic about the pending impeachment of President Clinton. Even though the House continued with the process and impeached Clinton, the Senate refused to remove him from office.

Elections are a means for citizens to evaluate the policy performance of government officials. The concept of retrospective voting is that citizens base their election decisions on their evaluation of the performance of incumbent officials. Indeed, the history of elections in America is one of the voters tossing officials out of office when they believe that government policies have failed, and reelecting incumbents when times are good. For example, an analysis of the 2006 midterm election suggests that the war in Iraq may have cost the Republican Party control of the U.S. Senate. According to a study conducted by political scientist Jeffrey E. Cohen, each additional death per 100,000 residents in a state reduced the Republican vote total by 14 percentage points. The 2006 midterm Senate elections were effectively a referendum on the president's Iraq War policy.[72]

# the THINKSPOT
www.thethinkspot.com

# TEST yourself

1. Luisa Cangelosi voted for the Republican candidate for president, the Democratic candidate for the U.S. Senate, and the Democratic candidate for the U.S. House. Ms. Cangelosi did which of the following?
   A. Violated the Voting Rights Act
   B. Voted in a presidential preference primary
   C. Voted a split ticket
   D. Voted in a primary election

2. State A limits primary voting to people who are registered party members. State A has which of the following?
   A. A closed primary
   B. An open primary
   C. A blanket primary
   D. A presidential preference primary

3. Which of the following elections is not conducted statewide at-large in most states?
   A. Election for governor
   B. Election for U.S. House
   C. Election for U.S. Senate
   D. Election for president

4. How often does reapportionment take place?
   A. Every ten years after the U.S. Census
   B. Every four years, to coincide with the presidential election
   C. Whenever population changes by more than 10 percent
   D. None of the above

5. *Baker v. Carr* (1962) and *Wesberry v. Sanders* (1964) dealt with which of the following issues?
   A. Gerrymandering
   B. Reapportionment
   C. Redistricting
   D. Voting Rights Act

6. Which of the following statements is true about the role of money in political campaigns?
   A. The candidate who spends the most money always wins.
   B. Advertising, especially television advertising, is the single largest expenditure in most campaign budgets.
   C. Candidates who provide most of their own campaign money usually win because they do not have to spend time fundraising.
   D. All of the above.

7. The Swift Boat Veterans for Truth is an example of which of the following?
   A. Interest group
   B. PAC
   C. 527 committee
   D. Political party

8. Federal funds are used to partially finance campaigns for which of the following offices?
   A. President
   B. U.S. House
   C. U.S. Senate
   D. All federal offices, including Congress and the president

9. Which of the following reasons helps explain why incumbent members of Congress typically win reelection?
   A. They usually have more money than their challenges.
   B. They are usually better known than their challengers.
   C. Many congressional districts are safe for one party or the other.
   D. All of the above.

10. Which of the following groups officially selected John McCain as the 2008 presidential nominee of the Republican Party?
    A. Delegates at the 2008 Republican National Convention by majority vote
    B. Electors from each state voting in the Electoral College
    C. Voters nationwide in an open primary
    D. Voters nationwide in a closed primary

11. How were the delegates to the 2008 Democratic National Convention chosen?
    A. They were chosen by the Congress.
    B. They were chosen by the Electoral College.
    C. They were chosen by each state party, either through a presidential preference primary or a party caucus.
    D. They were chosen in a national primary election.

12. Which of the following plays the most important role in selecting the presidential nominees of the Democratic and Republican parties?
    A. Party activists and party voters
    B. Party bosses
    C. Each party's congressional delegation
    D. Independent voters

**13** Why is doing well in the Iowa Caucus and the New Hampshire Primary important for candidates seeking their party's nomination for president?

A. Candidates who do well in both states benefit from large numbers of convention delegates.

B. Candidates who do well in both states benefit from a large amount of favorable publicity.

C. Candidates who do well in both states benefit from a large number of electoral votes.

D. All of the above.

**14** Which of the following statements about presidential electors is true?

A. They choose the party's presidential nominee at the national party convention.

B. They are elected officials, including members of Congress and state legislatures.

C. They are chosen by the state parties.

D. They select the president by a two-thirds vote.

**15** Alabama elects seven members of the House. How many electoral votes does Alabama have?

A. 7

B. 8

C. 9

D. 11

**16** Assume for the purpose of this question that a Democrat, a Republican, and a major independent candidate are running for president. In California, the Democrat gets 45 percent of the vote, the Republican gets 40 percent, and the independent receives the rest. How many of California's electoral votes will the Democratic candidate receive?

A. All of them

B. 45 percent of them

C. None of them

D. It depends on the outcome of the runoff between the Democrat and the Republican, the two top finishers.

**17** Under which of the following circumstances would Candidate A win the 2012 presidential election?

A. Candidate A wins a majority of the popular vote nationwide.

B. Candidate A carries more states than any other candidate.

C. Candidate A wins a plurality of the popular vote nationwide.

D. Candidate A wins a majority of the electoral vote.

**18** Which of the following is considered a red state?

A. New York

B. California

C. Texas

D. Illinois

**19** Which of the following statements is an expression of retrospective voting?

A. I voted for Candidate A because I like her promises and think she will do a good job in office.

B. I voted for Candidate B because he is a Republican and I am a Republican.

C. I voted for Candidate C because I agree with her on the issues.

D. I voted for Candidate D because I like the way things are going and he is the incumbent.

**20** Person A tells survey researchers that she is a committed Democrat who decided to vote for the Democratic nominee for president well before the party's national convention. Person A is an example of which of the following?

A. Base voter

B. Swing voter

C. Retrospective voter

D. Independent voter

## KNOW *the* **score**

18–20 correct: Congratulations! You are well informed!

15–17 correct: Your political knowledge is a bit low—be sure to review the key terms and visit TheThinkSpot.

<14 correct: Reread the chapter more thoroughly.

1. C; 2. A; 3. B; 4. A; 5. B; 6. B; 7. C; 8. A; 9. D; 10. A; 11. C; 12. A; 13. B; 14. C; 15. C; 16. A; 17. D; 18. C; 19. D; 20. A

# 10 CONGRESS

I n late 2005, the U.S. House of Representatives passed legislation aimed at enforcing the nation's immigration laws. A few months later, the U.S. Senate passed its own version of immigration reform.

Legislation cannot pass Congress unless both houses approve identical measures. When the House and Senate pass different bills addressing the same issue, congressional leaders often appoint a special congressional committee called a conference committee to negotiate differences on similar pieces of legislation passed by the House and Senate. The Senate was ready for the conference committee process on immigration reform, but the House leadership chose instead to hold a series of hearings and to attack the Senate bill. The Senate responded with hearings of its own, emphasizing the merits of the Senate approach. A few weeks before adjourning to campaign for the November 2006 election, Republican leaders in the House and Senate brought to a vote a bill to construct a 700-mile fence along the Mexican border and it passed easily. Congress failed to address other aspects of the issue.

The 2006 election failed to break the congressional deadlock over immigration reform. The Democratic Party won a majority of seats in both houses of Congress in the 2006 election, at least in part because of the failure of the Republicans to deal with illegal immigration. Nonetheless, the new Democratic Congress was no more willing or able to pass immigration reform legislation than the Republican Congress that preceded it.

The debate over immigration reform provides a backdrop for studying the U.S. Congress. It highlights the differences in the two chambers of Congress, illustrates the steps of the lawmaking process, and demonstrates the role of politics in the legislative process. This chapter examines the structure, membership, organization, and processes of the U.S. Congress. It explores the policymaking role of Congress using the struggle to pass immigration reform legislation to illustrate the dynamics of the process.

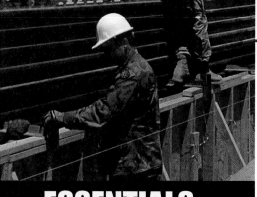

# bicameralism

**a**rticle I of the Constitution declares that the legislative power of the United States is vested in a **bicameral** (two-house) Congress, consisting of a Senate and a House of Representatives. Legislation does not pass Congress unless both the House and the Senate adopt it in identical form. The debate over immigration reform required policy agreement between the House and Senate, two distinctly different legislative bodies.

States enjoy equal representation in the U.S. Senate. The Constitution originally stipulated that each state be represented by two senators chosen by its state legislature. The Seventeenth Amendment, ratified in 1913, provided for the direct popular election of senators. Today, the 50 states elect 100 senators, running statewide to serve six-year staggered terms, with one-third of the Senate standing for reelection each election year. Because senators run for election statewide, they have more diverse constituencies than members of the House, most of whom run from relatively small districts.

The size of a state's delegation in the U.S. House depends on the state's population, but every state, no matter how small its population, must have at least one representative. In 1911, Congress capped the size of the House at 435 representatives. Today, the House membership also includes non-voting delegates from the District of Columbia, American Samoa, the Virgin Islands, and Guam, as well as a resident commissioner from Puerto Rico. Representatives run from districts for two-year terms, with the entire House standing for reelection every other year.

The Constitution assigns certain responsibilities exclusively to the Senate. The Senate ratifies treaties by a two-thirds vote. It confirms presidential appointments of federal judges, ambassadors, and executive-branch officials, all by majority vote. The only major appointment also requiring House approval is for the office of vice president. The Twenty-fifth Amendment provides that both the House and Senate

**bicameral** a two-house legislature.

The United States Capitol is the tallest building in Washington, D.C. In this photo of the East Front, the Senate is on the near right; the House of Representatives is at the other end of the building.

# HOUSE

**Members:** 435

Apportioned among the states by population

**Term length:** Two years

**Members must be:**
- 25 years old
- U.S. citizen for at least seven years
- Legal resident of their state

**Responsibilities:**
- Initiates revenue-raising bills
- Impeaches federal officials by majority vote

**Characteristics of Chamber:**
- Members are constituency specialists who are typically more partisan than are members of the Senate
- House is majoritarian in that it decides most issues by simple majority vote

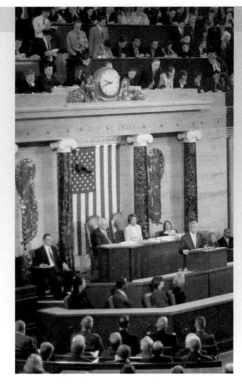

# SENATE

**Members:** 100

Two senators per state

**Term length:** Six years

**Members must be:**
- 30 years old
- U.S. citizen for at least nine years
- Legal resident of their state

**Responsibilities:**
- Ratifies treaties
- Confirms many presidential appointments
- Tries impeachment cases and can remove officials by a two-thirds vote

**Characteristics of Chamber:**
- Members are constituency generalists who are typically less partisan than are members of the House
- Senate frequently requires a super majority to conduct business

---

confirm the president's nominee for vice president if the office becomes vacant.

The Senate and House share other duties. Both chambers must vote by a two-thirds margin to propose constitutional amendments, and both houses must agree by majority vote to declare war. The government can neither raise nor spend money without majority approval of both chambers. The Constitution specifies that the House of Representatives can **impeach** (formally accuse) an executive or judicial-branch officeholder by majority vote. The accused official can be removed from office by a two-thirds vote of the Senate.

Because of their different constitutional structures and responsibilities, the House and Senate have developed into distinct legislative bodies. The Senate is often likened to a great debating society, where senators discuss the grand design of national policy. It is individualistic

think

**Would you rather be in the House or in the Senate? Why?**

and dependent on informally devised decision-making practices. Many of the decisions made in the Senate require the approval of a supermajority, a voting majority that is greater than a simple majority. Because the Senate conducts much of its business under agreements requiring the unanimous consent of its members, individual senators enjoy considerable power over the legislative process.[1] Furthermore, the rules of debate in the Senate allow a minority of 41 senators to extend debate endlessly, preventing a measure from ever coming to a vote.

The House of Representatives is a less prestigious body than the Senate. Members of the House have a reputation for devotion to technical expertise, personalized **constituency service**, and responsiveness to local political interests. Because of its size, the House is a relatively impersonal institution that depends on formal rules to structure the decision-

making process. In contrast to the Senate, the House makes decisions by majority vote. As long as a measure enjoys the support of a bare majority of the members of the House, its opponents are powerless to stop it.

The contrasting approaches taken to immigration reform by the House and Senate reflect the differences in the two legislative bodies. The Senate agreed on a balanced immigration reform plan because senators represent constituents holding a range of views. Most states include immigrant families concerned about the status of their relatives, business interests wanting to ensure an adequate supply of workers, low-skilled American workers worried about competition

**impeach** the act of formally accusing an official of the executive or judicial branches of an impeachable offense.

**constituency service** the action of members of Congress and their staffs attending to the individual, particular needs of constituents.

from illegal immigrants, and political activists on both sides of the issue. The Senate bill was able to attract enough votes to pass the Senate because it included something for everyone—tough border security, a pathway to legalization, employer verification of worker status, and a guest worker program. In contrast, the House passed a tough border security bill because most Republicans in the House were under heavy constituent pressure from conservative activists angry over illegal immigration. The Republican leadership in the House did not need to propose a balanced immigration reform bill or accept compromise because the chamber operates on a strict majority basis, and the leadership had enough votes to pass its bill. The House Republican leadership eventually decided that passing a bill to authorize construction of a fence along the border was preferable to passing a comprehensive immigration reform bill that would anger the party's core supporters.

# membership

the U.S. Constitution requires that members of the House be at least 25 years of age, American citizens for at least seven years, and residents of the state in which their district is located. Senators must be at least 30 years old, citizens for nine years, and residents of the state they represent. If disputes arise about qualifications or election results, each chamber of Congress determines the eligibility of its own members. The House and Senate can also expel a member for misconduct. In 2002, for example, the House of Representatives

think

**Are members of Congress fairly compensated for their service?**

voted to oust Ohio Congressman James Traficant, who had been convicted of corruption.

## Profile of the Membership

Because of the impact of the Voting Rights Act (VRA) and changing social and cultural values, Congress is more diverse than at any time in its history.[2] As recently as 1965, the year the VRA became law, only 6 African Americans and 4 Latinos served in Congress. In contrast, the 111th Congress, which took office in 2009, was relatively diverse. Sev-

Democrat Al Franken, a former *Saturday Night Live* cast member, won a U.S. Senate seat from Minnesota in 2008, defeating Republican Senator Norm Coleman by 312 votes out of more than 3 million ballots cast. Coleman contested the outcome in court, but conceded after the Minnesota Supreme Court unanimously upheld Franken's victory. Franken was sworn in to the Senate on July 7, 2009.

# Racial & Ethnic Makeup of the U.S. and Congress

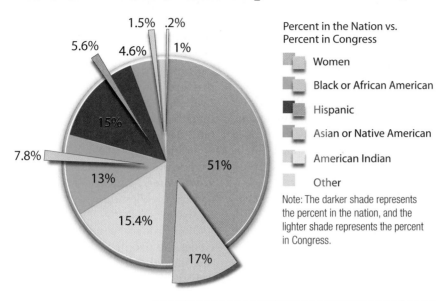

1.5%  .2%
5.6%  4.6%  1%
15%
7.8%
13%
15.4%
51%
17%

Percent in the Nation vs.
Percent in Congress

- Women
- Black or African American
- Hispanic
- Asian or Native American
- American Indian
- Other

Note: The darker shade represents the percent in the nation, and the lighter shade represents the percent in Congress.

In every case, minorities make up a larger percentage of the U.S. population than they represent in the current U.S. Congress.

enteen women, 2 Asian Americans, 3 Latinos, and 1 African American served in the Senate. The House of Representatives included 78 women, 39 African Americans, 27 Latinos, 7 Asian Americans, 1 Native American, 2 openly gay men, and 1 lesbian. Despite the influx of women and minority members over the last few decades, more than three-fourths of the members of the 111th Congress were white males of European ancestry.

Most members of Congress are older, affluent, established members of society. Almost every member of Congress is a college graduate and nearly two-thirds of the members hold advanced college degrees. Law and public service are the most popular professions, followed by business and education. Many members of the House and Senate are personally wealthy. The most commonly cited religious affiliations are Roman Catholic, Episcopalian, Methodist, Baptist, and Presbyterian. Most members of Congress have held elective office before coming to Congress. In the 111th Congress, the average age in the House was 57; it was 63 in the Senate.[3]

## Compensation

Congress determines the compensation of its members. In 2009, rank and file members of the House and Senate received $174,000 a year, with members of the leadership earning higher salaries. Under a federal law enacted in 1989, lawmakers get an annual cost of living raise unless both the House and Senate vote to block it.

In addition to their salaries, members of Congress have provided themselves with a number of perks. Senators and representatives have an allowance sufficient to cover regular trips home. They can also travel abroad for free on official business. Members enjoy free parking on Capitol Hill and at Washington, D.C. airports, free long-distance telephone use, and free postage for official correspondence—a perk known as the **franking privilege**. Members of Congress also benefit from a generous pension system.

## Personal Styles

Traditionally, members of Congress got things done and advanced their careers by building relationships with colleagues, deferring to senior members, and bargaining. New members of Congress, especially in the House, were expected to learn the ropes from more experienced members before speaking out on policy matters. They earned respect from their colleagues by specializing in a particular policy area rather than trying to have an impact on a broad range of issues. Members of Congress were expected to cooperate

**franking privilege** free postage provided to members of Congress.

## btw...

Congressional compensation is controversial. Some observers believe that high pay is needed to attract good people, but many critics argue that high salaries are unjustified considering the inability of Congress to solve some of the nation's most pressing problems. Although congressional salaries are more than adequate by most standards, senators and representatives earn less money than they would in private business, and most members of Congress must maintain two residences—one in Washington, D.C., and another in their district or state.

Senators Durbin and Schumer share this rowhouse with two congressmen to minimize expenses while they are in Washington.

# MEMBERS OF CONGRESS PERCEIVE MORE THAN ONE CONSTITUENCY WHOSE SUPPORT THEY CULTIVATE

with one another, exchanging favors and engaging in **logrolling**, an arrangement in which two or more members of Congress agree in advance to support each other's favored legislation. The ideal lawmaker was someone who regarded the House or Senate as a career rather than a stepping-stone to higher office.[4]

In today's Congress, individual members have greater latitude than did their predecessors. Some members are skilled media entrepreneurs, using policy issues to gain media coverage so they can establish themselves as national political figures. They are less interested in passing legislation than in advancing their own political careers. Other members use the media to promote their legislative agendas. Through news conferences, press releases, televised speeches on C-Span, and other staged media events, they influence the legislative agenda, define policy alternatives, and shape public opinion about proposed legislation.[5]

## Home Styles

Most members of Congress believe that they have a responsibility to "vote their district," that is, take policy positions in accordance with the views of the majority of their constituents. Senators and representatives know that if they stray too far and too frequently from the policy preferences of the majority of their constituents, they may pay the price at the ballot box. Future elec-

tion opponents will accuse them of "losing touch" with the folks back home and charge them with voting against the interests of the state or district.[6] Consequently, members of Congress stress their local ties, go home often, and spend considerable time in their districts.[7]

Political scientist Richard F. Fenno points out that members of Congress perceive more than one constituency whose support they cultivate. The Geographic Constituency includes everyone who lives within the boundaries of a state (for a senator) or congressional district (for a representative). In sheer numbers, the Geographic Constituency is the largest—but the least important—constituency to the member of Congress because it includes many people who do not vote or who consistently support candidates of the other party.

The Reelection Constituency is those voters who support the senator or representative at the polls in general elections. It consists of loyal party voters and swing voters, in-

cluding independents and people who identify with the other party but are willing to vote for candidates of the opposing party under certain circumstances. Incumbent members of Congress focus on this constituency, especially in districts that are competitive between the two major political parties. Representatives and senators who potentially face strong general election opposition often take moderate policy positions to win the support of swing voters, who are usually less conservative/less liberal than core party voters.

The Primary Constituency includes the people who would back the incumbent against a serious challenger in a party primary. Although any senator or member of Congress could face a primary election challenge, members of Con-

**logrolling** an arrangement in which two or more members of Congress agree in advance to support each other's favored legislation.

## SAFE DISTRICTS AND CONGRESSIONAL PARTISANSHIP

| ELECTION YEAR | NO. CLOSE HOUSE RACES (decided by a margin of 10 percentage points or less) | AVERAGE WINNING PERCENTAGE |
|---|---|---|
| 1992 | 111 | 64 |
| 1994 | 87 | 67 |
| 1996 | 80 | 64 |
| 1998 | 43 | 71 |
| 2000 | 42 | 69 |
| 2002 | 34 | 70 |
| 2004 | 31 | 69 |
| 2006 | 58 | 66 |

Congressional partisanship is more intense today than it was 20 or 30 years ago because most members of Congress win election from districts that are safe for candidates from their political party.

Center for Responsive Politics, www.opensecrets.org

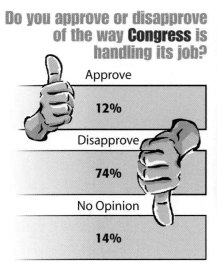

## Do you approve or disapprove of the way **Congress** is handling its job?

Approve
**12%**

Disapprove
**74%**

No Opinion
**14%**

Illinois Governor Rod Blagojevich was discussing his plan for filling President-elect Barack Obama's vacant Senate seat: "I've got this thing and it's [expletive] golden, and I'm just not giving it up for [expletive] nothing." Unfortunately for the governor, the FBI was recording the conversation as part of a criminal investigation into allegations that he was trying to sell the appointment. The FBI arrested Blagojevich and charged him with fraud and conspiracy to solicit bribes. According to the U.S. Constitution, the governor of a state with a Senate vacancy calls a special election. Alternatively, the state legislature can empower the governor to appoint a temporary replacement to serve until a permanent replacement is chosen in the next general election. After the governor's arrest, the Illinois legislature debated whether to impeach and remove Blagojevich so that a new governor could appoint a senator or pass legislation to hold a special election in 2009. Before the legislature acted, however, Blagojevich announced the appointment of former Illinois Attorney General Roland Burris, who had not been implicated in the bribery scheme. After some hesitation, the U.S. Senate accepted the appointment and Burris replaced Barack Obama, not just as a senator but as the body's only African American member.

gress who represent districts that are solidly Democratic or Republican are unlikely to have serious opposition in any election other than the primary. Consequently, GOP members of Congress from safe districts often take more conservative policy positions than Republicans from competitive districts because they want to cultivate the support of Republican primary voters, who tend to be more conservative than the electorate as a whole. For similar reasons, Democrats from safe districts are frequently more liberal than Democrats representing swing districts.[8] Congressional partisanship is more intense today than it was 20 or 30 years ago because most members of Congress win election from districts that are safe for candidates from their political party.[9]

Members of Congress shore up constituent support through constituency service, actions taken by members of Congress and their staffs to attend to the individual, particular needs of constituents. Citizens sometimes ask senators or representatives to resolve problems with federal agencies, such as the Social Security Administration (SSA) or the U.S. Citizenship and Immigration Services (USCIS). Constituents may ask members and their staffs to supply information about federal laws or regulations. Also, local civic clubs and other organizations frequently invite members of Congress to make

public appearances at functions in their districts or states and meet with various groups of constituents about problems of local concern. Studies show that constituency service boosts the standing of an incumbent member of Congress with constituents regardless of their party affiliation or political ideol-

## Do you approve or disapprove of the way **your representative** is handling his/her job?

Approve
**43%**

Disapprove
**31%**

No Opinion
**26%**

CBS NEWS/NEW YORK TIMES POLL,
October 14, 2008.
http://www.cbsnews.com/htdocs/pdf/
Oct08b-economy.pdf

ogy.[10] Furthermore, incumbents benefit from a ripple effect in increased popularity among people who hear about these services from friends, relatives, or neighbors.[11]

## Membership Turnover

Members of Congress seeking reelection are usually successful, especially members of the House. Over the last 50 years, the reelection rate is 93 percent for House members and 80 percent for senators.[12] Members of Congress win reelection despite the general unpopularity of Congress because the voters make a distinction between the performance of their representative and the performance of Congress as an institution. Polls consistently show that the voters like their own member of Congress even when they disapprove of the actions of Congress as a whole.[13]

Despite relatively high reelection rates, Congress experiences significant turnover. In the 111th Congress, the average tenure for members of the House was 11 years; it was 13 years for members of the

Senate.[14] Turnover is greater than statistics on incumbent reelection success rates suggest because many members decide not to seek reelection. Some members retire, some quit to run for higher office, and some leave Congress to pursue other opportunities, including work as lobbyists. For example, Representative Billy Tauzin of Louisiana, the former chair of the House Ways and Means Committee and the principle author of the Medicare prescription drug benefit, retired from Congress to become president of the Pharmaceutical Research and Manufacturers of America, the chief lobby group for brand-name drug companies. It was estimated that Tauzin would earn $2 million a year or more from his new job.[15]

# organization

the organization of the House and Senate is based on political party.

## Organization of the Floor

The "floor of the House" and "floor of the Senate" are the large rooms in which the members of each chamber assemble to do business. As a practical matter, the **floor** refers to the full House or full Senate taking official action. The organization of the floor refers to the structures that organize the flow of business conducted by the House or Senate as a whole.

The organization of the floor is based on party strength in each chamber. In the 111th Congress, the Democratic Party controlled both the House and the Senate. Democrats outnumbered Republicans in the House, 257 to 178. The party balance in the Senate was 58 Democrats, 40 Republicans, and two independents, both of whom voted with the Democrats to organize the chamber, effectively giving the Democrats a 60–40 advantage.

Although the Constitution designates the vice president as the Senate's presiding officer, the legislative role of the vice president is relatively unimportant. The vice president may not address the Senate without permission of the chamber and votes only in case of a tie, which is rare. During eight years as vice president, Al Gore cast only four tie-breaking votes in the Senate. More often than not, the vice president attends to other tasks, leaving the chore of presiding over the Senate to others.

The **Senate president pro tempore** is officially the presiding officer of the Senate in the vice president's absence. The Senate as a whole selects the president pro tempore, customarily electing the senator from the majority party with the greatest length of service, or **seniority**, in the chamber. The Senate president pro tempore in the 111th Congress was Democrat Robert Byrd of West Virginia. In practice, the post of Senate president pro tempore is more honorary than substantive, and the rather tedious chore of presiding in the Senate is usually left to junior members of the majority party.

The **Senate majority leader** and the **Speaker of the House** are the most important legislators in their respective chambers. The Senate majority leader and the Speaker appoint members to special committees and influence assignments to stand-

IN **SNL**'S '08 PRESIDENTIAL BASH,

Jason Sudeikis's Senator Joe Biden tells the audience that he has succeeded in the Senate because he has reached across the aisle to people like John McCain, whom he characterized as "a raging maniac . . . and a dear, dear friend." Senator Biden was head of the powerful Senate Foreign Relations Committee when he was elected vice president. The influential McCain has headed such important committees as the Senate Commerce Committee.

**floor** the full House or full Senate taking official action.

**Senate president pro tempore** the official presiding officer in the Senate in the vice president's absence.

**seniority** length of service.

# ORGANIZATION AND LEADERSHIP

## SENATE

## HOUSE

**VP** *JOE BIDEN*
**PRESIDENT *PRO TEMPORE*>**
*ROBERT BYRD*
**(D, WV)**

The vice president and Senate president *pro tempore* are constitutionally the presiding officers of the Senate, but, in practice, their role is more ceremonial than substantive.

**SPEAKER:** *NANCY PELOSI* >
**(D, CA)**

The Speaker of the House is the presiding officer. The entire House membership selects the Speaker, but because almost all members vote for their party's candidate, the Speaker is invariably the leader of the majority party.

**< MAJORITY LEADER**
*HARRY REID* **(D, NV)**

**MAJORITY WHIP**
*DICK DURBIN* **(D, IL)**

The majority leader controls the business of the Senate. The whip is an assistant floor leader.

**< MAJORITY LEADER**
*STENY HOYER* **(D, MD)**

**MAJORITY WHIP**
*JAMES E. CLYBURN* **(D, SC)**

The majority party also has a majority leader and a majority whip to direct the agenda and votes on the floor.

**MINORITY LEADER >**
*MITCH MCCONNELL* **(R, KY)**

**MINORITY WHIP**
*JON KYL* **(R, AZ)**

The minority leadership works to define a party program in their chamber, plan strategy, and, frequently, oppose the initiatives of the majority party leadership. The minority party in the Senate often has policy influence because of the filibuster, especially if it is united or the majority party is divided.

**MINORITY LEADER >**
*JOHN BOEHNER* **(R, OH)**

**MINORITY WHIP**
*ERIC CANTOR* **(R, VA)**

The minority party in the House seldom has policymaking influence, at least not if the majority party is united or nearly united, because the House works on a strictly majority basis. The minority party leadership speaks out on policy issues and plans strategy in hopes of eventually winning majority control of the chamber.

---

While the vice president and president *pro tempore* have largely ceremonial powers, the other congressional leaders have real power to direct how and when legislation reaches the floor.

---

ing committees. They refer legislation to committee and control the flow of business to the floor. These latter two powers are especially important for the Speaker, who can use them to control the timing of legislation and determine the policy options available to House members voting on the floor. Although the Speaker cannot force passage of unpopular legislation, he or she can usually prevent consideration of a measure that he or she opposes, even when the measure enjoys enough support to pass the full House if it were to come to a vote.

The Senate majority leader and the Speaker hold positions of high visibility and great prestige, both in Congress and the nation. As party leaders, they work with fellow party members in Congress to set policy goals and to assemble winning coalitions. They consult widely with various party factions, working to compromise differences among party members and to maintain party unity. As national political leaders, the Senate majority leader and Speaker publicize the achievements of Congress, promote their party's positions in the media, and react to presidential initiatives.

Because party leadership posts are elective, the Senate majority leader and Speaker maintain their power by helping members achieve their goals: reelection, influence in national politics, policy enactment, and election to higher office. Party leaders create political action committees (PACs) to raise and distribute campaign money to fellow party members running for reelection. By playing the campaign money game, party leaders can support their parties in Congress while building personal loyalty among party members.[16]

The Speaker and majority leader are political party leaders, working

**Senate majority leader** the head of the majority party in the Senate.

**Speaker of the House** the presiding officer in the House of Representatives and the leader of the majority party in that chamber.

**majority whip** the majority leader's first assistant.

**whips** assistant floor leaders in Congress.

**House majority leader** the second-ranking figure in the majority party in the House.

**minority leader** the head of the minority party in the House or Senate.

**minority whip** the minority leader's first assistant in the House or Senate.

to advance their parties' policy interests and to maintain their majority. Democrats favor liberal policies; Republicans prefer conservative policies. When the Democratic Party controls Congress, the leadership promotes liberal policy alternatives while preventing the consideration of conservative bills (and vice versa when Republicans control). Although a Democratic majority in Congress cannot ensure the enactment of liberal legislation, it can usually prevent the passage of conservative measures.[17]

Consider the fate of immigration reform legislation in 2006. The measure that passed the House was a Republican bill. Republican lawmakers supported the bill overwhelmingly, with 203 voting for it compared with 12 who voted against it. Only 36 Democrats voted for the measure compared with 164 who opposed it. In the Senate, immigration reform had bipartisan support although most Democrats voted for the bill and most Republicans voted against it. Senate Democrats supported the measure by a count of 38 to 4, whereas Republicans voted 23 in favor of the bill and 32 against it.[18] House Republican leaders refused to consider the Senate ver-

sion of immigration reform in a **conference committee** because they did not want to advance a bill that a majority of Republican members of the House opposed.

The majority leadership wants to avoid scheduling votes on legislation that divides the base of the party. Immigration reform proved too hot to handle for Democratic congressional leaders in 2007 and 2008 because the issue divided the party base. Many Latinos and liberal activists favor comprehensive

immigration reform that provides a pathway to citizenship for immigrant families that have lived in the United States for years. Many working-class white and African American Democrats are concerned about an influx of immigrant labor driving down wage rates. Democratic members of Congress preferred avoiding the issue to casting a vote that would upset important parts of their electoral base.

Members of Congress have a strong incentive to cooperate with their party leadership because their success is tied to the success of their political party, especially in the House. In the current Congress, Democrats want to maintain their majority, whereas Republicans want to become the majority. Members of the majority party chair all committees and subcommittees, and have a greater opportunity for input on the details of legislation, at least in the House where the majority party tightly controls deliberations in committee and on the floor. Furthermore, the election prospects of senators and members of the House from competitive districts depend at least in part on the standing of their political party in the eyes of the voters.[19]

The role of the minority party leadership in the House and Senate is similar to that of the majority party leadership with some important exceptions. The **minority leader** and the **minority whip**

**MEMBERS OF CONGRESS HAVE A STRONG INCENTIVE TO COOPERATE WITH THEIR PARTY LEADERSHIP BECAUSE THEIR SUCCESS IS TIED TO THE SUCCESS OF THEIR POLITICAL PARTY**

work to define a party program in their chamber, plan strategy, and unite party members behind party positions. As with the Senate majority leader and the Speaker, the Senate and House minority leaders may become media spokespersons for their party. In practice, minority party leaders spend

These two girls stare through the border fence from Mexico. They were separated from their parents, who had made it across the fence earlier.

a good deal of time working to help their party become the majority party by recruiting candidates, raising money, and planning strategy. Fundraising ability has even become an important criterion in each congressional party's leadership selection process.[20]

Because of their party's minority status, the leadership of the minority party lacks the influence that their majority party counterparts enjoy, especially in the House. Although the majority leader in the Senate and the Speaker of the House may consult with the minority party leadership on bill scheduling, the authority to control the flow of business to the floor lies with the majority party leadership. Furthermore, the ability of the minority leadership in the House and Senate to influence legislative policy is limited by their party's minority status, especially in the House of Representatives, where the rules enable a simple majority to conduct business. As long as the majority party in the House is united or nearly united, depending on the size of its majority, it can pass legislation without having to compromise with the minority party. Because the rules of the Senate allow a minority of senators, or sometimes even a single senator, to delay or defeat legislation, the minority party leadership plays a more substantive legislative role in the Senate than in the House. The immigration reform bill that passed the House was a Republican measure, written without Democratic input. In contrast, the Senate bill was a bipartisan compromise, supported by both Democrats and Republicans.

The style of party leadership in Congress depends to a large degree on the occupant of the White House. When the opposition party controls the White House, congressional leaders act independently from, and frequently in opposition to, the White House. They scrutinize presidential appointments, aggressively investigate policy missteps, and critically evaluate presidential initiatives. In contrast, Congressional leaders usually have a positive relationship when the same party controls both the legislative and executive branches of government. Republican congressional leaders worked closely with President Bush to enact his policy proposals, especially during his first term. The Senate approved most of the president's nominees and generally sheltered the administration from investigatory scrutiny over such matters as the war in Iraq and the government's response to Hurricane Katrina. Bush had considerably less success in his dealings with Congress in his second term because his public approval rating fell. Republicans in Congress decided that it was more important to take positions designed to help with their own reelections even if it meant failing to support their party's president. After the 2006 election, Bush faced a Congress controlled by the Democrats.

**conference committee** a special congressional committee created to negotiate differences on similar pieces of legislation passed by the House and Senate.

This stretch of the U.S.–Mexico border fence separates Nogales, Arizona, from Nogales, Mexico.

# The Indian Parliament

The Indian Parliament is bicameral. The lower chamber, which is called the Lok Sabha, has 545 members chosen from districts apportioned among the Indian states on the basis of population. Rajya Sadha, the upper chamber, has 250 members elected from the states also on the basis of population, except that small states enjoy somewhat more representation than their population would merit.

Lok Sabha is the more important of the two chambers. It has exclusive authority on bills dealing with spending, taxation, and borrowing. Lok Sabha more often than not gets its way on other measures as well. When the two chambers disagree on the content of legislation, they meet in joint session and decide by majority vote. The larger size of Lok Sabha gives it the advantage.

The Indian Parliament, similar to most legislative bodies in democracies other than the United States, does not usually initiate major legislative proposals. In a parliamentary system, most legislative proposals come from the prime minister and the cabinet. The legislative role of Parliament is limited to scrutinizing and revising the details of legislation. Parliament rarely defeats government-sponsored legislation because Indian law mandates party discipline. Legislators who vote against their party's official position lose their seats unless one-third or more of a party's members defect. The law then assumes that the party has split and a new party is formed.

Despite party discipline, the Indian Parliament has the ability to hold the government accountable for its actions. When Parliament is in session, the legislative day begins with an hour in which the members question cabinet ministers about government policies. The sessions allow opposition lawmakers the opportunity to criticize government policies and to put cabinet ministers on the spot. Furthermore, a majority of the members of Lok Sabha can bring down the government by voting "no confidence." A no-confidence vote leads to the dissolution of Parliament and the holding of new elections.

## Questions to Consider

1. In what way is the relationship between the two chambers of the Indian Parliament similar to the relationship between the U.S. House and Senate?

2. Would party discipline make the U.S. Congress more or less democratic?

3. Which legislative body plays the greater policymaking role, the U.S. Congress or the Indian Parliament? What is the basis of your answer?

Indian legislators walk past their parliament building in New Delhi, India's capital.

# Committee and Subcommittee Organization

The detailed work of Congress takes place in committees. The advantage of the committee system is that it allows Congress to divide legislative work among a number of subgroups while giving individual members the opportunity to specialize, developing expertise in particular policy areas. The disadvantage of the committee system is that the division of broad issues into smaller sub-issues may impede the development of comprehensive and coordinated national policy.

A **standing committee** is a permanent legislative committee with authority to draft legislation in a particular policy area or areas. The House Agriculture Committee, for example, deals with subjects related to agriculture, including rural economic conditions, crop insurance, agricultural trade, commodity futures trading, agricultural research and promotion, conservation, farm credit, welfare and food nutrition programs, and food safety inspection. The jurisdiction of the Senate Foreign Relations Committee includes matters relating to American national security policy, foreign policy, and international economic policy.

In addition to standing committees, Congress has special or select committees and joint committees. A **special or select committee** is a committee established for a limited time only. A **joint committee** is a committee that includes members from both houses of Congress. In contrast to standing committees, joint committees and special or select committees do not usually have the legislative authority to draft legislation. They can only study, investigate, and make recommendations.

Committees are divided into subcommittees. Not all committees have subcommittees, and not all bills are referred to subcommittee, but in the House in particular, subcommittees have become the center of legislative work. For example, the House Ways and Means Committee, which deals with tax issues, trade, and Social Security, has six subcommittees, each of which addresses a different aspect of the committee's responsibilities.

When senators and representatives are first elected, they request assignment to standing committees that they believe will 1) help them win re-election, 2) gain influence in national politics, and 3) affect policy. Committees dealing with money qualify

**standing committee** a permanent legislative committee with authority to draft legislation in a particular policy area or areas.

**special or select committee** a committee established for a limited time only.

**joint committee** a committee that includes members from both houses of Congress.

A bridge on Interstate 35W collapsed in Minneapolis, Minnesota, in August 2007. Federal officials fast-tracked the replacement bridge because of its importance as a transportation link. The Minnesota legislature voted a special gas tax to provide funding for the bridge's quick replacement.

on all three counts and are in great demand. The money committees in the Senate are Appropriations, Budget, and Finance. In the House, the committees dealing with money are Appropriations, Budget, and Ways and Means. The other Senate committees that are considered prestigious assignments are Foreign Relations, Armed Services, and Judiciary.[21] In the House, members want to serve on the Energy and Commerce Committee because it deals with a broad range of important legislation. The Transportation and Infrastructure Committee is popular as well, because members see it as a way to procure projects for their districts. Senators and representatives frequently request assignments on committees that deal with policy issues particularly relevant to their states and districts. Members of Congress from urban and financial centers are attracted to the banking committees; members from agricul-

**think**

**Which congressional committee would you choose? Explain your answer.**

tural states favor membership on the agricultural committees. Finally, some members of Congress request particular committee assignments for personal reasons. For example, members of the House with prior military service may seek membership on the Armed Services Committee.[22]

Party committees in each chamber make committee assignments for members of their party. Party leaders control these committees and, in theory, they could use them to reward friends and punish enemies. In practice, however, the party committees try to accommodate the preferences of members. If members are unhappy with a committee assignment, they may request a transfer when openings occur on committees they prefer. Committee switching is not especially common, particularly among senior members, because members who change

committees must start over on the seniority ladder of the new committee. Nonetheless, it is not unusual for members to request transfer to one of the really choice committees.

The majority party controls each committee and subcommittee. Before the 2006 election, the Republican Party was the majority party in the House and Senate. Republicans comprised a majority of the membership of each committee and subcommittee and chaired every committee and subcommittee in both chambers. In 2006, the Democrats won majorities in both houses of Congress and the roles of the parties reversed. Beginning in 2007, Democrats made up a majority of every committee and subcommittee and Democrats chaired every committee and subcommittee.

Each party has its own procedures for selecting committee chairs (for the majority party) and ranking members (for the minority party). Republican Party rules stipulate that the party committee that makes initial committee assignments nom-

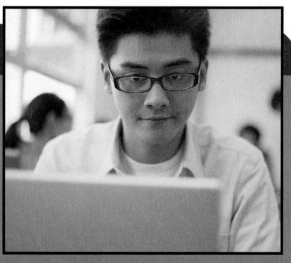

## takeaction

### IN-PERSON LEARNING >>

**Sending E-mail to Your U.S. Representative**

Your assignment is to participate in America's democracy by sending an e-mail message about a current policy issue to the man or woman who represents you in the U.S. House. You can find the name and e-mail address of your U.S. representative online at www.house.gov. The following guidelines will help you write an effective letter:

- Know what you are writing about. If you do not understand an issue, your message will have little impact. You may choose an issue discussed in the textbook or another topic in the news. Be sure, however, that you have researched the issue sufficiently to speak about it intelligently.
- Use correct grammar. E-mail messages filled with grammatical errors and misspelled words will not have a positive impact.

- Make your point clearly and succinctly. Present your opinion and give the reasons behind your position in no more than a few paragraphs. Long, rambling messages are ineffective.

Print the e-mail message and submit a copy to your instructor. Your instructor will not grade you on your point of view, but will evaluate your work on the criteria stated above.

inates chairs or ranking members with confirmation by the **party caucus**, which is all of the party members of a chamber meeting as a group. The Republicans select chairs or ranking members based on party loyalty and ability to raise campaign money for party candidates, rather than using seniority as the basis for selection.[23] Each Republican member of the House is expected to contribute money to the party's campaign fund. Party members who fail to meet their financial obligations will be passed over for leadership positions.[24] Democrats, meanwhile, provide for the selection of committee chairs and ranking members by a secret-ballot vote of the party caucus. The Democrat with the most seniority on a particular committee usually wins the vote, except on those rare occasions when a senior member has alienated his or her colleagues. Both parties limit chairs and subcommittee chairs to six-year terms.

Veteran Pennsylvania Senator Arlen Specter switched from the Republican Party to the Democratic Party in early 2009, primarily because he thought he would have a better chance to win reelection in 2010 running as a Democrat. Specter's defection gave the Democrats 60 seats, enough to halt a Republican filibuster if they all voted together.

**party caucus** all of the party members of the House or Senate meeting as a group.

# the legislative
## PROCESS

the traditional image of the legislative process is that a member introduces a bill, it is referred to committee, it goes from committee to the floor, from the floor to a conference committee, and, if it passes every step, to the president. Since the early 1990s, the legislative process has not conformed to the traditional to the traditional "bill-becomes-a-law" formula. Congress has adopted modifications in the traditional legislative process to pass major legislation. The key differences between the traditional model and the new model of legislative policymaking are the following:

- Major legislation is often written in the form of **omnibus bills**, which are complex, highly detailed legislative proposals covering one or more subjects or programs. The immigration reform measure that passed the House included border security provisions, criminalization of illegal immigration status, sanc-

tions against people who assist the undocumented, and a tighter worker verification process for employers. The Senate bill contained border security, a guest worker program, employee verification, and a pathway to citizenship for unauthorized residents. Congressional leaders assemble omnibus bills to attract as much support as possible.

- Major legislation is frequently referred to more than one standing committee. Involving several committees in the legislative process provides a measure's supporters with an opportunity to draft legislation that enjoys a broader base of support. Furthermore, the strategy avoids the danger of a hostile committee chair bottling up the bill, which

SINCE THE 1940s, THE LENGTH OF THE AVERAGE BILL HAS INCREASED FROM 2.5 PAGES TO MORE THAN 19 PAGES

sometimes happens to measures referred to only one committee.

- The legislative leadership, especially in the House, coordinates the work of the standing committees and sets timetables to move legislation through the committee stage.
- The legislative leadership, especially in the House, fashions the details of the legislation and develops a strategy for winning passage on the floor. Even after a bill clears committee, the leadership may change its provisions to broaden its base of support.
- A conference committee of dozens, maybe even hundreds, of members works out the final

**omnibus bills** complex, highly detailed legislative proposals covering one or more subjects or programs.

compromise language of the bill. Once again, the goal is to build a broad-enough coalition of support for the measure to ensure its passage.[25]

## Introduction

In the 110th Congress, members introduced 14,042 bills and resolutions—9,419 in the House and 4,623 in the Senate.[26] A **bill** is a proposed law. Except for revenue raising bills, which must begin in the House, any bill may be introduced in either chamber. A **resolution** is a legislative statement of opinion on a certain matter. Resolutions may be introduced in either chamber. A member who introduces a measure is known as its **sponsor**. Bills and resolutions may have multiple sponsors, known as co-sponsors. Over the years, legislative measures have grown longer and more complex. Since

the 1940s, the length of the average bill has increased from 2.5 pages to more than 19 pages.[27] Omnibus bills are far longer. The No Child Left Behind Act, the education reform measure enacted in 2002, was 670 pages long.[28]

## Committee and Subcommittee Action

Once a bill or resolution is introduced, it is assigned a number and referred to committee. A measure introduced in the House has the initials "H.R." for House of Representatives, whereas Senate measures begin with the "S." for Senate. The immigration reform measure passed by the House was H.R. 4437. (The number signifies the order in which a measure was introduced.) The sponsors of a bill also give it a popular title designed to put the measure in a favorable light. Representative James F. Sensenbrenner,

Jr., the House sponsor of immigration reform, called his bill the Border Protection, Antiterrorism, and Illegal Immigration Control Act. The chamber parliamentarian, working under the oversight of the Speaker of the House or the Senate majority leader, refers the measure to a committee based on the subject covered by the bill or resolution.

Complex issues such as healthcare, immigration reform, international trade, and homeland security often cut across committee jurisdictions. Sometimes committees develop arrangements to cooperate or

**bill** a proposed law.

**resolution** a legislative statement of opinion on a certain matter.

**sponsor** a member who introduces a measure.

**THE GATEKEEPERS**

**COMMITTEES ARE GATEKEEPERS** IN THE LAWMAKING PROCESS, KILLING MOST OF THE BILLS AND RESOLUTIONS REFERRED TO THEM. IN THE 110TH CONGRESS, CONGRESSIONAL COMMITTEES REPORTED 1,764 MEASURES TO THE FLOOR OF 14,042 BILLS AND RESOLUTIONS INTRODUCED, FOR A REPORT RATE OF 12.6 PERCENT. THE FOLLOWING MEASURES ARE MOST LIKELY TO RECEIVE DETAILED COMMITTEE AND SUBCOMMITTEE CONSIDERATION:

- MEASURES THAT COMMITTEE AND SUBCOMMITTEE CHAIRS PERSONALLY FAVOR.
- MEASURES THAT HAVE THE SUPPORT OF THE CONGRESSIONAL LEADERSHIP.
- MEASURES THAT ENJOY BROAD SUPPORT IN CONGRESS AS A WHOLE.
- MEASURES THAT BENEFIT FROM THE BACKING OF IMPORTANT INTEREST GROUPS.
- MEASURES THAT DEAL WITH ISSUES THAT MANY MEMBERS OF CONGRESS AND A LARGE SEGMENT OF THE GENERAL PUBLIC CONSIDER IMPORTANT.
- MEASURES THAT ARE PUSHED BY THE WHITE HOUSE.

IN CONTRAST, MEASURES THAT LACK SUPPORT, OR ARE OPPOSED BY THE COMMITTEE OR CONGRESSIONAL LEADERSHIP, SELDOM EMERGE FROM COMMITTEE.

# Congressional War Power

**Should Congress have more control over U.S. military power? If so, could this harm the United States' ability to act in times of immediate crisis?**

**Has history run its course in such a way that the executive should keep its increased war-making power? Is it necessary in times when the United States faces an enemy without borders and a conventional military?**

**Overview:** The American founders believed that the predisposition to engage in war lay with the executive power, and that it was through war that nations ended up in tyranny. The founders believed that the decision to go to war should be made by the legislative branch because, in democratic theory, it is the legislative branch that represents the will of the people.

The Constitution does not exactly delineate between congressional and executive war powers. The founders assumed that power would shift between the branches as conditions demanded, but over the course of American history, it is the president's office that has assumed considerable constitutional discretion in how the United States engages in war and diplomacy. For example, James Madison would not go to war with Great Britain in 1812 without a war declaration from Congress, yet the last seven major American conflicts (Korea, Vietnam, First Gulf War, Kosovo, war on terror, Afghanistan, and Iraq War) were and are conducted without declarations of war.

With the September 11, 2001 attacks on American soil, the U.S. government has fundamentally shifted traditional defense policy. The Bush Doctrine holds that the United States will use preemptive military force, if necessary, for national defense. Furthermore, it is undisputed that the United States is now considered the "hyperpower," that is, the sole nation capable of projecting military and economic might anywhere on the globe. This opens up many constitutional and moral questions. What is the proper forum for national debate in regard to this shift in defense strategy? How, then, will future American force be used? For all practical purposes, has the military power of the Congress been assumed by the executive branch? What is to be the role of Congress? These questions promise to be at the forefront of defense policy debate for the foreseeable future.

## supporting increased congressional control over military matters

**the founders believed the decision to go to war should be left to the American people.** With the exception of invasion or extraordinary circumstances, the founders believed Congress is the proper venue to discuss and debate matters of war and peace, as Congress is considered the direct representative of the American people.

**some American foreign policy has been harmful to American interests.** Executive use of the war power has harmed U.S. interests; take, for example, the Vietnam War. President Johnson used his authority to increase military involvement based on faulty intelligence, and President Nixon used U.S. military force against nations (Cambodia and Laos) with whom America was not at war.

**in the post-9/11, post–Cold War world, Congress more than ever needs to supervise U.S. military activity.** With the United States' new foreign policy doctrine of preemption, it is imperative that Congress be consulted to ensure that the use of military force is just and absolutely necessary.

## against increased congressional control over military matters

**declarations of war are a relic of the eighteenth century.** With the speed of modern conventional weapons, Congress does not have the time to respond to current military threats. Additionally, the nature of America's enemies has changed—for instance, how does a nation declare war on terrorist organizations whose political and military base transcends borders?

**Congress has not abdicated its military power; it has failed to exercise its constitutional prerogatives.** The Constitution gives Congress the authority to authorize military expenditures, thus limiting the war-making power of the executive. For example, the new Democratic-controlled House of Representatives passed a war funding bill linking military spending with a timetable to withdraw troops from Iraq.

**the Constitution does not explicitly state that a declaration of war is necessary for the use of American Forces.** Some constitutional scholars argue that simple congressional resolution is sufficient for Congress to satisfy its Article I obligations.

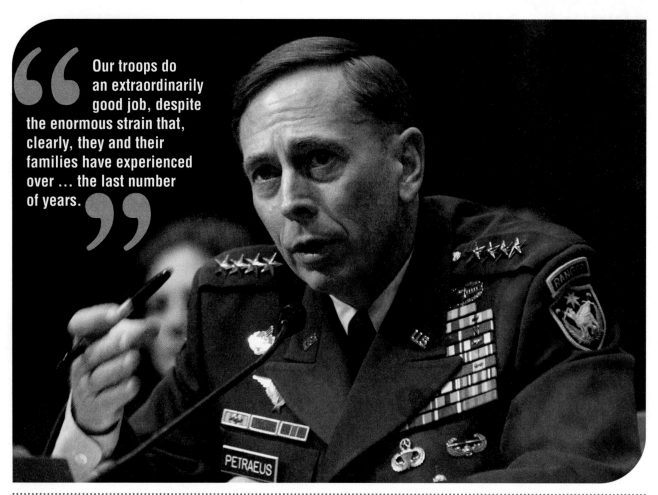

"Our troops do an extraordinarily good job, despite the enormous strain that, clearly, they and their families have experienced over ... the last number of years.

General David Petraeus testifies before Congress in support of continuing operations in the Iraq War. He was confirmed by the Senate as head of the Central military command, directing U. S. forces in East Africa, the Middle East, and Central Asia.

defer to one another.[29] At other times, the leadership employs **multiple referral of legislation,** which is the practice of assigning legislation to more than one committee. The Senate permits joint, sequential, and partial referrals of legislation. House rules allow only sequential and partial referrals, and one committee may be designated the committee of primary jurisdiction. The Speaker makes multiple referral decisions in the House. In the Senate, multiple referral of legislation requires the unanimous agreement of the chamber. Multiple referral of legislation is more common in the House than in the Senate and is more likely to be used for major legislation than routine measures. Although most multiple referrals go to only two committees, complex measures may be referred to several committees. Four com-

mittees considered immigration reform in the House, including Judiciary, Homeland Security, Education and the Workforce, and Ways and Means.

Committees and subcommittees do the detailed work of Congress. Once a measure is sent to committee or subcommittee, the chair and the ranking minority member ask their staffs to prepare separate reports on its merits. For major legislation, the committee or subcommittee chair schedules hearings to allow the measure's supporters and opponents a chance to make their case. Full committees generally conduct Senate hearings; subcommittees hold most hearings in the House.

The next step is **legislative markup**. This is the process in which legislators go over a measure line-by-line, revising, amending, or

rewriting it. In the House, markup usually takes place in subcommittee. Markup in the Senate generally occurs in full committee.

Once markup is complete, the subcommittee, and then the full committee, vote on whether to recommend passage. If the measure is voted down at either stage or members vote to **table** it (that is, postpone consideration), it is probably dead, at least for the session. If the measure is

**multiple referral of legislation** the practice of allowing more than one committee to consider legislation.
**legislative markup** the process in which legislators go over a measure line-by-line, revising, amending, or rewriting it.
**table** to postpone consideration of a measure during the legislative process.

approved in subcommittee and committee, the next step is the floor of the full House or Senate.

The rules of the House provide a mechanism for members to bring to the floor a bill that has been tabled or defeated in committee. However, the procedure is seldom used and almost never successful. A bill's supporters can compel a committee to report a measure to the floor by means of a **discharge petition**, in which a majority of the members of the House of Representatives force a committee to report a bill to the floor of the House. Since 1910, only three measures forced from committee through the use of a discharge petition eventually became law.[30] Most members of Congress are reluctant to sign a discharge petition because they do not want to undermine committee authority. Furthermore, the threat of a discharge petition is sometimes enough to stimulate a committee to act on stalled legislation.

## Floor Action

In the House, the process for moving measures from committee to the floor varies, depending on the type of measure involved. The House considers noncontroversial measures of relatively minor importance through a shortcut procedure on designated special days set aside for that purpose. Budget resolutions and **appropriation bills** may go directly from committee to the House floor.

The leadership may bring major pieces of legislation to the floor without committee consideration or with only cursory committee examination. If a measure was carefully studied in committee in the last session of Congress, the leadership may determine that no more committee work is necessary. Sometimes, the leadership wants to move quickly for political reasons. In 2005, the House leadership put legislation on a fast track to provide aid for people affected by Hurricane Katrina, moving it directly to the floor without committee consideration.[31]

## SOMETIMES THE LEADERSHIP WANTS TO MOVE QUICKLY FOR POLITICAL REASONS

Most measures that clear standing committee must go to the Rules Committee before going to the floor. The **House Rules Committee** is a standing committee that determines the rules under which a specific bill can be debated, amended, and considered on the House floor. Because more measures clear committee than the full House has time to consider, the Rules Committee determines which measures go forward. Measures that are not assigned rules are not considered on the House floor and therefore have no chance of passage unless supporters can succeed in forcing the legislation out of the Rules Committee by means of a discharge petition.

When the Rules Committee refers a bill to the floor, it sets a time limit for debate and determines the ground rules for amendments. Debate in the House is defined by the rule under which a measure is considered. The Rules Committee limited debate on the immigration reform bill to two hours, divided equally between proponents organized by the chair of the Judiciary Committee and opponents organized by the committee's ranking member. The Rules Committee also sets the terms for consideration of amendments, including identifying which amendments may be offered, who may propose amendments, and the order in which amendments may be considered. A rule that opens a measure to amendment on the House floor without restriction is an **open rule**. In contrast, a **closed rule** is a rule that prohibits floor consideration of amendments on the House floor. The measure must be voted up or down without amendment. In practice, both open rules and strict closed rules are rare. Nearly two-thirds of rules are at least somewhat restrictive. For most major pieces of legislation, the Rules Committee grants restrictive rules that limit the consideration of amendments to certain specific alternatives. Restrictive rules also determine the order of consideration for amendments.[32]

**discharge petition** a procedure whereby a majority of the members of the House of Representatives can force a committee to report a bill to the floor of the House.

**appropriation bill** a legislative authorization to spend money for particular purposes.

**House Rules Committee** a standing committee that determines the rules under which a specific bill can be debated, amended, and considered on the House floor.

**open rule** a rule that opens a measure to amendment on the House floor without restriction.

**closed rule** a rule that prohibits floor consideration of amendments on the House floor.

**think**

**Does the Rules Committee in the House have too much power?**

Rules are a means for structuring debate on the House floor. Rules allowing choice among comprehensive substitute bills focus debate on big choices rather than the details of legislation. Rules can also prevent a measure's opponents from forcing votes on the most unpopular provisions of a bill or offering amendments that the leadership opposes.[33] The Rules Committee is an important element of the Speaker's power. In contrast to other House committees, the Speaker personally appoints the majority party members of the Rules Committee subject to approval by the party caucus, thereby ensuring control. The Speaker uses the Rules Committee not only to determine which measures reach the floor, but also to structure the policy choices available to members on the floor.

**The Rules Committee is an important element of the Speaker's power.**

In the Senate, a measure typically reaches the floor through the mechanism of a unanimous consent agreement (UCA), which is a formal understanding on procedures for conducting Senate business that requires acceptance by every member of the chamber. UCAs, like rules from the Rules Committee in the House, limit debate and determine the amendments that can be offered. Because a single senator can prevent the adoption of an agreement, UCAs reflect negotiation between the Senate leadership and the membership to consider the needs of every member. A member who objects to a UCA is said to have placed a hold on the measure. Members can work through the Majority Leader's secretary to place holds anonymously, but that approach is rare. Often the purpose of a hold is to force some sort of concession, sometimes on an unrelated piece of legislation. The majority leader may choose to bring the measure to the floor despite the hold, but the motion to

proceed may face a **filibuster,** an attempt to defeat a measure through prolonged debate. If that fails, the bill itself may be filibustered.

Nonetheless, senators usually get their legislation to the floor. A senator can often obtain unanimous consent by accepting policy compromises or by threatening to oppose the legislation favored by the measure's opponents. A senator can also bring a measure to the floor by offering it as an amendment to another bill. Senate rules allow consideration of non-germane amendments, unrelated to the subject matter of the original measure. For example, Senator James N. Imhofe of Oklahoma offered an amendment to the Senate immigration reform bill to declare English the official language of the United States. The amendment passed.[34] Non-germane amendments are not allowed in the House.

Senators may offer a **killer amendment,** an amendment designed to make a measure so unattractive that it will lack enough support to pass. Opponents of term limitation, which Congress considered in 1995, offered an amendment that would count time already served in the calculation.

Prominent southern senators discuss strategy for their filibuster of the 1964 Civil Rights Act. The filibuster failed, and the Civil Rights Act was signed into law by President Lyndon Johnson.

If it passed, many members of Congress would effectively have voted themselves out office.[35] Senators sometimes propose unrelated amendments in order to promote their particular policy views or embarrass their political opponents.

Floor proceedings are more structured in the House than in the Senate. Although House members can delay action through parliamentary maneuvers, the Rules Committee system generally ensures that House proceedings move forward. In contrast, the rules of the Senate maximize the rights of individual senators. One senator or a group of senators may use these rules to produce chaos on the Senate floor.

Jimmy Stewart plays a filibustering senator in the 1939 classic film *Mr. Smith Goes to Washington.*

Indeed, senators sometimes take advantage of the rules to defeat legislation they oppose. Senate rules do not limit the amount of time a senator, or the chamber as a whole, can discuss a measure, so a bill's opponents may filibuster. Under Senate rules, each senator who wishes to speak must be recognized and cannot be interrupted without consent. The Senate cannot vote on a piece of legislation until every senator has finished speaking.[36]

The procedure for ending a filibuster is known as **cloture**. Senators wanting to halt a filibuster must announce their intentions and gather the signatures of a sixth of the Senate, 16 senators, to force a vote on cloture, which, in turn, requires a three-fifths vote of the Senate membership (60 votes) to succeed. Although Senate rules limit post-cloture debate to 30 hours, a measure's opponents often delay action even longer through parliamentary maneuvering.

Filibusters have grown more common. From 1955 to 1960, the Senate experienced only two filibusters.[37] In contrast, recent sessions of Congress have averaged 28

filibusters each, with half of all major pieces of legislation facing a filibuster or a serious threat of a filibuster.[38] The filibuster is a potent weapon. Since 1970, the passage rate for legislation subject to filibuster has been 54 percent compared to a 74 percent passage rate for measures not filibustered.[39]

The nature of the filibuster has changed as well. In the 1950s and 1960s, Senators conducting a filibuster engaged in long-winded debate. Today, classic filibusters are a thing of the past. Senators simply announce their intention to filibuster, and the Senate goes on with other business while the leadership works to gather sufficient support to invoke cloture. Sometimes, Senate leaders file a cloture petition to end debate even before a filibuster materializes. The Senate invoked cloture to end the debate on immigration reform despite the absence of an organized filibuster against the measure.

## Conference Committee Action

A measure does not pass Congress until it clears both the House and Senate in identical form. If the House and Senate pass similar, but not identical bills, the chamber that initially passed the measure can agree to the changes made by the other chamber, or the two houses can resolve their differences by adopting a series of reconciling amendments. When the differences between the two measures are too great for easy resolution, the two chambers create a conference committee. Although Congress resorts to the conference committee process for only about 10 percent of the measures that ultimately become law, conference committees are typical for major legislation.[40]

The Speaker and the Senate majority leader appoint the members of a conference committee (called **conferees**) from lists given to them by committee leaders. Although the Speaker and majority leader can appoint any member, they almost always select members of the standing committee or committees that considered the bill, including the committee chair(s) and ranking member(s). If the Speaker and majority leader are concerned that the conferees may not uphold the position of the majority party, they may also appoint members who are sympathetic to the party's position.[41] Because of omnibus bills, the size of conference committees has grown, sometimes including dozens or even hundreds of members.

A conference committee is sometimes called the third house of Congress because it writes the final version of legislation. The conferees are not bound to stick with the version of the measures passed by either the House or the Senate. The conference committee can delete

**Floor proceedings are more structured in the House than in the Senate.**

**cloture** the procedure for ending a filibuster.

**conferees** members of a conference committee.

ANYBODY ELSE CARE TA SEE IF AH'M RELEVANT?!!

S·CHIP

veto

THE SALT LAKE TRIBUNE  BAGLEY '07

President George Bush vetoed the State Children's Health Insurance Program, saying the bill was too costly.

provisions passed by both houses and include provisions passed by neither. In practice, the final version of major legislation reflects a compromise among the party leadership in each chamber, the president, and key interest groups. Each chamber's conferees vote separately. Once a majority agree on a compromise, the revised measure, called the conference report, goes back to the floor of the House and Senate. The first chamber to vote on the conference report has three options: to accept, reject, or return to conference for more negotiations. If the first chamber accepts the measure, the second chamber has two options, to adopt or reject. If both chambers accept the conference report, the measure goes to the president.

## SUCCESS RATE OF BILLS IN THE 110TH CONGRESS

INTRODUCED: 14,042
REPORTED: 1,764
(12.6% OF ALL INTRODUCED)
ENACTED INTO LAW: 416
(3% OF ALL INTRODUCED, 23.6% OF ALL REPORTED)

## Presidential Action

If the president signs a measure, it becomes law. If the president does not sign the measure, it becomes law anyway after ten days unless Congress is adjourned, in which case it dies. When a president allows a measure to die without signature after Congress has adjourned, it is known as a **pocket veto**.

If the president opposes a measure he can use his **veto,** the refusal to sign a measure passed by the legislature. A president vetoes a bill by returning it to Congress with a statement of objections. Congress needs a two-thirds vote of each house to override the president's veto and enact the measure into law. Should either house fall short of two-thirds, the veto is sustained, and the measure has failed. Over the last century, presidents have vetoed about 1 percent of the measures reaching their desks, with Congress overriding only about 7 percent of those vetoes.[42]

The president must accept or reject a measure in its entirety. Congress takes advantage of this situation by passing omnibus bills combining provisions the president wants with measures the president would veto were they standing alone. A **rider** is a provision, unlikely to become law on its own merits, which is attached to an important measure so that it will ride through the legislative process. Appropriation bills are favorite vehicles for riders because they are must-pass legislation. For example, Congress enacted a prohibition against smoking on commercial airline flights as a rider attached to an appropriation measure.[43]

Modifications in the legislative process adopted to increase the likelihood that major legislation will become law have been effective. Although the overall success rate for bills is poor, a majority of the major pieces of legislation considered by Congress become law. In the 110th Congress, only 416 bills out of 14,042 measures introduced in the House and Senate became law, for a success rate of 3 percent.[44] In contrast, major pieces of legislation fare much better. Over the last decade, 59 percent of major bills have become law.[45]

**pocket veto** the action of a president allowing a measure to die without signature after Congress has adjourned.

**veto** an action by the chief executive refusing to approve a measure passed by the legislature.

**rider** a provision, unlikely to become law on its own merits, that is attached to an important measure so that it will ride through the legislative process.

# CONCLUSION
# congress
# & PUBLIC POLICY

**a** long with the presidency, Congress is the foremost policymaking institution of American national government.

## Agenda Building
Congress plays an important role in agenda building. Although many of the issues that Congress addresses were first raised by other political actors, Congress increases an issue's visibility by holding hearings and conducting debates. In recent years, Congress has helped focus attention on such issues as immigration reform, campaign finance reform, global warming, and Internet privacy.

## Policy Formulation and Adoption
Congress formulates policy through the legislative process. The policy formulation process in Congress usually involves competition among political interests. The outcome of that process may reflect compromise among those interests or the triumph of one set of interests over other interests, depending on the relative political strength of competing groups.

Congress participates in policy adoption when it passes legislation, ratifies treaties, confirms appointments, and proposes constitutional amendments. In each of these situations, Congress shares policy adoption authority with other political actors. Legislation passed by Congress does not become law unless it is signed by the president or passed by a two-thirds margin over a presidential veto. Treaties cannot be ratified or appointees confirmed unless they are first proposed or nominated by the president. Constitutional amendments must be ratified by three-fourths of the states.

## Policy Implementation and Evaluation
Congress uses the authorization process and the budget process to influence policy implementation. Congress typically authorizes the creation of agencies or programs for a limited number of years, after which the agency or program must be reauthorized. Executive branch officials, knowing that their agencies and programs face periodic reauthorization, have an incentive to conform to the wishes of Con-

**CONGRESS PARTICIPATES IN POLICY ADOPTION WHEN IT PASSES LEGISLATION, RATIFIES TREATIES, CONFIRMS APPOINTMENTS, AND PROPOSES CONSTITUTIONAL AMENDMENTS**

gress as they implement policy.[46] Similarly, Congress uses the budget process to influence policy implementation. Executive officials want to stay on the good side of Congress because Congress controls their budgets.

Finally, Congress evaluates policy. Congress, as a whole, evaluates programs when problems persist or when the media publicize scandals in administration. Standing committees provide legislative oversight. The appropriation committees scrutinize agency spending. Congress sometimes uses the feedback from policy evaluation to formulate and adopt policy revisions.

# the THINK SPOT
## www.thethinkspot.com

225

# TEST yourself

1. What happens if the House and Senate pass different versions of a bill to address a particular policy issue but cannot agree on compromise legislation?
   A. The president creates a conference commission to negotiate a compromise.
   B. The measure fails because nothing passes Congress unless both the House and Senate pass it in identical form.
   C. The Supreme Court determines which measure becomes law.
   D. The House bill goes to the president for signature.

2. Which of the following statements better describes the House than it does the Senate?
   A. It makes decisions strictly by majority vote.
   B. It has a tradition as a great debating society where members enjoy broad freedom to voice their points of view.
   C. It is an individualistic body where one member has considerable influence on the legislative process.
   D. All of the above.

3. Which of the following statements better describes the Senate than the House?
   A. Every member stands for reelection every two years.
   B. A minority of members has the power to bring legislative business to a halt in the chamber.
   C. Members of this chamber sometimes run for seats in the other chamber.
   D. None of the above.

4. The office of Congresswoman Martinez helps a district resident resolve a problem with the Social Security Administration. The action was an example of which of the following?
   A. Filibuster
   B. Logrolling
   C. Closed rule
   D. Constituency service

5. Which of the following statements about congressional turnover is *not* true?
   A. Most members of Congress are reelected.
   B. The reelection rate for House members is higher than it is for senators.
   C. Congress experiences significant turnover because term limits restrict members of the House and Senate to no more than 12 consecutive years in office.
   D. Voters typically express a higher level of approval for their representative in Congress than they do for the institution as a whole.

6. In practice, which of the following officials is the most important leader in the U.S. Senate?
   A. Speaker of the House
   B. Senate president *pro tempore*
   C. Senate majority leader
   D. Vice president

7. Which of the following officials is the most important leader in the U.S. House?
   A. Speaker of the House
   B. Senate president *pro tempore*
   C. Senate majority leader
   D. Vice president

8. How is the Senate majority leader selected?
   A. By vote of the members of the majority party in the Senate
   B. By popular vote in a national election
   C. By the president
   D. He or she is the longest served member of the majority party in the Senate

9. What was the party affiliation of the chair of the House Ways and Means Committee in 2008?
   A. The chair could have been a Democrat or Republican depending on which member of the committee had the most seniority.
   B. The chair would be a Republican because the president was Republican.
   C. The chair would be a Democrat because Democrats won a majority in the House in the 2006 election.
   D. The chair could be a Democrat or a Republican depending on which member of the committee won a vote of the committee membership.

10. In the current Congress (elected in 2008), which of the following individuals is a Republican?
    A. Senate minority leader
    B. Speaker of the House
    C. Chair of the House Committee on Appropriations
    D. Each official could be either Republican or Democrat

11. Why do major legislative measures often take the form of omnibus bills, which are complex, highly detailed legislative proposals covering one or more subjects or programs?
    A. Complex problems require complex solutions.
    B. Government is so big that legislation must deal with a broad range of policy areas.
    C. Congress is in session only part of the year and omnibus bills enable it to get more done in a short period of time.
    D. Congressional leaders assemble omnibus bills in order to attract as much support as possible.

**12** Which of the following individuals has the authority to introduce a bill in the U.S. Senate?

A. A senator

B. A member of the House

C. The president

D. All of the above

**13** The detailed work of Congress takes place at which point in the legislative process?

A. On the floor

B. In committee

C. In conference committee

D. In the Rules Committee

**14** Legislative markup occurs at which stage of the legislative process?

A. On the floor

B. In committee

C. In conference committee

D. In the Rules Committee

**15** What is the purpose of a discharge petition?

A. It is the process that is used to end a filibuster.

B. It is a demand that a member of Congress be expelled for misconduct.

C. It is a procedure used to force a committee to report a bill to the floor of the House.

D. It is the beginning of the impeachment process.

**16** What is the purpose of a closed rule?

A. It prohibits consideration of amendments to a bill on the floor of the House.

B. It is a procedure for ending a filibuster.

C. It is a means of coordinating the work of committees when a bill is multiply referred.

D. It is a procedure used to force a committee to report a bill to the floor of the House.

**17** An amendment designed to make a measure so unattractive that it will lack enough support to pass is known as which of the following?

A. Discharge petition

B. Non-germane amendment

C. Killer amendment

D. Cloture petition

**18** The Senate is considering a controversial measure. How many votes will the measure's supporters need to ensure passage in the chamber?

A. Legislation passes by majority vote.

B. It takes a two-thirds vote to pass bills in the Senate.

C. It takes 60 votes to invoke cloture and overcome a filibuster.

D. It takes 40 votes to invoke cloture.

**19** A conference committee agrees on a conference report. It passes the House, but it fails to pass the Senate. What is the status of the bill?

A. The measure goes to the president.

B. The measure is dead unless Senate reconsiders it and passes it.

C. The House votes again on the measure and if it passes again, it goes to the president.

D. The president convenes a reconciliation committee involving the leadership of both the House and Senate.

**20** Congress passes a bill that the president generally favors with the exception of one provision. What are the president's options?

A. The president can ask a conference committee to rewrite the bill.

B. The president can ask the Supreme Court to revise the bill.

C. The president can veto the offensive provision while signing the rest into law.

D. The president can sign or veto the bill in its entirety.

1. B; 2. A; 3. B; 4. D; 5. C; 6. C; 7. A; 8. A; 9. C; 10. C; 11. A; 12. D; 13. B; 14. B; 15. C; 16. A; 17. C; 18. C; 19. B; 20. D

Mike Keefe THE DENVER POST 4·29·09

Few presidents have entered the White House facing as many pressing issues as Barack Obama. When Obama took office, he inherited a set of pressing problems from his predecessor, including:

- The most severe economic downturn since the Great Depression;
- A financial crisis threatening the solvency of the banking industry;
- The looming bankruptcy of the American automobile industry;
- A large and growing **budget deficit**, which is the amount by which annual budget expenditures exceed annual budget receipts; and
- Ongoing wars in Iraq and Afghanistan, as well as the continuing war on terror.

During the 2008 election campaign, Obama promised healthcare reform and action to address climate change in addition to promising to end the war in Iraq.

The challenge for the president was to determine how best to move forward. Should he tackle the most pressing problems left over from the Bush administration and postpone addressing healthcare reform and climate legislation, or should he attempt to address everything at once? On one hand, presidents are seldom more influential than they are in their first year in office. New presidents typically enjoy a period of good will from a public willing to give them the benefit of the doubt. On the other hand, tackling multiple complex problems at once poses the risk of policy overload. Could Congress and the White House formulate and adopt policies dealing with the economy, healthcare, climate change, and other issues in less than a year?[1]

President Obama decided to address all of the issues in his first year. The success of his presidency would likely depend on the outcome.

# PRESIDENCY

## ESSENTIALS...

*after studying Chapter 11, students should be able to answer the following questions:*

> What is the constitutional presidency in terms of qualifications and backgrounds, term of office, impeachment and removal, succession, and disability?

> What are the constitutional powers of the presidency, and how have those powers expanded beyond the constitutional outline of the office?

> What is the organization of the White House staff and the Executive Office of the President?

> What are the various perspectives on presidential leadership and presidential power taken by political scientists?

> What factors affect presidential popularity?

> What is the role of the presidency in America's policy process?

# the constitutional
## PRESIDENCY

the Constitution describes the office of the presidency in Article II.

## Qualifications and Backgrounds

The Constitution declares that the president must be at least 35 years of age, a natural-born American citizen (as opposed to a naturalized citizen), and a resident of the United States for at least 14 years. Before the 2008 election, all the nation's presidents had been white males of Western European ancestry. Two sets of presidents were father and son (John and John Quincy Adams and George and George W. Bush); two were grandfather and grandson (William Henry and Benjamin Harrison); and two were cousins (Theodore and Franklin D. Roosevelt). All but Roman Catholic John Kennedy have been Protestant Christians. Most presidents have been fairly wealthy; the majority of them have been experienced politicians. Most presidents have come from states outside the South. In recent years, however, social barriers have begun to fall as the nation has elected a Roman Catholic (Kennedy), three native Southerners (Jimmy Carter, Clinton, and George W. Bush), and a divorced person (Ronald Reagan) to the White House. The election of Barack Obama, the son of a white woman from Kansas and a black immigrant from Kenya, shattered the barriers of race and ethnicity. Furthermore, Hillary Clinton's strong showing in the race for the Democratic presidential nomination suggested that gender was no longer a major barrier to the White House. The myth that anyone born in the United States could grow up to become president came closer to reality than ever before in the nation's history.

## Term of Office

The president's constitutional term of office is four years. The Framers of the Constitution placed no limit on the number of terms presidents could serve, believing that the desire to remain in office would compel presidents to do their best. George Washington, the nation's first chief executive, established a custom of seeking no more than two terms, which every president honored until Franklin D. Roosevelt broke tradition in the early 1940s. After Roosevelt, a Democrat, won election to a third and then a fourth term, unhappy Republicans launched a drive to amend the Constitution to limit the president to two terms. They succeeded with the ratification of the Twenty-second Amendment in 1951.

The proponents of the two-term limit argued that it prevented a president from becoming too powerful. In contrast, critics believed that the two-term limit unnecessarily weakened the office of the presidency by making a second-term president a **lame duck**, an official whose influence is diminished because the official either cannot or

**budget deficit** the amount by which annual budget expenditures exceed annual budget receipts.

**lame duck** an official whose influence is diminished because the official either cannot or will not seek reelection.

**Should the United States consider amending the Constitution to allow naturalized (foreign-born) American citizens to become president?**

# You Must Be:
## At least 35 years old
## A natural-born American citizen
## A resident of the United States for at least 14 years

# BUT...
## Who have our presidents been?
### 60% were lawyers
### 80% received higher education
### 98% (all but one) were Protestant Christian
### 98% (all but one) were white!
### 100% were male!

will not seek reelection. The opponents of the Twenty-second Amendment also complained that it was undemocratic because it denied voters the right to reelect a president they admired.

## Impeachment and Removal

**Impeachment** is a process in which an executive or judicial official is formally accused of an offense that could warrant removal from office. The Constitution states that the president may be impeached for "treason, bribery, or other high crimes and misdemeanors." The founders foresaw two broad, general grounds on which a president could be impeached and removed from office. First, impeachment could be used against a president who abused the powers of office, thereby threatening to become a tyrant. Second, it could be employed against a presi-

dent who failed to carry out the duties of the office.[2] The House has impeached two presidents—Andrew Johnson in 1868 and Bill Clinton in 1998. Impeachment proceedings were begun against President Richard Nixon, but he resigned before the House could act.

The actual process of impeachment and removal involves both houses of Congress. The House drafts **articles of impeachment**, a document listing the impeachable offenses that the House believes the president committed. Technically, *impeach* means to accuse; so when the House impeaches the president by majority vote, it is accusing the president of committing offenses that may warrant removal from of-

fice. The Senate then tries the president, with the chief justice of the Supreme Court presiding. The Senate must vote by a two-thirds majority to remove the president from office. The Senate failed to remove either Johnson or Clinton from office.

**impeachment** a process in which an executive or judicial official is formally accused of an offense that could warrant removal from office.

**articles of impeachment** a document listing the impeachable offenses that the House believes the president committed.

# Impeaching a President

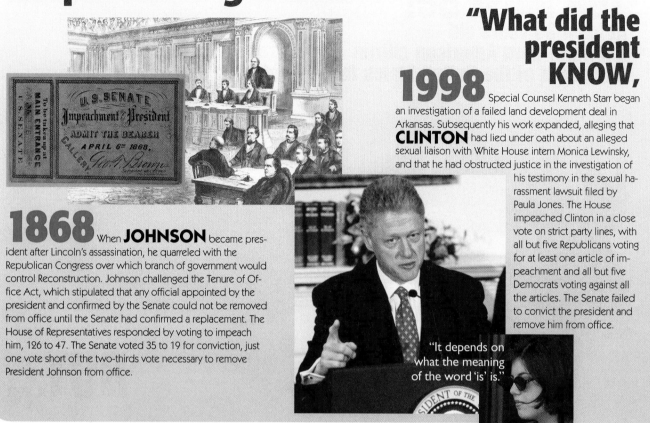

## "What did the president KNOW,

**1998** Special Counsel Kenneth Starr began an investigation of a failed land development deal in Arkansas. Subsequently his work expanded, alleging that **CLINTON** had lied under oath about an alleged sexual liaison with White House intern Monica Lewinsky, and that he had obstructed justice in the investigation of his testimony in the sexual harassment lawsuit filed by Paula Jones. The House impeached Clinton in a close vote on strict party lines, with all but five Republicans voting for at least one article of impeachment and all but five Democrats voting against all the articles. The Senate failed to convict the president and remove him from office.

"It depends on what the meaning of the word 'is' is."

**1868** When **JOHNSON** became president after Lincoln's assassination, he quarreled with the Republican Congress over which branch of government would control Reconstruction. Johnson challenged the Tenure of Office Act, which stipulated that any official appointed by the president and confirmed by the Senate could not be removed from office until the Senate had confirmed a replacement. The House of Representatives responded by voting to impeach him, 126 to 47. The Senate voted 35 to 19 for conviction, just one vote short of the two-thirds vote necessary to remove President Johnson from office.

## Presidential Succession and Disability

The vice president succeeds a president who is removed, resigns, or dies in office. After the vice president, the line of succession passes to the Speaker of the House, president *pro tempore* of the Senate, Secretary of State, and then through the cabinet in order of the creation of the cabinet department. In American history, nine vice presidents have succeeded to the presidency, but no Speakers or Senate presidents *pro tempore*. Furthermore, because of the Twenty-fifth Amendment, the order of succession probably will never extend beyond the office of vice president.

The Twenty-fifth Amendment was ratified in 1967, after Presiden Dwight Eisenhower's heart attack and President Kennedy's assassination focused attention on the issue of presidential succession and disability. The amendment authorizes

the president to fill a vacancy in the office of vice president, subject to majority confirmation by both houses of Congress. This procedure was first used in 1973, when President Nixon nominated Gerald Ford to replace Vice President Spiro Agnew, who resigned under accusation of criminal wrongdoing. When Nixon himself resigned in 1974, Ford moved up to the presidency and appointed former governor of New York Nelson Rockefeller to be the new vice president.

Other provisions of the Twenty-fifth Amendment establish procedures for the vice president to become acting president should the president become disabled and in-

capable of performing the duties of office. The president may declare disability by written notice to the Senate president *pro tempore* and the Speaker of the House. The vice president then becomes acting president until the president declares in writing the ability to resume the responsibilities of office. If the president is unable or unwilling to declare disability, the vice president can declare the president disabled in conjunction with a majority of the cabinet. Should the vice president/cabinet and president disagree on the question of the president's disability, Congress may declare the president disabled by two-thirds vote of each house.

think

**Do you think presidents should be permitted to run for more than two terms?**

**and WHEN did he know it?"**

**"I AM NOT A CROOK."**

**1974** In the Watergate scandal of 1972, five men, employed by the Committee to Reelect the President, broke into Democratic National Committee headquarters to plant electronic eavesdropping devices. **NIXON** called the affair a "two-bit burglary," but as the cover-up began to unravel (culminating in the discovery of tape recordings directly linking Nixon to the cover-up), the House Judiciary Committee recommended impeachment. In August 1974, in the face of these proceedings, Nixon resigned.

## The Vice Presidency

The Constitution gives the vice president two duties. The vice president is president of the Senate and votes in case of a tie. The vice president also becomes president of the United States if the office becomes vacant. For most of American history, however, the vice president was the forgotten person of Washington. In 1848, Daniel Webster, a prominent political figure of the time, rejected the vice presidential nomination of his party, by saying "I do not propose to be buried until I am dead."[3] Before the last half of the twentieth century, the vice president had no staff and few responsibilities. The vice president represented the nation at selected ceremonial occasions, such as the funeral of a foreign leader, but had no policy responsibilities.

Today, the vice presidency has become a more visible and important office. The death in office of President Franklin Roosevelt, Eisenhower's heart attack, Kennedy's assassination, Nixon's resignation, and the assassination attempt against Reagan all called attention to the possibility that the vice president could become president at any time. Furthermore, the vice presidency has become the most common path to the office of the presidency, either through succession or election. Since 1950, five presidents (Harry Truman, Lyndon Johnson, Nixon, Ford, and the elder Bush) held office as vice president prior to becoming president. Men and women of stature are now willing to serve as vice president.

Recent presidents have actively involved their vice presidents in their administrations. When George H. W. Bush became president, he appointed his vice president, Dan Quayle, to head a Council on Competitiveness that reviewed proposed regulations for their impact on business and the economy. President Clinton made Vice President Al Gore the chair of the National Performance Review Commission,

**RECENT PRESIDENTS HAVE ACTIVELY INVOLVED THEIR VICE PRESIDENTS IN THEIR ADMINISTRATIONS**

which was assigned the task of recommending reforms to make government more efficient and cost effective. He assigned Gore the task of debating Ross Perot on the North American Free Trade Agreement (NAFTA), which the administration favored and Perot opposed.

"YOU HAVE TO REMEMBER, CHENEY'S JOB IS TO BACK UP THE PRESIDENT..."
PATRICK ANDERSON GOPACTIVIST

The **North American Free Trade Agreement (NAFTA)** is an international accord among the United States, Mexico, and Canada to lower trade barriers among the three nations.[4] Although Vice President Richard Cheney was probably not a co-president, as some critics suggested, he almost certainly exercised more policy influence than any vice president in history.[5] President Bush preferred to focus on broad policy objectives and delegate authority to work out the details of policy to subordinates. Cheney developed great influence because he was detail-oriented and was willing to assert himself. Many observers believed he was Bush's most important advisor on energy policy, the war in Iraq, judicial nominations, and tax policy.[6]

**North American Free Trade Agreement (NAFTA)** an international accord among the United States, Mexico, and Canada to lower trade barriers among the three nations.

**think**

As the role of the vice president has grown, do you think we should reevaluate the current method for filling this important position?

In February 2009, Congress passed and President Obama signed a $787 billion stimulus package of tax cuts and spending initiatives aimed at helping the economy recover from the economic downturn. Vice President Joe Biden was put in charge of the committee responsible for overseeing the distribution of the funds.

# presidential
## POWERS

the powers of the presidency have developed through the give-and-take of the political process. Although the Constitution outlines the powers of the office in Article II, many of its provisions are not clearly defined.[7] This ambiguity has enabled presidents to expand the limits of presidential power beyond the initial understanding of the authority granted the office.[8]

## Diplomatic Powers

The Constitution gives the president, as **chief of state** (the official head of government), broad diplomatic authority to conduct foreign relations. The president has the power officially to recognize the governments of other nations and to receive and appoint ambassadors. The only constitutional limitation on the president's power of diplomatic recognition is that ambassadorial appointments must be approved by majority vote of the Senate.

The Constitution empowers the president to negotiate treaties with other nations, subject to a two-thirds vote of ratification by the Senate. Since 1789, the Senate has rejected only 21 of more than 1,500 treaties submitted to it, but that figure underestimates the role of the Senate in the ratification process. Most treaties that lack sufficient support to pass the Senate are either withdrawn from consideration by the president or bottled up in committee. The Senate may make its approval of a treaty conditional, depending on the acceptance of amendments, interpretations, understandings, or other reservations. The president and the other countries involved must then decide whether to accept the conditions, renegotiate the provisions, or abandon the treaty altogether.[9]

Presidents use executive agreements to expand their diplomatic authority beyond the treaty power. An **executive agreement**

### btw...

The United States broke off diplomatic relations with China after the communist takeover in 1949. More than 20 years later, President Richard Nixon stunned the world by flying to Beijing and beginning the process of normalization of diplomatic relations with the People's Republic of China. Nixon's visit was remarkable not just because of the longstanding enmity between the two nations but also because of Nixon's personal reputation as a staunch anti-communist. President Jimmy Carter completed the normalization process in 1979 and the two nations exchanged ambassadors.

is an international understanding between the president and foreign nations that does not require Senate ratification. Although the Constitution says nothing about executive agreements, the Supreme Court has upheld their use based on the president's diplomatic and military powers. Executive agreements are more numerous than treaties. The United States is currently a party to nearly 900 treaties and more than 5,000 executive agreements.[10] Many executive agreements involve relatively routine matters, such as the exchange of postal service between nations. Congress has passed legislation authorizing the executive branch to make executive agreements with other countries in certain fields, such as agriculture, trade, and foreign aid. Some executive agreements also require congressional participation because they involve changes in American law. Congress had to pass legislation authorizing NAFTA, even though it was an executive agreement, because it required changes in American trade laws.

**chief of state** the official head of government.

**executive agreement** an international understanding between the president and foreign nations that does not require Senate ratification.

## Military Powers

The Constitution names the president commander in chief of the armed forces. As commander in chief, the president makes military policy, including decisions involving the use of force, operational strategy, and personnel. President Franklin Roosevelt, for example, chose the time and place of the Normandy invasion during World War II. President George W. Bush ordered American forces to take military action against the Taliban government in Afghanistan and the al-Qaeda terrorists that it sheltered. He also ordered the American military to overthrow the government of Saddam Hussein in Iraq.

The president's role as commander in chief embodies the doctrine of **civilian supremacy of the armed forces,** which is the concept that the armed forces should be under the direct control of civilian authorities. The doctrine of civilian supremacy is based on the belief that military decisions should be weighed in light of political considerations. The concept of civilian supremacy also reflects the view that the preservation of representative democracy depends on keeping the military out of politics. In many nations, the armed forces are a powerful political force, and military men sometimes seize the reins of government from civilian authorities. The government of

**civilian supremacy of the armed forces**
the concept that the armed forces should be under the direct control of civilian authorities.

Burma (also known as Myanmar), for example, is a military government, headed by generals whose power depends on the support of the armed forces rather than the votes of the nation's people. In the United States, the president, a civilian, stands at the apex of the command structure of the armed forces. The government controls the military rather than the military controlling the government.

Presidents sometimes use their power as commanders in chief as the basis for exercising authority beyond the scope of direct military action. After Japan bombed Pearl Harbor in 1941 and the United States entered World War II, President Franklin

How was President Franklin Roosevelt able to round up American citizens of Japanese descent during World War II? Shouldn't the Constitution have protected the rights of these Americans, just as it did other citizens?

Several Japanese-Americans took legal action, and a case filed by Fred Korematsu eventually reached the Supreme Court. The Court upheld Roosevelt's exclusion order, ruling that the government's need to prevent espionage outweighed the individual rights of the Japanese Americans. The court did not, however, address the constitutionality of the detention orders. Eventually, public opinion turned against the detention and in favor of the internees. In 1988, Congress passed legislation to pay $20,000 in reparations to each surviving internee.[11]

After the 9/11 attacks, the Bush White House set up detainment camps at Guantanamo Bay, an American naval base in Cuba, and critics raised issues similar to those surrounding the Japanese internment. What about the writ of *habeas corpus*, which is guaranteed by the Constitution?

The Bush White House argued that habeas corpus did not apply to the individuals held at Guantanamo Bay because they were enemy combatants and they were not held on American soil.

In 2006, the U.S. Supreme Court ruled that the Guantanamo detainees were protected under the rules of war of the Geneva Convention.

In 2008, the Supreme Court ruled that the detainees have the right to challenge their detention in federal court.

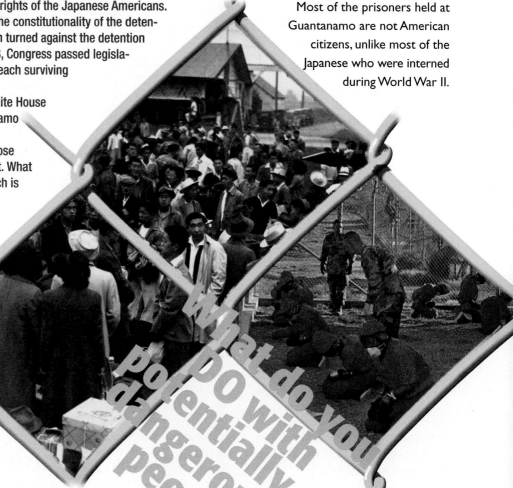

Most of the prisoners held at Guantanamo are not American citizens, unlike most of the Japanese who were interned during World War II.

What do you do with potentially dangerous people?

# The Russian Presidency

Russia elects a president to a four-year term by popular vote. If no candidate receives a majority in the first election, the two candidates with the most votes face each other in a runoff election a month later. Russia has no vice president. If the office of president becomes vacant, the prime minister becomes acting president for 90 days, and a special election is held.

The Russian Constitution makes the president the most powerful office in the government. The president appoints the prime minister to head the cabinet and to administer the government. The Duma, the lower chamber of the Russian parliament, must approve the president's choice for prime minister. If the Duma rejects the president's nominee three times, the president must either select a different prime minister or call for new parliamentary elections. In practice, the Duma is unlikely to reject a prime minister because its members would have to face reelection, whereas the president would not.

The Russian president plays a role in the legislative process somewhat similar to the role played by the American president in the legislative process. Measures passed by the parliament go to the president, who may sign or reject them. If the president rejects a bill, the parliament may vote to override the rejection by a two-thirds vote of both chambers. If the parliament cannot override the rejection, it creates a conciliation commission with representatives of the president in an attempt to reach compromise. The president also has the power to make laws by decree. The Russian Constitution declares that presidential decrees may not contradict existing laws. Furthermore, the parliament can rescind a presidential decree by majority vote.

The presidency was the dominant institution of Russian politics during the administration of Vladimir Putin, who served from 2000 through 2008. Putin crushed his opponents and consolidated power. President Putin won reelection in 2004 with 72 percent of the vote against several unknown opponents because the government disqualified on technicalities every candidate with enough support to seriously challenge Putin. The government also took control of the news media to ensure that Putin received flattering coverage while political opponents were either ignored or attacked. News editors who dared to exercise their independence were beaten or prosecuted for criticizing the government.[12]

The importance of the presidency in Russian government is now in decline, ironically, because of Putin. The Russian Constitution limits the president to two 4-year terms. Rather than attempting to change the Constitution to remain president, Putin promoted the candidacy of a handpicked successor, Dmitry Medvedev, a relatively unknown bureaucrat who won easily over token opposition. Putin then became prime minister. Many observers believed that the Russian system will evolve to resemble most parliamentary systems in which the real power is in the hands of the prime minister, whereas the president is the ceremonial head of state without significant decision-making influence.[13]

## Questions

1. Is there a difference between the Russian president ruling by decree and the American president issuing executive orders?

2. Could a future American political leader execute a maneuver similar to that accomplished by Putin to stay in power despite the end of a second term in the White House?

3. What keeps the American president from taking actions similar to those taken by Putin?

When Putin talks, Medvedev listens. Vladimir Putin is no longer president of Russia, but, as prime minister, he is apparently still the man with the power.

Vice President Dick Cheney and his legal counsel were instrumental in asserting the executive branch's inherent powers to designate enemy combatants and use aggressive interrogation techniques on them. The technique of waterboarding, or simulated drowning, has been banned in multiple countries and even prosecuted in the United States. In the above, human rights activists demonstrate the technique on a volunteer on Capitol Hill.

Roosevelt issued an executive order authorizing the military to relocate all persons of Japanese ancestry from the West Coast to inland relocation centers. More than 120,000 persons were interned, including 70,000 native-born American citizens. The U.S. Supreme Court upheld the constitutionality of the action.[14] After the terrorist attacks of September 11, 2001, President Bush exercised his authority as commander in chief to order the arrest and detention of persons suspected of involvement in terrorist activity.

Congress and the president have frequently quarreled over the authority of the legislative and executive branches to make military policy. Although the president is commander in chief, the Constitution grants Congress sole authority to declare war. The last war that Congress declared, however, was World War II. The president has initiated all subsequent American military actions, including the Korean War and the Vietnam War, without benefit of a congressional declaration of war. Although Congress authorized the use of force in Iraq before the U.S. invasion, it did not issue a declaration of war.

In 1973, during the war in Vietnam, Congress responded to what it considered an infringement of its constitutional power to declare war by enacting the **War Powers Act,** which limited the president's ability to commit American armed forces to combat abroad without consultation with Congress and congressional approval.[15] The measure includes a number of important provisions.

The War Powers Act is probably a less effective check on the president's military power than is public opinion. If a president's actions enjoy broad public support, as was the case with the first war in the Persian Gulf, Congress is unlikely to order a withdrawal of American forces. In contrast, the risk of adverse public reaction may deter some military

**War Powers Act** a law limiting the president's ability to commit American armed forces to combat abroad without consultation with Congress and congressional approval.

initiatives or cut short others. In 1983, for example, President Reagan ordered American forces withdrawn from Beirut, Lebanon, well in advance of a War Powers Act cutoff date, after several hundred marines were killed in a terrorist bombing. Perhaps more significantly, the ordered withdrawal came well in advance of the 1984 presidential election.

In 2008, a commission recommended that Congress and the president scrap the War Powers Act and replace it with legislation requiring the president and congressional leaders to consult before going to war. The commission, which was headed by two former secretaries of state, Republican James A. Baker III and Democrat Warren Christopher, declared the War Powers Act "ineffective at best and unconstitutional at worst."[16] The commission proposed a law that would create a new committee of congressional leaders and relevant committee chairs, with a full-time staff that would have access to military and foreign policy intelligence information. The president would be required to consult with this committee in advance of military action expected to take longer than a week (except in rare emergencies), and meet with it regularly during an extended conflict. Congress as a whole would be required to vote on an authorization resolution within 30 days of the initiation of hostilities. If the authorization resolution failed, any member of Congress could introduce a resolution of disapproval, which would have to pass both houses of Congress and be signed by the president to go into effect. A presidential veto would have to be overridden by a two-thirds vote before the resolution of disapproval had the force of law.[17]

## Inherent Powers

**Inherent powers** are those powers vested in the national government, particularly in the area of foreign and defense policy, which do not depend on any specific grant of authority by the Constitution, but rather, exist because the United

> **Would you agree that a dunk in the water is a no-brainer if it can save lives?**
>
> RADIO SHOW HOST SCOTT HENNEN:

> **It's a no-brainer for me, but for a while there I was criticized as being the vice president "for torture." WE DON'T TORTURE.**
>
> VICE PRESIDENT CHENEY:

States is a sovereign nation. Consider the **Louisiana Purchase,** which was the acquisition from France of a vast expanse of land stretching from New Orleans north to the Dakotas. President Thomas Jefferson justified his decision to acquire the territory on the basis of inherent powers because the Constitution says nothing about purchasing land from another country. Similarly, Lincoln claimed extraordinary powers to defend the Union during the Civil War on the basis of inherent powers. President George

W. Bush used the doctrine of inherent powers to justify the use of military tribunals to try enemy combatants captured in the war on terror, to designate U.S. citizens as enemy combatants, to send terror suspects to countries that practice torture, and to authorize eavesdropping on American citizens by the National Security Agency (NSA).[18]

Presidential assertions of inherent powers are almost invariably controversial because they involve an expansion of government authority and presidential power not authorized by the Constitution. Critics of the Louisiana Purchase, for example, called Jefferson a hypocrite because he had long argued that the authority of the national government was limited to powers clearly delegated by the Constitution. In recent years, critics accused President Bush of not just exceeding his power but violating the Constitution. They challenged his actions in Congress and in the courts.

**inherent powers** powers vested in the national government, particularly in the area of foreign and defense policy, which do not depend on any specific grant of authority by the Constitution, but rather exist because the United States is a sovereign nation.

**Louisiana Purchase** the acquisition from France of a vast expanse of land stretching from New Orleans north to the Dakotas.

## Judicial Powers

The president plays a role in judicial policymaking. The president nominates all federal judges pending majority-vote confirmation by the Senate. The Senate usually approves nominees, but not without scrutiny, especially for Supreme Court selections. The Senate rejected two consecutive Supreme Court appointments by President Nixon before confirming his third choice. Similarly, the Senate rejected President Reagan's nomination of Robert Bork to the Supreme Court.

**think** *Is the president's authority as commander in chief too broad?*

The power of appointment gives a president, especially a president who serves two terms, the opportunity to shape the policy direction of the judicial branch of American government. During his eight years in office, President Clinton appointed 374 federal judges, including two members of the Supreme Court. George W. Bush named more than 300 judges during his two terms in office. His appointments included two Supreme Court justices.[19]

The Constitution empowers the president to grant pardons and reprieves. A **pardon** is an executive action that frees an accused or convicted person from all penalties for an offense. A **reprieve** is an executive action that delays punishment for a crime. With some exceptions, such as President Ford's pardon of former President Nixon, most presidential pardons and reprieves have not been controversial.

## Executive Powers

The president is the nation's **chief executive**, that is, the head of the executive branch of government.

The Constitution grants the president authority to require written reports from department heads and enjoins the president to "take care that laws be faithfully executed." As head of the executive branch of government, presidents can issue executive orders to manage the federal bureaucracy. An **executive order** is a directive issued by the president to an administrative agency or executive department. Although the Constitution says nothing about executive orders, the courts have upheld their use based on law, custom, and the president's authority as head of the executive branch.

Presidents have used executive orders to enact important (and sometimes controversial) policies. President Lincoln, for example, used an executive order to issue the Emancipation Proclamation. President Eisenhower issued an executive order to send National Guard troops into Little Rock, Arkansas in 1957 to protect African American youngsters attempting to attend a whites-only public high school. The first President Bush issued executive orders to prohibit abortion counseling at federally funded family planning centers. President Clinton, in turn, used an executive order to reverse the Bush order.

The president's power to issue executive orders is not unlimited. Presidents may issue executive orders only when they fall within the scope of the president's constitutional powers and legal authority. In 1952, for example, during the Korean War, the U.S. Supreme Court overturned an executive order by President Truman seizing the nation's steel mills to head off a strike that would have disrupted steel production and hurt the war effort. The Court declared that the president lacked the legal authority to seize private property and that the

**pardon** an executive action that frees an accused or convicted person from all penalties for an offense.

**reprieve** an executive action that delays punishment for a crime.

**chief executive** the head of the executive branch of government.

**executive order** a directive issued by the president to an administrative agency or executive department.

Federal troops patrolled the grounds of Central High School in Little Rock, Arkansas after court-ordered integration began.

# Taking Sides

# Judicial Selection and Partisan Politics

## Should the judicial nomination process be reformed? If so, why? If not, why not?

## Should judicial nominees be selected based on judicial philosophy or political ideology? Is this what the founders intended?

Supreme Court Justice Stephen Breyer, a Clinton appointee, is regarded as one of the more liberal members of the Supreme Court.

**Overview:** Though the courts have always been a political institution, the increasing polarization of electoral politics over the last four decades has taught political parties and interest groups to view litigation and judicial decisions as tools to circumvent existing law and policy. With this in mind, the two major political parties have turned to further politicization of the federal judiciary in an attempt to shape its ideological leanings.

The 2000 election put the Republican Party in charge of Congress and the presidency for the first time in 40 years. President George W. Bush had promised that he would nominate judges who adhered to the strict-construction philosophy of judicial decision making—that is, he would appoint judges who believed in applying the letter of the law instead of trying to determine its meaning or spirit and attempting to order judicial remedies. The Democratic Party, for its part, instituted a political litmus test for judicial nominees, arguing that a president's nominees should be ideologically mainstream and not selected for their perceived political biases. To prevent President Bush from having his nominees confirmed, the

Senate Democrats, in a move used only once in American history, filibustered the president's judicial choices, thus preventing vacant judgeships from being filled.

President Bush avoided the Senate altogether and appointed some of his favored nominees to the federal bench through the process of the recess appointment. Article II of the Constitution gives the president the authority to temporarily appoint judges and officials when the Senate is not in session and, since 1789, over 300 judicial appointments have been made by this method. But questions still remain. Has the Senate's constitutional authority been undermined? What is the best way to ensure an independent and effective judiciary?

## supporting reform of the judicial selection process

**judicial nominations should be above politics.** An independent judiciary is essential to free government. Choosing judicial nominees based on political ideology or litmus tests further makes judges *de facto* tools of political parties and interest groups.

**the nature of judicial appointments makes it imperative that judges receive a full hearing.** Federal judges may sit on the bench for life, and they can wield considerable clout in determining how the Constitution is interpreted and applied. It follows that judicial appointments merit more open and public deliberation.

**Senate obstructionism may deny the judiciary qualified judges.** For example, Miguel Estrada was a Bush appointee who graduated with honors from Harvard Law School and clerked for Supreme Court Justice Anthony Kennedy. He withdrew his nomination to sit on the appeals court of the District of Columbia in frustration after two years of obstruction by the Senate.

## against reform of the judicial selection process

**it is Congress's prerogative to determine its rules of procedure.** Article I gives each chamber the authority to "determine the rules of its proceedings" and the historical evolution of Senate rules has provided stability and continuity in the nomination process.

**the Senate is an explicitly political institution.** Just as the president makes decisions based on political considerations, it is the Senate's appropriate function to ensure judicial nominations will not be too partisan and that judges adhere to moderate ideological and judicial views.

**recess appointments are a means for judicial relief.** The Constitution states that vacancies may be filled until an intervening midterm or general election. Should the election have a favorable outcome for the president, he may resubmit a nominee for the Senate's consideration.

president's power as commander in chief did not extend to labor disputes.[20] Congress can also overturn an executive order legislatively. Because the president would likely veto a measure reversing an executive order, Congress would need to vote to repeal the order and then to vote again by a two-thirds margin to override the veto.

## Legislative Powers

Finally, the Constitution grants the president certain tools for shaping the legislative agenda. From time to time, it says, the president shall "give to Congress information of the state of the Union, and recommend to their consideration such measures as he shall judge necessary and expedient." Traditionally, the president makes a State of the Union address each January before a joint session of Congress and a national television audience. The speech gives the president the opportunity to raise issues and frame the terms of their discussion. In 2005, for example, President George W. Bush used the address to promote his Social Security reform proposal. Although the State of the Union address allows the president the opportunity to present himself or herself as the nation's chief legislator, it may also create unrealistic public expectations. In practice, Congress approves only 43 percent of the policy initiatives included in the average State of the Union speech, either in whole or in part.[21]

The president can use the veto power to shape the content of legislation. The Constitution empowers the president to return measures to Congress along with objections. A vetoed measure can become law only if both the House and Senate vote to override by a two-thirds margin. The veto is a powerful weapon. In more than 200 years, Congress has overridden less than 1 percent of presidential vetoes.[22] Nonetheless, political scientists consider the actual use of the veto a sign of weakness rather than strength because influential presidents can usually prevent passage of measures they oppose by threatening a veto.[23] A **presidential signing statement** is a pronouncement issued by the president at the time a bill passed by Congress is signed into law. Presidents historically have used signing statements to comment on the bill they are signing, score political points, identify areas of disagreement with the measure, and discuss its implementation. President George W. Bush went further than any of his predecessors in using signing statements to expand the powers of his office. Bush signing statements identified more than 800 provisions in 500 measures that he signed into law but considered unconstitutional limitations on his authority as president. He asserted his intention to ignore these provisions or treat them as advisory. Bush declared, for example, that legislative provisions establishing qualifications for executive branch officials were advisory rather than mandatory because he believed that they unconstitutionally restricted the presidential power of appointment. He asserted his intention to withhold information from Congress and rejected legislative provisions that he believed would limit his power as commander in chief.

Presidential signing statements are controversial. Political scientist Phillip J. Cooper believes that President Bush used presidential signing statements as a vehicle for revising legislation without issuing a veto, which is subject to congressional override.[24] The American Bar Association (ABA) declares that Bush's use of signing statements is "contrary to the rule of law and our constitutional system of separation of powers" because the Constitution requires that the president sign legislation or veto it in its entirety.[25] In contrast, law professors Curtis A. Bradley and Eric A. Posner argue that signing statements are legal and useful because they provide a way for the president to disclose his or her views about the meaning and constitutionality of legislation.[26]

### THE PRESIDENT CAN USE THE VETO POWER TO SHAPE THE CONTENT OF LEGISLATION

## btw...

Reforming Social Security was the foremost priority of President George W. Bush's second term. Social Security faces a long-term financial crisis. With the retirement of the baby boom generation, the ratio of beneficiaries to workers paying taxes into the system will shrink from 33-to-1 in 2007, to 2.2-to-1 in 2030. The cost of providing benefits will exceed tax revenues in 2017. Bush proposed supplementing Social Security by allowing workers to invest some of the money they would have otherwise paid in Social Security taxes into private savings accounts. Even though the White House launched a public relations blitz to promote the idea, public support for private accounts fell. Congress did not seriously consider the proposed reform and Bush left office without accomplishing his goal.

**presidential signing statement** a pronouncement issued by the president at the time a bill passed by Congress is signed into law.

# the organization
## OF THE PRESIDENCY

the development of the modern presidency has been accompanied by a significant growth in the size and power of the presidential bureaucracy, that is, the White House staff and the Executive Office of the President. Early chief executives wrote their own speeches and even answered their own mail. They had only a few aides, whom they paid from their own funds. Thomas Jefferson, for example, had one messenger and one secretary. Eventually, Congress appropriated money for the president to hire aides and advisors, and the presidential bureaucracy grew. In the 1920s, the president had a staff of 30. By the 1950s, the number of presidential aides and advisors had grown to 250. Today, the combined staffs of the Executive Office and the White House number more than 2,000, and the president has grown to rely on them more and more.[27] The modern president spends time bargaining with Congress while dealing with the media and the public. Reelection campaigns begin almost from the first day in office. Presidents have responded to the demands of the office by hiring aides with specialized expertise.[28]

## The White House Staff

The White House staff consists of personal aides, assistants, and advisors to the president, including a chief of staff, press secretary, speechwriter, appointments secretary, national security advisor, legislative liaison, counselor to the president, and various special assistants. They give the president advice on policy issues and politics, screen key appointments, manage press relations, organize the president's workday, and ensure that the president's wishes are carried out. The president selects the White House staff without Senate confirmation. As with most presidential appointees (the exceptions are federal judges and regulatory commissioners), White House staff members serve at the president's pleasure, which means that the president can remove them at will.

Political and personal loyalty is usually the foremost criterion the president uses in selecting a staff. When George W. Bush became president, he recruited his staff primarily from his father's administration, his own administration as governor of Texas, and his presidential campaign. Andrew H. Card, Jr., the White House chief of staff during Bush's first term, was secretary of transportation in the first Bush administration. Similarly, President Obama selected Rahm Emanuel, a member of Congress from Chicago, Illinois, Obama's political home base, to serve as his chief of staff.

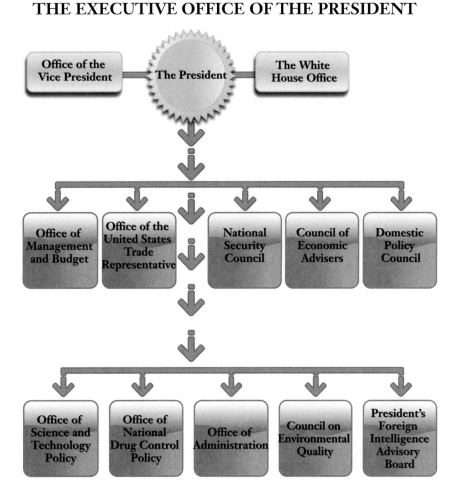

*How the*
# WHITE HOUSE RUNS:
### THE EXECUTIVE OFFICE OF THE PRESIDENT

Office of the Vice President — The President — The White House Office

- Office of Management and Budget
- Office of the United States Trade Representative
- National Security Council
- Council of Economic Advisers
- Domestic Policy Council

- Office of Science and Technology Policy
- Office of National Drug Control Policy
- Office of Administration
- Council on Environmental Quality
- President's Foreign Intelligence Advisory Board

## The Executive Office of the President

The **Executive Office of the President** is the group of White House offices and agencies that develop and implement the policies and programs of the president. Congress established the Executive Office in 1939 after a special investigative commission concluded that the responsibilities of the presidency were too great for any one individual. "The president needs help," the commission said. The legislation creating the Executive Office allowed the president to create and disband components without further congressional authorization. Consequently, the size and composition of the Executive Office changes somewhat from administration to administration. During the most recent Bush administration, the Executive Office had 17 units.[29]

The major agencies of the Executive Office are the National Security Council (NSC), Office of Management and Budget (OMB), Council of Economic Advisers (CEA), Council on Environmental Quality, Office of Science and Technology Policy, Office of the United States Trade Representative, and Domestic Policy Council. The first two are the most prominent. The **National Security**

The Council on Environmental Quality coordinates federal environmental policies and initiatives such as cap-and-trade legislation, a measure designed to reduce the emissions that cause global warming. Under cap and trade, the government distributes permits that cap the amount of pollution that can be emitted. Companies have an incentive to reduce their pollution below the caps because they can sell excess permits to firms that are unable to meet their targets.

**Council (NSC)** is an agency in the Executive Office of the President that advises the chief executive on matters involving national security. It includes the president, vice president, Secretaries of State and defense, and other officials the president may choose to include, such as the national security advisor, the head of the Joint Chiefs of Staff, and the director of the Central Intelligence Agency (CIA). The **Office of Management and Budget (OMB)** is an agency that assists the president in preparing the budget. The OMB is an important instrument of presidential control of the executive branch. It assists the president in preparing the annual budget to be submitted to Congress, screens bills drawn up by executive branch departments and agencies to ensure that they do not conflict with the president's policy goals, monitors expenditures by executive branch departments, and evaluates regulations proposed by executive agencies.

## The Presidential Bureaucracy and Presidential Influence

The presidential bureaucracy is essential to the effective operation of the modern presidency. An efficient, knowledgeable White House staff is an important element of presidential power. Members of the staff not only advise the president on policy issues and political strategy, but they often act on behalf of the president in dealing with Congress, members of the executive branch bureaucracy, and the media. An efficient, professional staff can further the president's policy goals and create an image of presidential competence. A White House staff that is accessible to members of Congress and maintains open lines of communication will help promote the president's policies while keeping the president well-informed enough to prevent surprises.[30] In contrast, an inefficient staff makes the president appear incompetent. During the first two years of the Clinton administration, a disorganized White House staff contributed to the president's penchant for putting off decisions and failing to stick to decisions once they were made. As a result, Clinton developed a reputation for indecision and inconsistency, a reputation that contributed to substantial Democratic losses in the 1994 con-

**Executive Office of the President** the group of White House offices and agencies that develop and implement the policies and programs of the president.

**National Security Council (NSC)** an agency in the Executive Office of the President that advises the chief executive on matters involving national security.

**Office of Management and Budget (OMB)** an agency that assists the president in preparing the budget.

gressional elections. Leon Panetta, whom Clinton named chief of staff in 1994, brought discipline to the White House, enabling the president to rehabilitate his image and win reelection in 1996.[31]

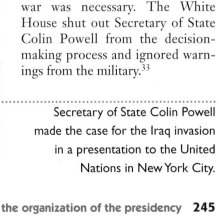

The tendency of newly elected presidents to select old friends and campaign aides who are unfamiliar with Washington politics to serve in the White House often undermines the president's effectiveness. The problem is made worse if the president is also inexperienced in national politics. Healthcare reform was the foremost goal of Clinton's first term in office. The president appointed a task force chaired by Hillary Clinton to hold hearings and develop a plan to be presented to Congress. Because the task force lacked broad-based representation and conducted much of its work in secret, it failed to develop a plan with enough support to pass Congress, and the effort became an embarrassing failure.

The challenge for a president is to develop a leadership style that del-

**An efficient, professional staff CAN FURTHER THE PRESIDENT'S POLICY GOALS and create an image of presidential competence**

egates neither too little nor too much. Because a president's time, energy, and abilities are limited, the president must delegate some tasks. To be effective, a president must know which tasks can be delegated and which cannot. The president must also have a strong enough grasp of policy issues to recognize when the proposals of subordinates make sense and when they do not.[32]

President George W. Bush's decision to go to war against Iraq was based on a flawed decision-making process within the administration. Bush ordered the overthrow of Saddam Hussein because he believed that Iraq possessed **weapons of mass destruction (WMD)**, nuclear, chemical, and biological weapons designed to inflict widespread military and civilian casualties. The United States had to act, the president declared, before Iraq gave WMD to terrorist groups that could then use them against the United States or its allies. The conclusion that Iraq possessed WMD, however, was wrong. The administration not only misinterpreted some of the intelligence it received, but also attempted to influence the nature of that intelligence to support its position. It sought evidence to prove that Iraq possessed WMD while ignoring information to the contrary. Furthermore, Bush decided to go to war without deliberating with his advisors as to whether war was necessary. The White House shut out Secretary of State Colin Powell from the decision-making process and ignored warnings from the military.[33]

Secretary of State Colin Powell made the case for the Iraq invasion in a presentation to the United Nations in New York City.

# theories of
# PRESIDENTIAL LEADERSHIP

**p**olitical scientists take different approaches to describing and explaining presidential leadership.

## Presidential Character

Political scientist James David Barber believes that a president's performance in office depends on personality traits formed primarily during childhood, adolescence, and early adulthood. Barber classifies personality along two dimensions. The first dimension involves the amount of energy an individual brings to the office. Active presidents throw themselves into their work, immersing themselves in the details of the office, whereas passive presidents devote relatively little energy and effort to the job. The second dimension to Barber's personality classification scheme involves the president's attitude toward the job. Positive presidents enjoy their work. They have an optimistic, positive attitude. Negative presidents feel burdened by the weight of the office. They tend to be pessimists.

Barber uses these two dimensions to create four general types of presidential personalities: active-positive, active-negative, passive-positive, and passive-negative. According to Barber, the best type of personality for a president is active-positive. This president is self-confident, optimistic, flexible, and enjoys the job. Barber believes that

## BARBER'S CLASSIFICATION OF
## PRESIDENTIAL CHARACTER

**Active-positive**
Self-confident, optimistic, flexible, and enjoys the job; uses the office as an "engine of power."

Franklin Roosevelt

**Active-negative**
Puts great energy into work, but derives little pleasure from it; tends to view political disputes in terms of personal success or failure.

Richard Nixon

**Passive-positive**
Indecisive and superficially optimistic; tends to react rather than initiate.

Ronald Reagan

**Passive-negative**
Is involved in politics out of a sense of duty; avoids conflict and uncertainty and just plain dislikes politics.

Dwight Eisenhower

# takeaction

## WHY DO THEY RUN? >>

Have you ever wondered why people seek political office? Do they want personal power? Do they hope to accomplish policy objectives? Are they motivated by a desire to serve the community?

Investigate the answers to these questions by interviewing an elected official in a city, county, township, school district, or special district unit of government in your area. Keep in mind that most public officials are busy, so it may be unrealistic to attempt to arrange an interview with the mayor of a large city or the county executive in a metropolitan area. Local judges, school board members, community college trustees, and city council members in small towns may prove more accessible to students. Once you decide on an official, call his or her office to introduce yourself and ask if the official is willing to set aside 15 minutes or so for an interview, either on the telephone or in person. If the official is unavailable, try another officeholder.

Before you conduct the interview, do your homework so you can make the most of the opportunity. Learn as much as you can about the office and the official. Study the questions you want to ask so you will be able to speak in a conversational tone of voice. Prepare to tape-record the interview if possible so you will not have to worry about taking notes.

Begin the interview by thanking the official for his or her time. Explain that you will report to your class on what you learn. Then, conduct the interview. The following questions can serve as a guideline. Remember, however, that these are general-purpose questions. You may want to add other ques-

tions of your own or rephrase these questions to put them in your own words.

- Is this the first elected office you have held? (If not, ask what other posts the official has held.)
- Why did you decide to seek this office?
- About how many hours a week do you spend on the job?
- Do you enjoy it?
- What do you like most about your position in local government?
- What do you like least about your position?
- Are you glad you sought this office and won? Why or why not?

Once you have completed the interview, thank the official again for his or her time. You will also want to write the official a thank-you letter for taking time to chat with you.

Prepare a short oral report for your class by listening to the tape of the interview, reviewing your notes, and organizing your information. Your report should include your impressions of the official in addition to relating what the official told you in the interview. Also, prepare to discuss whether you are interested in running for office yourself.

---

the most dangerous chief executive is the active-negative president. This type of president puts great energy into work, but derives little pleasure from it. Barber says that active-negative presidents suffer from low self-esteem and tend to view political disputes in terms of personal success or failure. They are pessimistic, driven, and compulsive. Active-negative presidents tend to overreact to crises and continue failed policies long after it is clear they do not work because to admit error would be to lose control. Barber classifies Richard Nixon as active-negative because he was personally insecure, combative, tough, and vindictive.

Scholars identify a number of weaknesses with Barber's classification scheme. It is not always clear in which category a president should be placed. President Reagan can be labeled *passive* because of his inattentiveness and willingness to allow aides to carry a good deal of his workload. Nonetheless, the Reagan administration had a substantial impact on public policy, taking important initiatives in a wide range of policy areas. Is that the record of a passive president? Some critics complain that Barber's categories are so broad as to be little help in differentiating among presidents. Barber puts Presidents Franklin Roosevelt,

Carter, and the first President Bush in the same category—active-positive. How helpful is Barber's classification scheme if such different presidents fit in the same category? Historians typically rank Franklin Roosevelt among the best of the nation's presidents, whereas Carter and George H. W. Bush are considered only average. Finally, Barber's scheme ignores the political climate in which a president serves. The success or failure of a chief executive depends on a number of factors in addition to the president's personality traits.[34]

## The Power to Persuade

Political scientist Richard Neustadt believes that presidents succeed or fail based on their skills as political bargainers and coalition builders. Although the presidency is regarded as a powerful office, Neustadt points out that presidents lack authority to command public officials other than the members of the White House staff, some executive branch appointees, and the members of the armed forces. Under America's

## POLITICS INVOLVES *NEGOTIATION, GIVE-AND-TAKE, AND* COMPROMISE

constitutional system, the members of Congress, federal judges, and state officials do not take orders from the president. Because presidents cannot command, they must convince other political actors to cooperate with them voluntarily. The power of the president, Neustadt says, is the power to persuade.

Presidents must bargain with other political actors and groups to try to win their cooperation. Presidents are brokers, consensus builders. In this task, presidents have several assets: They have a number of appointments at their disposal; they prepare the budget; they can help supporters raise money for reelection; and they can appeal to others on the basis of the national interest or party loyalty. To use these assets to their fullest, presidents must un-

derstand the dynamics of political power.[35]

Neustadt's approach can be used to explain the presidencies of Lyndon Johnson and Jimmy Carter. President Johnson learned as majority leader in the Senate how to build a political coalition to get legislation passed. In the White House, he put those skills to work and won passage for his legislative program, which was known as the **Great Society**. In contrast, President Carter never mastered the mechanics of political power. He ran for president as an outsider, someone who was not tainted by Washington politics. Once in office, Carter appeared standoffish. He had won the Democratic nomination and been elected president without having to bargain with the Washington establishment, and he thought he could govern without bargaining. He was wrong. Politics involves negotiation, give-and-take, and compromise. Carter never understood that and consequently failed to accomplish many of his goals.

## Going Public

Political scientist Samuel Kernell has updated the Neustadt approach. Kernell believes that contemporary presidents often must adopt a media-oriented strategy, which he calls "going public," if they are to

achieve their goals in today's political environment. In 1981, for example, President Reagan went on television to ask citizens to contact their representatives in Congress to support his economic program. The public responded and Congress approved the president's budget proposals.

Media-oriented approaches are not new—Franklin Roosevelt was famous for his fireside chats on the radio—but the strategy has become more common. Modern communications and transportation technologies make going public relatively easy. Furthermore, today's presidential selection process tends to favor people who are better at public appeals than political bargaining. Perhaps most important, going public has become an easier

**Great Society** the legislative program put forward by President Lyndon Johnson.

President Theodore Roosevelt was famous for the use he made of "the bully pulpit"—his ability to use his office to influence debate.

# Leadership *Style*

Some scholars believe that the ability of a president to use the powers of the office effectively depends on leadership style. Political scientist Fred I. Greenstein takes this approach by identifying six qualities associated with effective presidential leadership.

| | Public Communicator | Organizational Skills | Political Skills | Vision | Cognitive Skills | Emotional Intelligence |
|---|---|---|---|---|---|---|
| F. ROOSEVELT | ✔ | | | | | |
| TRUMAN | | ✔ | | | | |
| EISENHOWER | | ✔ | | ✔ | | ✔ |
| KENNEDY | ✔ | ✔ | | ✔ | | |
| JOHNSON | | | ✔ | | | |
| NIXON | | | | ✔ | ✔ | |
| FORD | | ✔ | | | | ✔ |
| CARTER | | | | ✔ | | |
| REAGAN | ✔ | | | ✔ | | |
| G. H. W. BUSH | | ✔ | | ✔ | | ✔ |
| CLINTON | ✔ | | | | | |
| G. W. BUSH | | | | | | ✔ |

and more efficient method for achieving political goals than bargaining. In the 1950s, a president pushing a policy agenda had to bargain with a handful of party leaders and committee chairs in Congress. Today, power in Congress is more fragmented and the number of interest groups active in Washington politics has increased. As a result, it has become easier for presidents to go public than to engage in political bargaining.[36]

The George W. Bush administration illustrates both the strengths and limitations of the going public strategy. Bush effectively used the going public strategy to bring the threat of Iraq to the top of the public agenda and put pressure on Congress to approve his war policy. Public concern over Iraq made Democrats in Congress wary about opposing the president on Iraq because Saddam Hussein was a highly unpopular figure. Many Democrats believed that Saddam actually did have WMD and was a threat to national security. Opposing Bush on Iraq could open them to the charge that they were soft on national defense. Nearly 40 percent of House Democrats and 57 percent of Senate Democrats joined nearly every Republican member of Congress in voting in favor of the resolution to authorize the use of military force in Iraq.[37] In contrast, the Bush administration's 60-stops-in-60-days strategy to promote Social Security private accounts was a failure. Although President Bush succeeded in elevating the issue to the top of the policy agenda, he failed to convince a majority of the public that private retirement accounts were a good idea. As a result, it was easy for Democrats in Congress to oppose the president on the issue and difficult for Republicans to support him. Going public is an ineffective strategy if the president's proposed initiative lacks public support.[38]

## Unilateral Tools of Presidential Power

Professor Christopher S. Kelley says that presidents have certain "power tools" that allow them to take unilateral action without direct congressional authorization or approval.[39] These tools include the following:

- **Executive orders**. They enable the president to adopt a number of important policies without legislative approval.

- **Executive agreements**. They give the president an important tool that does not require Senate ratification for conducting foreign relations.[40]

- **Presidential signing statements**. They enable the president to define the scope and limitations of legislation passed by Congress.

- **Recess appointments**. By filling vacancies during a period of time when Congress is in recess, the president can temporarily make appointments without the advice and consent of the Senate.[41]

# presidential POPULARITY

**P**residential popularity influences presidential power. A president's personal popularity affects the position of the president as a political broker and the ability of the president to appeal to the public for policy support. A president who is politically popular can offer more benefits and inducements to other political actors for their cooperation than can an unpopular chief executive. Campaign help from a popular president is more valuable, and support for legislative proposals is more effective. Similarly, a popular president can claim to speak for the national interest with greater credibility.

A popular president enjoys more success with Congress than an unpopular chief executive. After September 11, 2001, President Bush's approval rating soared. Republican members of Congress eagerly associated themselves with the president, whereas Democrats were reluctant to oppose him. Congress passed legislation embodying the president's policy proposals dealing with taxes, the budget, government reorganization, Iraq, and the war on terror. By 2006, however, Bush's approval rating had fallen below 40 percent and members of Congress from both parties found it easy to oppose the president's legislative agenda. Democrats attacked Bush at every opportunity while Republican members of Congress boasted of their independence from the White House.

New presidents are popular, at least for a few months. The tendency of a president to enjoy a high level of public support during the early months of an administration is known as the **honeymoon effect**. In the first few months of an administration, opposition political leaders and the press usually reserve judgment, waiting for the president to act before offering comment. Most voters, regardless of party affiliation, tell poll-takers that they approve of the president's performance in office because they have heard few complaints on which to base disapproval. Once an administration begins making controversial policy decisions, however, opposition leaders and the media begin to

**honeymoon effect** the tendency of a president to enjoy a high level of public support during the early months of an administration.

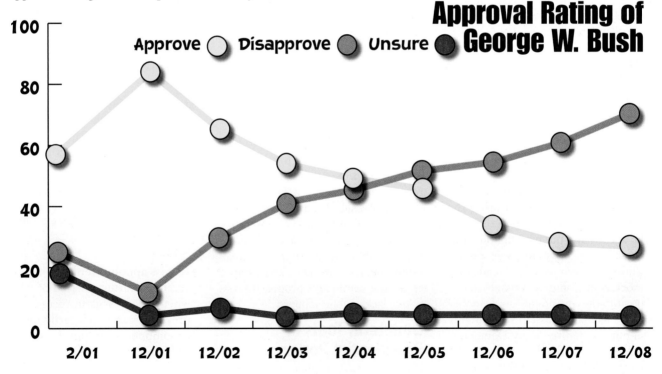

## Approval Rating of George W. Bush

Approve · Disapprove · Unsure

*Gallup Poll and USA Today/Gallup Poll*, available at http://www.pollingreport.com/BushJob1.htm.

criticize the president's performance. As the criticism mounts, the president's popularity invariably falls, especially among people who identify with the opposition political party.[42]

Presidential approval responds to events. In domestic policy matters, presidential popularity rises with good news and falls with bad news, especially news concerning the economy. Although President Reagan was called the "Teflon President"—regardless of what went wrong, no blame stuck to him—he was an unpopular president during the recession of 1982. Only when the economy began to recover did Reagan's popular standing again exceed the 50-percent approval mark.

Presidential popularity rises dramatically during times of international crisis because of the **rally effect,** which is the tendency of the general public to express support for the incumbent president during a time of international threat. Political scientist John Mueller defines the rally effect as "being associated with an event which 1) is international and 2) involves the United States and particularly the president

directly." Mueller says that the event must be "specific, dramatic, and sharply focused."[43] Mueller found that the "public seems to react to both 'good' and 'bad' international events in about the same way"—with a burst of heightened presidential approval.[44] For example, President George W. Bush's standing in the polls soared after September 11, 2001. The percentage of Americans who told survey researchers that they approved of Bush's performance in office leaped from 51 percent in early September to 90 percent later in the month.[45]

The appearance and size of a rally effect depends on how the crisis is presented to the public in terms of media coverage, comments from opposition political leaders, and statements from the White House.[46] When the nation appears threatened from abroad, the political criticism that generally accompanies presidential action is muted. The White House is able to get its interpretation of events before the public because opposition political leaders do not want to be accused of undermining the president during an international crisis. The public

tends to support the president because the only messages it hears about the president's handling of the crisis are positive messages, usually conveyed by the White House itself or the president's allies in Congress.[47] Even though 9/11 was a national disaster, President Bush's approval rating soared because no one, at least initially, publicly raised questions about the administration's failure to foresee or prevent the terrorist attacks. Instead, the media were filled with images of the president comforting the families of the victims and declaring that the United States would bring to justice the people responsible for the attacks.[48]

The public responds differently to a domestic crisis than it does to an international crisis. Whereas opposition political leaders and the press typically withhold judgment in an international crisis, they are quick to criticize if something goes

**rally effect** the tendency of the general public to express support for the incumbent president during a time of international threat.

wrong domestically. Consider the reaction to Hurricane Katrina in August 2005 and its impact on President Bush's standing in the polls. Within days of the hurricane's coming ashore, opposition political leaders and the news media were blasting the Bush administration for inadequately responding to the disaster. Between late August and October 2005, the president's popularity rating fell by five percentage points.[49]

Usually, a rally effect has only a short-term impact on presidential popularity. According to a study conducted by the Gallup organization, a president's approval rating reverts to previous levels within seven months of an international crisis unless other factors intervene, such as changing economic conditions.[50] At the beginning of an international crisis, the president enjoys near-unanimous support from members of the president's political party and strong support from independents and members of the other party. As the political climate returns to normal, the press and opposition party leaders begin voicing criticism, initially about domestic policy matters and eventually about foreign affairs, as well. Although members of the president's party usually continue to support the incumbent, members of the other party and independents began to register their displeasure with the president's performance and the president's overall standing in the polls falls.[51]

# the presidency
## & PUBLIC POLICY

the presidency is a major participant in every stage of the policymaking process.

## Agenda Building

No other figure in American politics is better positioned to influence the policy agenda than the president. Because the chief executive is always in the media spotlight, the president has a unique opportunity to direct attention to policy problems. President George W. Bush drew attention to his education reform proposal to require states to implement basic skills testing by visiting schools where similar reforms were already successfully in place. The president can discuss an issue during a State of the Union address, identify a problem during a press conference, or give a major speech to focus attention on an issue.[52] The president also has a number of spokespersons, including the vice president, members of the White House staff, and executive branch department heads, who can raise issues on behalf of the administration.

Research finds that the president has more influence in setting the domestic policy agenda than the agenda in foreign affairs. World events and media coverage of those events set the foreign policy agenda; the president just reacts. George W. Bush did not run for office expecting to fight a war on terror, but after September 11, 2001, the fight against terrorism became the primary focus of his administration. In contrast to foreign policy, the president has the opportunity to operate as an issue entrepreneur in domestic policy. If an issue is not already part of ongoing media coverage or congressional hearings, a president may be able to set the agenda of the television networks and Congress. President Clinton, for example, succeeded in making healthcare reform an important part of the policy agenda in his first term.[53] Furthermore, presidents can sometimes redefine issues already on the policy agenda. When George W. Bush took office, for example, education was already an important part of the nation's policy agenda. Bush succeeded in framing the issue in terms of basic skills testing.[54]

## THE PRESIDENT HAS MORE INFLUENCE IN SETTING THE DOMESTIC POLICY AGENDA THAN IN FOREIGN AFFAIRS

## Policy Formulation and Adoption

The president is involved in the formulation and adoption of a broad range of policies. Presidents propose legislation to Congress, sometimes drafting the actual bills in the White House or the executive branch. Presidential speeches inform members of Congress of the president's policy priorities.[55] Measures that reach the president for signature often reflect a compromise negotiated between the White House and congressional leaders, especially when the opposition party controls Congress. Because the veto power gives the president a formal role in legislative policymaking, the president can influence policy formulation. As long as one-third plus one member of either the House or Senate support the president's position on an issue, congressional leaders must negotiate with the White House over the content of legislation. The measure ultimately adopted may not totally reflect the president's policy preferences, but it will likely include some features the president favors and exclude some the president opposes.[56]

The president has the authority to adopt some policies without congressional participation. Presidents make policy when they negotiate executive agreements or issue executive orders. Although Congress has the authority to cancel or repeal an executive agreement or executive order legislatively, the action would be subject to a presidential veto. Over the years, especially during time of war, presidents have exercised extraordinary policymaking power based on their authority as commander in chief of the armed forces.

## Policy Implementation and Evaluation

As head of the executive branch, the president plays an important role in policy implementation. Congress frequently allows executive branch agencies a certain degree of discretion in implementing the nation's public policies. For example, the Environmental Protection Agency (EPA) may enforce the Clean Air Act more or less aggressively. President Carter contributed to the aggressive enforcement of environmental laws by appointing agency administrators who believed strongly in the agency's mission. Carter asked Congress for sufficient funding to support an aggressive enforcement effort. In contrast, President Reagan wanted the EPA to work more positively with the industries it regulates. He appointed critics of the EPA to head the agency and submitted budgets to Congress that cut money for enforcement activities.

The president also evaluates policies. The president can commission policy studies to identify weaknesses with current policies and then propose reforms. President George W. Bush, for example, appointed a commission to evaluate the Social Security system and to recommend changes to ensure its long-term financial stability. The president also engages in policy evaluation during the budgetary process, working primarily through the OMB.

# the THINK SPOT
## www.thethinkspot.com

# TEST yourself

1. After winning reelection in 2004, President George W. Bush was a lame duck. What does that phrase mean?
   A. President Bush was unpopular.
   B. President Bush was ineligible to run for reelection.
   C. President Bush had to deal with a Congress controlled by the opposition party.
   D. President Bush was facing impeachment charges.

2. Which of the following is *not* part of the impeachment process?
   A. The House drafts articles of impeachment.
   B. The House votes to impeach the president by majority vote.
   C. The chief justice presides over an impeachment trial in the Senate.
   D. The Senate votes to remove the president by majority vote.

3. Which of the following presidents was impeached and removed from office?
   A. Andrew Johnson
   B. Richard Nixon
   C. Bill Clinton
   D. None of the above

4. Which of the following statements about the vice presidency is true?
   A. The vice president votes in the Senate only to break a tie.
   B. The policymaking influence of the vice president today is significantly greater than it was 50 years ago.
   C. In case of presidential disability, the vice president can become acting president.
   D. All of the above.

5. Who is the chief of state of American government?
   A. The Senate president *pro tempore*
   B. The president
   C. The Speaker of the House
   D. The chief justice of the United States

6. What is the difference between an executive agreement and a treaty?
   A. Executive agreements do not require Senate ratification.
   B. Treaties are more numerous than executive agreements.
   C. The president negotiates treaties but members of Congress negotiate executive agreements.
   D. None of the above.

7. The Constitution gives the president all but which one of the following powers?
   A. To negotiate treaties
   B. To appoint ambassadors
   C. To declare war
   D. To fill judicial vacancies

8. Which of the following is an example of a check and balance on the powers of the presidency?
   A. Congress must ratify treaties.
   B. Congress must confirm judicial appointments.
   C. Congress must confirm ambassadorial appointments.
   D. All of the above.

9. Which of the following statements about the War Powers Act is true?
   A. It only applies to officially declared wars.
   B. It requires the president to consult with Congress whenever possible before committing American forces to combat.
   C. It has proved an effective check on the president's authority as commander in chief.
   D. None of the above.

10. What constitutional authority does the president have over the Supreme Court?
    A. The president can fill vacancies by appointment subject to Senate confirmation.
    B. The president can veto Supreme Court rulings subject to possible override by the Court.
    C. The president can initiate removal proceedings against justices.
    D. None of the above.

11. Suppose that President Obama disagrees with an executive order issued by President George W. Bush. What can he do?
    A. Obama can issue an executive order reversing Bush's executive order.
    B. Obama can ask Congress to repeal the Bush executive order.
    C. Obama can ask the Supreme Court to overturn the Bush order.
    D. Nothing.

12. Which of the following constitutional actions can a president take if Congress passes legislation the president opposes?

A. Nothing.

B. The president can veto the measure subject to a possible override.

C. The president can rewrite the legislation subject to a possible override.

D. The president can refuse to enforce the legislation.

13. A pronouncement issued by the president at the time a bill passed by Congress is signed into law is known as which of the following?

A. A veto statement

B. The State of the Union Address

C. A presidential signing statement

D. An executive order

14. Which of the following agencies is part of the Executive Office of the President?

A. Office of Management and Budget (OMB)

B. Department of Justice

C. Federal Communication Commission (FCC)

D. All of the above

15. Which of the following political scientists analyzes presidential performance based on the personality traits of the president?

A. Samuel Kernell

B. Richard Neustadt

C. Fred I. Greenstein

D. James David Barber

16. Which of the following political scientists analyzes presidential performance based on leadership style?

A. Samuel Kernell

B. Richard Neustadt

C. Fred I. Greenstein

D. James David Barber

17. Which of the following political scientists analyzes presidential performance based on the chief executive's skill as a political bargainer and coalition builder?

A. Samuel Kernell

B. Richard Neustadt

C. Fred I. Greenstein

D. James David Barber

18. Which of the following is an example of a unilateral tool of presidential power that does not require congressional approval?

A. Executive agreements

B. Recess appointments

C. Signing statements

D. All of the above

19. Soon after President Barack Obama took office, public opinion polls showed that he enjoyed a high approval rating. Which of the following terms would a political scientist use to describe Obama's high standing in the polls at the very beginning of his administration?

A. Two-presidencies thesis

B. Coat-tail effect

C. Honeymoon effect

D. Rally effect

20. President George W. Bush's approval rating soared after September 11, 2001. Which of the following terms would political scientists use to describe that phenomenon?

A. Two-presidencies thesis

B. Coat-tail effect

C. Honeymoon effect

D. Rally effect

KNOW *the* **score**

18–20 correct: Congratulations! You are well informed!

15–17 correct: Your political knowledge is a bit low—be sure to review the key terms and visit TheThinkSpot.

<14 correct: Reread the chapter more thoroughly.

1. B; 2. D; 3. D; 4. D; 5. B; 6. A; 7. C; 8. A; 9. B; 10. A; 11. A; 12. B; 13. C; 14. A; 15. D; 16. C; 17. B; 18. D; 19. C; 20. D

# 12 FEDERAL

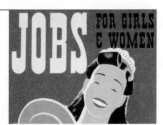

The World Health Organization (WHO) declared the HINI virus, commonly called swine flu, a pandemic in mid-2009.[1] The WHO made the designation because HINI was a new strain of the influenza virus that had infected people in more than 70 countries. By late 2009, more than a million swine flu cases had been reported in the United States, including cases in every state.[2] Although most cases were relatively mild, health officials worried that HINI could eventually pose a serious public health risk. The virus spreads easily from person to person and, because it was a new virus, people have little or no immunity to it. Furthermore, flu viruses mutate rapidly, so HINI could potentially develop into a more deadly illness than it had demonstrated by late 2009.[3] In 1918–1919, a new strain of the influenza virus killed 20 to 40 million people worldwide, including an estimated 675,000 Americans.[4]

Two federal agencies, the Centers for Disease Control and Prevention (CDC) and the Food and Drug Administration (FDA), led the response to the disease in the United States. The CDC tracked the illness, identifying cases and assessing their severity. It issued guidelines for responding to the disease, recommending, for example, when to close schools, and advising individuals as to the steps they could take to prevent contracting the illness. The FDA, meanwhile, approved both tests for the virus and antiviral treatments to counter its infection. The FDA also oversaw the development and approval of a vaccine that could be used to inoculate large numbers of people prior to the winter flu season.[5]

# BUREAUCRACY

# ESSENTIALS...

*after studying Chapter 12, students should be able to answer the following questions:*

> **How is the federal bureaucracy organized?**

> **What is the history of federal personnel policies?**

> **What are the steps of the rulemaking process?**

> **What perspectives and political resources do the president, Congress, interest groups, and bureaucrats have in the administrative process?**

> **How do subgovernments and issue networks affect bureaucratic policymaking?**

> **What is the role of the federal bureaucracy in the policymaking process?**

# organization of
## THE BUREAUCRACY

t he Constitution says nothing about the organization of the executive branch. Congress and the president through the legislative process have created the executive departments, commissions, agencies, and bureaus of the federal bureaucracy on a piecemeal basis over the last 220 years.

## Cabinet Departments

The **cabinet departments** are major administrative units of the federal government. They have responsibility for the conduct of a wide range of government operations. The 15 cabinet departments (in the order of their creation) are as follows: State, Defense, Treasury, Justice, Interior, Agriculture, Commerce, Labor, Housing and Urban Development (HUD), Transportation, Energy, Health and Human Services, Education, Veterans Affairs, and Homeland Security. The largest departments in terms of personnel are Defense and Veterans Affairs. In 2007, the Department of Defense had 673,722 civilian employees; the Department of Veterans Affairs employed 245,537 workers. In contrast, fewer than 4,500 employees worked for the Department of Education, the smallest department.[6] Each cabinet department includes a number of smaller administrative units. The Federal Emergency Management

Agency (FEMA), for example, is part of the Department of Homeland Security. Both the CDC and FDA are part of the Department of Health and Human Services. With the exception of the attorney general, who heads the Justice Department, the people who lead the cabinet departments are called secretaries. The Secretary of Defense, for example, heads the Department of Defense.

The president appoints the heads of the cabinet departments and their chief assistants, who are called undersecretaries, deputy undersecretaries, and assistant secretaries, pending Senate confirmation. Although the Senate confirms most presidential appointments, the approval process has grown increasingly time-consuming. The average time between presidential nomination and Senate confirmation for executive branch appointees has increased steadily from 2.35 months for the nominees of President John Kennedy[7] to 9 months for individuals nominated by President George W. Bush.[8] The Senate is more likely to reject or at least fail to confirm a nominee when one party holds the White House and the other controls the Senate. Confirmation delays have steadily increased, regardless of party control of Congress and the White House, because individual senators have more frequently been using a parliamentary procedure called a hold that allows an individual senator to privately delay a vote on a nomination.[9]

Presidents employ a number of criteria in selecting department heads. They look for knowledge, administrative ability, experience, loyalty, and congeniality. Some cabinet posts may be given to reward campaign assistance. Modern presidents want a cabinet that includes both men and women, and that reflects

**If you were president, what qualities would you look for in a cabinet secretary?**

**cabinet departments** major administrative units of the federal government that have responsibility for the conduct of a wide range of government operations.

The president's cabinet includes the Vice President and the heads of 15 executive departments—the Secretaries of Agriculture, Commerce, Defense, Education, Energy, Health and Human Services, Homeland Security, Housing and Urban Development, Interior, Labor, State, Transportation, Treasury, and Veterans Affairs, as well as the Attorney General.

**STATE** Conducts foreign policy, including negotiating treaties & executive agreements

**TREASURY** Manages government finance

**DEFENSE** Provides for national defense

**JUSTICE** Enforces the law

**INTERIOR** Manages the nation's natural resources, including wildlife & public lands

**AGRICULTURE** Promotes agriculture, implements food & nutrition programs

**COMMERCE** Assists businesses & conducts the U.S. Census

**LABOR** Administers labor laws

**HEALTH & HUMAN SERVICES** Implements health, welfare, & Social Security programs

**HOUSING AND URBAN DEVELOPMENT** Manages urban and housing programs

**TRANSPORTATION** Oversees national transportation system, including highway & mass transit programs

**ENERGY** Manages energy policy & research

**EDUCATION** Administers federal education policy, including No Child Left Behind

**VETERANS AFFAIRS** Administers programs aiding veterans

**HOMELAND SECURITY** Protects against terrorism & responds to natural disasters

the ethnic and racial diversity of the United States. Presidents also seek individuals who fit the style and image of the department and who will be acceptable to the interest groups with which the department works most closely. The secretary of the treasury, for example, is typically someone with a background in banking or finance. The secretary of agriculture is a farmer, usually from the Midwest.

The heads of the cabinet departments are part of the **president's cabinet**, a body that includes the executive department heads and other senior officials chosen by the president, such as the U.S. ambassador to the United Nations. The policymaking role of the cabinet varies from president to president. President Dwight Eisenhower delegated considerable responsibilities to cabinet members. He met with his cabinet two or three times a month. In contrast, contemporary presidents seldom convene their

# MOST DEPARTMENT HEADS DO NOT HAVE THE TIME TO CONCENTRATE ON THE DETAILS OF ADMINISTRATION

cabinets, relying instead on the White House staff, the Executive Office of the President, and individual department heads. President Bill Clinton, for example, convened his cabinet only seven times during his first year in office.[10] The traditional image of the cabinet is that its members are primarily responsible for advising the president on policy formulation and leading their departments in policy implementa-

tion. In practice, however, most executive department heads do not do much of either activity. Presidents usually turn to smaller groups of aides, advisers, and selected department heads for policy advice. Four cabinet officials—the secretary of state, secretary of defense, secretary of the treasury, and the attorney general—are known as the **inner cabinet** because of the importance of the policy issues their departments address.[11] Full cabinet meetings tend to become forums for presidential pep talks or show-and-tell sessions for cabinet members to discuss the latest developments in their departments. As for leading their departments, many secretaries soon learn that their departments are not easily led. Also, most department heads do not have the time to concentrate on the details of administration. They are too busy dealing with Congress, doing public relations work with their department's constituents, selling the president's program, and campaigning for the president's reelection.

## Independent Executive Agencies

Congress and the president have also created a number of **independent executive agencies,** executive branch agencies that are not part of any of the 15 cabinet-level departments. The Peace Corps, National Aeronautics and Space Administration (NASA), Central Intelligence Agency (CIA), Environmental Protection Agency (EPA), Social Security Administration (SSA), and the Small Business Administration (SBA) are independent executive agencies that are headed by individual administrators. The Federal Election Com-

**president's cabinet** an advisory group created by the president that includes the department heads and other officials chosen by the president.

**inner cabinet** the secretary of state, secretary of defense, secretary of the treasury, and the attorney general.

**independent executive agencies** executive branch agencies that are not part of any of the 15 cabinet-level departments.

## btw...

In the spring of 2008, hundreds of people across the United States fell ill with salmonella infection. The Food and Drug Administration, an agency of the Department of Health and Human Services, scrambled to trace the outbreak. Consumers were advised to avoid certain strains of tomatoes and peppers, and many restaurants stopped serving this produce. As months passed and the FDA was still unable to track down the exact source, the agency was widely criticized by farmers who experienced massive revenue losses because of the FDA's broad warnings against various kinds of produce. Agricultural interest groups are demanding that this case result in dramatic changes in the FDA.

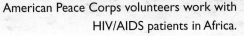

American Peace Corps volunteers work with HIV/AIDS patients in Africa.

Independent executive agencies perform a range of administrative and regulatory activities. The **Peace Corps,** for example, is an agency that administers an American foreign aid program under which volunteers travel to developing nations to teach skills and help improve living standards. The National Aeronautics and Space Administration (NASA) is the federal agency in charge of the space program. The Central Intelligence Agency (CIA) is the federal agency that gathers and evaluates foreign intelligence information in the interest of national security. The Environmental Protection Agency (EPA) is the federal agency responsible for enforcing the nation's environmental laws. The Social Security Administration (SSA) is a federal agency that operates the Social Security system. The Small Business Administration (SBA) is a federal agency established to make loans to small businesses and assist them in obtaining government contracts. The Federal Election Commission (FEC) is the agency that enforces federal campaign finance laws.

mission (FEC) is an independent executive agency headed by a multi-member commission. The president appoints both individual agency heads and board members, pending confirmation by the Senate. The heads of independent executive agencies report directly to the president and serve at the president's pleasure. FEMA was an independent executive agency before the creation of the Department of Homeland Security.

**Peace Corps** an agency that administers an American foreign aid program under which volunteers travel to developing nations to teach skills and help improve living standards.

## Government Corporations

Government corporations are organizationally similar to private corporations except that the government, rather than stockholders, owns them. Their organizational rationale is that an agency that makes a product or provides a service should be run by methods similar to those used in the private sector. For example, the Postal Service is a government corporation responsible for mail service. An 11-member board of governors appointed by the president to serve 9-year, overlapping terms leads the agency. The board names a postmaster general to manage the day-to-day operation of the service. In addition to the Postal Service, the list of government corporations includes the National Railroad Passenger Corporation (which is known as Amtrak), a federal agency that operates intercity passenger railway traffic; the Federal Deposit Insurance Corporation (FDIC), a federal agency established to insure depositors' accounts in banks and thrift institutions; and the Tennessee Valley Authority (TVA), a federal agency established to promote the development of the Tennessee River and its tributaries.

An important principle behind government corporations is that they should be self-financing, at least to a significant degree. In the case of the Postal Service, users pay most of the cost of operation by purchasing stamps and paying service charges. Not all government corporations, however, are financially self-sufficient. Amtrak requires a subsidy from Congress to keep its trains rolling. Amtrak's critics argue that the agency should be

If you were a member of Congress, would you vote in favor of government subsidies of AMTRAK?

forced to pay its own way or go out of business. If the demand for passenger rail is not sufficient to support Amtrak's operation, then the service should end. In contrast, the defenders of Amtrak believe that the agency provides an important service that should be continued. Furthermore, they point out that the government subsidizes automobile transportation by building highways and air transportation by constructing airports.

**The FCC fined CBS for a performance by Justin Timberlake and Janet Jackson at the 2004 Superbowl that included a "wardrobe malfunction" on national television.**

## Foundations and Institutes

Foundations and institutes administer grant programs to local governments, universities, nonprofit institutions, and individuals for research in the natural and social sciences or to promote the arts. These agencies include the National Science Foundation (NSF), a federal agency established to encourage scientific advances and improvements in science education, and the National Endowment for the Arts (NEA), a federal agency created to nurture cultural expression and promote appreciation of the arts. Foundations and institutes are governed by multimember boards appointed by the president with Senate concurrence from lists of nominees submitted by various scientific and educational institutions.

## Independent Regulatory Commissions

An **independent regulatory commission** is an agency outside the major executive departments that is charged with the regulation of important aspects of the economy. The Federal Trade Commission (FTC), for example, is an agency that regulates business competition, including enforcement of laws against monopolies and the protection of consumers from deceptive trade practices. The Federal Communications Commission (FCC) is an agency that regulates interstate and international radio, television, telephone, telegraph, and satellite communications, as well as licensing radio and television stations. The Securities and Exchange Commission (SEC) is an agency that regulates the sale of stocks and bonds as well as investment and holding companies. The Equal Employment Opportunity Commission (EEOC) is an agency that investigates and rules on charges of employment discrimination.

Congress has attempted to insulate independent regulatory commissions

The National Science Foundation supports a wide range of media and museum experiences to engage learners in science education. A recent popular traveling exhibit is "CSI: The Experience" in which participants can enter crime scene rooms and play the role of investigator. They learn scientific principles and real investigative techniques as they try to solve the crime in a given room.

from direct political pressure, especially from the White House. These agencies are headed by boards of three to seven members who are appointed by the president with Senate approval. In contrast to cabinet members and the heads of other executive departments, the president cannot remove regulatory commissioners. Instead, they serve fixed, staggered terms ranging from 3 to 14 years. As a result, a new president must usually wait several years before having much impact on the composition of the boards. Furthermore, the law generally requires that no more than a bare majority of board members be from the same political party.

Congress has designed independent regulatory commissions to provide closer, more flexible regulation than Congress itself can offer through **statutory law**, law written

by the legislature. Congress has delegated authority to these agencies to control various business practices using broad, general language. Congress has authorized the FTC, for example, to regulate advertising in the "public convenience, interest, or necessity." It has empowered the EEOC "to prevent any person from engaging in any unlawful employment practice."

**independent regulatory commission** an agency outside the major executive departments that is charged with the regulation of important aspects of the economy.

**statutory law** law that is written by the legislature.

## Quasi-Governmental Companies

A **quasi-governmental company** is a private, profit-seeking corporation created by Congress to serve a public purpose. For example, Congress created the Federal National Mortgage Association (Fannie Mae) and Federal Home Loan Mortgage Corporation (Freddie Mac) to increase the availability of credit to home buyers. Fannie Mae and Freddie Mac are profit-making corporations run by 18-member boards of governors appointed by the president with Senate confirmation. They are exempt from state and federal taxation and enjoy a line of credit at the U.S. Treasury.

Because of the perception that Congress would bail them out if they got in financial trouble, Fannie Mae and Freddie Mac pay lower interest rates than they would if they were strictly private enterprises. Lower rates benefit home buyers, some of whom would not be able to qualify to purchase a home at all without the lower interest rate.

In 2008, Congress passed, and the president signed, legislation to commit federal funds to Fannie Mae and Freddie Mac to ensure that they would not collapse under the weight of losses incurred in the housing foreclosure crisis. The federal government eventually took over the operation of Fannie Mae and Freddie Mac, at least temporarily, to prevent their financial collapse, which would have been catastrophic for the home mortgage industry. The action kept Fannie and Freddie in business, but potentially put taxpayers on the hook for billions of dollars in bad loans.

**quasi-governmental company** a private, profit-seeking corporation created by Congress to serve a public purpose.

# personnel

**t**he size of the federal civilian bureaucracy has grown dramatically since the early days of the nation. In 1800, only about 3,000 persons worked for the U.S. government. That figure grew to 95,000 by 1881 and half a million in 1925. Today, the federal bureaucracy is the largest civilian workforce in the Western world, with 2.7 million civilian employees stationed in every state and city in the country and in almost every nation in the world.[12]

As the figure on p. 265 indicates, the number of federal civilian employees has generally fallen since the early 1990s. Between 1991 and 2001, the federal payroll decreased from 3.1 million to 2.7 million, a decline of nearly 13 percent. After September 11, 2001, the number of federal employees inched up. Congress passed, and the president signed, legislation to make airport baggage screeners federal employees, adding thousands of people to the federal payroll. Employment in other federal agencies that deal with security issues, including the Border Patrol, increased as well. The post-9/11 surge in federal employment peaked in 2003. Thereafter, the size of the federal workforce began to decline again.

Although the official size of the federal workforce has generally declined since the early 1990s, the actual number of people employed directly and indirectly by the federal government has risen sharply over the same period of time. Political scientist Paul C. Light estimates that the true size of the federal civilian workforce is 14.6 million employees, not the 2.7 million on the official payroll.[13] In addition to civilian employees working directly for the federal government, Light's figure includes millions of contract workers, state and local government employees working on federally funded programs, and federal grant beneficiaries at colleges and universities. The federal government pays their salaries, but their names do not appear on federal personnel rosters. Contract workers collect

THE ACTUAL NUMBER OF PEOPLE EMPLOYED DIRECTLY AND **INDIRECTLY** BY THE FEDERAL GOVERNMENT HAS RISEN SHARPLY SINCE THE 1990s.

taxes, prepare budget documents, take notes at meetings, and perform hundreds of other governmental functions. The Department of Defense even hires private security guards to protect military bases in the United States.[14] Furthermore, Congress and the president rely on millions of state and local bureaucrats to administer federal programs, such as No Child Left Behind, Medicaid, and the Food Stamp Program.

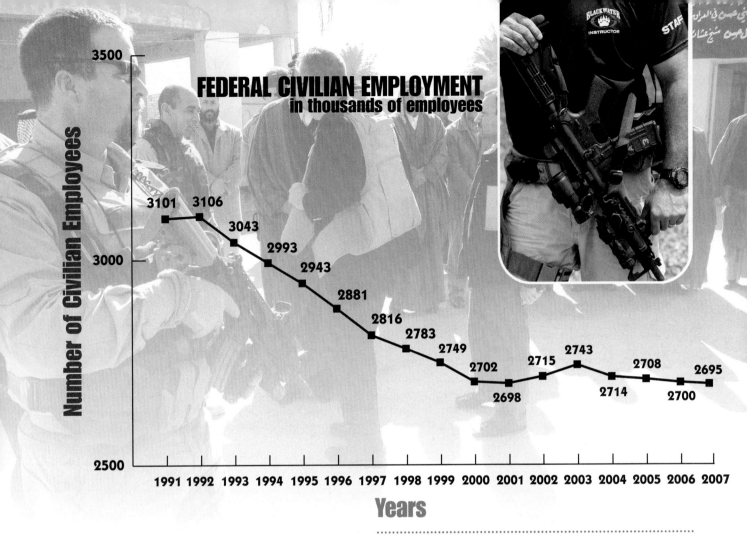

# FEDERAL CIVILIAN EMPLOYMENT
## in thousands of employees

**Number of Civilian Employees**

3500

3000

2500

3101 3106 3043 2993 2943 2881 2816 2783 2749 2702 2698 2715 2743 2714 2708 2700 2695

1991 1992 1993 1994 1995 1996 1997 1998 1999 2000 2001 2002 2003 2004 2005 2006 2007

**Years**

The number of federal civilian employees fell during the 1990s and has since leveled off at around 2.7 million.

## Employment Practices

Employment practices in the early days of the nation emphasized character, professional qualifications, and political compatibility with the administration in office. Under President Andrew Jackson (1829–1837), political considerations became paramount. A new president would fire many of the employees of the previous administration and replace them with friends and supporters. To the victor belonged the spoils they said, and federal jobs were the spoils. The method of hiring government employees from among the friends, relatives, and supporters of elected officeholders was known as the **spoils system**.

**think**

What are the advantages of civil service tests for federal employees?

When a disgruntled office seeker assassinated President James Garfield in 1881, Congress passed, and the new president signed, legislation to reform the federal hiring process. The legislation created a Civil Service Commission to establish a hiring system based on competitive examinations and to protect federal workers from dismissal for political reasons. Initially, the civil service system covered only about

10 percent of federal jobs, but Congress gradually expanded coverage to include more than 90 percent of federal workers.[15] In 1939, Congress enacted another reform, the **Hatch Act** (named after its author, Senator Carl Hatch of New Mexico), which was a measure designed to restrict the political activities of

**spoils system** the method of hiring government employees from among the friends, relatives, and supporters of elected officeholders.

**Hatch Act** a measure designed to restrict the political activities of federal employees to voting and the private expression of views.

# Where Do Federal Employees Work?

| GOVERNMENT AGENCIES | NUMBER OF EMPLOYEES |
| --- | --- |
| Postal Service | 753,254 |
| Department of Defense | 673,722 |
| Veterans Affairs | 245,537 |
| Homeland Security | 155,397 |
| Department of the Treasury | 111,577 |
| Department of Justice | 106,946 |
| Social Security Administration | 62,769 |

Source: Federal Civilian Employment by Branch and Agency: U.S. Census Bureau, *The 2008 Statistical Abstract*, available at www.census.gov.

federal employees to voting and the private expression of views. The rationale behind the law was to protect government workers from being forced by their superiors to work for particular candidates.

Although civil service ended the spoils system, it, too, became the target of criticism. Many observers charged that the civil service system was too inflexible to reward merit, punish poor performance, or transfer civil servants from one agency to another without having to scale a mountain of red tape. In 1978, Congress and the president responded to complaints against the civil service system by enacting a package of reforms. The legislation established a Senior Executive Service (SES) composed of approximately 8,000 top civil servants who would be eligible for substantial merit bonuses but who could be transferred, demoted, or fired more easily than other federal employees. The reform measure replaced the old Civil Service Commission with two new agencies: an Office of Personnel Management to manage the federal workforce and a

# Evolution of the FEDERAL BUREAUCRACY

**1789** | Congress authorizes the creation of the first federal agency, which it later renamed the Department of State.

**1881** | A disgruntled federal office seeker assassinates President James Garfield.

**1883** | Congress passes the Civil Service Reform Act, also called the Pendleton Act, to reform the federal hiring process on the basis of merit rather than patronage.

| 1780 | 1800 | 1820 | 1840 | 1860 | 1880 | 1900 | 1920 |
| --- | --- | --- | --- | --- | --- | --- | --- |

**1829** | President Andrew Jackson ushers in the spoils system, in which political considerations became paramount in hiring government employees.

**1933** | The size of the federal bureaucracy balloons during the New Deal era as President Franklin Delano Roosevelt and Congress create a series of federal agencies to regulate industry and to put Americans back to work during the Great Depression.

Merit Systems Protection Board to hear employee grievances.[16]

Congress and the president have given federal employees limited rights to organize. Federal workers won the right to form unions in 1912. Fifty years later, President John Kennedy signed an executive order giving federal workers the right to bargain collectively over a limited set of issues but not about pay or benefits. **Collective bargaining** is a negotiation between an employer and a union representing employees over the terms and conditions of employment. The civil service reform legislation adopted in 1978 guaranteed federal employees the right to bargain collectively over issues other than pay and benefits, but it prohibited federal workers from striking. In 1981, President Ronald Reagan fired more than 11,000 air traffic controllers for participating in a strike organized by the Professional Air Traffic Controllers Association (PATCO).

Democratic presidents typically have a more positive relationship with federal employee organizations than do Republican presidents. Labor unions in general are allied with the Democratic Party, whereas the GOP has stronger ties to management, and public employee unions are no exception to the pattern. President Bill Clinton, for example, issued an executive order directing federal agencies to develop partnerships with the employee unions. Clinton justified the approach as a means to reform government by making it more efficient. In contrast, President George W. Bush took an adversarial approach toward employee unions. He dissolved the partnership councils created during the Clinton administration and asked

**collective bargaining** a negotiation between an employer and a union representing employees over the terms and conditions of employment.

## Federal employees MAY:

be candidates for public office in nonpartisan elections

express opinions about candidates and issues

contribute money to political organizations

attend and be active in political fundraising functions, political rallies, and political party or club meetings

campaign for or against candidates in partisan elections

## Federal employees MAY NOT:

be candidates for public office in partisan elections

use their official authority or influence to affect the outcome of an election

knowingly encourage or discourage the political activity of any person who has business before the agency

engage in political activity while on duty, in any government office, while wearing an official uniform, or while using a government vehicle

Source: U.S. Special Counsel's Office

**1939** | Congress authorizes the establishment of the Executive Office of the President (EOP) to assist in managing the bureaucracy, and passes the Hatch Act, which restricts the political activities of federal employees.

SEVERE
SEVERE RISK OF TERRORIST ATTACKS

HIGH
HIGH RISK OF TERRORIST ATTACKS

ELEVATED
SIGNIFICANT RISK OF TERRORIST ATTACKS

GUARDED
GENERAL RISK OF TERRORIST ATTACKS

LOW
LOW RISK OF TERRORIST ATTACKS

**2002** | George W. Bush issues an executive order creating an Office of Homeland Security within the EOP, which is later elevated to a full cabinet department.

1940    1960    1980    2000

**1965** | Lyndon Johnson's Great Society programs result in the largest expansion of the federal bureaucracy since FDR's New Deal.

**1978** | Congress enacts a package of reforms, including the creation of two new agencies: an Office of Personnel Management to manage the federal workforce and a Merit Systems Protection Board to hear employee grievances.

Congress to change personnel policies in light of the war on terror.[17]

When Congress created the Department of Homeland Security, it gave President Bush authority to relax civil service rules to make it easier for the administration to hire, transfer, promote, cross-train, discipline, and fire employees in the new department without having to worry about union rules and civil service procedures. The president argued that the administration needed more flexibility over personnel than the old civil service system provided in order to create a modern workforce capable of responding to the threat of international terrorism. In particular, the administration wanted to base annual salary increases on performance tied to job

evaluations, rather than giving every employee an annual raise based on longevity. The American Federation of Government Employees and other employee unions adamantly opposed waiving civil service rules because they feared that some managers would use the authority to reward their friends and punish their enemies, without regard for the

performance of the workers.[18] But the unions lost, not just for the Department of Homeland Security, but for the whole federal government. Unless Congress changes the law, the federal government will adopt a pay-for-performance system for all federal agencies in 2009, replacing the old general schedule system with its 15 GS levels and 10 steps within each level. The new system will make it easier for managers to reward good work and punish poor performance while making it more difficult for unions to intervene on behalf of their members.[19] With Democrats in control of Congress and a Democrat in the White House in 2009, however, the new pay-for-performance system may never go into effect.

Federal civil service employees generally cannot strike, in part because the federal government does not want major transportation or economic systems disrupted. The 2005 New York City transit strike by employees of the local Metropolitan Transit Authority (MTA) suggests why. The $2^1/_2$ day strike by the transit workers (who are *not* federal employees) shut down buses and subways, stranding millions of commuters and putting thousands of people on foot.

# rulemaking

independent regulatory commissions and regulatory agencies in the executive branch do much of their work through the rulemaking process. When Congress passes regulatory legislation, it frequently delegates authority to the bureaucracy to make rules to implement the legislation. A **rule** is a legally binding regulation. **Rulemaking** is the regulatory process used by government agencies to enact legally binding regulations. The SEC, for example, makes rules governing corporate finance disclosure. On average, federal agencies produce between four and five thousand rules a year.[20]

The rulemaking process begins with an agency giving advance notice that it is considering issuing a rule in a particular policy area. The agency publishes the text of the proposed rule in the *Federal Register* and allows at least 30 days for the public to comment on the proposed rule. Concerned parties, usually interest groups affected by the proposed rule, submit written comments or offer testimony at public hearings. When an agency officially adopts a rule, it is published in the *Code of Federal Regulations*.

The Office of Management and Budget (OMB) is a regular participant in the rulemaking process. In 1981, President Ronald Reagan issued an executive order requiring that any executive branch agency issuing a new rule with an economic impact of $100 million or more must prepare a cost-benefit analysis and submit it to the OMB for approval. A **cost-benefit analysis** is an evaluation of a proposed policy or regulation based on a comparison of its expected benefits and anticipated costs. Reagan's order applied to executive branch agencies such as the EPA, but not to independent regulatory commissions such as the FCC. Although subsequent presidents have kept Reagan's requirement for a cost-benefit analysis of regulations, they have approached the issue from different perspectives. In Republican administrations, the OMB functions as an appeals court for business and trade groups worried about the impact of regulation on their activities. In contrast, environmentalists, consumer groups, and organized labor have more influence in the

**rulemaking** the regulatory process used by government agencies to enact legally binding regulations.
**rule** a legally binding regulation.
**cost-benefit analysis** an evaluation of a proposed policy or regulation based on a comparison of its expected benefits and anticipated costs.

## Mark CUBAN

Billionaire Mark Cuban has played a lot of roles in his life. He owned two different technology companies that he sold for huge profits. He owns the NBA's Dallas Mavericks (where he has continually aggravated the league with his frequent criticism of game officials and league policy). He was even a contestant on ABC's *Dancing with the Stars*. And soon, Cuban might have a new role if the SEC has its way: inmate. In November 2008, the SEC filed charges against Cuban for insider trading. They allege he dumped all his Mamma.com stock based on inside information about a coming company stock sale. Cuban stated pointedly: "The government's claims are false and they will be proven to be so." The case is pending.

OMB review process during Democratic administrations.[21]

Congress exercises oversight of agency rules. Agencies must submit all proposed new rules to Congress, which has 60 days to overturn it through the legislative process subject to a presidential veto and a possible override attempt. If Congress does not act within 60 days, the rule goes into effect.

Federal courts also play a role in the rulemaking process. Individuals and groups unhappy with agency decisions sometimes turn to the federal courts for relief. Courts hear challenges not just from business groups who believe that federal regulations have gone too far, but also from consumer and environmental groups who argue that regulations are not strict enough. In general, the courts have ruled that agency decisions must be supported by evidence and reasoned explanations, and that the agencies must follow statutory requirements to give notice, hold hearings, and consult with parties outside the affected industries.[22]

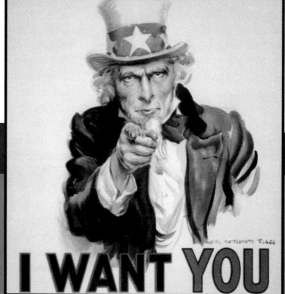

# politics and
## ADMINISTRATION

**b**ureaucratic policymaking is a complex process involving the president, Congress, interest groups, and the bureaucracy itself. Each of the participants has a perspective and a set of political resources for achieving its goals.

## The President

Presidents have an important stake in the faithful and efficient implementation of federal programs, but they must work to influence the administrative process—and their success is not assured. Being chief executive does not entitle a president to command the federal bureaucracy so much as it offers the opportunity to influence policy implementation. President Jimmy Carter once ordered relevant federal agencies to develop guidelines to implement the administration's policy of discouraging industrial and commercial development in areas subject to repeated flooding. More than two years later, only 15 of 37 agencies most directly involved had written guidelines. Thirteen agencies were still working on the assignment, and 12 agencies had done nothing at all![23]

Presidents face a continuous struggle to have a major impact on bureaucratic policymaking. The federal bureaucracy is too large and spread out for easy oversight from the White House, and many federal programs are administered by state and local officials or by private contractors over whom the president has little direct authority. Presidents often lack the time to manage the bureaucracy and may not be interested in trying. It is more glamorous and politically rewarding, at least in the short run, to propose new policy initiatives than to supervise the implementation of programs already in place.

Presidents have several tools for influencing the bureaucracy. The president has the authority to name most of the top administrators in the bureaucracy, including department secretaries and undersecretaries, agency heads, and regulatory commissioners. President George W. Bush ordered each executive branch agency to create a regulatory policy office run by a presidential appointee to ensure that rules and other actions taken by the agency conformed to the president's policy priorities.[24] Except for members of the independent regulatory commissions, presidents also have the power to dismiss their appointees.

The president can use the OMB to evaluate agency performance and screen rules proposed by executive branch agencies. The president proposes agency budgets and can ask Congress to reorganize the bureaucracy.

## Congress

Congress has strong legal authority to oversee the actions of the federal bureaucracy. Congress can abolish an agency, reorganize its structure, change its jurisdiction, cut its budget, audit its expenditures, investigate its performance, and overrule its decisions. In short, Congress has effective means for getting an agency's attention. The Smithsonian Institution is a national museum and educational institution chartered by Congress. When the Smithsonian's governing board failed to provide Congress with a satisfactory justification for an exclusive deal with Showtime Network to use materials in the Smithsonian collection to make films, the House

Since 2002, the airport screeners who check to ensure that passengers do not carry cigarette lighters, knives, and other prohibited items on airplanes have been federal employees.

Appropriations Committee cut $15 million from the agency's budget and sought a cap on salaries for agency administrators.[25]

Some political scientists believe that congressional oversight is generally ineffective. Congress is unable to provide clear, consistent policy oversight for the bureaucracy, they say, because Congress itself lacks consensus on administrative policy goals. Whereas some members of Congress will think an agency has gone too far, others will believe that it has not gone far enough. Furthermore, many political scientists believe that the increased attention of members of Congress to **constituency service** (the actions of members of Congress and their staffs attending to the individual, particular needs of constituents) has made senators and representatives more dependent on executive branch agencies for help in providing services to constituents. Members of Congress who have built mutually beneficial relationships with the bureaucracy are not going to undermine those relationships through aggressive oversight.[26]

In contrast, other political scientists believe that Congress has developed an effective method of oversight through a process that some observers call **fire-alarm oversight.** It is an indirect system of congressional surveillance of bureaucratic administration, characterized by rules, procedures, and informal practices that enable individual citizens and organized interest groups to examine administrative decisions, charge agencies with violating legislative goals, and seek remedies from agencies, courts, and the Congress itself. In other words, Congress exercises oversight when the media, interest groups, or citizens call attention to a problem. Congress reacted to complaints about FEMA's response to Hurricane Katrina because of the visibility of the issue.

## Interest Groups

Every agency has several, or perhaps dozens, of interest groups vitally concerned with the programs it administers. Broadcasters are concerned with the FCC. The airline industry, aircraft manufacturers, airline employee associations, and consumer groups have an interest in the Federal Aviation Administration (FAA). Western land interests and environmentalists monitor the activities of the Interior Department. Postal workers' unions, direct-mail advertisers, publishers, and consumer groups focus on the work of the Postal Service.

Interest groups have a number of tools for influencing the bureaucracy. Groups lobby bureaucratic agencies. They also lobby Congress to pressure the bureaucracy on their behalf. Sometimes groups file lawsuits to block or reverse an agency's decisions.

Critics charge that federal agencies often become **captured agencies,** that is, agencies that work to benefit the economic interests they regulate rather than to serve the public interest. The Federal Maritime Commission, for example, historically has worked closely with shippers. The Federal Power Commission has been accused of acting on behalf of the electric-utility industry. Proponents of the captured-agencies thesis point to what they describe as a revolving door between industry and the bureaucracy as evidence of the comfortable relationship between the regulatory commissions and industry. Presidents appoint corporate lawyers and industry executives to serve as commissioners. When the commissioners eventually leave government, they often take jobs in the industries they once regulated.

Many political scientists believe that the captured-agencies thesis is too simplistic. Studies have found that capture is not the norm, and when it does occur, it does not always last.[27] Instead, a range of factors, including presidential appointments, congressional committees and subcommittees, judicial actions, economic conditions, and agency staffs affect agency decisions.[28] Professor Steven P. Croley notes that government agencies do not always take the side of special interests against the public interest. The FTC, for example, adopted the National Do Not Call Registry despite the opposition of the telemarketing industry.[29] The captured agencies thesis assumes that the political environment for each government agency consists of a single set of interest groups with a similar perspective, but that is not usually the case. The debate over the adop-

**Interest groups have a number of tools for influencing the bureaucracy.**

**constituency service** the action of members of Congress and their staffs attending to the individual, particular needs of constituents.

**fire-alarm oversight** an indirect system of congressional surveillance of bureaucratic administration characterized by rules, procedures, and informal practices that enable individual citizens and organized interest groups to examine administrative decisions, charge agencies with violating legislative goals, and seek remedies from agencies, courts, and Congress itself.

**captured agencies** agencies that work to benefit the economic interests they regulate rather than serving the public interest.

tion of the National Do Not Call Registry involved not just an industry group, but also consumer organizations and the AARP.

## Bureaucrats

Each agency has two sets of administrators—a small group of presidential appointees, typically called political appointees, and a larger group of career civil servants. Nineteen presidential appointees and 284 SES managers lead the Department of Health and Human Services. Five presidential appointees and 20 SES managers head the EEOC.[30] In contrast to presidential employees who

their programs, and their budgets. Furthermore, agencies often attract employees who are personally committed to the mission of their department. Environmentalists work for the EPA, whereas people with agricultural backgrounds seek employment with the Department of Agriculture.

Career bureaucrats have resources for defending their turf. Sometimes career employees resort to subtle, behind-the-scenes resistance to policy changes they oppose, a sort of bureaucratic guerrilla warfare. In an organization as large as the federal bureaucracy, presidential initiatives can be opposed in

byists. By assisting key members of Congress with problems involving constituent complaints, agencies build friendships. Furthermore, most agencies have interest group constituencies that are willing to use their political resources on behalf of the agency. Teacher groups lobby for the Department of Education; defense contractors fight for the defense budget. Medical professionals support the Public Health Service.

Executive branch officials know that they are more likely to achieve their goals if they can find a way to connect their policy preferences with the self-interest of members of

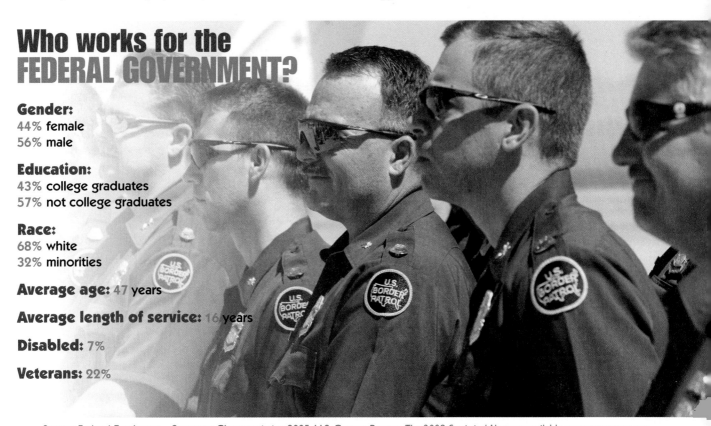

## Who works for the FEDERAL GOVERNMENT?

**Gender:**
44% female
56% male

**Education:**
43% college graduates
57% not college graduates

**Race:**
68% white
32% minorities

**Average age:** 47 years

**Average length of service:** 16 years

**Disabled:** 7%

**Veterans:** 22%

Source: Federal Employees—Summary Characteristics: 2005, U.S. Census Bureau, *The 2008 Statistical Abstract*, available at www.census.gov.

serve no more than four or eight years, depending on the number of terms of the president who appoints them, SES managers are career bureaucrats who stay with a single agency for most of their careers. SES managers have interests of their own that may differ from those of the president and political administrators appointed to run their agencies. Career SES managers typically want to preserve and enhance their positions,

a number of quiet ways. Changes may be delayed. Bureaucrats may follow the letter but not the spirit of directives. Officials may "forget" to pass along orders to subordinates. News of mistakes or internal bickering may be leaked to the press.[31]

Bureaucracy finds power in alliances with important members of Congress and interest groups. Executive branch agencies are some of the most vigorous and effective lob-

Congress. Consider NASA's successful strategy for winning congressional support for continued funding of the International Space Station (ISS). NASA distributed work on the ISS to 68 prime contractors and 35 major subcontractors in 22 states, including California, Texas, Florida, New York, Illinois, Ohio, and Pennsylvania—all states with large, politically influential congressional delegations.[32]

# 9/11 Commission

**Is the intelligence community truly to blame for the 9/11 attacks? Is it possible that no matter how effective and efficient a bureaucracy may be, there are just some things that will always lie outside its sphere of action?**

**Overview:** Bureaucracies are essential for the proper and efficient functioning of government, and one significant benefit—if not one of the most important benefits—of bureaucracies is that they provide expert policy analysis and policy proposals in their respective domains. One particular problem in governmental bureaucracies is that many within a given bureaucracy want to protect turf; that is, civil servants or agents do not want to share responsibility or policy with other agencies.

The September 11 attacks and the subsequent war in Iraq (with its missing weapons of mass destruction) have demonstrated to the American people and government that America's intelligence capabilities are woefully inade-

quate to address new threats found in the post–Cold War world. Questions remain as to what went wrong. To this end, a nonpartisan panel was commissioned to investigate how and why the September 11 attacks happened, and to propose policy changes and solutions in order to prevent further attacks. Among other things, one of the striking findings of the 9/11 Commission was the massive intelligence failure due to bureaucratic myopia, lack of communication between intelligence agencies, institutional rules and regulations that prohibited the sharing of information and analysis, and a lack of creative vision to address new strategies for a new foreign threat.

What the 9/11 Commission found was that rules and regulations in place

in the intelligence community prohibited those agencies from recognizing a developing threat. For example, a 1995 memorandum prevented the sharing of information between criminal investigations and intelligence gathering, even if the two collection activities were pursuing the same goal. Though this might not have prevented the 9/11 attacks, proper intelligence sharing might have given the government information that something disastrous was about to happen. The Commission recommended that intelligence activities be centralized, and it also advocated the creation of a new intelligence czar to help aid in efficient and timely intelligence gathering.

---

**supporting** | **implementing the 9/11 Commission's proposals**

**the creation of both the National Counterterrorism Center and an intelligence czar will help improve the United States' intelligence objectives.** The creation of these institutions will help facilitate information sharing and communication.

**restructuring the U.S. intelligence bureaucracies will provide an improved structure for decision making.** Former CIA director George Tenet testified that the American government "profoundly ... lacked capability to integrate foreign and domestic knowledge, data, operations, and analysis."

**a national intelligence directorate can streamline intelligence collection, analysis, and dissemination.** Right now, the various intelligence agencies operate with different rules and procedures, and this prevents effective information sharing and hinders cross-agency analysis. By standardizing rules and procedures, intelligence from different agencies can be quickly analyzed and reported to relevant end users.

---

**against** | **implementing the 9/11 Commission's proposals**

**a new, centralized intelligence bureaucracy would not be effective.** Over time, a new intelligence bureaucracy would fall prey to the same jurisdiction problems and groupthink that have plagued all American intelligence bureaucracies.

**a new intelligence bureaucracy is not needed.** The answer to America's intelligence collection problem is not more bureaucrats, agents, and institutions (with the associated red tape), but rather, more effective communication and information sharing between the bureaucracies that already exist.

**a new centralized intelligence bureaucracy may be harmful to civil liberties.** The American founders believed a large, powerful government would eventually use its strength to oppress. Splitting up and fragmenting intelligence organizations into competing agencies can help prevent a potential Big Brother from coming into existence.

# subgovernments and
## ISSUE NETWORKS

**P**olitical scientists use different concepts to explain administrative policymaking. One approach to understanding the administrative process is the concept of subgovernment, or iron triangles. A **subgovernment, or iron triangle** is a cozy, three-sided relationship among government agencies, interest groups, and key members of Congress in which all parties benefit.

- On one point of the subgovernment triangle, the bureaucracy and interest groups benefit from a special relationship. Agencies enhance the economic status of the interest group through favorable regulation or the awarding of government contracts. Interest groups return the favor by lobbying Congress on behalf of the agency.
- On the second point of the triangle, interest groups and members of Congress enjoy a mutu-

ally beneficial relationship. Interest groups assist senators and members of the House by contributing to their reelection campaigns. In return, members of Congress vote to appropriate money for programs the interest groups support.

- The third point of the triangle focuses on the interaction between agencies and members of Congress. Politically wise bureaucrats know that it is important to keep key members of Congress happy by providing all the information they request, by solving problems members of Congress bring to their attention, and by paying special notice to the needs of the home states and districts of key senators and representatives.

Consider the highway subgovernment. On one point of the highway triangle are interest groups that

benefit from highway construction: auto manufacturers, the United Auto Workers Union (UAW), tire companies, asphalt and cement dealers, road contractors, long-haul trucking firms, the Teamsters Union, and oil companies. The second point

> **think**
>
> **Do you think the influence of interest groups on government is good or bad? Explain your opinion.**

**subgovernment, or iron triangle** a cozy, three-sided relationship among government agencies, interest groups, and key members of Congress in which all parties benefit.

The United Auto Workers (UAW), major auto companies, environmental interest groups, and members of Congress from Michigan and other states with a heavy auto industry presence, are all part of the issue network for government policy dealing with the automobile industry.

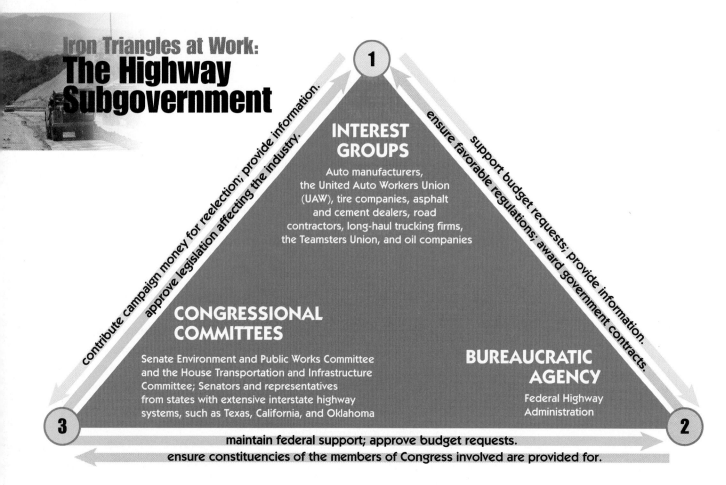

# Iron Triangles at Work: The Highway Subgovernment

**1** INTEREST GROUPS

Auto manufacturers, the United Auto Workers Union (UAW), tire companies, asphalt and cement dealers, road contractors, long-haul trucking firms, the Teamsters Union, and oil companies

CONGRESSIONAL COMMITTEES

Senate Environment and Public Works Committee and the House Transportation and Infrastructure Committee; Senators and representatives from states with extensive interstate highway systems, such as Texas, California, and Oklahoma

BUREAUCRATIC AGENCY

Federal Highway Administration

contribute campaign money for reelection; provide information. approve legislation affecting the industry.

ensure favorable regulations; award government contracts. support budget requests; provide information.

**3** maintain federal support; approve budget requests. **2**
ensure constituencies of the members of Congress involved are provided for.

is the Federal Highway Administration, which, of course, is interested in the preservation of the programs it administers. On the third point of the triangle are the congressional committees that consider highway-construction bills—the Environment and Public Works Committee in the Senate and the Committee on Transportation and Infrastructure in the House. Senators and representatives from states with extensive interstate highway systems, such as Texas, California, and Oklahoma, are also involved.

Each part of the subgovernment serves and is served by the other two. The members of Congress involved work to maintain federal support for highway construction and maintenance. The interest groups lobby Congress on behalf of highway programs, and their political action committees (PACs) contribute campaign money to members of Congress on key committees. The agency, meanwhile, makes sure that

the districts and states of the members of Congress involved get their share of new highways and bridges. Also, if some town in the district wants a special favor, local officials call their representative or senator, who passes the request along to the agency. The agency is eager to please and happy to give the member of Congress the credit.

The political scientists who study subgovernments believe that a great deal of public policy is made through behind-the-scenes understandings among interest groups, key members of Congress, and the federal bureaucracy. When issues arise, the participants in the subgovernment settle the matter, with little input from political actors outside the triangle, including the president. The result is that public policy is tailored to the wishes of those groups most closely associated with the policy itself. Energy policy, they say, reflects the interests of the oil and gas industry. Highway pro-

grams are geared to match the concerns of the highway lobby.

In recent years, however, many political scientists have concluded that although subgovernments exist in American politics, their influence is less than it was during the 1940s and 1950s. Subgovernments prospered in a time when public policy was the work of a relatively small number of fairly autonomous participants: a handful of powerful committee chairs, a small number of interest groups, and a few agency administrators. Furthermore, most policy decisions were made outside public view.

Today's policy environment has changed. Power in Congress is centralized in the party leadership. Committee chairs are less influential. Interest groups are more numerous. Furthermore, new issues have arisen for which it is all but impossible to identify clearly the dominant actors, including energy, consumer protection, illegal immigration, and the environment.[33]

# The Egyptian Bureaucracy

Egypt is a developing country, struggling to overcome problems of overpopulation, poverty, illiteracy, social inequality, unemployment, and foreign debt. The nation's economy depends on foreign aid (mostly from the United States), tourism, income earned by Egyptians working abroad, and borrowing. The Egyptian economy lacks a substantial industrial base. Furthermore, rapid population growth erases whatever economic gains the nation's economy makes.

The Egyptian government assumes responsibility for feeding, educating, and employing the populace. The government owns and operates 70 percent of the nation's industry and business enterprises, including hotels, airlines, the steel industry, and utility companies.[34] Consequently, the government bureaucracy runs not only the government, but many business enterprises as well.

The Egyptian bureaucracy does more to impede than promote economic development. It has a huge structure with a reputation for the selective enforcement of rules, mismanagement, and corruption. It is lethargic, inflexible, and rigid. Surveys of government workers show that they hold the general public in disdain. Because the government guarantees a job in the bureaucracy to all college graduates, the bureaucracy is overstaffed by a factor of more than three to one.[35] Anyone who wants to start a business must comply with dozens of rules and regulations and complete a sandstorm of forms. The only way for entrepreneurs to cut through the red tape is to pay a bribe to the bureaucrat overseeing the process.[36]

Bureaucratic reform will be difficult to achieve in Egypt. In order to streamline the bureaucracy, the government would have to lay off millions of government workers, swelling an already high unemployment rate. High unemployment, especially among educated professionals, would threaten the political survival of the Egyptian government.

## Questions

1. Does government in Egypt play a larger role in society than government in the United States?

2. In the United States, does government bureaucracy promote or hinder economic development? What is the basis of your answer?

3. Would democracy make bureaucratic reform more or less likely to take place in Egypt?

At Damietta, huge culverts are being built to carry sewage from the town to the sea.

Political scientist Hugh Heclo believes that the concept of issue networks more accurately describes administrative policymaking today than the concept of subgovernments. An **issue network** is a group of political actors concerned with some aspect of public policy. Issue networks are fluid, with participants moving in and out. They can include technical spe-

## Environmentalists worried about the effect of highway construction on the environment

cialists, members of Congress, journalists, the president, interest groups, bureaucrats, academic experts, and individual political activists. Powerful interest groups may be involved, but they do not control the process. Instead, policy in a particular area results from conflict among a broad range of political actors both in and out of government.[37]

Consider the fate of the Highway Trust Fund. A subgovernment once dominated federal highway policy, but that is no longer the case. During the 1970s, the number of interest groups concerned with highway construction grew. Environmentalists worried about the effect of highway construction on the environment. Minority rights groups became alarmed about the impact of freeway construction on minority neighborhoods. Groups advocating energy conservation argued that government should divert money from highways to mass transit. In the meantime, congressional committees and subcommittees with jurisdiction over highway programs began to include members of Congress allied to groups opposed to highway spending. As a result, fed-

eral highway policy is now made in a more contentious, uncertain environment than before.[38] In 1991, Congress passed and the president signed the Intermodal Surface Transportation Efficiency Act (ISTEA), granting states considerable leeway in deciding whether to spend federal transportation money for highways or mass transit. The legislation also required that states use a certain amount of money to fund "enhancement programs," which were local transportation-related projects designed to aid a community's quality of life, such as hike and bike trails. The passage of ISTEA reflected the participation of a broad range of interests concerned with transportation policy, not just the traditional set of interest groups involved with highway funding.[39]

**issue network** a group of political actors that is actively involved with policymaking in a particular issue area.

## ISSUE NETWORKS

TECHNICAL SPECIALIST

MEMBERS OF CONGRESS

BUREAUCRATS

JOURNALISTS

POLITICAL ACTIVISTS

ACADEMIC EXPERTS

INTEREST GROUPS

THE PRESIDENT

Issue networks are used to better explain the more complicated relationship among the parties involved in policymaking.

# FDA Regulates Tobacco, and Phillip Morris Cheers

BY NIV ELIS, *FORBES*

**JUNE 6, 2009**

WASHINGTON, D.C.—The Senate voted 79–17 Thursday to give the Food and Drug Administration regulatory authority over tobacco, giving Uncle Sam oversight of a product that kills 440,000 Americans each year.

And joining the chorus of hurrahs from more than 1,000 public health groups: the Marlboro Man.

The bill, already passed by the House of Representatives, will change the face of the tobacco industry by giving the FDA the authority to restrict tobacco product ingredients, impose nicotine caps and limit advertising campaigns. It solidifies the position of the producer with the greatest market share—Altria—which makes 50% of all cigarettes in the U.S.

Because the domestic cigarette market is shrinking every year, manufacturers are competing fiercely for customers. Companies like R.J. Reynolds and Lorillard Tobacco argue that under FDA regulation, they'll have trouble convincing people to switch to their brands because of stringent advertising restrictions. That means no more sponsorship of sports and entertainment events, color or photo ads in publications with significant teen readership, or free gifts with tobacco products.

Lorillard in particular has much at stake because its advertising strategies have helped boost sales of its popular Newport cigarettes and menthol brands. Lorillard officials were not immediately available for comment after Thursday's vote.

The bill will ding Altria in at least one regard: Tobacco regulation will be funded by fees levied on tobacco companies in proportion to market share. An Altria spokesman declined to comment on how much the new regulations will cost the company.

Congress' passage of the bill settles a decades-old dispute over how to regulate tobacco products, and it exposes makers of all tobacco products to higher standards. Tobacco foes and public health groups like the American Cancer Society and American Heart Association hailed the legislation.

It "attacks tobacco marketing, strengthens health warnings, eliminates misleading terms like 'low tar,' and prohibits unsubstantiated claims that some products are safer than others," argues Matthew L. Myers, president of the Campaign for Tobacco-Free Kids. Tobacco products will be prohibited from carrying an FDA logo to prevent them from appearing "safe," and will require large, graphic warnings covering 50% of the front packaging.

But the new oversight authority also raises a question about the FDA's ability to handle more oversight. Critics like Wyoming Sen. Mike Enzi, the top Republican on the Senate's health committee, argue that that the FDA is already overburdened with regulation of food, cosmetics, drugs and medical devices.

Not so, retorts Sen. Edward Kennedy, D-Mass., who sponsored the bill. "Not a single dollar will be diverted from FDA's existing responsibilities," he says. The Obama administration's budget proposal for fiscal year 2010 expands funding for the FDA by 19% to $3.2 billion—the largest increase in the agency's history.

## ⬈ CRITICAL THINKING QUESTIONS

- Why do public health groups favor FDA regulation of tobacco?
- Why does Altria, the parent company for Marlboro and other popular brands, also favor FDA regulation?
- If you were a member of Congress, would you have voted for this legislation? Why or why not?

**>> END**

# CONCLUSION
# the federal bureaucracy
# &PUBLIC POLICY

t he federal bureaucracy participates in every stage of the
policymaking process.

## Agenda Building

The actions of federal agencies
sometimes focus public attention on
issues. For example, the federal bureaucracy has done more to call
public attention to the health risks
of tobacco than either Congress or
the president. In 1964, the **surgeon
general,** an official in the Public
Health Service who advises the
president on health issues, released a
report summarizing research showing a link between smoking and cancer. That document, which was
called the *Surgeon General's Report on
Smoking and Health*, was the nation's
first official recognition that cigarette smoking causes cancer and
other serious illnesses. Over the
years, the surgeon general has issued
additional reports dealing with related issues, such as the effect of sec-
ond-hand smoke and preventing tobacco use among young people. The
initial report and each succeeding
report received a good
deal of attention,
sparking a public
debate about the
impact of tobacco
use on the public
health.

Agency reports
and official state-
ments can highlight
policy issues, espe-
cially if the media and the
general public perceive that agency
officials are acting on the basis of
their professional expertise rather
than political motives. Even though
surgeons general are presidential
appointees, they are held in respect

because they are physicians who
work in an agency dominated by
health professionals. The scientific
evidence presented in the various
reports released by the surgeon
general put the tobacco companies
on the defensive, making it difficult
for them to defeat proposals to restrict tobacco advertising and require health warnings on tobacco
products.

## Policy Formulation and Adoption

Federal agencies participate in policy formulation. Agency officials
work directly with the White
House and members of Congress
during the legislative process.
Agency officials may assist members
of Congress in drafting legislation
related to their departments. Agencies participate in the budget
process by making budget requests
to the president and testifying at
congressional budget hearings. Of-

ficials in the executive branch advise
the president on policy decisions.

Executive branch agencies do not
directly adopt policy, but they participate in policy adoption by lobbying the president and Congress.
Consider the role in policy adoption of the **Joint Chiefs of Staff,**
the military advisory body composed of the chiefs of staff of the
U.S. Army and Air Force, the chief
of naval operations, and sometimes
the commandant of the Marine

**surgeon general** an official in the Public
Health Service who advises the
president on health issues.

**Joint Chiefs of Staff** a military advisory
body that is composed of the chiefs of
staff of the U.S. Army and Air Force,
the Chief of Naval Operations, and
sometimes the Commandant of the
Marine Corps.

The surgeon general has issued a number of reports compiling
research showing a direct link between smoking and cancer.

Corps. The Joint Chiefs not only advise the president on defense policy, but they also lobby the White House and Congress on policies that concern the armed forces. When President Clinton attempted to end the policy of excluding gay men and lesbians from military service at the beginning of his first term, members of the Joint Chiefs lobbied Congress to oppose the president's initiative.

## Policy Implementation and Evaluation

The federal bureaucracy implements policy. The IRS, for example, enforces the nation's tax laws. The U.S. Armed Forces carry out the nation's military policies. The Department of Homeland Security implements domestic security policies. FEMA responds to natural disasters.

Congress delegates authority to federal agencies to implement policy. Sometimes Congress writes detailed legislation, giving agency administrators little enforcement discretion. At other times, Congress grants agencies broad regulatory discretion. Sometimes Congress gives agencies so much leeway that an argument can be made that the agencies are actually adopting policies themselves, rather than implementing policies adopted by Congress and the president through the legislative process.

Finally, federal agencies evaluate policy. Agencies gather data, conduct research, prepare reports, and recommend policy changes. The

# Congress delegates authority to federal agencies to implement policy

Department of Education, for example, conducts and compiles research on the effectiveness of teacher training programs and other educational programs. The Department of Defense researches the effectiveness of weapons systems. After the Katrina disaster, Homeland Security Secretary Chertoff asked Congress to enhance the capacity of FEMA to respond to crises by adding employees and expanding its regional offices.[40]

the **THINKSPOT**

**www.thethinkspot.com**

# TEST yourself

1. Which of the following agencies played the most important role in the government's response to the H1N1 virus (swine flu)?
   A. CDC
   B. FTC
   C. Department of State
   D. Department of Agriculture

2. The Department of Health and Human Services is an example of which of the following types of government agencies?
   A. Cabinet department
   B. Independent executive agency
   C. Government corporation
   D. Independent regulatory commission

3. Which of the following is *not* a cabinet department?
   A. Environmental Protection Agency (EPA)
   B. Department of Homeland Security
   C. Department of Defense
   D. Department of Justice

4. Which of the following cabinet departments has the largest number of civilian employees?
   A. Department of Homeland Security
   B. Department of Defense
   C. Department of Education
   D. Department of Justice

5. The attorney general heads which of the following departments?
   A. Department of Homeland Security
   B. Department of Defense
   C. Department of State
   D. Department of Justice

6. Which of the following is *not* an example of a government corporation?
   A. Amtrak
   B. CIA
   C. Postal Service
   D. FDIC

7. Which of the following agencies is expected to be self-financing?
   A. Department of the Treasury
   B. EPA
   C. FDIC
   D. Peace Corps

8. Which of the following agencies regulates business competition, including enforcement of laws against monopolies and the protection of consumers from deceptive trade practices?
   A. FCC
   B. FTC
   C. SEC
   D. EPA

9. Which of the following agencies regulates interstate and international radio, television, telephone, telegraph, and satellite communications, as well as licensing radio and television stations?
   A. FCC
   B. FTC
   C. SEC
   D. EPA

10. The president has the authority to remove all but which one of the following government officials?
    A. Attorney General
    B. Secretary of Defense
    C. SEC commissioner
    D. Secretary of Transportation

11. Which of the following agencies is an example of a quasi-governmental company?
    A. Postal Service
    B. CDC
    C. Amtrak
    D. Fannie Mae

12. The spoils system involved which of the following?
    A. Hiring friends, relatives, and political supporters to work for the government
    B. Giving government contracts to companies owned by friends, relatives, and political supporters
    C. Contracting out with private companies to implement government programs
    D. Forbidding government employees from engaging in political activities

13. Which of the following rights do federal employees enjoy?
    A. The right to form unions
    B. The right to vote for candidates of their choice
    C. The right to bargain collectively over issues other than pay and benefits
    D. All of the above

**14** Are private companies legally obligated to follow rules adopted by regulatory agencies?

A. No. Only Congress has the authority to enact legally binding regulations.

B. Yes, but only if the rules are ratified by Congress.

C. Yes. Rules are legally binding.

D. No, although many business follow them voluntarily.

**15** Suppose the president disagrees with the policy initiatives of a federal agency. What can the president do to exert control?

A. The president can ask Congress to cut the agency's budget.

B. The president can appoint administrators to head the agency that agree with the president's policy position.

C. The president can ask Congress to reorganize the agency.

D. All of the above.

**16** Suppose that a majority of the members of Congress disagree with the policy initiatives of a federal agency. What actions can Congress take to exert control?

A. Congress can cut the agency's budget.

B. Congress can change the legislation under which the agency operates.

C. Congress can reorganize the agency or merge it with another agency.

D. All of the above.

**17** Which of the following is an example of fire-alarm oversight?

A. Congress conducts periodic review of an agency's operation.

B. The president conducts periodic review of an agency's operation.

C. Congress responds to complaints about an agency's performance.

D. All of the above.

**18** An agency that is accused of working too closely with the interest groups it is supposed to be regulating is known as which of the following?

A. Issue network

B. Captured agency

C. Independent regulatory commission

D. Iron triangle

**19** Which of the following political actors is *not* part of a subgovernment or iron triangle?

A. President

B. Congress

C. Interest group

D. Government agency

**20** Which of the following is a group of political actors that is concerned with some aspect of public policy?

A. Issue network

B. Captured agency

C. Independent regulatory commission

D. Iron triangle

KNOW *the* **score**

18–20 correct: Congratulations! You are well informed!

15–17 correct: Your political knowledge is a bit low—be sure to review the key terms and visit TheThinkSpot.

<14 correct: Reread the chapter more thoroughly.

1. A; 2. A; 3. A; 4. B; 5. D; 6. B; 7. C; 8. B; 9. A; 10. C; 11. D; 12. A; 13. D; 14. C; 15. D; 16. D; 17. C; 18. B; 19. A; 20. A

# 13 THE FEDERAL

## > WHAT'S AHEAD

Judicial Policymaking
The Federal Court System
Power, Politics, and the Courts
Conclusion: The Courts
& Public Policy

President Barack Obama made history in 2009 by nominating Sonia Sotomayor, a justice serving on the U.S. Court of Appeals for the Second Circuit, to fill the Supreme Court vacancy created by the retirement of Associate Justice David Souter. When the U.S. Senate confirmed Sotomayor, she became the nation's first Hispanic justice and third female Supreme Court justice. Considering the age of the other justices, Obama may have the opportunity to make additional appointments. When Sotomayor began her service, the average age on the Court was 69, with five justices older than 70 years of age. The oldest member of the Court was Associate Justice John Paul Stevens, age 89.

Obama may be able to change the policymaking direction of the Supreme Court because it is closely divided philosophically. In recent sessions, the Court has decided many cases by the narrowest of margins. In the 2008–2009 session, the Court decided 23 cases by a five–four vote. In most of the closely divided cases, Justices Stevens, Souter, Stephen Breyer, and Ruth Bader Ginsburg—the so-called liberal wing of the Court—voted as a bloc. Four other justices—Chief Justice John Roberts and Associate Justices Antonin Scalia, Clarence Thomas, and Samuel Alito—voted together as the conservative wing of the Court. In 18 of 23 cases, Associate Justice Anthony Kennedy was the swing vote, siding with the conservatives on some issues and the liberals on other issues.[1] Depending on which additional seats become vacant during his tenure, Obama could maintain the current philosophical balance or move the Court in a liberal direction on such issues as abortion, gun control, affirmative action, capital punishment (the death penalty), and gay and lesbian rights.[2]

# COURTS

# judicial
## POLICYMAKING

**ESSENTIALS...**

*after studying Chapter 13, students should be able to answer the following questions:*

> What are the different approaches to judicial interpretation of the Constitution and to the proper role of judges?

> How is the judicial branch organized? What is the decision-making process of the Supreme Court?

> How much influence do the federal courts have on public policy?

> What is the role of the federal courts in the policymaking process?

Courts make policy by interpreting the law and the Constitution.[3] When courts interpret the law, they modify policies adopted by the executive and legislative branches by aggressively expanding or narrowly restricting the provisions of a law. When courts interpret the Constitution, they exercise **judicial review,** which is the power of courts to declare unconstitutional the actions of the other branches and units of government. From 1789 through 2006, the Supreme Court overturned at least one provision in 160 federal laws and 1,295 state laws and local ordinances.[4]

Controversy rages over the leeway courts should exercise in interpreting the Constitution. **Strict construction** is a doctrine of constitutional interpretation holding that the document should be interpreted narrowly. Advocates of strict construction believe that judges should stick closely to the literal meaning of the words in

*ED FISCHER*

the Constitution and place themselves in harmony with the purpose of the Framers. In contrast, **loose construction** is a doctrine of constitutional interpretation holding that the document should be interpreted broadly. Loose constructionists argue that strict construction is neither possible nor desirable. They point out that it is often difficult to ascertain original intent because no complete and accurate records exist to indicate what the authors of the Constitution had in mind. Furthermore, those records that exist show that the nation's founders often disagreed with each other about the Constitution's basic meaning.

A similar and related debate involves the role of judges. Conservative opponents of the Supreme Court sometimes accuse it of **judicial activism,** which is the charge that judges are going beyond

**judicial review** the power of courts to declare unconstitutional the actions of the other branches and units of government.

**strict construction** a doctrine of constitutional interpretation holding that the document should be interpreted narrowly.

**loose construction** a doctrine of constitutional interpretation holding that the document should be interpreted broadly.

**judicial activism** the charge that judges are going beyond their authority by making the law and not just interpreting it.

What do you think this cartoon is trying to say about the confirmation process for recent Supreme Court Justices?

their authority by making the law and not just interpreting it. For example, critics of *Roe v. Wade*, the Supreme Court's landmark abortion decision, call it an activist ruling because the U.S. Constitution does not specifically address the issue of abortion. Republican presidential candidates typically promise to nominate men and women to the Supreme Court who will practice **judicial restraint,** which is the concept that judges should defer to the policymaking judgment of the legislative and executive branches of government unless their actions clearly violate the law or the Constitution.

Many political scientists believe that the debate between judicial activism and judicial restraint is more about politics than judicial behavior. Professors Kermit Roosevelt III and Thomas M. Keck contend that the accusation of judicial activism is a convenient line of attack for people who disagree with a court ruling for whatever reason.[5] The real dispute is not between the advocates of

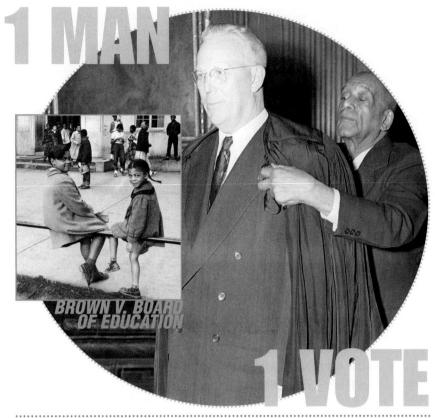

1 MAN

BROWN V. BOARD OF EDUCATION

1 VOTE

Chief Justice Earl Warren led the Supreme Court into new areas of law, helping to establish the one man, one vote doctrine, desegregating schools in *Brown v. Board of Education*, and creating the Miranda Warning ("You have the right to remain silent...").

**think** If you were a member of the Supreme Court, how would you approach the job?

judicial activism and judicial restraint, but between liberal and conservative activism. All judges regard the Constitution as a charter of fundamental principles that courts are pledged to uphold. The real controversy is that conservative and liberal judges disagree as to what those principles are.[6]

**judicial restraint** the concept that judges should defer to the policymaking judgment of the legislative and executive branches of government unless their actions clearly violate the law or the Constitution.

**trial** the formal examination of a judicial dispute in accordance with law before a single judge.

# the federal
## COURT SYSTEM

The figure on page 288 diagrams the federal court system. Trial courts make up the lowest tier of federal courts. A **trial** is the formal examination of a judicial dispute in accordance with law before a single judge. Trials involve attorneys, witnesses, testimony, evidence, judges, and, occasionally, juries. The U.S. district courts are the most important federal trial courts, hearing nearly all federal cases. The U.S.

Court of Federal Claims and the U.S. Court of International Trade are specialized trial courts, created to deal with some of the more complex areas of federal law. The U.S. Court of Federal Claims hears disputes over federal contracts and cases involving claims for monetary damages against the U.S. government; the U.S. Court of International Trade hears cases involving international trade and customs issues.

An **appeal** is the taking of a case to a higher court by the losing party

# The procedures of appeals courts differ notably from those of trial courts.

in a lower-court decision. The procedures of appeals courts differ notably from those of trial courts. In general, trial courts are concerned with questions of fact and the law as it applies to those facts. In contrast, appeals are based on issues of law and procedure. Appellate courts do not retry cases appealed to them. Instead, appellate court justices (juries do not participate in appellate proceedings) make decisions based on the law and the Constitution, the written and oral arguments presented by attorneys for the litigants in the lawsuit, and the written record of the lower-court proceedings. Also, appellate court justices usually make decisions collectively in panels of

three or more judges rather than singly, as do trial court judges.

The U.S. courts of appeals and the U.S. Supreme Court are primarily appellate courts. The courts of appeals hear appeals from the federal trial courts and administrative agencies. The U.S. Supreme Court stands at the apex of the American court system. Although it has authority to try a limited range of cases, it is in practice an appellate court, hearing appeals from both the federal and state court systems.

## District Courts

Congress has created 94 district courts, with at least one court in every state and one each in the District of Columbia, Guam, Northern Mariana Islands, Puerto Rico, and the Virgin Islands. Although only one judge presides in each courtroom, each of the districts has enough business to warrant more than one courtroom, each with its own judge. The number of judges per district ranges from 1 to 28. Altogether, 678 full-time judges and more than 100 semi-retired senior judges staff the district courts.[7]

**Jurisdiction.** The term **jurisdiction** refers to the authority of a court to hear and decide a case. The jurisdiction of district courts includes both civil and criminal matters. A **civil case** is a legal dispute concerning a private conflict between two parties—individuals, corporations, or government agencies. A **criminal case** is a legal dispute dealing with an alleged violation of a penal law. More than 80 percent of district court cases are civil disputes.[8] In sheer volume, the main chores of

**appeal** the taking of a case from a lower court to a higher court by the losing party in a lower-court decision.
**jurisdiction** the authority of a court to hear a case.
**civil case** a legal dispute concerning a private conflict between two parties—individuals, corporations, or government agencies.
**criminal case** a legal dispute dealing with an alleged violation of a penal law.

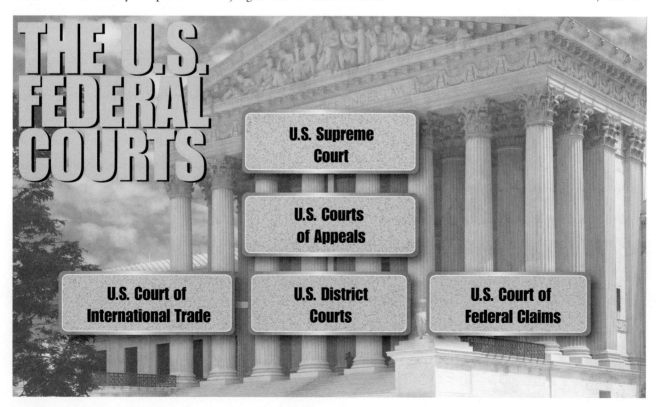

# THE U.S. FEDERAL COURTS

U.S. Supreme Court

U.S. Courts of Appeals

U.S. Court of International Trade

U.S. District Courts

U.S. Court of Federal Claims

# BARRYBONDS

**FEDERAL PROSECUTORS INDICTED BASEBALL PLAYER BARRY BONDS IN NOVEMBER 2007 ON PERJURY AND OBSTRUCTION OF JUSTICE CHARGES. THE FORMER SAN FRANCISCO GIANTS OUTFIELDER WAS ACCUSED OF LYING TO FEDERAL INVESTIGATORS AND OBSTRUCTING JUSTICE DURING A FEDERAL PROBE OF STEROID USE IN MAJOR LEAGUE BASEBALL. BONDS STAUNCHLY DENIED ANY USE OF STEROIDS, BUT GOVERNMENT INVESTIGATORS FOUND RECORDS OF HIS STEROID USE DURING THEIR PROBE. BONDS, WHO HOLDS THE ALL-TIME MAJOR LEAGUE BASEBALL HOME RUN RECORD, FACES UP TO 30 YEARS IN PRISON IF HE IS CONVICTED ON ALL COUNTS. A NUMBER OF OTHER BASEBALL STARS HAVE BEEN IMPLICATED IN THE STEROID INVESTIGATION, INCLUDING PITCHERS ROGER CLEMENS AND ANDY PETTITTE, AND INFIELDER MIGUEL TEJADA.**

the district courts are naturalizing new citizens and granting passport applications. District courts also have jurisdiction over bankruptcy cases filed under federal law, civil cases involving more than $75,000 in which the U.S. government is a party, and—if either litigant requests it—lawsuits in which the parties live in different states and in which more than $75,000 is at stake. In these latter types of cases, federal judges apply the laws of the applicable state rather than federal law. A Louisiana firm in a legal dispute with a Texas company over an oil and gas lease in Texas might prefer that the case be heard by a federal court rather than a state court in Texas. Unlike federal judges, Texas judges are all elected and may be the beneficiaries of generous campaign contributions from the Texas company involved in the dispute.

As for criminal matters, district courts try all cases involving violations of federal law as well as criminal offenses occurring on federal territory, federal reservations, or the high seas. District judges must also rule on *habeas corpus* petitions filed by inmates in both state and federal prisons. A **writ of *habeas corpus*** is a court order requiring government authorities either to release a person held in custody or demonstrate that the person is detained in accordance with law. *Habeas corpus* petitions allege that a prisoner is held contrary to law and ask a court to inquire into the matter. An inmate's attorney may charge, for example, that a state trial court erred in admitting certain evidence, thereby violating the Fourth and Fourteenth Amendments to the U.S. Constitution. If the judge sees merit in the petitioner's complaint, the judge can direct the jailer to reply, and a suit will be joined. Death row inmates often use *habeas corpus* petitions to avoid, or at least to delay, their execution. Litigants who lose their district court cases may appeal to a U.S. court of appeals. In practice, less than 20 percent of district court decisions are appealed.[9]

**Selection of Judges.** The president appoints federal judges subject to Senate confirmation by majority vote. **Senatorial courtesy**, the custom that senators from the president's party have a veto on judicial appointments from their states, determines the selection of most district judges. When district court vacancies occur, senators from the president's party submit names to the president, who makes the formal nomination. The president can reject a senator's recommendation, of course, but rarely does. If both of a state's senators belong to the president's political party, the senior senator makes the recommendations. When vacancies develop in states where neither

> **writ of *habeas corpus*** a court order requiring that government authorities either release a person held in custody or demonstrate that the person is detained in accordance with law.
>
> **senatorial courtesy** the custom that senators from the president's party have a veto on judicial appointments from their states.

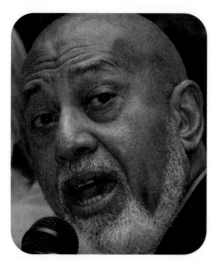

Alcee Lamar Hastings is living proof that impeachment does not necessarily end a career in public service. Hastings became a federal judge in 1979 when President Jimmy Carter appointed him as a judge on the U.S. district court for the Southern District of Florida. Hastings's career suffered a setback in 1981 when he was charged with accepting a bribe from a defendant in his court and then lying about it to federal prosecutors. Even though Hastings was acquitted of all charges, the U.S. House impeached him and in 1989 the U.S. Senate removed him from office. Nonetheless, three years later Hastings won election to Congress from the Twenty-third U.S. Congressional District in South Florida. Many of the voters in the district, which is majority African American, apparently believed that Congress had treated Hastings unfairly because he was impeached and removed from his judgeship despite his acquittal. Hastings has subsequently easily won reelection and continues to serve in the U.S. House alongside some of the members who voted to impeach him as a federal judge two decades earlier.

senator shares the president's party affiliation, the White House usually consults state party leaders and/or members of the House for their recommendations.

The Senate Judiciary Committee evaluates district court nominees. After the committee staff conducts a background check, the committee chair schedules a hearing to allow the nominee and interested parties an opportunity to be heard. The confirmation of district court judges is usually a quiet affair, with few nominees rejected. Confirmation is not necessarily speedy, however, especially when the Senate and White House are in the hands of different political parties. Toward the end of a presidential term, the chair of the Senate Judiciary Committee and the Senate majority leader will sometimes delay the confirmation process in hopes that the White House changes parties and the new president can then fill pending vacancies. Even early in a term, the confirmation process takes anywhere from four months to two years, or even longer.[10]

Presidents typically nominate judges whose party affiliation and political philosophy are compatible with their own. Democratic presidents appoint Democratic judges; Republican presidents select Republicans. Some presidents also seek judges with particular political philosophies. In general, Republican presidents choose judges with conservative political philosophies, whereas Democratic presidents select liberal judges. Conservative judges tend to favor government interests over criminal defendants, interpret narrowly the constitutional guarantees of equal rights for women and minorities, support corporate interests against the claims of individual workers or consumers, and rule against federal government involvement in local policy issues. In contrast, liberal judges are more inclined than their conservative counterparts to favor judicial underdogs, such as consumers, workers, criminal defendants, and members of minority groups. They tend to support the federal government in federalism disputes over the relative power of the states and the national government.[11]

Federal judges hold lifetime appointments, with "good behavior," as the Constitution puts it. They may not be retired involuntarily or removed for political reasons, but they are subject to impeachment by the House and removal by the Senate. Although members of Congress occasionally threaten to impeach judges with whom they have policy disagreements, impeachment is rare and always directed against judges who are accused of misconduct. In American history, only seven federal judges have been impeached and removed from office. Most judges who get in trouble resign rather than face the humiliation of impeachment.[12]

## Courts of Appeals

The U.S. courts of appeals (also known as circuit courts of appeals) are the primary intermediate appellate courts in the federal system. There are 13 courts of appeals, one

**In American history, only seven federal judges have been impeached and removed from office.**

for each of the 12 judicial circuits (or regions), and a thirteenth circuit called the U.S. Court of Appeals for the Federal Circuit. The latter court hears appeals in specialized cases, such as patent law, and cases appealed from the Court of International Trade and the Court of Federal Claims. The number of justices for each of the circuits ranges from 3 to 24. Altogether, 179 justices staff the courts of appeals along with another 40 senior justices.

**Jurisdiction.** The courts of appeals are exclusively appellate courts, usually hearing cases in panels of three justices each. They hear appeals from the U.S. district courts, the Court of International Trade, and the Court of Federal Claims. The courts of appeals also hear appeals on the decisions of the regulatory

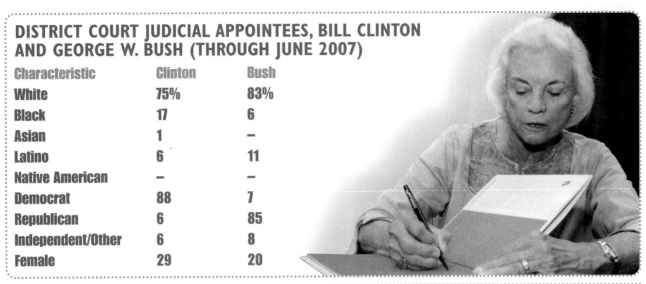

| DISTRICT COURT JUDICIAL APPOINTEES, BILL CLINTON AND GEORGE W. BUSH (THROUGH JUNE 2007) | | |
|---|---|---|
| Characteristic | Clinton | Bush |
| White | 75% | 83% |
| Black | 17 | 6 |
| Asian | 1 | – |
| Latino | 6 | 11 |
| Native American | – | – |
| Democrat | 88 | 7 |
| Republican | 6 | 85 |
| Independent/Other | 6 | 8 |
| Female | 29 | 20 |

Sandra Day O'Connor, appointed by President Ronald Reagan in 1981, was the first woman to serve on the Supreme Court.

Harold M. Stanley and Richard G. Niemi, *Vital Statistics on American Politics 2007–2008* (Washington, DC: CQ Press, 2008), p. 290.

commissions, with the rulings of the National Labor Relations Board (NLRB) producing the most appeals. The courts of appeals are generally not required to hold hearings in every case. After reading the legal briefs in a case (a **legal brief** is a written legal argument) and reviewing the trial court record, the appeals court may uphold the lower court decision without hearing formal arguments.

When an appeals court decides to accept an appeal, the court usually schedules a hearing at which the attorneys for the two sides in the dispute present oral arguments and answer any questions posed by the justices. Appeals courts do not retry cases. Instead, they review the trial-court record and consider legal arguments. After hearing oral arguments and studying legal briefs,

appeals court justices discuss the case and eventually vote on a decision, with a majority vote of the justices required to decide a case. The court may **affirm** (uphold) the lower court decision, reverse it, modify it, or affirm part of the lower court ruling while reversing or modifying the rest. Frequently, an appeals court may **remand** (return) a case to the trial court for reconsideration in light of the appeals court decision. The courts of appeals have the final word on more than 95 percent of the cases they hear because the Supreme Court rarely intervenes on appeal.[13]

**Selection of Justices.** The White House generally takes more care with nominations to the courts of appeals than it does with district court selections. Because the judicial circuits usually include several states, senatorial courtesy does not dictate the selection of justices on the courts of appeals.[14] When a vacancy occurs, a deputy attorney general gathers names of potential nominees, asking party leaders, senators, and members of the House for suggestions. Eventually, the deputy attorney general suggests a name or perhaps a short list of names for the president's consideration, and the president makes a choice. The Senate examines appel-

late court nominees more closely than it considers district court selections, especially when the opposition party controls the Senate. Furthermore, as with district court nominees, delays are not unusual. The length of confirmation delays depends on the size of the president's opposition in the Senate, the proximity of the next presidential election, and whether the nominee is a woman or minority. Appellate court nominees who are women or minorities take twice as long to confirm as do white males.[15] The Senate is more likely to reject nominees when the opposition party controls the Senate, and in the last year of a president's term. Since 1950, the Senate has confirmed 94 percent of district and appellate court appointees when the president's party controls the Senate but only 80

**Do you think that federal judges should be periodically subject to reappointment? Why or why not?**

**legal brief** a written legal argument.

**affirm** the action of an appeals court to uphold the decision of a lower court.

**remand** the decision of an appeals court to return a case to a lower court for reconsideration in light of an appeals court decision.

# Islamic Law in Nigeria

Nigeria is an ethnically and religiously diverse country. Its population includes several major ethnic groups (the Hausa-Fulani, Yoruba, and Igbo) as well as hundreds of smaller groups. The most important religions are Islam, Christianity, Orisha (the traditional Yoruba religion), and Animism, which is the belief that souls inhabit most bodies, including people, animals, plants, and even inanimate objects, such as stones.

After military rule ended in Nigeria in 1999 and the country established a federal system, 12 of the northern states adopted Sharia, Islamic law based on the Koran. Sharia addresses issues of sexual morality and alcohol consumption in addition to other crimes. Pun-

ishments under Sharia can be harsh. Adulterers may be stoned to death or flogged. Thieves may suffer the amputation of a hand. Public intoxication is punishable by flogging.

The adoption of Sharia in the northern states of Nigeria has been controversial. Even though Sharia applies only to Muslims, some aspects of it, including banning alcohol and prostitution, apply generally. Critics declare that the use of Sharia violates the principle of separation of state and religion. Furthermore, they charge that the status of women under Sharia and its imposition of harsh punishments cast the nation in an unfavorable light. They point to the 2002 case that provoked international outrage in which a divorced Muslim

woman was sentenced to death after having a child out of wedlock. Islamic courts eventually overturned the sentence on the basis of a technicality. Sharia courts have subsequently avoided high-profile controversial cases.[16]

## Questions

1. In a country as diverse as Nigeria, is it better for different regions to follow their own legal traditions or would it be preferable for the entire nation to have a uniform system?

2. Should a nation's laws be based on its religious traditions?

3. In what ways, if any, is American law grounded in Judeo-Christian legal traditions?

Amina Lawal and her lawyer appealed Lawal's Sharia sentence of death by stoning for adultery.
The court overturned the verdict and Lawal was freed.

percent of nominees when the opposition controls the Senate. The odds of confirmation in any event decline by 25 percent in a presidential election year.[17]

The nomination process for courts of appeals judges is contentious because so many of their decisions are final. In 2007, appellate courts decided more than 30,000 cases compared with fewer than a hundred decided by the U.S. Supreme Court, which agrees to hear relatively few appeals.[18]

## Supreme Court

The Supreme Court of the United States is the highest court in the land. Its rulings take precedence over the decisions of other federal courts. On matters involving federal law and the U.S. Constitution, the decisions of the U.S. Supreme Court take precedence over state court rulings as well.

The Constitution says nothing about the size of the Supreme Court, letting Congress and the president set its size legislatively. Through the years, the size of the Court has varied from five to ten justices. The present membership of nine justices has been in effect for more than a century. In the 1930s, President Franklin Roosevelt attempted to enlarge the Court in order to appoint new justices friendly to the New Deal, but his effort was popularly attacked as a court-packing plan and defeated by Congress. Since then, no serious efforts have been made to change the Court's size.

Today's Court includes a chief justice and eight associate justices. The justices are equal and independent, similar to nine separate law firms, but the chief justice is first among them. The chief presides over the Court's public sessions and private conferences. The chief justice can call special sessions of the Court and helps administer the federal court system. The chief justice also assigns justices the responsibility of writing the Court's majority opinion in cases when the chief

Senators John Warner of Virginia and John McCain of Arizona, and their aides, leave a meeting with Majority Leader Bill Frist. The senators represented a group of 14 senators who wanted to avoid the "nuclear option" threatened by Republican senators to force Democratic leadership to bring judicial appointments to the floor of the Senate.

**WHEN GEORGE W. BUSH WON** the White House in 2000, he was able to appoint judges to fill the vacancies left at the end of Clinton's term. During Bush's first term, Democrats filibustered 10 of 52 appellate court nominees, declaring that the judicial philosophies of the 10 were so conservative that they were outside the judicial mainstream. Republicans responded to the Democrats' tactic by threatening a procedure they labeled the "constitutional option." Democrats called it the "nuclear option." The strategy involved Republican senators asking the presiding officer of the Senate, Vice President Dick Cheney, to rule that it was unconstitutional to filibuster judicial nominees. Because a simple majority would be sufficient to uphold the vice president's ruling, Senate Republicans who outnumbered Democrats 55 to 45 would be able to end the Democratic filibuster and force a vote on Bush's nominations whose appointments had been blocked. Democrats responded to the Republican strategy by threatening to use various parliamentary maneuvers to shut down or at least seriously delay Senate business.[19] Eventually, a group of 14 senators—7 Democrats and 7 Republicans—brokered a compromise to allow the confirmation of some of the filibustered judicial nominees. The compromise defused the crisis temporarily but did not resolve the issue.

votes with the majority. Regular sessions of the Supreme Court run from the first Monday in October until the end of June or early July.

**Jurisdiction.** Technically, the Supreme Court can be both a trial court and an appellate court. The Constitution gives the Court a limited **original jurisdiction,** which is the set of cases a court may hear as a trial court. The Supreme Court may try "cases affecting ambassadors, other public ministers and consuls, and those in which a state shall be a party," except for cases initiated against a state by the citizens of another state or nation. In practice, however, the Court does not conduct

**original jurisdiction** the set of cases a court may hear as a trial court.

# THE U.S. SUPREME COURT IN 2009

| Justice | Year Born | Appointment Year | Political Party | Law School | Appointing President | Religion | Senate Confirmation Vote |
|---|---|---|---|---|---|---|---|
| John Paul Stevens | 1920 | 1975 | R | Chicago | Ford | Nondenominational | 98–0 |
| Antonin Scalia | 1936 | 1985 | R | Harvard | Reagan | Roman Catholic | 98–0 |
| Anthony Kennedy | 1936 | 1988 | R | Harvard | Reagan | Roman Catholic | 97–0 |
| Clarence Thomas | 1948 | 1991 | R | Yale | G. Bush | Roman Catholic | 52–48 |
| Ruth Bader Ginsburg | 1933 | 1993 | D | Columbia | Clinton | Jewish | 96–3 |
| Stephen Breyer | 1938 | 1994 | D | Harvard | Clinton | Jewish | 87–9 |
| John G. Roberts, Jr. | 1955 | 2005 | R | Harvard | G.W. Bush | Roman Catholic | 78–22 |
| Samuel A. Alito, Jr. | 1950 | 2006 | R | Yale | G.W. Bush | Roman Catholic | 58–42 |
| Sonia Sotomayor | 1954 | 2009 | I | Yale | Obama | Roman Catholic | 68–31 |

trials. The Court shares jurisdiction with the U.S. district courts on the matters included in its original jurisdiction and leaves most of those cases for the district courts to decide. Even for the few cases of original jurisdiction that the justices consider worthwhile, the Supreme Court does not hold a trial. Instead, the Court appoints a special master to conduct a hearing to determine the facts before it decides the legal issues.

The Court's appellate jurisdiction is set by law and, through the years, Congress has made the Supreme Court of the United States the nation's highest appellate court for both the federal and the state judicial systems. In the federal system, the courts of appeals generate the largest number of appeals by far. Cases may arise from the court of military appeals and special three-judge courts, which Congress has authorized to hear redistricting cases and some civil rights cases. Cases can also be appealed to the Supreme Court from the highest court in each state, usually the state supreme court.

Congress can reduce the jurisdiction of the Supreme Court if it chooses. After the Civil War, Congress removed the authority of the Court to review the constitutionality of Reconstruction legislation. Since then, Congress has been reluctant to tamper with the jurisdiction of the federal courts on grounds that it would interfere with the independence of the judicial branch. In recent years, most attempts to limit the jurisdiction of federal courts in cases involving such controversial issues as abortion, school prayer, busing, and the rights of criminal defendants have failed.[20]

**Selection of Justices.** Nominating individuals to the Supreme Court is one of the president's most important responsibilities. The formal procedures for appointment and confirmation of Supreme Court justices are similar to those for appellate court justices except that they are generally performed more carefully and receive considerably more publicity. The attorney general begins the task by compiling a list of

possible nominees. The president narrows the list to a few names and the FBI conducts background checks on each.

In selecting individuals to serve on the Supreme Court, presidents look for nominees who share their political philosophy: Conservative presidents prefer conservative justices, whereas liberal presidents want liberal justices. When President Franklin Roosevelt finally had the chance to make appointments to the Supreme Court, he was careful to select nominees sympathetic to the New Deal. In contrast, President Reagan screened nominees to ensure their political conservatism.

The Senate scrutinizes Supreme Court nominations more closely than lower-court appointments. The Judiciary Committee staff and the staffs of individual senators carefully examine the nominee's background and past statements on policy issues. The committee conducts hearings at which the nominee, interest group spokespersons, and other concerned parties testify. The Senate as a whole then debates the nomination on the floor before voting to confirm or reject.

The confirmation process is highly political, with the White House and interest groups conducting public relations campaigns in hopes of putting pressure on wavering senators to confirm or reject the president's choice.[21] For example, the nomination of Clarence Thomas by the first President Bush became a political tug-of-war between women's groups and the White House over

ceived as well-qualified and whose political views are close to those of their constituents. When nominees are less qualified or hold controversial views, the outcome of the confirmation vote depends to a large degree on the political environment.[23] The Senate is most likely to reject Supreme Court nominees when the opposition party controls the Senate and/or when a nomination is made in the last year of a president's term.[24] When both of these conditions apply, the failure

"good behavior," they can serve for life, and many have continued on the bench well past traditional retirement age. Associate Justice Hugo Black, for example, served until age 85; William O. Douglas stayed on the Court until he was 77, despite having had a debilitating stroke. Justices can be impeached and removed from office, but Congress is unlikely to act without clear evidence of misconduct. Politics or old age and ill health are probably not reason enough for Congress to

## CAN YOU IDENTIFY THE SUPREME COURT JUSTICES?

According to a December 2005 national survey conducted by FindLaw, only 43 percent of American adults can name at least one justice who is currently serving on the nation's highest court.

| SUPREME COURT JUSTICE | % WHO COULD NAME THE JUSTICE |
|---|---|
| SANDRA DAY O'CONNOR* | 27 |
| CLARENCE THOMAS | 21 |
| JOHN G. ROBERTS, JR. | 16 |
| ANTONIN SCALIA | 13 |
| RUTH BADER GINSBURG | 12 |
| ANTHONY KENNEDY | 7 |
| DAVID SOUTER | 5 |
| JOHN PAUL STEVENS | 3 |
| STEPHEN BREYER | 3 |

*Sandra Day O'Connor retired in 2005 and was replaced by Samuel A. Alito, Jr., in January 2006.

Incorrect responses from those surveyed as to who is currently serving on the U.S. Supreme Court included George W. Bush, Hillary Clinton, Thurgood Marshall, and Arnold Schwarzenegger.

Source: FindLaw's U.S. Supreme Court Awareness Survey

Thomas's fitness to serve, after Anita Hill, a former employee of Thomas at the Equal Employment Opportunity Commission (EEOC), accused him of sexual harassment. Thomas eventually won confirmation by a narrow margin.

The Senate confirms most Supreme Court nominees. Since 1789, the Senate has approved 122 of 151 nominations. In the twentieth century alone, the rate was 52 of 62.[22] Senators routinely vote to confirm nominees who are per-

rate for Supreme Court nominees is 71 percent. It is 19 percent when one condition applies and only 10 percent when neither condition exists.[25] Some political scientists believe that the frequency of divided government forces the president to nominate politically moderate, cautious justices who accept a rather limited role for the federal judiciary in the political process.[26]

Like other federal judges, members of the Supreme Court enjoy the ultimate in job security. With

initiate impeachment proceedings. Furthermore, because of advances in medicine, life tenure means more today than it did when the Constitution was written. Between 1789 and 1970, the average justice served less than 15 years, with vacancies occurring on average every two years. Since 1970, the average justice serves more than 26 years and a vacancy occurs every three years.[27]

**Deciding to Decide.** Supreme Court justices set their own agenda. Each year, litigants appeal 7,000 to

10,000 cases to the Supreme Court, far more cases than the Court can reasonably handle. As a result, the justices screen the cases brought to them to decide which ones merit their attention.

An important judicial ground rule is that the Supreme Court must wait for a case to be appealed to it before it can rule. The Supreme Court does not issue advisory opin-ions. Although the members of the Court decide themselves what cases they will hear, their choices are lim-ited to those cases that come to them on appeal. During the Civil War, for example, Chief Justice Taney, and perhaps a majority of the members of the Supreme Court, believed that the draft law was un-constitutional. They never had the opportunity to rule on the issue, however, because no case challeng-ing the law ever reached the Court.

The legal requirement that the Supreme Court can rule only when presented a case gives interest

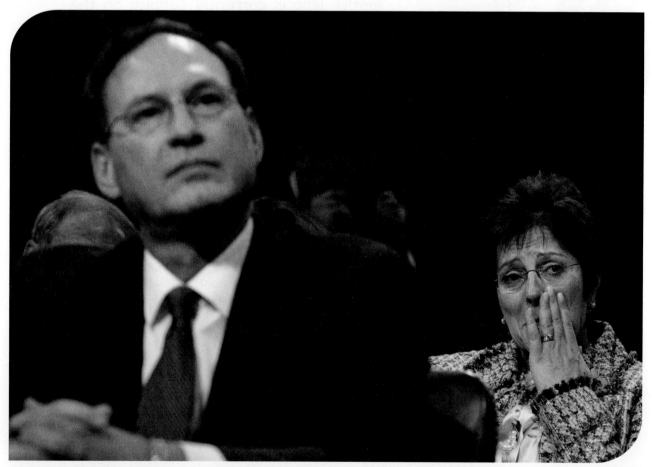

In the picture above, Martha-Ann Alito, the wife of Supreme Court nominee Samuel Alito, tears up as her husband faces aggressive questioning from Democratic members of the Senate Judiciary Committee. Critics suggested that Ms. Alito's appearance at the hearing and her emotional response were orchestrated by the Bush administration to solicit public sympathy for the controversial nominee.

groups an incentive to promote and finance **test cases**, lawsuits initiated to challenge the constitutionality of a legislative or executive act. *Brown v. Board of Education of Topeka*, for example, was a test case initiated by the NAACP. Linda Brown was a public school student who was prohibited by state law from attending a whites-only school near her home. The NAACP recruited the Brown family to file suit and provided the legal and financial resources necessary for carrying the case through the long and expensive process of trial and appeals.

Lawyers for losing parties in lower-court proceedings begin the process of appeal to the Supreme Court by filing petitions and submitting briefs explaining why their clients' cases merit review. Appellants must pay a filing fee and submit multiple copies of the paperwork, but the Court will waive these requirements when a litigant is too poor to hire an attorney or to cover the expenses of an appeal. The Court allows indigent appellants to file *in forma pauperis*, which is the process whereby an indigent litigant can file an appeal of a case to the Supreme Court without paying the usual fees. Frequently, pauper petitions come from prison inmates who study law books and prepare their own appeals. In 2006, 80 percent of the cases appealed to the Supreme Court were *in forma pauperis*.[29] The Court rejects most of these petitions, but a few make the Court's docket for full examination. When the Court decides to accept a case from the *in forma pauperis* docket, it appoints an attorney to prepare and argue the case for the indigent petitioner.

The actual selection process takes place in **conference**, a closed meeting attended by only the members of the Supreme Court. The justices decide which cases to hear based on the **Rule of Four**, a decision process used by the Supreme Court to determine which cases to consider on appeal, holding that the Court will hear a case if four of the nine justices agree to the review. In practice, the Supreme Court grants **certiorari**, or cert for short, which is the technical term for the Supreme Court's decision to hear arguments and make a ruling in a case, to only about 1 percent of all the cases appealed to it. In its 2006 term, the Court heard arguments on only 78 of 8,857 cases appealed to it.[30]

What kinds of cases does the Supreme Court accept? The justices choose cases with legal issues of national significance that the Court has not already decided, cases involving conflicts among courts of appeals or between a lower court and the Supreme Court, and cases in which the constitutionality of a state or federal law is under attack. The Court rejects cases it considers trivial or local in scope, and cases that raise issues already decided by earlier rulings. The Court will not accept appeals from state courts

NOW & THEN

**In 1789, the average life expectancy was about 40 years. Today, it's closer to 78 years.**

**As a result, Supreme Court justices today serve longer terms than their predecessors and presidents have fewer vacancies to fill.**

Supreme Court Justice John Paul Stevens (top) in 1975 and (below) at the age of 88.

**think**

Do you think federal judges should be appointed for life? Why or why not?

**per curiam opinion** an unsigned written opinion of a court.

**amicus curiae (friend of the court) brief** written legal arguments presented by parties not directly involved in the case, including interest groups and units of government.

**majority opinion** the official written statement of the Supreme Court that explains and justifies its ruling and serves as a guideline for lower courts when similar legal issues arise in the future.

unless the appellant can demonstrate that a substantial national constitutional question is involved.

In practice, the justices of the Supreme Court set their own rules for deciding which cases to accept, and then follow or interpret the rules as they see fit. For years, the Court refused to consider whether legislative districts that varied considerably in population size violated the Constitution. It was a political question, the justices said, declaring that the legislative and executive branches of government should address the issue rather than the judicial branch. In 1962, however, in *Baker v. Carr*, the Court chose to overlook its political-questions doctrine and rule on the dispute.[31]

**Deciding the Case.** The Supreme Court usually deals with the cases it chooses to hear in one of two ways. It decides some cases without oral arguments, issuing a ruling accompanied by an unsigned written opinion called a **per curiam opinion** that briefly explains the Court's decision. The justices may use this approach, for example, to reverse a lower-court ruling that is contrary to an earlier decision of the Court.

The Court gives full treatment to the remainder of the cases it accepts. The attorneys for the litigants submit briefs arguing the merits of the case, and the Court schedules oral arguments. The Court may also receive **amicus curiae** or **friend of the court briefs**, which are written legal arguments presented by parties not directly involved in the case, including interest groups and units of government. *Amicus* briefs offer the justices more input than they would otherwise receive and provide interest groups

**Cases appealed to the Supreme Court 8,857**

**Cases the Court agrees to hear 78**

and other units of government an opportunity to lobby the Court. The justices sometimes use information contained in *amicus* briefs to justify their rulings.[32]

Attorneys for the litigants present oral arguments publicly to the nine justices in the courtroom of the Supreme Court building. The

Court usually allows each side half an hour to make its case and to answer any questions the justices may ask. The members of the Court use the oral arguments to gather information about the case and to identify their policy options.[33] A few days after oral arguments, the justices meet in closed conference to discuss the case and to take a tentative vote. If the chief justice sides with the Court's majority on the initial vote, the chief either writes the majority opinion or assigns another justice the task. If the chief justice does not vote with the majority, the most senior justice in the majority is responsible for opinion assigning. The **majority opinion** is the official written statement of the Supreme

# HOW TO GET ON THE SUPREME COURT DOCKET

## CASE LOST IN LOWER COURT

Losing party files appeal to Supreme Court

Supreme Court holds conference to decide which cases to hear

Fewer than four justices agree to review

At least four justices agree to review

Appeal denied

Case placed on the docket

## Justice Kennedy Casts Decisive Vote

**By Tom Ramstack, Washington Times**
**FRIDAY, JUNE 27, 2008**

ONCE AGAIN, Justice Anthony M. Kennedy provided the "swing vote" in a tight contest among Supreme Court justices—this time deciding against the District's gun ban.

Thursday's 5–4 ruling pitted the court's conservatives, who said the ban was unconstitutional, against liberals, who called it a reasonable restriction for public safety. Justice Kennedy sided with the conservatives, resulting in a decision that will let more individuals own handguns for home protection.

One day earlier, his vote supported the liberal position in a 5–4 decision saying the death penalty could be imposed only when a criminal defendant kills another person but not for the rape of a child.

"The constitutional provision against excessive or cruel and unusual punishments mandates that punishment be exercised within the limits of civilized standards," said the opinion Wednesday written by Justice Kennedy, which overrides a Louisiana law allowing the death penalty for child rape.

He also sided with the liberals in the 5–4 opinion on June 12 that gives terrorist suspects held at the Guantanamo Bay, Cuba, military prison the right to court hearings, contrary to the stance of the Bush administration.

Some legal scholars refer to Justice Kennedy as a libertarian, whose decisions are guided by a desire to maximize individual liberties while minimizing the role of government. His most frequent critics are political conservatives who see him as unpredictable.

Justice Kennedy's swing votes have given him a powerful voice on the Supreme Court. While the other jurists stick with consistent conservative or liberal positions, Justice Kennedy is most likely to break the deadlock.

Justice Kennedy, 71, was appointed to the Supreme Court by President Reagan in 1988 after working as a private lawyer, a federal judge, and a law school professor. When he was appointed, he was living in the Sacramento, CA, house where he was raised as a child.

He taught constitutional law at the University of the Pacific's McGeorge School of Law from 1965 to 1988. He continues to teach legal seminars at the school.

On religious issues, Justice Kennedy—a Catholic—tends to be slightly conservative, favoring a "coercion test" that he explained in the case of *County of Allegheny v. ACLU*. A Christmas madonna and child display could be allowed on courthouse steps as long as no one "coerced" other people to accept their religious beliefs, he said.

However, his expansive support for Fourteenth Amendment due process rights has led him to support a constitutional right to abortion. He also voted to overturn a federal law forbidding "virtual" child pornography on the Internet, saying the law violated the First Amendment protection of free speech.

### CRITICAL THINKING QUESTIONS:

- How powerful is Anthony Kennedy? Is he more important than a member of Congress? Is he more important than the president?
- Would you prefer a Supreme Court that is closely divided philosophically as opposed to a Court that is consistently conservative or liberal? Why or why not?
- Will Kennedy go down in history as a great Supreme Court justice? What is the basis for your opinion?

Court, which explains and justifies its ruling and serves as a guideline for lower courts when similar legal issues arise in the future. The majority opinion is more important than the outcome of the case because the majority opinion establishes policy.

While the majority opinion is being drafted, other justices may be preparing and circulating concurring or dissenting opinions. A **concurring opinion** is a judicial statement that agrees with the Court's ruling but disagrees with the reasoning of the majority opinion. A justice may write a concurring opinion to point out what the Court did not do in the majority opinion and identify the issues that remain open for further litigation.[34] A **dissenting opinion** is a judicial statement that disagrees with the decision of the court's majority. Justices write dissenting opinions in order to note disagreement with the Court's ruling, to emphasize the limits of the majority opinion, and to express the conscience of the individual justice. Only the majority opinion of the Court has legal force.

**The Decision.** Eventually, the positions of the justices harden or coalesce, and the Supreme Court announces its decision. The announcement takes place in open court, and the final versions of the majority, concurring, and dissenting opinions are published in the *United States Reports*. The Court decides cases by majority vote—nine to zero, five to four, or anything in between, assuming, of course, that the Court is fully staffed and that every justice participates.

# THE MAJORITY OPINION IS MORE IMPORTANT THAN THE OUTCOME OF THE CASE BECAUSE THE MAJORITY OPINION ESTABLISHES POLICY.

Many observers believe that the strength of a Supreme Court decision depends on the level of agreement among the justices. *Brown v. Board of Education* was decided unanimously; the death or resignation of one or two justices was not going to reverse the majority on the issue should a similar case come before the Court in the near future. Furthermore, the Court issued only one opinion, the majority opinion written by Chief Justice Warren. The decision offered no comfort to anyone looking for a weakness of will on the Court. In contrast, the Court's decision in *Furman v. Georgia* (1972) was muddled. In *Furman*, the Court ruled that the death penalty, as then practiced, was discriminatory and hence unconstitutional. The Court did not say, however, that the death penalty, as such, was unconstitutional. The ruling's weakness, perhaps fragility, came from the closeness of the vote, five to four, and the number of opinions—four concurring and four dissenting opinions, besides the majority opinion. The justices could not agree on which facts were

**concurring opinion** a judicial statement that agrees with the Court's ruling but disagrees with the reasoning of the majority opinion.

**dissenting opinion** a judicial statement that disagrees with the decision of the Court's majority.

important in the case or what goals the Court should pursue.[35]

**Implementation.** Political scientists Charles Johnson and Bradley Canon divide the judicial policymaking process into three stages. (see chart below).

Although the implementation of Supreme Court rulings is not automatic, direct disobedience is rare because Court actions enjoy considerable symbolic legitimacy. When the Supreme Court ordered President Nixon to turn over key Watergate tapes to the special prosecutor, for example, Nixon complied. Had the president made a bonfire of them, as some observers suggested, he probably would have been impeached. Instead of defiance, unpopular Supreme Court decisions are often met with delay and subtle evasion. Ten years after the *Brown* ruling, there was not a single state in the Deep South where as many as 10 percent of African American students attended school with any white youngsters.[36] And evasion of the Supreme Court's rulings against government-sponsored school prayers is widespread.[37]

# STAGES OF THE JUDICIAL POLICYMAKING PROCESS

## FIRST
Higher courts, especially the U.S. Supreme Court, develop policies. Although major policy cases make headlines, the Supreme Court frequently clarifies and elaborates an initial decision with subsequent rulings on related issues.

## SECOND
Lower courts interpret the higher court rulings. In theory, lower federal courts apply policies formulated by the U.S. Supreme Court without modification. In practice, however, Supreme Court rulings are often general, leaving room for lower courts to adapt them to the circumstances of specific cases.

## THIRD
Relevant government agencies and private parties implement court decisions. For example, state legislatures had to rewrite death penalty statutes to comply with the *Furman* ruling. Local school boards had the task of developing integration plans to comply with the *Brown* decision.[38]

**Impact.** Supreme Court decisions have their greatest impact when the Court issues a clear decision in a well-publicized case and its position enjoys strong support from other branches and units of government, interest groups, and public opinion.[39] The figure below traces the impact of the Court's rulings on abortion. In 1973, when *Roe v. Wade* was decided, the abortion ratio, the number of abortions out of every hundred pregnancies resulting in an abortion or live birth, was 19.3. (Abortion was already legal in many states.) Four years later, the abortion ratio had risen to 28.6, and it continued climbing until 1983. During the same period, the number of adoptions was falling, apparently because legalized abortion was reducing the number of unwanted infants. In 1970, before *Roe v. Wade*, the total number of adoptions in the nation was 175,000. In 1975, after the decision, the number of adoptions had declined to 129,000.[40]

As the opponents to abortion have grown more aggressive and the Supreme Court has modified its policy position, the impact of *Roe v. Wade* has lessened. Compared with the mid-1970s, fewer physicians are performing abortions, and the number of hospitals and clinics offering abortion services has declined. Pro-life groups such as Operation Save America have picketed not only abortion clinics but also the homes of doctors who perform abortions. Some abortion clinics have been bombed and abortion providers threatened with violence. Several doctors who perform abortions have been shot and killed by abortion opponents. Furthermore, the Supreme Court has somewhat backed away from the *Roe* decision, allowing states more leeway to restrict access to abortion. Declining abortion rates may be due to other factors as well, including better access to contraceptives and pregnancy counseling, and changing attitudes about family size.[41]

# HOW THE COURT DECIDES:

- Attorneys for the litigants submit briefs.
- Other parties submit *amicus curiae* briefs.
- Attorneys for the litigants present oral arguments.
- Justices meet in closed conference to discuss and vote.
- Designated justice drafts majority opinion.
- Other justices in the majority may draft concurring opinions.
- Justices in the minority may draft dissenting opinions.
- Decision announced in open court.

# ABORTION RATES

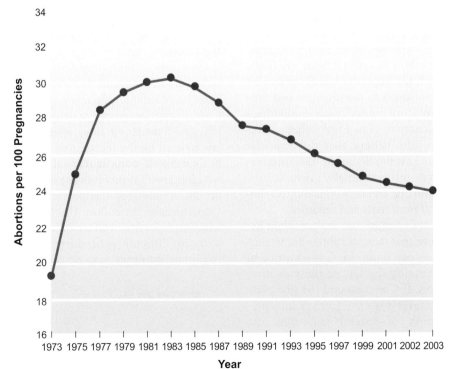

Abortions per 100 Pregnancies (y-axis, 16 to 34)

Year (x-axis): 1973 1975 1977 1979 1981 1983 1985 1987 1989 1991 1993 1995 1997 1999 2001 2002 2003

ARE ABORTION RATES DECLINING IN PART BECAUSE OF ABSTINENCE VOWS? Abstinence vows are increasingly common—and public—among celebrities and ordinary American youth. NBA star A.C. Green vowed to practice abstinence until marriage. *American Idol* winner Jordin Sparks is a proud virgin. So are the Jonas Brothers. *Friends* star Lisa Kudrow is another well-known star who waited until marriage. But Britney Spears also took the vow, which she later broke. New research suggests that girls who take chastity vows still have sex at the same rate as those who do not, but that they practice contraception at a lower rate than those who have not taken vows.

Abortion rates rose sharply in the years following *Roe v. Wade*, but have been slowly declining since 1983.

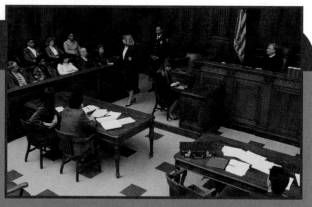

# power, politics,
## AND THE COURTS

**h**ow much influence do federal courts have in the policymaking process? How responsive are they to public concerns? On different occasions in American history, various groups and individuals have attacked the federal courts as both too powerful and undemocratic. In the early 1930s, liberals said that the members of the Supreme Court were "nine unelected old men" who abused their power and tried to unravel the New Deal, despite strong popular support for President Roosevelt's program. In the 1960s and 1970s, conservatives complained about court rulings that gave rights to accused criminals, atheists, and political protesters, while preventing state and local governments from outlawing abortion or controlling the racial balance of local schools.

Political scientists who study the judicial branch identify a number of restrictions on the power of the federal courts. Both the Constitution and the law check judicial authority. The president appoints federal judges, and the Senate confirms their appointments. In the long run, Franklin Roosevelt won his battle with the Supreme Court by waiting for justices to die or retire and then replacing them with individuals friendly to New Deal policies. Voters who believe that the Supreme Court is too liberal or too conservative can eventually reverse the Court by electing conservative/liberal presidents and senators.

If Congress and the president believe that judicial rulings are wrong, they can undo the Court's work by changing the law or the Constitution. If Congress and the president disagree with the Court's interpretation of federal law, they can rewrite the law. In 1978, for example, the Supreme Court ruled that the completion of a dam on the Little Tennessee River would violate the Endangered Species Act because it threatened a tiny fish called the snail darter.[42] The following year, Congress legislated to reverse the Court.

Congress and the president cannot overrule Supreme Court decisions based on interpretations of the Constitution by simply passing legislation. **Statutory law**, which is law written by the legislature, does not supersede **constitutional law**, which is law that involves the interpretation and application of the Constitution. Amending the Constitution to overturn court rulings is a more difficult procedure than changing statutory law, of course,

**statutory law** law that is written by the legislature.

**constitutional law** law that involves the interpretation and application of the Constitution.

but it has been done. The Twenty-sixth Amendment, giving 18-year-olds the right to vote, was passed and ratified after the Supreme Court held that Congress could not legislatively lower the voting age because of constitutional restrictions.[43] Congress and the states have overturned four Supreme Court decisions by enacting constitutional amendments.[44]

The power of the federal courts is also limited by the practical nature of the judicial process. Courts are reactive institutions. They respond to policies adopted in other branches and at other levels of government, and then only when presented with a case to decide. The Supreme Court cannot rule on the constitutionality of the War Powers Act, for example, until it has been given a case dealing with the issue.

Because the courts cannot enforce their own rulings, they must depend on the cooperation and compliance of other units of government and private parties to implement their decisions. Consider, for example, the difficulty in enforcing the Supreme Court's school prayer rulings. For years after the Court's original decision, a public high school in a suburb of Houston, Texas used a school song that was essentially a prayer set to music. It

asked God's blessing and guidance and ended with the phrase, "In Jesus' name we pray. Amen." Despite the Supreme Court's longstanding decision against government-prescribed official prayers in public school classrooms, the school was still using the song years later. Eventually, a federal judge ordered the use of the song discontinued, but the ruling came only after several offended parents brought a lawsuit to federal court. Had no one objected to the song and, just as importantly, had no one been willing to go to the expense and endure the publicity surrounding a lawsuit, the school would probably still be using

the song in official functions today.

Political scientist Robert Dahl believes that the courts are not out of step with Congress and the executive branch for long. Dahl conducted a study in which he traced the fate of 23 "important" laws that had been struck down by the Supreme Court. Three-fourths of the time, Dahl found that the original policy position adopted by Congress and the president ultimately prevailed. In most instances, Congress simply passed legislation similar to the measure that had been initially invalidated. The second time around, however, the Court ruled the legislation constitutional. The

## Overriding the Courts

*Congress and the states have overturned five Supreme Court decisions by enacting constitutional amendments:*

**The Eleventh Amendment**, ratified in 1795, overruled the Supreme Court decision in *Chisholm v. Georgia* (1793). The amendment upheld the sovereign immunity of each state by protecting states from lawsuits filed by the citizens of other states or by citizens of another country.

**The Fourteenth Amendment**, ratified in 1868, overruled the Supreme Court decision in *Dred Scott v. Sandford* (1857), which denied that slaves and their descendants had rights under the Constitution. The amendment defines citizenship broadly to include all persons born or naturalized in the United States.

**The Sixteenth Amendment**, ratified in 1913, overruled the Supreme Court decision in *Pollock v. Farmers' Loan & Trust Co.* (1895), which held the federal income tax unconstitutional. The amendment allows Congress to levy an income tax.

**The Nineteenth Amendment**, ratified in 1920, overruled the Supreme Court decision in *Minor v. Happersett* (1875) which had held that states could constitutionally deny women the right to vote. The amendment granted women the right to vote.

**The Twenty-sixth Amendment**, ratified in 1971, overruled the Supreme Court decision in *Oregon v. Mitchell* (1970), which held that states could set their own legal minimum voting age for state elections. The amendment established 18 as the national minimum legal voting age for all elections.

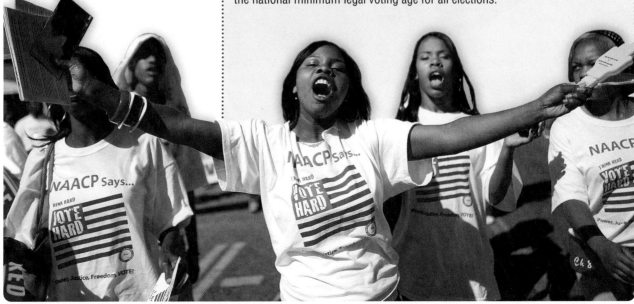

DESPITE THE SUPREME COURT'S LONGSTANDING DECISION AGAINST GOVERNMENT-PRESCRIBED OFFICIAL PRAYERS IN PUBLIC SCHOOL CLASSROOMS, THE SCHOOL WAS STILL USING THE SONG YEARS LATER

role of the courts, Dahl said, is to legitimize the policy decisions made by the elected branches of government rather than to make policy on their own.[45]

In contrast, other political scientists believe that Dahl underestimated the policy influence of the courts. They note that whereas Dahl examined issues that he considered important, many so-called unimportant decisions are not unimportant at all, particularly to the groups most directly affected. Even on important matters, Dahl admits that court rulings affect the timing, effectiveness, and details of policy.[46]

The role of the courts varies from issue to issue. In today's policy process, the courts are most likely to defer to the other branches of government on issues involving foreign and defense policy, and economic policy. The courts are least likely to follow the lead of other branches and units of government on matters dealing with civil rights and civil liberties.

Political scientist Jeffrey Rosen believes that the courts reflect the views of a majority of Americans on most issues. Judges can nudge the country in one policy direction or another, but they are sensitive to public opinion through pressure by Congress and the president. They recognize that their policy decisions will not be accepted by the country unless those decisions are perceived as being rooted in constitutional principles rather than the personal preferences of judges. On those occasions when courts stray too far away from mainstream public opinion, they get slapped down.[47]

**think** If you were a member of the Supreme Court, when, if ever, would you consider public opinion in making decisions?

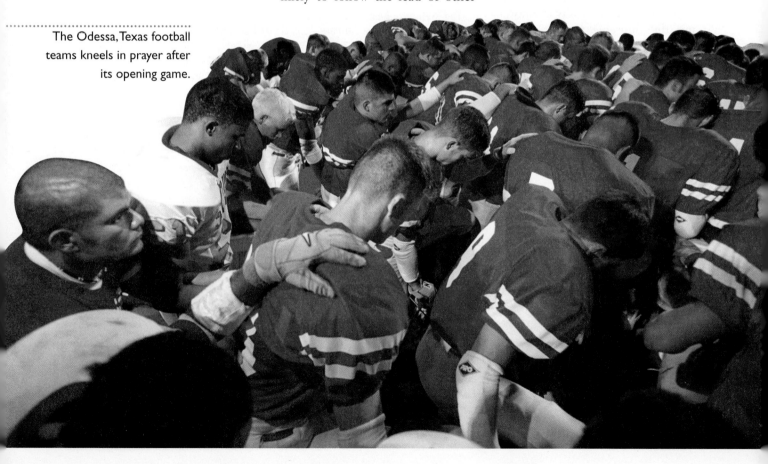

The Odessa, Texas football teams kneels in prayer after its opening game.

# Congressional Control over the Judiciary

**Should Congress exercise its authority to limit the power of the judiciary? Is this a proper role for Congress?**

**Have the courts taken too much constitutional power? If so, why? If not, why not?**

**Overview:** Today, commentators on both sides of the political spectrum complain that the Supreme Court oversteps its constitutional authority and acts in a political or lawmaking capacity, and—depending on one's point of view—the Court is either creating rights or restricting freedoms.

Currently, the debate over homosexual marriage and the definition of what constitutes a family has brought the constitutional question of Congress's authority into policy debate. Because of the possibility of majority tyranny, advocates of homosexual marriage and unions argue that the courts are the proper forum in which to make this judgment. Op-

ponents argue that this should be left to the states or Congress. What political institution has the authority to define rights? Opponents of homosexual unions introduced a bill (HR 724) in January 2007 that would prohibit the federal judiciary, including the Supreme Court, from hearing cases arising from the Defense of Marriage Act, which defines marriage as being between a man and a woman. As this would effectively bar federal courts from deciding on this particular issue, has Congress overstepped its authority or is it simply reasserting its prerogatives?

Like all constitutional powers, the authority of Congress to determine

appellate jurisdiction of the federal judiciary has provoked much debate and many interpretations. Nevertheless, the courts themselves have given broad interpretation to this congressional power and they have consistently affirmed this prerogative of Congress. Proponents of the bill argue that the states will be able to allow or ban gay unions abiding by the will of their citizens. Proponents of gay marriage argue that this is a civil right that should have constitutional protection, by stripping the courts of their authority, Congress is chipping away at the courts' obligation to secure individual rights.

## supporting congressional determination of federal appellate jurisdiction

**it is not the authority of the courts to determine rights.** Many believe that it is the role of legislatures, as representative of the wishes of the people, to determine individual rights, and the role of the judiciary to protect rights.

**the federal courts are exceeding their constitutional limits and encroaching on the constitutional prerogatives of other political institutions.** For example, a federal judge ordered the state of Missouri to spend over two billion dollars to improve the Kansas City school system, and ordered an increase in property taxes to help pay for the improvements. Critics argue that only elected officials should be able to write and execute tax policy; the judiciary was created to judge, not to enact policy.

**the founders envisioned a limited judiciary.** Alexander Hamilton writes in *The Federalist,* No. 78 that the judiciary is weak by design, and that Congress has the authority to limit the courts' jurisdiction to provide a check against judicial encroachment on the powers of the other two branches.

## against congressional determination of federal appellate jurisdiction

**it is the obligation of the federal courts to ensure that individual rights are protected.** History shows that at times, minority rights are denied by a majority. Take, as an example, the internment of Americans of Japanese descent during World War II. It is not the responsibility of Congress to define civil rights.

**congressional limitation of the courts' appellate jurisdiction violates the principle of separation of power.** The courts have the right to exercise judicial review to ensure that actions of the federal and state governments are constitutional. For example, should HR 724 become law, the courts would not be able to determine whether or not individual rights are being violated, since they have been denied the ability to exercise judicial review.

**allowing Congress the precedent to alter existing jurisdiction can create confusion among the 50 states.** Limiting the federal courts' appellate jurisdiction in certain matters will cause federal law and policy to be interpreted by 50 state courts. This undermines the principle of federalism because federal law is to provide consistent and fair national policy in certain domains.

# HOW WELL DO SUPREME COURT DECISIONS ON CONTROVERSIAL ISSUES REFLECT PUBLIC OPINION?

| Issue: | Case: | SC decision: | Public Opinion at time of decision |
|---|---|---|---|
| Should abortion be legal? | *Roe v. Wade* (1973) | Yes (7-2) | 67% support Roe decision |
| Is the death penalty constitutional? | *Gregg v. Georgia* (1976) | Yes (7-2) | 63% favor death penalty |
| Is flag burning constitutional? | *Texas v. Johnson* (1989) | Yes (5-4) | 57% favor amendment to overturn ruling |
| Should the Boy Scouts be able to ban gay troop leaders? | *Boy Scouts of America v. Dale* (2000) | Yes (5-4) | 64% agree with ruling |
| Should homosexual relations be legal? | *Lawrence v. Texas* (2003) | Yes (6-3) | 55% say homosexual relations should be legal |
| Is affirmative action constitutional? | *Grutter v. Bollinger* (2003) | Yes (5-4) | 50% support affirmative action |
| Should displaying the Ten Commandments on public property be legal? | *Van Orden v. Perry* (2005) | Yes (5-4) | 35% agree with school prayer decision |

## CONCLUSION
# the courts and
# & PUBLIC POLICY

the federal courts are important participants in the policymaking process.

## Agenda Building
The courts play a role in agenda building by tackling issues that might not otherwise be addressed by other levels and branches of government. For example, the U.S. Supreme Court made abortion a national issue in *Roe v. Wade*. Before *Roe*, state governments made abortion policy. Some states, such as New York, permitted abortion; other states, such as Texas, prohibited abortion except to preserve the life of the woman. After *Roe*, abor-

tion became a national policy issue not just for the courts, who continued to hear abortion cases, but also for the president and Congress, because the politics of judicial appointment and confirmation now became the politics of abortion as well. Other issues that have become part of the official policy agenda because of court decisions include legislative redistricting and school prayer.

## Policy Formulation and Adoption
The courts play an important role in policy formulation and adoption. Judges formulate policy when they

read legal briefs, listen to oral arguments, and negotiate rulings and opinions among themselves. Furthermore, court decisions affect policy formulation in the other branches and units of government. Members of Congress and state legislators formulating abortion policy, for example, must work within the guidelines established in *Roe* and subsequent abortion decisions or

**item veto** the power of an executive to veto sections or items of a tax or appropriation measure while signing the remainder of the bill into law.

face the likelihood of having any legislation they pass be overturned in federal courts.

Courts adopt policy when they make rulings and issue opinions. When the Supreme Court issued its decision in *Brown v. Board of Education of Topeka*, for example, it adopted a policy on racial desegregation of public schools. Most judicial policymaking involves civil liberties and civil rights policies. Political scientists concerned with public policies on capital punishment, government-sponsored prayer in public schools, affirmative action, and pornography regulation will spend a good deal of time reading Supreme Court opinions. In contrast, the judicial branch plays a relatively minor role in economic, regulatory, foreign, and defense policymaking.

## Policy Implementation and Evaluation

The federal courts play a role in policy implementation. Lower courts implement Supreme Court rulings by applying them to new cases as they arise. The courts also affect policy implementation when they interpret the law. Consider the implementation of the Americans with Disabilities Act (ADA), which is a federal law designed to end discrimination against persons with disabilities and to eliminate barriers to their full participation in American society. The law requires companies to make "reasonable accom-

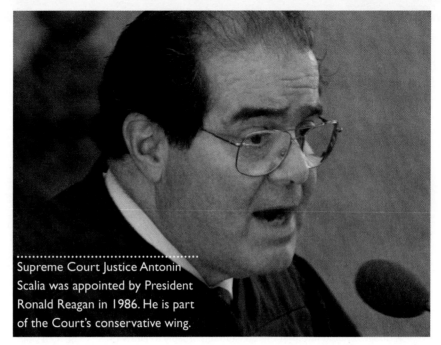

Supreme Court Justice Antonin Scalia was appointed by President Ronald Reagan in 1986. He is part of the Court's conservative wing.

modation" for otherwise qualified job applicants or current employees who happen to be disabled, unless the business can show that the accommodation would put an "undue hardship" on its operation. When Congress wrote the law, it did not define "reasonable accommodation" and "undue hardship." As a result, the federal courts have been heavily involved with the implementation of the ADA by interpreting its meaning in the context of specific controversies.

Finally, federal courts evaluate policies in light of the Constitution. In theory, at least, judges do not evaluate policies on their effectiveness or wisdom, but only on their constitutionality. In 1996, for example, Congress passed, and Presi-

dent Clinton signed, legislation granting the president the **item veto,** which is the power of an executive to veto sections or items of a tax or appropriation measure while signing the remainder of the bill into law. Two years later, a legal challenge to the policy reached the U.S. Supreme Court. The Court ruled that the law giving the president the item veto was unconstitutional because it legislatively made a fundamental change in the relationship between the executive and legislative branches of government. The Court held that changes of such constitutional significance must be made through the adoption of a constitutional amendment rather than through the legislative process.[48]

the THINK SPOT
www.thethinkspot.com

# TEST yourself

1. The power of the courts to declare unconstitutional the actions of the other branches and units of government is known as which of the following?
   A. Loose construction
   B. Judicial review
   C. Strict construction
   D. Civil liberties

2. Which of the following statements most closely reflects the philosophy of loose construction of the Constitution?
   A. Judges should interpret the Constitution broadly to allow it to change with the times.
   B. Judges should recognize that their role is to interpret the law rather than make the law.
   C. Judges should stick to the literal meaning of the Constitution.
   D. Judges should closely follow the intent of the Framers of the Constitution.

3. A doctrine of constitutional interpretation holding that the document should be interpreted narrowly is known as which of the following?
   A. Strict construction
   B. Loose construction
   C. Civil liberties
   D. Judicial review

4. Which of the following federal courts is exclusively a trial court?
   A. District court
   B. Courts of appeal
   C. Supreme Court
   D. None of the above

5. How are U.S. district judges selected?
   A. They are career civil servants, chosen through a merit hiring process.
   B. They are appointed by the president subject to confirmation by the Senate.
   C. They are elected by the voters in the states where they serve.
   D. They are appointed by the president subject to confirmation by the House and Senate.

6. Which of the following statements most accurately describes the principle of senatorial courtesy?
   A. The Senate almost always confirms the president's district court nominees.
   B. Senators will always confirm judicial nominees who have the support of the senators from their home states.
   C. Senators from the president's party have a veto on the confirmation of district judge nominees from their states.
   D. Senators agree not to filibuster judicial nominations.

7. A liberal judge is more likely than a conservative judge to take which of the following policy actions?
   A. To rule in favor of the government and against criminal defendants
   B. To rule in favor of workers and against corporate interests
   C. To rule in favor of state governments in federalism disputes with the federal government
   D. All of the above

8. What is the term of a federal district judge?
   A. Two years
   B. Four years
   C. Six years
   D. Life, with "good behavior"

9. The "nuclear option" involved which of the following actions?
   A. An attempt to increase the size of the Supreme Court
   B. An effort to amend the Constitution to restrict the president's authority as commander in chief
   C. An effort to eliminate the Senate filibuster for judicial nominees
   D. An attempt to limit the jurisdiction of the Supreme Court to prevent it from hearing abortion cases

10. According to the U.S. Constitution, how many justices serve on the Supreme Court?
    A. Seven
    B. Nine
    C. Eleven
    D. The Constitution says nothing about the size of the Supreme Court

11. The Supreme Court decides a case by a unanimous vote. Who writes the majority opinion?
    A. The chief justice
    B. The most senior justice
    C. The chief justice either writes the opinion or assigns it to another justice
    D. Opinion assignment is done randomly

12. Suppose that Congress passes controversial legislation that some people believe is unconstitutional. When, if ever, will the Supreme Court address the issue?
    A. The Supreme Court will decide the issue when and if it accepts a case that involves a challenge to the constitutionality of the legislation.
    B. The Supreme Court reviews legislation passed by Congress before it takes effect.
    C. The Supreme Court will only review the legislation if Congress requests a review.
    D. Never.

**13** Why was *Brown v. Board of Education* an example of a test case?

A. The Supreme Court reversed an earlier decision (the *Plessy* case) when it decided *Brown*.

B. The case was prepared, presented, and financed by an interest group.

C. An interest group submitted a legal brief that discussed issues raised by the case.

D. *Brown* is considered a landmark decision in constitutional law.

**14** Daryl Renard Atkins was convicted of murder in the state of Virginia and sentenced to death. Under which of the following circumstances would the U.S. Supreme Court hear an appeal of his case?

A. All death penalty cases are automatically appealed to the U.S. Supreme Court.

B. State cases such as the Atkins case cannot be appealed to the federal court system.

C. His attorneys would have to convince a majority of the justices of the Supreme Court that his case is interesting enough to review.

D. His attorneys raise national constitutional issues that at least four justices believe are worth considering.

**15** A Supreme Court justice agrees with the outcome of a case but disagrees with the legal reasoning presented in the majority opinion. Which of the following actions would the justice take?

A. File a friend of the court brief

B. Write a concurring opinion

C. Write a majority opinion

D. Write a dissenting opinion

**16** What is a friend of the court brief?

A. An opinion written by a member of a court who agrees with the court's ruling but disagrees with the reasoning behind it

B. A judicial order directing the government either to release someone in custody or to justify why the person is being help

C. A court case that is supported financially by an interest group

D. A brief submitted by an interest group not directly involved in a case that is attempting to influence the outcome of the case

**17** What is a dissenting opinion?

A. It is a legal brief written by an interest group attempting to influence the outcome of a case.

B. It is an opinion written by a justice on the Supreme Court who agrees with the outcome of a case but disagrees with the reasoning contained in the majority opinion.

C. It is a document written by an interest group that disagrees with a ruling issued by the Supreme Court.

D. It is an opinion written by a justice of the Supreme Court who disagrees with the majority ruling on a case.

**18** Suppose that a majority of the members of the Supreme Court believe that a recent action by the president violates the Constitution. What can they do?

A. They can do nothing until a case arises that involves the issue and the case is appealed to the Supreme Court.

B. Nothing. The Supreme Court can review the acts of Congress but not the actions of the president.

C. The Supreme Court can issue an opinion declaring the president's action unconstitutional.

D. The Supreme Court can invite parties to file a challenge against the president's action.

**19** What power does the Supreme Court have to enforce its rulings?

A. The Court can order law enforcement personnel to enforce its rulings.

B. The Court must rely on the other branches and units of government to enforce its rulings.

C. None. Court rulings are regularly ignored.

D. None of the above.

**20** Which of the following is a check on the power of the Supreme Court?

A. The president can appoint and the Senate can confirm new justices to fill vacancies on the Court.

B. The House and Senate can propose an amendment to the Constitution to overturn a judicial interpretation of the Constitution.

C. Congress and the president can rewrite a law to reverse a judicial interpretation of an act of Congress.

D. All of the above.

KNOW *the* **score**

18–20 correct: Congratulations! You are well informed!

15–17 correct: Your political knowledge is a bit low—be sure to review the key terms and visit TheThinkSpot.

<14 correct: Reread the chapter more thoroughly.

1. B; 2. A; 3. A; 4. A; 5. B; 6. C; 7. B; 8. D; 9. C; 10. D; 11. C; 12. A; 13. B; 14. D; 15. B; 16. D; 17. D; 18. A; 19. B; 20. D

# 14 ECONOMIC

Healthcare reform was the foremost legislative priority of President Barack Obama during his first year in office. The issue was important because more than 45 million Americans, 15.3 percent of the population, lack health insurance. African Americans (19.5 percent) and Latinos (32.1 percent) are more likely to be uninsured than are whites (10.4 percent). Insurance coverage also varies based on citizenship. The uninsured rate for native-born Americans is 12.7 percent, compared with 17.6 percent for naturalized citizens and 43.8 percent for non-citizens.[1] People without healthcare coverage must go without treatment, pay out of pocket for their health expenses, or seek care at a hospital emergency room. They are more likely than the insured to postpone care for injury or illness and to neglect preventive medical care, such as regular checkups and vaccinations. Meanwhile, a significant percentage of people filing bankruptcy or losing their homes to foreclosure do so because of catastrophic medical expenses.

Healthcare reform is important even to people with insurance coverage. Because healthcare expenses are increasing at twice the rate of inflation, insurance premiums are going up as well. Families and individuals are forced to cut back on other expenditures to cover the growing cost of insurance coverage. Rising health insurance premiums reduce employee take-home pay by driving up compensation costs for employers.

Rapidly rising healthcare costs threaten to bankrupt both the national government and the states. The Congressional Budget Office (CBO) estimates that federal expenditures for Medicare and Medicaid will increase from 4 percent of the Gross Domestic Product (GDP) in 2009 to 12 percent in 2050.[2] Because Medicaid requires the financial participation of state governments as well as the national government, it is

# POLICYMAKING

also a threat to the financial health of state governments. Healthcare expenditures in general are the largest and fastest growing expenditure for the federal government, larger than national defense and Social Security.

The action Congress and the president take to address healthcare reform will have long term consequences not just for individual Americans, but also for government finance and the economy as a whole.

# ESSENTIALS...

*after studying Chapter 14, students should be able to answer the following questions:*

> What are the principal goals of economic policy?

> What are the major sources of federal tax revenue? How is the tax burden distributed, and what were George W. Bush's tax reforms?

> What is the history of federal budget deficits and surpluses, and what impact do budget deficits have on the nation's economy?

> What are the goals and strategies of the Medicare, Medicaid, and Social Security programs? What are the concerns about their long-term financial viability?

> What is the process through which Congress and the president make fiscal policy?

> What is the role of the Federal Reserve in setting monetary policy?

> Who are the major players in the formulation, implementation, and evaluation of economic policymaking?

# the goals of ECONOMIC POLICY

**a**mericans disagree about the goals of economic policy.

## Fund Government Services

The most basic goal of economic policy is to fund government services. In fiscal year 2009, which ran from October 1, 2008 through September 30, 2009, the federal government spent $4.0 trillion funding government programs, including various healthcare programs, Social Security, and national defense.[3] Nonetheless, Americans disagree over spending priorities and the appropriate level of funding for federal government activity. In general, liberals believe that government can play a positive role in addressing the needs of society. They favor programs to improve the nation's health, education, and welfare, such as a government program to provide healthcare coverage for individuals and families not currently covered. In contrast, conservatives believe that the role of government should be lim-ited to the provision of basic services. They support spending for national defense and to promote economic development, but they are wary about spending for social programs, especially by the federal government, because they think that high taxes and big government suppress economic growth. They see the provision of tax credits to enable individuals to buy health insurance on the open market as a better approach to healthcare reform than a government program.

**think**

**Should the government subsidize farm production?**

American agricultural producers benefit from billions of dollars in subsidies.

# HEALTHCARE PROTESTERS: GRASSROOTS MOVEMENT OR ASTROTURF?

When members of Congress returned to their states and districts during the August 2009 recess, they faced protests from constituents, angry over the healthcare reform proposals before Congress. Town hall meetings around the nation turned into shouting matches between healthcare reform advocates and conservative opponents. A number of demonstrators accused the Obama administration of promoting socialism or equated Obama to Adolf Hitler and the Nazis.

Republicans and Democrats in Congress disagreed about the nature of the protests. Many of the opponents of reform were associated with the Tea Party Movement, a loose-knit network of conservative activists alarmed over the policies of the Obama administration. Tea Party organizers described the protests as a grassroots movement, locally organized through Facebook and Twitter rather than by a national leadership structure. Republicans in Congress declared that the protests were an indication that the American people had turned against healthcare reform. In contrast, Democrats ridiculed the healthcare reform protests, calling them Astroturf rather than grassroots because they were organized by pharmaceutical companies, healthcare insurance firms, and other powerful interest groups opposed to reform. The best assessment of the protests is that they reflect genuine citizen anger that is coordinated at least some extent by media figures such as Glenn Beck, a Fox Television talk show host, and organizations such as Freedom Works, a conservative advocacy group.

Views on Healthcare Reform Bill
Oct 1–4, 2009

## Encourage/Discourage Private Sector Activity

Congress and the president use economic policy to encourage some private sector activities while discouraging others. By making home mortgage interest and real estate taxes deductible, the federal government promotes housing construction and home ownership. Similarly, the government uses tax breaks to encourage people to give money to charity, save for retirement, and invest in state and local government bonds. Congress and the president also use tax policy to discourage certain activities. Increasing cigarette taxes, for example, reduces the smoking rate for teenagers. Raising gasoline taxes saves energy and decreases pollution by discouraging driving.

A **subsidy** is a financial incentive given by government to an individual or a business interest to accomplish a public objective. For example, the federal government operates a number of agricultural subsidy programs. It gives some farmers price-support loans. Farmers borrow money from the government, using their crops as collateral. The value of the crops, and hence, the amount of money the farmer can borrow, is determined by a target commodity price set by the U.S. Department of Agriculture (USDA). If the market price rises above the target price, the farmer sells the crop, repays the loan, and makes a profit. If the market price falls below the target price, the government pays farmers the difference between the two prices, either in cash or in certificates for government-stored commodities.

## The world's democracies tend to be countries with a large middle class

## Redistribute Income

**Income redistribution** involves government taking items of value, especially money, from some groups of people and then giving items of value, either in cash or services, to other groups of people. Those people who favor income redistribution believe that government has an obligation to reduce the income gap between the poorest and wealthiest income groups in the nation. They advocate the adoption of programs that provide benefits based on need and a tax structure whose burden falls most heavily on business and

**subsidy** a financial incentive given by government to an individual or a business interest to accomplish a public objective.

**income redistribution** government taking items of value, especially money, from some groups of people and then giving items of value, either in cash or services, to other groups of people.

# Should the government adopt policies designed to narrow the gap between the rich and the poor?

In the first episode of his reality TV show, *30 Days*, Morgan Spurlock and his fiancée spent thirty days living in Columbus, Ohio, trying to get by on minimum wage. Other shows, such as *The Hills*, glamorize the lives of the rich.

the wealthy. Furthermore, many scholars believe that extreme levels of income inequality are incompatible with democracy. They note that the world's democracies tend to be countries with a large middle class, whereas countries that are divided between a small group of very rich families and a huge group of the very poor typically do not have democratic governments. In contrast, the opponents of income redistribution believe that government should adopt tax systems and spending programs designed to foster economic development because, in the long run, economic development will benefit all segments of society, including low-income groups, more than programs designed to redistribute wealth. In practice, they warn, programs designed to redistribute wealth hinder economic development, hurting everyone. They believe that government has a role to ensure a level playing field in

which everyone can compete fairly to get ahead, but that government should not intervene to dictate economic winners and losers.

## Economic Growth with Stable Prices

Americans also disagree about the role the government should play in promoting economic growth. Some Americans think that the federal government can play a positive role in promoting economic growth with stable prices. They believe that the government should seek to avoid depression, minimize the severity of recession, and control inflation.[4] A **depression** is a severe and prolonged economic slump characterized by decreased business activity and high unemployment. A **recession** is an economic slowdown characterized by declining economic output and rising unemployment. A recession is less severe

than a depression. **Inflation** is a decline in the purchasing power of the currency. By controlling interest rates, taxes, and expenditures, they argue, government can promote a healthy economy. In contrast, other Americans believe that government does more harm than good when it attempts to manage the economy. In their view, the best government policies for promoting economic growth are low taxes, low spending, and minimal regulation.

**depression** a severe and prolonged economic slump characterized by decreased business activity and high unemployment.

**recession** an economic slowdown characterized by declining economic output and rising unemployment.

**inflation** a decline in the purchasing power of the currency.

# tax REVENUES

In 2009, the U.S. government raised $2.2 trillion in tax revenues. The figure on page 315 shows the relative importance of the major sources of tax revenue.

## Individual Income Tax

The individual income tax is the largest single source of revenue for the national government, generating 44.2 percent of the nation's total tax

**fiscal year** budget year.

revenue in **fiscal year** (budget year) 2009. The income tax system divides taxable income into brackets and applies a different tax rate to the portion of income falling into each bracket, with higher incomes taxed at higher rates than lower incomes. In 2009, the lowest individual rate, for income below $8,350, was 10 percent; the highest rate, for income more than $372,950, was 35 percent.

Because of tax preferences, not all income is taxable. A **tax preference** is a tax deduction or exclusion that allows individuals to pay less tax than they would otherwise. Tax preferences include tax exemptions, deductions, and credits. A **tax exemption** is the exclusion of some types of income from taxation. For example, veterans' benefits, pension contributions and earnings, and interest earned on state and local government bonds are exempt from the income tax. A **tax deduction** is an expenditure that can be subtracted from a taxpayer's gross income before figuring the tax owed. Taxpayers can itemize deductions for such expenditures as home mortgage interest payments, charitable con-

**tax preference** a tax deduction or exclusion that allows individuals to pay less tax than they would otherwise.

**tax exemption** the exclusion of some types of income from taxation.

**tax deduction** an expenditure that can be subtracted from a taxpayer's gross income before figuring the tax owed.

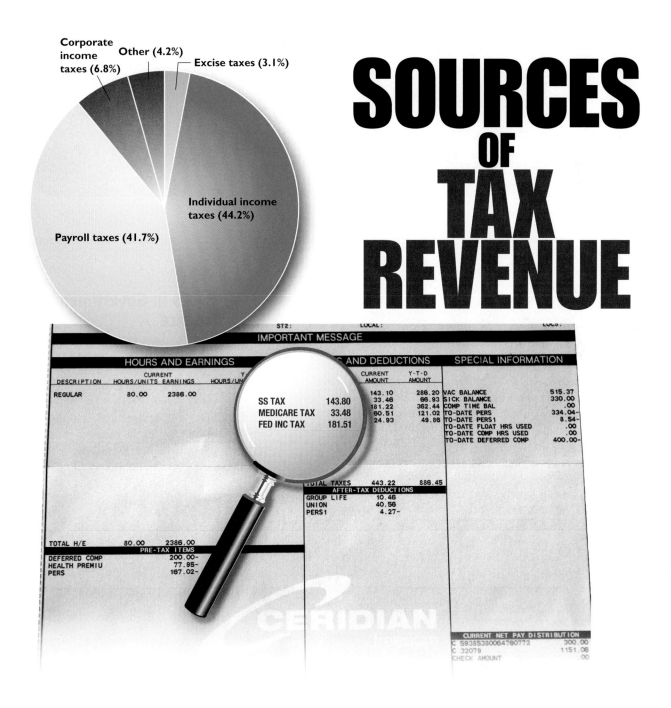

Corporate income taxes (6.8%)
Other (4.2%)
Excise taxes (3.1%)
Individual income taxes (44.2%)
Payroll taxes (41.7%)

# SOURCES OF TAX REVENUE

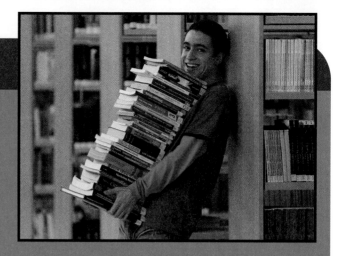

# **take**action

## TAX BREAKS FOR COLLEGE STUDENTS >>

The Hope Credit and Lifetime Learning Credit are tax breaks for college students. Your assignment is to research the tax rules to determine whether you or your parents can benefit from these credits. You can find information about the Hope Credit and the Lifetime Learning Credit from official publications available at the local IRS office or online at the IRS website, www.irs.gov. Research these tax breaks for college students, review your family's tax situation, and answer the following questions:

1. How do the Hope Credit and Lifetime Learning Credit programs differ?

2. Do you have to be a full-time student to benefit?

3. Are the credits available for both public and private schools or for public school students only?

4. If parents have two children in college at the same time, can they claim a tax credit for each of them?

5. Can you claim the cost of this textbook as an educational expense? Why or why not?

6. Do you or your parents qualify for either the Hope Credit or the Lifetime Learning Credit? Why or why not?

7. If you qualify for either the Hope Credit of the Lifetime Learning Credit, how will the credit affect your tax liability? Explain.

8. Did you or your parents claim a credit last year? Will you claim it next year?

tributions, and state and local real estate taxes. A tax credit is an expenditure that reduces an individual's tax liability by the amount of the credit. A tax credit of $500 reduces the amount of tax owed by $500.

## Payroll Taxes

As the figure on p. 315 indicates, payroll taxes are the second-largest source of federal tax revenue, producing 41.7 percent of total revenues in 2009. The payroll tax rate, which is levied on wages and salaries but not other sources of income, is 15.3 percent, with 7.65 percent withheld from the employee's paycheck and an equivalent 7.65 percent paid by the employer. The payroll tax funds both the Social Security and Medicare programs, with 12.4 percent going to finance Social Security and 2.9 percent set aside for Medicare. Wage earners and their employers paid Social Security payroll taxes on the first $106,800 of an employee's annual salary in 2009. They paid the Medicare payroll tax on all wage income.

## Corporate Income Taxes and Other Revenue Sources

In 2009, the national government derived 14.1 percent of its tax revenue from corporate income taxes, excise taxes, and miscellaneous revenue sources. The corporate income tax, which generated 6.8 percent of federal tax revenues in 2009, has four brackets—15 percent on the first $50,000 of taxable earnings, 25 percent on income between $50,000 and $75,000, 34 percent on earnings between $75,000 and $10 million, and 35 percent on income greater than $10 million. Because the 15 percent and 25 percent rates apply only to income below $75,000, most corporate profits are taxed at the higher rates. **Excise taxes** are taxes levied on the manufacture, transportation, sale, or consumption of a particular item or set of related items. The government assesses excise taxes on gasoline, alcohol, tobacco, tires, airplane tickets, and a number of other items. The govern-

ment also raises revenue through customs duties, fines, penalties, and inheritance taxes.

## Issues in Government Finance

Policymakers face a number of issues in government finance.

**Tax Burden.** Are taxes too high? Economists believe that the best way to evaluate the size of the nation's tax burden is to consider it in proportion to the nation's **gross domestic product (GDP),** which is the total value of goods and services

**excise taxes** taxes levied on the manufacture, transportation, sale, or consumption of a particular item or set of related items.

**gross domestic product** (GDP) the total value of goods and services produced by a nation's economy in a year, excluding transactions with foreign countries.

produced by a nation's economy in a year. Federal government tax receipts rose during the 1990s, peaking at 20.9 percent in 2000. Tax receipts fell during the early years of the twenty-first century both because of a recession in 2002 and because of tax cuts passed by Congress and signed into law by President Bush. In 2009, the federal tax burden stood at 15.1 percent of the nation's GDP. National, state, and local taxes combined represented 25.4 percent of GDP.[5]

Observers disagree about the weight of the nation's tax burden. Scholars who believe that the taxes are either too low or about right note that the tax burden in the United States is relatively light compared to the tax burden in many other industrialized nations. Italy, Canada, France, Germany, and the United Kingdom all allocate more than 40 percent of their gross domestic products to government compared with less than 30 percent for the United States.[6] In contrast, other scholars contend that Americans are overtaxed and they warn that high tax rates depress economic growth. In general, Republicans believe that high taxes undermine economic prosperity, whereas Democrats resist tax cuts because they want to ensure that the government has sufficient revenue to fund government services.

**Tax Incidence and Tax Fairness.** The term **tax incidence** refers to the point at which the actual cost of a tax falls. Using this concept, social scientists identify three general types of taxes: progressive, proportional, and regressive. A **progressive tax** is a levy that taxes people earning higher incomes at a higher rate than it does individuals making

# OBSERVERS DISAGREE ABOUT THE WEIGHT OF THE NATION'S TAX BURDEN.

less money. The federal income tax is a progressive tax because people earning higher incomes pay a higher tax rate than persons making less money. A **proportional tax** is a levy that taxes all persons at the same percentage rate, regardless of income, whereas a **regressive tax** is a levy whose burden falls more heavily on lower-income groups than on wealthy taxpayers. Economists generally classify sales and

# $2.80 PER GALLON

5.6% or about $0.17 went for federal taxes

9.4% or about $0.27 went for state taxes (on average)

10% or $0.28 spent for distribution and marketing

17% or about $0.48 spent on refining costs and company profits

58% or about $1.60 paid for the actual crude oil

excise taxes as regressive taxes because lower-income persons spend a greater proportion of their earnings on items subject to taxation than do upper-income persons.

Observers disagree about the fairest tax system. The advocates of progressive taxation often defend the concept on the basis of the **ability-to-pay theory of taxation**, which is the approach to government finance that holds that taxes should be based on an individual's ability to pay. Well-to-do persons can better afford taxes than lower-income individuals, so they should pay more.[7] Furthermore, the advocates of income redistribution point out that a progressive tax helps to narrow the income differential between the poor and the affluent.

Other experts on public finance believe that the best tax system is one that encourages economic growth. They favor sales and excise taxes because those levies discourage people from spending their money on consumer goods. They want people to save and invest their incomes. They also believe that progressive taxes such as the income tax are harmful to the economy because they reduce the amount of money middle- and upper-income individuals have available to invest in economic development.

## The Bush Tax Reforms

Shortly after taking office, President George W. Bush proposed, and Congress passed, a major income tax cut that would be phased in over the next ten years. They also agreed to repeal the **estate tax**, which is a tax levied on the value of an inheritance. In subsequent years, Congress and the president acceler-

**ability to pay theory of taxation** the approach to government finance that holds that taxes should be based on an individual's ability to pay.
**estate tax** a tax levied on the value of an inheritance.

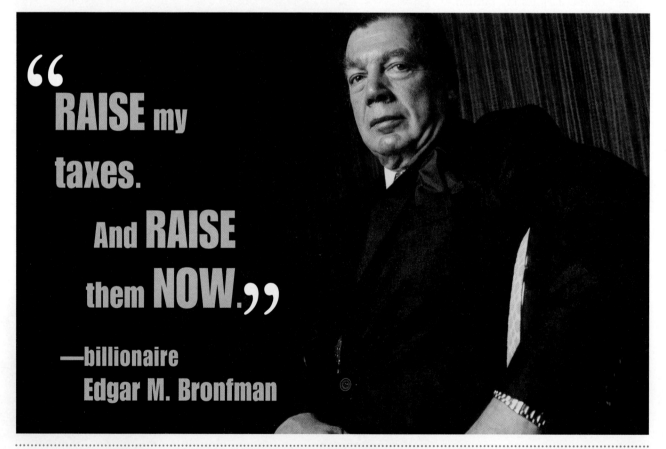

"RAISE my taxes. And RAISE them NOW."

—billionaire Edgar M. Bronfman

Billionaire and former head of Seagram's LTD Edgar Bronfman argued in a 2008 Huffington Post article that the rich and ultra-rich should pay higher taxes. Bronfman said that the Bush tax cuts had been fiscally disastrous and that President Barack Obama should not just let them expire, but actively seek to repeal them as quickly as possible.

ated the pace of the earlier tax cuts already adopted, reduced taxes on dividend income, and exempted or deferred taxes on interest income from savings.

The Bush tax reforms reflected the president's goal of increasing savings and investment. Bush focused the bulk of his tax cuts on upper-income taxpayers because they are more able to invest and save money than lower-income taxpayers. With more money available for business to expand, he reasoned, the economy would grow and everyone would be better off. Companies would hire more workers and investors would realize greater gains from investments. Even though lower-income people would not benefit directly from the tax reductions, the president argued that they would be better off in the long run because the economy would grow.[8]

The Bush tax cuts reflected **supply-side economics**, the economic theory that tax cuts, especially for business and the wealthy, will lead to savings and investment that will benefit everyone. Supply-side economists believe that high tax rates discourage investment and worker productivity. Why risk your savings on investments or work harder to earn more money if much of it goes to the government? Supply-side economists advocate tax reductions in order to stimulate investment and economic growth. In fact, some supply-siders believe that economic growth generated by tax reductions will be sufficient to produce an actual increase in tax receipts.

The tax policies adopted during the Bush administration dramatically changed the nation's tax structure by shifting the federal tax burden away from taxes on dividends, capital gains, and interest income to taxes on wages and salaries. If people make money from working, they pay taxes. If they make money as investors, they do not pay taxes.

The Bush tax reforms are controversial. Although everyone favors economic growth, not everyone agrees that policies designed to in-

**Warren Buffett, chairman and CEO of Berkshire Hathaway,** was ranked by *Forbes* as the richest man in the world in 2008. Mr. Buffet caused a media stir in both the financial and political sectors when he publicly criticized the U.S. tax system. He stated that his $46 million income was taxed at a rate of 17.7 percent, while his secretary's $60,000 was taxed at 30 percent. Several well-known business people countered Buffet's approach, saying that he was unfairly comparing Buffet's investment gains against his secretary's straight income. Said Randal J. Kirk, a wealthy pharmaceuticals businessman, "[H]is thesis here seems grossly simplistic. There are good reasons why investment returns are not taxed at the 'ordinary' income tax rate. If investment returns in the U.S. are reduced through the imposition of additional taxes, people will 'buy' less investment (because the price would have gone up)." According to this thinking, lower investment would hurt business and the economy as a whole.

crease the savings rate are the only way—or even the best way—to grow the economy. Bush's critics favor policies aimed at increasing consumption: The economy will grow if consumers increase their purchases of goods and services. Economists taking this approach favor increasing the minimum wage (because low-income people spend their money), cutting taxes for lower- and middle-income taxpayers, and adopting government spending programs. Many economists also warn that tax cuts that are not offset by spending reductions will eventually harm the economy because they create budget deficits.[9]

The Bush tax cuts were an issue in the 2008 election campaign because they are set to expire in 2010. John McCain proposed making the tax cuts permanent during the 2008

election campaign, arguing that allowing them to expire would harm the economy by increasing taxes. In contrast, Barack Obama declared that he would allow the cuts to expire for people making more than $250,000 a year while keeping—or even increasing—tax reductions for people earning less money. Meanwhile, many economists have warned that neither approach would address the problem of the federal budget deficit.[10]

**supply-side economics** the economic theory that tax cuts, especially for business and the wealthy, will lead to savings and investment that will benefit everyone.

# Tobacco Regulation

**Does government have the right to force tobacco companies to pay for public healthcare? Does this not open the door for similar regulation of other industries?**

**Is cigarette smoking an individual choice whose consequences require public care? If smoking is so damaging, shouldn't it be banned or strictly regulated?**

**Overview:** One function of government is to regulate goods and services that might damage public health—morning-after birth control, alcohol, all-terrain vehicles, and, especially, tobacco products. Cigarettes are responsible for high rates of lung cancer and related diseases, and studies show that smokers are less productive workers and have higher rates of absenteeism. The tobacco industry's products are harmful to public health, and they have a depressing effect on the economy.

In this light, it seems clear that the industry should be strictly regulated, but Congress has not done so. The states sued the tobacco industry, charging complicity in fraudulent claims made by tobacco marketers and deceptive statements concerning cigarette research. On November 23, 1998, the attorneys general of 46 states settled a lawsuit in which the tobacco industry will pay $206 billion over 25 years in exchange for the states' dropping future lawsuits. The industry agreed to end advertising on billboards, city buses, and T-shirts; ban cartoon characters in advertising; and to finance antismoking ads and research. The states, in their turn, claimed they would use settlement money to support healthcare programs addressing smoking-related diseases and problems, and for youth smoking prevention programs. In fact, most states used the monies for purposes other than these, and the tobacco industry successfully stalled increased regulation.

Because of Congress's inaction, the Clinton administration granted the Food and Drug Administration (FDA) the authority to declare nicotine an addictive drug, which gave the FDA the power to regulate tobacco. The tobacco industry sued the FDA, charging that it was subject to congressional authority to regulate its products. In *FDA v. Brown & Williamson* (2000) the U.S. Supreme Court agreed. If the federal government wishes to regulate the tobacco industry, the regulation must flow from Congress.

## supporting tobacco regulation and the tobacco settlement

**tobacco harms public health and should be strictly regulated.** Studies indicate that smoking claims more than 400,000 lives and smoking-related healthcare costs exceed $75 billion annually. According to the BBC, smokers take more sick time than nonsmokers, and smokers are considerably less productive. Regulating tobacco products will help reduce these public costs.

**the tobacco settlement holds cigarette makers accountable for past actions.** The tobacco settlement forced cigarette makers to admit their culpability and their responsibility to rectify the effects of past practices. Cigarette makers must pay out $206 billion dollars to help smokers quit, to provide healthcare to current and ex-smokers, and to reimburse the states for healthcare expenditures for tobacco-related diseases.

**the tobacco settlement is an example of regulation through the cooperation of private and public institutions.** The tobacco settlement calls for the cigarette industry to provide funds for "smoking cessation programs, healthcare, education, and programs benefiting children," and to limit its marketing in order to prevent America's youth from taking up smoking.

## against tobacco regulation and the tobacco settlement

**tobacco products are legal and consumers are responsible for their choices.** Cigarettes are legal and the choice is freely made. Industries and businesses should not be held responsible for the actions of individuals who choose to use their products.

**the tobacco industry should not be required to pay for public healthcare costs.** To force an industry to provide public benefits for the results of this freely made choice is a *de facto* tax. This is an impermissible encroachment of government on the private sphere. Constitutional theory holds that taxes should be raised and spent by elected legislative assemblies—not by deals cut between lawyers and state attorneys general.

# budget deficits
## AND SURPLUSES

the terms *budget deficit*, *budget surplus*, and *balanced budget* refer to the relationship between annual budget revenues and budget expenditures. A **budget deficit** is the amount of money by which annual budget *expenditures* exceed annual budget *receipts*, whereas a **budget surplus** is the sum by which annual budget *receipts* exceed annual budget *expenditures*. If budget receipts equal budget expenditures, the government has a **balanced budget**. Finally, the **national debt** is the accumulated indebtedness of the federal government. An annual budget deficit increases the debt by the amount of the deficit, whereas a surplus decreases the debt. In 2009, for example, federal budget receipts were $2.2 trillion compared with outlays of $4.0 trillion, for a budget deficit of $1.8 trillion.[11] As a result, the national debt grew by $1.8 trillion during 2009.

The 2009 federal budget deficit was well over a trillion dollars larger than the 2008 deficit ($1.8 trillion compared with $458 billion) because of the recession. With unemployment rising, expenditures for unemployment compensation and various welfare programs increased, while tax revenues, especially individual and corporate income tax revenues, declined. In the meantime, the president and Congress increased spending in hopes of stimulating an economic recovery. The billions of dollars spent bailing out the financial indus-

try and the auto manufacturers in late 2008 counted toward the 2009 deficit as did the $787 billion stimulus package adopted in early 2009. Budget analysts projected deficits in excess of $500 billion for years to come.[12]

How important is a balanced budget? Economists generally agree that small deficits probably do not matter, whereas big deficits probably do. The American economy is so large that deficits (or surpluses) of $100 billion or so are probably too small to have much effect. Similarly, most economists agree that

This National Debt Clock is located in New York City. It tracks the size of the national debt and tabulates how much of that debt is owed by each American family. The clock has recently run out of digits to keep up with our soaring debt!

having deficits so large that the national debt grows more rapidly than the nation's economy is dangerous—eventually the economy will be unable to support them. Funding the debt will sap the economy of resources and drive up interest rates, harming economic growth. Economists disagree about the importance of intermediate-size deficits. Some economists believe that persistent deficits will retard the nation's long-term economic growth because money that would otherwise be in-

vested to promote economic development goes instead to finance the deficit. In contrast, other economists think that deficits have little if any impact on economic growth.[13]

Nonetheless, many economists and policy analysts believe that the nation's return to deficit spending in the early 2000s came at a bad time. In FY 2009, the national government spent $143 billion on interest on the national debt.[14] The sizable budget surpluses of FY 2000 and 2001 offered the prospect that the government would pay off most or all of the national debt, cutting or eliminating the expense of paying interest from future budgets. The money saved could have been used to address the looming budget crisis brought on by the aging of the baby boom generation. With the OMB and the CBO now predicting years of future deficits, the government's opportunity to shore up Social Security, Medicare, Medicaid, and other programs without substantial reductions in benefit levels, major tax increases, or significant deficit spending is probably lost for good.

# government
## EXPENDITURES

**a** s the figure below shows, the most important spending priorities for the federal government in 2008 were healthcare, Social Security, national defense, income security, and interest on the debt.

### Healthcare

Health is the largest category, accounting for 19.6 percent of federal government spending. Although health expenditures include money for medical research and disease control, by far the largest federal health programs are Medicare and Medicaid. In 2009, 45 million people participated in the Medicare program at a cost of $468 billion, including premiums and deductibles paid by program participants, and general revenue expenditures, which, in 2009, were $185 billion.[15] Part A of Medicare is compulsory hospitalization insurance that covers the cost of inpatient care after beneficiaries pay a deductible. It is financed from premiums deducted from the Social Security checks of retirees and by a 2.9 percent payroll tax, divided evenly between workers and their employers. Medicare Part B is a voluntary medical insurance plan that covers certain physician fees and non hospital services after beneficiaries pay a deductible. It is funded by premiums deducted from the Social Security checks of retired persons who choose to participate. In 2009, the premium was $96.40 a month for most recipients. Medicare recipients earning more than $82,000 in adjusted annual income had to pay a surcharge. Affluent recipients will have to pay an amount equal to either 1.4 times, 2.6 times, or 3.2 times the standard premium, depending on

their income level.[16] Medicare Part D is a prescription drug benefit offered and managed by private insurers under contract with the government.

The Medicare program faces a long-term financial crisis that is more serious than the Social Security shortfall. The aging of the baby

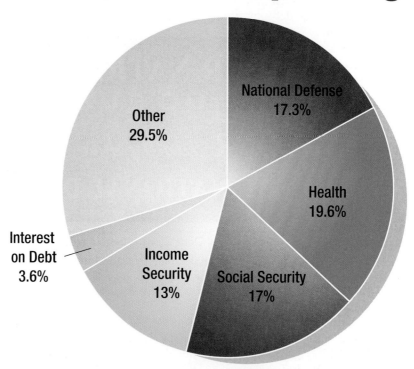

**Health** is the **largest category,** accounting for **19.6 percent** of federal government **spending.**

Federal Government Expenditures

Medicare recipients who choose to participate pay a monthly premium, which averaged $25 in 2008, along with various deductibles and copays.[17]

boom generation is a demographic time bomb for the Medicare program. Between 2010 and 2030, the Medicare rolls will more than double, adding huge costs to the

# Healthcare in Canada

**Canada provides its citizens** with universal healthcare provided on the basis of need rather than ability to pay. Canada administers its healthcare program through the nation's ten provinces, which are the Canadian equivalent of states, and its three territories. Because the provinces have some leeway to design their own plans, healthcare funding and delivery varies somewhat from one part of the nation to another. Some provinces assess their citizens a monthly premium or charge a fee for each visit to a physician, whereas others fund the program from tax money. Coverage also varies somewhat from province to province, and waits for services are longer in some areas than others.[18]

Although Canadian healthcare is publicly funded, it is privately provided. Citizens seeking medical services go to private physicians or visit hospitals and clinics that are either for-profit businesses or nonprofits governed by boards of trustees. Many Canadians also have supplemental insurance coverage, often provided through their employers, to pay for services not covered, or only partially covered, by the national health system, including dental, optical, and prescription drug service.

Is the Canadian healthcare system better than its counterpart in the United States? Proponents of the Canadian system point out that life expectancy is longer in Canada than it is in the United States and that infant mortality rates are lower. Furthermore, Canada devotes a smaller share of its GDP to healthcare than does the United States. In contrast, critics of the Canadian healthcare system complain that wait times for nonemergency services are sometimes long. Canadian medicine may also be relatively slow to adopt new treatments and technologies.[19]

## Questions

1. Would you prefer the Canadian healthcare system to that in the United States?

2. What individuals and groups in the United States would support moving to a system similar to the Canadian system? Which would oppose?

3. Would either the Obama or McCain healthcare proposals lead to a Canadian-style system in the United States? Why or why not?

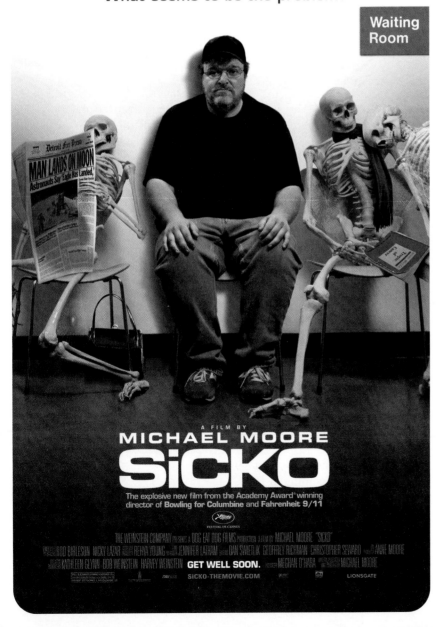

Filmmaker Michael Moore criticized the American healthcare system in his 2007 film *SiCKO*.

system.[20] Furthermore, inflation in the healthcare industry is driving up the cost of medical care faster than wages are rising to provide tax revenues to cover the cost. The addition of the prescription drug benefit to Medicare will make the program's financial crisis more severe because the cost of prescription drugs is rising more rapidly than healthcare costs in general. The cost of the prescription drug benefit, which was $33 billion in 2006 when the program began, will rise

increase by an average of 2.5 percent a year over the next ten years because of the aging of the baby boom generation. Rising Medicaid costs also reflect inflation in the healthcare industry, which has been greater than in the economy as a whole, particularly with the introduction of expensive new prescription drugs and technologies.[24]

## Social Security

**Social Security**, a federal pension and disability insurance program

adjustment (COLA) in their benefit checks because the CPI rose 6.2 percent in 2008. A **cost-of-living adjustment (COLA)** is a mechanism designed to regularly increase the size of a payment to compensate for the effects of inflation. In 2008, the average retired worker received a monthly Social Security check of $1,079.[25]

The Social Security program can most accurately be described as a tax on workers to provide benefits to elderly retirees and disabled persons. Contrary to popular belief, Congress did not create Social Security as a pension/savings plan in which the government would simply refund the money retirees contributed over the years. Instead, current payroll taxes pay the benefits for current recipients. Because the initial tax rate was relatively low, current retirees draw substantially more money in Social Security benefits than they paid in payroll taxes. The average retired person today gets back all the money he or she paid into Social Security, with interest, in about seven years. Because tax rates are higher today, workers who are now in their thirties will likely pay more money in taxes during their lifetimes than they will collect in benefits after they retire.

Even though payroll taxes were initially low, the Social Security trust funds maintained healthy surpluses into the early 1970s. With the baby boom generation coming

# The **Congressional Budget Office (CBO)** estimates that Medicaid costs will **double** over the next **decade.**

every year. In 2015, the annual cost is expected to be nearly $140 billion.[21] The Medicare Board of Trustees estimates that program expenditures will exceed assets in five years.[22]

Medicaid is another large and rapidly growing federal healthcare program. In 2009, Medicaid served 68 million people at a cost to the federal government of $255 billion. The poor—particularly pregnant women, mothers, and their young children—are the largest group of recipients, accounting for three-fourths of Medicaid beneficiaries. Nearly two-thirds of Medicaid spending, however, goes to the other 25 percent of recipients—the blind, disabled, and impoverished elderly—because their medical needs are greater, and therefore more expensive to meet. All told, Medicaid covers the cost of healthcare for one in every three children. It pays for 40 percent of births and funds two-thirds of the nursing home care in the country.[23]

The Congressional Budget Office (CBO) estimates that Medicaid costs will double over the next decade. The CBO projects that Medicaid enrollment of elderly persons will

funded through a payroll tax on workers and their employers, accounted for 17 percent of federal expenditures in 2009. Congress created the program in 1935 to provide limited coverage to workers in industry and commerce upon their retirement at age 65. Through the years, Congress has extended the program's scope and increased its benefits. Even before the first benefit checks were mailed, Congress expanded coverage to include the aged spouse and children of a retired worker, as well as the young children and spouse of a covered worker upon the worker's death. Congress subsequently added disability insurance to the package and provided for early retirement.

Congress and the president have also increased Social Security benefits, especially over the last 35 years. They raised benefits 15 percent in 1970, 10 percent in 1971, and 20 percent in 1972. Beginning in 1975, Congress and the president indexed benefits to the **consumer price index (CPI)**, a measure of inflation that is based on the changing cost of goods and services. In 2009, for example, Social Security recipients enjoyed a 6.2 percent cost-of-living

**Social Security** a federal pension and disability insurance program funded through a payroll tax on workers and their employers.

**consumer price index (CPI)** a measure of inflation that is based on the changing cost of goods and services.

**cost-of-living adjustment (COLA)** a mechanism designed to regularly increase the size of a payment to compensate for the effects of inflation.

of age and more women entering the workforce than ever before, the pool of workers paying taxes into the system grew more rapidly than did the number of retirees collecting benefits. Furthermore, the system benefited from a healthy economy and rising wages.

Eventually, demographic and economic changes combined with political decisions to drive the Social Security system into near bankruptcy. Early retirement, increased longevity, and falling birthrates served to swell the ranks of Social Security beneficiaries while slowing the increase in the number of em-

draws retirement benefits for 19 years.[26] In the meantime, Congress and the president increased benefits and pegged future increases in Social Security payments to the inflation rate. When the economy slumped and inflation soared in the late 1970s, the Social Security system faced a financial crisis.

In 1983, Congress and President Reagan responded to the situation by adopting a Social Security bailout plan that increased payroll taxes significantly while somewhat limiting future benefit payments. The plan provided for an increase in the retirement age by small an-

**think**

If you were a member of Congress, what actions would you favor to ensure the long-term solvency of the Social Security program?

# In 1950, 16 workers paid taxes for every person drawing benefits.

ployees paying taxes. When Social Security was created, the average worker retired at age 69 and lived another eight years. Today, the average worker retires at 64 and

nual increments after the year 2000 until the retirement age reaches 67. Also, the bailout legislation provided that half the benefits of upper-income recipients would be

counted as taxable income for income tax purposes. In 1993, Congress increased the share of taxable Social Security for middle- and upper-income recipients from 50 to 85 percent.

The goal of the Social Security bailout plan was not only to keep the program solvent for the short-term, but also to ensure its long-range stability despite unfavorable demographic trends. In 1950, 16 workers paid taxes for every person drawing benefits. In 2000, the ratio was down to 3 to 1. By the year 2030,

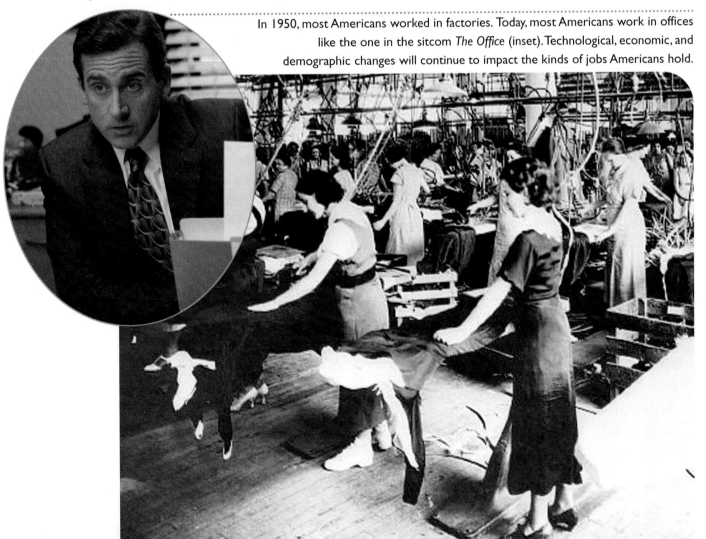

In 1950, most Americans worked in factories. Today, most Americans work in offices like the one in the sitcom *The Office* (inset). Technological, economic, and demographic changes will continue to impact the kinds of jobs Americans hold.

when the baby boom generation will have retired, the ratio of workers to retirees will be only 2 to 1.[27] The architects of the bailout plan hoped that the payroll tax increases would be sufficient to allow the Social Security trust funds to build up sizable surpluses that could be used to pay benefits well into the twenty-first century. In 2008, the Social Security trust funds held assets worth $2.4 trillion and were growing. During 2008, for example, the trust funds grew by $192 billion based on payroll tax revenues worth $708 billion and benefit outlays of $506 billion.[28]

Although the bailout plan has put Social Security in the black for now, the retirement of the baby boom generation threatens the system's long-term financial viability. Benefit payments begin to exceed payroll tax revenue in 2016, and the trust funds will be exhausted by 2037. At that point, payroll taxes will generate only 78 percent of the cost of the program.[29] Because trust fund assets are held in treasury notes, the key date for policymakers is 2016 rather than 2037. The Social Security trust funds are a record of funds transferred from one part of the government, the Social Security system, to other parts of the government. They contain no real assets. Consequently, from a practical financial perspective, it makes no difference whether the Social Security trust funds contain a paper balance of trillions of dollars or a balance of zero dollars.[30] Once the annual cost of Social Security benefits exceeds payroll tax revenues, Congress and the president will have to make up the shortfall by cutting other programs, raising taxes, borrowing, or reducing benefit rates.

## National Defense

National defense is the third-largest category of federal government expenditures, accounting for 17.3 percent of spending in 2009. This budget category includes funding for the Department of Defense as well as nuclear weapons-related activities of the Department of Energy and defense-related expenditures by several other agencies, such as the Coast Guard and the Federal Bureau of Investigation (FBI). Chapter 17 examines defense spending in detail.

## Income Security

Income security is the fourth-largest category of federal government spending, accounting for 13 percent of expenditures in 2009. It encompasses a variety of domestic spending programs, including unemployment insurance, federal retirement, and, with the major exception of Medicaid, most welfare programs. federal civilian retirement and federal military retirement collectively represent almost half the expenditures in the category. **Welfare programs**, which are government programs that provide benefits to individuals based on their economic status, account for most of the rest.

The most important welfare programs are the Earned Income Tax Credit (EITC), Food Stamps, Supplemental Security Income (SSI), Temporary Assistance to Needy Families (TANF), and Medicaid, which was discussed earlier in the chapter. The Earned Income Tax Credit (EITC) is designed to give cash assistance to low-income working families by refunding some or all of the taxes they pay and, if their wages are low, giving them a payment rather than assessing a tax. The Food Stamp program provides vouchers to low-income families and individuals to purchase food. Supplemental Security Income (SSI) provides money to low-income people who are elderly, blind, or disabled, and who do not qualify for Social Security benefits. Temporary Assistance to Needy Families (TANF) provides temporary financial assistance and work opportunities to needy families. EITC, Food

By the end of 2008, more than 28 million Americans were using food stamps. Massachusetts, which had previously had the lowest percentage of residents using food stamps, had the most rapidly growing food stamp program in the nation. Since the economy soured in 2008, at least 40 states have seen record increases in their food stamp enrollment.

In Michigan, where the unemployment rate is approaching 10%, one in eight residents is using food stamps.

**welfare programs** government programs that provide benefits to individuals based on their economic status.

**means-tested program** a government program that provides benefits to recipients based on their financial need.

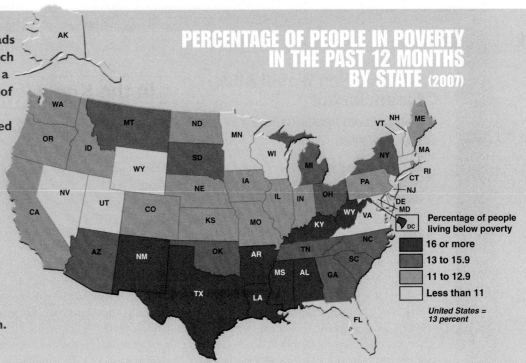

Human Services caseloads are at all-time highs. Much of Michigan's increase is a result of the steady loss of manufacturing jobs, a decline which has affected neighboring Illinois and Ohio as well.

As a percentage of the population, food stamp use peaked in 1994. The rebounding economy of the 1990s helped somewhat—but in the economic meltdown of 2008, the numbers are beginning to climb again.

Percentage of people living below poverty

- 16 or more
- 13 to 15.9
- 11 to 12.9
- Less than 11

*United States = 13 percent*

Stamps, SSI, TANF, and Medicaid are examples of a **means-tested program**, a government program that provides benefits to recipients based on their financial need.

Federal welfare policy changed in the mid-1990s with the adoption of welfare reform. Before 1996, the unofficial goal of the nation's welfare system was to provide welfare recipients with a minimum standard of living.[31] In 1996, Congress passed, and President Bill Clinton signed, sweeping welfare reform legislation that explicitly changed the underlying philosophy of American welfare policy. Instead of attempting to supply low-income individuals and families with cash and benefits sufficient to meet basic human needs, the goal of welfare reform was to move recipients from the welfare rolls to the workforce. The legislation limited the amount of time able-bodied adult recipients could draw benefits by placing a lifetime limit of five years on welfare assistance. Furthermore, childless adults between the ages of 18 and 50 could receive food stamps for no more than three months in any three-year period.

Welfare reform also instituted work requirements for welfare recipients. The heads of families on welfare would have to find work within two years, or the family would lose benefits. It reduced the amount of federal money available for public assistance programs. Welfare reform also included a number of provisions aimed at changing the behavior of welfare recipients. In order to collect benefits, unmarried teenage mothers would have to live at home and stay in school. States were given the option to deny assistance to children born to welfare recipients in order to discourage welfare mothers from having additional children. The measure even offered a cash prize to the states that were most successful in reducing the number of children born outside of marriage.

Welfare reform has shifted the focus of government assistance to the poor from cash benefits to services designed to help poor people get and keep jobs. Cash assistance now counts for less than half of all spending under TANF. Instead, states are using their welfare dollars to help meet the transportation needs of welfare recipients to get to work, to address drug abuse and mental health problems, and to provide childcare for single parents.[32]

Welfare reform has helped reduce the welfare rolls, but it has not eliminated poverty. The number of TANF recipients has fallen dramatically from 14.2 million in 1994 to 3.8 million in 2008. Government data show that most people leaving welfare find work and earn enough money so that they are better off than they were before.[33] Nonetheless,

Should states cut off welfare benefits to women who have children while on welfare?

# Obama Plan Would Alter Financial Aid

BY MADELINE REDDINGTON, *DAILY TROJAN*
**MARCH 5, 2009**

The budget plan released by the Obama administration last week included a proposal that could change the way many students pay for college by increasing the amount of financial aid funds available to students in federal grants and by restructuring federal student loan programs.

The plan would increase the maximum award given by the Federal Pell Grant program, expand the Perkins Loan Program and shift all federally guaranteed student loans into the direct loan program administered by the U.S. Department of Education, thereby ending private bank involvement in federal student loans.

The changes to the Pell Grant program would increase its maximum award from $4,731 for the 2008–09 school year to $5,550 for the 2010–11 school year and require the program to adjust the maximum each year for inflation.

According to Edie Irons, communications director of the Institute for College Access and Success in Berkeley, this change would help the program address some budgeting problems it has had in the past.

"This year, for example, there's been a shortfall in the funding, because the amount they budgeted turned out to be less than the demand," Irons said. "That's the danger of having it be part of appropriations and not be an entitlement."

Irons said the shift of the Pell Grant program from an appropriations program with a predetermined budget to an entitlement program—which would base funding on demonstrated need—would increase the amount of students who receive grants.

According to the American Council on Education website, the changes to the Perkins Loan Program would include restructuring the formula used to distribute the money and increasing funding from $1 billion to $5 billion.

Currently, about three-quarters of federally funded student loans are distributed by private banks like Citibank and Wells Fargo, with the remaining quarter distributed by the Department of Education, Irons said.

These lenders are participants of the Federal Family Education Loan Program, which has been providing loans since 1965, and they profit from the student loans they distribute, Irons said.

Obama's plan would eliminate the FFEL Program beginning in July 2010 and start all new loans through the direct loan program within the Department of Education.

"There's an argument that the direct loan program is more efficient because it cuts out the middle man," Irons said. "There's still profit to be made . . . [and] there seems to be interest in reinvesting [it] back into increased aid for students."

According to a Department of Education press release, the change will save the government $4 billion per year.

## ↗ CRITICAL THINKING QUESTIONS:

• What are entitlement programs? How would making federal financial aid an entitlement program instead of a budgeted program affect students?

• What is the downside of making financial aid an entitlement program?

• What are the most important arguments that could be made against ending the role of private banks in the student loan program and turning it over to the Department of Education?

**>> END**

most of the people who have left welfare still rely heavily on public assistance, especially EITC, which is now larger than TANF, Food Stamps, or SSI.[34] Most of the people who have made their way off welfare lack the skills necessary to get jobs that pay much more than $7 or $8 an hour. As a result, they remain dependent on government assistance. The impact of welfare reform has been to change from a system that subsidized families unconditionally to one that subsidizes families in work. Although people who have left welfare are no longer totally dependent on the government for their livelihood, most of them still rely on government assistance. The new welfare debate centers on how government can best help the working poor, especially single-parent families headed by women, to rise above poverty.[35]

## Interest on the Debt

Interest on the debt, which accounted for 3.6 percent of federal government expenditures in 2009, is the fifth-largest spending category. When the federal budget is in deficit, the Department of the Treasury borrows money to close the gap between revenues and expenditures. Much of the money needed to cover the deficit is borrowed from surplus funds in other federal accounts, such as the Old Age and Survivors Insurance (OASI) Trust Fund, which by law must be invested in U.S. Treasury securities. The government borrows the rest of the money from public sources, such as savings and loan institutions, corporations, insurance companies, commercial banks, state and local governments, foreign investors, foreign governments, and individual Americans. The national government does not have to pay interest on money borrowed from government accounts, but it does pay interest on debt that is held by the public. In mid-2009, the national debt stood at $11.6 trillion, including $7.3 trillion publicly held and $4.3 held in government accounts.[36] Because the federal budget deficit is growing, the share of the federal budget devoted to interest on the debt will likely increase relative to the budget as a whole for the near future.

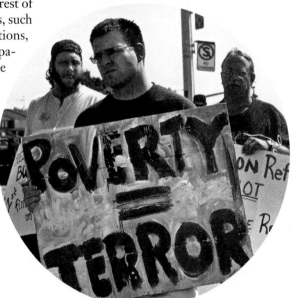

Protesters march to a rally in Detroit in support of welfare recipients.

# fiscal POLICYMAKING

**f**iscal **policy** is the use of government spending and taxation for the purpose of achieving economic goals.

## Ground Rules for Budgeting

Congress and the president must operate under certain ground rules as they formulate and adopt an annual budget.

**Entitlements.** An **entitlement program** is a government program providing benefits to all persons qualified to receive them under law. Social Security, Medicare, Medicaid, unemployment compensation, Food Stamps, federal retirement programs, and most agriculture programs are entitlements. Spending for entitlement programs depends on the number of recipients collecting benefits. Anyone who qualifies for Social Security, for example, is entitled to collect benefits regardless of the budget. Consequently, the amount of money Congress and the president include in the annual budget for each entitlement program is a prediction of how much money the government will actually spend on the program rather than a policy decision about spending levels. If Congress and the president underestimate the amount of money needed, the funds will be spent anyway. Entitlement programs consume more than half of the federal budget.

**Contractual Commitments.** The budgetary discretion of Congress and the president is limited by contractual commitments made in pre-

**fiscal policy** the use of government spending and taxation for the purpose of achieving economic goals.

**entitlement program** a government program providing benefits to all persons qualified to receive them under law.

vious years. Congress and the president often stretch weapons purchases over several years, contracting with the manufacturer to supply a certain number of ships or planes each year for several years. Money for each purchase must be included in each year's budget. Similarly, the federal government is legally committed to pay interest on the national debt.

**Budget Agreements.** Between 1990 and 2002, Congress and the president, first President George H. W. Bush and then President Clinton, prepared the annual budget on the basis of negotiated budget agreements that established spending limits for that part of the budget not predetermined by entitlements or prior contractual agreements. The negotiated budget agreements set bottom-line budget limits but did not mandate spending amounts for individual budget items. The budget agreement negotiated between the president and Congress covering the period from 1990 through 2002 set strict spending caps for three spending areas—domestic, defense, and international expenditures—and prohibited shifting money among the categories.[37] As a result, the annual budget debate revolved around the distribution of a predetermined amount of money among items within the three categories. Instead of debating spending

> **Congress** and the **president** consider how to **allocate budget resources** among budget items **within each category.**

priorities between domestic and defense spending, for example, Congress and the president considered how to allocate budget resources among budget items within each category. The budget agreements also included a **PAYGO** provision, which is a pay-as-you-go budget rule that requires that any tax cut or spending increase be offset by tax increases or spending cuts elsewhere in the budget. In 2002, however, Congress and the president allowed the budget agreement to expire so they could adopt tax cuts and increase spending without adopting corresponding tax increases and budget reductions. Without the discipline of a budget agreement, federal spending increased dramatically, from 18.5 percent of GDP in 2001 to 28.1 percent in 2009.[38] Spending associated with homeland security, the war on terror, and wars in Iraq and Afghanistan drove up the cost of government, of course, but the absence of a budget agreement

made it easier for Congress and the president to increase spending for education, agriculture, transportation, healthcare, and other programs. After winning control of Congress in the 2006 election, Democrats restored PAYGO, but Congress waived or circumvented the rule repeatedly rather than make tough decisions on spending and taxation.

## The Budget Process

The White House begins the process of formulating a budget in March, a year and a half before the start of the fiscal year, when the president sets economic goals and establishes overall revenue and expenditure levels. Once the president has set administration priorities, the OMB sends spending guidelines to the various departments of the executive branch and directs them to prepare detailed budgets. Several months later, the agencies send the

> **PAYGO** a pay-as-you-go budget rule that requires that any tax cut or spending increase be offset by tax increases or spending cuts elsewhere in the budget.

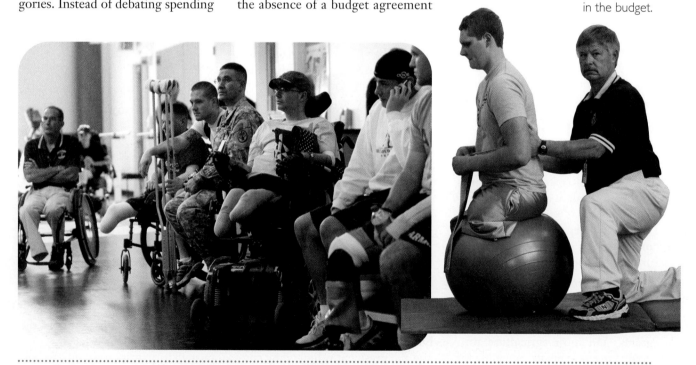

Caring for wounded veterans from the Iraq and Afghanistan wars represents a growing cost to the federal treasury.

OMB their budget proposals, which often exceed the original ceiling. The OMB questions the size of some of the spending requests, and the agencies respond by justifying their proposals. The head of the agency, the director of the OMB, and a member of the White House staff, and perhaps even the president, negotiate a final budget request for inclusion in a detailed budget proposal, which the president submits to Congress in January.

Budget expenditures are classified as mandatory or discretionary. **Mandatory spending** refers to budgetary expenditures that are mandated by law, including entitlements and contractual commitments made in previous years. Interest on the debt is also mandatory spending because the government has no choice but to pay interest on money it has borrowed. **Discretionary spending** includes budgetary expenditures that are not mandated by law or contract, including annual funding for education, the Coast Guard, space explo-

ration, highway construction, defense, foreign aid, and the Federal Bureau of Investigation (FBI). More than 60 percent of total government expenditures are mandatory. The 2008 budget included $1.1 trillion in discretionary spending and $1.8 billion in mandatory expenditures.[39]

Discretionary expenditures must be approved through the **appropriations process,** which is the procedure through which Congress legislatively provides money for a particular purpose. Appropriation bills begin in the appropriations committees in each house although, by tradition, the House Appropriations Committee takes the lead in the process. Congress appropriates money annually. Spending for entitlement programs is included in the budget but does not go through the appropriations process.

Spending programs must be authorized, regardless of whether they are entitlements or programs funded by discretionary spending. The **authorization process** is the

procedure through which Congress legislatively establishes a program, defines its general purpose, devises procedures for its operation, specifies an agency to implement the program, and indicates an approximate level of funding for the program (but does *not* actually provide money). The standing legislative committees in each chamber, such as Agriculture or Armed Services, consider authorization bills. Congress may authorize a program for one year only or for several years. The budget timetable calls for Congress and the president to complete work on the budget by October 1, the beginning of the fiscal year.

**btw...**

On November 14, 1995, the federal government was forced to close down because Congress and the White House had failed to agree on a budget bill. The closure made major portions of the federal government inoperative. Nearly 200,000 passports and visas were delayed, all national parks were closed, 212,000 Social Security cards were delayed, and more than 400,000 eligible Medicare recipients could not enroll in the program.

When polls showed that most voters blamed Speaker of the House Newt Gingrich and the Republicans in Congress for the budget crisis rather than President Clinton, the Republicans backed down. On January 6, 1996, Congress passed the budget, restoring full funding for government programs, and the government reopened for business.

**mandatory spending** budgetary expenditures that are mandated by law, including entitlements and contractual commitments made in previous years.

**discretionary spending** budgetary expenditures that are not mandated by law or contract, including annual funding for education, the Coast Guard, space exploration, highway construction, defense, foreign aid, and the Federal Bureau of Investigation (FBI).

**appropriations process** the procedure through which Congress legislatively allocates money for a particular purpose.

**authorization process** the procedure through which Congress legislatively establishes a program, defines its general purpose, devises procedures for its operation, specifies an agency to implement the program, and indicates an approximate level of funding for the program, but does not actually provide money.

Congress and the president adopt tax measures through the legislative process with the constitutional stipulation that revenue-raising bills must originate in the House. Consequently, tax legislation must pass the House before it passes the Senate. The Ways and Means Committee has jurisdiction over tax measures in the House. In the Senate, the Finance Committee considers tax bills.

# monetary
## POLICYMAKING

**I**nterest is money paid for the use of money. Most Americans are concerned about interest rates. Consumers pay interest on credit card debt and when they borrow money to purchase vehicles or homes. Investors earn interest on stimulate economic growth. The government affects interest rates through its control of the money supply. **Monetary policy** is the control of the money supply for the purpose of achieving economic goals.

## Many economists believe that the government can influence the performance of the nation's economy by adjusting interest rates.

the money they save. Interest rates also affect the economy. Low interest rates encourage companies to borrow money to expand their operations. Low interest rates for automobile loans and home mortgage interest promote consumer automobile and home purchases. In contrast, high interest rates promote savings and discourage borrowing by business and consumers alike.

Many economists believe that the government can influence the performance of the nation's economy by adjusting interest rates. Increasing interest rates can cool inflation by slowing down economic activity, whereas cutting interest rates can

The **Federal Reserve Board (Fed)** is an independent regulatory commission that makes monetary policy. A seven-member board of governors is appointed by the president with Senate confirmation to serve fixed, overlapping terms of 14 years. His board heads the Fed, as the agency is often called. The president designates one member of the board as the chair to serve a four-year term, pending Senate confirmation. Alan Greenspan, who was first appointed by President Reagan, chaired the Fed from 1987 to 2006, having been re-appointed by president George H. W. Bush, President Clinton, and President George W.

Bush. When Greenspan retired, President Bush appointed, and the Senate confirmed, economist Ben Bernanke as the new Fed chair.

Congress has ordered the Fed to make policy with two goals: full employment and price stability. The **Federal Open Market Committee (FOMC)** is a committee of the Federal Reserve that meets eight times a year to review the economy and to adjust monetary policy to achieve the goals. The FOMC is a 12-member group that includes the seven members of the Federal Reserve board, the president of the Federal Reserve Bank of New York, and four of the eleven other Federal Reserve Bank presidents who serve on a rotating basis. If the FOMC determines that the demand for goods and services is growing faster than businesses can supply them, it tightens monetary supply to fight inflation. It does this by reducing the funds available to banks for loans and by raising interest rates to make businesses and individuals less willing to borrow

President George W. Bush appointed Ben Bernanke (center) to head the Fed in 2006 after Allan Greenspan retired.

money. In contrast, if the FOMC believes that businesses are not selling as many goods and services as they can produce and fewer people have jobs than want them, it eases monetary policy to prevent recession. It lowers interest rates by increasing the funds that banks can lend, hoping to encourage businesses and consumers to borrow to make purchases.

## CONCLUSION
# economic
# POLICYMAKING

the most important elements of the environment for economic policymaking are public opinion, the strength of the economy, and party control of the executive and legislative branches of government. Conventional wisdom holds that people "vote their pocketbooks." That is, they reelect incumbent officeholders if the economy is strong, but turn them out of office if the economy is weak. In this case, political science research supports the conventional wisdom. Economic conditions have an important impact on voter choices.[40] Furthermore, many Americans are part of attentive publics for specific economic policy issues, such as Social Security, Medicare, tax reform, and agriculture policy.

The strength of the economy expands or limits the policy options available to economic policymakers. A growing economy generates revenue that can be used to fund new

Barack Obama speaks about healthcare reform to a crowd in Texas during his successful campaign for the White House in 2008.

spending programs or provide tax cuts. Strong economic growth in the mid- and late-1990s did at least as much to eliminate the budget deficit as the policy choices of elected officials. In contrast, economic decline reduces the options available to policymakers.

It matters which party controls Congress. Democrats generally back policies designed to assist their traditional support groups: organized labor, inner-city voters, and lower- and middle-income families. Republicans, meanwhile, steer economic policy to benefit their support groups: business people and professionals, suburban voters, and middle- and upper-income families. When Congress and the presidency are in the hands of different parties, economic policy typically reflects compromise between the parties.

## Agenda Building

A number of political actors participate in elevating economic issues to the official policy agenda. Candidates often highlight economic issues during election campaigns.

Ross Perot made deficit reduction a major talking point when he ran for president as an independent in 1992 and 1996. Bill Clinton stressed welfare reform when he first ran for president, promising to "end welfare as we know it." George W. Bush promised to cut taxes during his presidential campaign in 2000. Barack Obama stressed healthcare reform.

Interest groups frequently emphasize economic issues. The **AARP**, an interest group representing the interests of older Americans, stresses the need to preserve Social Security and Medicare. Business groups are concerned about tax issues and government regulation. Farm groups, such as the American Farm Bureau, lobby for farm support programs.

## Policy Formulation and Adoption

Economic policy formulation takes place in congressional committees, executive branch agencies, and the White House. It involves officials

from all levels of government as well as a wide range of interest group participants. The president and the president's staff, department heads, and the OMB prepare detailed budget proposals for submission to Congress. The appropriations committees in each house draft budget legislation; standing committees work on authorization measures. The Ways and Means Committee in the House and the Finance Committee in the Senate deal with tax measures. Conference committees iron out the final details for most appropriation bills, tax measures, and authorization bills. The Federal Reserve Board formulates monetary policy.

Individual members of Congress focus on issues important to their states and districts. Farmbelt senators and representatives pay special attention to legislation affecting agriculture. Members with defense bases or defense industries in their districts are concerned with the defense appropriation. Senators and representatives are also interested in special projects that benefit their states and districts. **Earmarks** are provisions that direct that funds be spent for particular purposes. In 2008, Congress earmarked almost $8 billion for special projects, including money for water resource development, local transportation projects, tourist attractions, and special projects for colleges and universities.[41] The opponents of earmarks charge that they are nothing more than **pork-barrel spending,** expenditures to fund local projects

**AARP** an interest group representing the concerns of older Americans.

**earmarks** provisions that direct that funds be spent for particular purposes.

**pork-barrel spending** expenditures to fund local projects that are not critically important from a national perspective.

that are not critically important from a national perspective. John McCain promised to end earmarking when he ran for president in 2008. Other members of Congress defend earmarks, noting that they have funded many worthwhile projects, including most federal breast cancer research and the Boys & Girls Clubs of America. Moreover, the congressional leadership uses earmarks to win support for appropriation bills that might not otherwise pass.[42]

Interest groups also take part in policy formulation. Corporations lobby Congress to affect the impact of tax policies on their firms. Weapons manufacturers attempt to influence decisions on defense spending. The AARP participates in negotiations over reform of the Medicare program and changes in Social Security.

The executive and legislative branches of American national government are primarily responsible for the adoption of fiscal policy. The judiciary plays a relatively small role. Congress and the president create government programs and appropriate money to fund them. They raise funds through taxation and borrowing. In the meantime, the Fed adopts monetary policies through its rulemaking process.

## Policy Implementation and Evaluation

The implementation of economic policy involves nearly the whole of government in America. The Treasury Department, especially the IRS, is responsible for tax collection and borrowing. The Federal Reserve and its member banks implement monetary policy. Money is spent by the agencies of the executive branch and, through federal programs, by an array of state and local governments. State governments, for example, are responsible

## economic policy involves nearly the whole of government in America

for implementing federal transportation policies, Medicaid, and most welfare programs.

Congress and the president often leave considerable discretion to officials who implement economic policies. Welfare reform initially allowed states considerable flexibility to design their welfare programs. In general, the legislation set goals and allowed state governments to develop their own strategies for achieving the goals. States which met the goals would receive financial rewards; states falling short of goals would suffer penalties. When Congress reauthorized welfare reform in 2006, however, it tightened the definitions of work and work-related activities, reducing state flexibility.[43]

Both the executive and legislative branches of American government have mechanisms for evaluating economic policy. The OMB assesses the operation of programs within the executive branch for the president, whereas the Government Accountability Office (GAO) performs a similar role for Congress, investigating agency activities and auditing expenditures. Outside of the GAO, however, efforts at oversight are haphazard and unsystematic. Furthermore, when they do occur, they tend to focus on nickel-and-dime matters, such as expense accounts and limousine use, or on well-publicized abuses, such as cost overruns on weapons systems purchased by the Pentagon.

the THINKSPOT

www.thethinkspot.com

# TEST yourself

1. A financial incentive given by government to an individual or a business interest to accomplish a public objective is known by which of the following terms?
   - A. Entitlement
   - B. Welfare program
   - C. Subsidy
   - D. Progressive taxation

2. "The nation is suffering a severe economic slump. Many companies have gone out of business and unemployment is at a record high." This statement describes which of the following?
   - A. Inflation
   - B. Recession
   - C. Depression
   - D. *Laissez-faire*

3. "Prices just keep going up. It sure seems like a dollar doesn't go as far these days as it used to." This statement describes which of the following?
   - A. Inflation
   - B. Recession
   - C. Depression
   - D. Supply-side economics

4. Which of the following is the most important tax source of revenue for the U.S. government?
   - A. Sales tax
   - B. Payroll tax
   - C. Corporate income tax
   - D. Individual income tax

5. Which of the following taxes is assessed on wage earnings but not on income generated by stock dividends and interest?
   - A. Individual income tax
   - B. Excise tax
   - C. Corporate income tax
   - D. Payroll tax

6. Federal payroll taxes fund which of the following government programs?
   - A. Social Security
   - B. Medicaid
   - C. Education
   - D. All of the above

7. Federal taxes on gasoline, tires, and airplane tickets are examples of which of the following?
   - A. Progressive tax
   - B. Excise tax
   - C. Payroll tax
   - D. Tax preference

8. The federal income tax is an example of which of the following?
   - A. Progressive tax
   - B. Regressive tax
   - C. Proportional tax
   - D. Excise tax

9. Which of the following was a goal of the tax reforms associated with President George W. Bush?
   - A. Increase personal savings and investment
   - B. Increase taxes on upper income earners
   - C. Increase the estate tax
   - D. Make the federal income tax system more progressive

10. Assume that federal government revenues are $2.6 trillion and expenditures are $2.9 trillion. Which of the following statements is accurate?
    - A. The budget is balanced.
    - B. The government ran a surplus of $0.3 trillion.
    - C. The government ran a deficit of $0.3 trillion.
    - D. The national debt is $0.3 trillion.

11. How does a deficit of $400 billion affect the national debt?
    - A. It has no impact on the national debt.
    - B. It increases the national debt by $400 billion.
    - C. It decreases the national debt by $400 billion.
    - D. The national debt is $400 billion.

12. Which of the following is *not* one of the top five major expenditure categories in the federal budget?
    - A. Foreign aid
    - B. Social Security
    - C. National defense
    - D. Healthcare

**13** Which of the following is a factor negatively affecting the future of the Social Security program?

A. People are living longer.

B. The baby boom generation is beginning to retire.

C. The generation following the baby boom generation is smaller than its predecessor.

D. All of the above.

**14** Which of the following is an example of a means-tested program?

A. Social Security

B. Medicare

C. Medicaid

D. All of the above

**15** Which of the following is *not* a result of welfare reform?

A. The number of welfare recipients has fallen.

B. The number of people living in poverty has decreased.

C. Most people leaving welfare have found work.

D. Most people leaving welfare still depend on the government for assistance.

**16** Which of the following is an example of an entitlement program?

A. Social Security

B. Medicare

C. Medicaid

D. All of the above

**17** Which of the following is *not* an example of mandatory spending?

A. Social Security expenditures

B. Interest on the debt

C. Spending for education

D. Payment for a weapons system contracted for in a prior year

**18** Which of the following is primarily responsible for setting monetary policy?

A. Federal Reserve Board

B. Office of Management and Budget

C. Department of the Treasury

D. Congress

**19** The Federal Open Market Committee (FOMC) makes decisions that directly impact which of the following?

A. Tax rates

B. Fiscal policy

C. Interest rates

D. Social Security

**20** An appropriation bill includes money to fund a mining museum for a small city in Alaska. This provision is an example of which of the following?

A. Entitlement

B. Means-tested program

C. Privatization

D. Earmark

---

## KNOW *the* score

18–20 correct: Congratulations! You are well informed!

15–17 correct: Your political knowledge is a bit low—be sure to review the key terms and visit TheThinkSpot.

<14 correct: Reread the chapter more thoroughly.

1. C; 2. C; 3. A; 4. D; 5. D; 6. A; 7. B; 8. A; 9. A; 10. C; 11. B; 12. A; 13. D; 14. C; 15. B; 16. D; 17. C; 18. A; 19. C; 20. D

# 15 CIVIL LIBERTIES

Assume for a moment that you are the president of the United States. Although the terror attacks of 9/11 took place almost a decade ago, the nation remains in danger. The director of the Central Intelligence Agency (CIA) has informed you that American forces have captured an individual believed to be a high-level al-Qaeda operative, someone who may know about plans for future attacks against the United States. What would you do?

In early 2002, President George W. Bush approved the use of aggressive interrogation methods, including waterboarding, sleep deprivation, and temperature manipulation. Spokespersons for the Bush administration defended the action as legal, necessary, and effective. "With many thousands of lives potentially in the balance," argued former Vice President Dick Cheney, "we did not think it made good sense to let the terrorists answer questions in their own good time."[1]

Shortly after taking office, Obama signed an executive order banning the use of waterboarding and other harsh interrogation techniques. "I believe that waterboarding was torture," declared the president. "We have to be true to our ideals," he said, arguing that harsh interrogation techniques serve as a recruitment tool for al-Qaeda, on balance making the United States less secure.[2] Some critics of the use of torture also argue that it is ineffective because people make up information.[3]

The controversy over the use of harsh interrogation techniques in the war on terror illustrates the dilemma of a democracy at war. How can a free society protect itself against its enemies without compromising the principles of civil liberties and human rights that it holds dear?

# POLICYMAKING

# the constitutional basis of civil liberties POLICYMAKING

**C**ivil liberties concern the protection of the individual from the unrestricted power of government. Civil liberties policymaking takes place within the context of the U.S. Constitution and, to a lesser but still important extent, state constitutions as well.

## The U.S. Constitution

The Bill of Rights and the Fourteenth Amendment are the most important constitutional provisions affecting civil liberties policymaking. The **Bill of Rights**, which is contained in the first ten amendments to the Constitution, is a constitutional document guaranteeing individual rights and liberties. Initially, the Bill of Rights restricted the national government but not the states. It prohibited Congress from passing laws abridging the freedom of speech, for example, but it did not affect the actions of state and local governments.

The Due Process Clause of the Fourteenth Amendment provided the mechanism by which the U.S. Supreme Court eventually applied most of the provisions of the Bill of Rights to the states. Section 1 of the Fourteenth Amendment reads as follows: "No State shall . . . deprive any person of life, liberty, or property, without due process of law." The Supreme Court has interpreted the word *liberty* in the Due Process Clause to include most of the individual rights and liberties protected by the Bill of Rights. As a result, most of the provisions of the Bill of Rights now apply not just to the national government but to state and local governments as well. The process through which the U.S. Supreme Court interpreted the Due Process Clause of the Fourteenth Amendment to apply most of the provisions of the national Bill of Rights to the states is known as the **selective incorporation of the Bill of Rights**.

The Supreme Court has held that the guarantees of the Bill of Rights are not absolute. Note the wording of the Due Process Clause: "No State shall . . . deprive any person of life, liberty, or property, *without due process of law*" (emphasis added). The government can restrict indi-

**civil liberties** the protection of the individual from the unrestricted power of government.

**Bill of Rights** the first ten amendments to the U.S. Constitution.

**selective incorporation of the Bill of Rights** the process through which the U.S. Supreme Court interpreted the Due Process Clause of the Fourteenth Amendment of the U.S. Constitution to apply most of the provisions of the national Bill of Rights to the states.

## SHOULD SCHOOL OFFICIALS BE ALLOWED TO DISCIPLINE STUDENTS WHO POST ENTRIES ON MYSPACE OR FACEBOOK THAT MAY DISRUPT SCHOOL CLASSES?
### YES—50%
### NO—44%

Source: *The State of the First Amendment 2008 Survey,* www.firstamendmentcenter.org.

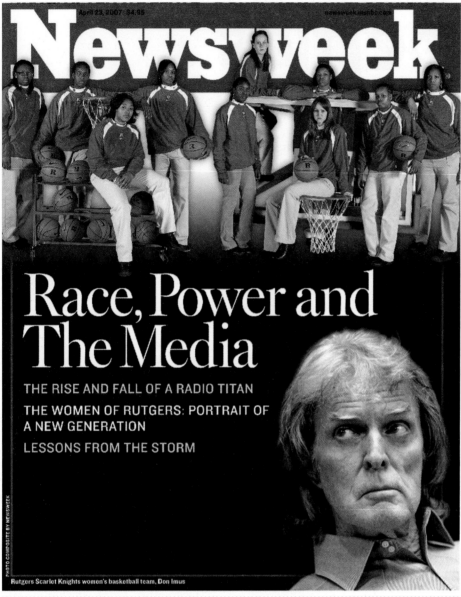

Rutgers Scarlet Knights women's basketball team, Don Imus

PHOTO COMPOSITE BY NEWSWEEK

# Newsweek
April 23, 2007 $4.95

newsweek.msnbc.com

## Race, Power and The Media

THE RISE AND FALL OF A RADIO TITAN

THE WOMEN OF RUTGERS: PORTRAIT OF A NEW GENERATION

LESSONS FROM THE STORM

Radio talk-show host Don Imus lost his job after referring to the Rutgers University women's basketball team as "nappy-headed hos."

vidual rights and liberties when it can demonstrate sufficient reason. Furthermore, the Bill of Rights applies only to the actions of government, not to those of individuals or private employers. Consider the controversy surrounding Don Imus, the former radio talk-show host of *Imus in the Morning*. CBS canceled his show after Imus referred to the members of the Rutgers University women's basketball team as "nappy-headed hos." Because of the First Amendment's guarantee of freedom of expression, the government could not fine Imus or put him in

jail because of his views. The Constitution did not protect him, however, from losing his job because of his statements.

The Supreme Court has determined that some rights are more important than other rights. A **fundamental right** is a constitutional right that is so important that government cannot restrict it unless it can demonstrate a compelling or overriding public interest for so doing. To restrict rights that are not fundamental, government need show only that it is acting in pursuit of a legitimate public purpose. Sup-

pose a city government prohibited both holding political rallies and drinking alcoholic beverages in a public park. Because the U.S. Supreme Court has recognized freedom of expression as a fundamental right, the city would have to show a compelling or overriding public interest in prohibiting political rallies for that policy to survive legal challenge. In contrast, because the Supreme Court has not held that drinking alcoholic beverages is a fundamental right, the city government would need to demonstrate only a legitimate public purpose to justify its policy on alcohol consumption.

## State Constitutions

State constitutions affect civil liberties policymaking as well. In America's federal system of government, states must grant their residents all the rights guaranteed by the U.S. Constitution (as interpreted by the Supreme Court). If state governments so choose, they may offer their residents *more* rights than are afforded by the U.S. Constitution.[4] All state constitutions include bills of rights, many of which are longer and use more expansive language than the national document. Since 1970, state supreme courts around the nation have issued hundreds of rulings in which they have granted broader rights protection under state constitutions than the U.S. Supreme Court has allowed under the U.S. Constitution.

**fundamental right** a constitutional right that is so important that government cannot restrict it unless it can demonstrate a compelling or overriding public interest for so doing.

# civil liberties
## ISSUES AND POLICIES

Civil liberties policies reflect judicial response to policy initiatives taken by legislatures and executives at the state and national levels of government. Although Congress, the president, federal agencies, states, and local governments are all involved in civil liberties policymaking, the judicial branch of government, particularly the Supreme Court of the United States, establishes the limits of policy by formulating and adopting constitutional law for each policy area. **Constitutional law** is law that involves the interpretation and application of the Constitution. It is the highest form of law, superseding both **statutory law**, law written by a legislature, and **administrative law**, administrative rules adopted by regulatory agencies.

### Government and Religion

The First Amendment addresses the relationship between church and state with these well-known words: "Congress shall make no law respecting an establishment of religion, or prohibiting the free exercise thereof." The provision has two separate and distinct elements. On one hand, the First Amendment prohibits the establishment of religion. It concerns the degree to which the government may constitutionally support religion or promote religious belief. On the other hand, the First Amendment prohibits the government from interfering with the free exercise of religion. It addresses the extent to which government actions may constitutionally interfere with individual religious practice.

**Establishment of Religion.**
The First Amendment prohibits government from making laws "respecting an establishment of religion. " Historians agree that the authors of this provision intended to prohibit the naming of an official state church, but they disagree as to

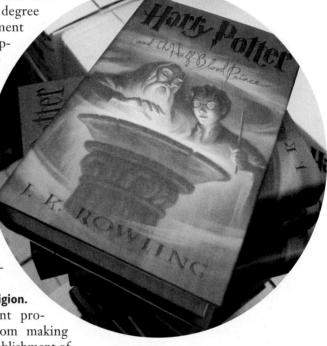

what other forms of church/state involvement constitute "establishment." Some experts believe that the Framers intended to build a wall of separation between church and state so that the affairs of government and the affairs of religion should never intermix. In contrast, other scholars argue that the founders never envisioned so ex-

**constitutional law** law that involves the interpretation and application of the Constitution.

**administrative law** administrative rules adopted by regulatory agencies.

**statutory law** law that is written by the legislature.

## How do you stack up?
### "Books that contain dangerous ideas should be banned from public school libraries."

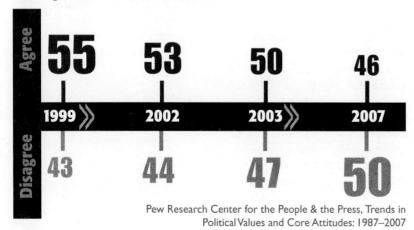

| | Agree | Disagree |
|---|---|---|
| 1999 | 55 | 43 |
| 2002 | 53 | 44 |
| 2003 | 50 | 47 |
| 2007 | 46 | 50 |

Pew Research Center for the People & the Press, Trends in Political Values and Core Attitudes: 1987–2007

**think**

Do you believe in the strict separation of government and religion, or should the government accommodate the interests of religion?

treme an interpretation of the Establishment Clause. They believe that the authors of the Constitution favored a society in which government would accommodate the interests of religion, especially Christian religion.[5]

The Supreme Court has adopted a middle ground on the issue of establishment of religion, attempting to balance the concerns of groups favoring a strict separation of church and state and the values of groups calling for accommodation between government and religion.[6] Consider the controversy over state aid to parochial schools. In 1941, the New Jersey legislature authorized school districts to subsidize the transportation of students to

and from school and, if districts chose, to extend the aid to parochial school students as well. When Ewing Township did just that, a taxpayer named Arch R. Everson sued, challenging the constitutionality of the action. The Supreme Court decided in *Everson v. Board of Ewing Township* that New Jersey's transportation plan was constitutional because it had a "secular legislative purpose"—safe transportation for school children—and "neither advance[d] nor inhibit[ed] religion." Thus, the Court created a standard for determining the constitutionality of state aid to parochial schools: Aid that serves a public purpose is constitutional; aid that serves a religious purpose is not.[7]

**parental choice** an educational reform aimed at improving the quality of schools by allowing parents to select the school their children will attend.

The controversy over parental choice and school vouchers is a recent manifestation of the battle over public funding for church-related schools. **Parental choice** is an educational reform aimed at improving the quality of schools by allowing parents to select the school their children will attend. The theory behind the concept is that public schools will have to improve in order to hang onto students and funding. Under a parental choice program, the state gives parents a voucher that provides a type of scholarship to be paid to the school that the parents choose for their child to attend. Some parental choice programs allow parents to select not only among public schools but also among private schools, including parochial schools. For example, the state of Ohio created a parental choice program for low-income families residing in the Cleveland City school district. Students who qualified could attend the private school of their parents' choice or a public school in an adjacent district and receive tuition assistance grants from

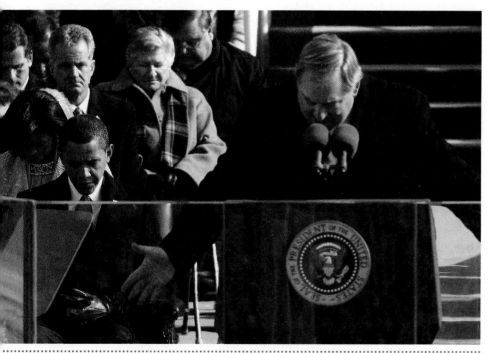

The Reverend Rick Warren gave the invocation before President Barack Obama took the oath of office in January 2009. Some liberal activists criticized Obama for inviting Warren to participate in the inauguration because of Warren's opposition to abortion rights and support for the successful ballot initiative to overturn gay marriage in California. Ironically, some conservatives criticized Warren for accepting the invitation because of Obama's support for abortion rights and gay and lesbian rights.

## Which Should Have **More Influence** on U.S. Laws?

*The Will of the American People* **63%**

*The Bible* **32%**

*Don't Know* **5%**

Source: The Pew Forum on Religion and Public Life. "More Americans Question Religion's Role in Politics," Aug. 21, 2008.

**civil liberties issues and policies    343**

the state. Although the overwhelming majority of private schools chosen by parents for student transfer were religiously affiliated, the U.S. Supreme Court ruled the program constitutional. The Court upheld the program because it had a valid secular purpose (providing educational assistance to poor children in a weak school system), it was neutral toward religion (parents could choose any private school or even another public school), and it provided assistance to families rather than to the schools.[8]

School prayer is perhaps the most controversial Establishment Clause issue. In *Engel v. Vitale* (1962), the Supreme Court ruled that the daily classroom recitation of a prayer written by New York's State Board of Regents violated the First Amendment. "[I]t is no part of the business of government to compose official prayers for any group of the American people to recite as part of a religious program carried on by the government," declared the Court. Furthermore, it was irrelevant that the prayer was voluntary and students were not forced to recite it. "When the power, prestige, and financial support of government [are] placed behind a particular religious belief," the Court said, "the indirect coercive pressure upon religious minorities to conform to the prevailing officially approved religion is plain."[9]

The Supreme Court has consistently ruled against government efforts to introduce religious observances into the public schools. Consider the school prayer controversy in Santa Fe, Texas. The school district allowed students at Santa Fe High School to vote on whether to

have an "invocation" before home football games and then held a second election to select a student to deliver the prayer. Two families—one Mormon and the other Catholic—sued the school district, and the case reached the Supreme Court in 2000. The Court ruled that the invocation was an unconstitutional infringement on the Establishment Clause, rejecting the school district's argument that the student delivering the invocation was exercising her free speech rights. "The delivery of a message such as the invocation here—on school property, at school-sponsored events, over the school's public address system, by a speaker representing the student body, under the supervision of school faculty, and pursuant to a school policy that explicitly and implicitly encourages public prayer—is not properly characterized as 'private' speech."[10]

**Free Exercise of Religion.** The First Amendment prohibits the adoption of laws interfering with the free exercise of religion. In practice, disputes concerning free exercise fall under two general categories. The first category involves the deliberate effort of government to restrict the activities of small, controversial religious groups. Many localities have also enacted local laws aimed at preventing Jehovah's Witnesses and other religious groups from distributing religious literature door-to-door. The Supreme Court has upheld these sorts of restric-

> School prayer is perhaps the most controversial Establishment Clause issue.

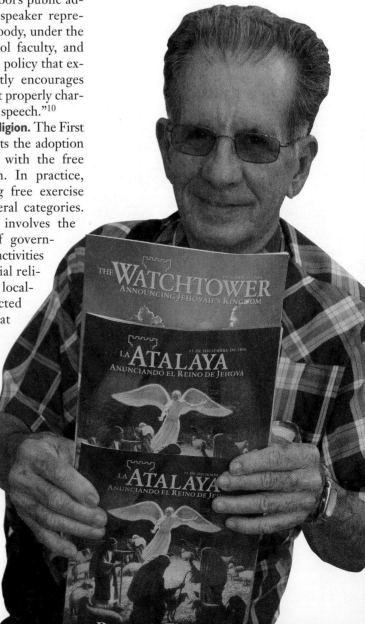

**think**

Do you agree with the Supreme Court's decision in *Engel v. Vitale*? Why/or why not?

tions on religious practice only when the government has been able to justify its action on the basis of a compelling or overriding government interest that could not be achieved in a less restrictive fashion. Because the compelling interest test is a high standard, the Supreme Court more often than not has

The First Amendment protects the right of Jehovah's Witnesses, Mormons, and other religious believers to go door-to-door to spread their faith.

Kara Neumann of Weston, Wisconsin died from a treatable form of diabetes after her parents prayed for her healing rather than seek medical treatment. The parents argued they were exercising their constitutional right to religious freedom, but they were convicted of second-degree reckless homicide. They were placed on 10 years' probation and ordered to spend 30 days in jail each year for the next six years.

struck down laws and regulations aimed against particular religions or religious practices.[11]

The second category of disputes concerns the impact on religious practice of general laws and government procedures that are otherwise neutral with respect to religion. Prison inmates who are Muslim or Jewish, for example, demand that they be provided meals that do not violate the dietary restrictions imposed by their religious faiths. Amish parents protest school attendance laws. For years, the Supreme Court subjected these sorts of incidental restrictions on religious practice to the compelling government interest test. Since *Employment Division v. Smith* (1990), however, the Supreme Court has held that states can enact laws that have an incidental impact on religious freedom so long as they serve a valid state purpose and are not aimed at inhibiting any particular religion. The *Smith* case involved a decision by the state

of Oregon to deny unemployment benefits to state employees who were fired because they used peyote, which is a hallucinogenic drug, in Native American religious practices. The Court upheld the firing and denial of unemployment benefits because the law under which they were dismissed served a valid state purpose, was not aimed at any particular religion, and had only an incidental impact on religious belief.[12]

## Freedom of Expression

The First Amendment guarantees freedom of expression. "Congress shall make no law . . . abridging the freedom of speech, or of the press; or the right of the people peaceably to assemble to petition the government for a redress of grievances."

**Anti-Government Speech.** Constitutional law holds that the government can restrict political expression only if it has a compelling interest that cannot be achieved by less restrictive means. In practice, the com-

pelling interest standard is so difficult to meet that most laws limiting expression are unconstitutional. Consider the case of Clarence Brandenburg, a Ku Klux Klan leader from Ohio, who was convicted under an Ohio law for making a speech at a Klan cross-burning rally in which he threatened the president, Congress, and the Supreme Court for suppressing the white race. In 1969, the Supreme Court overturned Brandenburg's conviction, saying that the mere advocacy of lawless action was not sufficient to sustain a conviction because the state does not have a compelling interest in outlawing "mere abstract teaching." Instead, the state must prove that the "advocacy is directed to inciting or producing imminent lawless action and is likely to incite or produce such action."[13]

**Expression That Threatens the Public Order.** Can the government punish expression that may lead to a disruption of public order?

Consider the controversy generated by Paul Cohen and his jacket. In 1968, during the Vietnam War, Cohen wore a jacket into the Los Angeles County Courthouse upon which the words "F___ the Draft" were clearly visible. Cohen was arrested and subsequently convicted by a local court for disturbing the peace. The judge reasoned that the jacket might provoke others to commit acts of violence and sentenced Cohen to 30 days in jail. Cohen appealed, and the case eventually reached the Supreme Court, which overturned the conviction. The Court held that government cannot forbid shocking language that is not legally obscene and that is not directed at an individual listener (or reader) in such a way as to provoke violence.[14]

**Hate-crimes Legislation.** A **hate-crimes law** is a legislative measure that increases penalties for persons convicted of criminal offenses motivated by prejudice based on race,

Supporters rally against hate crimes at a vigil to commemorate the anniversary of the death of Matthew Shepard. Shepard, a gay student at the University of Wyoming, was beaten and left to die outside of Laramie.

religion, national origin, gender, or sexual orientation. Suppose a group of young white men beat up an African American man who has just moved his family into a predominantly white neighborhood. During the assault, the white men use racial slurs and warn the man to move out of the area. The white men could be charged with the crime of assault. Because they acted out of racial animosity, they could also be charged with a hate crime. In recent years, many states have adopted hate-crimes legislation, enhancing penalties for persons convicted of crimes motivated by bias.

Hate-crimes legislation is controversial. Critics charge that hate-crimes laws infringe on freedom of expression. They also believe that hate-crimes provisions inhibit expression because they rely on speech as evidence of biased motive. In contrast, the proponents of hate-crimes laws claim they are justified because crimes motivated by hate inflict not only physical harm but also psychological damage on their victims. Furthermore, they argue that violent crimes aimed at groups of persons are more threatening to society than crimes against particular individuals because they increase racial and social divisions.[15]

The Supreme Court has upheld hate-crimes legislation, drawing a distinction between speech and action. Although biased speech is constitutionally protected, violent behavior motivated by bias is not. "A physical assault is not by any stretch of the imagination ... protected by the First Amendment," said the Court. Because hate crimes are perceived as inflicting "greater individual and societal harm" than ordinary crimes, states are justified in pro-viding greater penalties for their commission.[16]

**Symbolic Expression.** Symbolic expression, such as flying the flag or burning a cross, enjoys the same constitutional protection as speech or written communication. Congress and the states can restrict symbolic expression only when they can demonstrate a compelling government interest that cannot be achieved in a less restrictive fashion. Consider the issue of flag burning. In 1989, the Supreme Court overturned a Texas flag desecration law under which Gregory Lee Johnson was convicted for burning an American flag at the 1984 Republican convention in Dallas, ruling that Johnson's action was a form of symbolic speech. "If there is any bedrock principle underlying the First Amendment," wrote Justice William Brennan in the majority opinion, "it is that the government may not prohibit the expression of an idea simply because society finds the idea itself offensive or disagreeable."[17] Congress responded to the uproar over the Court's decision by passing a federal anti-flag burning statute, which, a year later, the Court also declared unconstitutional.[18]

## Privacy Rights

Do Americans enjoy a constitutional right of privacy? Although the Constitution does not specifically mention privacy, the Supreme Court has interpreted the Due Process Clause of the Fourteenth Amendment to include a right of privacy. In 1965, the Court struck down a seldom-enforced Connecticut law that prohibited the use of contraceptives and the dispensing of birth control information, even to married couples, on the grounds that its enforcement would involve government's invading "the privacy of the bedroom." The Court declared that various constitutional guarantees found in the Bill of Rights create "zones of privacy." The Third Amendment's prohibition against quartering soldiers in private homes and the Fourth Amendment's protection against unreasonable searches and seizures imply a right of privacy.[19] In contrast, conservative legal scholars believe that the Supreme Court simply invented a right of privacy that does not exist in the Constitution because a majority of the justices disagreed with the Connecticut law and wanted to find an excuse to strike it down. Although few conservatives want to defend Connecticut's statute against contraception, which some label "an uncommonly silly law," they have been outraged that the Court has used the right of privacy as the basis for major decisions involving abortion and gay rights.

The Supreme Court based *Roe v. Wade*, its landmark abortion decision, on a right of privacy. The case dealt with a challenge by an anonymous Dallas woman, "Jane Roe," to a Texas law prohibiting

**think** Do people who commit crimes out of prejudice deserve more severe punishment than other criminals or should similar crimes be punished similarly regardless of motive? Why or why not?

THE SUPREME COURT HAS UPHELD HATE-CRIMES LEGISLATION, DRAWING A DISTINCTION BETWEEN SPEECH AND ACTION.

**hate-crimes law** a legislative measure that increases penalties for persons convicted of criminal offenses motivated by prejudice based on race, religion, national origin, gender, or sexual orientation.

# Taking Sides

# Flag-Burning Amendment

Can burning a flag be considered proper political speech? What is the intent behind flag burning?

Should the Constitution be amended to alter the Bill of Rights? If this movement is successful, is it likely there will be other attempts to constitutionally limit liberties?

**Overview:** The business of determining and defining rights is one of the most important functions of government in a liberal, rights-based society. The discovery or determination of rights and liberties is problematic because rights usually come into conflict with other liberties. Take, for example, the debate over whether to amend the Constitution to prohibit flag burning. There are many who argue that burning a flag is a form of political expression. In this instance, the right to political speech comes into conflict with the right of a state to protect political and historical symbols and icons. Indeed, some argue that the patriotism and civic pride encouraged by the flag, the Pledge of Allegiance, the National Anthem, and so on, should have state protection. Furthermore, some hold that flag burning is tantamount to anti-Americanism.

The Supreme Court has held that the right to political expression transcends spoken or written speech. The speech, press, and association clauses of the First Amendment were written to guarantee Americans the constitutional protection to express their displeasure with government policy and law. The Supreme Court struck down flag-protection statutes in 48 states, as well as a 1968 and 1990 federal flag- protection statute in *Texas v. Johnson* (1989) and *U.S. v. Eichman* (1990), but Congress has debated the merits of a flag-burning amendment in almost every session since 1990. In fact, the House of Representatives overwhelmingly passed proposed constitutional amendments to prohibit flag desecration in 1995, 1997, 1999, 2001, 2003, and 2005. And the Senate voted on the proposed amendment in 1995 and 2000, but fell short of the two-thirds vote needed to send the proposed amendment to the state legislatures for ratification.

## supporting the flag-burning amendment

**the flag represents American values and principles and, as such, should be protected.** The flag symbolizes a shared history and common heritage of the pursuit of equal rights, duties, and self-government. A government reserves the right to protect those symbols and artifacts which represent its guiding principles.

**veneration of symbols is necessary for good citizenship.** At a flag raising at Independence Hall in 1861, Abraham Lincoln expressed his view that honoring the flag helps foster "the spirit [of freedom] that animated" the founders. The flag reminds Americans to respect the rights of others, to behave as good constitutional citizens, and to honor and protect the country in times of turmoil and danger.

**an amendment to ban flag burning reflects the will of the majority.** Most major public opinion polls show that roughly 63 to 72 percent of all Americans favor an amendment to ban flag burning. Both Democratic– and Republican Party–controlled Congresses have introduced flag-burning amendments.

## against the flag-burning amendment

**the Constitution should not be amended to prohibit political speech.** The First Amendment guarantees freedom of speech and expression, no matter how offensive some may find such speech. Freedom of expression is necessary for vigorous debate and dissent to prevent the abuse of governmental power.

**flag burners should be held to the same standard as those who damage their own property.** Most flag burners purchase or are given their own flags, and thus they should be subject to the same laws that regulate the burning or destruction of private property. Should people burn a flag that is not their own, they should be held to the same standard to which we hold people when they burn property that is not their own.

**flag burning is not a hate crime.** Representative Henry Hyde argued during floor debate that flag burning is a hate crime because "burning the flag is an expression of contempt for the moral unity of the American people," but hate crimes can be directed only against individuals, not against symbols or political principles.

abortion except to save the life of a woman. The Court found the Texas statute unconstitutional, declaring that a woman's right to personal privacy under the U.S. Constitution included her decision to terminate a pregnancy. The Court said, however, that a woman's right to privacy was not absolute and must be balanced against the state's interest in protecting health, medical standards, and prenatal life.

The Supreme Court balanced these competing interests by dividing a pregnancy into trimesters. During the first trimester, state governments could not interfere with a physician's decision, reached in consultation with a pregnant patient, to terminate a pregnancy. In the second trimester, the state could regulate abortion, but only to protect the health of a woman. In the third trimester, after

**think**

**Should privacy be a constitutional right? Why or why not?**

the fetus had achieved viability (the ability to survive outside the womb), the Court ruled that state governments could prohibit abortion except when it was necessary to preserve the life or health of a woman.[20]

Since *Roe*, the Supreme Court has upheld its original decision while allowing states leeway to regulate abortion. In 1989, the Court upheld a Missouri law limiting access to abortion. The statute prohibited the use of public em-

ployees or facilities to perform or assist an abortion except to save a woman's life, and outlawed the use of public funds, employees, or facilities to encourage or counsel a woman to have an abortion not necessary to save her life. Citing recent medical advances, the Court abandoned the trimester system adopted in *Roe* by allowing Missouri to require physicians to perform medical tests to determine fetal viability beginning at 20 weeks.[21] The Court subsequently ruled that a state could regulate access to abortion as long as the regulations did not place an "undue burden" on a woman's right to choose. The Court's majority defined an undue burden as one that presented an "absolute obstacle or severe limitation" on the right to decide to have an abortion. State regulations that simply "inhibited" that right were permissible.

The Court has upheld a number of restrictions on abortion, including the following:

- Women seeking abortions must be given information about fetal development and alternatives to ending their pregnancies.

# Abortion Should Be:
**Legal in all cases–17%**
**Legal in most cases–37%**
**Illegal in most cases–26%**
**Illegal in all cases–15%**
**Don't know–5%**

An abortion opponent kneels amid mock cemetery crosses to dramatize the loss of life through abortion. Pew Research Center Survey, August 2008.

- Women must wait at least 24 hours after receiving that information before having an abortion.
- Doctors must keep detailed records on each abortion performed.
- Abortion records are subject to public disclosure.
- Unmarried girls under the age of 18 must get the permission of one of their parents or the certification of a state judge that they are mature enough to make the decision on their own.

The only provision in the law that the Court considered an undue burden was a requirement that married women notify their husbands of their plans to have an abortion.[22]

The Supreme Court's most recent application of the right of privacy involved a legal challenge to the Texas sodomy law, which criminalized private, consensual sexual conduct between two adults of the same gender. When police in Houston, Texas, arrived at the home of John Lawrence because of an unrelated call, they found Lawrence and another man engaged in sexual in-

*"FREEDOM OF SPEECH SHOULD NOT EXTEND TO GROUPS THAT ARE SYMPATHETIC TO TERRORISTS."*

**AGREE 45%**
**DISAGREE 50%**
**UNSURE 5%**

Pew Research Poll, 2008

tercourse. They arrested the men and charged them with violating the Texas homosexual conduct law for "engaging in deviate sexual intercourse with another person of the same sex." In *Lawrence v. Texas*, the Court ruled that the Texas law violated the Due Process Clause of the Fourteenth Amendment because it intruded into the personal and private lives of individuals without furthering a legitimate state interest.[23]

## Due Process of Law and the Rights of the Accused

Several provisions of the Bill of Rights, including the better part of the Fourth, Fifth, and Eighth Amendments, protect the rights of persons under investigation or accused of crimes. The key constitutional phrase is found in the Fifth Amendment and repeated in the Fourteenth Amendment: No person shall be deprived of "life, liberty, or property, without due process of law." **Due process of law** is the constitutional

provision that declares that government must follow fair and regular procedures in actions that could lead to an individual's suffering loss of life, liberty, or property. Neither the national government nor the states may resort to stacked juries, coerced confessions, self-incrimination, denial of counsel, cruel and unusual punishments, or unreasonable searches and seizures.

**Searches and Seizures.** The Fourth Amendment guarantees the "right of the people to be secure in their persons, houses, papers, and effects, against unreasonable searches and seizures . . . and no warrants shall issue, but upon probable cause . . . and particularly describing the place to be searched, and the persons or things to be seized." In general, this provision means that the police need a **warrant** (that is, an official authorization issued by a judicial officer) for most searches of persons or property. Judges or other magistrates issue warrants after the law-enforcement authorities have shown probable cause that certain

**due process of law** the constitutional principle holding that government must follow fair and regular procedures in actions that could lead to an individual's suffering loss of life, liberty, or property.

**warrant** an official authorization issued by a judicial officer.

Actor Tommy Chong during his "Light Up America" tour, supporting the legalization of marijuana.

*"THE POLICE SHOULD BE ALLOWED TO SEARCH THE HOUSES OF PEOPLE WHO MIGHT BE SYMPATHETIC TO TERRORISTS WITHOUT A COURT ORDER."*

**AGREE 37%**
**DISAGREE 61%**
**UNSURE 2%**

Pew Research Poll, 2008

# Population Policy in China

## around THE WORLD

With a population of more than 1.3 billion people, China is the most populous country in the world. Because of medical advances and nutritional improvements, life expectancy in China has increased dramatically, and the population has more than doubled since 1949. Chinese families have traditionally been large because Chinese couples want children to care for them when they are old. Male children are especially prized because sons traditionally live near their parents, whereas daughters marry and leave home. Chinese couples want to bear sons because their daughters-in-law will care for them in their old age, whereas their daughters will be caring for someone else.[24]

The Chinese government believes that population control is a prerequisite for economic development. Rapid population growth strains the nation's agricultural resources and contributes to the shortage of adequate housing. Substantial economic growth is necessary just to provide jobs for the growing population.

Since the 1980s, the government has implemented a one-child policy. Couples are to bear no more than one child, unless they receive permission from the government based on special circumstances. Some local officials have taken drastic steps to enforce the policy, including forced abortions, sterilization for women who have too many children, and destroying the assets of families that are too large. Because of the cultural preference for male children, some families abort female children. According to Chinese demographic figures, the ratio of male to female children under the age of five in China is 117 to 100. According to the International Planned Parenthood Federation, China aborts seven million fetuses a year and about 70 percent are female. Chinese families apparently abandon millions of other girls to state-run orphanages.[25]

The population policy has worked more effectively in urban centers than in rural areas. In urban areas, women average only one child, whereas rural women have two or more children.[26] Urban couples more readily comply with the policy because they are more subject to government sanctions than are people living in the countryside. Traditional cultural practices are also stronger in rural China than they are in urban centers.

## Questions

1. How does China's population policy compare and contrast with America's abortion policy?

2. Would you expect a democracy to adopt a population policy similar to China's policy?

3. Do you believe that the need for economic development is sufficient to justify China's population policy?

A billboard beside a Xining, China, apartment house promotes the official one-child policy.

items will be found. **Probable cause** is the reasonable suspicion based on evidence that a particular search will uncover contraband.

Through the years, the Supreme Court has permitted a number of exceptions to the basic warrant requirement. The police do not need a warrant, for example, to search suspects who consent to be searched or to search suspects after valid arrests. If police officers have a reasonable suspicion of criminal activity, they may stop and search suspicious individuals. The Court has ruled, for example, that the police are justified in searching an individual in a high-crime area who flees when the police appear.[27] The authorities can also search luggage in airports and may fingerprint suspects after arrests.

The Supreme Court has been more willing to authorize searches of automobiles without warrants than it has offices and homes. Consider the 1982 case, *United States v. Ross*. An informant tipped off the District of Columbia police about a narcotics dealer known as Bandit, who sold drugs from the trunk of his purplish-maroon Chevrolet Malibu. When the police spotted a car fitting the description, they pulled it over and searched the trunk, even though they did not have a warrant. Sure enough, they found heroin and cash in the trunk. The car's driver, Albert Ross, Jr., was subsequently tried and convicted of possession of narcotics with intent to distribute. He appealed his case to the Supreme Court. Did the police search of Ross's car trunk without a warrant violate his constitutional rights? The Court said that it did not because the police had legitimately stopped the car and had

## CIVIL LIBERTIES AND TERRORISM
### In order to curb terrorism in this country, do you think it will be necessary for the average person to give up some civil liberties?

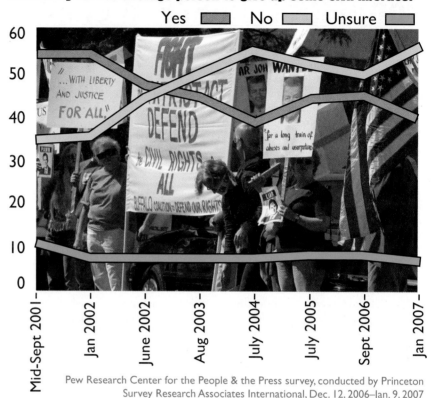

Yes ▭ No ▭ Unsure ▭

Pew Research Center for the People & the Press survey, conducted by Princeton Survey Research Associates International, Dec. 12, 2006–Jan. 9, 2007

probable cause to believe it contained contraband. As a result, the police could search the vehicle as thoroughly as if they had a warrant. The Court added, however, that a search "must be limited by its object," that is, the police cannot conduct a general search to see what might turn up.[28]

**The Exclusionary Rule.** The **exclusionary rule** is the judicial doctrine stating that when the police violate an individual's constitutional rights, the evidence obtained as a result of police misconduct or error cannot be used against the defendant in a criminal prosecution. In 1914, the Supreme Court estab-

lished the exclusionary rule in federal prosecutions in the *Weeks v. United States* case. The police arrested Fremont Weeks at his place of business and then searched his home. Both of these actions were taken without a warrant. Papers and articles seized in the search were used in federal court against Weeks, and he was convicted. He appealed his conviction, arguing that the judge should not have admitted into

**probable cause** the reasonable suspicion based on evidence that a particular search will uncover contraband.

**exclusionary rule** the judicial doctrine stating that when the police violate an individual's constitutional rights, the evidence obtained as a result of police misconduct or error cannot be used against the defendant.

*think*

**If the police obtain evidence in an unlawful search that conclusively proves a defendant guilty, should the evidence be used to prosecute the defendant? Why or why not?**

evidence illegally seized materials. The Supreme Court agreed. In 1961, the Supreme Court extended the exclusionary rule to the states in the case of *Mapp v. Ohio*.[29]

The exclusionary rule is controversial. Its defenders say that is a necessary safeguard to ensure that police authorities do not intentionally violate individual rights. In contrast, critics point out that the United States is the only country to take the position that police misconduct must automatically result in the suppression of evidence. In other countries, the trial judge determines whether the misconduct is serious enough to warrant the exclusion of the evidence.[30]

In recent decades, the Supreme Court has weakened the exclusionary rule without repealing it by carving out major exceptions to its application. In 1984, the Court adopted a "good faith" exception to the exclusionary rule requirement, allowing the use of illegally seized evidence in criminal prosecutions as long as the police acted in good faith.[31] Subsequently, the Court added a "harmless error" exception, allowing a criminal conviction to stand despite the use of illegally obtained evidence when other evidence in the case was strong enough to convict the defendant anyway.[32] In 2009, the Court ruled that evidence obtained from an unlawful arrest based on careless record keeping rather than intentional police misconduct could be used in a prosecution.[33]

**The Miranda Warning.** Ernesto Miranda was an Arizona man arrested for kidnapping and raping a young woman. Under questioning, Miranda confessed. On appeal, Miranda challenged the use of his confession as a violation of the Fifth Amendment's guarantee against self-incrimination because the police had not informed him of his constitutional rights to remain silent and consult an attorney.

The Supreme Court reversed Miranda's conviction. The Court's majority held that the prosecution could not use a statement against an

# **take**action
## TALKING ABOUT *MIRANDA*

Is the *Miranda* warning a meaningful constitutional safeguard or a technical formality that has no impact on justice? Do police officers take it seriously? Do suspects understand its meaning? The class project is to research the implementation of the *Miranda* warning by interviewing one or more police officers. Some students may know police officers as friends, neighbors, or relatives. Students may also be able to interview members of the campus police at your college.

Before conducting the interviews, prepare a set of questions designed to focus on the following topics:

- Police training. How do police academies cover the topic of *Miranda*? Is it presented as a necessary evil or as an important element of civil liberties in a free society?
- Police supervision. How seriously does management take the *Miranda* warning? Do police supervisors frequently review implementation procedures or is that left to the discretion of individual officers?
- *Miranda* implementation. When, if ever, do officers recite the *Miranda* warning to suspects? Do they read the warning from a card, or do they have it memorized? What steps, if any, do officers take to ensure that suspects understand the meaning of the warning?
- *Miranda* impact. Do law enforcement officers believe that the *Miranda* warning has an impact on their work?

Do they think the warning discourages guilty persons from confessing? Do they believe that *Miranda* plays a positive role in law enforcement by reminding innocent people of their constitutional rights? Or do they believe that the *Miranda* warning is meaningless, a waste of time to satisfy the courts that has no impact in the real world of law enforcement?

After the interviews are complete, students should organize their notes and prepare to participate in class discussion. The instructor will ask students not just about the content of the interviews and their reaction to them, but also about the *Miranda* warning in general. In particular, the instructor will invite students to discuss their assessment of the *Miranda* warning. Is it harmful or beneficial, or is it just a meaningless technicality that neither police officers nor criminal suspects take seriously?

accused person in a court of law unless the authorities observe adequate procedural safeguards to ensure that the statement was obtained "voluntarily, knowingly, and intelligently." Before questioning, accused persons must be warned that 1) they have a right to remain silent, 2) that any statements they give may be used against them, and 3) that they are entitled to the presence of an attorney, either retained or appointed.[34]

they know their rights. *Miranda* protects poor, uneducated, and first-time offenders from police coercion.

The Supreme Court has weakened the *Miranda* ruling without reversing it. The Court has held that in cross-examining defendants, prosecutors can use statements that do not meet the *Miranda* standard.[36] The Court has also ruled that police need not give the *Miranda* warning before questioning a suspect when

acquittal in an earlier prosecution. No person shall be "twice put in jeopardy of life and limb" for the same criminal offense, the amendment declares. The goal of this provision is to protect individuals from the harassment of repeated prosecutions on the same charge after an acquittal. Because of the Double Jeopardy Clause, no one who has been acquitted of an offense can be retried for the same crime even if incontrovertible evidence of the person's guilt is discovered.

The Supreme Court has held that the Double Jeopardy Clause does not protect persons convicted of child molestation from involuntary commitment to mental hospitals after they have served their prison sentences. Consider the case of *Kansas v. Hendricks*. Leroy Hendricks was a pedophile, an adult who sexually abuses children. He had five convictions for child molestation in the state of Kansas and admitted that he could not stop trying to have sex with children. In 1994, after Hendricks finished serving his most recent sentence for child molestation, the state of Kansas transferred him to a mental health facility, where he was confined indefinitely under provisions of the state's Sexually Violent Predator Act. A state judge ruled that Hendricks was "mentally abnormal" and likely to commit additional crimes. Hendricks and his attorneys filed suit against the state, charging that his continued confinement was a sort of double jeopardy in that he was tried and punished twice for the same crime. The case eventually reached the U.S. Supreme Court, which declared that Hendricks could be confined against his will because he was being held in a mental institution rather than a prison. Technically, he was no longer being punished.[39] Although no one was

In June 2009, the Supreme Court ruled in *Safford Unified School District v. Redding* that a strip search of middle-schooler Savana Redding, suspected of distributing prescription drugs, violated her Fourth Amendment right to be secure against "unreasonable searches and seizures."

The Court's *Miranda* ruling has sparked an ongoing debate. Critics say that it makes law enforcement more difficult by preventing police from interrogating suspects quickly before they have a chance to concoct an alibi or reflect on the consequences of telling the truth.[35] In contrast, *Miranda*'s defenders call it the "poor person's Fifth Amendment." Educated, middle-class defendants do not need the *Miranda* warning—

the public safety is immediately and directly threatened.[37] The Court even upheld a conviction when the police refused to allow an attorney hired by a suspect's relatives to see him because the suspect had not asked to see a lawyer.[38]

**Double Jeopardy.** The Fifth Amendment prohibits **double jeopardy**, which involves the government trying a criminal defendant a second time for the same offense after an

**double jeopardy** the government trying a criminal defendant a second time for the same offense after an acquittal in an earlier prosecution.

**Should child molesters be kept in confinement even after they have served their criminal sentences? Why or why not?**

sympathetic with Hendricks, a number of observers worried about the precedent set by the case. "Today we're dealing with sexual predators," said Steven Shapiro of the ACLU. "Who is it tomorrow that we're going to label as abnormal and potentially dangerous?"[40]

**Fair Trial.** A number of provisions in the Sixth Amendment are aimed at guaranteeing that defendants receive a fair trial. The amendment promises a speedy and public trial. Although the Supreme Court has been reluctant to set timetables for trials, the federal government and many states have adopted "speedy trial laws" to ensure that justice will not be long delayed. As for the public trial requirement, the Supreme Court has held that the public (and the press) may not be excluded from the courtroom except in rare circumstances.[41] Furthermore, the Court has said that states may permit the unobtrusive use of television in a courtroom if they wish.[42]

The Sixth Amendment guarantees trial by an impartial jury. Although juries are traditionally 12 persons, the Supreme Court has said that juries with as few as 6 people are acceptable.[43] The Court has also held that jury selection processes must ensure that the jury pool represents a cross-section of the community, holding, for example, that prosecutors may not systematically exclude racial minorities from jury service.[44]

The Sixth Amendment grants defendants the right to legal counsel. In *Gideon v. Wainwright*, the Supreme Court ruled that states must provide attorneys for indigent defendants charged with serious crimes.[45] The Court has also held that assigned counsel must meet a standard of reasonable competence.[46]

# Executions in the United States

| Year | Executions |
|------|-----------|
| 1988 | 11 |
| 1989 | 16 |
| 1990 | 23 |
| 1991 | 14 |
| 1992 | 31 |
| 1993 | 38 |
| 1994 | 31 |
| 1995 | 56 |
| 1996 | 45 |
| 1997 | 74 |
| 1998 | 68 |
| 1999 | 98 |
| 2000 | 85 |
| 2001 | 66 |
| 2002 | 71 |
| 2003 | 65 |
| 2004 | 59 |
| 2005 | 60 |
| 2006 | 53 |
| 2007 | 42 |
| 2008 | 37 |

Lethal injection is replacing (clockwise from top left) a firing squad, the electric chair, hanging, or the gas chamber in various U.S. states.

**Cruel and Unusual Punishments.** Should mentally retarded offenders be held fully accountable for their crimes? Daryl Renard Atkins is a murderer, convicted and sentenced to death by the state of Virginia for the robbery and slaying of a U.S. airman in 1996. Atkins is also severely retarded, at least according to his defense attorneys. Would executing Atkins violate the prohibition against cruel and unusual punishments contained in the Eighth Amendment to the U.S. Constitution? In general, the Supreme Court has interpreted this provision to mean that the punishment must fit the crime. The Court, for example, has held that a life sentence without the possibility of parole for a series of nonviolent petty offenses is cruel and unusual.[47] The Court has also ruled that it is unconstitutional to impose the death penalty on a defendant who rapes a child but does not kill the victim.[48]

No issue has generated more controversy under the Eighth Amendment than the death penalty (**capital punishment**). In 1972, the opponents of capital punishment won a temporary victory in the case of *Furman v. Georgia*. By a 5–4 vote, the Supreme Court declared that the death penalty, *as then applied*, was unconstitutional because it allowed too much discretion, thereby opening the door to discriminatory practices. Which crimes and individuals received the death penalty was so arbitrary, the Court said, that it was similar to being struck by lightning.[49]

Many state legislatures responded to *Furman* by adopting new capital punishment laws designed to satisfy the Court's objections. As the states implemented their new death penalty statutes, cases began to make their way through the court system. In 1976, the U.S. Supreme Court ruled in the case of *Gregg v.*

**capital punishment** the death penalty.

*Georgia*, which involved a constitutional challenge to Georgia's new death penalty statute, that capital punishment was constitutional.[50] Thirty-eight states and the federal government adopted capital punishment statutes, and 32 states carried out executions, with Texas taking the lead, carrying out more than a third of the nation's executions.[51] The federal government carried out one execution, Timothy McVeigh, the convicted Oklahoma City bomber. As the figure on p. 355 shows, the number of executions increased during the 1990s, peaking at 98 in 1999.

The increased rate of executions was accompanied by increased controversy. The opponents of the death penalty charged that the process of trials and appeals was so flawed that innocent people might face execution. A study published by Columbia University law professor James S. Liebman found that two-thirds of the death sentences given by American courts between 1973 and 1995 were overturned on appeal. When death penalty cases were retried, 7 percent of defendants were found not guilty.[52] Furthermore, the critics of the death penalty argued that it was inefficient because only 5 percent of death sentences were actually carried out and then only after years of evaluation.[53] In contrast, the proponents of capital punishment defended the process, saying that it was scrupulously fair. They pointed out that people given the death penalty were entitled to an appeals process that lasts for years. According to the Bureau of Justice Statistics, the average time on death row for the convicted murderers before their executions is more than 12 years, long enough for their cases to be thoroughly examined for error.[54]

The renewed debate over capital punishment has been accompanied by a decline in the implementation of the death penalty. As the figure on p. 355 shows, the number of people executed in the United States has fallen since peaking in 1999. In some states, executive officials slowed or halted capital punishment because of concerns about efficacy. New Jersey repealed its death penalty statute entirely, and 18 states adopted laws to prohibit the execution of mentally retarded criminals.[55]

In this context, the U.S. Supreme Court declared that the execution of mentally retarded defendants violated the Cruel and Unusual Punishment Clause of the Eighth Amendment. The Court argued that a national consensus had developed against executing the mentally retarded and reversed the position it had taken in 1989 when only two states excluded mentally retarded individuals from the death penalty.[56] The Court returned the Atkins case to a trial court in Virginia to determine whether the defendant was indeed mentally retarded. Ironically, a jury found Atkins mentally competent, and a judge sentenced him to death. His case is once again on appeal.

## Executive Authority, Civil Liberties, and the War on Terror

Executive authority grows during wartime, sometimes at the expense of civil liberties. In the midst of war, presidents exercise extraordinary

# Capital Punishment by State

Green states employ the death penalty. Yellow numerals show the number of death row inmates as of January 1, 2007. White numerals show the number of executions carried out between 1976 and December 2007.

http://pewforum.org/docs/?DocID=273

powers and declare that their actions are necessary to defend the nation and win the war. Although civil libertarians often challenge the president's actions as infringements on personal liberty, other political actors and the general public either support the president's initiatives or mute their criticism for fear of being accused of failing to stand up to the enemy. Over time, public passions over the war recede and either a new administration or the other branches of government reverse the policies that compromised civil liberties.[57]

lenged his detention, the U.S. Supreme Court upheld the constitutionality of the executive order.[58] The U.S. government eventually began to regard the Japanese internment with regret. In 1988, Congress passed and President Ronald Reagan signed legislation officially apologizing for the internment and providing reparation payments of $20,000 each to the survivors or their heirs.

After 9/11, President George W. Bush took actions that critics charged threatened civil liberties. He approved wiretapping of overseas telephone calls without benefit of court

intent to try some enemy combatants in military tribunals without many of the civil liberties guarantees afforded by civilian courts.

The U.S. Supreme Court and the Obama administration overturned or modified many of the Bush administration's actions. In a case involving Yaser Esam Hamdi, an American citizen who was taken into custody in Afghanistan, the Court held that the president could not deprive detainees of their right to due process.[59] The Court ruled against Bush's plan to put detainees on trial before military tribunals because Congress had

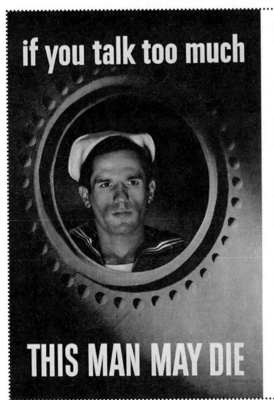

if you talk too much

THIS MAN MAY DIE

# Civil Liberties in Times of War

**1861 (Civil War)** President Lincoln suspends the writ of *habeas corpus* to protect troop movements along the railroad lines.

**1918 (WWI)** Congress passes the Sedition Act, which makes it a crime to say or publish anything "disloyal, profane, scurrilous, or abusive" about the government or the military.

**1942 (WWII)** President Roosevelt issues Executive Order 9066, which forces nearly 120,000 people of Japanese ancestry—70,000 of them American citizens—from their homes and businesses into internment camps until the war's conclusion in 1945.

**1950 (Cold War)** Congress passed the Subversive Activities Control Act (also known as the McCarran Act), which authorized the president to detain without the benefit of *habeas corpus* anyone considered likely to engage in espionage or sabotage.

**2001 (war on terror)** Congress passes the USA PATRIOT Act, which loosened restrictions on domestic surveillance, investigations without probable cause, and detention without judicial review when there is deemed to be a threat to national security.

Consider the Japanese internment during World War II. In early 1942, shortly after the Japanese attack on Pearl Harbor, President Franklin Roosevelt issued an executive order to forcibly relocate nearly 120,000 people of Japanese ancestry living on the West Coast into internment camps until the end of the war. Most were American citizens. The president justified the order as necessary to prevent sabotage and espionage. When Fred Korematsu, an American citizen of Japanese descent, chal-

order. He ordered terror suspects captured in the war on terror to be held at Guantánamo Bay, Cuba, without benefit of prisoner-of-war status or the rights of suspected criminals under the U.S. Constitution. The president authorized the use of aggressive interrogation techniques against terror suspects, and had some detainees transported to third countries where they were allegedly tortured. American citizens suspected of terrorism were held indefinitely without trial. Bush also declared his

not authorized the action.[60] The Supreme Court also declared that terror suspects held at Guantánamo have a constitutional right to seek their release in federal court.[61] Similarly, President Obama reversed many Bush administration policies concerning the war on terror. In addition to banning the use of aggressive interrogation techniques, Obama ordered the closure of the Guantánamo prison within a year and halted trials of terror suspects pending review.

# CONCLUSION

# civil liberties
## POLICYMAKING

Constitutional law is the most important environmental factor affecting civil liberties policymaking. Civil liberties questions are constitutional questions. Policy debates over prayer in public schools and capital punishment are invariably debates about constitutional law. Did the founders intend for the Establishment Clause to prohibit organized spoken prayer in public schools? Is it cruel and unusual punishment under the Eighth Amendment to execute convicted murderers who are mentally retarded? The Constitution and its interpretation affect every stage of the civil liberties policy process.

Because of the constitutional nature of civil liberties policymaking, judges, especially the men and women who serve on the Supreme Court of the United States, are the most important civil liberties policymakers. Liberal judges are more likely than conservative judges to rule in favor of unpopular litigants, such as atheists, Jehovah's Witnesses, members of the Ku Klux Klan, criminal defendants, and prison inmates. During the 1960s, a liberal bloc of justices led by Chief Justice Earl Warren dominated the Supreme Court. Many of the decisions of that era, including *Engel v. Vitale* and *Miranda v. Arizona*, reflected their policy preferences. In contrast to liberal members of the judiciary, judges with conservative policy preferences tend to decide cases in favor of the police, criminal prosecutors, majority religious preferences, and traditional values. The Supreme Court today is closely divided on civil liberties issues and many cases are decided by the narrowest margin.

Civil liberties policymaking is affected by the presence of interest groups and other organizations capable of participating in the policy process. The American Civil Liberties Union (ACLU) is a frequent participant in civil liberties policymaking. Other interest groups involved with various civil liberties issues include the National Organization for Women (NOW), Planned Parenthood, NARAL Pro-Choice America, the National Rifle Association (NRA), and the National Right to Life Committee.

Public opinion affects the civil liberties policymaking process. Legislatures and executives respond to public demands by enacting death penalty statutes, school prayer requirements, and other measures related to civil liberties. At times, judges seem to respond to public opinion. Historically, the Supreme Court has been more willing to support presidential actions to limit civil liberties during wartime than it is after the war is over.

In the long run, the policy preferences of the president affect civil liberties policymaking because the president appoints judges. Republican presidents tend to select conservative judges, whereas Democratic presidents appoint liberals. Because federal judges enjoy lifetime appointments, a president's influence on judicial policymaking will be slow to materialize but can continue well after the president leaves office.

"It is a fair summary of history to say that the safeguards of liberty have been forged in controversies involving not very nice people."
—Felix Frankfurter, U.S. Supreme Court Justice (1939–1962)

In the early years of the twenty-first century, former Presidents Reagan, Bush, and Clinton continue to affect the judicial branch of government because their appointees still serve on the Court. The survival of the *Roe* precedent depends on future presidential and senatorial elections.

## Agenda Building

A number of political actors help set the agenda for civil liberties policymaking. Interest groups and other organizations are particularly important. Conservative groups call on the government to get tough on pornography and crime, and to limit access to abortion. Groups with unpopular views, such as Nazis and members of the Ku Klux Klan, stimulate debate on the First Amendment by attempting to march and demonstrate. A **test case** is a lawsuit initiated to assess the constitutionality of a legislative or executive act. Many of the civil liberties disputes reaching the Supreme Court are test cases initiated by groups such as the ACLU or the Jehovah's Witnesses. The latter have been responsible for more than 50 cases involving religious liberty, winning 90 percent of them.[62] Interest groups ranging from the Chamber of Commerce to B'nai B'rith, a Jewish organization, join other civil liberties cases by means of the *amicus* brief. An **amicus curiae** or **friend of the court brief** is a written legal argument presented by a party not directly involved in a case.

Individuals can add civil liberties issues to the public agenda. Many criminal justice disputes arise from appeals filed by convicted felons, such as Ernesto Miranda. Other individuals raise civil liberties issues on the basis of principle. Madalyn Murray O'Hair, for example, was famous for initiating test cases to challenge what she regarded as unconstitutional government support of religion.

## Policy Formulation and Adoption

Many civil liberties policies are formulated and adopted in the executive and legislative branches of government, both at the national level and in the states. After the terrorist attacks of September 11, 2001, for example, Congress passed, and President George W. Bush signed, the USA PATRIOT Act, which makes it easier for federal officials to get wiretapping orders from judges to investigate terrorism, and authorizes nationwide search warrants for computer information in terrorism investigations.[63] State governments adopt policies dealing with the death penalty, state aid to parochial schools, abortion, and other civil liberties issues.

The courts become involved in civil liberties policymaking only when a civil liberties policy adopted by another unit of government is challenged on constitutional grounds. The U.S. Supreme Court has addressed the issue of school prayer because of legal challenges filed against state and local policies. Court rulings then serve as guidelines for other institutions of government.

If the Supreme Court overturns *Roe v. Wade*, the issue of abortion will return to the states. Before *Roe*, states set their own abortion policies. Some states allowed abortion, whereas other states prohibited it except when necessary to protect the life of the woman. In *Roe*, the Supreme Court ruled that women have a constitutional right to an abortion during the first trimester. States could regulate second trimester abortions; they could prohibit late-term abortions. If the Supreme Court overturns the *Roe*

> THE COURTS BECOME INVOLVED IN CIVIL LIBERTIES POLICYMAKING ONLY WHEN A CIVIL LIBERTIES POLICY IS CHALLENGED ON CONSTITUTIONAL GROUNDS.

precedent, some states, such as South Dakota, will prohibit abortion except when the woman's life is in jeopardy, whereas others will allow most abortions. Other states will likely take a moderate approach, allowing abortion under certain circumstances but prohibiting abortions otherwise.

## Policy Implementation and Evaluation

A broad range of government entities participates in the implementation of civil liberties policy. The Supreme Court's willingness to allow states to enact school voucher programs may not necessarily lead to the adoption of voucher programs, at least not in all states. Some state legislatures will adopt programs, but other legislatures will not. The Supreme Court's decision effectively moves the policymaking arena from the courthouse to the legislature, the governor's mansion, and the school district.

Scholars have completed a number of studies evaluating certain aspects of civil liberties policy. For example, research suggests that the primary impact of the *Miranda* decision has been psychological and that the ruling has had little appreciable effect on confessions and convictions.[64] Another observer concludes that *Miranda* has had no measurable impact on reducing police misconduct.[65] The Liebman study of capital punishment was designed to assess the effectiveness of the death penalty.

**test case** a lawsuit initiated to assess the constitutionality of a legislative or executive act.

**amicus curiae or friend of the court brief** written legal arguments presented by parties not directly involved in the case, including interest groups and units of government.

# TEST yourself

1. The protection of the individual from the unrestricted power of government is the definition for which of the following?
   A. Selective incorporation of the Bill of Rights
   B. Fundamental rights
   C. Civil rights
   D. Civil liberties

2. Where is the Bill of Rights found?
   A. It is the first ten amendments to the Constitution
   B. It is found in Article I, Section 8 of the Constitution
   C. It is part of the Declaration of Independence
   D. It is part of the Articles of Confederation

3. The Bill of Rights initially restricted the power of which of the following levels of government?
   A. Neither the national government nor state governments
   B. Both the national government and state governments
   C. The national government but not state governments
   D. State governments but not the national government

4. The selective incorporation of the Bill of Rights against the states is based on which of the following?
   A. Due Process Clause of the Fourteenth Amendment
   B. First Amendment
   C. Equal Protection Clause of the Fourteenth Amendment
   D. Thirteenth Amendment

5. Which of the following is the reason why China has adopted a one-child policy?
   A. To increase the size of the nation's population
   B. To balance the population between men and women
   C. To limit population growth in order to promote economic development
   D. To force people to move to urban areas

6. Your friend, who works at a local construction company, was fired because his boss disagreed with him over a bumper sticker for a presidential candidate. Does your friend have any legal recourse under the U.S. Constitution or federal law?
   A. Yes, he can sue for his job back based on his boss's violating his freedom of expression.
   B. No, he cannot sue because the First Amendment protects freedom of speech, and bumper stickers are not speech.
   C. No, the First Amendment does not apply to private employers.
   D. Yes, your friend can sue his former boss for age discrimination.

7. Which of the following statements about constitutional rights is true?
   A. All rights are equally important.
   B. Rights are absolute, meaning that government cannot abridge rights guaranteed by the Constitution.

C. State constitutions can guarantee more rights than those found in the federal constitution.
   D. All of the above.

8. Which of the following statements is true about the fundamental rights protected by the Bill of Rights?
   A. They are absolute and may never be abridged by the government.
   B. They are guidelines, but government officials can abridge them when they determine it is in the public interest.
   C. They can be abridged, but only when the government can demonstrate a plausible justification.
   D. They cannot be abridged unless the government can demonstrate a compelling or overriding public interest for so doing.

9. The Parker family is suing the local public school district. The Parkers, who are Mormons, complain that their children's school principal recites prayers over the school intercom and that the prayers are contrary to the family's religious beliefs. Which of the following statements is NOT true about this dispute?
   A. The Parker's lawsuit would be based on the First and Fourteenth Amendments of the U.S. Constitution.
   B. The principal would likely successfully defend against the suit because he has the freedom of religion to express his religious views and that is protected by the Constitution.
   C. The ACLU might be willing to assist the Parkers in their lawsuit.
   D. The Parkers would probably sue in federal court rather than state court.

10. *Engel v. Vitale* dealt with which of the following issues?
    A. Abortion
    B. Freedom of religion
    C. Freedom of speech
    D. Establishment of religion

11. A federal district judge rules that the display of a Ten Commandments monument on the grounds of the county courthouse violates the Establishment Clause. What, if anything, can be done to challenge his decision?
    A. Nothing. Federal court rulings are not subject to reversal because federal judges are appointed for life.
    B. The state legislature and the governor could pass a law to overturn the decision.
    C. Congress and the president could pass a law to overturn the decision.
    D. The county could appeal the decision to a higher court.

12. Which of the following is an example of a hate crime?
    A. A group of white and Latino men break into the home of an Asian family. While robbing the family, they use racial/ethnic slurs, threatening the Asian family with

violence if they don't move out of the neighborhood.

B. A woman publishes a newsletter in which she attacks homosexuals as "godless pagans who spread disease."

C. A white man who is fleeing from the scene of a crime shoots and wounds a police officer who is African American.

D. All of the above.

**13** Which of the following statements is true regarding a right to privacy?

A. The First Amendment guarantees people the right to personal privacy.

B. The Supreme Court has interpreted various provisions of the Bill of Rights to create "zones of privacy."

C. A right to privacy is the basis for *Brown v. Board of Education*.

D. All of the above.

**14** Which of the following statements is true about *Roe v. Wade*?

A. It is based on a constitutional right of privacy.

B. It prohibited states from regulating abortion under all circumstances.

C. The Supreme Court has subsequently overturned major parts of *Roe*.

D. All of the above.

**15** The constitutional principle that government cannot deprive someone of life, liberty, or property without following fair and regular procedures is known as which of the following?

A. Selective incorporation

B. Parental choice

C. Exclusionary rule

D. Due process of law

**16** What is the rationale for the exclusionary rule?

A. If the evidence proves a defendant's guilt, then the evidence should be used against the defendant regardless of how the evidence was obtained.

B. If the government is allowed to use evidence that was obtained illegally, then the government has no incentive to follow the law in collecting evidence.

C. Defendants should be informed of their rights so they can knowingly choose to exercise them or not to exercise them.

D. All of the above.

**17** *Mapp v. Ohio* is associated with which of the following?

A. Prior restraint

B. The *Miranda* warnings

C. Double jeopardy

D. Exclusionary rule

**18** The right to a counsel is associated with which of the following cases?

A. *Gideon v. Wainwright*

B. *Engel v. Vitale*

C. *Miranda v. Arizona*

D. *Mapp v. Ohio*

**19** *Employment Division v. Smith* dealt with which of the following issues?

A. Establishment of religion

B. Freedom of religion

C. School prayer

D. Abortion rights

**20** What branch of government has had the greatest impact on civil liberties policy formulation and adoption?

A. Judicial branch

B. Executive branch

C. Legislative branch

D. State governments have been more important than the national government

---

**KNOW** *the* **score**

18–20 correct: Congratulations! You are well informed!

15–17 correct: Your political knowledge is a bit low–be sure to review the key terms and visit TheThinkSpot.

<14 correct: Reread the chapter more thoroughly.

---

1. D; 2. A; 3. C; 4. A; 5. C; 6. C; 7. C; 8. D; 9. B; 10. D; 11. D; 12. A; 13. B; 14. A; 15. D; 16. B; 17. D; 18. A; 19. B; 20. A

# 16 CIVIL RIGHTS

The University of Michigan Law School is one of the most prestigious law schools in the nation. Each year it receives more than 3,500 applications, from which it selects a first-year class of 350 students. The law school looks for capable students who seem to promise success in the classroom and in the future profession of law. It also strives to admit a mixture of students with varying backgrounds and experiences who will learn from each other. In particular, the law school attempts to ensure that its student body is racially and ethnically diverse by enrolling a critical mass of students from groups that have historically suffered discrimination—especially African Americans, Latinos, and Native Americans. In order to achieve its admissions goals, the law school rejects some academically strong applicants in favor of other applicants who add diversity to its student body. Barbara Grutter was one such student rejected by the law school. Grutter, a white woman, had a college grade point average of 3.8 and a high score on the Law School Admissions Test (LSAT). When the law school rejected her application, Grutter accused it of favoring minority applicants who were less qualified academically. She filed suit, charging that the school discriminated against her on the basis of race in violation of the Fourteenth Amendment and the Civil Rights Act of 1964.[1] Did the University of Michigan Law School illegally discriminate against Barbara Grutter? We will explore the answer to that question as we study civil rights policy in Chapter 16.

# POLICYMAKING

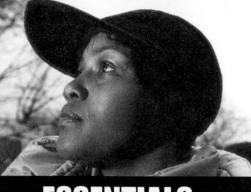

# the constitutional basis of civil rights POLICYMAKING

## ESSENTIALS...

after studying Chapter 16, students should be able to answer the following questions:

> What is the constitutional basis of civil rights policymaking?

> What is the history and current status of constitutional law regarding equality before the law, voting rights and representation, freedom from discrimination, sexual harassment, and affirmative action?

> What are the major factors affecting civil rights policymaking?

both the U.S. Constitution and state constitutions affect civil rights policymaking. The most important provisions dealing with civil rights in the U.S. Constitution are the Fourteenth and Fifteenth Amendments. The Fourteenth Amendment includes the **Equal Protection Clause:** "No State shall . . . deny to any person within its jurisdiction the equal protection of the laws." The Fifteenth Amendment declares that the right to vote "shall not be denied or abridged by the United States or by any State on account of race, color, or previous condition of servitude." Both the Fourteenth and Fifteenth Amendments contain sections granting Congress authority to pass legislation to enforce their provisions.

Most state constitutions include provisions prohibiting discrimination and/or guaranteeing equal protection of the laws. In recent years, a number of state supreme courts have interpreted their state constitutions to require equitable funding for public schools, guarantee equal rights for women, and, in Massachusetts and Connecticut, grant marriage rights to same-sex couples. In each of these cases, state courts adopted policy positions embracing a more expansive interpretation of civil rights than were taken at the time of writing either the U.S. Constitution or federal law.

**Equal Protection Clause** a provision of the Fourteenth Amendment of the U.S. Constitution that declares that "No State shall . . . deny to any person within its jurisdiction the equal protection of the laws."

Congress has a variety of caucuses, including (from left to right) the Asian Caucus, the Hispanic Caucus (with then-candidate Barack Obama), and the Black Caucus. These groups take a special interest in laws and programs that affect their constituents.

# civil rights issues
## AND POLICIES

**C**ivil rights is the protection of the individual from arbitrary or discriminatory acts, either by government or by other individuals, based on an individual's group status, such as race or gender. Whereas civil liberties issues involve individual rights, civil rights issues concern group rights. Civil liberties policy issues revolve around the rights of individuals to be free from unwarranted government restrictions on expression, religious belief, and personal liberty. Civil rights policy issues concern the relationship of the government to individuals based on their status as members of a group.

> THE COURT HAS RECOGNIZED THAT MOST DISTINCTIONS ARE NECESSARY AND DESIRABLE, AND HENCE PERMISSIBLE UNDER THE CONSTITUTION.

Civil rights issues are similar to civil liberties issues in that they are often constitutional issues. Although executives, legislatures, bureaucracies, interest groups, and political parties are all involved in civil rights issues, the courts, especially the Supreme Court of the United States, usually have the last word on the parameters of policymaking. Consequently, any discussion of civil rights issues focuses heavily on **constitutional law**, that is, law that involves the interpretation and application of the Constitution.

## Equality Before the Law

Although the Fourteenth Amendment guarantees individuals equal protection under the law, the Supreme Court has never required that laws deal with everyone and everything in precisely the same fashion. By their nature, laws distinguish among groups of people, types of property, and kinds of actions. The Court has recognized that most distinctions are necessary and desirable, and hence permissible under the Constitution. Only certain types of classifications that the Court considers arbitrary and discriminatory violate the Equal Protection Clause.

The Supreme Court has ruled that policy distinctions among persons based on their race, ethnicity, and citizenship status are **suspect classifications,** distinctions among persons that must be justified on the basis of a compelling government interest. The Supreme Court has

**civil rights** the protection of the individual from arbitrary or discriminatory acts by government or by individuals based on that person's group status, such as race and gender.

**constitutional law** law that involves the interpretation and application of the Constitution.

**suspect classifications** distinctions among persons that must be justified on the basis of a compelling government interest that cannot be achieved in a less restrictive fashion.

Even though Latinos, African Americans, and Asian Americans together make up 30 percent of the nation's population, only 15 percent of the members of Congress are minority.

declared that it will apply "strict judicial scrutiny" to any law that distinguishes among persons based on their race and ethnicity or citizenship. **Strict judicial scrutiny** is the judicial decision rule holding that the Supreme Court will find a government policy unconstitutional unless the government can demonstrate a compelling interest justifying the action. In other words, government cannot constitutionally adopt policies that treat people differently on the basis of race or citizenship status unless it can demonstrate an overriding public interest in making

that distinction. Furthermore, the government must prove that a policy that distinguishes among persons based on their race, ethnicity, or citizenship status is the least restrictive means for achieving the compelling policy objective.

The Supreme Court has chosen not to look so closely at laws that discriminate against persons on grounds other than race and ethnicity or citizenship status. It has held that government need only demonstrate some "reasonable basis" in order to justify public policies that distinguish among persons on the basis of such

factors as relative wealth, physical ability, marital status, residency, or sexual orientation. As for gender, the Court has ruled that the government must offer an "exceedingly persuasive justification" that gender-based distinctions are necessary to achieve some "important governmental objective." Commentators see this standard as somewhere between "compelling government interest" and "reasonable basis."[2]

**Racial Equality.** Although the Equal Protection Clause of the Fourteenth Amendment was intended to protect the civil rights of freed slaves, it initially did little to shelter African Americans from discrimination. In the late nineteenth and early twentieth centuries, southern state legislatures enacted **Jim Crow laws,** which were legal provisions requiring the social segregation of African Americans in separate and generally unequal facilities. Jim Crow Laws prohibited blacks from sharing schools, hospitals, hotels, restaurants, passenger railcars, and a wide range of other services and public facilities with whites.

Did Jim Crow laws violate the Equal Protection Clause? The U.S. Supreme Court addressed the question in 1896 in the famous case of *Plessy v. Ferguson.* Homer Plessy, an African American, purchased a first-class ticket on the East Louisiana Railway to travel from New Orleans to Covington, Louisiana, and took a seat in the rail car reserved for whites. He was arrested and charged

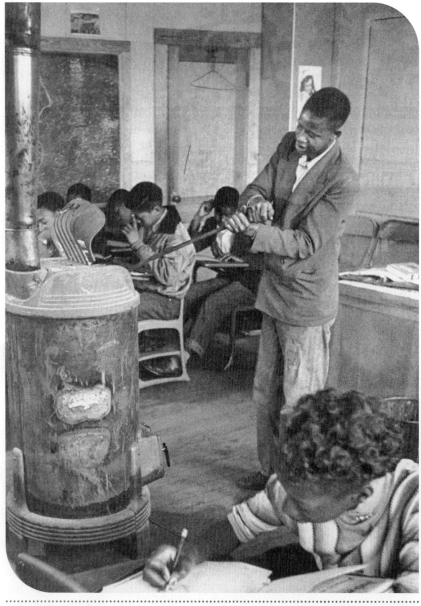

"Separate but Equal" schools were never equal for African American students. They were underfunded and neglected by white-run school boards.

**strict judicial scrutiny** the judicial decision rule holding that the Supreme Court will find a government policy unconstitutional unless the government can demonstrate a compelling interest justifying the action.

**Jim Crow laws** legal provisions requiring the social segregation of African Americans in separate and generally unequal facilities.

with violating a state law that prohibited members of either race from occupying accommodations set aside for the other. Plessy contended that the Louisiana law violated his rights under the U.S. Constitution to equal

**How important is it for children to attend schools that are racially diverse?**

protection. By an 8–1 vote, the U.S. Supreme Court ruled that the law was a reasonable exercise of the state's power, holding that states can require separate facilities for whites and African Americans as long as the facilities are equal. Thus, the Court adopted the policy known as **separate but equal,** the judicial doctrine holding that separate facilities for whites and African Americans satisfy the equal protection requirement of the Fourteenth Amendment... as long as the facilities are the same.[3]

The Supreme Court began to reassess the constitutional status of racial segregation in the late 1930s. The Court started chipping away at the *Plessy* precedent in 1938 in *Missouri ex rel Gaines v. Canada*, the beginning of a long line of test cases brought by the National Association for the Advancement of Colored People (NAACP). A **test case** is a lawsuit initiated to assess the constitutionality of a legislative or executive act. Gaines, who was an African American citizen of Missouri, applied to attend the University of Missouri law school. The state denied him admission, but offered to pay his tuition at a law school in a neighboring state where he could be accepted. Gaines sued, charging that

the arrangement violated the Equal Protection Clause, and the Court agreed. Separate but equal had to be in the same state.[4]

The Supreme Court further undermined *Plessy* in two cases decided in 1950. In *Sweatt v. Painter*, it ruled that Texas's hasty creation of an African American law school did not satisfy the constitutional criterion of equal protection.[5] In *McLaurin v. Oklahoma State Regents*, the Court ruled against segregation within an institution. The University of Oklahoma admitted G. W. McLaurin, an African American

**separate but equal** the judicial doctrine holding that separate facilities for whites and African Americans satisfy the equal protection requirement of the Fourteenth Amendment.

**test case** a lawsuit initiated to assess the constitutionality of a legislative or executive act.

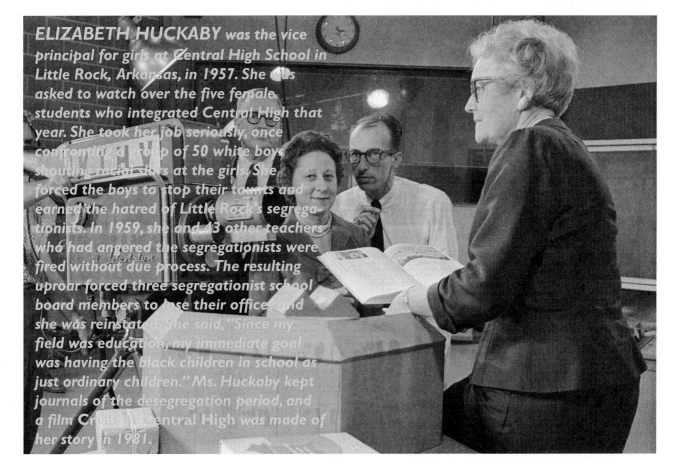

ELIZABETH HUCKABY *was the vice principal for girls at Central High School in Little Rock, Arkansas, in 1957. She was asked to watch over the five female students who integrated Central High that year. She took her job seriously, once confronting a group of 50 white boys shouting racial slurs at the girls. She forced the boys to stop their taunts and earned the hatred of Little Rock's segregationists. In 1959, she and 43 other teachers who had angered the segregationists were fired without due process. The resulting uproar forced three segregationist school board members to lose their offices, and she was reinstated. She said, "Since my field was education, my immediate goal was having the black children in school as just ordinary children." Ms. Huckaby kept journals of the desegregation period, and a film Crisis at Central High was made of her story in 1981.*

man, to graduate school but forced him to sit in a particular seat, study in a particular carrel in the library, and eat at a particular table in the cafeteria—all labeled, "Reserved for Colored." The Supreme Court ordered that McLaurin be treated like other students.[6]

In 1954, the Court took the final step, unanimously overturning *Plessy* with the landmark decision known as *Brown v. Board of Education of Topeka*. The case involved a lawsuit brought by the parents of Linda Brown, an African American youngster who was denied admission to a "whites only" school near her home. The Court ruled that racial segregation mandated by law denied African American students equal educational opportunity. "Segregation of white and colored children in public schools has a detrimental effect upon the colored children," wrote Chief Justice Earl Warren in the Court's majority opinion. The Court declared that "separate but equal" was a contradiction in terms. Once the law requires racial separation, it stamps the badge of inferiority on the minority race.[7]

The *Brown* decision may have been the most important judicial ruling of the twentieth century, but it left two important questions unanswered. One concerned the distinction between *de jure* and *de facto* segregation. **De jure segregation** means racial separation required by law, whereas **de facto segregation** is racial separation resulting from factors other than law, such as housing patterns. In *Brown*, the Court ruled that *de jure* segregation was unconstitutional, but it left the issue of *de facto* segregation undecided. The second problem left unsettled by *Brown* was implementation. How was desegregation to be achieved

and at what pace? The Court delayed its implementation decision until 1955, when it ordered the lower federal courts to oversee the transition to a nondiscriminatory system "with all deliberate speed."[8]

For years, *Brown* was a hollow victory for civil rights forces. Congress did nothing. President Dwight Eisenhower stood silent. The president finally took action in 1957, ordering federal troops into Little Rock, Arkansas, to enforce a school desegregation order against a stubborn Governor Orval Faubus and an angry mob. Nonetheless, a decade after the *Brown* decision, only 1 percent of African American students living in the South attended public schools that were not racially segregated.[9]

**THE END OF LEGAL SEGREGATION HAS NOT NECESSARILY BROUGHT ABOUT MEANINGFUL RACIAL INTEGRAGATION.**

The civil rights movement of the 1960s succeeded in rallying support for the cause of African American civil rights. African American protest demonstrations, vividly displayed on the television evening news, moved public opinion to support the cause. Presidents John Kennedy and Lyndon Johnson called for action, and Congress responded with the Civil Rights Act of 1964, which authorized the government to cut off federal money to school districts practicing segregation. The department set guidelines and some progress took place. Furthermore, the Supreme Court lost patience with the slow pace of school desegregation, declaring an end to "all deliberate speed" and ordering immediate

**de jure segregation** racial separation required by law.

**de facto segregation** racial separation resulting from factors other than law, such as housing patterns.

PUBLIC SCHOOL ENROLLMENT BY RACE/ETHNICITY

| | White | Black | Latino | Asian | American Indian |
|---|---|---|---|---|---|
| 1990–1991 | 67% | 16% | 12% | 4% | 1% |
| 2005–2006 | 57% | 17% | 20% | 5% | 1% |

NCES Common Core of Data

# U.S. Black Student Population:
## Percentage in Intensely Segregated Minority Schools (less than 10% white)

| Year | % |
|------|-----|
| 1968 | 64 |
| 1980 | 33 |
| 1988 | 32 |
| 1991 | 34 |
| 2005 | 38 |

More than 50 years after *Brown v. Board of Education*, many public schools, especially in urban areas, remain racially segregated.

NCES Common Core of Data

Orfield, Gary and Lee, Chungmei. "Historic Reversals, Accelerating Resegregation, and the Need for New Integration Strategies." A report of the Civil Rights Project, UCLA, August 2007.

desegregation.[10] By the 1972–1973 school year, a majority of African American students living in the South attended integrated schools.[11]

The Court's decision to order an end to racial segregation forced the justices to deal with the issues left unresolved by the original *Brown* case. How could integration be achieved? In *Swann v. Charlotte-Mecklenburg Board of Education* (1971), the Court unanimously held that busing, racial quotas, school pairing or grouping, and gerrymandered attendance zones could all be used to eliminate the vestiges of state-supported segregation.[12] Two years later, the Court expanded the definition of *de jure* segregation to include segregation fostered by administrative policies even in the absence of segregation laws. Consequently, the Court ordered the integration of Denver schools, not because they were segregated by force of law, but because the local school board had manipulated attendance zones to create one-race schools.[13]

Today, racial segregation no longer has a legal basis. Few issues of constitutional law are more firmly established than the principle that any law or procedural requirement compelling the physical separation of people by race or ethnicity is unconstitutional. The old Jim Crow laws are now all gone, either repealed or rendered unenforceable by court rulings.

Nonetheless, the end of legal segregation has not necessarily brought about meaningful racial integration in the public schools. Today, African American and Latino students have less contact with white students than their counterparts had in 1970, and most African American and Latino children attend schools where their racial/ethnic group is in the majority.[14] Racial segregation in the schools is growing because of a major increase in enrollment by minority students, continued migration of white families from urban neighborhoods, and housing patterns that isolate racial and ethnic groups.

Furthermore, the Supreme Court is no longer willing to order state and local officials to act aggressively to achieve racial integration.[15] In *Millikin v. Bradley* (1974), the Court ruled that a district judge in Michigan lacked authority to order student busing between Detroit's predominantly African American inner-city school district and 53 predominantly white suburban school districts. Suburban school districts could not be forced to help desegregate a city's schools unless the suburbs had been involved in illegally segregating them in the first place.[16]

In *Missouri v. Jenkins* (1995), the Supreme Court overturned a district court order requiring the state of Missouri to pay for a plan to upgrade predominantly African American schools in Kansas City, Missouri. The goal of the district court order had been to improve the inner-city schools in hopes of enticing white parents who live in the suburbs to voluntarily send their children to the inner city. The Supreme Court held that local desegregation plans could not go beyond the purpose of eliminating racial discrimination.[17]

Finally, in *Parents Involved in Community Schools v. Seattle School District No. 1* (2007), a closely divided Supreme Court struck down a Seattle school assignment procedure that used race as a "tiebreaker" in making student assignments to high schools, even though the goal of the plan was to achieve racial integration rather than segregation.[18] Instead of using the *Brown* precedent to further efforts to achieve racial integration of public schools, the Court declared that *Brown* required school districts to follow color-blind school assignment policies.

**Other Equal Protection Issues.** Not all equal-protection claims involve African Americans or school desegregation. The Supreme Court has declared that citizenship status is a suspect classification similar to race, justifiable only by a compelling government interest. For example, the Court has struck down state laws that prohibited non-citizen permanent residents from becoming lawyers, engineers, or notary publics, and ruled that states may not deny legal residents who are not

IN 1996, THE SUPREME COURT ISSUED ITS FIRST EQUAL-PROTECTION RULING FAVORING GAY AND LESBIAN RIGHTS.

citizens the opportunity to apply for financial aid for higher education.[19] In each case, the Court ruled that the government had failed to establish that it had a compelling interest in making the distinction. In contrast, the Court has held that states do indeed have a compelling interest in excluding non-citizens from playing a role in government, either by voting, running for office, or working as police officers.

Over the last 30 years, the Supreme Court has begun to look closely at claims of gender discrimination. Although the Court has not added gender to its list of suspect classifications, it has required that

**Is the male-only draft registration requirement gender discrimination?**

state governments prove that sex-based distinctions are necessary to achieve some "important governmental objective." The Court has also declared that the government must offer an "exceedingly persuasive justification" for gender-based distinctions if they are to be held constitutional.[20] The Court ruled, for example, that the Virginia Military Institute (VMI), a state-supported military university, could not constitutionally exclude women, and that the state's offer to create a separate military college for women was unacceptable. The Court held that the state of the Virginia had failed to show an exceedingly persuasive justification for maintaining a male-only university.[21] Nonetheless, the Court still upholds some gender-based laws, such as Congress's decision to exclude women from having to register for military service, on the basis of traditional attitudes about the respective roles of men and women in society.[22]

In 1996, the Supreme Court issued its first equal-protection ruling favoring gay and lesbian rights in the case of *Romer v. Evans*. The legal dispute concerned a challenge to an amendment to the constitution of Colorado approved by state voters in 1992. Amendment Two, as it was known, not only repealed all local ordinances and statewide policies protecting gay men and lesbians

from discrimination, but also prohibited the future enactment of similar measures. The Supreme Court declared that the state of Colorado would have to demonstrate that the amendment bore a rational relationship to some legitimate end in order to meet the requirements of the Equal Protection Clause. The amendment was so broadly drawn, however, that the only logical explanation for its enactment was animosity toward gay men and lesbians. The real purpose of the measure was evidently "to make homosexuals unequal to everyone else," which, the Court said, is not a legitimate goal of state government. Consequently, Amendment Two violated the Equal Protection Clause of the Fourteenth Amendment.[23]

## Voting Rights and Representation

Although the right to vote is a fundamental civil right, universal adult **suffrage** (the right to vote) is a relatively recent development in the United States. The original Constitution (Article I, Section 2) allowed the states to establish voter qualifications, and initially most states limited the right to vote to adult white males who owned property. Popular pressure forced states to drop the property qualification in the early decades of the nineteenth century. Women won the right to vote with the ratification of the Nineteenth Amendment in 1920.

The struggle for voting rights for African Americans was particularly difficult despite the Fifteenth Amendment, which declared that the right to vote could not be abridged on account of race or

**suffrage** the right to vote.

# Taking Sides

JAMES BYRD, JR.
MAY 2, 1949
JUNE 7, 1998
MY BELOVED SON

# Hate-Crimes Legislation

**Is hate-crimes legislation necessary? Is it acceptable to punish people for their thoughts or feelings?**

**What are other possible ways to prevent crimes that are motivated by hate or ignorance? Is education the answer?**

**Overview:** On June 7, 1998, James Byrd was dragged to death behind a pickup truck simply because he was black. On October 12, 1998, Matthew Shepard was brutally beaten and left to die of exposure in the cold Wyoming night air because he was gay. On December 7, 2000, in Wichita, Kansas, two black brothers began a week-long crime spree that resulted in the vicious murders of five white victims. The common thread connecting these brutal crimes is that they occurred, or were made worse, because of race or sexual orientation of the victims.

It follows that hate-crimes legislation may provide a deterrent and could help prevent crimes against others based on race, sex, religion, or sexual orientation. Americans have a right to be secure in their person and identity. Hate-crimes legislation helps secure these rights.

Should hate-crimes legislation be enforced by the federal government? The U.S. Supreme Court gave sanction to hate-crimes legislation in *Wisconsin v. Mitchell* (1993) when it upheld Wisconsin's statute imposing harsher sentences if the victim was chosen due to race, religion, national origin, and so forth. A further 44 states have hate-crimes legislation in place. Does the principle of federalism give the states the right to determine and enforce criminal statutes? If so, how can minorities have protection and security and be treated equally? Did it not take federal action to ensure social and political equality?

## supporting hate-crimes legislation

**hate crimes have a unique character compared to other crimes.** Enhancement and hate crimes statutes recognize that hate crimes have a special psychological and emotional impact not only on victims, but on the victim's community as well. Hate crimes intimidate, induce fear and anxiety, and leave minority communities feeling isolated and vulnerable.

**in a pluralistic society, hate crimes cannot be tolerated.** Hate crimes violate the social contract and have the effect of fragmenting society. In a society based on the principles of tolerance and equality, tacit acceptance of hate crimes can lead to the idea that some communities are somehow inferior and not worthy of majority protection.

**hate-crimes legislation is necessary in post–9/11 America.** As we have learned from the internment of Japanese Americans during World War II, legislation is necessary to protect the rights and freedoms of Americans of Middle Eastern descent in post-9/11 America. During times of national crisis, such as the war on terror, it is imperative that all Americans be protected from the misguided ideas and passions of a certain few.

## against hate-crimes legislation

**in many cases it is difficult to prove hateful motivation for a criminal act.** Instead of legislation defining hateful acts and crimes, it is the proper role of juries to determine intent when an offender commits a crime.

**those who perpetrate hate crimes are punished for their actions.** The murderers of James Byrd, Matthew Shepard, and the five innocents in Wichita have been sentenced either to death or to life in prison. How can hate-crimes legislation be a deterrent when, depending on the state, the maximum penalties for violent crime are already the death penalty and life in prison?

**hate-crimes legislation violates the principle of freedom of thought.** A crime is a crime no matter what the thought behind the action. No matter how distasteful or offensive, bigoted or racist thought is, hate-crimes legislation has the effect of criminalizing thought, which is a violation of basic freedom.

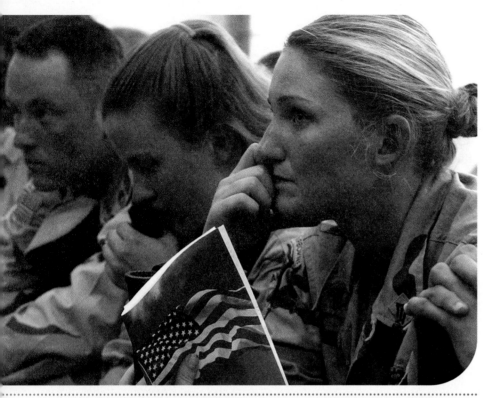

These female GIs are stationed at Wagram Air Base near Kabul, Afghanistan. Women, who make up 15 percent of military personnel, now serve in most areas of the U.S. military, but they are prohibited from serving in ground combat units, including armor, artillery, infantry, and special forces units.

color. In the late nineteenth and early twentieth centuries, Southern white authorities adopted an array of devices designed to prevent African Americans from exercising meaningful voting rights. Disfranchisement methods included tests of understanding, literacy tests, the white primary, grandfather clauses, and poll taxes. **Disfranchisement** is the denial of voting rights.

The **white primary** was an electoral system used in the South to prevent the participation of African Americans in the Democratic primary. (A **primary election** is an intra-party election held to select party candidates for the general-election ballot.) Because Democrats dominated Southern politics from the 1870s through the 1950s, the Democratic Party primary was, by far, the most important election in most Southern states. By excluding African Americans from the Democratic primary, Southern officials effectively prevented them from participating meaningfully in

state politics. The Supreme Court invalidated the white primary in 1944.[24]

Tests of understanding, literacy tests, and poll taxes were often used in combination with a grandfather clause. A **test of understanding** was a legal requirement that citizens must accurately explain a passage in the United States or state constitution before they could register to vote. A **literacy test** was a legal requirement that citizens demonstrate an ability to read and write before they could register to vote. A **poll tax** was a tax levied on the right to vote. A **grandfather clause** was a provision that exempted those persons whose grandfathers had been eligible to vote at some earlier date from tests of understanding, literacy tests, and other difficult-to-achieve voter qualification requirements. The effect of the grandfather clause was to allow prospective white voters to escape voter requirements used to discourage or disqualify prospective African American voters.

**disfranchisement** the denial of voting rights.

**white primary** an electoral system used in the South to prevent the participation of African Americans in the Democratic primary.

**primary election** an election held to determine a party's nominees for the general election ballot.

**test of understanding** a legal requirement that citizens must accurately explain a passage in the U.S. Constitution or state constitution before they could register to vote.

**literacy test** a legal requirement that citizens demonstrate an ability to read and write before they could register to vote.

**poll tax** tax levied on the right to vote.

**grandfather clause** a provision that exempted those persons whose grandfathers had been eligible to vote at some earlier date from tests of understanding, literacy tests, and other difficult-to-achieve voter qualification requirements.

Although the Supreme Court invalidated the grandfather clause in 1915,[25] tests of understanding, literacy tests, and poll taxes survived constitutional challenge for decades. The Court finally knocked down the use of tests of understanding in 1965, holding that they were often used to deny African Americans the right to vote.[26] In the same year, Congress passed, and the president signed, legislation that suspended the use of literacy tests throughout the South. Five years later, Congress extended the ban on literacy tests to the entire nation. The poll tax lasted until the mid-1960s. The Twenty-fourth Amendment, ratified in 1964, eliminated the use of poll taxes for elections to federal office.

In 1966, the Supreme Court held that the poll tax was an unconstitutional requirement for voting in state and local elections as well.[27]

## Freedom from Discrimination

Civil rights concerns the protection of the individual, not just against government action, but also against discrimination by *private* parties, such as hotels, restaurants, theaters, and business firms. Most individual rights claims against private discrimination are based on **statutory law,** law written by a legislature, rather than constitutional law.

After the Civil War, Congress enacted two important laws designed to protect the civil rights of former slaves. The Civil Rights Act of 1866 declared that citizens "of every race and color" were enti-

tled "to make and enforce contracts, to sue . . ., give evidence, to inherit, purchase, lease, sell, hold, and convey real and personal property."[28] The Civil Rights Act of 1875 declared that "all persons within the jurisdiction of the United States shall be entitled to the full and equal enjoyment of the accommodations . . . of inns, public conveyances on land or water, theaters, and other places of public amusement."[29]

In the *Civil Rights Cases* (1883), however, the U.S. Supreme Court found the Civil Rights Act of 1875 unconstitutional. These cases involved disputes over theaters that would not seat African Americans, hotels and restaurants that would

not serve African Americans, and a train that refused to seat an African American woman in the "ladies" car. The Court held that the Fourteenth Amendment protected individuals from discrimination by government but not by private parties.[30] The Court's decision in the *Civil Rights Cases* opened the door for private individuals, businesses, and organizations to discriminate in housing, employment, and a broad range of public accommodations.

It took civil rights forces more than 80 years to overcome the precedent set in the *Civil Rights Cases*.

**statutory law** law that is written by the legislature.

# VOTiNG RiGHTS

**1776 | most states limit suffrage to white men with property.**

**1920 | the Nineteenth Amendment, adopted by Congress on June 4, 1919, is ratified by the states, giving women the right to vote.**

**1944 | the U.S. Supreme Court rules in *Smith v. Allwright* that the white primary system in Texas is unconstitutional.**

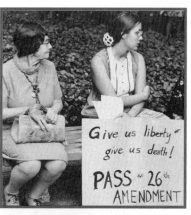

**1971 | the Twenty-sixth Amendment gives 18-year-olds the right to vote.**

| 1776 | 1870 | 1915 | 1920 | 1944 | 1964 | 1965 | 1971 |

**1870 | the Fifteenth Amendment is ratified by the states, guaranteeing male freed slaves and other African American men the right to vote.**

**1915 | the U.S. Supreme Court rules in *Guinn v. United States* that Oklahoma's "grandfather clause," which is used to disfranchise black men, is unconstitutional.**

**1964 | poll taxes are outlawed with the adoption of the Twenty-fourth Amendment.**

**Congress passes and President Lyndon B. Johnson signs the Civil Rights Act of 1964, making it illegal to discriminate on the basis of race, national origin, religion, or gender in voting, public accommodations, the workplace, and schools.**

**1965 | Congress passes and President Johnson signs the Voting Rights Act into law, permanently barring direct barriers to political participation by racial and ethnic minorities.**

Consider the problem of **racially restrictive covenants,** which were private deed restrictions that prohibited property owners from selling or leasing property to African Americans or other minorities. The NAACP finally succeeded in undercutting restrictive covenants in *Shelley v. Kraemer,* a test case that reached the Supreme Court in 1948. The Court held that private contracts calling for discrimination could be written, but state courts could not constitutionally enforce them because enforcement would make the state a party to discrimination.[31]

Civil rights forces used litigation and legislation to attack other forms of private discrimination. In the late 1950s and early 1960s, African American activists staged sit-ins at segregated dime store lunch counters and refused to leave until served. Local police would arrest the protesters, charging them with disturbing the peace or breaking a local Jim Crow ordinance. With NAACP legal assistance, the demonstrators would appeal their convictions to

## Civil rights forces used litigation and legislation to attack other forms of private discrimination.

the federal courts, where they would be reversed and the local segregation ordinance overturned. This case-by-case approach desegregated many public facilities, but it was slow and expensive.

The Civil Rights Act of 1964 was a more efficient tool for fighting discrimination. Title II of the act outlawed discrimination based on race, religion, color, sex, or national origin in hotels, restaurants, gas stations, and other public accommodations. Congress based Title II on the Interstate Commerce Clause in order to overcome the precedent set in the *Civil Rights Cases* that the Fourteenth Amendment prohibits discrimination by the government but not discrimination by private individuals and firms. The **Interstate Commerce Clause** is the constitutional provision giving Congress authority to "regulate commerce . . . among the several states." Because hotels, restaurants, gas stations, and the like serve individuals traveling from state to state, and because they purchase products that have been shipped in interstate commerce, Congress reasoned that they are part of interstate commerce and, consequently, subject to regulation by Congress. In *Heart of Atlanta Motel v. United States* and *Katzenbach v. McClung* (1964), the Supreme Court upheld the constitutionality of Congress's action.[32]

Congress and the president have enacted legislation extending civil rights protection to groups based on criteria other than race, religion, color, gender, or national origin. The **Americans with Disabilities Act (ADA)** is a federal law in-

tended to end discrimination against disabled persons and to eliminate barriers to their full participation in American society. Other federal legislation prohibits age discrimination and protects families with children from housing discrimination. Title IX of the Education Amendments of 1972 is a federal law that prohibits gender discrimination in programs at educational institutions that receive federal funds. Because of Title IX, high schools, colleges, and universities have expanded athletic opportunities for women.

The Civil Rights Act of 1991 dealt with hiring practices that are not overtly discriminatory but which, nonetheless, limit employment opportunities for women and minorities. Suppose a city government requires prospective police officers to stand at least 5'5" tall. That requirement would disproportionately reduce the number of women eligible to apply for jobs because women are typically shorter than

**racially restrictive covenants** private deed restrictions that prohibited property owners from selling or leasing property to African Americans or other minorities.

**Interstate Commerce Clause** the constitutional provision giving Congress authority to "regulate commerce . . . among the several states."

**Americans with Disabilities Act (ADA)** a federal law designed to end discrimination against persons with disabilities and eliminate barriers to their full participation in American society.

men. The Civil Rights Act of 1991 declared that hiring practices that have a disproportionate impact on women and minorities must be "job-related for the position in question and consistent with business necessity." The city's height requirement for police officers would

be illegal unless the city could show that a height of at least 5'5" was necessary to do the job. Furthermore, the Civil Rights Act of 1991 allowed women, minorities, and the disabled to sue for monetary damages in cases of intentional job discrimination and harassment.

State and local governments have also adopted policies protecting various groups from discrimination. Many state and local governments offer protections from discrimination based on race, ethnicity, gender, age, color, national origin, and

disability, similar to those contained in federal law. Some state and local governments go beyond federal law, offering protection from discrimination based on sexual orientation and sexual identify (to protect transgendered persons from discrimination). A number of states have

In 2008, **Congress passed, and** President George W. Bush signed, **the** Genetic Information Non-discrimination Act. It prohibited health insurance companies **from using genetic information to deny benefits or to raise premiums. It also** prohibited employers **from using genetic information to make employment decisions.**

enacted legislation to allow gay men and lesbians to form **civil unions,** legal partnerships between two men or two women that give the couple all the benefits, protections, and responsibilities under law that are granted to spouses in a traditional marriage. Other states allow same-sex couples and opposite sex

couples to create a **domestic partnership,** a legal status similar to civil unions in that it confers rights similar to marriage. Connecticut and Massachusetts allow gay marriage.

## Sexual Harassment

The male chief executive officer (CEO) of a large organization invites a young, female employee of the organization to meet him in private. He allegedly exposes his genitals to her and asks for sexual favors. The young woman refuses. The alleged incident is a one-time-only event. The CEO does not threaten the female employee with retaliation, and, in fact, she continues her career in the organization without suffering any apparent penalty. Does the alleged event constitute sexual harassment under the law?

The legal concept of sexual harassment is based on federal laws prohibiting gender discrimination in employment.[33] The courts have held

**civil union** a legal partnership between two men or two women that gives the couple all the benefits, protections, and responsibilities under law as are granted to spouses in a traditional marriage.

**domestic partnership** a legal status similar to civil unions in that it confers rights similar to marriage.

**btw...**

Harvey Milk, as played by Sean Penn in 2008's *Milk*, was the first openly gay man to be elected to public office in the United States. Largely through his efforts on the San Francisco County Board of Supervisors, the city council passed a gay rights ordinance in 1978 that protected gay men and lesbians from employment discrimination.

# Women's Rights in Saudi Arabia

Women in Saudi Arabia have limited legal rights. Under Saudi law, which is based on a conservative interpretation of Islam, women are socially and legally dependent on their male guardians—their fathers at birth and their spouses upon marriage. Women cannot even have their own legal identity cards. Their names are added to their father's identify card when they are born and transferred to their husband's identity card when they marry. As a result, a woman cannot travel, purchase property, or enroll in college without the written permission of a male relative.[34]

The Saudi government encourages women to be stay-at-home mothers. Women must cover themselves fully in public and wear a veil. They cannot attend classes with men or work with men. Women's education is aimed at making women better wives and mothers.

Women cannot study law or become pilots. Instead, they are directed toward occupations deemed suitable for their gender, such as teaching in a girls' school. Women are not allowed to vote or to drive a vehicle. Women who fail to conform to societal norms are subject to harassment by the religious police. They may be arrested, imprisoned, and even caned.

Nonetheless, Saudi Arabia has a women's rights movement. Many Saudi women are aware of the status of women in other countries, including Muslim countries, because of the Internet, satellite TV, and travel abroad, and they are demanding better treatment. Young Saudi women in particular, who are better educated than most of the older women, are challenging their society's conservative interpretation of Islam. They are demanding access to education and employment opportunities.

The Saudi government has made some concessions to women's rights. Women are now permitted to stay in a hotel alone without the presence of a male relative. Even though some leading universities continue to admit only men, women now constitute a majority of university students.[35] The Saudi government is also reportedly considering lifting the ban against women driving.[36]

## Questions

1. Is the treatment of women in Saudi Arabia a concern for people around the world, or should it be an internal matter for the Saudis alone to address?

2. Should the United States pressure Saudi Arabia to improve the status of women?

3. Do you think most women in Saudi Arabia are comfortable with their legal and social status?

Although Saudi women cannot drive, they can own cars. These two saleswomen work in a women-only car dealership in Saudi Arabia.

that employers who sexually harass their employees or permit sexual harassment in the workplace are guilty of illegal employment discrimination. Sexual harassment can be male–female, female–male, male–male, or female–female.[37]

The federal courts have identified two categories of sexual harassment: *quid pro quo* harassment and harassment based on a hostile environment. *Quid pro quo* harassment involves a supervisor threatening an employee with retaliation unless the employee submits to sexual advances. "You either sleep with me, or you are fired," is a clear and blatant example of *quid pro quo* sexual harassment. Defining sexual harassment based on a hostile environment is more difficult. Even though no sexual demands are made, an employer may be guilty of sexual harassment if an employee is subjected to sexual conduct and comments that are pervasive and severe enough to affect the employee's job performance. A supervisor who continues to ask a subordinate for a date despite repeated rejections may be guilty of creating a hostile work environment.

Was the CEO in our above example guilty of sexual harassment if, of course, the alleged incident actually occurred? A federal judge threw the case out of court, declaring that the alleged incident, even if true, did not constitute illegal sexual harassment. No threat of retaliation occurred, so the incident could not have constituted *quid pro quo* harassment. Because the alleged incident was an isolated occurrence, the judge ruled that the employee was not subjected to a hostile work environment. The woman appealed the ruling, however, and rather than risk losing on appeal, the CEO agreed to pay her a settlement of $850,000 in exchange for her dropping the lawsuit. Incidentally, the CEO of the large organization was Bill Clinton, who was then governor of Arkansas. The young female employee was Paula Jones.

## Affirmative Action

**Affirmative action,** which refers to steps taken by colleges, universities, and employers to remedy the effects of past discrimination, is controversial. The proponents of race- and gender-based preferences believe they are necessary to remedy the effects of past discrimination. Colleges and universities assert that they benefit from a diverse student body. Employers value a diverse workforce. In contrast, the opponents of racial and gender preferences argue that the only fair way to determine college admissions and employment decisions is merit. It is wrong, they say, to hire or promote someone simply because of race or gender.

Federal government efforts to remedy the effects of discrimination began in the early 1960s. Presidents Kennedy and Johnson ordered affirmative action in federal employment and hiring by government contractors, but their orders had little practical effect until the late 1960s, when the Department of Labor began requiring government contractors to employ certain percentages of women and minorities. For the following decade, affirmative action took on a momentum all its own. For some, affirmative action meant nondiscrimination. For others, it required seeking out qualified women and minorities. For still others, affirmative action stood for hiring set percentages of women and minorities—a quota system. All the while, employers kept careful records of how many women and minority group members were part of their operations.

The election of Ronald Reagan as president in 1980 was a major setback for the proponents of affirmative action. During the Reagan administration, the Equal Employment Opportunity Commission (EEOC), under the leadership of Clarence Thomas, dismantled affirmative action programs and anything that resembled a quota system for women and minorities. In Reagan's view, civil rights laws should offer relief, not to whole

> colleges and universities **assert** that they benefit from a *diverse student body*

## The Gender Gap in Wages

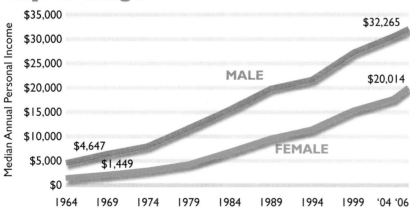

Despite significant gains over the last half century, the median annual income for women is still approximately $12,000 less than that of men.

U.S. Census Bureau, "Median Income of People in Current and Constant (2006) Dollars by Race and Hispanic Origin," *The 2009 Statistical Abstract*, available at www.census.gov.

**affirmative action** steps taken by colleges, universities, and private employers to remedy the effects of past discrimination.

groups of people, but only to specific individuals who could prove that they were victims of discrimination. Hiring goals, timetables, and racial quotas, the administration argued, were reverse discrimination against whites. Reagan's most lasting impact on affirmative action was in the judicial branch of government. Reagan appointees, later reinforced by justices appointed by President George H. W. Bush, created a Supreme Court majority that shared Reagan's conservative philosophy on affirmative action issues.

In *City of Richmond v. J. A. Croson Co.* (1989), the Supreme Court put many affirmative policies in constitutional jeopardy. The *Croson* case dealt with a minority business set-aside program for municipal construction contracts established by the city of Richmond, Virginia. A **minority business set-aside** is a legal requirement that firms receiving government grants or contracts allocate a certain percentage of their purchases of supplies and services to businesses owned or controlled by members of minority groups. Even though African Americans constituted half of Richmond's population, less than 1 percent of city government construction dollars had typically gone to minority-owned firms. In light of this history, the city council passed an ordinance requiring that prime contractors awarded city construction contracts over the following five years must subcontract at least 30 percent of the dollar amount of their contracts to one or more minority-business enterprises.

**minority business set-aside** a legal requirement that firms receiving government grants or contracts allocate a certain percentage of their purchases of supplies and services to businesses owned or controlled by members of minority groups.

Richmond's minority business set-aside program soon became the target of litigation. J. A. Croson Co., a contracting company whose bid for a city project was rejected for failing to meet the minority set-aside, filed suit against the ordinance, charging that it was unconstitutional. The U.S. Supreme Court ruled that Richmond's set-aside ordinance unconstitutionally violated the Equal Protection Clause of the Fourteenth Amendment because it denied, based solely on their race, certain persons an opportunity to compete for a fixed percentage of city contracts. The most significant aspect of the *Croson* decision was that the Court applied strict judicial scrutiny to race-conscious efforts to remedy the effects of past discrimination. The Court's majority opinion declared that although minority set-aside programs can be justified as a remedy for discrimination in some instances, the Richmond city council failed to demonstrate a specific history of discrimination in the city's construction industry sufficient to justify a race-based program of relief. The mere fact that few city construction contracts had gone to minority firms was not sufficient evidence to prove discrimination either by the city government or in the city's construction industry. The Court also held that Richmond's set-aside program was constitutionally unacceptable because it was not narrowly tailored to achieve any goal except "outright racial balancing." The plan gave absolute preference to minority entrepreneurs from anywhere in the country, not just the Richmond area. Furthermore, the Court said, the program made no effort to determine whether particular minority businesspersons seeking a racial preference had themselves suffered the effects of discrimination.[38]

The Supreme Court dealt with affirmative action in college admissions in *Regents of the University of California v. Bakke* (1978). Allan Bakke, a white male, sued the university after he was denied admission to medical school. The university had a minority admissions program in which it set aside 16 of 100 places each year for minority applicants. Because he was not allowed to compete for any of the slots reserved for minority applicants, Bakke charged that he was the victim of illegal racial discrimination, and the Court agreed. The Court ordered Bakke admitted, saying that a numerical quota for minority admissions violated the Equal Protection Clause of the Fourteenth Amendment. The Court added, however, that race and ethnicity could be considered as one of several factors in admissions decisions as a "plus factor" in an individualized admissions process.[39]

The Supreme Court reaffirmed the *Bakke* precedent in the University of Michigan Law School case discussed in the introduction to this chapter. The Court ruled that the university, which is a government agency, could consider race in its admissions program because the government has a compelling interest in promoting racial and ethnic diversity in higher education. Ms. Grutter lost her case.[40] In the meantime, the Court struck down an undergraduate admissions program at the same university because it assigned applicants a set number of points if they happened to be members of an underrepresented minority group—Latinos, African Americans, or Native Americans. The Court ruled that the undergraduate admissions process violated the Constitution because, unlike the law school process, it was not narrowly tailored to achieve the goal of diversity.[41]

| Population | White | Black | Hispanic |
|---|---|---|---|
| Population | 198.7 million | 36.7 million | 44.3 million |
| % married couples (of households) | 52.7 | 28.9 | 50.4 |
| % adults 25+ with college degree | 30 | 17 | 12 |
| % births to unmarried women | 24 | 66 | 37 |
| % homeowner (of households) | 74 | 46.5 | 49.3 |
| Median household income | $52,423 | $31,969 | $37,781 |
| Poverty rate for individuals | 8.2 | 24.3 | 20.6 |
| % of population | 66 | 12 | 15 |
| % of prison inmates | 36 | 40 | 20 |

Source: U.S. Census Bureau 2006 Population Estimates, 2006 American Community Survey, U.S. Justice Department, 2006

# where do we stand today?

# CONCLUSION
# civil rights
# POLICYMAKING

the Constitution is the most important environmental factor affecting civil rights policymaking, just as it is for civil liberties. Affirmative action, school integration, voting rights, and other civil rights concerns are constitutional issues. Consequently, civil rights policies reflect the parameters of constitutional law.

The policy preferences of federal judges affect civil rights policymaking. Liberal judges are more likely than conservative judges to rule in favor of women and members of minority groups. In contrast, conservative judges are hesitant to expand constitutional rights. The appointment of relatively more conservative justices by recent Republican presidents has created a Supreme Court majority almost as skeptical of racial, ethnic, and gender preferences as it is of racial, ethnic, and gender discrimination. Because the current Court is closely divided on a number of civil rights issues, including affirmative action, the retirement of

one or two justices could have a major policy impact, depending, of course, on the judicial philosophy of their replacements.

Civil rights policymaking is affected by the presence of organized groups concerned with civil rights issues. For example, the adoption of policies favorable to gay and lesbian rights coincides with the appearance of homosexual rights organizations, such as the Human Rights Campaign. Laws protecting gay and lesbian rights are least common in the South, where conservative Christian groups opposed to gay and lesbian rights are influential.

Public opinion is another important element of the environment for civil rights policymaking. Survey research shows that Americans have grown more tolerant of racial and cultural diversity. As recently as the 1940s, a majority of white Americans supported racial segregation and discrimination, both in principle and in practice. By the 1970s, support for overt discrimination

## public opinion on affirmative action

"We should make every effort to improve the position of blacks and minorities, even if it means giving preferential treatment."

64 68 61 56 57

29 27
13 17 19

1987 1991 1993 1997 1999 2002 2007

african american agreement
white agreement

African Americans are considerably more likely to favor preferential treatment for minorities than are whites.

## public opinion on affirmative action

**White support for affirmative action is greater now than it was a decade ago, but it still lags well behind the level of support for affirmative action expressed by African Americans.**

### Favor affirmative action:

|  | 1995 | 2007 | % change |
|---|---|---|---|
| **TOTAL POP.** | 58 | 70 | +12 |
| **Black** | 94 | 93 | -1 |
| **White** | 53 | 65 | +12 |

Pew Research Center, *Trends in Political Values and Core Attitudes: 1987-2007*

had virtually vanished. Today, polls find that large majorities of Americans of all races and both genders oppose discrimination.[42] Nonetheless, whites and African Americans do not see eye to eye on the rate of minority progress. A recent public opinion survey found that 61 percent of African Americans say that there has been "no real progress for blacks in the last few years," compared with 31 percent of white Americans who take that position.[43]

## Agenda Building
Individuals, as well as groups, political parties, and the media, participate in setting the agenda for civil

rights policymaking. Susan B. Anthony, for example, was a leader of the movement for women's suffrage. Dr. Martin Luther King, Jr., was the foremost spokesperson for civil rights for African Americans during the 1960s. Linda Brown advanced the cause of civil rights issues by participating in a lawsuit.

gather signatures to put their pet policy issues on the ballot in states with the **initiative process,** which is a procedure available in some states and cities whereby citizens can propose the adoption of a policy measure by gathering a prerequisite number of signatures. Voters must then approve the measure before it

**initiative process** a procedure whereby citizens can prepare the adoption of a policy measure by gathering a prerequisite member of signatures. Voters must then approve the measure before it can take effect.

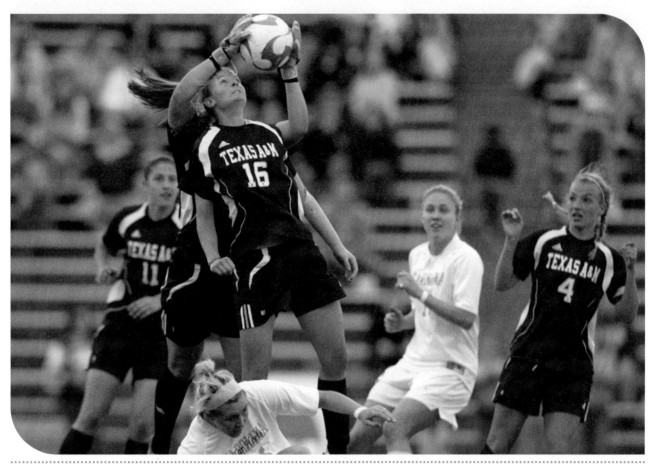

Title IX is a federal law that prohibits gender discrimination in programs at educational institutions that receive federal funds. Since Title IX became law in the early 1970s, the number of women on athletic scholarships at Division I colleges and universities has increased from fewer than a hundred to more than 65,000.

A number of groups help set the agenda for civil rights issues. The NAACP Legal Defense Fund, Mexican American Legal Defense and Education Fund (MALDEF), the National Organization for Women (NOW), and other groups raise civil rights issues by supporting lawsuits as test cases. Large national membership organizations, such as NOW, the NAACP, and the League of United Latin American Citizens (LULAC), lobby elected officials at the state and national levels to address their policy concerns. Groups

can take effect. After the Supreme Court upheld the University of Michigan Law School's affirmative action program, Barbara Gutter and other opponents of racial preferences gathered signatures to put the issue on the ballot and won. In November 2006, Michigan voters approved an amendment to the state constitution to prohibit state agencies and institutions from operating affirmative action programs that grant preferences based on race, color, ethnicity, national origin, or gender.[44]

Political parties often promote civil rights causes. The modern Democratic Party has adopted platforms supporting school integration, affirmative action, women's rights, equal employment opportunity, and gay and lesbian rights. All of these positions reflect alliances between the party and various interest groups and blocs of voters. African American, Latino, female, and gay and lesbian voters are a major part of the base of the Democratic Party. Although the Republican Party favors equal opportunity and

When an exam used to qualify firefighters for promotions in New Haven, CT, resulted in no eligible black candidates, the city threw out the results based on the test's disparate impact on a protected racial minority. The firefighters who passed the exam sued the city, and in its June 2009 decision in *Ricci v. DeStefano*, the Supreme Court held 5–4 that New Haven's decision to ignore the test results violated Title VII of the Civil Rights Act of 1964.

opposes discrimination based on race, ethnicity, or gender, the GOP is generally against affirmative action and opposes gay and lesbian rights. The Republican position reflects the views of the middle-income whites, who compose the core of GOP voters, and the conservative Christian groups that ally with the party.

The media play a role in setting the agenda for civil rights. News reports and media coverage of political demonstrations highlight issues that might otherwise receive relatively little notice. During the 1960s, for example, media coverage of political demonstrations in favor of black civil rights and the violent reaction to those demonstrations helped mobilize northern white public opinion in favor of the protesters.

## Policy Formulation and Adoption

Civil rights policy formulation and adoption may involve action by the president, Congress, the bureaucracy, local governments, private in-

dividuals, corporations, and the courts. Civil rights policies often take the form of legislation or executive orders. The ADA, for example, is a federal law which was passed by Congress and signed by the president. State and local governments adopt affirmative action plans, such as Richmond's minority business set-aside plan. Colleges and universities formulate and adopt admissions policies. Civil rights policies may sometimes take the form of executive orders. President Truman, for example, issued an executive order to racially integrate the armed forces.

Judicial decisions are not necessarily the last word in civil rights policymaking, especially when the courts base their rulings on the interpretation of statutory law. Congress, after all, can rewrite laws to overcome judicial objections. In 1984, for example, the Supreme Court severely restricted the impact of federal laws prohibiting discrimination on the basis of gender, race, age, or disability by institutions receiving federal

funds. The Court ruled that the law prohibited discrimination only by the *direct* recipient of the money.[45] Thus, if a university's chemistry department received federal funds but its athletic department did not, the latter would not be covered. Congress responded to the Court's decision by rewriting the law (and overriding President Reagan's veto in the process). Because athletic programs receive little if any federal money, most college athletic departments did not take Title IX seriously until Congress rewrote the law. In theory, a college or university that fails to comply with Title IX in athletics could lose federal funding for student scholarships and research grants.

## Policy Implementation and Evaluation

The implementation of civil rights policy falls to the executive branch of the national government, lower federal courts, state and local governments, individuals, and private businesses. The Equal Employment Opportunity Commission (EEOC) enforces laws prohibiting employment discrimination. The implementation of school desegregation policy takes place under the supervision of federal district judges.

Interest groups, individuals, and their attorneys play a major role in civil rights policy implementation by suing or threatening to sue. Individuals who think that they have been denied a job or promotion because of illegal bias can file suit. In practice, many companies devise hiring and promotion procedures with the goal of protecting themselves against discrimination lawsuits.

Consider the implementation of Title IX. Congress voted to prohibit discrimination on the basis of gender without specifying how that prohibition would apply to college athletic programs. In fact, southern conservatives added Title IX to the measure, hoping Congress would defeat the entire bill rather than enact legislation to prohibit discrimi-

nation on the basis of gender. They were wrong; the legislation passed anyway. The details of implementation of Title IX were left to the federal bureaucracy, universities, and the courts. In practice, each university takes steps to implement Title IX based on federal court decisions, guidelines set by the Department of Education, and the resources at hand. Individuals and groups who believe that a university has failed adequately to implement the law can file suit, asking a federal court to issue an **injunction,** or court order, directing the university to take additional steps to comply with the law. People can also ask a court to award financial damages.

The evaluation of civil rights policies involves both factual analyses and analyses based on values. Consider the impact of the elimination of affirmative action in university admissions after the passage of California's Proposition 209, a state ballot measure passed in 1996 designed to eliminate affirmative action in the state by banning prefer-

ential treatment of women and minorities in public hiring, contracting, and education. The number of African American students admitted to law school at the University of California, Berkeley, fell 81 percent. Latino admissions dropped 50 percent. Minority enrollment grew, however, at less-prestigious law schools in the state.[46] The critics of Proposition 209 worry that the state's best colleges and universities will have student bodies composed almost entirely of white and Asian students. In contrast, other observers believe that ending affirmative action helps well-qualified African American and Latino students who are admitted to the best schools because no one will question whether they really belong. Minority students who are not as well-prepared will benefit as well because they will not be placed in situations where they cannot effectively compete.

**injunction** a court order.

the
THINKSPOT
www.thethinkspot.com

# TEST yourself

1. Which of the following constitutional provisions has the greatest impact on civil rights policymaking?
   A. Equal Protection Clause of the Fourteenth Amendment
   B. First Amendment
   C. Second Amendment
   D. Due Process Clause of the Fourteenth Amendment

2. Which of the following is a good description of the meaning of civil rights?
   A. The right of an individual to be protected from the power of government when it comes to such matters as freedom of expression and freedom of religion
   B. The right of an individual not to be harmed or disadvantaged because of the individual's membership in a group based on race, ethnicity, gender, etc.
   C. The right of an individual to be protected from the oppressive power of government
   D. All of the above

3. Which of the following branches of government plays the greatest role in civil rights policymaking?
   A. Legislative branch
   B. Executive branch
   C. Judicial branch
   D. The three branches are equally involved

4. Does the Constitution require that government treat all persons identically, regardless of their race, ethnicity, gender, etc.?
   A. Yes. The Equal Protection Clause requires that everyone be treated identically by government.
   B. Yes. The Bill of Rights requires that the government not make distinctions among persons on the basis of race, gender, or religion.
   C. No. The Supreme Court has long recognized that the government can make distinctions among persons if it can justify the distinctions.
   D. No. The Constitution does not address the issue of equal treatment.

5. Under what if any circumstances can the government treat people of different races or ethnicities differently?
   A. The government must demonstrate an overriding public interest in making the distinction and prove that it is achieving the compelling public interest in the least restrictive way possible.
   B. The government must have a reasonable basis for making the distinction.
   C. The government must prove that the distinction is necessary to achieve an important governmental objective.
   D. The government must treat all persons identically. The Constitution is color-blind.

6. Which of the following distinctions among persons is not a suspect classification?
   A. Ethnicity
   B. Race
   C. Citizenship status
   D. Sexual orientation

7. The judicial decision rule holding that the Supreme Court will find a government policy unconstitutional unless the government can demonstrate a compelling interest justifying the action is known as which of the following?
   A. Strict judicial scrutiny
   B. Separate but equal
   C. Civil liberties
   D. Civil rights

8. Under what circumstances would it be constitutionally permissible for the government to deal differently with individuals based on whether they smoke? (For example, the government might prohibit smokers from becoming foster parents.)
   A. Under no circumstances—the government must treat everyone alike.
   B. The government must demonstrate a compelling government interest to treat people differently.
   C. Because smoking status is not a suspect classification, the government need only demonstrate a reasonable basis for making the distinction.
   D. The government must offer an exceedingly persuasive justification for making the distinction.

9. The doctrine of "separate but equal" concerned what issue?
   A. Separation of powers with checks and balances
   B. Affirmative action
   C. Voting rights for African Americans
   D. Whether laws requiring separate facilities for whites and blacks satisfy the Equal Protection Clause

10. Which of the following statements about *Brown v. Board of Education* is/are true?
    A. It was a test case promoted by the NAACP.
    B. It overturned *Plessy v. Ferguson*.
    C. It outlawed *de jure* segregation but not *de facto* segregation.
    D. All of the above.

11. Why is it that many public schools in the United States have student bodies that are all, or almost all, members of the same racial/ethnic group?
    A. The Supreme Court overturned *Brown v. Board of Education* in *Parents Involved in Community Schools v. Seattle School District No. 1*.
    B. The federal courts no longer enforce the *Brown* decision.

C. Housing patterns in many cities isolate racial and ethnic groups.

D. Public opinion is heavily opposed to racial integration in public schools.

**12** Suppose the government reinstates the military draft, but drafts only men and not women. Would it be possible for the government to adopt the policy constitutionally?

A. Yes, but it would have to demonstrate a rational basis for making the distinction.

B. Yes, but it would have to offer an "exceedingly persuasive justification" to make the distinction.

C. Yes, but it would have to demonstrate a compelling government interest in making the distinction.

D. No. Because of the Equal Protection Clause, any draft would have to include both men and women.

**13** A state university decides to limit graduate student enrollment in its space physics program to American citizens, excluding permanent residents. Is such an action constitutional?

A. It is, if the university can demonstrate a compelling governmental interest in making the distinction between citizens and non-citizen permanent residents.

B. It is, if the university can state a rational basis for the distinction.

C. Yes. Permanent residents do not have the rights of citizens.

D. No. The Constitution prohibits distinctions based on citizenship status. Everyone must be treated equally.

**14** How did the white primary discriminate against African American voters?

A. African Americans were allowed to vote in primary elections but not general elections, thus minimizing their electoral influence.

B. African Americans were prevented from voting in the Democratic primary. Because the South was a one-party Democratic region, the white primary prevented African Americans from voting in the only election that really mattered.

C. African Americans were prevented from voting in the Republican primary. Because the South was a one-party Republican region, the white primary prevented African Americans from voting in the only election that really mattered.

D. African Americans had to pay a tax in order to vote and that discouraged their electoral participation.

**15** What was the purpose of a grandfather clause?

A. To exempt white people from voting restrictions placed on African Americans

B. To limit voting to older people

C. To prevent older people from voting

D. To establish different voting requirements based on age

**16** What is the current status of deed restrictions that prevent property owners from selling their homes to members of racial and ethnic minority groups?

A. They still apply because they are private agreements, and anti-discrimination laws do not apply to private agreements.

B. They are illegal because of the Voting Rights Act (VRA).

C. The Supreme Court ruled them unenforceable in *Brown v. Board of Education*.

D. The Supreme Court ruled them unenforceable in *Shelley v. Kraemer*.

**17** Does the federal government have the authority to outlaw discrimination against racial and ethnic minorities in private businesses such as restaurants and hotels?

A. Yes. The Supreme Court has ruled that Congress can legislate on the basis of its constitutional authority to regulate interstate commerce.

B. Yes. The Supreme Court has ruled that Congress can legislate as part of its authority to enforce the Equal Protection Clause of the Fourteenth Amendment.

C. Yes. The First Amendment gives the federal government the authority to prohibit discrimination.

D. No. These are state issues, not federal issues.

**18** What is the basis for sexual harassment law?

A. Federal laws prohibiting gender discrimination in employment

B. First Amendment

C. Equal Protection Clause of the Fourteenth Amendment

D. Voting Rights Act

**19** Which of the following cases dealt with affirmative action?

A. *Shelley v. Kraemer*

B. *Brown v. Board of Education*

C. *City of Richmond v. J. A. Croson Company*

D. All of the above

**20** Why did the U.S. Supreme Court uphold the admissions program at the University of Michigan law school?

A. The Court ruled that the government has a compelling interest in promoting racial and ethnic diversity in higher education.

B. The admissions program did not establish a quota system for admissions.

C. The admissions program did not award a set number of points to applicants based on their race or ethnicity.

D. All of the above.

1. A; 2. B; 3. C; 4. C; 5. A; 6. D; 7. A; 8. C; 9. D; 10. D; 11. C; 12. B; 13. A; 14. B; 15. A; 16. D; 17. A; 18. A; 19. C; 20. D

# 17 FOREIGN

Soon after taking office, President George W. Bush declared that Iran, Iraq, and North Korea were an "axis of evil," seeking to develop **weapons of mass destruction (WMD)**, which are nuclear, chemical, and biological weapons designed to inflict widespread military and civilian casualties. The United States went to war against Iraq to overthrow the government of Saddam Hussein and to prevent Iraq from developing nuclear weapons or giving biological or chemical weapons to terrorist groups. American forces quickly defeated the Iraqi military and toppled the government, but, ironically, found no WMD.

Iran and North Korea responded to the American invasion of Iraq by speeding up their own weapons-development programs. Iran has been acquiring the materials and developing the expertise necessary to build nuclear weapons. Furthermore, the Iranian government has failed to cooperate with the International Atomic Energy Agency (IAEA), denying it access to nuclear sites. North Korea is further along in its nuclear program than Iran.

President Bush declared that Iran and North Korea are **rogue states**, nations that threaten world peace by sponsoring international terrorism and promoting the spread of weapons of mass destruction. American policymakers worry that Iran and North Korea, armed with nuclear weapons, would bully their neighbors, perhaps setting off regional arms races as neighboring states rush to acquire nuclear weapons to counter the Iranian or North Korean threat. They might even use a nuclear weapon against the United States or its allies.

The threat of nuclear weapons development in Iran and North Korea is a major foreign and defense policy challenge for the United States. The United States went to war against

# AND DEFENSE POLICYMAKING

Iraq to defuse a threat that, in retrospect, was less serious than the threats posed by the Iranians and North Koreans. Does the United States have a realistic military option for dealing with either nation now? Can the United States and its allies convince Iran and North Korea to abandon their nuclear ambitions through negotiations? Will the United States simply have to learn to live with a nuclear Iran and a nuclear North Korea?

# the international COMMUNITY

Since the seventeenth century, the nation-state has been the basic unit of the international community. A **nation-state** is a political community, occupying a definite territory, and having an organized government. Other nations recognize its independence and respect the right of its government to exercise authority within its boundaries, free from external interference. Today, the world's community of nations comprises more than 190 countries.

Political scientists divide the world's nations into three groups based on their level of economic development. The United States, Canada, Japan, and the countries of Western Europe are **postindustrial societies,** nations whose economies are increasingly based on services, research, and information rather than on heavy industry. India, China, South Korea, Brazil, and a number of other countries are modernizing industrial states that are emerging as important economic powers. Finally, many of the countries of Asia, Africa, and Latin America are pre-industrial states with an average standard of living well below that in postindustrial societies.[1]

The United States has diplomatic relations with almost all of the world's nations. The term **diplomatic relations** refers to a system

**nation-state** a political community occupying a definite territory and having an organized government.

**postindustrial societies** nations whose economies are increasingly based on services, research, and information rather than heavy industry.

**diplomatic relations** a system of official contacts between two nations in which the countries exchange ambassadors and other diplomatic personnel and operate embassies in each other's country.

Kim Jong-il, the leader of North Korea, commands the fifth-largest standing army in the world. The United States believes that a nuclear North Korea would be a threat to world peace.

of official contacts between two nations in which the countries exchange ambassadors and other diplomatic personnel and operate embassies in each other's country. North Korea, Iran, Cuba, and Libya are among the few nations with which the United States does not have formal diplomatic relations.

In addition to the governments of the world, more than a hundred

bers disagree on how best to approach the problem.

Some of the UN's most important accomplishments have come in the areas of disaster relief, refugee relocation, agricultural development, loans for developing nations, and health programs. The UN has several agencies that carry out these and other tasks, including the International Monetary Fund and the World

ments charged to member nations. The amount of each nation's contribution depends, in general, on the strength of the nation's economy. Although every nation, even small and very poor nations, must support the work of the UN financially, the United States has the largest assessment because the American economy is the world's largest. As a result, the United States is also the

THE NEW AMERICAN EMBASSY IN BAGHDAD, WITH ITS COMPLEX OF 21 BUILDINGS ON 104 ACRES ALONG THE TIGRIS RIVER, IS THE WORLD'S LARGEST EMBASSY. IT ALSO EMPLOYS THE LARGEST STAFF: 5,500 PEOPLE. CRITICS OF THE NEW EMBASSY, ESPECIALLY IRAQIS, SEE IT AS A SYMBOL OF WHO HAS THE REAL POWER IN IRAQ. DEFENDERS SAY THAT THE SIZE OF THE EMBASSY SHOWS THAT THE UNITED STATES IS MAKING A HUGE COMMITMENT TO REBUILD THE WAR-TORN COUNTRY. THE EMBASSY HAS COST ABOUT $730 MILLION AND WILL HAVE ITS OWN POWER AND WATER. IT ALSO HAS REINFORCED WALLS TO PROTECT IT FROM ROCKET ATTACKS IN THE EVENT OF STREET FIGHTING. THE EMBASSY WILL OFFICIALLY OPEN IN 2009.

transnational (or multinational) organizations are active on the international scene. The best known of these is the **United Nations (UN)**, an international organization founded in 1945 as a diplomatic forum to resolve conflicts among the world's nations. In practice, the UN has not always been effective at maintaining the peace. The UN Security Council, the organization charged with maintaining peace and security among nations, has frequently been unable to act because each of its five permanent members (Russia, China, Britain, France, and the United States) has a veto on its actions. The Security Council has been unable to persuade either Iran or North Korea to give up its nuclear weapons program, at least in part, because the permanent mem-

Health Organization. The **International Monetary Fund (IMF)** is an international organization created to promote economic stability worldwide. It provides loans to nations facing economic crises, usually on the condition that they adopt and implement reforms designed to bring long-term economic stability. The World Health Organization (WHO) is an international organization created to control disease worldwide. The WHO is a world clearinghouse for medical and scientific information. It sets international standards for drugs and vaccines and, at government request, helps fight disease in any country. The WHO is in the forefront of the battle against the spread of AIDS in the developing world.

The UN and its affiliated agencies are funded through dues and assess-

UN's most influential member. Nonetheless, the United States has often been highly critical of some UN procedures, especially those associated with budgeting. Congress has sometimes made payment of American dues contingent on the UN agreeing to internal reforms to improve its operations.[2]

**United Nations (UN)** an international organization founded in 1945 as a diplomatic forum to resolve conflicts among the world's nations.

**International Monetary Fund (IMF)** the international organization created to promote economic stability worldwide.

Chris Klein (left) and Julian Valentin, members of the Los Angeles Galaxy Major League Soccer team, publicize a UN "Nothing but Nets" workshop at UCLA. The goal of the program is to eradicate malaria in Africa through the distribution and use of mosquito nets.

A number of other international organizations are important to American foreign and defense policies. The **North Atlantic Treaty Organization (NATO)** is a regional military alliance consisting of the United States, Canada, and most of the European democracies. The United States and its allies formed NATO after World War II to defend against the threat of a Soviet attack on Western Europe. With the collapse of the Soviet Union, NATO

**Should the United States pull out of the UN?**

has expanded to include some of the nations that were once part of the Soviet bloc: Poland, Hungary, the Czech Republic, Bulgaria, Estonia, Latvia, Lithuania, Romania, Slovakia, and Slovenia. The United States, Canada, and the established democracies of Western Europe hope that the inclusion of these nations in the NATO alliance will strengthen their commitment to democratic institutions and capitalist economic structures. In the meantime, NATO has changed its military focus to take into account the changing international environment by creating a multinational force that can be deployed quickly. The United States wants NATO to become a global security organization that is capable either of taking military action or of providing humanitarian relief anywhere in the world. In

2005, for example, NATO gave assistance to earthquake victims in Pakistan and Kashmir.[3]

The **World Trade Organization (WTO)** is an international organization that administers trade laws, and provides a forum for settling trade disputes among nations. It promotes international trade by sponsoring negotiations to reduce tariffs and

**North Atlantic Treaty Organization (NATO)**

a regional military alliance consisting of the United States, Canada, and most of the European democracies.

**World Trade Organization (WTO)** an international organization that administers trade laws and provides a forum for settling trade disputes among nations.

other barriers to trade. (A **tariff** is a tax on imported goods.) The WTO also arbitrates disputes over trade among its 145 member nations. For example, the WTO has sponsored negotiations to allow modernizing countries to make generic versions of lifesaving drugs for their own use and for export to countries too poor either to make the drugs themselves or to purchase them from pharmaceutical companies. Wealthy nations, led by the United States, want to sharply limit the number of diseases covered by the drugs in order to protect the intellectual property rights of pharmaceutical companies. In contrast, developing nations, such as Brazil, China, and India, argue that governments should have the right to determine which diseases constitute public health crises in their countries.[4]

**Nongovernmental organizations (NGOs)** are international organizations committed to the promotion of a particular set of issues. Greenpeace, Friends of the Earth, World Wide Fund for Nature, and the Nature Conservancy are NGOs that address environmental issues. Save the Children is an NGO concerned with the welfare of children. Al-Qaeda and other international terrorist organizations are also NGOs.[5] NGOs vary in their relationship to the international community. NGOs such as the International Red Cross and Doctors Without Borders work in partnership with national governments to assist the victims of natural disasters

**tariff** a tax levied on imported goods.

**nongovernmental organizations (NGOs)** international organizations committed to the promotion of a particular set of issues.

or political turmoil. Other NGOs lobby national governments over policy issues such as the effort to ban the importation of genetically modified foods. Some NGOs encourage consumers to boycott retailers who sell goods produced under exploitative working conditions in developing countries. They organize protests at international meetings of the WTO to push for the incorporation of health and safety conditions in international trade agreements.[6]

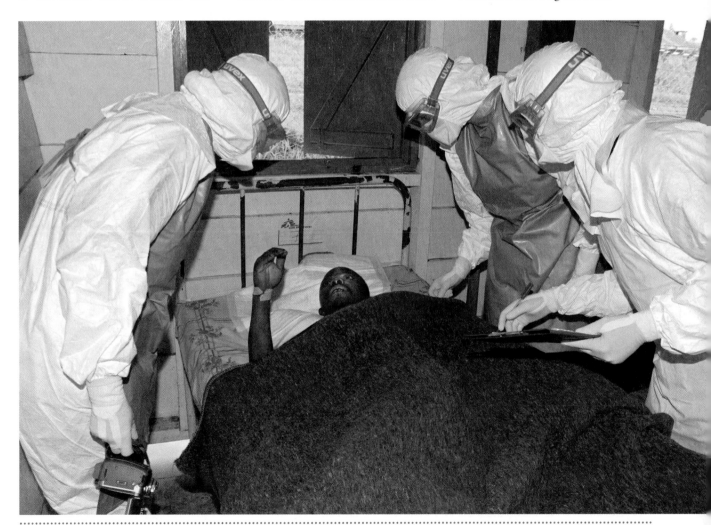

The NGO *Médecins Sans Frontières* (Doctors Without Borders) is an international humanitarian aid organization that provides emergency medical assistance to populations in danger in more than 80 countries. Here MSF doctors in Uganda examine a man thought to be carrying the Ebola virus.

# the ends and means of
## AMERICAN POLICY

the United States has consistently pursued three foreign and defense policy goals throughout its history: national security, economic prosperity, and the projection of American values abroad.[7] The foremost goal of American foreign and defense policies is national security. A basic aim of the foreign policy of any nation is to preserve its sovereignty and to protect its territorial integrity. No nation wants to be overrun by a foreign power or dominated by another nation. During the **Cold War**, which was the period of international tension between the United States and the Soviet Union lasting from the late 1940s through the late 1980s, American foreign policy was premised on the goal of protecting the nation from communist aggression. Although the United States is today the world's foremost military power, it still has national security concerns. The terrorist attacks of September 11, 2001 demonstrated the vulnerability of the United States to attack by a terrorist group. Although neither Iran nor North Korea would be able to mount a direct attack on the United States, they could threaten American interests in their regions of the world. They could also give or sell nuclear weapons to terrorist groups.

National prosperity is another goal of American foreign and defense policy. This goal includes encouraging free markets, promoting international trade, and protecting American economic interests and investments abroad. Because the American economy is closely entwined with the global economy, it is essential to the nation's economic health that the United States has access both to foreign suppliers of goods and services, and to foreign markets for American products. The nation's military involvement in the Persian Gulf, for example, has been motivated at least in part by a desire by the United States to protect access to the region's oil fields.

**think**

Do the economic gains from trade outweigh the costs? Would you spend more money to purchase goods that were made in the United States?

| Period | Total Exports | Total Imports | Balance |
|---|---|---|---|
| 1960 | 25,940 | 22,432 | 3,508 |
| 1965 | 35,285 | 30,621 | 4,664 |
| 1970 | 56,640 | 54,386 | 2,254 |
| 1975 | 132,585 | 120,181 | 12,404 |
| 1980 | 271,834 | 291,241 | -19,407 |
| 1985 | 289,070 | 410,950 | -121,880 |
| 1990 | 535,233 | 616,097 | -80,864 |
| 1995 | 794,387 | 890,771 | -96,384 |
| 2000 | 1,070,597 | 1,450,432 | -379,835 |
| 2005 | 1,283,753 | 1,995,320 | -711,567 |
| 2008 | 1,826,596 | 2,522,532 | -695,936 |

**INTERNATIONAL TRADE** VALUE IN MILLIONS OF DOLLARS

The table above shows the monetary value of American imports and exports as well as the balance of trade, which is the difference between the value of imports and exports. As the table shows, the value of goods and services traded between the United States and other countries has risen dramatically, especially in the last decade. Because imports have risen more rapidly than exports, the United States has a sizable trade deficit.

U.S. Census Bureau, Foreign Trade Division.

International trade has grown increasingly important to the economy of the United States. Trade now accounts for 28 percent of the nation's output of goods and services compared to only 11 percent in 1970. The United States exported $1.6 trillion worth of goods and services in 2007 while importing $2.3 trillion worth. The nation's leading trading partners were, in order of importance, Canada, Mexico, China, and Japan.[8]

Trade is controversial in the United States because it produces winners and losers. Consumers benefit from trade because they have the opportunity to purchase a broad range of goods at competitive prices. American manufacturers of medical instruments, farm equipment, pharmaceuticals, oil drilling equipment, and electronics benefit because they sell their products abroad. In contrast, inefficient small farmers, old steel mills, and the nation's clothing and textile manufacturers suffer because they do not compete effectively against international competition. Some liberal groups in the United States also oppose international trade because they believe it rewards international corporations that exploit low-wage workers in developing countries and that it leads to environmental degradation around the globe.

Recent administrations of both political parties have favored the growth of trade because they believe that the economic gains from trade outweigh the costs. President Bill Clinton, despite the opposition of a majority of the members of his own political party, won congressional support for the **North American Free Trade Agreement (NAFTA)**, an international accord among the United States, Mexico, and Canada to lower trade barriers among the three nations. The George W. Bush administration negotiated the Central America Free Trade Agreement (CAFTA) with Nicaragua, Honduras, Costa Rica, El Salvador, and Guatemala to phase out tariffs among participating nations on manufactured goods, agricultural commodities, chemicals, and construction equipment.

A final general goal of American foreign and defense policy is the promotion of American ideas and ideals abroad. Historically, American policymakers have justified military interventions as efforts to protect freedom and promote democracy. Many of the nation's foreign policies today are designed to further the causes of democracy, free-market capitalism, and human rights. For years, the United States has attempted to isolate Cuba economically and diplomatically in hopes of either driving the Castro regime out of power or of forcing Castro to bring democracy and free-market capitalism to the island.

Spreading democracy was at the center of the foreign policy of the George W. Bush administration. When American forces failed to uncover WMD in Iraq, President Bush offered the promotion of democracy as the new justification for the invasion. Democracies are stronger economically and more stable politically than undemocratic governments, he declared. Consequently, their residents have few incentives to join terrorist organizations. Bush also endorsed the theory of the **democratic peace**, which is the concept that democracies do not wage war against other democracies.[9]

> An additional goal of **American foreign and defense policy** is the promotion of American ideas and ideals abroad.

**North American Free Trade Agreement (NAFTA)** an international accord among the United States, Mexico, and Canada to lower trade barriers among the three nations.

**democratic peace** the concept that democracies do not wage war against other democracies.

# THE SELLING OF
# AMERICAN ARMS

ONE AMERICAN EXPORT that has proved durable is military equipment. In 2006 alone, the U.S. sold more than $21 billion worth of the F-16 fighter jets, mostly to friendly governments in South Asia and the Middle East. The U.S. government must approve all sales of military equipment to prevent unfriendly powers from getting sophisticated technology. In 2006–2007, the U.S. sold $37.2 billion worth of weapons and weapons systems to 174 governments.

Critics of the Bush administration warn that an emphasis on democratization is unrealistic, naïve, and counterproductive. Implanting democracy in countries without a democratic tradition may be impossible because people may be unwilling to make the compromises necessary for democracy to work. The various tribal and religious factions in Iraq fought with each other despite the introduction of democracy after the fall of Saddam. Furthermore, democracy may result in the election of regimes hostile to American interests. In much of the Arab world, including Egypt and Saudi Arabia, free elections would likely produce the selection of distinctly anti-American Islamic regimes. Finally, American pressure to democratize may alienate allies in the war on terror. The United States depends on the cooperation of undemocratic regimes in Egypt and Saudi Arabia to combat terrorism.

The United States pursues its foreign and defense policy goals through military, economic, cultural, and diplomatic means. Since the end of World War II, the Armed Forces of the United States have intervened militarily in Korea, Lebanon, the Dominican Republic, Indochina, Grenada, Panama, Kuwait, Afghanistan, the Serbian province of Kosovo, Iraq, and Liberia. The United States has also given military assistance in the form of arms and advisors to friendly governments fighting against forces hostile to the interests of the United States. For example, the United States has provided military aid to the government of Colombia in its war against guerrilla forces supported by international narcotics traffickers. After September 11, 2001, the United States supplied military aid, including American advisors, to the government of the Philippines in its war against insurgent forces, which may have ties to al-Qaeda.

Besides the actual use of military force, the United States has pursued its policy goals by forming defense alliances and transferring military hardware to other nations. Since the end of World War II, the United States has participated in a number of defense alliances, including NATO and SEATO (the Southeast Asia Treaty Organization). America is also the world's major distributor of weapons, accounting for more than 45 percent of world arms sales. Egypt, Israel, Saudi Arabia, South Korea, and Taiwan are among the major purchasers of American arms.[10] Some international arms sales are private transactions between American firms and foreign governments. Most sales, however, are government-to-government transactions in which the U.S. Department of Defense acts as a purchasing agent for a foreign government wanting to buy American-made weapons.

The United States also attempts to achieve foreign policy goals through economic means, such as trade and foreign aid. Trade can be used to improve international relations. One method the United States employed to improve relations with China was to encourage a trade relationship. In contrast, America has erected trade barriers against foreign governments it wishes to pressure or punish. The United States attempts to isolate Cuba and North Korea economically. In fact, Congress passed, and President Clinton signed, legislation designed to punish third countries that violate the American embargo against Cuba by trading with the island nation. The measure, which was called the Helms-Burton Act, named for former Senator Jesse Helms (R-NC) and Representative Dan Burton (R-IN), provoked accusations of

> **Trade can be used to improve international relations.**

hypocrisy from Canada and Europe. While the United States tries to punish Cuba, they said, it disregards human rights abuses in China, a country that is a major trading partner of the United States.

The United States also uses foreign aid to achieve foreign policy goals. Although the United States is the world's largest donor, its level of giving as a share of national income is among the lowest of the developed nations, less than half that of European countries.[11] The size of the foreign aid budget is also relatively small, less than one percent of the federal budget—and most of this money goes to further the nation's foreign policy aims. The top two recipients of American foreign aid are Israel and Egypt, nations that are close allies of the United States. Both countries receive more money in military aid than they do in economic assistance. Colombia is the third-ranking foreign aid recipient. Furthermore, since September 11, 2001, the United States has increased aid to countries, such as Jordan, Pakistan, Turkey, and postwar Afghanistan, whose assistance America needs in the war on terror.[12] The United States has also made it clear to countries such as

Yemen and the Philippines that their ability to get loans from the IMF depends on their cooperation in the war on terror. Even though the IMF is an international organization, the United States has considerable influence on its loan decisions because it is the organization's largest source of funds.

Foreign policy goals can sometimes be realized through cultural means, including the promotion of tourism and student exchanges, goodwill tours, and international athletic events. The process of improving relations between the United States and China, for example, was facilitated by cultural exchanges. In fact, one of the first contacts between the two nations was the visit of an American table tennis team to China—"ping-pong diplomacy," the pundits called it. The Olympic Games, meanwhile, are not just a sporting event but also a forum for nations to make political statements. The United States boycotted the 1980 Moscow Olympics to protest the Soviet invasion of Afghanistan. The Soviet Union returned the favor in 1984 by staying

home when the games were held in Los Angeles.

Finally, foreign policy goals can also be achieved through **diplomacy,** which is the process by which nations carry on political relations with each other. Ambassadors and other embassy officials stationed abroad provide an ongoing link between governments. The UN, which is headquartered in New York City, offers a forum in which the world's nations can make diplomatic contacts, including countries that may

American soldiers listen intently to a speech by President George W. Bush.

not have diplomatic relations with one another. Diplomacy can also be pursued through special negotiations or summit meetings among national leaders.

**diplomacy** the process by which nations carry on political relations with each other.

# foreign POLICY

**t**he events of September 11, 2001 provide the backdrop for American foreign policy in the post-Cold War world. American policymakers generally agree that the

United States must be closely engaged in world affairs not only to protect its economic interests abroad but also to guard the American homeland against assault by terrorist

groups or rogue states. Policymakers also concur that the United States should exert leadership in international affairs because it is the world's foremost military and economic power. As former Secretary of State Madeleine Albright phrased it, the United States is the world's "indispensable nation" in that its participation is essential to solving the world's military, economic, and humanitarian problems.[13] Policymakers disagree, however, on how closely the United States should work with its allies and the other nations of the world.

**think**

Should the United States focus its foreign aid expenditures on humanitarian assistance to poor nations, or should it use aid primarily to further its own foreign policy objectives?

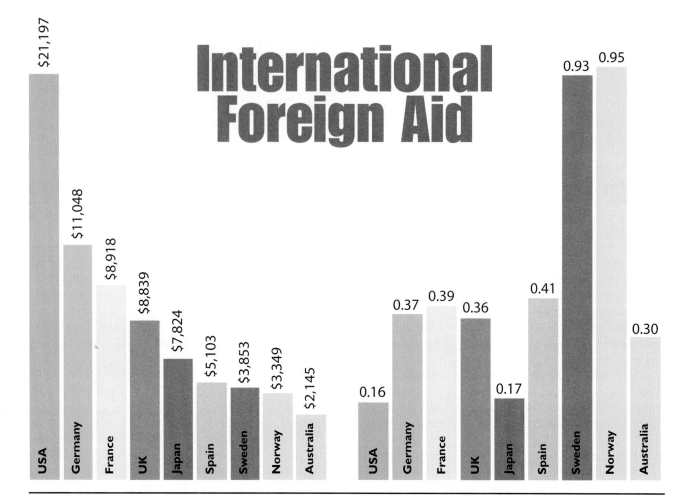

# International Foreign Aid

| | Foreign aid in millions of U.S. dollars |
|---|---|
| USA | $21,197 |
| Germany | $11,048 |
| France | $8,918 |
| UK | $8,839 |
| Japan | $7,824 |
| Spain | $5,103 |
| Sweden | $3,853 |
| Norway | $3,349 |
| Australia | $2,145 |

| | Foreign aid as a percentage of GDP |
|---|---|
| USA | 0.16 |
| Germany | 0.37 |
| France | 0.39 |
| UK | 0.36 |
| Japan | 0.17 |
| Spain | 0.41 |
| Sweden | 0.93 |
| Norway | 0.95 |
| Australia | 0.30 |

**Foreign aid in millions of U.S. dollars**

**Foreign aid as a percentage of GDP**

The United States gives more money in foreign aid than any other country, but the amount is relatively small measured as a percentage of each nation's GDP.

Source: Organization for Economic Co-operation and Development

Some policymakers believe that the United States should take an internationalist approach to achieving its foreign policy goals by working in close concert with the global community. After World War II, the United States and its allies established the UN, NATO, the IMF, and other international institutions to keep the peace, deter aggression, and promote economic development. The advocates of an internationalist approach to American foreign policy believe that the United States should work with these institutions and with its allies to address the problems of international terrorism, nuclear proliferation, and rogue states. Consider the challenges presented by nuclear weapons development in Iran and

North Korea. The United States can take the lead in addressing each nation, but it needs the support of other nations if it hopes to convince either nation to forego weapons development.

Other policymakers, however, believe that the United States should follow a unilateralist approach to achieving its foreign policy goals, acting alone if necessary. President George W. Bush justified attacking Iraq without UN support because his administration believed that Saddam Hussein had weapons of mass destruction that he could have given to terrorists, who could then have used them to kill tens of thousands of Americans. The advocates of the unilateralist approach argue that the United

States should cooperate with international agreements only as far as they benefit America. Because the United States has the world's most powerful military and largest economy, it can assert itself internationally. Other nations will have no choice but to accept the leadership of the United States and adapt to American preferences.[14]

Contemporary American foreign policies reflect both internationalist and unilateralist impulses, indicating, perhaps, that American policymakers are not firmly committed to either approach. On one hand, the United States has worked with the international community to combat terrorism. The United States organized an international coalition to overthrow the Taliban government

**think**

Should the United States act on its own to achieve its foreign policy and defense goals, even if its allies disagree with the action?

in Afghanistan that had harbored the al-Qaeda terrorist network, and it has enlisted the support of countries around the globe to track down terrorist cells. The United States has found support not just from traditional allies in Western Europe but also from other countries, such as Yemen, that had long been regarded as safe havens for terrorists. On the other hand, the United States government has rejected a series of global agreements that enjoy overwhelming international support, including the **Global Warming Treaty,** an international agreement to reduce the worldwide emissions of carbon dioxide and other greenhouse gases, because it believed that the treaty put too much of the burden for reducing emissions on the United States.

The war against Iraq illustrates the ambivalence of American policy. The United States initially worked with the UN to force Iraq to submit to UN inspection in order to ensure its compliance with UN resolutions to disarm. Eventually, however, the United States grew impatient with the pace of inspection, arguing that the Iraqi government was not honestly cooperating with the process. When the UN Security Council refused to adopt a new resolution giving Iraq a shorter deadline for full and complete disclosure, President Bush set his own deadline and then ordered military action when the deadline was not met to the president's satisfaction.

By the end of the Bush administration, the approach of the United States in dealing with rogue states had shifted from focusing on regime change, which it applied in Iraq, to behavior change. With American forces tied down, fighting insurgencies in Iraq and Afghanistan, the United States was in no position to take military

**Global Warming Treaty** an international agreement to reduce the worldwide emissions of carbon dioxide and other greenhouse gases.

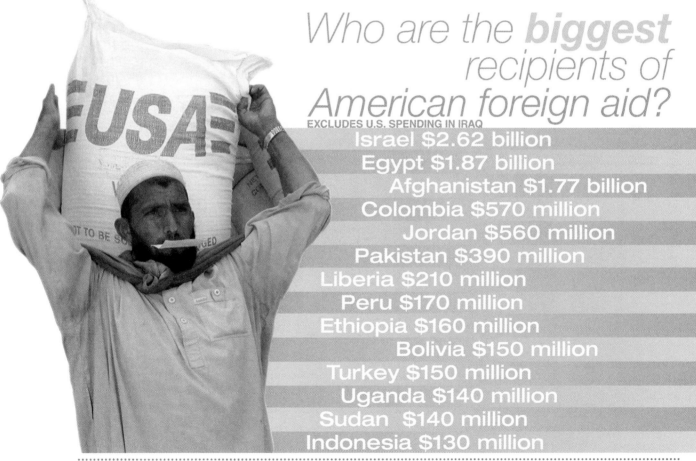

## Who are the **biggest** recipients of American foreign aid?

EXCLUDES U.S. SPENDING IN IRAQ

Israel $2.62 billion
Egypt $1.87 billion
Afghanistan $1.77 billion
Colombia $570 million
Jordan $560 million
Pakistan $390 million
Liberia $210 million
Peru $170 million
Ethiopia $160 million
Bolivia $150 million
Turkey $150 million
Uganda $140 million
Sudan $140 million
Indonesia $130 million

This Afghan man carries a bag of wheat donated by United States Agency for International Development (USAID) to his family in a refugee camp in Pakistan.

Source: Congressional Research Service

In 2009, North Korea continued to defy the international community by conducting another nuclear test and test firing a missile capable of reaching Hawaii.

action against other rogue states. Libya, a North African country associated with international terrorism, demonstrated the utility of this approach when it renounced efforts to develop WMD in exchange for assurances that the United States would not seek regime change. The United States and its European allies have been working through the IAEA to pressure Iran to abandon its nuclear program. They have threatened economic sanctions if the Iranians do not cooperate, but their leverage against Iran is dimin-

## Global Greenhouse Emissions

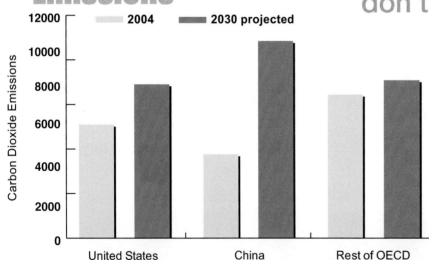

*The Organization for Economic Cooperation and Development (OECD) is an international organization of 30 nations committed to democracy and the market economy. Members include the majority of the European Union as well as a number of other countries, including Japan, Australia, Mexico, and South Korea.

The above figure shows the increase in greenhouse gases projected to be released by 2030. The U.S. has rejected global warming treaties, believing they put too much of the burden for reducing greenhouse gas emissions on the U.S. China, which is undergoing rapid industrialization, is projected to release more carbon dioxide emissions in 2030 than the entire European Union.

Source: The Organization for Economic Cooperation and Development.

*"When it comes to our security, we really don't need anybody's permission."* [15]

*President George W. Bush*

ished because Russia and China have a strong trading relationship with Iran and are reluctant to reduce those ties. Meanwhile, the Bush administration, after initially refusing to engage in direct talks with the North Koreans, agreed to participate in six-party talks (the United States, North Korea, Japan, China, Russia, and South Korea) to resolve the crisis over North Korea's nuclear program.[16] In 2009, the Obama administration announced that it was willing to hold talks with North Korea, offering the possibility of establishing diplomatic relations and providing economic assistance if the North Koreans abandoned their nuclear program. Otherwise, the United States said it would press forward with UN-mandated sanctions designed to cripple the North Korean economy.[17]

# The "Clash of Civilizations"

**Does Huntington's thesis have merit? If so, why? If not, why not?**

**Do democratization and modernization foster community and human rights? If this is true, what is the best way to further these values?**

**Overview:** In 1993, political scientist Samuel Huntington stirred a spirited academic and foreign policy debate with his controversial "clash of civilizations" thesis. Huntington argued that the world is divided into seven or eight civilizations and that these civilizations are in continual conflict. Furthermore, Huntington argued that this clash is inevitable and that there is a particularly hostile tension between Islamic and Western cultures. After the events of September 11, 2001, political commentators revisited Huntington's theory. But how compelling is his thesis?

In the year prior to Huntington's essay, Francis Fukuyama published *The End of History and the Last Man*, in which he argued that with liberal democracy and global modernization, humanity had discovered a social and political arrangement that most nationalities would eventually find attractive. Essentially, the world would be governed by democracies with varying degrees of market capitalism, and there could be a sort of world peace due to the fact that all peoples shared basic social and political values. It seems democratic values are in accord with the basic

human desire for equality and recognition.

The war on terror has illuminated the similarities and differences between nations and peoples. Evidence does suggest that modernization happens and that most people are attracted to some form of representative democracy and markets. Evidence also does suggest there is, for whatever reasons, conflict between Middle Eastern and Western cultures (as well as others). Is the policy of democratization a realistic or possible goal? Or are conflict and insecurity simply part of humanity's natural condition?

## supporting Huntington's thesis

**combatants in the war on terror generally follow those described by Huntington.** The terror visited upon New York (in 1993 and 2001) and on Washington D.C., as well as the massacres in Madrid, Spain, Beslan, Russia, and in Bali, Indonesia, were all perpetrated by Islamic extremists against a real or perceived threat from Western-style societies. Huntington's thesis also helps explain the tension between China and Japan and between India and Pakistan.

**instead of fostering a global community, modernization only helps nations go to war more effectively and efficiently.** For example, the Internet helps terrorist networks organize, communicate, and plan attacks, with an increasing ability to create and use weapons of mass destruction (based upon improved technology).

**proponents of democratization neglect to consider other strong global values and trends.** In addition to democratic and market values, there are other ways of viewing human society and organization. Some civilizations have long histories and deep traditional roots that may be more important than general Western values.

## against Huntington's thesis

**most major conflict in the twentieth century occurred within civilizations.** For example, the Nazi Holocaust, the horrible purges and genocides perpetrated by Stalin's Soviet Union and Cambodia's ruthless Pol Pot, the Korean War, and so on, occurred within the same civilizations. Furthermore, the First Gulf War pitted Arabic nations against one another, and much conflict in the Middle East is between the Shia and Sunni sects (and their offshoots) over questions of legitimacy. If conflict is inevitable, it is difficult to discern the true and justifiable reasons for any particular conflict.

**the United States has good relations with Islamic countries.** Though sometimes turbulent, the United States retains solid relations with states such as Turkey, Qatar, Kuwait, Jordan, and the United Arab Emirates. Additionally, the United States is working closely with Pakistan and other nations in Central Asia in prosecuting the war on terror. It is incorrect to say that future conflict will fall along civilizational fault lines.

**the process of modernization is bringing nations and peoples together.** Improved communications and transportation technologies are bringing global communities together, and this will help spread the values of human rights, representative democracy, and fair economic systems based on merit and social justice.

# defense
## POLICY

the nineteenth-century military strategist Karl von Clausewitz once described war as "diplomacy by other means." He meant that defense concerns and foreign policy issues are closely related. Foreign policy goals determine defense strategies. Military capabilities, meanwhile, influence a nation's foreign policy by expanding or limiting the options available to policymakers.

## Defense Spending

The figure below depicts United States defense spending from 1960 through 2008 as a percentage of the **gross domestic product (GDP)**, the total value of goods and services produced by a nation's economy in a year, excluding transactions with foreign countries. In general, defense spending rises during wartime and falls during peacetime. Defense

expenditures peaked relative to the size of the economy during the Korean War in the early 1950s and the Vietnam War in the late 1960s. After the end of both the Korean and Vietnam conflicts, defense spending fell. The only exception to the pattern of rising defense spending during wartime and falling defense expenditures during peacetime occurred during the early 1980s when President Reagan proposed and Congress passed the largest peacetime increase in military spending in the nation's history. Defense spending fell again in the 1990s after the collapse of the Soviet Union and the end of the Cold War. Since September 11, 2001, defense expenditures have increased as Congress and the president fund the war on terror as well as military operations in Afghanistan and Iraq.

## Defense Forces and Strategy

America's defense strategy is based on **strategic** (nuclear) and **conventional** (non-nuclear) **forces**.

**Strategic Forces.** The United States has more than 10,000 nuclear weapons. More than half are currently active and deployed, ready to be carried to their targets through a variety of delivery systems. The Air

**gross domestic product (GDP)** the total value of goods and services produced by a nation's economy in a year, excluding transactions with foreign countries.

**strategic forces** nuclear forces.

**conventional forces** non-nuclear forces.

Force can deliver at least 320 nuclear missiles by plane—B-52s or B-2s. The Navy has more than 2,000 nuclear missiles on submarines, with at least a third of the subs on patrol at any one time. The Army has 1,450 nuclear weapons configured for cruise missile delivery. Other missiles sit in silos located in 12 states and 6 European countries, ready for launch.[18]

Many defense theorists believe that nuclear weapons actually promoted world peace during the Cold War because no national leader acting rationally would risk initiating a nuclear holocaust. This concept was formalized in the doctrine of **mutual assured destruction (MAD)**, which was the belief that the United States and the Soviet Union would be deterred from launching a nuclear assault against each other for fear of being destroyed in a general nuclear war. MAD can be explained more fully by defining first- and second-strike capability. A first strike is the initial offensive move of a general nuclear war, aimed at knocking out the other side's ability to retaliate. A second strike is a nuclear attack in response to an adversary's first strike. **First-strike capability** is the capacity of a nation to launch an initial nuclear assault sufficient to cripple an adversary's ability to retaliate. **Second-strike capability** is the capacity of a nation to absorb an initial nuclear attack and retain sufficient nuclear firepower to inflict unacceptable damage on its adversary. According

**mutual assured destruction (MAD)** the belief that the United States and the Soviet Union would be deterred from launching a nuclear assault against each other for fear of being destroyed in a general nuclear war.

**first-strike capability** the capacity of a nation to launch an initial nuclear assault sufficient to cripple an adversary's ability to retaliate.

**second-strike capability** the capacity of a nation to absorb an initial nuclear attack and retain sufficient nuclear firepower to inflict unacceptable damage on its adversary.

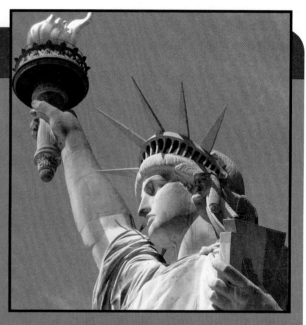

# **take**action

## AMERICA IN THE EYES OF THE WORLD >>

What do people in other countries think about the United States? Do they love America or hate it? Do they fear it or respect it? Are they envious or admiring? The class project is to interview international students and other foreign nationals about the perceptions of people in their home countries about the United States. Note that the assignment is not to ask international students *their own* opinion about the United States because they may be uncomfortable expressing anything other than positive points of view. Instead, class members should ask international students about the attitudes of people back home in their countries. International students who are part of the class can take the lead, interviewing their friends and helping American students understand the information they receive.

The interviews should focus on the following subject areas:

- Culture.   How influential is American culture (television, films, music, etc.) in your country? Do people admire American culture, or does it offend them? Do people worry that American culture will overwhelm their own culture?

- Economics.   Do people in your country believe that they benefit from the economic power of the United States, or do they think that they are hurt economically by the United States?

- Foreign policy.   What do people in your country think about American foreign policy? Do they consider the United States to be a force for good, or do they believe the United States acts unfairly in its own interest? Do they think that the United States is a bully?

After the interviews are complete, your instructor will ask students to discuss what they learned from the activity. In which of the three areas (culture, economics, and foreign policy) were attitudes about the United States the most positive? In which area were they least positive? How did points of view vary from region to region? Finally, why might people from other nations think as they do about the United States?

to the principles of MAD, America's best defense against nuclear attack and best deterrent to nuclear war hinge on maintaining a second-strike capability.

**Deterrence** was the organizing principle of American defense policy during the Cold War. It was the ability of a nation to prevent an attack against itself or its allies by destroying the other. Deterrence worked to prevent nuclear war during the Cold War because both the United States and the Soviet Union believed that the other side possessed an effective second-strike capability. The Soviet Union did not dare launch an attack against the United States (and vice versa) because Soviet leaders believed that cause they lack a home base that the United States could attack.[19]

President George W. Bush responded to the terrorist attacks of September 11, 2001 by announcing that the United States had adopted the policy of **military preemption**, which is the defense policy that declares that the United States will attack nations or groups

Tom Hanks and Julia Roberts star in *Charlie Wilson's War* (2007). In the 1980s, Texas Congressman Charlie Wilson conspired with a CIA anti-communism operative to arm and organize the Afghan Mujahedeen guerrilla fighters in their resistance to the Soviet occupation of Afghanistan.

threat of **massive retaliation,** the concept that the United States will strike back against an aggressor with overwhelming force. American leaders often explained the concept of deterrence with the phrase "peace through strength." By preparing for war, the United States would ensure the peace. Weaker nations would be deterred from attacking the United States because America enjoyed military superiority. In the meantime, the United States and the Soviet Union would be deterred from attacking each other because both countries possessed nuclear arsenals capable of enough American nuclear forces would survive the initial Soviet strike to destroy their country.

Deterrence does not fit the post-Cold War world because of rogue states and, especially, terrorist organizations. Although deterrence continues to be an effective defense strategy against the threat of nuclear attack by Russia or China, some defense analysts believe that it may be ineffective against rogue states whose leaders are sometimes prone to engage in high-risk behavior. Terrorist organizations, meanwhile, are unlikely to be deterred by the threat of massive retaliation be-

**deterrence** the ability of a nation to prevent an attack against itself or its allies by threat of massive retaliation.

**massive retaliation** the concept that the United States will strike back against an aggressor with overwhelming force.

**military preemption** the defense policy that declares that the United States will attack hostile nations or groups that represent a potential threat to the security of the United States.

# Is preemptive force justified?

## support for preemptive military action

| preemptive force can be justified... | may 2003 | jan 2007 |
|---|---|---|
| often | 22% | 16% |
| sometimes | 45% | 39% |
| rarely | 17% | 24% |
| never | 13% | 17% |
| don't know | 3% | 4% |

The first poll was taken a few months after the invasion of Iraq.

Support for preemptive war declined in the face of the failure to find WMD in Iraq and the continued insurgency.

Pew Research Center for the People & the Press, Trends in Political Values and Core Attitudes: 1987–2007

that represent a potential threat to the security of the United States. Under certain circumstances, preemption could even involve the United States using nuclear weapons against a potential enemy threat. President Bush justified the policy of preemption as follows:

> Given the goals of rogue states and terrorists, the United States can no longer solely rely on a reactive posture as we have in the past. The inability to deter a potential attacker, the immediacy of today's threats, and the magnitude of potential harm that could be caused by our adversaries' choice of weapons do not permit that option. We cannot let our enemies strike first.[20]

The American attack against Iraq to overthrow the regime of Saddam Hussein was the first application of the doctrine of military preemption. The United States went to war not because Iraq posed an immediate threat to national security, but because of the possibility that Iraq could give weapons of mass destruction to terrorists. "The people of the United States will not live at the mercy of an outlaw regime that threatens the peace with weapons of mass murder," said President Bush.

The policy of military preemption is controversial. Critics question the assertion that deterrence is ineffective against rogue states. The leaders of North Korea, Iran, and other enemies of the United States are not suicidal. Overwhelming military force deters rogue states as effectively as it does other nations. Just because American policymakers may not always understand North Korean or Iranian politics does not mean that those nations or their leaders behave irrationally.[21] Saddam Hussein was an evil dictator, but was he really an immediate threat to the United States? Critics also warn that the consistent application of the doctrine of preemption would involve the United States in perpetual war. Iran and North Korea have greater weapons capability than Iraq had. Does the United States plan to go to war against those nations as it did Iraq? Finally, the critics of preemption worry that other nations will use the doctrine of preemption to justify attacking their neighbors.[22]

**Conventional Forces.** For decades, the United States maintained a large standing army in order to defend against a possible conventional arms attack by the Soviet Union in Western Europe. More than two million men and women served in the U.S. Armed Forces through the 1980s. After the end of the Cold War, the United States scaled back its conventional forces, cutting the size of its Armed Forces sharply in the early

## IS MILITARY STRENGTH THE BEST WAY TO ENSURE PEACE?

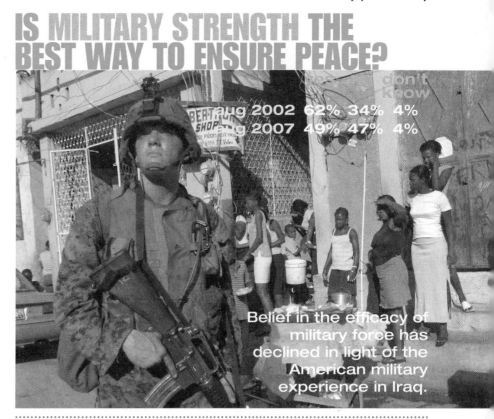

| | | | |
|---|---|---|---|
| Aug 2002 | 62% | 34% | 4% |
| 2007 | 49% | 47% | 4% |

Belief in the efficacy of military force has declined in light of the American military experience in Iraq.

A U.S. soldier patrols the streets of Port-au-Prince, Haiti, following unrest in 2004.

Pew Research Center for The People & The Press, Trends in Political Values and Core Attitudes: 1987–2007

1990s. With the dissolution of the Soviet Union, the chances of great armies clashing on the scale of World War II were remote. Nonetheless, the United States kept the basic structure of a large military intact, with 1.4 million troops in uniform. Pentagon planners believed that substantial military forces were still needed to fulfill the mission of fighting regional wars, promoting regional stability, keeping the peace, and participating in humanitarian relief efforts.

Donald Rumsfeld, the secretary of defense in the George W. Bush administration from 2001 through the end of 2006, advocated restructuring the U.S. military. He believed that the U.S. Armed Forces could rely on speed, mobility, and firepower rather than the giant armies characteristic of twentieth century warfare.[23] Rumsfeld put his theory into action in Afghanistan, where American airpower, including an unmanned aircraft called the Predator, defeated Taliban and al-Qaeda forces by using precision weapons operating at extremely long range, with targeting information gathered on the ground, in the air, and from space. American troops on the ground initially served as spotters for airpower and acted as liaisons to local Afghan militia. The United States employed the same strategy in Iraq, using highly mobile ground forces to slice through Iraqi defenses by use of overwhelming firepower, much of it delivered by air.

**think** Should gay men and lesbians be allowed to serve openly in the Armed Forces of the United States?

Rumsfeld's critics believe that the United States still needs substantial conventional forces and that, in fact, the U.S. military is too small. Although firepower and mobility enabled the United States to defeat the Taliban and the Iraqi Army in short order, American forces were insufficient to stabilize either nation. As a result, the United States and its allies remained embroiled in protracted warfare against insurgent forces in both Afghanistan and Iraq years after the initial invasion. Conditions in Iraq finally began to improve when the United States adopted a surge strategy, increasing troop strength in Iraq, especially in Baghdad, the nation's capital. The goal of the strategy was to establish order to buy time for Iraqi forces to develop the capacity to take over the defense of their own country while allowing the nation's political factions the opportunity to reconcile their divisions.

The United States is restructuring its conventional forces in response to the threats posed by the post-9/11 world. The U.S. Navy is expanding its fleet to add a number of small, fast vessels that can operate in relatively shallow coastal waters against terrorists while maintaining 11 aircraft carriers and other major vessels to counter the growth of Chinese naval power.[24] Meanwhile, the Department of Defense is reconfiguring the Army toward dealing with rogue states and terrorist threats. The goal is to develop mobile forces capable of defeating terrorists in dozens of countries at once, to counter the threat of WMD, and to deter China, Russia, and India from becoming adversaries.[25]

**AFTER THE END OF THE COLD WAR, THE UNITED STATES SCALED BACK ITS CONVENTIONAL FORCES.**

# Nuclear Weapons in Pakistan

around THE WORLD

Pakistan became a nuclear power in 1998 when it successfully tested several nuclear weapons. International observers believe that it has now produced enough fissile material to make as many as 50 nuclear devices.[26] Pakistan has also purchased or developed medium-range ballistic missiles that are capable of striking cities in neighboring India.

Pakistan developed nuclear weapons to achieve military parity with India and to gain international prestige as a nuclear power. Pakistan and India are longstanding enemies, having fought three wars since 1948. The two nations remain locked in a bitter dispute over control of the border region of Kashmir. Pakistan began a nuclear program in the early 1970s to match India's nuclear program and to offset India's advantage in conventional weapons. By developing nuclear weapons, Pakistan hopes to establish itself as a regional power and to claim leadership of the Muslim world as the first Muslim nation to have the bomb.

The United States opposes Pakistan's nuclear weapons program because of the danger that the next war between Pakistan and India will be a nuclear war and because of the fear that Pakistani nuclear weapons may fall into the hands of terrorists. The government of Pakistan is unstable, and senior officials in the Pakistani military are known to be sympathetic to the former Taliban government of Afghanistan and Osama bin Laden. The United States responded to Pakistan's nuclear tests in 1998 by imposing economic sanctions in hopes of convincing the Pakistani government that the price of nuclear weapons was too high, but Pakistan refused to change course. After September 11, 2001, the United States lifted the sanctions in exchange for Pakistani cooperation in the war against the Taliban government of Afghanistan and the fight against Osama bin Laden's terrorist network.[27]

## Questions

1. Does Pakistan having nuclear weapons make war between Pakistan and India more likely or less likely?

2. Is the United States hypocritical to oppose nuclear weapons in Pakistan, considering that the United States is the world's foremost nuclear power?

3. Is a nuclear Pakistan a threat to world peace? Why or why not?

Protesters in Karachi, Pakistan, burn an Indian flag. Tensions increased between the two countries in December 2008 after a terrorist attack on Mumbai, India. The Indian government charged that the attack was supported by Pakistanis.

# CONCLUSION

# foreign and defense
## POLICYMAKING

nternational events are the most important environmental factors affecting foreign and defense policymaking. During the Cold War, American foreign and defense policies were adopted and evaluated in light of the perceived threat of international communism. The Cold War shaped international diplomacy, alliances, defense budgets, and defense strategy. Today, the most important event shaping American foreign and defense policy are the terrorist attacks of September 11, 2001.

Survey research shows that the general public is more cautious about American involvement abroad than are foreign policy leaders in government, the media, business, and academia. For example, the general public is less supportive of foreign aid and immigration than are policy leaders. The public is also less willing to endorse the use of the American military to defend U.S. interests abroad.[28]

## Agenda Building

Events, public opinion, the media, interest groups, Congress, and the president all play a role in setting the agenda for foreign and defense policymaking. Some issues become important items on the policy agenda because of media coverage, such as the bombing of Pearl Harbor, or the terrorist attacks of September 11, 2001. Events affect the agenda for foreign and defense policymaking because of their impact on elite and mass public opinion.

Many interest groups participate in foreign and defense policymaking. Dozens of corporations and their employee unions lobby on behalf of weapons systems in which they have a financial interest. Cor-

porate and trade groups focus on trade policy, seeking protection from foreign competition or working against restrictive trade policies that threaten their businesses. Environmental groups emphasize international environmental issues. Ethnic groups—Cuban Americans, Arab Americans, and Jewish Americans—take an interest in foreign policies affecting regions of the world that are of particular interest to them. The American Jewish community, for example, is concerned about policy toward Israel. Cuban Americans focus on United States policy toward Cuba.

Historically, the president has taken the lead in foreign and defense policy matters.[29] During the 1960s and 1970s, a series of presidents worked to persuade Congress and the nation of the importance of American intervention in Vietnam. After September 11, 2001, President George W. Bush announced a new American policy of preemption and focused on disarming Iraq. Bush used his second inaugural address to focus attention on democratization as a principal goal of American foreign policy.

During the Cold War, presidents could generally count on bipartisan support for foreign policy issues. **Bipartisanship** is the close cooperation and general agreement between the two major political parties in dealing with foreign policy matters. Democrats and Republicans alike agreed that Soviet expansion was the primary threat to American interests and that deterrence and containment were the appropriate strategy to counter the threat. Congressional consensus on foreign policy and defense policy issues has become much less frequent

since the war in Vietnam.[30] Since 9/11, there has been consensus on the importance of eliminating al-Qaeda, but disagreement over how best to deal with rogue states.[31] When the president ordered the U.S. military to invade Iraq to overthrow Saddam Hussein, Congress offered support and voted to provide additional money to fund the war and to help rebuild Iraq. As the situation in Iraq worsened and public opinion began to turn against the war, individual members of Congress spoke out against administration policies and Congressional committees initiated investigations.

## Policy Formulation and Adoption

The president and Congress share constitutional authority to formulate and adopt foreign and defense policy. The president negotiates treaties, but the Senate must ratify them. The president has the power of diplomatic recognition, but the Senate must confirm ambassadorial appointments. The president can request money for foreign aid and defense, but Congress must appropriate the funds. The president is commander in chief of the Armed Forces, but Congress declares war. Congress also has the constitutional authority to raise and support armies and a navy.

The president often initiates foreign and defense policies, with Congress acting to modify or, occasionally, reject policies formulated in the executive branch. This divi-

**bipartisanship** the close cooperation and general agreement between the two major political parties in dealing with foreign policy matters.

sion of labor has developed for a number of reasons. First, the executive branch is better equipped to deal with international crises. The executive branch is unitary, under the authority of a single person, the president. Congress is a bicameral institution that often seems to speak with 535 separate voices. While the president can respond quickly to international events, Congress often reacts slowly and without unity.

Second, the president has an advantage in that secret national security information from the Central Intelligence Agency (CIA), military, Federal Bureau of Investigation (FBI), and diplomatic corps flows directly to the White House. The president can keep Congress in the dark about foreign and defense developments or can release information selectively to justify policies.

Third, the general public expects the president to lead in foreign and defense policymaking. As a rule, the public is neither well-informed nor particularly attentive to foreign affairs. In times of international crisis, Americans tend to rally around the president. Presidents typically enjoy a surge of popularity for roughly a 30-day period following the visible use of military force.[32] Immediately after September 11, 2001, for example, the percentage of Americans who told survey researchers that they approved of President Bush's performance in office leaped from 51 percent in early September to 90 percent later in the month. Bush's approval rating stayed well above the 60-percent level for more than a year, significantly strengthening the president's hand on foreign and defense policy issues.[33]

Finally, the president has often had considerable influence on foreign and defense policymaking because Congress has allowed it. Many members of Congress are not interested in overall foreign policy and defense strategy. Congress as an institution is decentralized, focusing on the parts of policy but seldom the big picture. Individual members focus primarily on the big issues

that gain national attention, or with issues of primary importance to their constituents.

Some foreign and defense policies can be adopted in the executive branch alone, but most require congressional action as well. Foreign aid and defense budgets must journey through the regular appropriations process. The Senate must ratify treaties and confirm presidential appointments. In practice, Congress more frequently modifies than blocks executive-branch initiatives in foreign and defense policy. In the 1970s, for example, the Senate ratified the Panama Canal

Treaty after tacking on 24 amendments, reservations, conditions, and understandings.

In general, Congress is more likely to support presidential initiatives in foreign and defense policy when the president's party controls Congress, when the president enjoys a relatively high approval rating, and during times of international crisis. President Clinton, for example, had to contend with a Congress controlled by the Republican Party for the last six years of his presidency. In contrast, after September 11, 2001, President George W. Bush benefited

from an atmosphere of international crisis and strong public support on foreign and defense policy issues. Furthermore, the Republican Party controlled the House and the Senate during the first few months of 2000, and then again after the 2002 election. As a result, Bush won congressional support for his proposals. Congress also granted the president authority to negotiate trade agreements that would not be subject to congressional amendment. Even after public opinion began to turn against administration policy, congressional criticism of the administration was muted because Republi-

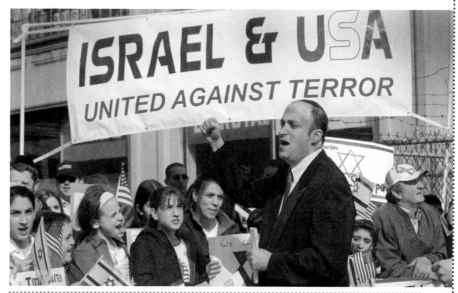

Certain groups of Americans, based on their ethnicity or religion, get involved in American foreign policy regarding nations that are of special interest to them. In this photo, a rabbi leads a pro-Israeli demonstration before a speech given by President George W. Bush.

can leaders did not want to challenge a president from their own party.

The controversy over gay men and lesbians serving in the armed forces illustrates the dynamic political nature of foreign and defense policy formulation. When President Clinton announced shortly after taking office that he was preparing an executive order to end the Pentagon's ban on gay men and lesbians in the military, he was taking a principled stand and fulfilling a campaign promise as well. Clinton argued that men and women who are serving their country honorably should be judged on the basis of their behavior rather than their sexual orientation. People who play by the rules should be allowed to serve without discrimination. Clinton's

President Bush stands strong with a NYC firefighter at the ruins of the World Trade Center.

promise to end the ban also fulfilled a campaign promise to a key group of political supporters. Gay men and lesbians are an important voter bloc, especially in the large states of California and New York. Furthermore, gay and lesbian rights groups raised millions of dollars for the Clinton campaign during the 1992 election season.

President Clinton's proposal generated a firestorm of controversy. The **Joint Chiefs of Staff,** a group of military advisors composed of the chiefs of staff of the U.S. Army and Air Force, the chief of naval operations, and sometimes the commandant of the Marine Corps, strongly disagreed with the president's plan. The Joint Chiefs warned that allowing openly gay men and lesbians to serve in the armed forces would undermine morale and threaten unit cohesion.

Democratic Senator Sam Nunn, who was then the chair of the Armed Services Committee, was the most effective opponent of the president's proposal. Nunn's committee staged televised hearings on the issue, allowing critics of the president's proposal a public forum to attack the plan while giving groups and individuals who favored the president's position little opportunity to make their case. Nunn even took the committee on a fact-finding tour of an aircraft carrier, showing television reporters the close quarters where service men and women live and work.

Clinton eventually compromised on the issue because he recognized that had he signed an executive order lifting the ban, Congress would have quickly passed legislation writing the original policy into law. The compromise, which pleased few, was called the "don't ask, don't tell policy." The military would not ask new recruits about their sexual orientation and would stop conducting investigations aimed at identifying and discharging homosexuals, but it would discharge service members who revealed their sexual orientation. Gay men and women who stayed "in the closet" could continue their service.

## Policy Implementation and Evaluation

The executive branch is primarily responsible for the implementation of foreign policy. The Department of State, Department of Defense, and CIA are prominently involved, but many other agencies and departments play a role as well. The Department of Agriculture, for example, promotes the sale of American agricultural products abroad. The Department of Education administers student-exchange programs.

Foreign and defense policies may not always be implemented the way the president and Congress originally intended or expected. Bureaucrats sometimes have priorities of their own. Also, large bureaucracies tend to develop standard operating procedures (SOPs) that they follow in performing their tasks.

The implementation of the "don't ask, don't tell" policy demonstrates that official policy changes do not always lead to changes in policy implementation; in fact, the military has actually become more diligent at discharging suspected homosexuals from the armed services. The military dismissed 1,227 people in 2001 for being gay or lesbian, far more people than were discharged for homosexuality in 1993. The number of people forced out of the military because of their sexual orientation fell significantly in subsequent years, but most observers believed that the decline reflected the military's need to hold onto qualified personnel.[34]

The government has no systematic, ongoing mechanism for evaluating foreign and defense policies. Congress monitors expenditures, but often limits its policy oversight to high-profile issues, or issues that affect members' home districts. Scandals also receive considerable attention. Other efforts at evaluation take place in the executive branch, in academia, and by the news media.

In general, foreign and defense policies are probably more difficult to evaluate than policies in other areas. It is not always possible to determine whether policy goals have been met. In the absence of war, for example, any evaluation of the effectiveness of particular defense strategies has to be at least somewhat speculative. Another problem is that many of the details of policy implementation are secret. Only now is information available so that historians can begin to evaluate American foreign policy in the years following World War II.

**Joint Chiefs of Staff** a military advisory body that is composed of the chiefs of staff of the U.S. Army and Air Force, the chief of naval operations, and sometimes the commandant of the Marine Corps.

# President Obama's Speech in Egypt

By Mckenzie Cassidy, *Suite 101*

JUNE 4, 2009

**President Barack Obama delivered a historic speech in Cairo, Egypt on June 3 in an attempt to mend the relationship between the United States and the Islamic world**

The speech received a tremendous amount of publicity after some controversial figures were invited, but overall the 55-minute speech stressed tolerance and partnership between East and West.  Seven million Muslims currently reside in the United States and Obama stressed that Islam is a vital part of the country—with a total of 1,200 mosques, and at least one in every state. The goal of the speech was to address vicious stereotypes and ideally get both sides working together against religious extremism and violence. "I've come here to Cairo to seek a new beginning between the United States and Muslims around the world, one based on mutual interest and mutual respect, and one based upon the truth that America and Islam are not exclusive and need not be in competition," said Obama.

## Conquering Stereotypes

Islamic extremists throughout the world have declared war or "jihad" on the United States because they believe that Americans are imperialists looking to dominate the Middle East. Obama wanted to debunk this notion. "Just as Muslims do not fit a crude stereotype, America is not the crude stereotype of a self-interested empire," said Obama.

Of course, any stereotype goes both ways. Obama, a Christian who came from a Muslim family in Kenya and lived in Indonesia for a few years as child, said he will also never stop working to counteract negative stereotypes of Muslims in the United States.

## Working Together Against Extremism

Obama pointed out that tensions exist between the United States and Muslim world, but rather than pretend they don't exist he suggested they take the tensions head on. The White House has been reaching out to countries such as Pakistan to work together in finding extremists. While the events of September 11 were traumatic for the American people, he told the Muslim world that continued operations in Afghanistan were only to root out extremist groups, such as Al Qaeda, that not only kill Americans but Muslim civilians. He added that if these dangerous groups didn't exist in Afghanistan than U.S. forces would not be present.  Obama described the War in Iraq as a "war of choice," and said all troops were slated to leave in 2012.

Other topics covered in the speech included relations between Israel and Palestine, religious freedom, the development of democracy and economic opportunities.

## ⬈CRITICAL THINKING QUESTIONS

- What are the sources of tension between the United States and the Muslim world?
- Why do you think President Obama decided to deliver the speech in Egypt rather than in the United States or in a Muslim country such as Indonesia, which is considered a democracy?
- Do you think that Obama is naïve to reach out to the Muslim world or do you believe that his speech will lead to better relations between Muslim countries and the United States?

>> END

# TEST yourself

1. Why does the United States oppose the development of nuclear weapons in Iran?
   A. Iran could provide a nuclear weapon to a terrorist group.
   B. Iran could use nuclear weapons against American interests in the Middle East or against allies of the United States.
   C. Iran could use its possession of nuclear weapons to bully its neighbors.
   D. All of the above.

2. Nations that threaten world peace by sponsoring international terrorism and promoting the spread of weapons of mass destruction are known as which of the following?
   A. Rogue states
   B. Nongovernmental organizations
   C. United Nations
   D. Postindustrial societies

3. Which of the following is an international organization created to promote economic stability worldwide?
   A. NATO
   B. United Nations
   C. WHO
   D. IMF

4. Which of the following organizations would be involved in international efforts to control avian influenza (bird flu)?
   A. NATO
   B. United Nations
   C. WHO
   D. IMF

5. Which of the following is a defense alliance?
   A. NATO
   B. United Nations
   C. WHO
   D. IMF

6. Which of the following organizations would be most likely to mediate a trade dispute?
   A. NATO
   B. WTO
   C. WHO
   D. IMF

7. Greenpeace, Friends of the Earth, World Wide Fund for Nature, and the Nature Conservancy are all examples of which of the following?
   A. Nation-states
   B. Rogue states
   C. Nongovernmental organizations
   D. All of the above

8. Which of the following statements about foreign aid is *not* true?
   A. Foreign aid makes up about 10 percent of the federal budget.
   B. Israel is a major beneficiary of American foreign aid.
   C. Egypt is a major beneficiary of American foreign aid.
   D. The United States has increased aid to countries whose assistance it needs in the war on terror.

9. Which of the following is an argument offered by those people who believe that the United States should take an internationalist approach to foreign policy?
   A. The United States should act in its own best interests rather than compromising with other nations.
   B. As the world's most powerful nation, the United States does not have to accommodate the interests of other countries.
   C. The United States needs the support of other nations if it hopes to accomplish its foreign policy goals.
   D. All of the above.

10. Which of the following statements is true about American defense spending?
    A. In general, defense spending rises during wartime and falls during peacetime.
    B. As a percentage of GDP, defense spending is much less today than it was in the 1960s.
    C. Defense spending has been rising in recent years because of the war on terror and the wars in Afghanistan and Iraq.
    D. All of the above.

11. "The Soviet leaders did not dare to launch a nuclear attack against the United States because the American counterattack would have destroyed the Soviet Union and vice versa." This statement is an expression of which of the following?
    A. Preemption
    B. Democratic peace
    C. Mutual assured destruction (MAD)
    D. "Don't ask, don't tell" policy

12. The capacity of a nation to absorb an initial nuclear attack and retain sufficient nuclear firepower to inflict unacceptable damage on its adversary is known as which of the following?
    A. Second-strike capability
    B. Mutual assured destruction (MAD)
    C. Deterrence
    D. Preemption

13. Why did Pakistan develop nuclear weapons?
    A. To prevent the United States from attacking it
    B. To sell weapons to other countries, including North Korea and Iran
    C. To threaten surrounding countries in order to spread Islam throughout the region
    D. To counter the development of nuclear weapons by neighboring India

14. "The North Koreans would not be a threat to the United States, even if they acquired nuclear weapons, because they are not suicidal. They realize that the United States would easily be able to wipe them off the face of the Earth." This statement is an expression of which of the following concepts?
    A. Second-strike capability
    B. Mutual assured destruction (MAD)
    C. Deterrence
    D. Preemption

15. "The United States needs to attack Iran to eliminate its nuclear capacity before it has the opportunity to attack us or to provide weapons of mass destruction to terrorists." This statement is an expression of which of the following concepts?
    A. Second-strike capability
    B. Mutual assured destruction (MAD)
    C. Deterrence
    D. Preemption

16. Which president is most closely associated with the concept of preemption?
    A. Richard Nixon
    B. George W. Bush
    C. Bill Clinton
    D. Ronald Reagan

17. Which of the following statements best summarizes Defense Secretary Donald Rumsfeld's approach to conventional forces?
    A. Rumsfeld believed that U.S. Armed Forces could best accomplish their goals by relying on speed, mobility, and firepower.
    B. Rumsfeld favored relying on nuclear weapons for the defense of the United States while depending on the conventional forces of allies to achieve defense goals.
    C. Rumsfeld favored reintroducing the military draft because the volunteer army was not large enough to accomplish defense goals.
    D. Rumsfeld believed that the United States should reduce its presence abroad so that its forces would not be exposed to terrorist attack.

18. Which of the following officials historically has taken the lead in foreign and defense policymaking?
    A. Secretary of defense
    B. Speaker of the House
    C. Chief justice of the Supreme Court
    D. President

19. The "don't ask, don't tell" policy deals with which of the following issues?
    A. The interrogation of terror suspects held in American custody
    B. Gay men and lesbians serving in the U.S. Armed Forces
    C. The ability of the armed forces to attract enough volunteers to staff the volunteer army
    D. Intelligence leaks over American policy in the war on terror

KNOW *the* **score**

18–19 correct: **Congratulations! You are well informed!**

15–17 correct: **Your political knowledge is a bit low—be sure to review the key terms and visit TheThinkSpot.**

<14 correct: **Reread the chapter more thoroughly.**

1. D; 2. A; 3. D; 4. C; 5. A; 6. B; 7. C; 8. A; 9. C; 10. D; 11. C; 12. A; 13. D; 14. C; 15. D; 16. B; 17. A; 18. D; 19. B

**the THINKSPOT**
**www.thethinkspot.com**

# the declaration
## OF INDEPENDENCE

## In Congress, July 4, 1776

*The unanimous Declaration of the thirteen united States of America.*

When in the Course of human events, it becomes necessary for one people to dissolve the political bands which have connected them with another, and to assume among the Powers of the earth, the separate and equal station to which the Laws of Nature and of Nature's God entitle them, a decent respect to the opinions of mankind requires that they should declare the causes which impel them to the separation.

We hold these truths to be self-evident, that all men are created equal, that they are endowed by their Creator with certain unalienable Rights, that among these are Life, Liberty and the pursuit of Happiness. That to secure these rights, Governments are instituted among Men, deriving their just powers from the consent of the governed. That whenever any Form of Government becomes destructive of these ends, it is the Right of the People to alter or to abolish it, and to institute new Government, laying its foundation on such principles and organizing its powers in such form, as to them shall seem most likely to effect their Safety and Happiness. Prudence, indeed, will dictate that Governments long established should not be changed for light and transient causes; and accordingly all experience hath shown, that mankind are more disposed to suffer, while evils are sufferable, than to right themselves by abolishing the forms to which they are accustomed. But when a long train of abuses and usurpations, pursuing invariably the same Object evinces a design to reduce them under absolute Despotism, it is their right, it is their duty, to throw off such Government, and to provide new Guards for their future security. Such has been the patient sufferance of these Colonies; and such is now the necessity which constrains them to alter their former Systems of Government. The history of the present King of Great Britain is a history of repeated injuries and usurpations, all having in direct object the establishment of an absolute Tyranny over these States. To prove this, let Facts be submitted to a candid world.

He has refused his Assent to Laws, the most wholesome and necessary for the public good.

He has forbidden his Governors to pass Laws of immediate and pressing importance, unless suspended in their operation till his Assent should be obtained; and when so suspended, he has utterly neglected to attend to them.

He has refused to pass other Laws for the accommodation of large districts of people, unless those people would relinquish the right of Representation in the Legislature, a right inestimable to them and formidable to tyrants only.

He has called together legislative bodies at places unusual, uncomfortable, and distant from the depository of their Public Records, for the sole purpose of fatiguing them into compliance with his measures.

He has dissolved Representative Houses repeatedly, for opposing with manly firmness his invasions on the rights of the people.

He has refused for a long time, after such dissolutions, to cause others to be elected; whereby the Legislative Powers, incapable of Annihilation, have returned to the People at large for their exercise; the State remaining in the mean time exposed to all the dangers of invasion from without, and convulsions within.

He has endeavoured to prevent the population of these States; for that purpose obstructing the Laws for Naturalization of Foreigners; refusing to pass others to encourage their migrations hither, and raising the conditions of new Appropriations of Lands.

He has obstructed the Administration of Justice, by refusing his Assent to Laws for establishing Judiciary Powers.

He has made Judges dependent on his Will alone, for the tenure of their offices, and the amount and payment of their salaries.

He has erected a multitude of New Offices, and sent hither swarms of Officers to harass our people, and eat out their substance.

He has kept among us, in times of peace, Standing Armies without the Consent of our legislatures.

He has affected to render the Military independent of and superior to the Civil Power.

He has combined with others to subject us to a jurisdiction foreign to our constitution, and unacknowledged by our laws; giving his Assent to their acts of pretended Legislation:

For quartering large bodies of armed troops among us:

For protecting them, by a mock Trial, from Punishment for any Murders which they should commit on the inhabitants of these States:

For cutting off our Trade with all parts of the world:

For imposing taxes on us without our Consent:

For depriving us in many cases, of the benefits of Trial by Jury:

For transporting us beyond Seas to be tried for pretended offences:

For abolishing the free System of English Laws in a neighbouring Province, establishing therein an Arbitrary government, and enlarging its Boundaries so as to render it at once an example and fit instrument for introducing the same absolute rule into these Colonies:

For taking away our Charters, abolishing our most valuable Laws, and altering fundamentally the Forms of our Governments:

For suspending our own Legislature, and declaring themselves invested with Power to legislate for us in all cases whatsoever.

He has abdicated Government here, by declaring us out of his Protection and waging War against us.

He has plundered our seas, ravaged our Coasts, burnt our towns, and destroyed the lives of our people.

He is at this time transporting large armies of foreign mercenaries to compleat the works of death, desolation and tyranny, already begun with circumstances of Cruelty and perfidy scarcely paralleled in the most barbarous ages, and totally unworthy the Head of a civilized nation.

He has constrained our fellow Citizens taken Captive on the high Seas to bear Arms against their Country, to become the executioners of their friends and Brethren, or to fall themselves by their Hands.

He has excited domestic insurrections amongst us, and has endeavoured to bring on the inhabitants of our frontiers, the merciless Indian Savages, whose known rule of warfare, is an undistinguished destruction of all ages, sexes and conditions.

In every stage of these Oppressions We have Petitioned for Redress in the most humble terms: Our repeated Petitions have been answered only by repeated injury. A Prince, whose character is thus marked by every act which may define a Tyrant, is unfit to be the ruler of a free people.

Nor have we been wanting in attentions to our British brethren. We have warned them from time to time of attempts by their legislature to extend an unwarrantable jurisdiction over us. We have reminded them of the circumstances of our emigration and settlement here. We have appealed to their native justice and magnanimity, and we have conjured them by the ties of our common kindred to disavow these usurpations which, would inevitably interrupt our connections and correspondence. They too have been deaf to the voice of justice and of consanguinity. We must, therefore, acquiesce in the necessity, which denounces our Separation, and hold them, as we hold the rest of mankind, Enemies in War, in Peace Friends.

We, therefore, the Representatives of the United States of America, in General Congress, Assembled, appealing to the Supreme Judge of the world for the rectitude of our intentions, do, in the Name, and by authority of the good People of these Colonies, solemnly publish and declare, That these United Colonies are, and of Right ought to be Free and Independent States; that they are Absolved from all Allegiance to the British Crown, and that all political connection between them and the State of Great Britain, is and ought to be totally dissolved; and that as Free and Independent States, they have full Power to levy War, conclude Peace, contract Alliances, establish Commerce, and to do all other Acts and Things which Independent States may of right do. And for the support of this Declaration, with a firm reliance of the Protection of Divine Providence, we mutually pledge to each other our Lives, our Fortunes and our sacred Honor.

# the constitution
## OF THE UNITED STATES OF AMERICA

*We the people of the United States, in Order to form a more perfect Union, establish justice, insure domestic Tranquility, provide for the common defence, promote the general Welfare, and secure the Blessings of Liberty to ourselves and our Posterity, do ordain and establish this Constitution for the United States of America.*

## Article I

### Section 1

All legislative Powers herein granted shall be vested in a Congress of the United States, which shall consist of a Senate and House of Representatives.

### Section 2

The House of Representatives shall be composed of Members chosen every second Year by the People of the several States, and the Electors in each State shall have the Qualifications requisite for Electors of the most numerous Branch of the State Legislature.

No person shall be a Representative who shall not have attained to the Age of twenty five Years, and been seven Years a Citizen of the United States, and who shall not, when elected, be an Inhabitant of that State in which he shall be chosen.

Representatives and direct Taxes shall be apportioned among the several States which may be included within this Union, according to their respective Numbers, which shall be determined by adding to the whole Number of free Persons, including those bound to Service for a Term of Years, and excluding Indians not taxed, three fifths of all other Persons.* The actual Enumeration shall be made within three years after the first Meeting of the Congress of the United States, and within every subsequent Term of ten Years, in such Manner as they shall by Law direct. The Number of Representatives shall not exceed one for every thirty Thousand, but each State shall have at Least one Representative; and until such enumeration shall be made, the State of New Hampshire shall be entitled to chuse three, Massachusetts eight, Rhode-Island and Providence Plantations one, Connecticut five, New-York six, New Jersey four, Pennsylvania eight, Delaware one, Maryland six, Virginia ten, North Carolina five, South Carolina five, and Georgia three.

When vacancies happen in the Representation from any State, the Executive Authority thereof shall issue Writs of Election to fill such Vacancies.

The House of Representatives shall chuse their Speaker and other Officers; and shall have the sole Power of Impeachment.

### Section 3

The Senate of the United States shall be composed of two Senators from each State, chosen by the Legislature thereof, for six Years; and each Senator shall have one Vote.

Immediately after they shall be assembled in Consequence of the first Election, they shall be divided as equally as may be into three Classes. The Seats of the Senators of the first Class shall be vacated at the Expiration of the second Year, of the second Class at the Expiration of the fourth Year, and of the third Class at the Expiration of the sixth Year, so that one third may be chosen every second Year; and if Vacancies happen by Resignation, or otherwise, during the Recess of the Legislature of any State, the Executive thereof may make temporary Appointments until the next Meeting of the Legislature, which shall then fill such Vacancies.†

No Person shall be a Senator who shall not have attained to the Age of thirty Years, and been nine Years a Citizen of the United States, and who shall not, when elected, be an Inhabitant of that State in which he shall be chosen.

The Vice President of the United States shall be President of the Senate, but shall have no Vote, unless they be equally divided.

The Senate shall chuse their other Officers, and also a President pro tempore, in the Absence of the Vice President, or when he shall exercise the Office of the President of the United States.

The Senate shall have the sole Power to try all impeachments. When sitting for that Purpose, they shall be on Oath or Affirmation. When the President of the United States is tried, the Chief Justice shall preside: And no person shall be convicted without the Concurrence of two thirds of the Members present.

Judgment in Cases of Impeachment shall not extend further than to removal from Office, and disqualification to hold and enjoy any Office of honor, Trust or Profit under the United States; but the Party convicted shall nevertheless be liable and subject to Indictment, Trial, Judgment and Punishment, according to Law.

*Other persons being black slaves. Modified by Amendment XIV, Section 2.

†Provisions changed by Amendment XVII.

## Section 4

The Times, Places and Manner of holding Elections for Senators and Representatives, shall be prescribed in each State by the Legislature thereof; but the Congress may at any time by Law make or alter such Regulations, except as to the Places of chusing Senators.

The Congress shall assemble at least once in every Year, and such Meeting shall be on the first Monday in December, unless they shall by Law appoint a different Day.*

## Section 5

Each House shall be the Judge of the Elections, Returns and Qualifications of its own Members, and a Majority of each shall constitute a Quorum to do Business; but a smaller number may adjourn from day to day, and may be authorized to compel the Attendance of absent Members, in such Manner, and under such Penalties as each House may provide.

Each House may determine the Rules of its Proceedings, punish its Members for disorderly Behaviour, and, with the Concurrence of two thirds, expel a Member.

Each House shall keep a Journal of its Proceedings, and from time to time publish the same, excepting such Parts as may in their Judgment require Secrecy; and the Yeas and Nays of the Members of either House on any question shall, at the Desire of one fifth of those Present, be entered on the Journal.

Neither House, during the Session of Congress, shall, without the Consent of the other, adjourn for more than three days, nor to any other Place than that in which the two Houses shall be sitting.

## Section 6

The Senators and Representatives shall receive a Compensation for their Services, to be ascertained by Law, and paid out of the Treasury of the United States. They shall in all Cases, except Treason, Felony and Breach of the Peace, be privileged from arrest during their Attendance at the Session of their respective Houses, and in going to and returning from the same; and for any Speech or Debate in either House, they shall not be questioned in any other Place.

No Senator or Representative shall, during the Time for which he was elected, be appointed to any civil Office under the Authority of the United States, which shall have been created, or the Emoluments whereof shall have been encreased, during such time; and no Person holding any Office under the United States shall be a Member of either House during his Continuance in Office.

## Section 7

All Bills for raising Revenue shall originate in the House of Representatives; but the Senate may propose or concur with Amendments as on other Bills.

Every Bill which shall have passed the House of Representatives and the Senate, shall, before it become a Law, be presented to the President of the United States;

If he approves he shall sign it, but if not he shall return it, with his Objections, to that House in which it shall have originated, who shall enter the Objections at large on their Journal, and proceed to reconsider it. If after such Reconsideration two thirds of that House shall agree to pass the Bill, it shall be sent, together with the Objections, to the other House, by which it shall likewise be reconsidered, and if approved by two thirds of that House, it shall become a Law. But in all such Cases the Votes of both Houses shall be determined by Yeas and Nays, and the Names of the Persons voting for and against the Bill shall be entered on the Journal of each House respectively. If any Bill shall not be returned by the President within ten Days (Sundays excepted) after it shall have been presented to him, the Same shall be a Law, in like Manner as if he had signed it, unless the Congress by their Adjournment prevent its Return, in which Case it shall not be a Law.

Every Order, Resolution, or Vote to which the Concurrence of the Senate and House of Representatives may be necessary (except on a question of Adjournment) shall be presented to the President of the United States; and before the Same shall take Effect, shall be approved by him, or being disapproved by him, shall be repassed by two thirds of the Senate and House of Representatives, according to the Rules and Limitations prescribed in the Case of a Bill.

## Section 8

The Congress shall have Power To lay and collect Taxes, Duties, Imposts and Excises, to pay the Debts and provide for the common Defence and general Welfare of the United States; but all Duties, Imposts and Excises shall be uniform throughout the United States;

To borrow Money on the credit of the United States;

To regulate Commerce with foreign Nations, and among the several States, and with the Indian Tribes;

To establish a uniform Rule of Naturalization, and uniform Laws on the subject of Bankruptcies throughout the United States;

To coin Money, regulate the Value thereof, and of foreign Coin, and fix the Standard of Weights and Measures;

To provide for the Punishment of counterfeiting the Securities and current Coin of the United States;

To establish Post offices and post Roads;

To promote the Progress of Science and useful Arts, by securing for limited Times to Authors and Inventors the exclusive Right to their respective Writings and Discoveries;

To constitute Tribunals inferior to the supreme Court;

To define and punish Piracies and Felonies committed on the high Seas, and Offences against the Law of Nations;

To declare War, grant Letters of Marque and Reprisal, and make Rules concerning Captures on Land and Water;

*Provisions changed by Amendment XX, Section 2.

To raise and support Armies, but no Appropriation of Money to that Use shall be for a longer Term than two Years;

To provide and maintain a Navy;

To make Rules for the Government and Regulation of the land and naval Forces;

To provide for calling forth the Militia to execute the Laws of the Union, suppress Insurrections and repel Invasions;

To provide for organizing, arming, and disciplining, the Militia, and for governing such Part of them as may be employed in the Service of the United States, reserving to the States respectively, the Appointment of the Officers, and the Authority of training the Militia according to the discipline prescribed by Congress;

To exercise exclusive Legislation in all Cases whatsoever, over such District (not exceeding ten Miles square) as may, by Cession of particular States, and the Acceptance of Congress, become the Seat of Government of the United States, and to exercise like Authority over all Places purchased by the Consent of the Legislature of the State in which the Same shall be, for the Erection of Forts, Magazines, Arsenals, dock-Yards, and other needful Buildings;—And

To make all Laws which shall be necessary and proper for carrying into Execution the foregoing Powers, and all other Powers vested by this Constitution in the Government of the United States, or in any Department or Officer thereof.

## Section 9

The Migration or Importation of such Persons as any of the States now existing shall think proper to admit, shall not be prohibited by the Congress prior to the Year one thousand eight hundred and eight, but a Tax, or duty may be imposed on such Importation, not exceeding ten dollars for each Person.

The privilege of the Writ of Habeas Corpus shall not be suspended, unless when in Cases of Rebellion or Invasion the public Safety may require it.

No Bill of Attainder or ex post facto Law shall be passed.

No Capitation, or other direct, Tax shall be laid, unless in Proportion to the Census or Enumeration herein before directed to be taken.

No Tax or Duty shall be laid on Articles exported from any State.

No Preference shall be given by any Regulation of Commerce or Revenue to the Ports of one State over those of another; nor shall Vessels bound to, or from, one State, be obliged to enter, clear, or pay Duties in another.

No Money shall be drawn from the Treasury, but in Consequence of Appropriations made by Law; and a regular Statement and Account of the Receipts and Expenditures of all public Money shall be published from time to time.

No Title of Nobility shall be granted by the United States: And no Person holding any Office of Profit or Trust under them, shall, without the Consent of the Congress, accept of any present, Emolument, Office, or Title, of any kind whatever, from any King, Prince, or foreign State.

## Section 10

No State shall enter into any Treaty, Alliance, or Confederation; grant Letters of Marque and Reprisal; coin Money; emit Bills of Credit; make any Thing but gold and silver Coin a Tender in Payment of Debts; pass any Bill of Attainder, ex post facto Law, or Law impairing the Obligation of Contracts, or grant any Title of Nobility.

No State shall, without the Consent of the Congress, lay any Imposts or Duties on Imports or Exports, except what may be absolutely necessary for executing its inspection Laws: and the net Produce of all Duties and Imposts, laid by any State on Imports or Exports, shall be for the Use of the Treasury of the United States; and all such Laws shall be subject to the Revision and Control of the Congress.

No State shall, without the Consent of Congress, lay any Duty of Tonnage, keep Troops, or Ships of War in time of Peace, enter into any Agreement or Compact with another State, or with a foreign Power, or engage in War, unless actually invaded, or in such imminent Danger as will not admit of delay.

## Article II

### Section 1

The executive Power shall be vested in a President of the United States of America. He shall hold his Office during the Term of four Years, and, together with the Vice President, chosen for the same Term, be elected, as follows:

Each State shall appoint, in such Manner as the Legislature thereof may direct, a Number of Electors, equal to the whole Number of Senators and Representatives to which the State may be entitled in the Congress; but no Senator or Representative, or Person holding an Office of Trust or Profit under the United States, shall be appointed an Elector.

The Electors shall meet in their respective States, and vote by Ballot for two Persons, of whom one at least shall not be an Inhabitant of the same State with themselves. And they shall make a List of all the Persons voted for, and of the Number of Votes for each; which List they shall sign and certify, and transmit sealed to the Seat of the Government of the United States, directed to the President of the Senate. The President of the Senate shall, in the Presence of the Senate and House of Representatives, open all the Certificates, and the Votes shall then be counted. The Person having the greatest Number of Votes shall be the President, if such Number be a Majority of the whole Number of Electors appointed; and if there be more than one who have such Majority, and have an equal Number of Votes, then the House of Representatives shall immediately chuse by Ballot one of them for President; and if no Person have a Majority, then from the five highest on the List the said House shall in like Manner chuse the President. But in chusing the President, the Votes shall be taken by States, the Representation from each State having one Vote; a quorum for this Purpose shall consist of a Member or Members from two thirds of the States, and a Majority of all the States shall be necessary to a Choice. In every Case, after the Choice of the President, the Person having the greatest Number of Votes of the Electors shall be the Vice President. But if there should remain two or more who have equal Votes, the Senate shall chuse from them by Ballot the Vice President.*

The Congress may determine the Time of chusing the Electors, and the Day on which they shall give their Votes; which Day shall be the same throughout the United States.

No Person except a natural born Citizen, or a Citizen of the United States, at the time of the Adoption of this Constitution, shall be eligible to the Office of President; neither shall any Person be eligible to that Office who shall not have attained to the Age of thirty five Years, and been fourteen Years a Resident within the United States.

In Case of the Removal of the President from Office, or of his Death, Resignation, or Inability to discharge the Powers and Duties of the said Office, the Same shall devolve on the Vice President, and the Congress may by Law provide for the Case of Removal, Death, Resignation or Inability, both of the President and Vice President, declaring what Officer shall then act as President, and such Officer shall act accordingly, until the Disability be removed, or a President shall be elected.

The President shall, at stated Times, receive for his Services, a Compensation, which shall neither be encreased nor diminished during the Period for which he shall have been elected, and he shall not receive within that Period any other Emolument from the United States, or any of them.

Before he enter on the Execution of his Office, he shall take the following Oath or Affirmation:—"I do solemnly swear (or affirm) that I will faithfully execute the Office of President of the United States, and will to the best of my Ability, preserve, protect and defend the Constitution of the United States."

## Section 2

The President shall be Commander in Chief of the Army and Navy of the United States, and of the Militia of the several States, when called into the actual Service of the United States; he may require the Opinion, in writing, of the principal Officer in each of the executive Departments, upon any Subject relating to the Duties of their respective Offices, and he shall have Power to grant Reprieves and Pardons for Offences against the United States, except in Cases of Impeachment.

He shall have Power, by and with the Advice and Consent of the Senate, to make Treaties, provided two thirds of the Senators present concur; and he shall nominate, and by and with the Advice and Consent of the Senate, shall appoint Ambassadors, other public Ministers and Consuls, Judges of the supreme Court, and all other Officers of the United States, whose Appointments are not herein otherwise provided for, and which shall be established by Law: but the Congress may by Law vest the Appointment of such inferior Officers, as they think proper in the President alone, in the Courts of Law, or in the Heads of Departments.

The President shall have Power to fill up all Vacancies that may happen during the Recess of the Senate, by granting Commissions which shall expire at the end of their next Session.

## Section 3

He shall from time to time give to the Congress Information of the State of the Union, and recommend to their Consideration such Measures as he shall judge necessary and expedient; he may, on extraordinary occasions, convene both Houses, or either of them, and in Case of Disagreement between them, with Respect to the Time of Adjournment, he may adjourn them to such Time as he shall think proper; he shall receive Ambassadors and other public Ministers; he shall take Care that the Laws be faithfully executed, and shall Commission all the Officers of the United States.

## Section 4

The President, Vice President and all civil Officers of the United States, shall be removed from Office on Impeachment for, and Conviction of, Treason, Bribery, or other high Crimes and Misdemeanors.

# Article III

## Section 1

The judicial Power of the United States, shall be vested in one supreme Court, and in such inferior Courts as the Congress may from time to time ordain and establish. The Judges, both of the supreme and inferior Courts, shall hold their Offices during good Behaviour, and shall, at stated Times, receive for their Services, a Compensation, which shall not be diminished during their Continuance in Office.

## Section 2

The judicial Power shall extend to all Cases in Law and Equity, arising under this Constitution, the Laws of the United States, and Treaties made, or which shall be made, under their Authority;—to all Cases affecting

*Provisions superseded by Amendment XII.

Ambassadors, other public Ministers and Consuls;—to all cases of admiralty and maritime Jurisdiction;—to Controversies to which the United States shall be a Party;—to Controversies between two or more States;—between a State and Citizens of another State;—between Citizens of different States;—between Citizens of the same State claiming Lands under Grants of different States, and between a State, or the Citizens thereof, and foreign States, Citizens or Subjects.*

In all Cases affecting Ambassadors, other public Ministers and Consuls, and those in which a State shall be Party, the supreme Court shall have original Jurisdiction. In all the other Cases before mentioned, the supreme Court shall have appellate Jurisdiction, both as to Law and Fact, with such Exceptions, and under such Regulations as the Congress shall make.

The Trial of all Crimes, except in Cases of Impeachment, shall be by Jury; and such Trial shall be held in the State where the said Crimes shall have been committed, but when not committed within any State, the Trial shall be at such Place or Places as the Congress may by law have directed.

## Section 3

Treason against the United States, shall consist only in levying War against them, or in adhering to their Enemies, giving them Aid and Comfort. No person shall be convicted of Treason unless on the Testimony of two Witnesses to the same overt Act, or on Confession in open Court.

The Congress shall have Power to declare the Punishment of Treason, but no Attainder of Treason shall work Corruption of Blood, or Forfeiture except during the Life of the Person attained.

## Article IV

### Section 1

Full Faith and Credit shall be given in each State to the public Acts, Records, and judicial Proceedings of every other State. And the Congress may by general Laws prescribe the Manner in which such Acts, Records and Proceedings shall be proved, and the Effect thereof.

### Section 2

The Citizens of each State shall be entitled to all Privileges and Immunities of Citizens in the several States.

A Person charged in any State with Treason, Felony, or other Crime, who shall flee from Justice, and be found in another State, shall on Demand of the executive Authority of the State from which he fled, be delivered up, to be removed to the State having Jurisdiction of the Crime.

No Person held to Service or Labour in one State, under the Laws thereof, escaping into another, shall, in Consequence of any Law or Regulation therein, be discharged from such Service or Labour, but shall be delivered up on Claim of the Party to whom such Service or Labour may be due.

*Clause changed by Amendment XI.

### Section 3

New States may be admitted by the Congress into this Union; but no new State shall be formed or erected within the Jurisdiction of any other State; nor any State be formed by the Junction of two or more States, or Parts of States, without the Consent of the Legislatures of the States concerned as well as of the Congress.

The Congress shall have Power to dispose of and make all needful Rules and Regulations respecting the Territory or other Property belonging to the United States; and nothing in this Constitution shall be so construed as to Prejudice any Claims of the United States, or of any particular State.

### Section 4

The United States shall guarantee to every State in this Union a Republican Form of Government, and shall protect each of them against Invasion; and on Application of the Legislature, or of the Executive (when the Legislature cannot be convened) against domestic Violence.

## Article V

The Congress, whenever two thirds of both Houses shall deem it necessary, shall propose Amendments to this Constitution, or, on the Application of the Legislatures of two thirds of the several States, shall call a Convention for proposing Amendments, which, in either Case, shall be valid to all Intents and Purposes, as Part of this Constitution, when ratified by the Legislatures of three fourths of the several states, or by Conventions in three fourths thereof, as the one or the other Mode of Ratification may be proposed by the Congress; Provided that no Amendment which may be made prior to the Year One thousand eight hundred and eight shall in any Manner affect the first and fourth Clauses in the Ninth Section of the first Article; and that no State, without its Consent, shall be deprived of its equal Suffrage in the Senate.

## Article VI

All Debts contracted and Engagements entered into, before the Adoption of this Constitution, shall be as valid against the United States under this Constitution, as under the Confederation.

This Constitution, and the Laws of the United States which shall be made in Pursuance thereof; and all Treaties made, or which shall be made, under the Authority of the United States, shall be the supreme Law of the Land; and the Judges in every State shall be bound thereby, any Thing in the Constitution or Laws of any State to the Contrary notwithstanding.

The Senators and Representatives before mentioned, and the Members of the several State Legislatures and all executive and judicial Officers, both of the United States and of the several States, shall be bound by Oath or Affirmation to support this Constitution; but no religious

Test shall ever be required as a Qualification to any Office or public Trust under the United States.

## Article VII

The Ratification of the Conventions of nine States shall be sufficient for the Establishment of this Constitution between the States so ratifying the Same.

Done in Convention by the Unanimous Consent of the States present the Seventeenth Day of September in the Year of our Lord one thousand seven hundred and Eighty seven and of the Independence of the United States of America the Twelfth.* In Witness whereof We have hereunto subscribed our Names.

*The Constitution was submitted on September 17, 1787, by the Constitutional Convention, was ratified by the conventions of several states at various dates up to May 29, 1790, and became effective on March 4, 1789.

# amendments
## TO THE CONSTITUTION
### (The First Ten Amendments Form the Bill of Rights)

### Amendment I [1791]

Congress shall make no law respecting an establishment of religion, or prohibiting the free exercise thereof; or abridging the freedom of speech, or of the press, or the right of the people peaceably to assemble, and to petition the Government for a redress of grievances.

### Amendment II [1791]

A well regulated Militia being necessary to the security of a free State, the right of the people to keep and bear Arms, shall not be infringed.

### Amendment III [1791]

No Soldier shall, in time of peace, be quartered in any house, without the consent of the Owner, nor in time of war, but in a manner to be prescribed by law.

### Amendment IV [1791]

The right of the people to be secure in their persons, houses, papers, and effects, against unreasonable searches and seizures, shall not be violated, and no Warrants shall issue, but upon probable cause, supported by Oath or affirmation, and particularly describing the place to be searched, and the persons or things to be seized.

### Amendment V [1791]

No person shall be held to answer for a capital or otherwise infamous crime, unless on a presentment or indictment of a Grand Jury, except in cases arising in the land or naval forces, or in the Militia, when in actual service in time of War or public danger; nor shall any person be subject for the same offence to be twice put in jeopardy of life or limb; nor shall be compelled in any criminal case to be a witness against himself, nor be deprived of life, liberty, or property, without due process of law; nor shall private property be taken for public use, without just compensation.

### Amendment VI [1791]

In all criminal prosecutions, the accused shall enjoy the right to a speedy and public trial, by an impartial jury of the State and district wherein the crime shall have been committed, which district shall have been previously ascertained by law, and to be informed of the nature and cause of the accusation; to be confronted with the witnesses against him; to have compulsory process for obtaining witnesses in his favor, and to have the Assistance of Counsel for his defence.

### Amendment VII [1791]

In Suits at common law, where the value in controversy shall exceed twenty dollars, the right of trial by jury shall be preserved, and no fact tried by a jury, shall be otherwise reexamined in any court of the United States, than according to the rules of the common law.

### Amendment VIII [1791]

Excessive bail shall not be required, nor excessive fines imposed, nor cruel and unusual punishments inflicted.

### Amendment IX [1791]

The enumeration in the Constitution, of certain rights, shall not be construed to deny or disparage others retained by the people.

### Amendment X [1791]

The powers not delegated to the United States by the Constitution, nor prohibited by it to the States, are reserved to the States respectively, or to the people.

## Amendment XI [1798]

The Judicial power of the United States shall not be construed to extend to any suit in law or equity, commenced or prosecuted against one of the United States by Citizens of another State, or by Citizens of Subjects of any Foreign State.

## Amendment XII [1804]

The Electors shall meet in their respective states and vote by ballot for President and Vice-President, one of whom, at least, shall not be an inhabitant of the same state with themselves; they shall name in their ballots the person voted for as President, and in distinct ballots the person voted for as Vice-President, and they shall make distinct lists of all persons voted for as President, and of all persons voted for as Vice-President, and of the number of votes for each, which lists they shall sign and certify, and transmit sealed to the seat of the government of the United States, directed to the President of the Senate;—The President of the Senate shall, in the presence of the Senate and House of Representatives, open all the certificates and the votes shall then be counted;—The person having the greatest number of votes for President, shall be the President, if such number be a majority of the whole number of Electors appointed; and if no person have such majority, then from the persons having the highest numbers not exceeding three on the list of those voted for as President, the House of Representatives shall choose immediately, by ballot, the President. But in choosing the President, the votes shall be taken by states, the representation from each state having one vote; a quorum for this purpose shall consist of a member or members from two-thirds of the states, and a majority of all the states shall be necessary to a choice. And if the House of Representatives shall not choose a President whenever the right of choice shall devolve upon them, before the fourth day of March next following, then the Vice-President shall act as President, as in the case of the death or other constitutional disability of the President.—The person having the greatest number of votes as Vice-President, shall be the Vice-President, if such number be a majority of the whole number of Electors appointed, and if no person have a majority, then from the two highest numbers on the list, the Senate shall choose the Vice-President; a quorum for the purpose shall consist of two-thirds of the whole number of Senators, and a majority of the whole number shall be necessary to a choice. But no person constitutionally ineligible to the office of President shall be eligible to that of Vice-President of the United States.

## Amendment XIII [1865]

### Section 1

Neither slavery nor involuntary servitude, except as a punishment for crime whereof the party shall have been duly convicted, shall exist within the United States, or any place subject to their jurisdiction.

### Section 2

Congress shall have power to enforce this article by appropriate legislation.

## Amendment XIV [1868]

### Section 1

All persons born or naturalized in the United States, and subject to the jurisdiction thereof, are citizens of the United States and the State wherein they reside. No State shall make or enforce any law which shall abridge the privileges or immunities of citizens of the United States; nor shall any State deprive any person of life, liberty, or property, without due process of law; nor deny to any person within its jurisdiction the equal protection of the laws.

### Section 2

Representatives shall be apportioned among the several States according to their respective numbers, counting the whole number of persons in each State, excluding Indians not taxed. But when the right to vote at any election for the choice of electors for President and Vice President of the United States, Representatives in Congress, the Executive and Judicial officers of a State, or the members of the Legislature thereof, is denied to any of the male inhabitants of such State being twenty-one years of age, and citizens of the United States or in any way abridged, except for participation in rebellion or other crime, the basis of representation therein shall be reduced in the proportion which the number of such male citizens shall bear to the whole number of male citizens twenty-one years of age in such State.

### Section 3

No person shall be a Senator or Representative in Congress, or elector of President and Vice President, or hold any office, civil or military, under the United States or under any State, who, having previously taken an oath, as a member of Congress, or as an officer of the United States, or as a member of any State legislature or as an executive or judicial officer of any State to support the Constitution of the United States, shall have engaged in insurrection or rebellion against the same, or given aid or comfort to the enemies thereof. But Congress may by a vote of two-thirds of each House, remove such disability.

### Section 4

The validity of the public debt of the United States, authorized by law, including debts incurred for payment of pensions and bounties for services in suppressing insurrection or rebellion, shall not be questioned. But neither the United States nor any State shall assume or pay any debt or obligation incurred in aid of insurrection or rebellion against the United States, or any claim for the loss or emancipation of any slave; but all such debts, obligations and claims shall be held illegal and void.

## Section 5
The Congress shall have the power to enforce, by appropriate legislation, the provisions of this article.

## Amendment XV [1870]

### Section 1
The right of citizens of the United States to vote shall not be denied or abridged by the United States or by any State on account of race, color, or previous condition of servitude.

### Section 2
The Congress shall have power to enforce this article by appropriate legislation.

## Amendment XVI [1913]

The Congress shall have power to lay and collect taxes on incomes, from whatever source derived, without apportionment among the several States, and without regard to any census or enumeration.

## Amendment XVII [1913]

The Senate of the United States shall be composed of two Senators from each State, elected by the people thereof, for six years; and each Senator shall have one vote. The electors in each State shall have the qualifications requisite for electors of the most numerous branch of the State legislatures.

When vacancies happen in the representation of any State in the Senate, the executive authority of such State shall issue writs of election to fill such vacancies: *Provided,* That the legislature of any State may empower the executive thereof to make temporary appointments until the people fill the vacancies by election as the legislature may direct.

This amendment shall not be so construed as to affect the election or term of any Senator chosen before it becomes valid as part of the Constitution.

## Amendment XVIII [1919]

### Section 1
After one year from the ratification of this article the manufacture, sale, or transportation of intoxicating liquors within, the importation thereof into, or the exportation thereof from the United States and all territory subject to the jurisdiction thereof for beverage purposes is hereby prohibited.

### Section 2
The Congress and the several States shall have concurrent power to enforce this article by appropriate legislation.

### Section 3
This article shall be inoperative unless it shall have been ratified as an amendment to the Constitution by the legislatures of the several States, as provided in the Constitution, within seven years from the date of the submission hereof to the States by the Congress.

## Amendment XIX [1920]

The right of citizens of the United States to vote shall not be denied or abridged by the United States or by any State on account of sex.

Congress shall have power to enforce this article by appropriate legislation.

## Amendment XX [1933]

### Section 1
The terms of the President and Vice President shall end at noon on the 20th day of January, and the terms of Senators and Representatives at noon on the 3rd day of January, of the years in which such terms would have ended if this article had not been ratified; and the terms of their successors shall then begin.

### Section 2
The Congress shall assemble at least once in every year, and such meeting shall begin at noon on the 3rd day of January, unless they shall by law appoint a different day.

### Section 3
If, at the time fixed for the beginning of the term of the President, the President elect shall have died, the Vice President elect shall become President. If a President shall not have been chosen before the time fixed for the beginning of his term, or if the President elect shall have failed to qualify, then the Vice President elect shall act as President until a President shall have qualified; and the Congress may by law provide for the case wherein neither a President elect nor a Vice President elect shall have qualified, declaring who shall then act as President, or the manner in which one who is to act shall be selected, and such person shall act accordingly until a President or Vice President shall have qualified.

### Section 4
The Congress may by law provide for the case of the death of any of the persons from whom the House of Representatives may choose a President whenever the right of choice shall have devolved upon them, and for the case of the death of any of the persons from whom the Senate may choose a Vice-President whenever the right of choice shall have devolved upon them.

### Section 5
Sections 1 and 2 shall take effect on the 15th day of October following the ratification of this article.

### Section 6
This article shall be inoperative unless it shall have been ratified as an amendment to the Constitution by the legislatures of three-fourths of the several States within seven years from the date of its submission.

## Amendment XXI [1933]

### Section 1

The eighteenth article of amendment to the Constitution of the United States is hereby repealed.

### Section 2

The transportation or importation into any State, Territory, or possession of the United States for delivery or use therein of intoxicating liquors, in violation of the laws thereof, is hereby prohibited.

### Section 3

This article shall be inoperative unless it shall have been ratified as an amendment to the Constitution by conventions in the several States, as provided in the Constitution, within seven years from the date of the submission hereof to the States by the Congress.

## Amendment XXII [1951]

### Section 1

No person shall be elected to the office of the President more than twice, and no person who has held the office of President, or acted as President, for more than two years of a term to which some other person was elected President shall be elected to the office of the President more than once. But this Article shall not apply to any person holding the office of President when this Article was proposed by the Congress, and shall not prevent any person who may be holding the office of President or acting as President, during the term within which this Article becomes operative from holding the office of President or acting as President during the remainder of such term.

## Amendment XXIII [1961]

### Section 1

The District constituting the seat of Government of the United States shall appoint in such manner as the Congress may direct:

A number of electors of President and Vice President equal to the whole number of Senators and Representatives in Congress to which the District would be entitled if it were a State, but in no event more than the least populous State; they shall be in addition to those appointed by the States, but they shall be considered, for the purposes of the election of President and Vice President, to be electors appointed by a State; and they shall meet in the District and perform such duties as provided by the twelfth article of Amendment.

### Section 2

The Congress shall have power to enforce this article by appropriate legislation.

## Amendment XXIV [1964]

### Section 1

The right of citizens of the United States to vote in any primary or other election for President or Vice President, for electors for President or Vice President, or for Senator or Representative in Congress, shall not be denied or abridged by the United States or any State by reason of failure to pay any poll tax or other tax.

### Section 2

The Congress shall have the power to enforce this article by appropriate legislation.

## Amendment XXV [1967]

### Section 1

In case of the removal of the President from office or his death or resignation, the Vice President shall become President.

### Section 2

Whenever there is a vacancy in the office of the Vice President, the President shall nominate a Vice President who shall take the office upon confirmation by a majority vote of both houses of Congress.

### Section 3

Whenever the President transmits to the President pro tempore of the Senate and the Speaker of the House of Representatives his written declaration that he is unable to discharge the powers and duties of his office, and until he transmits to them a written declaration to the contrary, such powers and duties shall be discharged by the Vice President as Acting President.

### Section 4

Whenever the Vice President and a majority of either the principal officers of the executive departments or of such other body as Congress may by law provide, transmit to the President pro tempore of the Senate and the Speaker of the House of Representatives their written declaration that the President is unable to discharge the powers and duties of his office, the Vice President shall immediately assume the powers and duties of the office as Acting President.

Thereafter, when the President transmits to the President pro tempore of the Senate and the Speaker of the House of Representatives his written declaration that no inability exists, he shall resume the powers and duties of his office unless the Vice President and a majority of either the principal officers of the executive department or of such other body as Congress may by law provide, transmit within four days to the President pro tempore of the Senate and the Speaker of the House of Representatives their written declaration that the President is unable to discharge the powers and duties of his office. Thereupon Congress shall decide the issue, assembling within 48 hours for that purpose if not in session. If the Congress, within 21 days after receipt of the latter written declaration, or, if Congress is not in session, within 21 days after Congress is required to assemble, determines by two-thirds vote of both houses that the President is unable to discharge the powers and duties of his office, the Vice President shall continue to discharge the same as Acting President; otherwise, the President shall resume the powers and duties of his office.

## Amendment XXVI [1971]

### Section 1
The right of citizens of the United States, who are 18 years of age or older, to vote shall not be denied or abridged by the United States or any state on account of age.

### Section 2
The Congress shall have the power to enforce this article by appropriate legislation.

## Amendment XXVII [1992]

No law varying the compensation for the service of Senators and Representatives shall take effect until an election of Representatives shall have intervened.

# choosing
## THE PRESIDENT

| Election Year | Elected to Office | | | | |
|---|---|---|---|---|---|
| | **President** | **Party** | **Vice President** | **Party** | |
| 1789 | George Washington | | John Adams | Parties not yet established | |
| 1792 | George Washington | | John Adams | Federalist | |
| 1796 | John Adams | Federalist | Thomas Jefferson | Democratic-Republican | |
| 1800 | Thomas Jefferson | Democratic-Republican | Aaron Burr | Democratic-Republican | |
| 1804 | Thomas Jefferson | Democratic-Republican | George Clinton | Democratic-Republican | |
| 1808 | James Madison | Democratic-Republican | George Clinton | Democratic-Republican | |
| 1812 | James Madison | Democratic-Republican | Elbridge Gerry | Democratic-Republican | |
| 1816 | James Monroe | Democratic-Republican | Daniel D. Tompkins | Democratic-Republican | |
| 1820 | James Monroe | Democratic-Republican | Daniel D. Tompkins | Democratic-Republican | |
| 1824 | John Quincy Adams Elected by House of Representatives because no candidate received a majority of electoral votes. | National Republican | John C. Calhoun | Democratic | |
| 1828 | Andrew Jackson | Democratic | John C. Calhoun | Democratic | |
| 1832 | Andrew Jackson | Democratic | Martin Van Buren | Democratic | |
| 1836 | Martin Van Buren | Democratic | Richard M. Johnson First and only vice president elected by Senate (1837), having failed to receive a majority of electoral votes. | Democratic | |

| Major Opponents | | Electoral Vote | | Popular Vote |
| --- | --- | --- | --- | --- |
| **For President** | **Party** | | | |
| | | Washington | 69 | Electors selected by |
| | | Adams | 34 | state legislatures |
| George Clinton | Democratic- | Washington | 132 | Electors selected by |
| | Republican | Adams | 77 | state legislatures |
| | | Clinton | 50 | |
| Thomas Pinckney | Federalist | Adams | 71 | Electors selected by |
| Aaron Burr | Democratic- | Jefferson | 68 | state legislatures |
| | Republican | Pinckney | 59 | |
| John Adams | Federalist | Jefferson | 73 | Electors selected by |
| Charles Cotesworth | Federalist | Adams | 65 | state legislatures |
| Pinckney | | | | |
| Charles Cotesworth | Federalist | Jefferson | 162 | Electors selected by |
| Pinckney | | Pinckney | 14 | state legislatures |
| Charles Cotesworth | Federalist | Madison | 122 | Electors selected by |
| Pinckney | | Pinckney | 47 | state legislatures |
| George Clinton | Eastern Republican | | | |
| De Witt Clinton | Democratic- | Madison | 128 | Electors selected |
| | Republican | Clinton | 89 | by state legislatures |
| | (antiwar faction) | | | |
| | and Federalist | | | |
| Rufus King | Federalist | Monroe | 183 | Electors selected by |
| | | King | 34 | state legislatures |
| | | Monroe | 231 | Electors selected by |
| | | John Quincy Adams | 1 | state legislatures |
| Andrew Jackson | Democratic | Adams | 84 | 113,122 |
| Henry Clay | Democratic- | Jackson | 99 | 151,271 |
| | Republican | Clay | 37 | 47,531 |
| William H. Crawford | Democratic- | Crawford | 41 | 40,856 |
| | Republican | | | |
| John Quincy Adams | National | Jackson | 178 | 642,553 |
| | Republican | Adams | 83 | 500,897 |
| Henry Clay | National Republican | Jackson | 219 | 701,780 |
| William Wirt | Anti-Masonic | Clay | 49 | 482,205 |
| | | Wirt | 7 | 100,715 |
| | | Floyd | 11 | Delegates chosen by |
| | | | | South Carolina |
| | | | | legislature |
| Daniel Webster | Whig | Van Buren | 170 | 764,176 |
| Hugh L. White | Whig | Harrison | 73 | 550,816 |
| William Henry | Anti-Masonic | White | 26 | 146,107 |
| Harrison | | Webster | 14 | 41,201 |
| | | Mangum | 11 | Delegates chosen |
| | | | | by South Carolina |
| | | | | legislature |

| Election Year | Elected to Office | | | | |
|---|---|---|---|---|---|
| | **President** | **Party** | **Vice President** | **Party** |
| 1840 | William Henry Harrison Died in 1841; succeeded by John Tyler. | Whig | John Tyler Assumed presidency in 1841; vice president's office was left vacant. | Whig |
| 1844 | James K. Polk | Democratic | George M. Dallas | Democratic |
| 1848 | Zachary Taylor Died in 1850; succeeded by Millard Fillmore. | Whig | Millard Fillmore Assumed presidency in 1850; vice president's office was left vacant. | Whig |
| 1852 | Franklin Pierce | Democratic | William R. King | Democratic |
| 1856 | James Buchanan | Democratic | John C. Breckenridge | Democratic |
| 1860 | Abraham Lincoln | Republican | Hannibal Hamlin | Republican |
| 1864 | Abraham Lincoln Died in 1865; succeeded by Andrew Johnson. | National Union/ Republican | Andrew Johnson Assumed presidency in 1865; vice president's office was left vacant. | National Union/ Republican |
| 1868 | Ulysses S. Grant | Republican | Schuyler Colfax | Republican |
| 1872 | Ulysses S. Grant | Republican | Henry Wilson | Republican |
| 1876 | Rutherford B. Hayes Contested result settled by special election commission in favor of Hayes. | Republican | William A. Wheeler | Republican |
| 1880 | James A. Garfield Died in 1881; succeeded by Chester A. Arthur. | Republican | Chester A. Arthur Assumed presidency in 1881; vice president's office was left vacant. | Republican |
| 1884 | Grover Cleveland | Democratic | Thomas A. Hendricks | Democratic |
| 1888 | Benjamin Harrison | Republican | Levi P. Morton | Republican |
| 1892 | Grover Cleveland | Democratic | Adlai Stevenson | Democratic |

| Major Opponents | | Electoral Vote | | Popular Vote |
| --- | --- | --- | --- | --- |
| **For President** | **Party** | | | |
| Martin Van Buren | Democratic | Harrison | 234 | 1,274,624 |
| James G. Birney | Liberty | Van Buren | 60 | 1,127,781 |
| | | | | |
| Henry Clay | Whig | Polk | 170 | 1,338,464 |
| James G. Birney | Liberty | Clay | 105 | 1,300,097 |
| | | Birney | — | 62,300 |
| Lewis Cass | Democratic | Taylor | 163 | 1,360,967 |
| Martin Van Buren | Free-Soil | Cass | 127 | 1,222,342 |
| | | Van Buren | — | 291,263 |
| | | | | |
| Winfield Scott | Whig | Pierce | 254 | 1,601,117 |
| John P. Hale | Free-Soil | Scott | 42 | 1,385,453 |
| | | Hale | — | 155,825 |
| John C. Fremont | Republican | Buchanan | 174 | 1,832,955 |
| Millard Fillmore | American | Fremont | 114 | 1,339,932 |
| | (Know-Nothing) | Fillmore | 8 | 871,731 |
| John Bell | Constitutional Union | Lincoln | 180 | 1,865,593 |
| Stephen A. Douglas | Democratic | Breckinridge | 72 | 848,356 |
| John C. Breckinridge | Democratic | Douglas | 12 | 1,382,713 |
| | | Bell | 39 | 592,906 |
| George B. McClennan | Democratic | Lincoln | 212 | 2,218,388 |
| | | McClennan | 21 | 1,812,807 |
| | | Eleven secessionist states did not participate. | | |
| Horatio Seymour | Democratic | Grant | 286 | 3,598,235 |
| | | Seymour | 80 | 2,706,829 |
| | | Texas, Mississippi, and Virginia did not participate. | | |
| Horace Greeley | Democratic and | Grant | 286 | 3,598,235 |
| | Liberal Republican | Greeley | 80 | 2,834,761 |
| Charles O'Connor | Democratic | Greeley died before the Electoral | | |
| James Black | Temperance | College met. His electoral votes were divided among the four minor candidates. | | |
| Samuel J. Tilden | Democratic | Hayes | 185 | 4,034,311 |
| Peter Cooper | Greenback | Tilden | 184 | 4,288,546 |
| Green Clay Smith | Prohibition | Cooper | — | 75,973 |
| Winfield S. Hancock | Democratic | Garfield | 214 | 4,446,158 |
| James B. Weaver | Greenback | Hancock | 155 | 4,444,260 |
| Neal Dow | Prohibition | Weaver | — | 305,997 |
| James G. Blaine | Republican | Cleveland | 219 | 4,874,621 |
| John P. St. John | Prohibition | Blaine | 182 | 4,848,936 |
| Benjamin F. Butler | Greenback | Butler | — | 175,096 |
| | | St. John | — | 147,482 |
| Grover Cleveland | Democratic | Harrison | 233 | 5,447,129 |
| Clinton B. Fisk | Prohibition | Cleveland | 168 | 5,537,857 |
| Alson J. Streeter | Union Labor | | | |
| Benjamin Harrison | Republican | Cleveland | 277 | 5,555,426 |
| James B. Weaver | Populist | Harrison | 145 | 5,182,600 |
| John Bidwell | Prohibition | Weaver | 22 | 1,029,846 |

| | President | Party | Vice President | Party |
|---|---|---|---|---|
| 1896 | William McKinley | Republican | Garret A. Hobart | Republican |
| 1900 | William McKinley Died in 1901; succeeded by Theodore Roosevelt. | Republican | Theodore Roosevelt Assumed presidency in 1901; vice president's office was left vacant. | Republican |
| 1904 | Theodore Roosevelt | Republican | Charles W. Fairbanks | Republican |
| 1908 | William Howard Taft | Republican | James S. Sherman | Republican |
| 1912 | Woodrow Wilson | Democratic | Thomas R. Marshall | Democratic |
| 1916 | Woodrow Wilson | Democratic | Thomas R. Marshall | Democratic |
| 1920 | Warren G. Harding Died in 1923; succeeded by Calvin Coolidge. | Republican | Calvin Coolidge Assumed presidency in 1923; vice president's office was left vacant. | Republican |
| 1924 | Calvin Coolidge | Republican | Charles G. Dawes | Republican |
| 1928 | Herbert C. Hoover | Republican | Charles Curtis | Republican |
| 1932 | Franklin D. Roosevelt | Democratic | John N. Garner | Democratic |
| 1936 | Franklin D. Roosevelt | Democratic | John N. Garner | Democratic |
| 1940 | Franklin D. Roosevelt | Democratic | Henry A. Wallace | Democratic |
| 1944 | Franklin D. Roosevelt Died in 1945; succeeded by Harry S. Truman. | Democratic | Harry S. Truman Assumed presidency in 1945; vice president's office was left vacant. | Democratic |
| 1948 | Harry S. Truman | Democratic | Alben W. Barkley | Democratic |
| 1952 | Dwight D. Eisenhower | Republican | Richard M. Nixon | Republican |
| 1956 | Dwight D. Eisenhower | Republican | Richard M. Nixon | Republican |

| Major Opponents | | Electoral Vote | | Popular Vote |
| --- | --- | --- | --- | --- |
| **For President** | **Party** | | | |
| William Jennings Bryan | Democratic, Populist, and National Silver Republican | McKinley | 271 | 7,102,246 |
| | | Bryan | 176 | 6,492,559 |
| Joshua Levering | Prohibition | | | |
| John M. Palmer | National Democratic | | | |
| William Jennings Bryan | Democratic and Fusion Populist | McKinley | 292 | 7,218,039 |
| | | Bryan | 155 | 6,358,345 |
| Wharton Barker | Anti-Fusion Populist | Woolley | — | 209,004 |
| Eugene V. Debs | Social Democratic | Debs | — | 86,935 |
| John G. Woolley | Prohibition | | | |
| Alton B. Parker | Democratic | Roosevelt | 336 | 7,626,593 |
| Eugene V. Debs | Socialist | Parker | 140 | 5,082,898 |
| Silas C. Swallow | Prohibition | Debs | — | 402,489 |
| | | Swallow | — | 258,596 |
| William Jennings Bryan | Democratic | Taft | 321 | 7,676,258 |
| Eugene V. Debs | Socialist | Bryan | 162 | 6,406,801 |
| Eugene W. Chafin | Prohibition | Debs | — | 420,380 |
| | | Chafin | — | 252,821 |
| William Howard Taft | Republican | Wilson | 435 | 6,296,547 |
| Theodore Roosevelt | Progressive (Bull Moose) | Roosevelt | 88 | 4,118,571 |
| Eugene V. Debs | Socialist | Taft | 8 | 3,486,720 |
| Eugene W. Chafin | Prohibition | | | |
| Charles E. Hughes | Republican | Wilson | 277 | 9,127,695 |
| Allen L. Benson | Socialist | Hughes | 254 | 8,533,507 |
| J. Frank Hanly | Prohibition | | | |
| Charles W. Fairbanks | Republican | | | |
| James M. Cox | Democratic | Harding | 404 | 16,133,314 |
| Eugene V. Debs | Socialist | Cox | 127 | 9,140,884 |
| | | Debs | — | 913,664 |
| John W. Davis | Democratic | Coolidge | 382 | 15,717,553 |
| Robert M. LaFollette | Progressive | Davis | 136 | 8,386,169 |
| | | LaFollette | 13 | 4,184,050 |
| Alfred E. Smith | Democratic | Hoover | 444 | 21,391,993 |
| Norman Thomas | Socialist | Smith | 87 | 15,016,169 |
| Herbert C. Hoover | Republican | Roosevelt | 472 | 22,809,638 |
| Norman Thomas | Socialist | Hoover | 59 | 15,758,901 |
| Alfred M. Landon | Republican | Roosevelt | 523 | 27,752,869 |
| William Lemke | Union | Landon | 8 | 16,674,665 |
| Wendell L. Wilkie | Republican | Roosevelt | 449 | 27,263,448 |
| | | Wilkie | 82 | 22,336,260 |
| Thomas E. Dewey | Republican | Roosevelt | 432 | 25,611,936 |
| | | Dewey | 99 | 22,013,372 |
| Thomas E. Dewey | Republican | Truman | 303 | 24,105,182 |
| J. Strom Thurmond | States' Rights Democratic | Dewey | 189 | 21,970,065 |
| | | Thurmond | 39 | 1,169,063 |
| Henry A. Wallace | Progressive | Wallace | — | 1,157,326 |
| Adlai E. Stevenson | Democratic | Eisenhower | 442 | 33,936,137 |
| | | Stevenson | 89 | 27,314,649 |
| Adlai E. Stevenson | Democratic | Eisenhower | 457 | 35,585,245 |
| | | Stevenson | 73 | 26,030,172 |

| Election Year | Elected to Office | | | |
|---|---|---|---|---|
| | **President** | **Party** | **Vice President** | **Party** |
| 1960 | John F. Kennedy Died in 1963; succeeded by Lyndon B. Johnson | Democratic | Lyndon B. Johnson Assumed presidency in 1963; vice president's office was left vacant. | Democratic |
| 1964 | Lyndon B. Johnson | Democratic | Hubert H. Humphrey | Democratic |
| 1968 | Richard M. Nixon | Republican | Spiro T. Agnew | Republican |
| 1972 | Richard M. Nixon Resigned in 1974; succeeded by Gerald R. Ford. | Republican | Spiro T. Agnew Resigned in 1974; replaced by Gerald R. Ford, who was in turn replaced by Nelson Rockefeller. | Republican |
| 1976 | James E. Carter | Democratic | Walter Mondale | Democratic |
| 1980 | Ronald Reagan | Republican | George Bush | Republican |
| 1984 | Ronald Reagan | Republican | George Bush | Republican |
| 1988 | George H. Bush | Republican | J. Danforth Quayle | Republican |
| 1992 | William J. Clinton | Democratic | Albert Gore, Jr. | Democratic |
| 1996 | William J. Clinton | Democratic | Albert Gore, Jr. | Democratic |
| 2000 | George W. Bush | Republican | Richard Cheney | Republican |
| 2004 | George W. Bush | Republican | Richard Cheney | Republican |
| 2008 | Barack Obama | Democratic | Joseph Biden | Democratic |

| Major Opponents | | Electoral Vote | | Popular Vote |
| --- | --- | --- | --- | --- |
| **For President** | **Party** | | | |
| Richard M. Nixon | Republican | Kennedy | 303 | 34,227,096 |
| | | Nixon | 219 | 34,108,546 |
| | | Byrd (Ind. Dem.)* | 15 | — |
| Barry M. Goldwater | Republican | Johnson | 486 | 43,126,584 |
| | | Goldwater | 52 | 27,177,838 |
| Hubert H. Humphrey | Democratic | Nixon | 301 | 31,770,237 |
| George C. Wallace | American | Humphrey | 191 | 31,270,533 |
| | Independent | Wallace | 46 | 9,906,141 |
| George S. McGovern | Democratic | Nixon | 520 | 46,740,323 |
| | | McGovern | 17 | 28,901,598 |
| | | Hospers (Va.) | 1 | — |
| Gerald R. Ford | Republican | Carter | 297 | 40,830,763 |
| Eugene McCarthy | Independent | Ford | 240 | 39,147,793 |
| | | McCarthy | — | 756,631 |
| James E. Carter | Democratic | Reagan | 489 | 43,899,248 |
| John B. Anderson | Independent | Carter | 49 | 35,481,435 |
| Ed Clark | Libertarian | Anderson | — | 5,719,437 |
| Walter Mondale | Democratic | Reagan | 525 | 54,451,521 |
| David Bergland | Libertarian | Mondale | 13 | 37,565,334 |
| Michael Dukakis | Democratic | Bush | 426 | 47,946,422 |
| | | Dukakis | 112 | 41,016,429 |
| George H.W. Bush | Republican | Clinton | 370 | 44,908,233 |
| H. Ross Perot | Independent | Bush | 168 | 39,102,282 |
| | | Perot | — | 19,217,213 |
| Robert Dole | Republican | Clinton | 379 | 45,590,703 |
| H. Ross Perot | Independent | Dole | 159 | 37,816,307 |
| | | Perot | — | 7,866,284 |
| Albert Gore, Jr. | Democratic | Bush | 271 | 50,456,141 |
| Ralph Nader | Green | Gore | 266 | 50,996,039 |
| Patrick Buchanan | Reform | Nader | — | 2,882,807 |
| | | Buchanan | — | 448,868 |
| John Kerry | Democratic | Bush | 286 | 62,028,194 |
| Ralph Nader | Green | Kerry | 252 | 59,027,612 |
| Michael Badnarik | Libertarian | Nader | — | 460,650 |
| | | Badnarik | — | 396,888 |
| John McCain | Republican | Obama | 365 | 69,456,897 |
| Ralph Nader | Green | McCain | 173 | 59,934,814 |
| | | Nader | | |

*Byrd received 15 electoral votes although he was not a candidate for the presidency.

# >glossary

**527 committees**   Organizations created by individuals and groups to influence the outcomes of elections by raising and spending money that candidates and political parties cannot legally raise.

**AARP**   An interest group representing the concerns of older Americans (formerly known as the American Association of Retired Persons).

**Ability-to-pay theory of taxation**   The approach to government finance that holds that taxes should be based on an individual's ability to pay.

**Absolute monarchy**   A country ruled by one person, usually a king or queen.

**Administrative law**   Administrative rules adopted by regulatory agencies.

**Access**   The opportunity to communicate directly with legislators and other government officials in hopes of influencing the details of policy.

**Adversary proceeding**   A legal procedure in which each side presents evidence and arguments to bolster its position while rebutting evidence that might support the other side.

**Advocacy groups**   Organizations created to seek benefits on behalf of groups of persons who are in some way incapacitated or otherwise unable to represent their own interests.

**Affirm**   The action of an appeals court to uphold the decision of a lower court.

**Affirmative action**   Steps taken by colleges, universities, and private employers to remedy the effects of past discrimination.

**Agenda building**   The process through which problems become matters of public concern and government action.

**Agents of socialization**   Those factors that contribute to political socialization by shaping formal and informal learning.

**Air war**   Campaign activities that involve the media, including television, radio, and the Internet.

**American Bar Association (ABA)**   An interest group representing the concerns of lawyers.

**American Civil Liberties Union (ACLU)**   A group organized to protect the rights of individuals as outlined in the U.S. Constitution.

**American Federation of Labor-Congress of Industrial Organization (AFL-CIO)**   A labor union federation.

**American Indian Movement (AIM)**   A group representing the views of Native Americans.

**American Medical Association (AMA)**   An interest group representing the concerns of physicians.

**Americans with Disabilities Act (ADA)**   A federal law designed to end discrimination against persons with disabilities and eliminate barriers to their full participation in American society.

***Amicus curiae*** or **friend of the court brief**   Written legal argument presented by parties not directly involved in the case, including interest groups and units of government.

**Anti-clericalism**   A movement that opposes the institutional power of religion, and the involvement of the church in all aspects of public and political life.

**Antifederalists**   Americans opposed to the ratification of the new Constitution because they thought it gave too much power to the national government.

**Appeal**   The taking of a case from a lower court to a higher court by the losing party in a lower-court decision.

**Apportionment**   The allocation of legislative seats among the states.

**Appropriation bill**   A legislative authorization to spend money for a particular purpose.

**Appropriations process**   The procedure through which Congress legislatively allocates money for a particular purpose.

**Articles of impeachment**   A document listing the impeachable offenses that the House believes the president committed.

**At-large election**   A method for choosing public officials in which the citizens of an entire political subdivision, such as a state, vote to select officeholders.

**Attack journalism**   An approach to news reporting in which journalists take an adversarial attitude toward candidates and elected officials.

**Authorization process**   The procedure through which Congress legislatively establishes a program, defines its general purpose, devises procedures for its operation, specifies an agency to implement the program, and indicates an approximate level of funding for the program but does not actually provide money.

**Baby boom generation**   The exceptionally large number of Americans born during the late 1940s, 1950s, and early 1960s.

**Balance of power**   A system of political alignments in which peace and security may be maintained through an equilibrium of forces between rival groups of nations.

**Balance the ticket**   An attempt to select a vice-presidential candidate who will appeal to different groups of voters than the presidential nominee.

**Balanced budget**   Budget receipts equal budget expenditures.

**Base voters**   Rock-solid Republicans or hardcore Democrats, firmly committed to voting for their party's nominee.

**Battleground states** Swing states in which the relative strength of the two major-party presidential candidates is close enough so that either candidate could conceivably carry the state.

**Biased question** A survey question that produces results tilted to one side or another.

**Biased sample** A sample that tends to produce results that do not reflect the true characteristics of the universe because it is unrepresentative of the universe.

**Bicameral legislature** A two-house legislature.

**Bicameralism** The division of the legislative branch of government into two chambers.

**Bill** A proposed law.

**Bill of attainder** A law declaring a person or a group of persons guilty of a crime and providing for punishment without benefit of a judicial proceeding.

**Bill of rights** A constitutional document guaranteeing individual rights and liberties.

**Bill of Rights** The first ten amendments to the U.S. Constitution.

**Bipartisan Campaign Reform Act (BCRA)** A campaign finance reform law designed to limit the political influence of "big money" campaign contributors.

**Bipartisanship** The close cooperation and general agreement between the two major political parties.

**Blanket primary** A primary election system that allows voters to select candidates without regard for party affiliation.

**Block grant program** A federal grant program that provides money for a program in a broad, general policy area, such as childcare or job training.

**Blue states** States that vote Democratic, symbolized by the color blue on the electoral college map.

**Brady Act** A federal gun control law that requires a background check on an unlicensed purchaser of a firearm in order to determine whether the individual can legally own a weapon.

**Broadcast media** Television, radio, and the Internet.

**Budget deficit** The amount by which annual budget expenditures exceed annual budget receipts.

**Budget surplus** The sum by which annual budget receipts exceed annual budget expenditures.

**Bundling** A procedure in which an interest group gathers checks from individual supporters made out to the campaigns of targeted candidates.

**Cabinet departments** Major administrative units of the federal government that have responsibility for the conduct of a wide range of government operations.

**Capital punishment** The death penalty.

**Capitalism** An economic system characterized by individual and corporate ownership of the means of production and a market economy based on the supply and demand of goods and services.

**Captured agencies** Agencies that work to benefit the economic interests they regulate rather than serving the public interest.

**Categorical grant program** A federal grant program that provides funds to state and local governments for a fairly narrow, specific purpose, such as removing asbestos from school buildings or acquiring land for outdoor recreation.

**Caucus method of delegate selection** A procedure for choosing national party convention delegates that involves party voters participating in a series of precinct and district or county political meetings.

**Cause groups** Organizations whose members care intensely about a single issue or small group of related issues.

**Central Intelligence Agency (CIA)** The federal agency that gathers and evaluates foreign intelligence information in the interest of national security.

***Certiorari* or cert** The technical term for the Supreme Court's decision to hear arguments and make a ruling in a case.

**Chamber of Commerce** A business federation representing the interests of businesses of all sizes, sectors, and regions.

**Checks and balances** The overlapping of the powers of the branches of government designed to ensure that public officials limit the authority of one another.

**Chief executive** The head of the executive branch of government.

**Chief of state** The formal head of a national state as distinguished from the head of the government.

**Citizen groups** Organizations created to support government policies that they believe will benefit the public at large.

**Civil case** A legal dispute concerning a private conflict between two parties—individuals, corporations, or government agencies.

**Civil liberties** The protection of the individual from the unrestricted power of government.

**Civil rights** The protection of the individual from arbitrary or discriminatory acts by government or by individuals based on that person's group status, such as race and gender.

**Civil union** A legal partnership between two men or two women that gives the couple all the benefits, protections, and responsibilities under law as are granted to spouses in a traditional marriage.

**Civilian supremacy of the armed forces** The concept that the armed forces should be under the direct control of civilian authorities.

**Class action lawsuits** Lawsuits brought by one or more people on behalf of themselves and others who are similarly situated.

**Closed primary** An election system that limits primary election participation to registered party members.

**Closed rule** A rule that prohibits floor consideration of amendments on the House floor.

**Cloture** The procedure for ending a filibuster.

**Club for Growth** A cause group that favors a low-tax and limited government agenda.

**Coattail effect** A political phenomenon in which a strong candidate for one office gives a boost to fellow party members on the same ballot seeking other offices.

**Cold War** The period of international tension between the United States and the Soviet Union lasting from the late 1940s through the late 1980s.

**Collective bargaining** The negotiation between an employer and a union representing employees over the terms and conditions of employment.

**Commerce Clause** The constitutional provision giving Congress authority to "regulate commerce . . . among the several states."

**Common Cause** A group organized to work for campaign finance reform and other good-government causes.

**Compulsory voting** The legal requirement that citizens participate in national elections.

**Concurrent powers** Those powers of government that are jointly exercised by the national government and state governments.

**Concurring opinion** A judicial statement that agrees with the Court's ruling but disagrees with the reasoning of the majority opinion.

**Confederation** A league of nearly independent states, similar to the United Nations today.

**Conferees** Members of a conference committee.

**Conference** A closed meeting attended only by the members of the Court.

**Conference committee** A special congressional committee created to negotiate differences on similar pieces of legislation passed by the House and Senate.

**Conference report** A revised bill produced by a conference committee.

**Conservatism** The political philosophy that government power undermines the development of the individual and diminishes society as a whole.

**Constituency** The district from which an officeholder is elected.

**Constituency service** The action of members of Congress and their staffs attending to the individual, particular needs of constituents.

**Constituents** The people an officeholder represents.

**Constitution** The fundamental law by which a state or nation is organized and governed, and to which ordinary legislation must conform.

**Constitutional amendment** A formal, written change or addition to the nation's governing document.

**Constitutional law** Law that involves the interpretation and application of the Constitution.

**Constitutional monarchy** A country in which the powers of the ruler are limited to those granted under the constitution and the laws of the nation.

**Consumer price index (CPI)** A measure of inflation that is based on the changing cost of goods and services.

**Containment** The American policy of keeping the Soviet Union from expanding its sphere of control.

**Conventional forces** Non-nuclear forces.

**Convergence theory** The view that communism and capitalism were evolving in similar ways, or converging.

**Corporation for Public Broadcasting** A government agency chartered and funded by the U.S. government with the goal of promoting public broadcasting.

**Cost-benefit analysis** An evaluation of a proposed policy or regulation based on a comparison of its expected benefits and anticipated costs.

**Cost-of-Living Adjustment (COLA)** A mechanism designed to regularly increase the size of Social Security benefits to compensate for the effects of inflation.

**Criminal case** A legal dispute dealing with an alleged violation of a penal law.

***De facto* segregation** Racial separation resulting from factors other than law, such as housing patterns.

***De jure* segregation** Racial separation required by law.

**Defense of Marriage Act** The federal law stipulating that each state may choose either to recognize or not recognize same-sex marriages performed in other states.

**Defense policy** Public policy that concerns the Armed Forces of the United States.

**Delegated or enumerated powers** The powers explicitly granted to the national government by the Constitution.

**Democracy** A system of government in which ultimate political authority is vested in the people.

**Democratic peace** The concept that democracies do not wage war against other democracies.

**Depression** A severe and prolonged economic slump characterized by decreased business activity and high unemployment.

**Détente** A period of improved communications and visible efforts to relieve tensions between the two superpowers.

**Deterrence** The ability of a nation to prevent an attack against itself or its allies by threat of massive retaliation.

**Developing countries** Nations with relatively low levels of per capita income.

**Diplomacy** The process by which nations carry on political relations with each other.

**Diplomatic relations** A system of official contacts between two nations in which the countries exchange ambassadors and other diplomatic personnel and operate embassies in each other's country.

**Direct democracy** A political system in which the citizens vote directly on matters of public concern.

**Discharge petition** A procedure whereby a majority of the members of the House of Representatives can force a committee to report a bill to the floor of the House.

**Discretionary spending** Budgetary expenditures that are not mandated by law or contract, including annual funding for education, the Coast Guard, space exploration, highway construction, defense, foreign aid, and the Federal Bureau of Investigation (FBI).

**Disfranchisement**   The denial of voting rights.

**Dissenting opinion**   A judicial statement that disagrees with the decision of the court's majority.

**District election**   A method for choosing public officials that divides a political subdivision, such as a state, into geographic areas called districts and each district elects one official.

**Divided government**   The phenomenon of one political party controlling the legislative branch of government while the other holds the executive branch.

**Doctrine of natural rights**   The belief that individual rights transcend the power of government.

**Domestic partnership**   A legal status similar to civil unions in that it confers rights similar to marriage.

**Don't ask, don't tell policy**   The official policy for dealing with gay men and lesbians in the U.S. armed forces. The military would not ask new recruits about their sexual orientation and would stop conducting investigations aimed at identifying and discharging homosexuals, but it would discharge service members who revealed their sexual orientation.

**Double jeopardy**   A procedural defense that forbids a defendant from being tried twice for the same crime using the same set of facts.

**Due Process Clause**   The constitutional provision that declares that no state shall "deprive any person of life, liberty, or property, without due process of law."

**Due process of law**   The constitutional principle holding that government must follow fair and regular procedures in actions that could lead to an individual's suffering loss of life, liberty, or property.

**Earmarks**   Legislative provisions that direct that funds be spent for particular purposes.

**Earned Income Tax Credit (EITC)**   A federal program designed to give cash assistance to low-income working families by refunding some or all of the taxes they pay and, if their wages are low, giving them an additional refund.

**Election campaign**   An attempt to get information to voters that will persuade them to elect a candidate or not elect an opponent.

**Electoral College**   The system established in the Constitution for indirect election of the president and vice president.

**Electors**   Individuals selected in each state to officially cast that state's electoral votes.

**Emily's List**   Emily's list is a PAC, the goal of which is the election of pro-choice Democratic women to office.

**Empirical analysis**   A method of study that relies on experience and scientific observation.

**Employment Non-Discrimination Act (ENDA)**   A proposed federal law that would protect Americans from employment discrimination on the basis of sexual orientation.

**Entitlement program**   A government program providing benefits to all persons qualified to receive them under law.

**Environmental Protection Agency (EPA)**   The federal agency responsible for enforcing the nation's environmental laws.

**Equal Employment Opportunity Commission (EEOC)**   An agency that investigates and rules on charges of employment discrimination.

**Equal Protection Clause**   A provision of the Fourteenth Amendment of the U.S. Constitution that declares that "No State shall . . . deny to any person within its jurisdiction the equal protection of the laws."

**Equal Rights Amendment (ERA)**   A proposed amendment guaranteeing equality before the law, regardless of sex.

**Equal-time rule**   An FCC regulation requiring broadcasters to provide an equivalent opportunity to opposing political candidates competing for the same office.

**Estate tax**   A tax levied on the value of an inheritance.

*Ex post facto* **law**   A retroactive criminal statute, which operates to the disadvantage of accused persons.

**Excise taxes**   Taxes levied on the manufacture, transportation, sale, or consumption of a particular item or set of related items.

**Exclusionary rule**   The judicial doctrine stating that when the police violate an individual's constitutional rights, the evidence obtained as a result of police misconduct or error cannot be used against the defendant.

**Executive agreement**   An international understanding between the president and foreign nations that does not require Senate ratification.

**Executive Office of the President**   The group of White House offices and agencies that develop and implement the policies and programs of the president.

**Executive order**   A directive issued by the president to an administrative agency or executive department.

**Executive power**   The power to enforce laws.

**Exit polls**   Surveys based on random samples of voters leaving polling places.

**External political efficacy**   The assessment of an individual of the responsiveness of government to his or her concerns.

**Externalities**   Costs or benefits not taken into account by private decision-makers.

**Extradition**   The return from one state to another of a person accused of a crime.

**Factions**   Special interests who seek their own good at the expense of the common good.

**Fairness Doctrine**   An FCC regulation requiring broadcasters to present controversial issues of public importance and to present them in an honest, equal, and balanced manner.

**Faith-based initiative**   A program designed to make federal grant money available to religiously based charitable groups on the same basis as other social service providers.

**Federal Communications Commission (FCC)**   An agency that regulates interstate and international radio, television, telephone, telegraph, and satellite communications, as well as grants licenses to radio and television stations.

**Federal Deposit Insurance Corporation (FDIC)**   A federal agency established to insure depositors' accounts in banks and thrift institutions.

**Federal Election Commission (FEC)**   The agency that enforces federal campaign finance laws.

**Federal grant program**   A program through which the national government gives money to state and local governments to spend in accordance with set standards and conditions.

**Federal mandate**   A legal requirement placed on a state or local government by the national government requiring certain policy actions.

**Federal Open Market Committee (FOMC)**   A committee of the Federal Reserve that meets eight times a year to review the economy and adjust monetary policy to achieving the net goals.

**Federal preemption of state authority**   An act of Congress adopting regulatory policies that overrule state policies in a particular regulatory area.

**Federal Reserve Board (Fed)**   An independent regulatory commission that makes monetary policy.

**Federal system**   *See* Federation or federal system.

**Federal Trade Commission (FTC)**   An agency that regulates business competition, including enforcement of laws against monopolies and the protection of consumers from deceptive trade practices.

**Federalism**   The distribution of power in an organization between a central authority and the constituent units.

**Federalist Papers**   A series of essays written by James Madison, Alexander Hamilton, and John Jay advocating the ratification of the Constitution.

**Federalists**   Americans who supported the ratification of the Constitution.

**Federation** or **federal system**   A political system that divides power between a central government, with authority over the whole nation, and a series of state governments.

**Feedback**   The impact of the results of policy evaluation on the policy process.

**Filibuster**   An attempt to defeat a measure through prolonged debate.

**Fire-alarm oversight**   An indirect system of bureaucratic oversight that enables individual citizens and organized interest groups to examine administrative decisions, charge agencies with violating legislative goals, and seek remedies from agencies, courts, and the Congress.

**First strike**   The initial offensive move of a general nuclear war, aimed at knocking out the other side's ability to retaliate.

**First-strike capability**   The capacity of a nation to launch an initial nuclear assault sufficient to cripple an adversary's ability to retaliate.

**Fiscal policy**   The use of government spending and taxation for the purpose of achieving economic goals.

**Fiscal year**   Budget year.

**Flat tax**   An income tax that assesses the same percentage tax rate on all income levels above a personal exemption while allowing few, if any, deductions.

**Floor**   The full House or full Senate taking official action.

**Food Stamp Program**   A federal program that provides vouchers to low-income families and individuals that can be used to purchase food from grocery stores.

**Foreign policy**   Public policy that concerns the relationship of the United States to the international political environment.

**Formula grant program**   A grant program that awards funding on the basis of a formula established by Congress.

**Framing**   The process by which a communication source, such as a news organization, defines and constructs a political issue or public controversy.

**Franking privilege**   Free postage provided to members of Congress.

**Free-rider barrier**   The concept that individuals will have little incentive to join a group and contribute resources to it if the group's benefits go to members and nonmembers alike.

**Friendly Incumbent Rule**   A policy whereby an interest group will back any incumbent who is generally supportive of the group's policy preferences, without regard for the party or policy views of the challenger.

**Frostbelt**   The northeastern and midwestern regions of the United States.

**Full Faith and Credit Clause**   The constitutional provision requiring that states recognize the official acts of other states, such as marriages, divorces, adoptions, court orders, and other legal decisions.

**Fundamental right**   A constitutional right that is so important that government cannot restrict it unless it can demonstrate a compelling or overriding public interest for so doing.

**Gender gap**   Differences in party identification and political attitudes between men and women.

**General election**   An election to fill state and national offices held in November of even-numbered years.

**Gerrymandering**   The drawing of legislative district lines for political advantage.

**Global economy**   The integration of national economies into a world economic system in which companies compete worldwide for suppliers and markets.

**Global warming**   The gradual warming of the Earth's atmosphere reportedly caused by the burning of fossil fuels and industrial pollutants.

**Global Warming Treaty**   An international agreement to reduce the worldwide emissions of carbon dioxide and other greenhouse gases.

**Governing party**   The political party or party coalition holding the reins of government in a democracy.

**Government**   The institution with authority to set policy for society.

**Grand Old Party (GOP)**   Nickname of the Republican Party.

**Grandfather clause**   A provision that exempted those persons whose grandfathers had been eligible to vote at some earlier date from tests of understanding, literacy tests, and other difficult-to-achieve voter qualification requirements.

**Great Society**   The legislative program put forward by President Lyndon Johnson.

**Gross domestic product (GDP)**   The total value of goods and services produced by a nation's economy in a year, excluding transactions with foreign countries.

**Ground war**   Campaign activities featuring direct contact between campaign workers and citizens, such as door-to-door canvassing and personal telephone contacts.

***Habeas corpus,* writ of**   A court order requiring that government authorities either release a person held in custody or demonstrate that the person is detained in accordance with law.

**Hard money**   Campaign funds which are subject to federal contribution and expenditure limitations.

**Hatch Act**   A measure designed to restrict the political activities of federal employees to voting and the private expression of views.

**Hate-crimes law**   A legislative measure that increases penalties for persons convicted of criminal offenses motivated by prejudice based on race, religion, national origin, gender, or sexual orientation.

**Honeymoon effect**   The tendency of a president to enjoy a high level of public support during the early months of an administration.

**House majority leader**   The second-ranking figure in the majority party in the House.

**House Rules Committee**   A standing committee that determines the rules under which a specific bill can be debated, amended, and considered on the House floor.

**Human Rights Campaign (HRC)**   An organization formed to promote gay and lesbian rights.

**Impeach**   The act of formally accusing an official of the executive or judicial branches of an impeachable offense.

**Impeachment**   A process in which an executive or judicial official is formally accused of an offense that could warrant removal from office.

**Implied powers**   Those powers of Congress not explicitly mentioned in the Constitution, but derived by implication from the delegated powers.

***In forma pauperis***   The process whereby an indigent litigant can file an appeal of a case to the U.S. Supreme Court without paying the usual fees.

**Income redistribution**   The government taking items of value, especially money, from some groups of people

and then giving items of value, either in cash or services, to other groups of people.

**Incumbent**   Current officeholder.

**Independent executive agencies**   Executive branch agencies that are not part of any of the 15 cabinet-level departments.

**Independent expenditures**   Money spent in support of a candidate but not coordinated with the candidate's campaign.

**Independent regulatory commission**   An agency outside the major executive departments that is charged with the regulation of important aspects of the economy.

**Inflation**   A decline in the purchasing power of the currency.

**Inherent powers**   Those powers vested in the national government, particularly in the area of foreign and defense policy, which do not depend on any specific grant of authority by the Constitution, but rather exist because the United States is a sovereign nation.

**Initiative process**   A procedure whereby citizens can prepare the adoption of a policy measure by gathering a prerequisite number of signatures. Voters must then approve the measure before it can take effect.

**Injunction**   A court order.

**Inner cabinet**   The secretary of state, secretary of defense, secretary of the treasury, and the attorney general.

**Interest**   Money paid for the use of money.

**Interest group**   An organization of people who join together voluntarily on the basis of some interest they share for the purpose of influencing policy.

**Internal political efficacy**   The assessment by an individual of his or her personal ability to influence the policymaking process.

**International Monetary Fund (IMF)**   The international organization created to promote economic stability worldwide.

**Interstate Commerce Clause**   The constitutional provision giving Congress authority to "regulate commerce … among the several states."

**Isolationism**   The view that the United States should stay out of the affairs of other nations.

**Issue network**   A group of political actors that is actively involved with policymaking in a particular issue area.

**Item veto**   The power of an executive to veto sections or items of a tax or appropriation measure while signing the remainder of the bill into law.

**Jim Crow laws**   Legal provisions requiring the social segregation of African Americans in separate and generally unequal facilities.

**Joint Chiefs of Staff**   A military advisory body that is composed of the chiefs of staff of the U.S. Army and Air Force, the chief of naval operations, and sometimes the commandant of the Marine Corps.

**Joint committee**   A committee that includes members from both houses of Congress.

**Judicial activism**   The charge that judges are going beyond their authority by making the law and not just interpreting it.

**Judicial power**   The power to interpret laws.

**Judicial restraint**   The concept that judges should defer to the policymaking judgment of the legislative and executive branches of government unless their actions clearly violate the law or the Constitution.

**Judicial review**   The power of courts to declare unconstitutional the actions of the other branches and units of government.

**Jurisdiction**   The authority of a court to hear a case.

**Killer amendment**   An amendment designed to make a measure so unattractive that it will lack enough support to pass.

***Laissez-faire***   The economic philosophy that government should not interfere with the free-market forces that drive a healthy economy.

**Lame duck**   An official whose influence is diminished because the official either cannot or will not seek reelection.

**Latent opinion**   What public opinion would be at election time if a political opponent made a public official's position on the issue the target of a campaign attack.

**League of United Latin American Citizens (LULAC)**   A Latino interest group.

**Left wing**   Liberal.

**Legal brief**   A written legal argument.

**Legal writs**   Written orders issued by a court directing the performance of an act or prohibiting some act.

**Legislative markup**   The process in which legislators go over a measure line-by-line, revising, amending, or rewriting it.

**Legislative power**   The power to make laws.

**Libel**   False written statements that lower a person's reputation or expose a person to hatred, contempt, or ridicule.

**Liberalism**   The political philosophy that favors the use of government power to foster the development of the individual and promote the welfare of society.

**Limited government**   The constitutional principle that government does not have unrestricted authority over individuals.

**Literacy test**   A legal requirement that citizens demonstrate an ability to read and write before they could register to vote.

**Lobbying**   The communication of information by a representative of an interest group to a government official for the purpose of influencing a policy decision.

**Logrolling**   An arrangement in which two or more members of Congress agree in advance to support each other's favored legislation.

**Loose construction**   A doctrine of constitutional interpretation holding that the document should be interpreted broadly.

**Louisiana Purchase**   The acquisition from France of a vast expanse of land stretching from New Orleans north to the Dakotas.

**Majority-minority district**   Legislative district whose population is more than 50 percent African American and Latino.

**Majority opinion**   The official written statement of the Supreme Court that explains and justifies its ruling and serves as a guideline for lower courts when similar legal issues arise in the future.

**Majority whip**   The majority leader's first assistant.

***Mandamus*, writ of**   A court order directing a public official to perform a specific act or duty.

**Mandatory spending**   Budgetary expenditures that are mandated by law, including entitlements and contractual commitments made in previous years.

**Margin of error** or **sample error**   A statistical term that refers to the accuracy of a survey.

**Marshall Plan**   The American program that provided billions of dollars to the countries of Western Europe to rebuild their economies after World War II.

**Massive retaliation**   The concept that the United States will strike back against an aggressor with overwhelming force.

**Matching funds requirement**   The legislative provision that the national government will provide grant money for a particular activity only on the condition that the state or local government involved supplies a certain percentage of the total money required for the project or program.

**Means-tested program**   A government program that provides benefits to recipients based on their financial need.

**Medicaid**   A federal program designed to provide health insurance coverage to low-income persons, people with disabilities, and elderly people who are impoverished.

**Medicare**   A federally funded health insurance program for the elderly.

**Mid-cycle redistricting**   The practice of redrawing legislative districts outside the regular redistricting cycle in order to gain political advantage.

**Military preemption**   The defense policy that declares that the United States will attack nations or groups that represent a potential threat to the security of the United States.

**Minimum wage**   The lowest hourly wage that an employer can legally pay covered workers.

**Minority business set-aside**   A legal requirement that firms receiving government grants or contracts allocate a certain percentage of their purchases of supplies and services to businesses owned or controlled by members of minority groups.

**Minority leader**   The head of the minority party in the House or Senate.

**Minority-vote dilution**   The drawing of election district lines so as to thinly spread minority voters among several districts, thus reducing their electoral influence in any one district.

**Minority-vote packing** The drawing of electoral district lines so as to cluster minority voters into one district or a small number of districts, thus reducing their overall electoral influence.

**Minority whip** The minority leader's first assistant in the House or Senate.

**Monetary policy** The control of the money supply for the purpose of achieving economic goals.

**Monroe Doctrine** A declaration of American foreign policy opposing any European intervention in the Western Hemisphere and affirming the American intention to refrain from interfering in European affairs.

**Mothers Against Drunk Driving (MADD)** An interest group that supports the reform of laws dealing with drunk driving.

**Moveon.org** An advocacy group that raises money for Democratic candidates.

**Multiparty system** The division of voter loyalties among three or more major political parties.

**Multiple referral of legislation** The practice of allowing more than one committee to consider legislation.

**Mutual assured destruction (MAD)** The belief that the United States and the Soviet Union would be deterred from launching a nuclear assault against each other for fear of being destroyed in a general nuclear war.

**NARAL Pro-Choice America** An organization that favors abortion rights.

**Nation-state** A political community occupying a definite territory and having an organized government.

**National Aeronautics and Space Administration (NASA)** The federal agency in charge of the space program.

**National Association for the Advancement of Colored People (NAACP)** An interest group organized to represent the concerns of African Americans.

**National debt** The accumulated indebtedness of the federal government.

**National Endowment for the Arts (NEA)** A federal agency created to nurture cultural expression and promote appreciation of the arts.

**National Organization for Women (NOW)** A group organized to promote women's rights.

**National Public Radio (NPR)** A nonprofit membership organization of radio stations.

**National Railroad Passenger Service Corporation (AMTRAK)** A federal agency that operates intercity passenger railway traffic.

**National Rifle Association (NRA)** An interest group organized to defend the rights of gun owners and defeat efforts at gun control.

**National Right to Life Committee** An organization opposed to abortion.

**National Science Foundation (NSF)** A federal agency established to encourage scientific advances and improvements in science education.

**National Security Council (NSC)** An agency in the Executive Office of the President that advises the chief executive on matters involving national security.

**National Supremacy Clause** The constitutional provision that declares that the Constitution and laws of the United States take precedence over the constitutions and laws of the states.

**National Voter Registration Act (NVRA)** A federal law designed to make it easier for citizens to register to vote by requiring states to allow mail registration and provide an opportunity for people to register when applying for or renewing driver's licenses or when visiting federal, state, or local agencies, such as welfare offices.

**Natural monopoly** A monopoly bestowed by nature on a geographical area, or one that, because of the nature of an enterprise, would make competition wasteful.

**Necessary and Proper Clause** or **Elastic Clause** The Constitutional provision found in Article I, Section 8 that declares that "[Congress shall have the power] to make all laws which shall be necessary and proper for carrying into execution the foregoing powers, and all other powers vested by this Constitution in the government of the United States, or in any department or office thereof." It is the basis for much of the legislation passed by Congress because it gives Congress the means to exercise its delegated authority.

**New Deal** A legislative package of reform measures proposed by President Franklin Roosevelt for dealing with the Great Depression.

**New media** A term used to refer to alternative media sources, such as the Internet, cable television, and satellite radio.

**Nixon Doctrine** The corollary to the policy of containment enunciated by President Richard Nixon providing that, although the United States would help small nations threatened by communist aggression with economic and military aid, those countries must play a major role in their own defense.

**Non-germane amendments** Amendments that are unrelated to the subject matter of the original measure.

**Nongovernmental organizations (NGOs)** International organizations committed to the promotion of a particular set of issues.

**Normative analysis** A method of study that is based on certain values.

**North American Free Trade Agreement (NAFTA)** An international accord among the United States, Mexico, and Canada to lower trade barriers among the three nations.

**North Atlantic Treaty Organization (NATO)** A regional military alliance consisting of the United States, Canada, and most of the European democracies.

**Nuclear Non-Proliferation Treaty** An international agreement designed to prevent the spread of nuclear weapons.

**Objective journalism** A style of news reporting that focuses on facts rather than opinion, and presents all sides of controversial issues.

**Office of Management and Budget (OMB)**   An agency that assists the president in preparing the budget.

**Omnibus bills**   Complex, highly detailed legislative proposals covering one or more subjects or programs.

**One person, one vote**   The judicial ruling that the Equal Protection Clause of the Fourteenth Amendment to the U.S. Constitution requires that legislative districts be apportioned on the basis of population.

**Open primary**   An election system that allows voters to vote in the party primary of their choice without regard to their party affiliation.

**Open rule**   A rule that opens a measure to amendment on the House floor without restriction.

**Opposition party**   The political party out of power in a democracy.

**Original jurisdiction**   The set of cases a court may hear as a trial court.

**Pardon**   An executive action that frees an accused or convicted person from all penalties for an offense.

**Parental choice**   An educational reform aimed at improving the quality of schools by allowing parents to select the school their children will attend.

**Parliament**   The British legislature.

**Parliamentary system**   A system of government in which political power is concentrated in a legislative body and a cabinet headed by a prime minister.

**Party caucus**   All of the party members of the House or Senate meeting as a group.

**Party era**   A period of time characterized by a degree of uniformity in the nature of political party competition.

**Party faction**   An identifiable subgroup within a political party.

**Party-line votes**   Votes in Congress in which a majority of the members of each party in a chamber vote on opposite sides of an issue.

**Party realignment**   A change in the underlying party loyalties of voters that ends one party era and begins another.

**Party platform**   A statement of party principles and issue positions.

**PAYGO**   A pay-as-you-go budget rule that requires that any tax cut or spending increase be offset by tax increases or spending cuts elsewhere in the budget.

**Peace Corps**   An agency that administers an American foreign aid program under which volunteers travel to developing nations to teach skills and help improve living standards.

**Per capita**   Per person.

***Per curium* opinion**   Unsigned written opinion of a court.

**Plurality election system**   A method for choosing public officials that awards office to the candidate with the most votes; favors a two-party system.

**Pocket veto**   The action of a president allowing a measure to die without signature after Congress has adjourned.

**Policy adoption**   The official decision of a government body to accept a particular policy and put it into effect.

**Policy evaluation**   The assessment of policy.

**Policy formulation**   The development of strategies for dealing with the problems on the official policy agenda.

**Policy implementation**   The stage of the policy process in which policies are carried out.

**Policymaking environment**   The complex of factors outside of government that has an impact, either directly or indirectly, on the policymaking process.

**Political action committee (PAC)**   An organization created to raise and distribute money in election campaigns.

**Political culture**   The widely held, deeply rooted political values of a society.

**Political campaign**   An attempt to get information to voters that will persuade them to elect a candidate or not elect an opponent.

**Political efficacy**   The extent to which individuals believe they can influence the policymaking process.

**Political elites**   Persons that exercise a major influence on the policymaking process.

**Political left**   Liberalism.

**Political legitimacy**   The popular acceptance of a government and its officials as rightful authorities in the exercise of power.

**Political participation**   An activity that has the intent or effect of influencing government action.

**Political party**   A group of individuals who join together to seek government office in order to make public policy.

**Political patronage**   The power of an officeholder to award favors, such as government jobs, to political allies.

**Political right**   Conservatism.

**Political socialization**   The process whereby individuals acquire political knowledge, attitudes, and beliefs.

**Politics**   The process that determines who shall occupy the roles of leadership in government and how the power of government shall be exercised.

**Poll tax**   A tax levied on the right to vote.

**Pork barrel spending**   Expenditures to fund local projects that are not critically important from a national perspective.

**Postindustrial societies**   Nations whose economies are increasingly based on services, research, and information rather than heavy industry.

**Poverty threshold**   The amount of money an individual or family needs to purchase basic necessities, such as food, clothing, healthcare, shelter, and transportation.

**Power of the purse**   The control of the finances of government.

**Preclearance**   A requirement of the Voting Rights Act that state and local governments in areas with a history of voting discrimination must submit redistricting plans to the federal Department of Justice for approval *before* they can go into effect.

**President's cabinet**   An advisory group created by the president that includes the department heads and other officials chosen by the president.

**Presidential preference primary**   An election in which party voters cast ballots for the presidential candidate they favor and in so doing help determine the number of national convention delegates that candidate will receive.

**Presidential signing statement**   A pronouncement issued by the president at the time a bill passed by Congress is signed into law.

**Primary election**   An election held to determine a party's nominees for the general election ballot.

**Print media**   Newspapers and magazines.

**Prior restraint**   Government action to prevent the publication or broadcast of objectionable material.

**Privatization**   A process that involves the government contracting with private business to implement government programs.

**Privileges and Immunities Clause**   The constitutional provision prohibiting state governments from discriminating against the citizens of other states.

**Probable cause**   The reasonable suspicion based on evidence that a particular search will uncover contraband.

**Progressive tax**   A levy that taxes people earning higher incomes at a higher rate than it does individuals making less money.

**Project grant program**   A grant program that requires state and local governments to compete for available federal money.

**Proportional representation (PR)**   An election system that awards legislative seats to each party approximately equal to its popular voting strength.

**Proportional tax**   A levy that taxes all persons at the same percentage rate, regardless of income.

**Prospective voting**   The concept that voters evaluate the incumbent officeholder and the incumbent's party based on their expectations of future developments.

**Public Broadcasting Service (PBS)**   A nonprofit private corporation that is jointly owned by hundreds of member television stations throughout the United States.

**Public opinion**   Combined personal opinions of adults toward issues of relevance to government.

**Public policy**   The response or lack of response of government decision-makers to an issue.

**Public policy approach**   A comprehensive method for studying the process through which issues come to the attention of government decision-makers and through which policies are formulated, adopted, implemented, and evaluated.

**Public utility**   A privately owned business that performs an essential service for the community.

**Quasi-governmental company**   A private, profit-seeking corporation created by Congress to serve a public purpose.

**Racially restrictive covenants**   Private deed restrictions that prohibited property owners from selling or leasing property to African Americans or other minorities.

**Rally effect**   The tendency of the general public to express support for the incumbent president during a time of international threat.

**Random sample**   A sample in which each member of a universe has an equal likelihood of being included.

**Ranking member**   The leader of the minority party on a committee or subcommittee.

**Reagan Doctrine**   A corollary to the policy of containment enunciated by President Reagan calling for the United States to offer military aid to groups attempting to overthrow communist governments anywhere in the world.

**Realignment**   A change in the underlying party loyalties of voters that ends one party era and begins another.

**Reapportionment**   The reallocation of legislative seats.

**Recession**   An economic slowdown characterized by declining economic output and rising unemployment.

**Reconstruction**   The process whereby the states that had seceded during the Civil War were reorganized and reestablished in the Union.

**Red states**   States that vote Republican, symbolized by the color red on the Electoral College map.

**Redistricting**   The process through which the boundaries of legislative districts are redrawn to reflect population movement.

**Regressive tax**   A levy whose burden falls more heavily on lower-income groups than on wealthy taxpayers.

**Regulatory negotiation**   A structured process by which representatives of the interests that would be substantially affected by a rule, including employees of the regulatory agency, negotiate agreement on the terms of the rule.

**Religious left**   Individuals who hold liberal views because of their religious beliefs.

**Religious right**   Individuals who hold conservative views because of their religious beliefs.

**Remand**   The decision of an appeals court to return a case to a lower court for reconsideration in light of an appeals-court decision.

**Representative democracy** or **republic**   A political system in which citizens elect representatives to make policy decisions on their behalf.

**Reprieve**   An executive action that delays punishment for a crime.

**Republic**   A representative democracy in which citizens elect representatives to make policy decisions on their behalf.

**Reserved** or **residual powers**   The powers of government left to the states.

**Resolution**   A legislative statement of opinion on a certain matter.

**Responsible party**   A political party that clearly spells out issue positions in its platform and, when in office, faithfully carries them out.

**Retrospective voting**    The concept that voters choose candidates based on their perception of an incumbent candidate's past performance in office or the performance of the incumbent party.

**Rider**    A provision, unlikely to become law on its own merits, that is attached to an important measure so that it will ride through the legislative process.

**Right-to-work laws**    Statutes that prohibit union membership as a condition of employment.

**Right wing**    Conservative.

**Rogue states**    Nations that threaten world peace by sponsoring international terrorism and promoting the spread of weapons of mass destruction.

**Rose Garden strategy**    A campaign approach in which an incumbent president attempts to appear presidential rather than political.

**Rule**    A legally binding regulation.

**Rule of four**    A decision process used by the Supreme Court to determine which cases to consider on appeal, holding that the Court will hear a case if four of the nine justices agree to the review.

**Rule of law**    The constitutional principle that holds that the discretion of public officials in dealing with individuals is limited by the law.

**Rulemaking**    The regulatory process used by government agencies to enact legally binding regulations.

**Runoff**    An election between the two candidates receiving the most votes when no candidate got a majority in an initial election.

**Sales tax**    A levy assessed on the retail sale of taxable items.

**Sample**    A subset of a universe.

**School Lunch Program**    A federal program that provides free or reduced-cost lunches to children from poor families.

**Second strike**    A nuclear attack in response to an adversary's first strike.

**Second-strike capability**    The capacity of a nation to absorb an initial nuclear attack and retain sufficient nuclear firepower to inflict unacceptable damage on its adversary.

**Securities and Exchange Commission (SEC)**    An agency that regulates the sale of stocks and bonds as well as investment and holding companies.

**Selective incorporation of the Bill of Rights**    The process through which the U.S. Supreme Court interpreted the Due Process Clause of the Fourteenth Amendment of the U.S. Constitution to apply most of the provisions of the national Bill of Rights to the states.

**Senate majority leader**    The head of the majority party in the Senate.

**Senate president *pro tempore***    The official presiding officer in the Senate in the vice president's absence.

**Senatorial courtesy**    The custom that senators from the president's party have a veto on judicial appointments from their states.

**Seniority**    Length of service.

**Separate but equal**    The judicial doctrine holding that separate facilities for whites and African Americans satisfy the equal protection requirement of the Fourteenth Amendment.

**Separation of powers**    The division of political power among executive, legislative, and judicial branches of government.

**Shield law**    A statute that protects journalists from being forced to disclose confidential information in a legal proceeding.

**Sierra Club**    An environmental organization.

**Signaling role**    A term that refers to the accepted responsibility of the media to alert the public to important developments as they happen.

**Slander**    False spoken statements that lower a person's reputation or expose a person to hatred, contempt, or ridicule.

**Small Business Administration (SBA)**    The federal agency established to make loans to small businesses and assist them in obtaining government contracts.

**Social Security**    A federal pension and disability insurance program funded through a payroll tax on workers and their employers.

**Social Security Administration (SSA)**    The federal agency that operates the Social Security system.

**Soft money**    The name given to funds that are raised by political parties that are not subject to federal campaign finance regulations.

**Solid South**    A phrase used to refer to the usual Democratic Party sweep of the electoral votes of the southern states in presidential elections.

**Sound bite**    A short phrase taken from a candidate's speech by the news media for use on newscasts.

**Sovereign immunity**    The legal concept that individuals cannot sue the government without the government's permission.

**Sovereignty**    The authority of a state to exercise its legitimate powers within its boundaries, free from external interference.

**Speaker of the House**    The presiding officer in the House of Representatives and the leader of the majority party in that chamber.

**Special** or **select committee**    A committee established for a limited time only.

**Split ticket ballot**    Voters casting their ballots for the candidates of two or more political parties.

**Split ticket voting**    Voters casting their ballots for the candidates of two or more political parties.

**Spoils system**    The method of hiring government employees from among the friends, relatives, and supporters of elected officeholders.

**Sponsor**    A member who introduces a measure.

***Sputnik***    The world's first satellite, launched by the Soviet Union.

**Standard of living**    A term that refers to the goods and services affordable by and available to the residents of a nation.

**Standing committee**   A permanent legislative committee with authority to draft legislation in a particular policy area or areas.

**States' rights**   An interpretation of the Constitution that favors limiting the authority of the federal government while expanding the powers of the states.

**Statutory law**   Law that is written by the legislature.

**Straight ticket ballot**   Voters selecting the entire slate of candidates of one party only.

**Straight ticket voting**   Citizens casting their ballots only for the candidates of one party.

**Strategic forces**   Nuclear forces.

**Strict construction**   A doctrine of constitutional interpretation holding that the document should be interpreted narrowly.

**Strict judicial scrutiny**   The judicial decision rule holding that the Supreme Court will find a government policy unconstitutional unless the government can demonstrate a compelling interest justifying the action.

**Subgovernment** or **iron triangle**   A cozy, three-sided relationship among government agencies, interest groups, and key members of Congress in which all parties benefit.

**Subpoena**   A legally binding order requiring an individual to appear before a committee to testify and bring requested information.

**Subsidy**   A financial incentive given by government to an individual or a business interest to accomplish a public objective.

**Suffrage**   The right to vote.

**Sunbelt**   The southern and western regions of the United States.

**Superdelegates**   Democratic Party officials and officeholders selected to attend the national party convention on the basis of the offices they hold.

**Supermajority**   A voting margin that is greater than a simple majority.

**Supplemental Security Income (SSI)**   A federal program that provides money to low-income people who are elderly, blind, or disabled who do not qualify for Social Security benefits.

**Supply-side economics**   The economic theory that tax cuts, especially for business and the wealthy, will lead to savings and investment that will benefit everyone.

**Surgeon general**   An official in the Public Health Service who advises the president on health issues.

**Survey research**   The measurement of public opinion.

**Suspect classifications**   Distinctions among persons that must be justified on the basis of a compelling government interest that cannot be achieved in a less restrictive fashion.

**Swing voters**   Citizens who could vote for either party in an election.

**Table**   To postpone consideration of a measure during the legislative process.

**Tariffs**   Taxes levied on imported goods.

**Tax credit**   An expenditure that reduces an individual's tax liability by the amount of the credit.

**Tax deduction**   An expenditure that can be subtracted from a taxpayer's gross income before figuring the tax owed.

**Tax exemption**   The exclusion of some types of income from taxation.

**Tax incidence**   The point at which the actual cost of a tax falls.

**Tax preference**   A tax deduction or exclusion that allows individuals to pay less tax than they would otherwise.

**Temporary Assistance for Needy Families (TANF)**   A federal program that provides temporary financial assistance and work opportunities to needy families.

**Tennessee Valley Authority (TVA)**   A federal agency established to promote the development of the Tennessee River and its tributaries.

**Term limitation**   The movement to restrict the number of terms public officials may serve.

**Test cases**   Lawsuits initiated to assess the constitutionality of a legislative or executive act.

**Test of understanding**   A legal requirement that citizens had to accurately explain a passage in the U.S. Constitution or state constitution before they could register to vote.

**Third party**   A minor party in a two-party system.

**Trade associations**   Organizations representing the interests of firms and professionals in the same general field.

**Triad**   The three methods the United States employs to deliver nuclear warheads to their targets. It includes intercontinental ballistic missiles (ICBMs) stored in missile silos and ready for launch, nuclear-powered submarines roaming the world's oceans armed with sea-launched ballistic missiles (SLBMs), and heavy bombers capable of delivering a nuclear payload to targets halfway around the globe.

**Trial**   The formal examination of a judicial dispute in accordance with law before a single judge.

**Truman Doctrine**   The foreign policy put forward by President Harry Truman calling for American support for all free peoples resisting communist aggression by internal or outside forces.

**Two-party system**   The division of voter loyalties between two major political parties.

**Two Presidencies Thesis**   The concept that the president enjoys more influence over foreign policy than domestic policy.

**Tyranny of the majority**   The abuse of the minority by the majority.

**Unanimous consent agreement**   A formal understanding on procedures for conducting business in the Senate that requires the acceptance of every member of the chamber.

**Unfunded mandate** A requirement imposed by Congress on state or local governments without providing federal funding to cover its cost.

**Unicameral legislature** A one-house legislature.

**Unitary government** A governmental system in which political authority is concentrated in a single national government.

**United Nations (UN)** An international organization founded in 1945 as a diplomatic forum to resolve conflicts among the world's nations.

**United States Postal Service** A government corporation responsible for mail service.

**Universe** The population survey researchers wish to study.

**Veto** An action by the chief executive refusing to approve a measure passed by the legislature.

**Voter activation** The process of inducing particular, finely targeted portions of the electorate to participate in politics.

**Voter mobilization** The process of motivating citizens to vote.

**Voting age population (VAP)** The number of U.S. residents who are 18 years of age or older.

**Voting eligible population (VEP)** The number of U.S. residents who are eligible to vote.

**Voting Rights Act (VRA)** A federal law designed to protect the voting rights of racial and ethnic minorities.

**War Powers Act** A law limiting the president's ability to commit American Armed Forces to combat abroad without consultation with Congress and congressional approval.

**Warrant** An official authorization issued by a judicial officer.

**Watergate** A scandal that involved the abuse of the powers of the presidency by President Richard Nixon and members of his administration that led to his resignation in 1974.

**Weapons of mass destruction (WMD)** Nuclear, chemical, and biological weapons that are designed to inflict widespread military and civilian casualties.

**Weblog or blog** An online personal journal or newsletter that is regularly updated.

**Wedge issue** A sharply divisive political issue raised by a candidate or party in hopes of attracting a portion of an opponent's customary supporters.

**Welfare programs** Government programs that provide benefits to individuals based on their economic status.

**Welfare state** A government that takes responsibility for the welfare of its citizens through programs in public health, public housing, old-age pensions, unemployment compensation, and the like.

**Whips** Assistant floor leaders in Congress.

**Whistleblowers** Workers who report wrongdoing or mismanagement.

**White primary** An electoral system used in the South to prevent the participation of African Americans in the Democratic primary.

**World Health Organization (WHO)** An international organization created to control disease worldwide.

**World Trade Organization (WTO)** An international organization that administers trade laws and provides a forum for settling trade disputes among nations.

**YouTube** A video sharing Internet website where users can upload, view, and share video clips.

**Zone of acquiescence** The range of policy options acceptable to the public on a particular issue.

# >notes

## Introduction

[1] Civil Rights Division, U.S. Department of Justice, "A Guide to Disability Rights Laws," September 2005, available at www.usdoj.gov.

[2] Office of Management and Budget, "Total Government Receipts in Absolute Amounts and as a Percentage of GDP: 1948–2006," *The Budget for Fiscal Year 2008, Historical Tables*, available at www.omb.gov.

[3] David Easton, "Political Science in the United States," in David Easton, John G. Gunnell, and Luigi Graziano, eds., *The Development of Political Science* (London: Routledge, 1991), p. 275.

[4] Thomas A. Birkland, *An Introduction to the Policy Process: Theories, Concepts, and Models of Public Policy Making* (Armonk, NY: M.E. Sharpe, 2001), pp. 4–5.

[5] Thomas A. Birkland, *An Introduction to the Policy Process: Theories, Concepts, and Models of Public Policy Making*, 2nd ed. (Armonk, NY: M. E. Sharpe, 2005), p. 6.

[6] Roger W. Cobb and Marc Howard Ross, "Agenda Setting and the Denial of Agenda Access: Key Concepts," in Cobb and Ross, eds., *Cultural Strategies of Agenda Denial: Avoidance, Attack, and Redefinition* (Lawrence, KS: University of Kansas Press, 1997), pp. 19–20.

[7] David A. Rochefort and Roger W. Cobb, "Problem Definition: An Emerging Perspective," in Rochefort and Cobb, eds., *The Politics of Problem Definition: Shaping the Policy Agenda* (Lawrence, KS: University of Kansas Press, 1994), pp. 1–31.

[8] Jack M. McNeil, *Employment, Earnings, and Disability*, U.S. Bureau of the Census, 2000, available at www.census.gov.

[9] Civil Rights Division, "A Guide to Disability Rights Laws."

[10] U.S. Equal Employment Opportunity Commission, Department of Justice, Civil Rights Division, *The Americans with Disabilities Act: Questions and Answers*, available at www.usdoj.gov.

[11] U.S. Equal Employment Opportunity Commission, "Charge Statistics FY 1997 through FY 2006," available at www.eeoc.gov.

[12] U.S. Equal Employment Opportunity Commission, "Selected Enforcement Guidelines and Other Policy Documents on the ADA," available at www.eeoc.gov.

[13] National Resource Center on AD/HD, "Workplace and Higher Education Issues," available at www.help4adhd.org.

[14] Christine H. Rossell, "Using Multiple Criteria to Evaluate Public Policies: The Case of School Desegregation," *American Politics Quarterly* 21 (April 1993): p. 162.

[15] Jill Smolowe, "Noble Aims, Mixed Results," *Time*, July 31, 1995, p. 55.

[16] U.S. Equal Employment Opportunity Commission, "ADA Charge Data by Impairments/Bases—Merit Factor Resolutions, 1997–2007," available at www.eeoc.gov.

[17] David C. Stapleton and Richard Burkhauser, eds., *Decline in Employment of People with Disabilities: A Policy Puzzle* (Kalamazoo, MI: W.E. Upjohn Institute, 2003).

## Chapter 1

[1] U.S. Census Bureau, "Resident Population Projection by Sex and Age: 2010–2050," 2008 Statistical Abstract, available at www.census.gov.

[2] "Vietnam Gears Up for Single-Party Election," May 18, 2002, available at cnn.com.

[3] Michael Slackman, "Testing Egypt, Mubarak Rival Is Sent to Jail," *New York Times*, December 25, 2005, available at www.nytimes.com.

[4] Robert A. Dahl, *Polyarchy: Participation and Opposition* (New Haven, CT: Yale University Press, 1971), p. 3.

[5] Stockholm International Peace Research Institute, "Fifteen Major Spenders in 2006," available at www.sipri.org.

[6] U.S. Census Bureau, "Census Bureau Data Show Key Population Changes Across Nation," available at www.census.gov.

[7] U.S. Citizenship and Immigration Services (USCIS), *Fiscal Year 2004 Yearbook of Immigration Statistics*, available at http://uscis.gov/graphics.

[8] Steven A. Camerota and Karen Jensenius, "Homeward Bound: Recent Immigration Enforcement and the Decline in the Illegal Immigration Population," Center for Immigration Studies, July 2008, available at www.cis.org.

[9] Jeffrey S. Passel, "Unauthorized Migrants: Numbers and Characteristics," Pew Hispanic Center Report, June 2005, available at http://pewhispanic.org.

[10] Christopher Rudolph, *National Security and Immigration: Policy Develops in the United States and Western Europe Since 1945* (Stanford, CA: Stanford University Press, 2006), pp. 126–142.

[11] Mari-Claude Blanc-Chaléard, "Old and New Migrants in France: Italians and Algerians," in Leo Lucassen, David Feldman, and Jochen Oltmer, eds., *Paths of Integration: Migrants in Western Europe (1880–2004)* (Amsterdam: Amsterdam University Press, 2006), p. 54.

[12] Alec G. Hargreaves, *Multi-Ethnic France: Immigration, Politics, Culture, and Society* (NY: Routledge, 2007), p. 201.

[13] U.S. Census Bureau, "Annual Estimates of the Resident Population by Sex, Race, and Hispanic Origin of the United States," available at www.census.gov.

[14] U.S. Census Bureau, The Population Profile of the United States: 2000, available at www.census.gov.

[15] U.S. Census Bureau, "Resident Population by Region, Race, and Hispanic Origin: 2000," 2001 Statistical Abstract of the United States, available at www.census.gov.

[16] Bureau of Economic Analysis, "Current Dollar and 'Real' Gross Domestic Product," available at www.bea.gov.

[17] Tim Weiner, "Free Trade Accord at 10: Growing Pains Are Clear," *New York Times*, December 27, 2003, available at www.nytimes.com.

[18] Gary Schneider, "Another Kind of Homeland Security," *Washington Post National Weekly Edition*, February 9–15, 2004, p. 16.

[19] Ibid.

[20] David Finkel, "The American Dream, Revisited," *Washington Post National Weekly Edition*, December 22, 2003–January 4, 2004, p. 19.

[21] Robert H. Frank, "Income Inequality and the Protestant Ethic," in Victor Nee and Richard Swedberg, eds., *Capitalism* (Stanford, CA: Stanford University Press, 2007), pp. 73–79.

[22] U.S. Census Bureau, "Income, Poverty, and Health Insurance Coverage in the United States: 2008," available at www.census.gov.

[23] U.S. Department of Health and Human Services, "2008 Annual Update of the HHS Poverty Guidelines," available at www.hhs.gov.

[24] U.S. Census Bureau, "Income, Poverty, and Health Insurance Coverage in the United States: 2008," available at www.census.gov.

[25] U.S. Census Bureau, "Income, Poverty, and Health Insurance Coverage in the United States: 2008," available at www.census.gov.

[26] Ibid.

[27] Passel, "Unauthorized Migrants: Numbers and Characteristics."

## Chapter 2

[1] Gordon S. Wood, *The Creation of the American Republic 1776–1787* (Chapel Hill, NC: University of North Carolina Press, 1969), pp. 131–148.

[2] Donald S. Lutz, "The Changing View of the Founding and a New Perspective on American Political Theory," *Social Science Quarterly* 68 (December 1987): 669–686.

[3] Wood, pp. 601–14.

[4] Lutz, p. 677.

[5] Paul Finkelman, "James Madison and the Bill of Rights: A Reluctant Paternity," in Gerhard Casper, Dennis J. Hutchison, and David Strauss, eds., *The Supreme Court Review* (Chicago, IL: University of Chicago Press, 1990), pp. 309–11.

[6] Richard Labunski, *James Madison and the Struggle for the Bill of Rights* (New York: Oxford University Press, 2006), pp. 96–255.

[7] *The Federalist*, no. 51.

[8] Ibid.

[9] Robert A. Dahl, *A Preface to Democratic Theory*, expanded edition (Chicago, IL: University of Chicago Press, 2006), p. 137.

[10] Edward C. Carmines and Lawrence C. Dodd, "Bicameralism in Congress: The Changing Partnership," in Lawrence C. Dodd and Bruce I. Oppenheimer, eds., *Congress Reconsidered*, 3rd ed. (Washington, DC: Congressional Quarterly Press, 1985), pp. 414–436.

[11] Leonard Levy, *Judgments: Essays on American Constitutional History* (Chicago, IL: Quadrangle Books, 1972), p. 17.

[12] *Marbury v. Madison*, 1 Cranch 137 (1803).

[13] Richard H. Fallon, Jr., *The Dynamic Constitution: An Introduction to American Constitutional Law* (New York: Cambridge University Press, 2004), p. 193.

[14] *Plessy v. Ferguson*, 163 U.S. 537 (1896).

[15] *Brown v. Board of Education of Topeka*, 347 U.S. 483 (1954).

[16] Thomas A. Birkland, *An Introduction to the Policy Process: Theories, Concepts, and Models of Public Policy Making* (Armonk, NY: M.E. Sharpe, 2001), p. 39.

[17] Charles A. Beard, *An Economic Interpretation of the Constitution of the United States* (New York: Macmillan, 1913).

[18]James L. Sundquist, *Constitutional Reform and Effective Government*, rev. ed. (Washington, DC: Brookings Institution, 1986), pp. 5–6.

[19]Peter F. Nardulli, "The Constitution and American Politics: A Developmental Perspective," in Peter F. Nardulli, ed., *The Constitution and American Political Development* (Chicago, IL: University of Chicago Press, 1992), p. 12.

[20]Jeffrey M. Jones, "Majority Continues to Consider Iraq War a Mistake," February 6, 2008, available at www.gallup.com.

## Chapter 3

[1]Kenneth Wong and Gail Sunderman, "Education Accountability as a Presidential Priority: No Child Left Behind and the Bush Presidency," *Publius: The Journal of Federalism* 37 (Summer 2007): 333–350.

[2]Public Law 107–110.

[3]Claudia Wallis and Sonja Steptoe, "How to Fix No Child Left Behind," *Time*, June 4, 2007, p. 36.

[4]Diana Jean Schemo, "Failing Schools Strain to Meet U.S. Standard," *New York Times*, October 16, 2007, available at www.nytimes.com.

[5]*McCulloch v. Maryland*, 4 Wheaton 316 (1819).

[6]*Dred Scott v. Sandford*, 19 Howard 393 (1857).

[7]*United States v. Lopez*, 514 U.S. 549 (1995).

[8]*Printz v. United States*, 521 U.S. 98 (1997).

[9]*United States v. Morrison*, 529 U.S. 598 (2000).

[10]Larry N. Gerston, *American Federalism: A Concise Introduction* (Armonk, NY: M.E. Sharpe, 2007), p. 69.

[11]Karen Adelberger, "Federalism and Its Discontents: Fiscal and Legislative Power-Sharing in Germany, 1948–1999," *Regional and Federal Studies* 11 (Summer 2000): 43–68.

[12]Jan Erk, *Explaining Federalism: State, Society and Congruence in Austria, Belgium, Canada, Germany, and Switzerland* (New York: Routledge, 2008), pp. 58–70.

[13]Frances E. Lee, "Bicameralism and Geographic Politics: Allocating Funds in the House and Senate," *Legislative Studies Quarterly* 29 (May 2004): 185–214.

[14]Frances E. Lee and Bruce I. Oppenheimer, *Sizing Up the Senate: The Unequal Consequences of Equal Representation* (Chicago: University of Chicago Press, 1999), pp. 203–224.

[15]*Characteristics of Federal Grant Programs to State and Local Governments: Grants Funded 1995* (Washington, DC: Advisory Commission on Intergovernmental Relations, 1995).

[16]David B. Walker, *The Rebirth of Federalism* (Chatham, NJ: Chatham House, 1995), p. 242.

[17]Trinity D. Tomsic, "Managing Medicaid in Tough Times," *State Legislatures*, June 2002, pp. 13–17.

[18]Paul Posner, "The Politics of Coercive Federalism in the Bush Era," *Publius: The Journal of Federalism* 37 (Summer 2007): p. 399.

[19]Gerston, *American Federalism: A Concise Introduction*, p. 20.

[20]Molly Stauffer and Carl Tubbesing, "The Mandate Monster," *State Legislatures*, May 2004, pp. 22–23.

[21]Julia Preston, "Surge in Immigration Laws Around U.S.," *New York Times*, August 6, 2007, available at www.nytimes.com.

[22]Pam Belluck, "Massachusetts Sets Health Plan for Nearly All," *New York Times*, April 5, 2006, available at www.nytimes.com.

[23]Joseph F. Zimmerman, "The Nature and Political Significance of Preemption," *PS: Political Science & Politics* (July 2005): 361.

[24]Jonathan Walters, "Save Us from the States!'" *Governing*, June 2001, p. 20.

## Chapter 4

[1]*New York Times*/CBS News Poll, Obama's 100th Day in Office, April 22–26, 2009, available at www.nytimes.com.

[2]Edward Greenberg, "Orientations of Black and White Children to Political Activity," *Social Science Quarterly* 5 (December 1970): 561–571.

[3]David O. Sears and Nicholas A. Valentino, "Politics Matters: Political Events as Catalysts for Pre-adult Socialization," *American Political Science Review* 91 (March 1997): 45–65.

[4]M. Kent Jennings, "Political Knowledge Over Time and Across Generations," *Public Opinion Quarterly* 60 (Summer 1996): 228–252.

[5]Eric Plutzer, "Becoming a Habitual Voter: Inertia, Resources, and Growth in Young Adulthood," *American Political Science Review* 96 (March 2002): 54.

[6]Richard G. Niemi and Jane Junn, *Civic Education: What Makes Students Learn* (New Haven, CT: Yale University Press, 1998), p. 148.

[7]Cynthia Gordon, "Al Gore's Our Guy: Linguistically Constructing a Family Political Identity," *Discourse and Society* 15 (2004): 607–631.

[8]Paul Allen Beck and M. Kent Jennings, "Family Traditions, Political Periods, and the Development of Partisan Orientations," *Journal of Politics* 53 (August 1991): 742–763.

[9]Niemi and Junn, *Civic Education*, p. 148.

[10]Edward Metz and James Youniss, "A Demonstration that School-Based Required Service Does Not Deter—But Heightens—Volunteerism," *PS: Political Science & Politics* (April 2003): 281–286.

[11]Molly W. Andolina, Krista Jenkins, Cliff Zukin, and Scott Keeter, "Habits from Home, Lessons from School: Influences on Youth Civic Engagement," *Social Education* 67 (October 2003): 278–279.

[12]Edgar Lott, "Civic Education, Community Norms, and Political Indoctrination," *American Sociological Review* 28 (February 1963): 69–75.

[13]Robert Wuthnow, "Mobilizing Civic Engagement: The Changing Impact of Religious Involvement," in Theda Skocpol and Morris P. Fiorina, eds., *Civic Engagement in American Democracy* (Washington, DC: Brookings Institution Press, 1999), p. 352.

[14]Frederick C. Harris, "Something Within: Religion as a Mobilizer of African American-Political Activism," *Journal of Politics* 56 (February 1994): 42–68.

[15]Kenneth D. Wald, Dennis E. Owen, and Samuel S. Hill, Jr., "Churches as Political Communities," *American Political Science Review* 82 (June 1988): 531–548.

[16]Kenneth D. Wald, Dennis E. Owen, and Samuel S. Hill, Jr., "Political Cohesion in Churches," *Journal of Politics* 52 (February 1990): 197–215.

[17]Katharine Q. Seelye and Janet Elder, "Strong Support Is Found for Ban on Gay Marriage," *New York Times*, December 21, 2003, available at www.nytimes.com.

[18]Paul Allen Beck, Russell J. Dalton, Steven Greene, and Robert Huckfeldt, "The Social Calculus of Voting: Interpersonal, Media, and Organizational Influences on Presidential Choices," *American Political Science Review* 96 (March 2002): 57–73.

[19]Herbert P. Hyman, *Political Socialization* (Glencoe, IL: Free Press, 1959), pp. 109–115.

[20]Clyde Wilcox, "Feminism and Anti-Feminism Among Evangelical Women," *Western Political Quarterly* 42 (March 1989): 147–160.

[21]Ibid., p. 185.

[22]Shanto Iyengar and Donald R. Kinder, *News That Matters: Television and American Opinion* (Chicago: University of Chicago Press, 1987), pp. 112–113.

[23]Jon A. Krosnick and Donald R. Kinder, "Altering the Foundations of Support for the President Through Priming," *American Political Science Review* 84 (June 1990): 497–512.

[24]John R. Alford, Carolyn L. Funk, and John R. Hibbing, "Are Political Orientations Genetically Transmitted?" *American Political Science Review* 99 (May 2005): 153–167.

[25]Jeffrey M. Stonecash, *Political Polling: Strategic Information in Campaigns* (Lanham, MD: Rowman & Littlefield, 2003), pp. 141–143.

[26]Richard Morin, "Look Who's Talking," *Washington Post National Weekly Edition*, July 19–25, 1993, p. 37.

[27]Megan Thee, "Cellphones Challenge Poll Sampling," *New York Times*, December 7, 2007, available at www.nytimes.com

[28]Herbert Asher, *Polling and the Public: What Every Citizen Should Know*, 6th ed. (Washington, DC: CQ Press, 2004), pp. 82–86.

[29]Adam J. Berinsky, "The Two Faces of Public Opinion," *American Journal of Political Science* 43 (October 1999): 1209–1230.

[30]Larry M. Bartels, "Democracy with Attitudes," in Michael B. Mac Kuen and George Rabinowitz, eds., *Electoral Democracy* (Ann Arbor, MI: University of Michigan Press, 2003), pp. 56–57.

[31]Frank Newport, "Six Out of 10 Americans Say Homosexual Relations Should Be Recognized as Legal," May 15, 2003, available at www.gallup.com.

[32]Asher, *Polling and the Public*, p. 61.

[33]John Zaller and Stanley Feldman, "A Simple Theory of the Survey Response: Answering Questions versus Revealing Preferences," *American Journal of Political Science* 36 (August 1992): 579–616.

[34]Richard Morin, "What Informed Public Opinion?" *Washington Post National Weekly Edition*, April 10–16, 1995, p. 36.

[35]Howard Schuman and Jean Converse, "The Effects of Black and White Interviewers on Black Response in 1968," *Public Opinion Quarterly* 35 (Spring 1971): 44–68; and Shirley Hatchett and Howard Schuman, "White Respondents and Race of Interviewer Effects," *Public Opinion Quarterly* 39 (Winter 1975): 523–528.

[36]Asher, *Polling and the Public*, p. 96.

[37]*Gallup Poll Monthly*, July 1992, pp. 8–9.

[38]W. Russell Neuman, *The Paradox of Mass Politics: Knowledge and Opinion in the American Electorate* (Cambridge, MA: Harvard University Press, 1986), ch. 1.

[39]Richard Morin, "Tuned Out, Turned Off," *Washington Post National Weekly Edition*, February 5–11, 1996, p. 6.

[40]Morin, "Tuned Out, Turned Off," p. 7.

[41]Quoted in Morin, "Tuned Out, Turned Off," p. 8.

[42]"Homosexual Relations," available at www.gallup.com.

[43]Samuel A. Stouffer, *Communism, Conformity, and Civil Liberties: A Cross Section of the Nation Speaks Its Mind* (Garden City, NY: Doubleday, 1955), pp. 28–42.

[44]James W. Prothro and C. W. Grigg, "Fundamental Principles of Democracy: Bases of Agreement and Disagreement," *Journal of Politics* 22 (Spring 1960): 276–294.

[45]Robert Chandler, *Public Opinion: Changing Attitudes on Contemporary Social and Political Issues*, A CBS News Reference Book (New York: R. R. Bowker, 1972), pp. 6–13.

[46]Clyde Z. Nunn, Harry J. Crockett, Jr., and J. Allen Williams, Jr., *Tolerance for Nonconformity: A National Survey of Americans' Changing Commitment to Civil Liberties* (San Francisco: Jossey-Bass, 1978); James A. Davis, "Communism, Conformity, Cohorts, and Categories: American Tolerance in 1954 and 1972–73," *American Journal of Sociology* 81 (November 1975): 491–513.

[47]Jeffrey J. Mondak and Mitchell S. Sanders, "Tolerance and Intolerance, 1976–1998," *American Journal of Political Science* 47 (July 2003): 492–502.

[48]Donald Philip Green and Lisa Michele Waxman, "Direct Threat and Political Tolerance," *Public Opinion Quarterly* 51 (Summer 1987): 149–165.

[49]James L. Gibson, "Enigmas of Intolerance: Fifty Years after Stouffer's *Communism, Conformity, and Civil Liberties*," *Perspectives on Politics* 4 (March 2006): 21–34.

[50]David G. Barnum and John L. Sullivan, "The Elusive Foundations of Political Freedom in Britain and the United States," *Journal of Politics* 52 (August 1990): 719–739.

[51]Dennis Chong, "How People Think, Reason, and Feel about Rights and Liberties," *American Journal of Political Science* 37 (August 1993): 867–899.

[52]Timothy E. Cook and Paul Gronke, "The Skeptical American: Revisiting the Meanings of Trust in Government and Confidence in Institutions," *Journal of Politics* 67 (August 2005): 784–803.

[53]"The NES Guide to Public Opinion and Electoral Behavior," available at www.electionstudies.org

[54]Ibid.

[55]Ruy A. Teixeira, *Why Americans Don't Vote: Turnout Decline in the United States 1960–1984* (New York: Greenwood Press, 1987), p. 78.

[56]William G. Jacoby, "The Sources of Liberal-Conservative Thinking: Education and Conceptualization," *Political Behavior* 10 (Winter 1988): 316–332.

[57]"The NES Guide to Public Opinion and Electoral Behavior," available at www.electionstudies.org

[58]Albert H. Cantril and Susan Davis Cantril, *Reading Mixed Signals: Ambivalence in American Public Opinion About Government* (Washington, DC: Woodrow Wilson Center Press, 1999), pp. 10–14.

[59]Ibid., p. 20.

[60]The Gallup Poll, available at www.gallup.com.

[61]Eugene R. Wittkopf and Michael R. Maggiotto, "Elites and Masses: A Comparative Analysis of Attitudes Toward America's World Role," *Journal of Politics* 45 (May 1983): 303–334.

[62]Richard Morin, "It's Not as It Seems," *Washington Post National Weekly Edition*, July 16–22, 2001, p. 34.

[63]Frank Newport, "Blacks as Conservative as Republicans on Some Moral Issues," *Gallup Poll*, December 3, 2008, available at www.gallup.com.

[64]Caryle Murphy and Alan Cooperman, "Seeking to Reclaim the Moral High Ground," *Washington Post National Weekly Edition*, May 29–June 4, 2006, p. 12.

[65]James L. Guth, John C. Green, Corwin E. Smith, and Margaret M. Poloma, "Pulpits and Politics: The Protestant Clergy in the 1988 Presidential Election," in Guth and Green, eds., *The Bible and the Ballot Box* (Boulder, CO: Westview Press, 1991), pp. 73–93.

[66]Allen D. Hertzke and John David Rausch, Jr., "The Religious Vote in American Politics: Value Conflict, Continuity, and Change," in Craig, *Broken Contract?*, p. 191.

[67]Steven A. Peterson, "Church Participation and Political Participation: The Spillover Effect," *American Politics Quarterly* 20 (January 1992): 123–139.

[68]Amy Goldstein and Richard Morin, "The Squeaky Wheel Gets the Grease," *Washington Post National Weekly Edition*, October 28–November 3, 2002, p. 34.

[69]Nicholas L. Danigelis and Stephen J. Cutler, "Cohort Trends in Attitudes about Law and Order: Who's Leading the Conservative Wave?" *Public Opinion Quarterly* 55 (Spring 1991): 24–49.

[70]Thomas C. Wilson, "Trends in Tolerance Toward Rightist and Leftist Groups, 1976–1988," *Public Opinion Quarterly* 58 (Winter 1994): 539–556.

[71]Laurel Elder and Steven Greene, "The Myth of 'Security Moms' and 'Nascar Dads,' Parenthood, Political Stereotypes, and the 2004 Election," *Social Science Quarterly* 88 (March 2007), p. 11.

[72]Karen M. Kaufmann, "The Gender Gap," *PS: Political Science & Politics* (July 2006): 447–453.

[73]V. O. Key, Jr., *Public Opinion and American Democracy* (New York: Alfred Knopf, 1961), p. 499.

[74]James A. Stimson, *Public Opinion in America: Moods, Cycles, and Swings* (Boulder, CO: Westview Press, 1991), pp. 19–21.

[75]Kenneth D. Wald, James W. Button, and Barbara A. Rienzo, "The Politics of Gay Rights in American Communities: Explaining Antidiscrimination Ordinances and Policies," *American Journal of Political Science* 40 (November 1996): 1152–1178.

## Chapter 5

[1]David Mark, "2008 Could See Turnout Tsunami," March 24, 2008, available at www.politico.com.

[2]Michael P. McDonald, United States Election Project, available at http://elections.gmu.edu.

[3]"The ANES Guide to Public Opinion and Electoral Behavior," available at www.electionstudies.org.

[4]John R. Petrocek and Daron Shaw, "Nonvoting in America: Attitudes in Context," in William Crotty, ed., *Political Participation and American Democracy* (New York: Greenwood Press, 1991), p. 83.

[5]McDonald, United States Election Project.

[6]Sidney Verba, Kay Lehman Schlozman, and Henry E. Brady, *Voice and Equality: Civic Volunteerism in American Politics* (Cambridge, MA: Harvard University Press, 1995), p. 51.

[7]André Blais, *To Vote or Not to Vote?* (Pittsburgh: University of Pittsburg Press, 2000), pp. 12–13.

[8]Henry E. Brady, Sidney Verba, Kay Lehman Schlozman, "Beyond SES: A Resource Model of Political Participation," *American Political Science Review* 89 (June 1995): 3.

[9]Andrea Louise Campbell, "Self-Interest, Social Security, and the Distinctive Participation Patterns of Senior Citizens," *American Political Science Review* 96 (September 2002): 565–574.

[10]Ibid.

[11]Verba, Schlozman, and Brady, *Voice and Equality: Civic Volunteerism in American Politics*, p. 354.

[12]Michael Luo, "Obama Hauls in Record $750 Million for Campaign," *New York Times*, December 4, 2008, available at www.nytimes.com.

[13]Thomas M. Holbrook and Scott D. McClurg, "The Mobilization of Core Supporters: Campaigns, Turnout, and Electoral Composition in the United States Presidential Elections," *American Journal of Political Science* 49 (October 2005): 689–703.

[14]Donald P. Green, Alan S. Gerber, and David W. Nickerson, "Getting Out the Vote in Local Elections: Results from Six Door-to-Door Canvassing Experiments," *Journal of Politics* 65 (November 2003): 1083–1096.

[15]Alan S. Gerber and Donald P. Green, "The Effects of Canvassing, Telephone Calls, and Direct Mail on Voter Turnout: A Field Experiment," *American Political Science Review* 94 (September 2000): 653–63.

[16]Blais, *To Vote or Not to Vote?* p. 13.

[17]U.S. Census Bureau, "Voting and Registration in the Election of November 2008," available at www.census.gov.

[18]APSA Task Force Report, "American Democracy in an Age of Rising Inequality," p. 656.

[19]U.S. Census Bureau, "Voting and Registration in the Election of November 2008."

[20]Verba, Schlozman, and Brady, *Voice and Equality: Civic Volunteerism in American Politics*, pp. 332–38.

[21]U.S. Census Bureau, "Voting and Registration in the Election of November 2008."

[22]Jeff Manza and Christopher Uggen, *Locked Out: Felon Disenfranchisement and American Democracy* (NY: Oxford University Press, 2006), pp. 76–80.

[23]Matt A. Barreto, "¡Sí Se Puede! Latino Candidates and the Mobilization of Latino Voters," *American Political Science Review* 101 (August 2007): 425–441.

[24]U.S. Census Bureau, "Voting and Registration in the Election of November 2008."

[25]Verba, Schlozman, and Brady, *Voice and Equality: Civic Volunteerism in American Politics*, p. 255.

[26]Richard Morin, "Tuned Out, Turned Off," *Washington Post National Weekly Edition*, February 5–11, 1996, p. 6.

[27]James G. Gimpel, Karen M. Kaufmann, and Shanna Pearson-Markowitz, "Battleground States Versus Blackout States: The Behavioral Implications of Modern Presidential Campaigns," *Journal of Politics* 69 (August 2007): 786–797.

[28]U.S. Census Bureau, "Voting and Registration in the Election of November 2004."

[29]International Institute for Democracy and Electoral Assistance, available at www.idea.int.

[30]U.S. Census Bureau, "Voting and Registration in the Election of November 2004," available at www.census.gov.

[31]Gary W. Cox, "Electoral Rules and the Calculus of Mobilization," *Legislative Studies Quarterly* 24 (August 1999): 387–419.

[32]G. Bingham Powell, Jr., "American Voter Turnout in Comparative Perspective," *American Political Science Review* 80 (March 1986): 17–43.

[33]Mark N. Franklin, "Electoral Engineering and Cross-National Turnout Differences: What Role of Compulsory Voting?" *British Journal of Political Science* 29 (January 1999): 205.

[34]Australian Electoral Commission, "2007 Federal Election Voter Turnout by Division," available at www.aec.gov.au.

[35]M. Mackerras and I. McAllister,"Compulsory Voting, Party Stability, and Electoral Advantage in Australia," *Electoral Studies*, 18 (June 1999): 217–33.

[36]Petrocek and Shaw, "Nonvoting in America: Attitudes in Context," pp. 71–72.

[37]Gary C. Jacobson, *A Divider, Not a Uniter: George W. Bush and the American People* (New York: Pearson Longman, 2007).

[38]Peter L. Francia, Rachel E. Goldberg, John C. Green, Paul S. Herrnson, and Clyde Wilcox, "Individual Donors in the 1996 Federal Elections," in John C. Green, ed., *Financing the 1996 Election* (Armonk, NY: M. E. Sharpe, 1999), p. 128.

[39]Theda Skocpol, *Diminished Democracy: From Membership to Management in American Civic Life* (Norman, OK: University of Oklahoma Press, 2003), pp. 6–13, 224–244.

[40]APSA Task Force Report, "American Democracy in an Age of Rising Inequality," p. 657.

[41]*Adarand Constructors v. Pena*, 515 U.S. 200 (1995).

## Chapter 6

[1]Jose Antonio Vargas, "Obama Raised Half a Billion Online," *Washington Post*, November 20, 2008, available at www.washingtonpost.com.

[2]Elizabeth Gorman, "Obama Cashes in On-Line Political Capital for Sotomayor," ABC News, May 29, 2009, available at www.abcnews.com.

[3]Quoted in *Texas Observer*, June 12, 2009, p. 15.

[4]Project for Excellence in Journalism, available at www.stateofthenewsmedia.org.

[5]"2006 Annual Report," available at www.tribune.com.

[6]"The State of the News Media 2006," available at www.stateofthenewsmedia.org.

[7]Pew Center for the People & the Press, available at http://people-press.org.

[8]Stephen J. Farnsworth and S. Robert Lichter, *The Nightly News Nightmare: Television's Coverage of U.S. Presidential Elections, 1988–2004*, 2nd ed. (Lanham, MD: Rowman & Littlefield, 2007), p. 25.

[9]Philip N. Howard, *New Media Campaigns and the Managed Citizen* (New York, NY: Cambridge University Press, 2006), p. 27.

[10]"Cuba—Annual Report 2007," available at www.rsf.org.

[11]Ibid.

[12]Erika Franklin Fowler and Kenneth M. Goldstein, eds., "Free Media in Campaigns," in Stephen C. Craig, ed., *The Electoral Challenge: Theory Meets Practice* (Washington, DC: CQ Press, 2006), pp. 112–115.

[13]Martha Joynt Kumar, "Managing the News: The Bush Communications Operation," in George C. Edwards III and Desmond S. King, eds., *The Polarized Presidency of George W. Bush* (New York, NY: Oxford University Press, 2007), pp. 353–354.

[14]Bruce Miroff, "The Presidential Spectacle," in Michael Nelson, ed., *The Presidency and the Political System*, 8th ed. (Washington, DC: CQ Press, 2006), p. 277.

[15]White House Press Release, "President Arrives in Alabama, Briefed on Hurricane Katrina," September 2, 2005, available at www.whitehouse.gov.

[16]S. Robert Lichter, Linda S. Lichter, and Stanley Rothman, *The Media Elite: America's New Powerbrokers* (Bethesda, MD: Adler and Adler, 1986), pp. 54–71.

[17]Farnsworth and Lichter, *The Nightly News Nightmare*, pp. 118–161.

[18]Jonathan S. Morris, "Slanted Objectivity? Perceived Media Bias, Cable News Exposure, and Political Attitudes," *Social Science Quarterly* 88 (September 2007): 707–728.

[19]Kim Fridkin Kahn and Patrick J. Kenney, "The Slant of the News: How Editorial Endorsements Influence Campaign Coverage and Citizens' Views of Candidates," *American Political Science Review* 96 (June 2002): 381–394.

[20]Tim Groeling and Samuel Kernell, "Is Network News Coverage of the President Biased?" *Journal of Politics* 60 (November 1998): 1063–1087; Larry Sabato, "Is There an Anti-Republican, Anti-Conservative Media Tilt?" *Campaigns and Elections*, September 1993, p. 16.

[21]Thomas E. Patterson, "Bad News, Period," *PS: Political Science and Politics* (March 1996): 17–20.

[22]Elizabeth A. Skewes, *Message Control: How News Is Made on the Presidential Campaign Trail* (Lanham, MD: Rowman & Littlefield Publishers, 2007), p. 13.

## Chapter 7

[1]Jeffrey M. Jones, "Public Believes Americans Have Right to Own Guns," March 27, 2008, available at www.gallup.com.

[2]Anthony J. Nownes, *Total Lobbying: What Lobbyists Want (and How They Try to Get It)*, (New York, NY: Cambridge University Press, 2006), p. 13.

[3]Center for Responsive Politics, available at www.opensecrets.org.

[4]"Labor Union Membership by Sector," *2009 Statistical Abstract*.

[5]*Dukes v. Wal-Mart, Inc.*, 04-16688 (9th Cir. Feb. 6, 2007).

[6]Peter L. Francia, "Protecting America's Workers in Hostile Territory: Unions and the Republican Congress," in Paul S. Herrnson, Ronald G. Shaiko, and Clyde Wilcox, eds., *The Interest Group Connection: Electioneering, Lobbying, and Policymaking in Washington*, 2nd ed. (Washington, DC: CQ Press, 2005), p. 214.

[7]Amy Joyce, "Divided Unions," *Washington Post National Weekly Edition*, August 1–7, 2005, p. 20.

[8]Caryle Murphy and Alan Cooperman, "Seeking to Reclaim the Moral High Ground," *Washington Post National Weekly Edition*, May 29–June 4, 2006, p. 12.

[9]John C. Green and Nathan S. Bigelow, "The Christian Right Goes to Washington: Social Movement Resources and the Legislative Process," in Herrnson, Shaiko, and Wilcox, eds., *The Interest Group Connection*, pp. 191–206.

[10]John C. Green, Mark J. Rozell, and Clyde Wilcox, eds., *The Values Campaign? The Christian Right and the 2004 Election* (Washington, DC: Georgetown University Press, 2006), p. 4.

[11]Roderi Ai Camp, *Politics in Mexico: The Democratic Consolidation* (New York, NY: Oxford University Press, 2007), p. 89.

[12]Ibid., pp. 144–145.

[13]Daniel C. Levy and Kathleen Bruhn, *Mexico: The Struggle for Democratic Development*, 2nd ed. (Berkeley, CA: University of California Press, 2006), pp. 123–124.

[14]Camp, Politics in Mexico, p. 146.

[15]Center for Responsive Politics, available at www.opensecrets.org.

[16]Federal Election Commission, "PAC Financial Activity, 2007–2008," available at www.fec.gov.

[17]Professor James A. Thurber, quoted in Jeffrey H. Birnbaum, "Mickey Goes to Washington," *Washington Post National Weekly Edition*, February 25–March 2, 2008, p. 6.

[18]Ronald G. Shaiko, "Making the Connection: Organized Interests, Political Representation, and the Changing Rules of the Game in Washington Politics," in Herrnson, Shaiko, and Wilcox, eds., *The Interest Group Connection*, p. 32.

[19]Rogan Kersh, "The Well-Informed Lobbyist: Information and Interest Group Lobbying," in Ciglar and Loomis, ed., *Interest Group Politics*, pp. 390–406.

[20]John R. Wright, "Contributions, Lobbying, and Committee Voting in the U.S. House of Representatives," *American Political Science Review* 84 (June 1990): 417–38.

[21]Thomas B. Edsall, "A Chill but Not the Cold Shoulder," *Washington Post National Weekly Edition*, January 16–22, 2006, p. 15.

[22]Dan Clawson, Alan Neustadtl, and Mark Weller, *Dollars and Votes: How Business Campaign Contributions Subvert Democracy* (Philadelphia: Temple University Press, 1998), pp. 67–69.

[23]Ruth Markus and Charles R. Babcock, "Feeding the Election Machine," *Washington Post National Weekly Edition*, February 17, 1997, p. 7.

[24]*District of Columbia v. Heller*, 554 U.S. _____ 208 (2008).

[25]Richard Monastersky, "Protesters Fail to Slow Animal Research," *Chronicle of Higher Education*, April 18, 2008, pp. A1, A26–A28.

[26]Diana Evans, "Before the Roll Call: Interest Group Lobbying and Public Policy Outcomes in House Committees," *Political Research Quarterly* 49 (June 1996): 287–304.

[27]Marcella Ridlan Ray, *The Changing and Unchanging Face of U.S. Civil Society* (New Brunswick, NJ: Transaction Publishers, 2002), pp. 2–3.

[28]Richard M. Skinner, *More Than Money: Interest Group Action in Congressional Elections* (Lanham, MD: Rowman & Littlefield, 2007), pp. 165–167.

[29]Lydia Saad, "Public Divided on 'Pro-Choice' versus 'Pro-Life' Abortion Labels," Gallup News Service, May 21 2007, available at www.gallup.com.

[30]Americans for Tax Reform, available at www.atr.org.

## Chapter 8

[1]Center for Responsive Politics.

[2]A. James Reichley, "The Future of the American Two-Party System at the Beginning of a New Century," in John C. Green and Rick Farmer, eds., *The State of the Parties: The Changing Role of Contemporary American Parties*, 4th ed. (Lanham, MD: Rowman & Littlefield, 2003), pp. 20–21.

[3]Asher Arian, *Politics in Israel: The Second Republic*, 2nd ed. (Washington, DC: CQ Press, 2005), p. 203.

[4]Octavio Amorim Neto and Gary W. Cox, "Electoral Institutions, Cleavage Structures, and the Number of Parties," *American Journal of Political Science* 41 (January 1997): 149–74.

[5]Michael Toner, "The Impact of the New Campaign Finance Law on the 2004 Presidential Election," in Larry Sabato, ed., *Divided States of America: The Slash and Burn Politics of the 2004 Presidential Election* (New York, NY: Pearson Longman, 2006), p. 197.

[6]Timothy P. Nokken, "Ideological Congruence versus Electoral Success: Distribution of Party Organization Contributions in Senate Elections, 1990–2000," *American Politics Research* 31 (January 2003): 3–26.

[7]Pew Center for the People & the Press, "Fewer Voters Identify as Republicans," March 20, 2008, available at http://pewresearch.org.

[8]Exit poll data, available at www.cnn.com.

[9]Ibid.

[10]Juan Castillo, "Latinos Deliver on Potential, Turn Out Big for Obama," *Austin American-Statesman*, November 6, 2008, available at www.statesman.com.

[11]David L. Leal, Stephan A. Nuño, Jongho Lee, and Rodolpho O. de la Garza, "Latinos, Immigration, and the 2006 Midterm Election," *PS: Political Science & Politics* (April 2008): 312.

[12]Exit poll data.

[13]Ibid.

[14]Ibid.

[15]Ibid.

[16]Ibid.

[17]Exit poll data.

[18]Morris P. Fiorina, *Culture War? The Myth of a Polarized America*, 2nd ed. (New York, NY: Pearson Education, 2006), pp. 61–70.

[19]Jongho Lee and Harry P. Pachon, "Leading the Way: An Analysis of the Effect of Religion on the Latino Vote," *American Politics Research* 35 (March 2007): 252–272.

[20]John C. Green, Lyman A. Kellstedt, Corwin E. Smidt, and James L. Guth, "How the Faithful Voted: Religious Communities and the Presidential Vote," in David E. Campbell, ed., *A Matter of Faith: Religion in the 2004 Presidential Election* (Washington, DC: Brookings Institution Press, 2007), pp. 1–28.

[21]Exit poll data.

[22]Frank Newport, "Church Attendance and Party Identification," Gallup News Service, May 18, 2005, available at www.gallup.com.

[23]Exit poll data.

[24]Ibid.

[25]Joel H. Silbey, "Divided Government in Historical Perspective, 1789–1996," in Peter F. Golderisi, ed., *Divided Government: Change, Uncertainty, and the Constitutional Order* (Lanham, MD: Rowman & Littlefield, 1996), pp. 9–34.

[26]Morris Fiorina, *Divided Government*, 2nd ed. (Cambridge, MA: Harvard University Press, 1996), p. 7.

[27]Andrew E. Busch, *Horses in Midstream: U.S. Midterm Elections and Their Consequences, 1894–1998* (Pittsburgh: University of Pittsburgh Press, 1999), pp. 15–22.

[28]After the 2000 election, the Senate was evenly divided between the two parties and the vote of Republican Vice President Richard Cheney enabled the GOP to claim majority status. In 2001, however, Republican Senator James Jeffords of Vermont switched his party allegiance from Republican to independent to allow the Democrats to claim the majority.

[29]John R. Petrocik and Joseph Doherty, "The Road to Divided Government: Paved Without Intention," in Golderisi, ed., *Divided Government: Change, Uncertainty, and the Constitutional Order*, p. 105.

[30]Gary C. Jacobson, "The Persistence of Democratic House Majorities," in Gary W. Cox and Samuel Kernell, eds., *The Politics of Divided Government* (Boulder, CO: Westview, 1991), pp. 57–84.

[31]Gary C. Jacobson, "Divided Government and the 1994 Elections," in Golderisi, ed., *Divided Government: Change, Uncertainty, and the Constitutional Order*, p. 62.

[32]Barry C. Burden and David C. Kimball, "A New Approach to the Study of Ticket Splitting," *American Political Science Review* 92 (September 1998): 533–44.

[33]Walter R. Mebane, Jr., "Combination, Moderation, and Institutional Balancing in American Presidential Elections," *American Political Science Review* 94 (March 2000): 37–57.

[34]Richard D. Forgette, *Congress, Parties, and Puzzles: Politics as a Team Sport* (New York, NY: Peter Lang, 2004), p. 176.

## Chapter 9

[1]Robert E. Cushman and Robert F. Cushman, *Cases in Constitutional Law*, 3rd ed. (New York: Appleton-Century-Crofts, 1968), p. 42.

[2]*Baker v. Carr*, 369 U.S. 186 (1962) and *Wesberry v. Sanders*, 376 U.S. 1 (1964).

[3]Mark Monmonier, *Bushmanders and Bullwinkles: How Politicians Manipulate Electronic Maps and Census Data to Win Elections* (Chicago, IL: University of Chicago Press, 2001), p. 62.

[4]David Lublin and D. Stephen Voss, "Racial Redistricting and Realignment in Southern State Legislatures," *American Journal of Political Science* 44 (October 2000): 792–810.

[5]David T. Canon, *Race, Redistricting, and Representation: The Unintended Consequences of Black Majority Districts* (Chicago, IL: University of Chicago Press, 1999), p. 257.

[6]*Reno v. Bossier Parish School Board*, 528 U.S. 320 (2000).

[7]*Georgia v. Ashcroft*, 539 U.S. 461 (2003).

[8]Thomas L. Wyrick, "Management of Political Influence: Gerrymandering in the 1980s," *American Politics Quarterly* 19 (October 1991): 396–416.

[9]Michael P. McDonald, "Redistricting and Competitive Districts," in Michael P. McDonald and John Samples, eds., *The Marketplace of Democracy: Electoral Competition and American Politics* (Washington, DC: Cato Institute, 2006), p. 225.

[10]Richard G. Niemi and Laura R. Winsky, "The Persistence of Partisan Redistricting Effects in Congressional Elections in the 1970s and 1980s," *Journal of Politics* 54 (May 1992): 565–72.

[11]Center for Responsive Politics.

[12]John Mintz and Ruth Marcus, "Bush's Bucks Have a High Burn Rate," *Washington Post National Weekly Edition*, March 6, 2000, p. 11.

[13]Ken Herman, "Campaigns Spend Millions to Seek Yet More Millions," *Austin American-Statesman*, August 22, 2004, available at www.statesman.com.

[14]Center for Responsive Politics, available at www.opensecrets.org.

[15]Federal Election Commission, available at www.fec.gov.

[16]Richard A. Oppel, Jr., "Campaign Documents Show Depth of Bush Fund-Raising," *New York Times*, May 5, 2003, available at www.nytimes.com.

[17]Wayne Slater, "Elite Donors Lifted Bush," *Dallas Morning News*, May 5, 2003, available at www.dallasnews.com.

[18]Kirsten A. Foot and Steven M. Schneider, *Web Campaigning* (Cambridge, MA: MIT Press, 2006), pp. 197–198.

[19]Center for Responsive Politics.

[20]Michael J. Malbin, *The Election After Reform: Money, Politics, and the Bipartisan Campaign Reform Act* (Lanham, MD: Rowman & Littlefield, 2006), pp. 3–4.

[21]Glen Justice and Jim Rutenberg, "Advocacy Groups Step Up Costly Battle of Political Ads," *New York Times*, September 25, 2004, available at www.nytimes.com.

[22]Kerwin C. Swint, *Mudslingers: The Top 25 Negative Political Campaigns of All Time* (Westport, CT: Praeger, 2006), p. 47.

[23]Richard R. Lau and Gerald M. Pomper, "Effectiveness of Negative Campaigning in U.S. Senate Elections," *American Journal of Political Science* 46 (January 2002): 47–66.

[24]David E. Damore, "Candidate Strategy and the Decision to Go Negative," *Political Research Quarterly*, 55 (September 2002): 669–685.

[25]Stephen Ansolabehere and Shanto Iyengar, "Winning Through Advertising: It's All in the Context," in James A. Thurber and Candice J. Nelson, eds., *Campaigns and Elections American Style* (Boulder, CO: Westview, 1995), p. 109.

[26]Paul R. Abramson, John H. Aldrich, and David Rohde, *Change and Continuity in the 2004 and 2006 Elections* (Washington, DC: CQ Press, 2007), pp. 265–266.

[27]Center for Responsive Politics.

[28]Ibid.

[29]Robert S. Erikson and Gerald C. Wright, "Voters, Candidates, and Issues in Congressional Elections," in Lawrence C. Dodd and Bruce I. Oppenheimer, eds., *Congress Reconsidered*, 7th ed. (Washington, DC: CQ Press, 2001), p. 72.

[30]David J. Samuels, "Incentives to Cultivate a Party Vote in Candidate-Centric Electoral Systems: Evidence from Brazil," *Comparative Political Studies* 32 (June 1999): 487–518.

[31]Barry Ames, "Electoral Rules, Constituency Pressures, and Pork Barrel: Bases of Voting in the Brazilian Congress," *Journal of Politics* 57 (May 1995): 324–343.

[32]Secretary of State of New Hampshire, available at www.sos.nh.gov.

[33]John S. Jackson, Nathan S. Bigelow, and John C. Green, "The State of Party Elites: National Convention Delegates, 1992–2000," in John C. Green and Rick Farmer, eds., *The State of the Parties: The Changing Role of Contemporary American Parties* (Lanham, MD: Rowman & Littlefield, 2003), pp. 54–78.

[34]Paul R. Abramson, John H. Aldrich, Phil Paolino, and David W. Rohde, "Sophisticated Voting in the 1988 Presidential Primaries," *American Political Science Review* 86 (March 1992): 55–69.

[35]"State-by-state Election Results," available at www.govote.com.

[36]John M. Bruce, John A. Clark, and John H. Kessel, "Advocacy Politics in Presidential Politics," *American Political Science Review* 85 (December 1991): 1091–1105.

[37]Barbara Norrander, "Nomination Choices: Caucus and Primary Outcomes, 1976–88," *American Journal of Political Science* 37 (May 1993): 343–64.

[38]Federal Election Commission.

[39]Mark Z. Barabak, "How Obama Went from Underdog to Alpha," *Los Angeles Times*, June 4, 2008, available at www.latimes.com.

[40]Jackie Calmes, "Clinton Braces for Second Loss; Union, Senators May Back Obama," *Wall Street Journal*, January 8, 2008, available at www.wsj.com.

[41]Gerald M. Pomper, "Parliamentary Government in the United States: A New Regime for a New Century?" in Green and Farmer, eds., *The State of the Parties*, p. 273.

[42]Exit Poll Data, available at www.cnn.com.

[43]Ibid.

[44]David W. Abbott and James P. Levine, *Wrong Winner: The Coming Debacle in the Electoral College* (New York, NY: Praeger, 1991), p. 32.

[45]Lawrence D. Longley and Neal R. Peirce, *The Electoral College Primer 2000* (New Haven, CT: Yale University Press, 1999), p. 24.

[46]George C. Edwards III, *Why the Electoral College is Bad for America* (New Haven, CT: Yale University Press, 2004), p. 150.

[47]Ann N. Crigler, Marion R. Just, and Edward J. McCaffery, *Rethinking the Vote: The Politics and Prospects of American Electoral Reform* (New York: Oxford University Press, 2004).

[48]Daron R. Shaw, *The Race to 270: The Electoral College and the Campaign Strategies of 2000 and 2004* (Chicago: University of Chicago Press, 2006), p. 143.

[49]Kim J. Fridkin, Patrick J. Kenney, Sarah Allen Gershon, Karen Shafer, and Gina Serignese Woodall, "Capturing the Power of a Campaign Event: The 2004 Presidential Debate in Tempe," *Journal of Politics* 69 (August 2007): 770–785.

[50]Michael Dimock, April Clark, and Juliana Menasce Horowitz, "Campaign Dynamics and the Swing Vote in the 2004 Election," in William G. Mayer, ed., *The Swing Voter in American Politics* (Washington, DC: Brookings Institution, 2008), p. 58.

[51]Exit Poll Data.

[52]Mayer, ed., *The Swing Voter in American Politics*, p. 19.

[53]Ibid.

[54]Exit Poll Data.

[55]Warren E. Miller, "Party Identification, Realignment, and Party Voting: Back to the Basics," *American Political Science Review* 85 (June 1991): 557–68.

[56]John R. Petrocik, "Reporting Campaigns: Reforming the Press," in Thurber and Nelson, eds., *Campaigns and Elections American Style*, p. 128.

[57]Stephen Ansolabehere, Jonathan Rodden, and James M. Snyder, Jr., "The Strength of Issues: Using Multiple Measures to Gauge Preference Stability, Ideological Constraint, and Issue Voting," *American Political Science Review*, 102 (May 2008): 215–232.

[58]Scott J. Basinger and Howard Lavine, "Ambivalence, Information, and Electoral Choice," *American Political Science Review* 99 (May 2005): 169–184.

[59]Thomas M. Holbrook, "Do Campaigns Matter?" in Craig, ed., *The Electoral Challenge: Theory Meets Practice*, pp. 12–13.

[60]Edward Roeder, "Not Only Does Money Talk, It Often Calls the Winners," *Washington Post National Weekly Edition*, September 26–October 2, 1994, p. 23.

[61]Brian F. Schaffner, "Priming Gender: Campaigning on Women's Issues in U.S. Senate Elections," *American Journal of Political Science* 49 (October 2005): 803–817.

[62]Alan I. Abramowitz, "Can McCain Overcome the Triple Whammy?" May 29, 2008, Larry J. Sabato's Crystal Ball 2008, available at www.centerforpolitics.org.

[63]Exit Poll Data.

[64]David Karol and Edward Miguel, "The Electoral Cost of War: Iraq Casualties and the 2004 U.S. Presidential Election," *Journal of Politics* 69 (August 2007): 633–648.

[65]Exit Poll Data.

[66]Brad Lockerbie, "Prospective Voting in Presidential Elections, 1956–1988," *American Politics Quarterly* 20 (July 1992): 308–325.

[67]Michael B. MacKuen, Robert S. Erikson, and James A. Stimson, "Peasants or Bankers? The American Electorate and the U.S. Economy," *American Political Science Review* 86 (September 1992): 597–611.

[68]Tracy Sulkin, *Issue Politics in Congress* (New York, NY: Cambridge University Press, 2005), pp. 168–175.

[69]Evan J. Ringquist and Carl Dasse, "Lies, Damned Lies, and Campaign Promises? Environmental Legislation in the 105th Congress," *Social Science Quarterly* 85 (June 2004): 400–419.

[70]James A. Stimson, Michael B. McKuen, and Robert S. Erikson, "Dynamic Representation," *American Political Science Review* 89 (September 1995): 543–65.

[71]Lawrence J. Grossback, David A. M. Peterson, and James A. Stimson, *Mandate Politics* (New York, NY: Cambridge University Press, 2007), pp. 179–192.

[72]Jeffrey E. Cohen, "The Polls: Presidential Referendum Effects in the 2006 Midterm Elections," *Presidential Studies Quarterly* 37 (September 2007): 545–557.

## Chapter 10

[1]Charles B. Cushman, Jr., *An Introduction to the U.S. Congress* (Armonk, NY: M.E. Sharpe, 2006), p. 5.

[2]Robert V. Remini, *The House: The History of the House of Representatives* (New York, NY: HarperCollins, 2006), p. 496.

[3]Mildred Amer and Jennifer E. Manning, "Membership in the 111th Congress: A Profile," Congressional Research Service, December 31, 2008, available at http://assets.opencrs.com.

[4]Donald R. Matthews, *U.S. Senators and Their World* (New York, NY: Vintage Books, 1960), pp. 116–117.

[5]Burdett Loomis, *The New American Politician: Ambition, Entrepreneurship, and the Changing Face of Political Life* (New York, NY: Basic Books, 1988), pp. 233–244.

[6]Brandice Canes-Wrone, David W. Brady, and John F. Cogan, "Out of Step, Out of Office: Electoral Accountability and House Members' Voting," *American Political Science Review* 96 (March 2002): 127–140.

[7]Sally Friedman, *Dilemmas of Representation: Local Politics, National Factors, and the Home Styles of Modern U.S. Congress Members* (Albany, NY: State University of New York Press, 2007), pp. 223–225.

[8]Richard F. Fenno, *Home Style* (Boston, MA: Little, Brown, 1978), p. 18.

[9]Richard G. Forgette, *Congress, Parties, and Puzzles: Politics as a Team Sport* (New York, NY: Peter Lang, 2004), p. 174.

[10]Robert A. Bernstein, "Determinants of Differences in Feelings Toward Senators Representing the Same State," *Western Political Quarterly* 45 (September 1992): 701–725.

[11]George Serra, "What's in It for Me? The Impact of Congressional Casework on Incumbent Evaluation," *American Politics Quarterly* 22 (October 1994): 403–420.

[12]Roger H. Davidson and Walter J. Oleszek, *Congress and Its Members*, 8th ed. (Washington, DC: CQ Press, 2004), p. 60.

[13]John R. Hibbing and Christopher W. Larimer, "What the American Public Wants Congress to Be," in Lawrence C. Dodd and Bruce I. Oppenheimer, eds., *Congress Reconsidered*, 8th ed. (Washington, DC: CQ Press, 2005), p. 63.

[14]"Membership of the 110th Congress: A Profile."

[15]Robert Pear, "House's Author of Drug Benefit Joins Lobbyists," *New York Times*, December 16, 2004, available at www.nytimes.com.

[16]Kristin Kanthak, "Crystal Elephants and Committee Chairs: Campaign Contributions and Leadership Races in the U.S. House of Representatives," *American Politics Research* 35 (May 2007): 389–406.

[17]Gary W. Cox and Mathew D. McCubbins, *Setting the Agenda: Responsible Party Government in the U.S. House of Representatives* (New York, NY: Cambridge University Press, 2005), pp. 1–9.

[18]Library of Congress, available at http://thomas.loc.gov.

[19]Gary W. Cox and Mathew D. McCubbins, *Legislative Leviathan: Party Government in the House*, 2nd ed. (New York, NY: Cambridge University Press, 2007), pp. 256–257.

[20]Eric S. Heberlig and Bruce A. Larson, "Party Fundraising, Descriptive Representation, and the Battle for Majority Control: Shifting Leadership Appointment Strategies in the U.S. House of Representatives, 1990–2002," *Social Science Quarterly* 88 (June 2007): 404–421.

[21]Laura W. Arnold, "The Distribution of Senate Committee Positions: Change or More of the Same?" *Legislative Studies Quarterly* 26 (May 2001): 227–248.

[22]Scott A. Frisch and Sean Q. Kelly, *Committee Assignment Politics in the U.S. House of Representatives* (Norman, OK: University of Oklahoma Press, 2006), pp. 328–330

[23]Paul R. Brewer and Christopher J. Deering, "Musical Chairs: Interest Groups, Campaign Fund-Raising, and Selection of House Committee Chairs," in Paul S. Herrnson, Ronald G. Shaiko, and Clyde Wilcox, eds., *The Interest Group Connection: Electioneering, Lobbying, and Policymaking in Washington*, 2nd ed. (Washington, DC: CQ Press, 2005), pp. 141–146.

[24]Jeff Zeleny, "Of Party Dues and Deadbeats on Capitol Hill," *New York Times*, October 1, 2006, available at www.nytimes.com.

[25]Barbara Sinclair, *Unorthodox Lawmaking: New Legislative Processes in the U.S. Congress*, 3rd ed. (Washington, DC: Congressional Quarterly Press, 2007), pp. 5–8.

[26]Congressional Record, Daily Digest, "Résumé of Congressional Activity, 110th Congress," available at www.senate.gov/reference/resources/pdf/110_1.pdf.

[27]Roger H. Davidson and Walter J. Oleszek, *Congress and Its Members*, 7th ed. (Washington, DC: CQ Press, 2000), p. 31.

[28]Public Law 107–110, January 2002.

[29]John Baughman, *Common Ground: Committee Politics in the U.S. House of Representatives* (Stanford, CA: Stanford University Press, 2006), pp. 175–179.

[30]Davidson and Oleszek, *Congress and Its Members*, 7th ed. p. 242.

[31]Sinclair, *Unorthodox Lawmaking*, p. 19.

[32]Ibid., p. 22.

[33]Ibid., p. 32.

[34]Library of Congress, available at http://thomas.loc.gov.

[35]John D. Wilerson, "'Killer' Amendments in Congress," *American Political Science Review* 93 (September 1999): 535–552.

[36]Gregory J. Wawro and Eric Schickler, *Filibuster: Obstruction and Lawmaking in the U.S. Senate* (Princeton, NJ: Princeton University Press, 2006), pp. 13–14.

[37]Christopher J. Deering, "Leadership in the Slow Lane," *PS: Policy and Politics* (Winter 1986): 37–42; Bruce I. Oppenheimer, "Changing Time Constraints on Congress: Historical Perspectives on the Use of Cloture." in Lawrence C. Dodd and Bruce I. Oppenheimer, eds., *Congress Reconsidered*, 4th ed. (Washington, DC: Congressional Quarterly Press, 1989), pp. 393–413.

[38]Sinclair, *Unorthodox Lawmaking*, p. 69.

[39]Barbara Sinclair, "The '60-Vote Senate': Strategies, Process, and Outcomes," in Bruce I. Oppenheimer, ed., *U.S. Senate Exceptionalism* (Columbus, OH: Ohio State University Press, 2002), pp. 258–259.

[40]Sinclair, *Unorthodox Lawmaking*, p. 76.

[41]Jeffrey Lazarus and Nathan W. Monroe, "The Speaker's Discretion: Conference Committee Appointments in the 97th through 106th Congresses," *Political Research Quarterly* 60 (December 2007): 593–606.

[42]Samuel B. Hoff, "Saying No: Presidential Support and Veto Use, 1889–1989," *American Politics Quarterly* 19 (July 1991): 317.

[43]Dan Morgan, "Along for the Rider," *Washington Post National Weekly Edition*, August 19–25, 2002, p. 15.

[44]"Résumé of Congressional Activity, 110th Congress."

[45]Sinclair, *Unorthodox Lawmaking*, p. 272.

[46]James H. Cox, *Reviewing Delegation: An Analysis of the Congressional Reauthorization Process* (NY: Praeger, 2004), p. 124.

## Chapter 11

[1]Paul Krugman, "The Obama Agenda," November 7, 2008, *New York Times*, available at www.nytimes.com.

[2]Michael J. Gerhardt, *The Federal Impeachment Process: A Constitutional and Historical Analysis* (Princeton, NJ: Princeton University Press, 1995), p. 105.

[3]Quoted in Michael Nelson, "Choosing the Vice President," *PS: Political Science and Politics* (Fall 1988): 859.

[4]Joseph A. Pike, "The Vice Presidency: New Opportunities, Old Constraints," in Michael Nelson, ed., *The Presidency and the Political System*, 5th ed. (Washington, DC: Congressional Quarterly Press, 1998), pp. 548–54,

[5]Jody C. Baumgartner, *The American Vice Presidency Reconsidered* (Westport, CT: Praeger, 2006), p. 133.

[6]Barton Gellman and Jo Becker, "A 'Surrogate Chief of Staff,'" *Washington Post National Weekly Edition*, July 9–15, 2007, pp. 6–12.

[7]Harold J. Krent, *Presidential Powers* (New York, NY: New York University Press, 2005), pp. 215–216.

[8]Ryan J. Barilleaux, "Venture Constitutionalism and the Enlargement of the Presidency," in Christopher S. Kelley, *Executing the Constitution: Putting the President Back Into the Constitution* (Albany, NY: State University of New York, 2206), pp. 40–42.

[9]"Learning About the Senate: Treaties," available at www.senate.gov.

[10]Ibid.

[11]*Korematsu v. United States*, 323 U.S. 214, (1944).

[12]M. Steven Fish, *Democracy Derailed in Russia: The Failure of Open Politics* (New York, NY: Cambridge University Press, 2005), pp. 30–80.

[13]Clifford J. Levy, "With Tight Grip on Ballot, Putin Is Forcing Foes Out," *New York Times*, October 14, 2007, available at www.nytimes.com.

[14]*Korematsu v. United States*, 323 U.S. 214 (1944).

[15]Public Law 93–148 (1973).

[16]James A. Baker III and Warren Christopher, "Put War Powers Back Where They Belong," *New York Times*, July 8, 2009, available at www.nytimes.com.

[17]John M. Broder, "Report Urges Overhaul of the War Powers Law," *New York Times*, July 9, 2008, available at www.nytimes.com.

[18]Louis Fisher, "The Scope of Inherent Powers," in Edwards and King, *The Polarized Presidency of George W. Bush*, p. 53.

[19]Administrative Office of the U.S. Courts, "Federal Judicial Vacancies," available at www.uscourts.gov.

[20]*Youngstown Sheet and Tube Co. v. Sawyer*, 343 U.S. 579 (1952).

[21]Donna R. Hoffman and Alison D. Howard, *Addressing the State of the Union: The Evolution and Impact of the President's Big Speech* (Boulder, CO: Lynne Rienner, 2006), p. 194.

[22]Andrew Rudalevige, "The Executive Branch and the Legislative Process," in Joel D. Aberbach and Mark A. Peterson, eds., *The Executive Branch* (New York, NY: Oxford University Press, 2005), p. 373.

[23]Rebecca A. Deen and Laura W. Arnold, "Veto Threats as a Policy Tool: When to Threaten?" *Presidential Studies Quarterly* 32 (March 2002): 30–45.

[24]Phillip J. Cooper, "George W. Bush, Edgar Allan Poe, and the Use and Abuse of Presidential Signing Statements," *Presidential Studies Quarterly* 35 (September 2005): 515–532.

[25]Robert Pear, "Legal Group Faults Bush for Ignoring Parts of Bills," *New York Times*, July 24, 2006, available at www.nytimes.com.

[26]Curtis A. Bradley and Eric A. Posner, "Presidential Signing Statements and Executive Power," *Constitutional Commentary* 23 (Winter 2006): 307–364.

[27]John P. Burke, "The Institutional Presidency," in Michael Nelson, ed., *The Presidency and the Political System*, 8th ed. (Washington, DC: CQ Press, 2006), p. 386.

[28]Matthew J. Dickinson and Matthew J. Lebo, "Reexamining the Growth of the Institutional Presidency, 1940–2000," *Journal of Politics* 69 (February 2007): 206–219.

[29]The Executive Office of the President, available at http://first.gov/Agencies/Federal/Executive/EOP.shtml.

[30]Dickinson and Lebo, "Reexamining the Growth of the Institutional Presidency, 1940–2000," pp. 206–219.

[31]Paul J. Quirk, "Presidential Competence," in Nelson, *The Presidency and the Political System*, 8th ed. pp. 156–158.

[32]Ibid., pp. 179–89.

[33]James. P. Pfiffner, "Intelligence and Decision Making Before the War with Iraq," in Edwards and King, *The Polarized Presidency of George W. Bush*, p. 235.

[34]Michael Nelson, "The Psychological Presidency," in Nelson, ed., *The Presidency and the Political System*, 8th ed., pp. 170–194.

[35]Richard E. Neustadt, *Presidential Power: The Politics of Leadership* (New York, NY: Wiley, 1980).

[36]Samuel Kernell, *Going Public: New Strategies of Presidential Leadership*, 3rd ed. (Washington, DC: Congressional Quarterly Press, 1997).

[37]Scott B. Blinder, "Going Public, Going to Baghdad: Presidential Agenda-Setting and the Electoral Connection in Congress," in Edwards and King, eds., *The Polarized Presidency of George W. Bush*, pp. 336–344.

[38]Brandice Canes-Wrone, *Who Leads Whom? Presidents, Policy, and the Public* (Chicago, IL: University of Chicago Pres, 2006), p. 185.

[39]Kelly, *Executing the Constitution*, pp. 4–5.

[40]Steven A. Shull, *Policy by Other Means: Alternative Adoption by Presidents* (College Station, TX: Texas A&M University Press, 2006), pp. 30–35.

[41]Ryan C. Black, Anthony J. Madonna, Ryan J. Owens, and Michael S. Lynch, "Adding Recess Appointments to the President's 'Tool Chest' of Unilateral Powers," *Political Research Quarterly* 60 (December 2007): 645–654.

[42]Raymond Tatalovich and Alan R. Gitelson, "Political Party Linkages to Presidential Popularity: Assessing the 'Coalition of Minorities' Thesis," *Journal of Politics* 52 (February 1990): 241.

[43]John E. Mueller, *War, Presidents, and Public Opinion* (New York, NY: Wiley, 1973), p. 208.

[44]Ibid., p. 212.

[45]Jeffrey M. Jones, "Bush's High Approval Ratings Among Most Sustained for Presidents," *Gallup Poll Monthly*, November 2001, p. 32.

[46]William D. Baker and John R. O'Neal, "Patriotism or Opinion Leadership? The Nature and Origins of the 'Rally 'round the Flag' Effect," *Journal of Conflict Resolution* 45 (October 2001): 661–687.

[47]Richard Brody, "International Crises: A Rallying Point for the President?" *Public Opinion*, December/January 1984, pp. 41–43, 60.

[48]Marc J. Hetherington and Michael Nelson, "Anatomy of a Rally Effect: George W. Bush and the War on Terrorism," *PS: Political Science and Politics* (January 2003): 37–42.

[49]Gallup Poll, "Presidential Job Approval in Depth," available at www.gallup.com.

[50]*Gallup Poll Monthly*, June 1991, p. 27.

[51]Frank Newport, "Bush Job Approval Update," Gallup News Service, July 29, 2002, available at www.gallup.com.

[52]Roger T. Larocca, *The Presidential Agenda: Sources of Executive Influence in Congress* (Columbus, OH: Ohio University Press, 2006), pp. 5–6.

[53]George C. Edwards III and B. Dan Wood, "Who Influences Whom? The President, Congress, and the Media," *American Political Science Review* 93 (June 1999): 327–344.

[54]Jeffrey E. Cohen and Ken Collier, "Public Opinion: Reconceptualizing Going Public," in Steven A. Shull, *Presidential Policymaking: An End of the Century Assessment* (Armonk, NY: M.E. Sharpe, 1999), p. 43.

[55]Matthew Eshbaugh-Soha, *The President's Speeches: Beyond "Going Public"* (Boulder, CO: Lynne Rienner, 2006), p. 157.

[56]David W. Brady and Craig Volden, *Revolving Gridlock: Politics and Policy from Jimmy Carter to George W. Bush*, 2nd ed. (Boulder, CO: Westview Press, 2006), pp. 32–33.

## Chapter 12

[1]World Health Organization, Pandemic (H1N1) 2009, available at http://www.who.int/csr/disease/swineflu/en/.

[2]Centers for Disease Control and Prevention, "H1N1 Flu," available at www.cdc.gov.

[3]Ibid.

[4]"The Influenza Pandemic of 1918," available at http://virus.stanford.edu.

[5]Food and Drug Administration, "2009 H1N1 Flu Virus (Swine Flu)," available at www.fda.gov.

[6]U.S. Census Bureau, "Federal Civilian Employment by Branch and Agency," *The 2009 Statistical Abstract*, available at www.census.gov.

[7]G. Calvin MacKenzie, "The Real Invisible Hand: Presidential Appointees in the Administration of George W. Bush," *PS: Political Science & Politics* (March 2002): 28.

[8]Paul C. Light, "Late for Their Appointments," *New York Times*, November 16, 2004, available at www.nytimes.com.

[9]Nolan McCarty and Rose Razaghian, "Advice and Consent: Senate Responses to Executive Branch Nominations, 1885–1996," *American Journal of Political Science* 43 (October 1999): 1122–1143.

[10]Shirley Anne Warshaw, "The Formation and Use of the Cabinet," in Phillip G. Henderson, ed., *The Presidency Then and Now* (Lanham, MD: Rowman & Littlefield, 2000), p. 137.

[11]Joseph A. Pika and John Anthony Maltese, *The Politics of the Presidency*, 6th ed. (Washington, DC: CQ Press, 2004), p. 230.

[12]"Federal Civilian Employment, by Branch and Agency: 1990 to 2006," *Statistical Abstract of the United States 2000*.

[13]Paul C. Light, "The New True Size of Government," Robert F. Wagner Graduate School, New York University, available at http://wagner.nyu.edu.

[14]Scott Shane and Ron Nixon, "In Washington, Contractors Take on Biggest Role Ever," *New York Times*, February 4, 2007, available at www.nytimes.com.

[15]O. Glenn Stahl, *Public Personnel Administration*, 8th ed. (New York, NY: Harper & Row, 1983), p. 42.

[16]Joel D. Aberbach and Bert A. Rockman, "Senior Executives in a Changing Political Environment," in James P. Pfiffner and Douglas A. Brook, eds., *The Future of Merit: Twenty Years After the Civil Service Reform Act* (Washington, DC: Woodrow Wilson Center Press, 2000), pp. 81–97.

[17]James R. Thompson, "Federal Labor-Management Relations Under George W. Bush: Enlightened Management or Political Retribution?" in James S. Bowman and Jonathan P. West, eds., *American Public Service: Radical Reform and the Merit System* (Boca Raton, FL: RC Press, 2007), p. 240

[18]Christopher Lee, "An Overhaul, Not a Tune-Up," *Washington Post National Weekly Edition*, June 16–22, 2003, p. 30.

[19]Ann Gerhart, "Homeland Insecurity," *Washington Post National Weekly Edition*, April 4–10, 2005, pp. 6–7.

[20]Cornelius M. Kerwin, *Rulemaking: How Government Agencies Write Law and Make Policy*, 3rd ed. (Washington, DC: CQ Press, 2003), p. 21.

[21]Terry M. Moe, "The Presidency and the Bureaucracy: The Presidential Advantage," in Michael Nelson, ed., *The Presidency and the Political System*, 6th ed. (Washington, DC: CQ Press, 2000), pp. 465–468.

[22]Alan B. Morrison, "Close Reins on the Bureaucracy: Overseeing the Administrative Agencies," in Herman Schwartz, ed., *The Burger Years* (New York, NY: Viking, 1987), pp. 191–205.

[23]Ron Duhl, "Carter Issues an Order, But Is Anybody Listening?" *National Journal*, June 14, 1979, pp. 1156–1158.

[24]Robert Pear, "Bush Directive Increases Sway on Regulation," *New York Times*, January 30, 2007, available at www.nytimes.com.

[25]Edward Wyatt, "House Panel Challenges Smithsonian," *New York Times*, May 11, 2006, available at www.nytimes.com.

[26]Michael D. Reagan and John G. Salzone, *The New Federalism*, 2nd ed. (New York: Oxford University Press, 1981), chap. 3.

[27]Schlozman and Tierney, *Organized Interests and American Democracy*, pp. 341–346.

[28]Terry M. Moe, "Control and Feedback in Economic Regulation: The Case of the NLRB," *American Political Science Review* 79 (December 1985): 1094–1116; Jeffrey E. Cohen, "The Dynamics of the 'Revolving Door' on the FCC," *American Journal of Political Science* 30 (November 1986): 689–708.

[29]Steven P. Croley, *Regulation and Public Interests: The Possibility of Good Regulatory Government* (Princeton, NJ: Princeton University Press, 2008), pp. 214–230.

[30]Colin Campbell, "The Complex Organization of the Executive Branch: The Legacies of Competing Approaches to Administration," in Joel D. Aberbach and Mark A. Peterson, eds., *The Executive Branch* (New York, NY: Oxford University Press, 2005), p. 254.

[31]Dennis D. Riley and Bryan E. Brophy-Baermann, *Bureaucracy and the Policy Process* (Lanham, MD: Rowman & Littlefield Publishers, 2006), p. 98.

[32]Jeffrey Kluger, "Space Pork," *Time*, July 24, 2000, pp. 24–26.

[33]Jeffrey M. Berry, "Subgovernments, Issue Networks, and Political Conflict," in Richard A. Harris and Sidney M. Milkis, *Remaking American Politics* (Boulder, CO: Westview Press, 1989), pp. 239–260.

[34]Jamil E. Jreisat, *Politics Without Process: Administering Development in the Arab World* (Boulder, CO: Lynne Rienner, 1997), pp. 97–101.

[35]Monte Palmer, Ali Leila, and El Sayed Yassin, *The Egyptian Bureaucracy* (Syracuse, NY: Syracuse University Press, 1988), p. 151.

[36]Jreisat, *Politics Without Process*, p. 110.

[37]Hugh Heclo, "Issue Networks and the Executive Establishment," in Anthony King, ed., *The New American Political System* (Washington, DC: American Enterprise Institute, 1978), pp. 87-124

[38]John R. Provan, "The Highway Trust Fund: Its Birth, Growth, and Survival," in Theodore W. Taylor, ed., *Federal Public Policy* (Mt. Airy, MD: Lomond Publications, 1984), pp. 221–258.

[39]Jonathan Walters, "Revenge of the Highwaymen," *Governing*, September 1997, p. 13.

[40]Hsu, "Pondering FEMA's Future," p. 13.

## Chapter 13

[1]Jeffrey Rosen, "Supreme Agreement," *Time*, July 14, 2008, pp. 36–37.

[2]Robert Barnes, "It 'Sits on a Knife's Edge,'" *Washington Post National Weekly Edition*, July 7–13, 2008, p. 33.

[3]Richard L. Pacelle, Jr., *The Role of the Supreme Court in American Politics: The Least Dangerous Branch* (Boulder, CO: Westview, 2002), p. 35.

[4]Harold W. Stanley and Richard G. Niemi, *Vital Statistics on American Politics 2007–2008* (Washington, DC: Congressional Quarterly Press, 2008), p. 301.

[5]Kermit Roosevelt III, *The Myth of Judicial Activism: Making Sense of Supreme Court Decisions* (New Haven, CT: Yale University Press, 2006), p. 3.

[6]Thomas M. Keck, *The Most Activist Supreme Court in History: The Road to Modern Judicial Conservatism* (Chicago, IL: University of Chicago Press, 2004), pp 286–289.

[7]Robert A. Carp, Ronald Stidham, and Kenneth L. Manning, *Judicial Process in America*, pp. 43–44.

[8]Ibid., p. 52.

[9]Ibid., p. 53.

[10]Karl Derouen, Jr., Jeffrey S. Peake, and Kenneth Ward, "Presidential Mandates and the Dynamics of Senate Advice and Consent, 1885–1996," *American Politics Research* 33 (January 2005): 106–131.

[11]Cass R. Sunstein, David Schkade, Lisa M. Ellman, and Andres Sawicki, *Are Judges Political? An Empirical Analysis of the Federal Judiciary* (Washington, DC: Brookings Institution, 2006), pp. 147–149.

[12]Ibid., p. 141.

[13]Joan Biskupic, "Barely a Dent on the Bench," *Washington Post National Weekly Edition*, October 24–30, 1994, p. 31.

[14]Ashlyn Kuersten and Donald Songer, "Presidential Success through Appointments to the United States Courts of Appeal," *American Politics Research* 31 (March 2003): 119.

[15]David C. Nixon and David L. Gross, "Confirmation Delay for Vacancies on the Circuit Courts of Appeal," *American Politics Research* 29 (May 2001): 246–274.

16John N. Paden, Muslim Civic Cultures and Conflict Resolution: The Challenge of Democratic Federalism in Nigeria (Washington, DC: Brookings Institution Press, 2005), pp. 139–174.

17Sarah A. Binder and Forrest Maltzman, "Congress and the Politics of Judicial Appointments," in Lawrence C. Dodd and Bruce I. Oppenheimer, Congress Reconsidered, 8th ed. (Washington, DC: CQ Press, 2205), pp. 302–305.

18R. Jeffrey Smith, "Back-Bench Politics," Washington Post National Weekly Edition, December 15-21, 2008, p. 7.

19Helen Dewar and Mike Allen, "GOP May Target Use of Filibuster," Washington Post, December 13, 2004, p. A01.

20Charles Gardner Geyh, When Courts and Congress Collide: The Struggle for Control of America's Judicial System (Ann Arbor, MI: University of Michigan Press, 2006), p. 19.

21Quoted in Henry J. Abraham, Justices and Presidents: A Political History of Appointments to the Supreme Court (New York, NY: Oxford University Press, 1974), p. 246.

22Timothy R. Johnson and Jason M. Roberts, "Presidential Capital and the Supreme Court Confirmation Process," Journal of Politics 66 (August 2004): 663–683.

23Updated data, based on Lawrence Baum, The Supreme Court (Washington, DC: CQ Press, 1981), p. 25.

24Charles M. Cameron, Albert D. Cover, and Jeffrey A. Segal, "Senate Voting on Supreme Court Nominees: A Neoinstitutional Model," American Political Science Review 84 (June 1990): 525–34.

25Keith E. Whittington, "Presidents, Senates, and Failed Supreme Court Nominations," 2006 The Supreme Court Review (Chicago, IL: University of Chicago Press, 2006), pp. 412–422.

26John Massaro, Supremely Political: The Role of Ideology and Presidential Management in Unsuccessful Supreme Court Nominations (Albany, NY: State University of New York Press, 1990), p. 136.

27Mark Silverstein, "Bill Clinton's Excellent Adventure: Political Development and the Modern Confirmation Process," in Howard Gillman and Cornell Clayton, eds., The Supreme Court in American Politics: New Institutional Interpretation (Lawrence, KS: University of Kansas Press, 1999), p. 145.

28Linda Greenhouse, "New Focus on the Effects of Life Tenure," New York Times, September 10, 2007, available at www.nytimes.com.

29U.S. Supreme Court, "2007 Year-End Report on the Federal Judiciary," available at www.supremecourtus.gov.

30Ibid.

31Baker v. Carr, 369 U.S. 186 (1962).

32Lee Epstein and Jack Knight, "Mapping Out the Strategic Terrain: The Informational Role of Amici Curiae," in Cornell W. Clayton and Howard Gillman, Supreme Court Decision-Making, New Institutional Approaches (Chicago, IL: University of Chicago Press, 1999), p. 229.

33Timothy R. Johnson, "Information, Oral Arguments, and Supreme Court Decision Making," American Politics Research 29 (July 2001): 331–351.

34David O. Stewart, "A Chorus of Voices," ABA Journal (April 1991): 50.

35Furman v. Georgia, 408 U.S. 238 (1972).

36Harrell R. Rodgers, Jr., and Charles S. Bullock III, Law and Social Change (New York, NY: McGraw-Hill, 1977), p. 75.

37H. Frank Way, Jr., "Survey Research on Judicial Decisions: The Prayer and Bible Reading Cases," Western Political Quarterly 21 (June 1968): 189–205.

38Charles A. Johnson and Bradley C. Canon, Judicial Policies: Implementation and Impact (Washington, DC: Congressional Quarterly Press, 1984), ch. 1.

39Gerald N. Rosenberg, The Hollow Hope: Can Courts Bring About Social Change? (Chicago, IL: University of Chicago Press, 1991), pp. 336–338.

40Statistical Abstract of the United States, 1991, 111th ed. (Washington, DC: U.S. Department of Commerce, 1991), p. 71.

41Naseem Sowti, "Fewer Abortions," Washington Post National Weekly Edition, July 25–31, 2006, p. 29.

42Tennessee Valley Authority v. Hill, 437 U.S. 153 (1978).

43Oregon v. Mitchell, 400 U.S. 112 (1970).

44Carp, Stidham, and Manning, Judicial Process in America, p. 371.

45Robert Dahl, "Decision-Making in a Democracy: The Supreme Court as a National Policy-Maker," Journal of Public Law 6 (Fall 1957): 279–295.

46Johnson and Canon, Judicial Policies, pp. 231–232.

47Rosen, The Most Democratic Branch, pp. 7–8.

48Clinton v. City of New York, 524 U.S. 417 (1998).

## Chapter 14

1U.S. Census Bureau, "Income, Poverty, and Health Insurance Coverage in the United States: 2007," available at www.census.gov.

2Congressional Budget Office, "Key Issues in Analyzing Major Health Insurance Proposals," December 2008, available at www.cbo.gov.

3"A New Era of Responsibility: The President's Budget, FY2010," available at www.whitehouse.gov.

4Chris J. Dolan, John Frendreis, and Raymond Tatalovich, The Presidency and Economic Policy (Lanham, MD: Rowman & Littlefield, 2008), p. 3.

5"A New Era of Responsibility: The President's Budget, FY2010," available at www.whitehouse.gov.

6U.S. Census Bureau, "Gross Public Debt, Expenditures, and Receipts by Country: 1990–2006," The 2008 Statistical Abstract, available at www.census.gov.

7Anthony J. Cataldo II and Arline A. Savage, U.S. Individual Federal Income Taxation: Historical, Contemporary, and Prospective Policy Issues (Oxford, UK: Elsevier Science, 2001), pp. 39–40.

8Wojciech Bienkowski, Josef C. Brada, and Mariusz-Jan Radto, Reaganomics Goes Global: What Can the EU, Russia, and Other Transition Countries Learn from the USA? (New York, NY: Palgrave MacMillan, 2006), p. 69.

9Lori Montgomery, "The Bush Tax Cuts, Revisited," Washington Post National Weekly Edition, April 7–13, 2008, p. 23.

10Larry Rohter and Michael Cooper, "3 Candidates with 3 Financial Plans, but One Deficit," New York Times, April 27, 2008, available at www.nytimes.com.

11Congressional Budget Office, available at www.cbo.gov.

12David Leonhardt, "For U.S., a Sea of Perilous Red Ink, Years in the Making," New York Times, June 10, 2009, available at www.nytimes.com.

13Michael E. Bradley, "The Inexorable Rise of the National Debt," in Phillip John Davies, ed., An American Quarter Century: U.S. Politics from Vietnam to Clinton (Manchester, UK: Manchester University Press, 1995), pp. 59–61.

14"A New Era of Responsibility: The President's Budget, FY2010," available at www.whitehouse.gov.

15Congressional Budget Office, "CBO's March 2008 Baseline: Medicare," available at www.cbo.gov.

16Robert Pear, "Medicare Costs to Increase for Wealthier Beneficiaries," New York Times, September 11, 2006, available at www.nytimes.com.

17Centers for Medicare and Medicaid Services, available at www.cms.hhs.gov.

18Health Canada, available at www.hc-sc.gc.ca.

19Gerard W. Boychuk, National Health Insurance in the United States and Canada (Washington, DC: Georgetown University Press, 2008), pp. 3–21.

20Congressional Budget Office, "Budget Options," available at www.cbo.gov.

21Edmund L. Andrews, "Sharp Increase in Tax Revenue Will Pare U.S. Deficit," New York Times, July 13, 2005, available at www.nytimes.com.

22Social Security and Medicare Boards of Trustees 2008 Annual Reports, available at www.ssa.gov.

23Congressional Budget Office, "Fact Sheet for CBO's March 2009 Baseline: Medicaid," available at www.cbo.gov.

24Donald B. Marron, "Medicaid Spending Growth and Options for Controlling Costs," Testimony before the Senate Select Committee on Aging, available at www.cbo.gov.

25Social Security Administration, available at www.ssa.gov.

26Jesse J. Holland, "Raise Retirement Age to Save Social Security?" Business Week, August 1, 2008, available at www.businessweek.com.

27Social Security and Medicare Boards of Trustees 2008 Annual Reports.

28Social Security Administration, Trust Fund Data, available at www.ssa.gov.

29Social Security and Medicare Boards of Trustees 2008 Annual Reports.

30June O'Neill, "The Trust Fund, the Surplus, and the Real Social Security Problem," in Michael D. Tanner, ed., Social Security and its Discontents: Perspectives on Choice (Washington, DC: CATO Institute, 2004), pp. 37–38.

31William A. Kelso, Poverty and the Underclass: Challenging Perceptions of the Poor in America (New York, NY: New York University Press, 1994), p. 4.

32Robert Pear, "Welfare Spending Shows Huge Shift from Checks to Services," New York Times, October 13, 2003, available at www.nytimes.com.

33U.S. Department of Health and Human Services, Office of Family Assistance, Temporary Assistance for Needy Families, Sixth Annual Report to Congress, November 2004, available at www.acf.hhs.gov.

34Congressional Budget Office, "The Budget and Economic Outlook: An Update," available at www.cbo.gov.

35Jonathan Walters, "Is Welfare Working?" Governing, February 2008, pp. 28–33.

36Bureau of the Public Debt, available at www.treasurydirect.gov.

37Roger H. Davidson and Walter J. Oleszek, Congress and Its Members, 7th ed. (Washington, DC: CQ Press, 2000), p. 372.

38Office of Management and Budget, Budget of the United States Government, Fiscal Year 2009.

39Ibid.

[40]Alan I. Abramowitz, "Can McCain Overcome the Triple Whammy?" May 29, 2008, Larry J. Sabato's Crystal Ball 2008, available at www.centerforpolitics.org.

[41]Carl Hulse, "Congress is Still Pursuing Earmarks," *New York Times*, December 20, 2007, available at www.nytimes.com.

[42]Jonathan Weisman, "Bush Puts the Kibosh on Lawmakers' Pet Projects—Later," *Washington Post National Weekly Edition*, February 4–10, 2008, p. 7.

[43]Sheri Steisel and Jack Tweedle, "TANF Rules Tough on States," *State Legislatures*, March 2006, p. 23.

## Chapter 15

[1]Quoted in Mark Silva, "Cheney Defends Waterboarding, Says Guantanamo Prison Essential," May 21, 2009, *Los Angeles Times*, available at www.latimes.com.

[2]Quoted in "Obama Stands by End to Torture," April 29, 2009, available at www.upi.com.

[3]John McCain, "Torture's Terrible Toll," November 25, 2005, *Newsweek*, available at www.newsweek.com.

[4]*Pruneyard Shopping Center v. Robins*, 447 U.S. 74 (1980).

[5]Richard H. Fallon, Jr., *The Dynamic Constitution: An Introduction to American Constitutional Law* (New York, NY: Cambridge University Press, 2004), pp. 60–61.

[6]Patrick M. Garry, *Wrestling with God: The Court's Tortuous Treatment of Religion* (Washington, DC: Catholic University of America Press, 2006), pp. 70–72.

[7]*Everson v. Board of Ewing Township*, 330 U.S. 1 (1947).

[8]*Zelman v. Simmons-Harris*, 536 U.S. 639 (2002).

[9]*Engel v. Vitale*, 370 U.S. 421 (1962).

[10]*Santa Fe School District v. Doe*, 530 U.S. 290 (2000).

[11]*Cantwell v. Connecticut*, 310 U.S. 296 (1940) and *Martin v. Struthers*, 319 U.S. 141 (1943).

[12]*Employment Division, Oregon Department of Human Resources v. Smith*, 493 U.S. 378 (1990).

[13]*Brandenburg v. Ohio*, 395 U.S. 444 (1969).

[14]*Cohen v. California*, 403 U.S. 15 (1971).

[15]"Hate is Not Speech: A Constitutional Defense of Penalty Enhancement for Hate Crimes," *Harvard Law Review* 106 (April 1993): 1314–31.

[16]*Wisconsin v. Mitchell*, 508 U.S. 47 (1993).

[17]*Texas v. Johnson*, 491 U.S. 397 (1989).

[18]*United States v. Eichman*, 396 U.S. 310 (1990).

[19]*Griswold v. Connecticut*, 381 U.S. 479 (1965).

[20]*Roe v. Wade*, 410 U.S. 113 (1973).

[21]*Webster v. Reproductive Health Services*, 492 U.S. 490 (1989).

[22]*Planned Parenthood of Southeastern Pennsylvania v. Casey*, 505 U.S. 833 (1992).

[23]*Lawrence v. Texas*, 539 US 558 (2003).

[24]Alan Hunter and John Sexton, *Contemporary China* (London: MacMillan Press, 1999), pp. 59–60.

[25]Beth Nonte Russell, "The Mystery of the Chinese Baby Shortage," *New York Times*, January 23, 2007, available at www.nytimes.com.

[26]Cecilia Nathansen Milwertz, *Accepting Population Control: Urban Chinese Women and the One-Child Family Policy* (Richmond Surrey, UK: Curzon Press, 1997), p. 11.

[27]*Illinois v. Wardlow*, 528 U.S. 119 (2000).

[28]*United States v. Ross*, 456 U.S. 798 (1982).

[29]*Mapp v. Ohio*, 367 U.S. 643 (1961).

[30]Adam Liptak, "U.S. Alone in Rejecting All Evidence if Police Err," *New York Times*, July 19, 2008, available at www.nytimes.com.

[31]*Massachusetts v. Shepherd*, 468 U.S. 981 (1984) and *United States v. Leon*, 468 U.S. 897 (1984).

[32]*Arizona v. Fulminante*, 499 U.S. 270 (1991).

[33]*Herring v. United States*, 7-513 (2009).

[34]*Miranda v. Arizona*, 384 U.S. 436 (1966).

[35]Gary L. Stuart, *Miranda: The Story of America's Right to Remain Silent* (Tucson, AR: University of Arizona Press, 2004), p.100.

[36]*Harris v. New York*, 401 U.S. 222 (1971).

[37]*New York v. Quarles*, 467 U.S. 649 (1984).

[38]*Moran v. Burdine*, 475 U.S. 412 (1986).

[39]*Kansas v. Hendricks*, 521 U.S. 346 (1997).

[40]Quoted in *Time*, July 7, 1997, p. 29.

[41]*Globe Newspaper Co. v. Superior Court*, 457 U.S. 596 (1982).

[42]*Chancler v. Florida*, 449 U.S. 560 (1981).

[43]*Williams v. Florida*, 399 U.S. 78 (1970).

[44]*Snyder v. Louisiana*, No. 06-10119 (2008).

[45]*Gideon v. Wainwright*, 372 U.S. 335 (1963).

[46]*Tollett v. Henderson*, 411 U.S. 258 (1973).

[47]*Solem v. Helm*, 463 U.S. 277 (1983).

[48]*Kennedy v. Louisiana*, No. 07-343 (2008).

[49]*Furman v. Georgia*, 408 U.S. 238 (1972).

[50]*Gregg v. Georgia*, 428 U.S. 153 (1976).

[51]Bureau of Justice Statistics, "Capital Punishment Statistics," available at www.ojp.usdoj.gov.

[52]James S. Leibman, *A Broken System: Error Rates in Capital Cases, 1973–1995*, available at www.thejusticeproject.org.

[53]Ibid.

[54]Bureau of Justice Statistics, "Capital Punishment 2005," available at www.ojp.usdoj.gov.

[55]"Supreme Court Bars Executing Mentally Retarded," June 20, 2002, available at cnn.com.

[56]*Atkins v. Virginia*, 536 U.S. 304 (2002).

[57]Otis H. Stephens, Jr., "Presidential Power, Judicial Deference, and the Status of Detainees in an Age of Terrorism," in David B. Cohen and John W. Wells, eds., *American National Security and Civil Liberties in an Era of Terrorism* (NY: Palgrave MacMillan, 2004), p. 82.

[58]*Korematsu v. United States*, 323 U.S. 214 (1944).

[59]*Hamdi v. Rumsfeld*, 542 U.S. 507 (2004).

[60]*Hamdan v. Rumsfeld*, 548 U.S. 557 (2006).

[61]*Boumediene v. Bush*, 553 U.S. ___ (2008).

[62]Henry J. Abraham and Barbara A. Perry, *Freedom and the Court*, 7th. ed. (New York, NY: Oxford University Press, 1998), p. 236.

[63]Ranata Lawson Mack and Michael J. Kelly, *Equal Justice in the Balance: America's Legal Responses to the Emerging Terrorist Threat* (Ann Arbor, MI: University of Michigan Press, 2004), p. 238.

[64]Otis H. Stephens, Jr., *The Supreme Court and Confessions of Guilt* (Knoxville, TN: University of Tennessee Press, 1973).

[65]Donald L. Horowitz, *The Courts and Social Policy* (Washington, DC: Brookings Institution, 1977), p. 223.

## Chapter 16

[1]*Grutter v. Bollinger*, 539 U.S. 306 (2003).

[2]Elder Witt, *The Supreme Court and Individual Rights*, 2nd ed. (Washington, DC: Congressional Quarterly Press, 1988), pp. 223–26.

[3]*Plessy v. Ferguson*, 163 U.S. 537 (1896).

[4]*Missouri ex rel Gaines v. Canada*, 305 U.S. 337 (1938).

[5]*Sweatt v. Painter*, 399 U.S. 629 (1950).

[6]*McLaurin v. Oklahoma State Regents*, 339 U.S. 637 (1950).

[7]*Brown v. Board of Education of Topeka*, 347 U.S. 483 (1954).

[8]*Brown v. Board of Education of Topeka*, 349 U.S. 294 (1955).

[9]Gerald Rosenberg, "Substituting Symbol for Substance: What Did *Brown* Really Accomplish?" *P.S. Political Science & Politics* (April 2004): 205.

[10]*Alexander v. Holmes County Board of Education*, 396 U.S. 19 (1969).

[11]Rosenberg, "Substituting Symbol for Substance," p. 206.

[12]*Swann v. Charlotte-Mecklenburg Board of Education*, 402 U.S. 1 (1971).

[13]*Keyes v. School District #1, Denver, Colorado*, 413 U.S. 189 (1973).

[14]Greg Winter, "Schools Resegregate, Study Finds," *New York Times*, January 21, 2003, available at www.nytimes. com.

[15]"School Segregation on the Rise," *Harvard Gazette News*, July 19, 2001, available at www.new.harvard.edu/gazette.

[16]*Millikin v. Bradley*, 418 U.S. 717 (1974).

[17]*Missouri v. Jenkins*, 515 U.S. 70 (1995).

[18]*Parents Involved in Community Schools v. Seattle School District No. 1*, 551 U.S. ___ (2007).

[19]*In re Griffiths*, 413 U.S. 717 (1973); *Examining Board of Engineers, Architects and Surveyors v. de Otero*, 426 U.S. 572 (1976); *Bernal v. Fainter*, 467 U.S. 216 (1984).

[20]Philippa Smith, "The Virginia Military Institute Case," in Sibyl A. Schwarzenbach and Patricia Smith, eds., *Women and the Constitution: History, Interpretation, and Practice* (New York, NY: Columbia University Press, 2003), p. 343.

[21]*United States v. Virginia*, 518 U.S. 515 (1996).

[22]*Rostker v. Goldberg*, 453 U.S. 57 (1981).

[23]*Romer v. Evans*, 517 U.S. 620 (1996).

[24]*Smith v. Allwright*, 321 U.S. 649 (1944).

[25]*Guinn v. United States*, 238 U.S. 347 (1915).

[26]*Louisiana v. United States*, 380 U.S. 145 (1965).

[27]*Harper v. State Board of Elections*, 383 U.S. 663 (1966).

[28]Quoted in Alfred H. Kelley and Winfred A. Harbison, *The American Constitution: Its Origins and Development* (New York, NY: Norton, 1970), p. 460.

[29]Quoted in Witt, *The Supreme Court and Individual Rights*, p. 247.

[30]*Civil Rights Cases*, 109 U.S. 3 (1883).

[31]*Shelley v. Kraemer*, 334 U.S. 1 (1948).

[32]*Heart of Atlanta Motel v. United States*, 379 U.S. 241; and *Katzenbach v. McClung*, 379 U.S. 294 (1964).

[33]Augustus B. Cochran III, *Sexual Harassment and the Law* (Lawrence, KS: University of Kansas Press, 2004), p. 114.

[34]Stephen Schwartz, "Shari'a in Saudi Arabia, Today and Tomorrow," in Paul Marshall, ed., *Radical Islam's Rules: The Worldwide Spread of Extreme Shari'a Law* (Lanham, MD: Rowman & Littlefield, 2005), pp. 33–34.

[35]Mai Yamani, "Muslim Women and Human Rights in Saudi Arabia," in Eugene Cotran and Mai Yamani, eds., *The Rule of Law in the Middle East and the Islamic World: Human Rights and the Judicial Process* (London, UK: I. B. Tauris, 2000), pp. 137–145.

[36]Damien McElroy, "Saudi Arabia to Lift Ban on Women Drivers," Daily Telegraph, January 21, 2008, available at www.telegraph.co.uk.

[37]*Oncale v. Sundowner Offshore Services, Inc.*, 523 U.S. 75 (1998).

[38]*City of Richmond v. J. A. Croson Co.*, 488 U.S. 469 (1989).

[39]*Regents of the University of California v. Bakke*, 438 U.S. 265 (1978).

[40]*Grutter v. Bollinger*, 539 U.S. 306 (2003).

[41]*Gratz v. Bollinger*, 539 U.S. 244 (2003).

[42]Gallup, "Race Relations," available at www.gallup.com.

[43]The Pew Center for the People & the Press, "The Black and White of Public Opinion," October 2005, available at www.people-press.org.

[44]Peter Schmidt, "Michigan Overwhelmingly Adopts Ban on Affirmative-Action Preferences," *Chronicle of Higher Education*, November 17, 2006, p. A23.

[45]*Grove City College v. Bell*, 465 U.S. 555 (1984).

[46]*Time*, June 23, 1997, p. 34.

## Chapter 17

[1]Robert Cooper, *The Postmodern State and the World Order* (London: Demos, 2000), p. 22.

[2]Courtney B. Smith, *Politics and Process at the United Nations: The Global Dance* (Boulder, CO: Lynne Rienner, 2006), p. 28.

[3]Jim Hoagland, "A Transformative NATO," *Washington Post National Weekly Edition*, December 12–18, 2005, p. 5.

[4]Elizabeth Becker, "Trade Talks Fail to Agree on Drugs for Poor Nations," *New York Times*, December 21, 2002, available at www.nytimes.com.

[5]Michael E. Brown, ed., *Grave New World: Security Challenges in the 21st Century* (Washington, DC: Georgetown University Press, 2003), p. 307.

[6]Jonathan P. Doh and Hildy Teegan, *Globalization and NGOs: Transforming Business, Government, and Society* (Westport, CT: Praeger, 2003), pp. 3–9, 206–219.

[7]Terry L. Deibel, *Foreign Affairs Strategy: Logic for American Statecraft* (New York, NY: Cambridge University Press, 2007), p. 271.

[8]"United States Foreign Trade Highlights," International Trade Administration, U.S. Department of Commerce, available at www.ita.doc.gov.

[9]Marvin Zonis, "The 'Democracy Doctrine' of President George W. Bush," in Stanley A. Renshon and Peter Suedfeld, eds., *Understanding the Bush Doctrine: Psychology and Strategy in an Age of Terrorism* (New York, NY: Routledge, 2007), p. 232.

[10]Congressional Research Service, *Conventional Arms Transfers to Developing Nations, 1996–2003*, August 26, 2004, available at www.fas.org/man/crs.

[11]Celia W. Dugger, "U.S. Challenged to Increase Aid to Africa," *New York Times*, June 5, 2005, available at www.nytimes.com.

[12]Budget of the United States Government, Fiscal Year 2003, available at www.omb.gov.

[13]Robert J. Lieber, *Eagle Rules? Foreign Policy and American Primacy in the Twenty-First Century* (Upper Saddle River, NJ: Pearson, 2002), pp. 5–6.

[14]Joseph S. Nye, Jr., *The Paradox of American Power: Why the World's Only Superpower Can't Go it Alone* (New York, NY: Oxford University Press, 2002), p. 156.

[15]Quoted in G. John Ikenberry, "Is American Multilateralism in Decline?" *Perspectives on Politics* 1 (September 2003): 534.

[16]Robert S. Litwak, *Regime Change: U.S. Strategy Through the Prism of 9/11* (Baltimore, MD: Johns Hopkins University Press, 2007), pp. 2–10.

[17]John Herskovitz, "U.S. Ready for Talks and Sanctions with North Korea," *Washington Post*, July 18, 2009, available at www.washingtonpost.com.

[18]Isaiah Wilson III, "What Weapons Do They Have and What Can They Do?" *PS: Political Science & Politics* (July 2007): 473.

[19]Willie Curtis, "Illusionary Promises and Strategic Reality: Rethinking the Implications of Strategic Deterrence in a Post 9/11 World," in Renshon and Suedfeld, eds., *Understanding the Bush Doctrine*, pp. 133–143.

[20]Ibid.

[21]Steven Mufson, "Rogue States: A Real Threat?" *Washington Post National Weekly Edition*, June 12, 2000, p. 15.

[22]John Dumbrell, "The Bush Doctrine," in George C. Edwards III and Philip John Davies, *New Challenges for the American Presidency* (New York: Longman, 2004), pp. 232–234.

[23]Thomas E. Ricks, "A New Way of War," *Washington Post National Weekly Edition*, December 10–16, 2001, p. 6.

[24]David S. Cloud, "Navy to Expand Fleet with New Enemies in Mind," *New York Times*, December 5, 2005, available at www.nytimes.com.

[25]Ann Scott Tyson, "A Road Map for Resources," *Washington Post National Weekly Edition*, February 13–19, 2006, p. 29.

[26]David Albright, "Securing Pakistan's Nuclear Weapons Complex," Institute for Science and International Security," October 2001, available at www.isisonline.org/publications/terrorism/stanleypaper.html.

[27]Farzana Shaikh, "Pakistan's Nuclear Bomb: Beyond the Non-Proliferation Regime," *International Affairs* 78 (January 2002): 29–48.

[28]Richard Morin, "A Gap in Worldviews," *Washington Post National Weekly Edition*, April 19, 1999, p. 34.

[29]Cecil V. Crabb, Jr., Glenn J. Antizzo, and Leila E. Serieddine, *Congress and the Foreign Policy Process* (Baton Rouge, LA: Louisiana State University Press, 2000), p. 189.

[30]James Meernik, "Presidential Support in Congress: Conflict and Consensus on Foreign and Defense Policy," *Journal of Politics* 55 (August 1993): 569–87.

[31]Litwak, *Regime Change*, p. 48.

[32]Richard J. Stoll, "The Sound of the Guns," *American Politics Quarterly* 15 (April 1987): 223–37.

[33]Jeffrey M. Jones, "Bush's High Approval Ratings Among Most Sustained for Presidents," *Gallup Poll Monthly*, November 2001, p. 32.

[34]Evelyn Nieves and Ann Scott Tyson, "'Don't Tell' Because We Need You Now," *Washington Post National Weekly Edition*, February 21–27, 2005, p. 29.

# >credits

## TEXT CREDITS

"2010 Census Count Called Vital for Texas," The Associated Press, June 9, 2009. Reprinted with permission.

Bowman, Karlyn. From "Gay Marriage And Public Opinion," by Karlyn Bowman, Forbes, April 27, 2009. Reprinted by permission of Forbes.com © 2009 Forbes LLC.

Cassidy, Mckenzie. From "President Obama's Speech in Egypt," by Mckenzie Cassidy, June 4, 2009. Published with permission.

Chen Delos, Robin. From "Beyond Obama-mania: Will Young People Stay Involved Post-election?" by Robin Chen Delos, *Diverse Online*, December 1, 2008. Reprinted with permission from Diverse Issues in Higher Education, www.diverseeducation.com.

Doyle, Pat. From "More Guns, Safer Campus?" by Pat Doyle, Minneapolis-St. Paul Star Tribune, April 16, 2008. Reprinted with permission.

Elis, Niv. From "FDA Regulates Tobacco, and Phillip Morris Cheers," by Niv Elis, Forbes, June 11, 2009. Reprinted by permission of Forbes.com © 2009 Forbes LLC.

Gallup, George H. "How Many Americans Know U.S. History? Part I" by George H. Gallup, Jr. October 21, 2003, www.gallup.com. Courtesy of Gallup News Service.

Isaacs, Julia B. From "Economic Mobility of Men and Women" by Julia B. Isaacs, www.brookings.edu. Reprinted by permission of The Brookings Institution.

Maloney, Jennifer. From "College presidents want drinking age lowered to 18" by Jennifer Maloney, *Newsday*, August 19, 2008. Copyright © 2008 Newsday. Used by permission.

The National Entertainment State. From "10th Anniversary The National Entertainment State." Reprinted with permission from the July 3, 2006 issue of *The Nation*. For subscription information, call 1-800-333-8536. Portions of each week's *Nation* magazine can be accessed at http://www.thenation.com.

Ramstack, Tom. "Justice Kennedy casts decisive vote" by Tom Ramstack, *The Washington Times*, June 27, 2008. Copyright © 2008 The Washington Times LLC. This reprint does not constitute or imply an endorsement or sponsorship of any product, service, company or organization. Reprinted by permission.

Reddington, Madeline. From "Obama Plan Would Alter Financial Aid," by Madeline Reddington, Daily Trojan, Thursday, March 5, 2009.

Saad, Lydia. From "Religion is Very Important to Majority of Americans" by Lydia Saad, December 5, 2003, www.gallup.com. Courtesy of Gallup News Service.

*Trends in Higher Education Series: Trends in Student Aid, 2007*, www.collegeboard.com. Used by permission of The College Board.

## PHOTO CREDITS

### Front Matter

iv (l): Cedric Joubert/AP Photo; (c):Afton Almaraz/AP Photos; (r): vario images GmbH & Co.KG/Alamy; v (l): Mark Peterson/CORBIS; (c): Tammie Arroyo/AP Photo; (r): ROBERT GALBRAITH/Reuters/Corbis; vi (l): The Everett Collection; (c): Amy Sancetta/AP Photo; (r): Reuters/CORBIS; vii (l): David Maung/AP Photo; (c): Bettmann/CORBIS; (r): Tim Sloan/AFP/Getty Images; viii (l): LUC GNAGO/Reuters/Landov; (c): Lara Porzak Photography via Getty Images; (r): Jim West/The Image Works; ix (l): Susan Steinkamp/CORBIS; (c): Emilio Morenatti/AP Photo; (r): NatalieHelbert/istockphoto.com.

### Introduction

2–3 UPI Photo/Michael Kleinfield/Newscom; 3 (tr): James Pinsky/U.S. Navy/ZUMA/CORBIS; 4 (t): UPI Photo/Michael Kleinfield/Newscom; (b): James Pinsky/U.S. Navy/ZUMA/CORBIS; (inset): Jerry Grayson/Helifilms Australia PTY Ltd/Getty Images; 5 Sascha Burkard/Used under license from Shutterstock; 7 Gerald Herbert/AP Photo; 8 Bill Fritsch/Brand X/Corbis; 9 Alfred Eisenstaedt/Time & Life Pictures/Getty Images.

### Chapter 1

14 The Granger Collection; 15 Bettmann/CORBIS; 15 (tr): Solus-Veer/Corbis; 16 The Granger Collection (T), (b), Judy Ben Joud/Used under license from Shutterstock; 17 Molly Riley/Reuters/Landov; 18 Greg Baker/AP Photo; 19 Solus-Veer/Corbis; 20 Justin Sullivan/Getty Images; 21 Cedric Joubert/AP Photo; 22 *Reagan, Nixon, Johnson*: Bettmann/CORBIS; *George H.W. Bush*: Bachrach/Getty Images; *George W. Bush*: Brooks Kraft/Corbis; *Clinton*: Alex Wong/Getty Images; *Carter*: Wally McNamee/CORBIS; 23 (t): VisionsofAmerica/Joe Sohm/Getty Images; (b): Michael Silver Editorial/Alamy; 24 (t): Koji Sasahara/AP Photo; (b): magicoven/Used under license from Shutterstock. 25 (t): Sherwin Crasto/Reuters/CORBIS; (b): Tim Boyle/Getty Images; 26 Damian Dovarganes/AP Photo; 27 (l): EMMANUEL DUNAND/AFP/Getty Images; (r): Chip Somodevilla/Getty Images; 28 HANS DERYK/Reuters/Landov; 29 (t): Leah Nash/The New York Times/Redux Pictures; (b): Rolf Haid/dpa/Landov; 31 Amy Sancetta/AP Photo.

### Chapter 2

34–35 Karen Kasmauski/CORBIS; 35 (tr): Craig Brewer/Photodisc/Getty Images; 36 (t): Karen Kasmauski/CORBIS; (b): Colonial Williamsburg Foundation; 37 (t): Mike Bentley/istockphoto.com; (b): David Frazier/PhotoEdit; 38 Courtesy, PETA; 39 The Everett Collection; 41 Laurie Asseo/Bloomberg News/Landov; 42 Craig Brewer/Photodisc/Getty Images; 43 (l): Hulton Archive/Getty Images; (r): AP Photo; 44 Stock Montage/Getty Images; 45 Bob Daemmrich/The Image Works; 47 (bkgd): Toby Melville/WPA rota/PA Wire URN:5316105/AP Photos; (inset): REUTERS/Suzanne Plunkett/Landov; 48 Afton Almaraz/AP Photos; 49 Joe Fudge/Daily Press/AP Photo; 50 Bettmann/CORBIS; 51 culliganphoto/Alamy; 52 Ken James/UPI Photo/Landov; 53 Bettmann/CORBIS; 54 AP Photos; 55 Ron Edmonds/AP Photos.

### Chapter 3

58–59 STEPHEN McGEE/The New York Times/Redux Pictures *This photo has been altered slightly from the original. Writing on the blackboard has been removed.*; 59 (tr): vario images GmbH & Co.KG/Alamy; 60 STEPHEN McGEE/The New York Times/Redux Pictures (detail); 61 vario images GmbH & Co.KG/Alamy; 62 Greg Wahl-Stephens/AP Photo; 64 Tom Grill/CORBIS; 65 Eric Draper/AP Photo; 66 (t): A. Radzkou/Used under license from Shutterstock; (bl):Photos.com; (br): Yellowj/Used under license from Shutterstock; 68 quaxelc/Used under license from Shutterstock; 69 Kuttig-People/Alamy; 70 Pakhnyushcha/Used under license from Shutterstock; 72 Kapu/Used under license from Shutterstock.

### Chapter 4

76–77 Damian Dovarganes/AP Photo; 77 (tr): Paul Tomas; 78 (tl): Damian Dovarganes/AP Photo; (b): Mark Peterson/CORBIS; 79 John Sundlof/Alamy; 82 (l): Jeff Siner/The Charlotte Observer/AP Photo; (r): Dan Wagner; 83 (t): Stockbyte/Getty Images; (b): Clifford K. Berryman/The National Archives and Records Administration; 84 Bonnie Schiffman/CORBIS; 87 (t): Baltimore Sun, Jed Kirschbaum/AP Photo; (bl): Library of Congress Prints and Photographs Division Washington, D.C. [LC-USZCN4-189]; (br): AP Photo; 88 Izzy Schwartz/Photdisc/Getty Images; 89 David Hoffman Photo Library; 90 Michael Newman/Photo Edit; 91 (b): Paul Tomas; (tl): KAREN BLEIER/AFP/Getty Images; (cr): Kimberly White/Reuters; 92 Bettmann/CORBIS; 93 Pete Stone/CORBIS; 94 Digital Vision/Getty Images; 95 Gene Blevins/LA Daily News/CORBIS.

### Chapter 5

100–101 AP Photo; 101 (tr): Mike Wintroath/AP Photo; 102 (t): AP Photo; (b): Matt Rourke/AP Photo; 103 (l): Matt Stroshane/Getty Images; (r): Tammie Arroyo/AP Photo; 104 Paul Hawthorne/Getty Images; 105 (t): MR. MONOPOLY © 1935, 2009 Hasbro. All rights reserved. (b): Andresr/Used under license from Shutterstock; 106 Chuck Burton/AP Photo; 107 (tl): Wally McNamee/CORBIS; (tr): Alex Wong/Getty Images; (bl): Bettmann/CORBIS; (br): Sean Adair/Reuters/Landov; 108 suravid/Used under license from Shutterstock; 109 Mick Tsikas/Reuters; 110 Mike Wintroath/AP Photo; 111 Andrew Lichtenstein/Sygma/Corbis; 112 B.S.P.I./CORBIS; 113 Jeff Greenberg/The Image Works.

### Chapter 6

116–117 Rick Bowmer/AP Photo; 117 (tr): Damian Dovarganes/AP Photo; 118 (t): Rick Bowmer/AP Photo; (b): REUTERS/Ethan Miller/CORBIS; 119 Roger Ressmeyer/CORBIS; 120 (t): Lynn Goldsmith/Corbis; (b): Dell/Dreamstime.com; 121 Jose Goitia/AP Photo; 122 (tl): Robert Maass/CORBIS; (bl): James A Isbell/Shutterstock; (tr): Lou Dematteis/REUTERS; (br): Courtesy, The Drudge Report; 123 (t): Mark Mainz/AP Images for Fox; (cl): Keyur Khamar/Bloomberg News/Landov; (c): Reuters/CORBIS; (cr): Ted S. Warren/AP Photo; (bc): Philippe Wojazer/REUTERS; (br): Cafe Press/AP Photo; 124 © 2008 Wikimedia Foundation Inc.; 125 (t): Damian Dovarganes/AP Photo; (b): ROBERT GALBRAITH/Reuters/Corbis; 126 Comedy Central/Courtesy the Everett Collection; 127 (t): Shutterstock; (b): Courtesy, ESPN; 128 Paramount Pictures/Photofest; 129 CHUCK KENNEDY/MCT/Landov.

### Chapter 7

132–133 Reuters/CORBIS; 133 (tr): The Everett Collection; 134 Reuters/CORBIS; 135 *montage* Joshua Lott/AP Photo; Peter M. Fredin/AP Photo; John Russell/AP Photo; Peter Cosgrove/AP Photo; Brandon Thibodeaux/Dallas Morning News/Corbis; Nam Y. Huh/AP Photo; Mark Gilliland/AP Photo; Scott Olson/Getty Images; PRNewsFoto/Mothers Against DrunkDriving/newscom; 136 (t): J.D. Pooley/Getty Images; (b): Jerry S. Mendoza/AP Photo; 137 Amy Sancetta/AP Photo; 138 (l): Alex Wong/Getty Images; (r): Patti Longmire/AP Photo; 139 Gregory Bull/AP Photo; 140 (l): Chuck Savage/Corbis; (r): Peter Hvizdak/The Image Works; 141 Brendan Smialowski/AFP/Getty Images; 142 Matt Rourke/AP Photo; 143 (t): Gerald Herbert/AP Photo; (b): Scott Maxwell/LuMaxArt 2008/Used under license from Shutterstock.com; 144 Tatiana Popova 2008/Used under license from Shutterstock.com;

**145** Richard Lord/The Image Works; **146** (t): Jason Kempin/WireImage/Getty Images; (b): The Everett Collection; **147** Rick Wilking/Reuters/Corbis; **148** Diane Bondareff/AP Photo.

## Chapter 8
**152–153** Lynn Goldsmith/CORBIS; **153** (tr): Cory Ryan/Getty Images; **154** Lynn Goldsmith/CORBIS; **155** (tr): Jason Kirk/Getty Images; (tl): Cynthia Johnson/Getty Images; (cl): Dirck Halstead/Time Life Pictures/Getty Images; (bl): Justin Sullivan/Getty Images; **156** Shai Ginott/CORBIS; **157** Cory Ryan/Getty Images; **159** Wally McNamee/CORBIS; **160** (l): Chip Somodevilla/Getty Images; (r): Chip Somodevilla/Getty Images; **161** (t): Dennis Van Tine/Abaca Press/MCT/Newscom; (b): NBC-TV/THE KOBAL COLLECTION/EDELSON DANA/The Picture Desk; **162** Courtney Perry/Dallas Morning News/Corbis; **163** Stephen Saks Photography/Alamy; **165** David Coleman/Alamy; **167** Joshua Roberts/Bloomberg News/Landov.

## Chapter 9
**170–171** Gabriel Buoys/AFP/Getty Images; **171** (tr): John Moore/Getty Images; **172** (t): Gabriel Buoys/AFP/Getty Images; b Probate Court Jefferson County, AL; **173** UPI Photo/A.J. Sisco/Landov; **175** Eric Gay/AP Photo; **176** North Wind Picture Archives; **177** Obama Campaign/AP Photo; **178** (l): SwagHouse Media/Getty Images; (r): Reuters/CORBIS; **179** Jim McIsaac/Getty Images; **180** Randy Faris/Corbis; **181** Courtesy, Matthew Sheldon; **182** Vahan Shirvanian/Cartoonstock.com; **183** John Moore/Getty Images; **184** J. Scott Applewhite/AP Photo; **185** Silvia Izquierdo/AP Photo; **187** Dave Weaver/AP Photo; **188–189** (bkgd): Daniel Mandic/Used under license from Shutterstock; *Edwards:* Ethan Miller/Getty Images; *Biden:* Alex Wong/Getty Images; *Giuliani:* Moose/AdMedia/Newscom; *Romney:* Soren McCarty/WireImage/Getty Images; *Clinton:* Chris Fitzgerald/CandidatePhotos/Newscom; *McCain:* Yoan Valat/epa/Corbis; *Paul:* David McNew/Getty Images; *Obama:* Stefan Zaklin/epa/Corbis; *Huckabee:* TOSHIFUMI KITAMURA/AFP/Getty Images; *Gravel:* Alex Wong/Getty Images; **190** (tl): Brooks Kraft/Corbis; (tr): Steve Pope/epa/Corbis; (bl): Brendan Smialowski/Getty Images; (br): Rick Friedman/Corbis; **191** (l): Jiri Moucka/Shutterstock; (r): Jiri Moucka/Shutterstock; **192** The Granger Collection, New York; **194** BETH A. KEISER/AP Photo; **195** Bettmann/CORBIS; **197** Richard Drew/AP Photo; **198** Namir Noor-Eldeen RCS/AH/Reuters.

## Chapter 10
**202–203** David Maung/AP Photo; **203** (tr): Lauren Victoria Burke/AP Photo; **204** (t): David Maung/AP Photo; (b): MANDEL NGAN/AFP/Getty Images; **205** Tim Sloan/AFP/Getty Images; **206** Craig Lassig/epa/Corbis; **207** Doug Mills/The New York Times/Redux Pictures; **209** Seth Perlman/AP Photo; **210** Dana Edelson/NBCU Photo Bank via AP Images; **211** (tl): Jeff Gentner/AP Photo; (tr): Lauren Victoria Burke/AP Photo; (cl): Brendan Hoffman/Getty Images; (cr): Susan Walsh/AP Photo; (bl): Dennis Cook/AP Photo; (br): Susan Walsh/AP Photo; **212–213** Diane Cook and Len Jenshel/Getty Images; **213** (t): LM Otero/AP Photo; **214** AP Photo; **215** (l): Scott Cohen/Reuters; (r): Jim Mone/AP Photo; **216** Michael Hall Photography Pty Ltd/Corbis; **217** Matthew Cavanaugh/CORBIS; **218** The Everett Collection; **219** istera/Used under license from Shutterstock; **220** Susan Walsh/AP Photo; **222** Bettmann/CORBIS; **223** SuperStock Inc.; **224** Pat Bagley/www.caglecartoons.com.

## Chapter 11
**228–229** www.intoon.com; **229** (tr): Bettmann/CORBIS; **230** www.intoon.com; **231** *T. Roosevelt, Eisenhower, Kennedy:* Bettmann/CORBIS; *Reagan:* Wally McNamee/CORBIS; *Clinton:* Alex Wong/Getty Images; **232** (tl): David J. & Janice L. Frent Collection/CORBIS; (tr): CORBIS; (bl): Martin H. Simon/Corbis; (br): AFP/Getty Images; **233** Popperfoto/Getty Images; **234** (t): Paul Szep; (b): Scott Shaw/AP Photo; **235** (t): Paul Szep; **236** (l): Seattle Post-Intelligencer Collection; Museum of History and Industry/CORBIS; (r): U.S. Navy, Shane T. McCoy/AP Photo; **237** Alexander Natruskin/Pool/epa/Corbis; **238** Matthew Cavanaugh/epa/Corbis; **240** Bettmann/CORBIS; **241** Shawn Thew/epa/Corbis; **242** Brendan Smialowski/AFP/Getty Images;. **244** Gerd Ludwig/CORBIS; **245** Frank Franklin II/AP Photo; **246** (tl,bl): Bettmann/CORBIS; (tr): Popperfoto/Getty Images; (br): AP Photo; **247** Frank Micelotta/Getty Images; **248** Bettmann/CORBIS; **251** Mary Ellen Matthews/NBCU Photo B via AP Images; **253** Nick Ut/AP Photo.

## Chapter 12
**256–257** Mona Reeder/CORBIS; **257** (tr): Library of Congress Prints and Photographs Division Washington D.C. [LC-USZC4-1587]; **258** Mona Reeder/CORBIS; **259** Brooks Kraft/CORBIS; **260** David Scharf/Peter Arnold Inc.; **261** (both): Courtesy of the Peace Corps; **262** Jeff Kravitz/FilmMagic/Getty Images; **263** (l): National Science Foundation; (r): © CBS/Courtesy: Everett Collection; **265** (bkgd): Scott Peterson/Getty Images; (inset): Gerry Broome/AP Photo; **266** (t): David R. Frazier/The Image Works; (bl): Bettmann/CORBIS; (br): Library of Congress Prints and Photographs Division Washington D.C. [LC-USZC4-1587]; **267** Joe Marquette/AP Photo; **268** (t): SETH WENIG/Reuters/Landov; (b): Mario Tama/Getty Images; **269** AP Photo/David J. Phillip; **270** Library of Congress. Washington D.C. [LC-USZC4-3859]; **271** (l): AP Photo/Portland Police Department; (cl): David Toase/Getty Images; (cr): Juergen Becker/zefa/Corbis; (bl): Steven

Puetzer/Getty Images; bc dkey/A.collection/Getty Images; (br): George Doyle/Getty Images; **273** Jack Kurtz/ZUMA/Corbis; **274** Ron Sachs/CNP/Sygma/Corbis; **275** Carlos Osorio File/AP Photo; **276** AP Photo/Damian Dovarganes; **277** Reza/Webistan/Corbis; **278** (t): Cindy Charles/PhotoEdit; (cl): Congressional Quarterly/Getty Images; (c): Eric Rowley/AP Photo; (cr): MANDEL NGAN/AFP/Getty Images; (b): Tony Gutierrez/AP Photo; **280** David Young-Wolff/PhotoEdit.

## Chapter 13
**284–285** Michael Geissinger/The Image works; **285** (tr): LUC GNAGO/Reuters/Landov; **286** (t): Michael Geissinger/The Image Works; (b): www.cartoonstock.com; **287** (bkgd): Bettmann/CORBIS; (inset): Time & Life Pictures/Getty Images; **288** Travelpix Ltd/Getty Images; **289** ROBERT GALBRAITH/Reuters/Landov; **290** SERGEI KARPUKHIN/Reuters/Corbis; **291** Jack Kurtz/ZUMA/Corbis; **292** LUC GNAGO/Reuters/Landov; **293** Joe Raedle/Getty Images; **295** (bkgd): AP Photo/J. Scott Applewhite; (fgd): Roslen Mack/Used under license from Shutterstock; **296** (t): Time & Life Pictures/Getty Images; (b): Charles Dharapak/AP Photo; **297** (t): CORBIS; (b): AFP/Getty Images; **301** Mark Blinch/Reuters/Corbis; **302** Comstock/Jupiter Images; **303** Mario Tama/Getty Images; **304** Joe Raedle/Newsmakers/Getty Images; **305** Lara Porzak Photography via Getty Images; **306** Tony Savino/Corbis; **307** Bob Daemmrich/Corbis.

## Chapter 14
**310–311** Todd Bigelow/Aurora Photos; **311** (tr): Ryan Donnell/The New York Times/Redux; **312** (t): Todd Bigelow/Aurora Photos; (b): Rick Lew/Getty Images; **313** Orjan F. Ellingvag/CORBIS; **314** (l): Doug Hyun © F/X Network/Everett Collection; (r): MTV/THE KOBAL COLLECTION/Picture Desk; **315** Bonnie Kamin/PhotoEdit; **316** Commercial Eye/Getty Images; **317** Robert Llewellyn/Jupiter Images; **318** Marc Asnin/CORBIS SABA; **319** (t): Matthew Cavanaugh/epa/Corbis; **320** Richard Baker/Corbis; **321** Kathy Willens/AP Photo; **323** DOG EAT DOG FILMS/WEINSTEIN COMPANY/THE KOBAL COLLECTION/Picture Desk; **325** (bkgd): Bettman/Corbis; (inset): NBC-TV/THE KOBAL COLLECTION/Picture Desk; **326** (t): Ryan Donnell/The New York Times/Redux; (b): Getty Images; **329** Jim West/The Image Works; **330** (both): Gerald Herbert/AP Photo; **331** Wilfredo Lee/AP Photo; **333** J. Scott Applewhite/AP Photo; **334** Tony Gutierrez/AP Photo.

## Chapter 15
**338–339** Brooks Kraft/CORBIS **339** (tr): Susan Steinkamp/CORBIS; **340** Brooks Kraft/CORBIS; **341** PRNewsFoto/Newsweek/Newscom; **342** John Gress JG/CCK/Reuters; **343** Ron Edmonds/AP Photo; **344** Jeff Greenberg/PhotoEdit; **345** Wausau Daily Herald Butch McCartney/AP Photo; **346** (t): Andy Wong/AP Photo; (b): LISS STEVE/CORBIS SYGMA; **348** HIROKO MASUIKE/AFP/Getty Images; **349** Susan Steinkamp/CORBIS; **350** Tim Mosenfelder/Corbis; **351** Bohemian Nomad Picturemakers/CORBIS; **352** AP Photo/Don Heupel; **353** © NBC/Courtesy: Everett Collection.; **354** Evan Vucci/AP Photo; **355** (tl): Douglas C. Pizac/AP Photo; (tr): Nati Harnik/AP Photo; (bl): Mark Jenkinson/Corbis; (br): Jeffrey Coolidge/Ionica/Getty Images; **357** Northwestern University Library [http://www.library.northwestern.edu/govpub/collections/wwii-posters/img/ww1646-72]; **358** Christina Dicken/Chronicle-Tribune/AP Photo.

## Chapter 16
**362–363** Najlah Feanny/CORBIS SABA; **363** (tr): Emilio Morenatti/AP Photo; **364** (t): Najlah Feanny/CORBIS SABA; (bl): Alex Brandon/AP Photo; (br): Lawrence Jackson/AP Photo; **365** Manuel Balce Ceneta/AP Photo; **366** Time & Life Pictures/Getty Images; **367** Bettmann/Corbis; **368** Flying Colours Ltd/Getty Images; **369** David Churchill/Arcaid/Corbis; **370** James Dawson/Jupiter Images; **371** F. Carter Smith/Sygma/Corbis; **372** Emilio Morenatti/AP Photo; **373** (tl): Bettman/Corbis; (tr,br): Hulton Archive/Getty Images; (bl): North Wind Picture Archives; **374** Bettman/Corbis; **375** (t): Jean Claude Revy ISM/Phototake; (b): FOCUS FEATURES/THE KOBAL COLLECTION/Picture Desk; **376** Donna Abu-Nasr/AP Photo; **378** Henry Griffin/AP Photo; **379** (t): Michael Newman/PhotoEdit; (bl): Don Hammond/Design Pics/Corbis; (bc): AFP/Getty Images; (br): Tomas Van Houtryve/Corbis; **381** Andy Mead/Icon SMI/Corbis; **382** Steph Goranick/Getty Images.

## Chapter 17
**386–387** Nikoo Harf Maher/Document Iran/Corbis; **387** (tr): Transtock/Corbis; **388** (t): Nikoo Harf Maher/Document Iran/Corbis; (b): STR/AFP/Getty Images; **389** AP Photo; **390** (bkgd): AP Images for U.N. Foundation; (inset): Andy Crump TDR WHO/Photo Researchers Inc.; **391** Claude Mahoudeau/AFP/Getty Images; **392** Diego Lezama Orezzoli/Corbis; **393** Alejandro Ernesto/epa/Corbis; **394** Transtock/Corbis; **395** LARRY DOWNING/Reuters/Corbis; **397** Javed Khan/AP Photo; **398** Getty Images; **399** epa/Corbis; **401** Natalie Helbert/istockphoto.com; **402** UNIVERSAL PICTURES/THE KOBAL COLLECTION/DUHAMEL FRANCOIS/Picture Desk; **404** Les Stone/Zuma; **404** Courtesy, The Point Foundation; **405** RIZWAN TABASSUM/AFP/Getty Images; **407** Connecticut Post Brian A. Pounds/AP Photo; **408** Doug Mills/AP Photo.

General Motors (GM), 26, 134, 144
generations, opinion differences and, 96
Genetic Information Non-discrimination Act, 375
Geneva Convention, 236, 357
Geographic Constituency, 208
Georges, John, 173
Georgia, 22, 172, 175, 356
Germany, 20, 24, 69, 89, 108, 396
Gerry, Elbridge, 176
gerrymandering, 176
get-out-the-vote (GOTV) campaigns, 107
Giamatti, Paul, 39
*Gibbons v. Ogden*, 66
*Gideon v. Wainright*, 43, 355
Gil Party, 156
Gingrich, Newt, 331
Ginsburg, Ruth Bader, 285, 294, 295
*Gitlow v. New York*, 43
Glaxo-Smith-Kline, 135
Glazer, Matt, 117
global economy, 25–26
global warming, 65, 92
Global Warming Treaty, 397
GM (General Motors), 26, 134, 144, 311–312
*Gonzales v. Oregon*, 66
*Gonzales v. Ralch*, 66
GOP (Grand Old Party). *See* Republican Party
Gore, Al, 110, 122, 155, 192, 193, 195, 234
GOTV campaigns, 107
governing party, 167
government. *See also* federal bureaucracy
    definition, 5
    expenditures, 321–322, 324–329
    finance issues, 316–318
    healthcare, 322–324
    impact on individuals, 8
    importance of, 4–5
    income security, 326–327, 329
    interest on the debt, 329
    national defense, 326
    and politics, 5
    powers, 60–62
    public policy approach, 6–9
    regulations, 4
    religion and, 342–345
    services, 4–5, 312
    shut-down, 331
    Social Security. *See* Social Security
    taxes, 4–5
Government Accountability Office (GAO), 335
government agencies, 8–9
government corporations, 262
Government Responsiveness Index, 90
Grand Old Party (GOP). *See* Republican Party
grandfather clause, 372, 373
grant programs, federal. *See* federal grant programs
grassroots, party politics and, 161
Gravel, Mike, 189
Great Britain
    civil unions, 89
    colonial period of U.S. and, 36–37
    defense spending, 18

foreign aid, 396
GDP, 24
    immigration and, 20
    religious beliefs, 79
    UN Security Council, 389
    voting rates, 108
Great Depression, 54, 64, 82, 266
Great Plains, 162, 195
Great Society, 248, 267
Greater Houston Partnership, 28
Green, A.C., 301
Green Party, 154
greenhouse emissions, 398
Greenpeace, 391
Greenspan, Alan, 332, 333
Greenstein, Fred I., 249
*Gregg v. Georgia*, 306, 356
Grenada, 392
Grigg, C.W., 87
gross domestic product (GDP), 5, 24, 311, 316–317, 400
ground war, 181
Groves, Robert, 28
growth rate of American population, 19
Grutter, Barbara, 363, 379, 381
*Grutter v. Bollinger*, 306
Guam, 204
Guantanamo Bay, 236, 299, 357
Guatemala, 19, 393
Guiliani, Rudy, 184, 186–187, 188
*Guinn v. United States*, 373
Gulf War, 85, 219, 238, 397
gun control laws, 66, 111, 133, 149, 163, 164, 299
gun ownership, 163
Gun-Free School Zones Act of 1990, 64
*habeas corpus*, 41–42, 236, 289, 357
H1N1, 257
Hadash Party, 156
Haiti, 401
Halliburton, 134
Hamdi, Yawer Esam, 357
Hamilton, Alexander, 37, 45, 53, 305
hanging, 355
Hank, the Angry, Drunken Dwarf, 82
hard money, 179
HarperCollins, 119
Harrison, Benjamin, 192, 230
Harrison, William Henry, 230
Hasselbeck, Elizabeth, 103
Hastings, Alcee Lamar, 290
Hatch Act, 265, 267
hate-crimes legislation, 347, 371
Hayes, George E.C., 50
Hayes, Rutherford B., 192
head coverings, 21
Health and Human Service, Department of, 258–259, 260, 273
health insurance, 30, 311
healthcare
    in Canada, 323
    costs, 72
    government expenditures, 322–324
    Obama and, 229, 311
    in party platforms, 164
    poverty and, 30
    reform of, 245, 252, 311, 313, 334
    universal, 73, 323
*Heart of Atlanta Hotel v. United States*, 374
Heclo, Hugh, 278

Helms, Jesse, 394
Helms-Burton Act, 394
Hennen, Scott, 239
high school graduates, 160
highway subgovernment, 275–276, 278
Highway Trust Fund, 278
Hill, Anita, 295
*The Hills*, 314
Hilton, Paris, 178
Hispanic Caucus, 364
Hispanics, 22, 23, 26, 28, 29–30
Holder, Eric, 259
home style of congressional members, 208–209
Homeland Security Committee, 220
Homeland Security, Department of, 257, 258–259, 261, 266, 268, 281
Homeland Security, Office of, 267
homosexuality. *See* gay and lesbian rights
Honduras, 19, 393
honeymoon effect, 250
Hope Credit, 316
House and Urban Development, Department of (HUD), 258–259
House majority leader, 211
House majority whip, 211
House minority leader, 211, 213
House minority whip, 211
House of Commons, 47
House of Lords, 47
House of Representatives, 46, 111, 173, 174, 182–183, 203, 205. *See also* Congress
House Rules Committee, 221–222
House Transportation and Infrastructure Committee, 276
household income, 26, 29
Hoyer, Steny, 211
HRC (Human Rights Campaign), 140, 380
Huckabee, Mike, 184, 186–187, 189
Huckaby, Elizabeth, 367
HUD (House and Urban Development, Department of), 258–259
Huffington, Arianna, 120
*Huffington Post*, 120, 318
Hull, Blair, 176
human rights activists, 238
Human Rights Campaign (HRC), 140, 380
Humphrey, Hubert, 192
Hungary, 390
Hunter, Duncan, 188
Huntington, Samuel, 399
Hurricane Katrina, 65, 125, 126, 129, 221, 252, 281
Hussein, Saddam, 236, 245, 249, 385, 396, 403
Hyde, Henry, 348
IAEA (International Atomic Energy Agency), 385, 398
Ichud Leumi-Mafdal Party, 156
Illinois, 174, 189, 273, 327
IMF (International Monetary Fund), 389, 395
Imhofe, James N., 222
immigrant rights, 94
immigration
    illegal, 19–20, 31

policy and politics, 21
    reform of, 164, 203, 212–213, 220
impeachment, 49, 205, 231–233, 290
implied powers, 61, 64
imports, 392
Imus, Don, 341
"Imus in the Morning," 341
*in forma pauperis*, 297
income
    distribution, 26, 29
    as a factor in political participation, 104–105
    inequality of, 314
    redistribution, 313–314
    voting patterns and, 160
income security, 322, 326–327, 329
income tax, 26, 314–316
incumbency, 182–183
incumbent, 127
independent executive agencies, 260–261
independent regulatory commissions, 263
independents, 154, 155, 158
India, 19, 25, 214, 388, 390, 405
Indiana, 195
individual income tax, 26, 314–316
Indochina, 394
Indonesia, 25, 397
IndyMac, 253
inflation, 314
influence, presidential, 244–245
information, alternative sources of, 17
information superhighway, 122
inherent powers, 239
initiative process, 381
injunction, 383
inner cabinet, 260
in-person politics, 183
insider trading, 269
Institute for College Access and Success, 253
institutes and foundations, 263
Institutional Revolutionary Party (PRI), 139
Intel Corporation, 135
intelligence czar, 274
interest, 332
interest groups, 132–149
    alliances, 147
    business groups, 134–135
    citizen/advocacy/cause groups, 138, 140
    congressional voting scorecards, 141
    creating public pressure, 144
    electioneering, 140–142
    federal bureaucracy and, 272–273
    iron triangles and, 275–276, 278
    issue networks and, 8, 275–276, 278
    labor unions, 135–136, 267
    litigation, 146
    lobbying, 143–144
    opposition from other groups, 147
    political violence, 146
    professional associations, 136
    protest demonstrations. *See* protest demonstrations
    public opinion, 147
    public policy, 147–148
    racial/ethnic minority rights groups, 137
    religious groups, 137–138

margin of error, 81

marijuana, 66, 350

Marine Corps, 280–281

Marlboro, 279

marriage rights, 48, 65, 83, 89, 94, 305, 375

Marshall, John, 64

Marshall, Thurgood, 50

Maryland, 64

Massachusetts, 73, 364, 375

massive retaliation, 402

matching funds requirement, 70, 72

Matthews, Chris, 84

Mayer, William G., 195

McCain, John
  2008 election, 84, 196–197, 199
  advertising, 178
  campaign fundraising, 176
  in Congress, 210
  convention speech, 123
  Dobson and, 138
  endorsements, 140
  federal matching funds and, 194
  first-time voters and, 105
  nomination phase, 184, 186–187, 189–190
  presidential campaign, 153
  as Senator, 293
  supporters of, 118, 160, 162, 163
  vice presidential selection, 190

"McCain-Feingold" campaign finance law, 178–179

McCarran Act, 357

McCarthy, Carolyn, 111

McConnell, Mitch, 141, 211

McCulloch, James W., 64

McCulloch v. Maryland, 63, 64, 66

McDonald's restaurants, 25

McGeorge School of Law, 299

McLaurin, G.W., 367–368

McLaurin v. Oklahoma State Regents, 367–368

McVeigh, Timothy, 356

means-tested program, 327

Médecins San Frontiérs, 391

media, 116–129
  as agent of political socialization, 80
  biases in, 126–128
  consolidation of, 119, 122
  covering the news, 122–126
  in Cuba, 121
  government control of, 121
  Internet and, 124
  landscape of, 118–121
  presidential campaigns and, 122
  public policy, 128–129
  sources, 80
  traditional, 124
  types of, 118–119
  use of polling data as news, 95

Medicaid, 15, 30, 67, 72, 265, 311, 321–322, 324, 326

Medical Society, 135

Medicare, 15, 30, 311, 316, 321–322, 324

Medvedev, Dmitry, 237

"meetups," 180

menorah sculpture, 156

mentally retarded, execution of, 49

Meretz Party, 156

Merit Systems Protection Board, 266, 267

Methodists, 163, 207

Metropolitan Transit Authority (MTA), 268

Mexican American Legal Defense and Education Fund (MALDEF), 381

Mexican Americans, 160

Mexican Constitution, 139

Mexico
  church/state relations, 139
  immigration and, 19, 213
  NAFTA and, 234
  purchasing power, 24
  trade with, 393
  voter turnout, 108

Michael D. Palm Center, 409

Michigan, 174, 194, 326, 369

Microsoft Corp., 123, 134

Middle East, 409

midterm elections, 165–166, 199, 203

Midwest, voting patterns, 195

migrant workers, 137

military healthcare, 30

military powers, 236, 238–239

military preemption, 402–403

military service, 281, 407–408

Milk, 375

Milk, Harvey, 375

Millikin v. Bradley, 369

minimum wage, 136, 144

Minneapolis, Minnesota, 215

Minneapolis-St. Paul Star Tribune, 149

Minnesota State University, 149

Minor v. Happersett, 303

minority business set-aside, 378–379

minority groups, 29–30, 365

minority leader, 212–213

minority rights groups, 278

minority whip, 213

Miranda, Ernesto, 353, 359

Miranda v. Arizona, 358, 359

Miranda warning, 287, 353

Miroff, Bruce, 125

"Mission Accomplished," 125

Mississippi, 257

Missouri, 305

Missouri ex rel Gaines v. Canada, 367

Missouri v. Jenkins, 369–370

modernization, 397

modernizing industrial states, 388

monetary policymaking, 332–333

money, role of in elections, 176–179

Montesquieu, Baron de, 44

Moore, Michael, 323

Mormons, 163, 344

morning network shows, 80

mosquito nets, 390

Mothers Against Drunk Driving (MADD), 71, 102, 135, 140

Motor Voter Act, 73

Mousavi, Mir-Hossein, 118

MoveOn.org, 123, 141, 142

movies, politics and, 146

"Mr. Smith Goes to Washington," 223

MSNBC network, 119

MTA (Metropolitan Transit Authority), 268

Mueller, John, 251

multiparty system, 156

multiple referral of legislation, 220

Murphy v. United Parcel Service, 7

Muslims, 21, 345, 399, 409

mutual assured destruction (MAD), 401–402

Myanmar, 236

Myers, Matthew L., 279

mypoliscilab.com, 97

MySpace, 117, 340

NAACP (National Association for the Advancement of Colored People), 137, 297, 367, 381

Nabrit, James M., 50

Nader, Ralph, 155

NAFTA (North American Free Trade Agreement), 234, 235, 393

name recognition, 181

Napolitano, Janet, 259

NARAL Pro-Choice America, 140, 141, 358

NASA (National Aeronautics and Space Administration), 260, 261, 273

National Aeronautics and Space Administration (NASA), 260, 261, 273

National Association for the Advancement of Colored People (NAACP), 137, 297, 367, 381

National Association of Realtors, 142

National Conference on State Legislatures, 72

National Counterterrorism Center, 274

national curriculum, 69

national debt, 321, 329

National Debt Clock, 321

national defense, 322, 326. See also foreign and defense policymaking

National Democratic Assembly Party, 156

National Do Not Call Registry, 272–273

National Drug Control Policy, Office of, 243

National Education Association, 142

National Election Studies (NES), 93

National Endowment for the Arts (NEA), 263

national government powers, 60–62, 64

national government supremacy, 63

National Labor Relations Board (NLRB), 291

National Organization for Women (NOW), 135, 140, 141, 358, 381

national party chair, 157

national party committee, 157

National Performance Review Commission, 234

national powers, 63

National Public Radio (NPR), 118, 122

National Railroad Passenger Service Corporation (Amtrak), 262

National Rifle Association (NRA), 102, 133, 134, 140, 141, 142, 144, 146, 149, 358

National Right to Life Committee, 140, 144, 149, 358

National Science Foundation (NSF), 70, 263

national security adviser, 244

National Security Agency (NSA), 239

National Security Council (NSC), 243, 244

National Supremacy Clause, 62, 64

national supremacy vs. states' rights, 66

National Voter Registration Act, 73

nation-state, 388

Native Americans, 137, 143, 207, 345

Native Hawaiians, 22, 28

NATO (North Atlantic Treaty Organization), 390, 394

Natural Law Party, 154

natural rights interpretation, of Constitution, 53

Nature Conservancy, 389

Nazi Holocaust, 397

NBC network, 119

NCLB (No Child Left Behind), 55, 59, 67–68, 72–73, 218, 265

NEA (National Endowment for the Arts), 263

Nebraska, 191, 196

Necessary and Proper Clause, 61

negative campaigning, 181

negative press, 179

NES (National Election Studies), 93

Netherlands, 89

network evening news, 120

network television, 119

Neuman, W. Russell, 86

Neumann, Kara, 345

Neustadt, Richard, 248

Nevada, 160, 195

New Deal, 64, 266–267, 293, 302

New Hampshire, 186, 188–189, 195

New Haven, Connecticut, 382

New Jersey, 189, 343, 356

new media, 118–119

New Mexico, 160, 195

"New Offshore Drilling Not a Quick Fix, Analysts Say" (Wangsness), 279

New Orleans, 4

New York, 22, 174, 189, 190, 192, 194, 273, 344

New York City transit strike, 268

New York Times, 122

News America Marketing Group, 119

newsmagazines, 119

newspapers, 80, 119

Newsweek, 84, 119

NGO (Nongovernmental organizations), 391

Nicaragua, 19, 393

Nielson ratings, 122

Nigeria, 292

9/11 Commission, 274. See also September 11 terrorist attacks

Nineteenth Amendment, 303, 370

Ninth Amendment, 42

Nixon, Richard
  1960 election, 113
  character of, 246–247
  China and, 235
  debate with Kennedy, 194, 195
  election of, 192
  leadership style of, 249
  media coverage of, 128
  midterm elections and, 166
  pardon of, 240
  resignation of, 231, 233
  Sunbelt and, 22
  Supreme Court and, 300